FOURTH EDITION

W9-APU-782

The St. Martin's Guide to Writing

RISE B. AXELROD

California State University,
San Bernardino

CHARLES R. COOPER

University of California,
San Diego

ST. MARTIN'S PRESS

New York

Editor of The St. Martin's Guide to Writing: Marilyn Moller
Project Manager: Denise Quirk
Acquisitions Editors: Karen Allanson, Nancy Lyman
Editorial Assistants: Susan Cottenden, Steven Kutz
Art Director: Sheree Goodman
Text and Cover Design: Anna George

Library of Congress Catalog Card Number: 92-63068
Copyright © 1994 by St. Martin's Press, Inc.
All rights reserved. No part of this book may be reproduced,
stored in a retrieval system, or transmitted by any form or
by any means, electronic, mechanical, photocopying, recording,
or otherwise, except as may be expressly permitted by the
applicable copyright statutes or in writing by the Publisher.
Manufactured in the United States of America.
8 7 6 5 4
f e d c b

For information, write:
St. Martin's Press, Inc.
175 Fifth Avenue
New York, NY 10010

ISBN: 0-312-07541-3

Acknowledgments

Maya Angelou. "Uncle Willie." From *I Know Why the Caged Bird Sings* by Maya Angelou. Copyright © 1969 by Maya Angelou. Reprinted by permission of Random House, Inc.

David Ansen. "Searing, Nervy, and Very Honest." From *Newsweek*, July 3, 1989. © 1989 Newsweek, Inc. All rights reserved. Reprinted by permission.

Carolyn Anthony. "A Four Blade Case," © 1989 by Clyde Edgerton, from *Family Portraits* by Carolyn Anthony. Used by permission of Doubleday, a division of Bantam Doubleday Dell Publishing Group, Inc.

Robert Bellah et al. "Mythic Individualism." From *Habits of the Heart; Individualism and Commitment in America* by Robert Bellah, et al., pp. 144–147. Copyright © 1985 by The Regents of the University of California. Reprinted by permission.

"brave." By permission. From Webster's New Dictionary of Synonyms © 1984 by Merriam-Webster Inc., publisher of the Merriam-Webster® dictionaries.

"brave." Copyright © 1988 by Houghton Mifflin Company. Reprinted by permission from *Roget's II New Thesaurus, Expanded Edition.*

Janice Castro. "Contigent Workers." Originally titled "Disposable Workers." Copyright 1993 Time Inc. Reprinted by permission.

Sandra Cisneros. "The Monkey Garden." From *The House on Mango Street.* Copyright © 1989 by Sandra Cisneros. Published in the United States by Vintage Books, a division of Random House, Inc., New York, and distributed in Canada by Random House of Canada Limited, Toronto. Originally published in somewhat different form by Arte Publico press in 1984 and revised in 1989. Reprinted by permission of Susan Bergholz Literary Services, New York

K. C. Cole. "Why There Are So Few Women in Science." Copyright © 1981 by The New York Times Company. Reprinted by permission.

Annie Dillard. "Handed My Own Life," from *An American Childhood* by Annie Dillard. Copyright © 1987 by Annie Dillard. Reprinted by permission of HarperCollins Publishers, Inc.

Barbara Ehrenreich. "The Wretched of the Hearth." Reprinted by permission of author.

Entry 91×2727. (Mayberry, Maralee & Knowles, J. Gary. Article from *Urban Review*), *Sociological Abstracts*, April 1991. Reprinted with permission.

Amitai Etzioni. "Hate Speech." From *The Spirit of Community* by Amitai Etzioni. Copyright © 1993 by Amitai Etzioni. Reprinted by permission of Crown Publishers, Inc.

Victor Fuchs, "Suicide among Young People." Excerpted by permission of the publishers from *How We Live* by Victor Fuchs, Cambridge, MA: Harvard University Press, Copyright © 1983 by the President and Fellows of Harvard College.

Acknowledgments and copyrights are continued at the back of the book on page 772, which constitutes an extension of the copyright page.

Writing is the act of saying *I*, of imposing onese[n] *listen to me, see it my way, change your mind.*

A writer...is someone who has found a process that wil[l] new things....   —Willi[am]

...I think best with a pencil in my hand....   —Anne Morrow Lindbergh

I am never as clear about any matter as when I have just finished writing about it.
                                                                —James Van Allen

Writing keeps me from believing everything I read.   —Gloria Steinem

Don't tear up the page and start over when you write a bad line—try to write your way out of it. Make mistakes and plunge on....Writing is a means of discovery, always....   —Garrison Keillor

To the Instructor

When we first wrote *The St. Martin's Guide to Writing*, we tried to design a composition textbook that would be a versatile classroom tool for instructors and a helpful guide for students. We took what we had learned from classical rhetoric as well as from contemporary composition theory and research and did our best to put it into teachable form. We wanted to write a book that would teach students to write, not one that just talked about writing. The enthusiastic reception of the *Guide* in its first three editions testifies to the dedication and seriousness of many instructors who share our conviction that writing can and should be taught. We are deeply grateful to everyone who has helped make it the most widely used college rhetoric today.

While the *Guide* has changed over the years, our basic goals remain unchanged. From the beginning, we have tried to continue the classical tradition of teaching writing not only as a method of composing rhetorically effective prose but also as a powerful heuristic for thinking creatively and critically. To the best insights from that tradition, we have with each new edition added what we believed to be some promising developments in composition theory and research. In particular, we have tried to emphasize the idea that writing is both a social act and a way of knowing. We try to teach students that form emerges from context as well as content, that writing knowledge comes not from studying static forms alone but by participating in a community of writers and readers. Writing and reading different kinds of discourse prepares students to write effectively and read critically in all their academic work. By writing and reading in other disciplines, students will learn both what counts as knowledge in a discipline and how to join the disciplinary conversation.

Our principal aim, then, is to demystify writing and authorize students as writers. To this end, we seek to teach students how to use the composing process as a means of seeing what they know as well as how they know it. We want students to learn to use writing to think critically and communicate effectively with others. Finally, we hope to inspire students with the desire to question their own certainties and provide them with the tools for doing so.

AN OVERVIEW OF THE BOOK

As a rhetoric, reader, and handbook, *The St. Martin's Guide* can serve as a comprehensive introduction to discursive practice. It comprises several parts:

Part I. Writing Activities presents nine different essay assignments, all reflecting actual writing situations that students may encounter both in and out of college, kinds of discourse that they should learn to read critically and to write intelligently. Among the types of essays included are autobiography, explanation, position paper, proposal, and literary interpretation.

You may choose among these chapters and teach them in any sequence you wish, though they are sequenced here to move students from writing based on personal experience and observation to academic types of writing calling for the analysis and synthesis of ideas and information derived from a variety of sources.

Each chapter follows the same organizational plan:

- several brief scenarios identifying the kind of discourse covered in the chapter and suggesting the range of occasions when such writing is done
- an activity for group inquiry that gets students working with the kind of discourse taught in that chapter
- a set of readings accompanied by a critical apparatus designed to help students explore pertinent readerly and writerly questions
- a summary of the purpose and audience and the features basic to writing of this kind
- a flexible guide to writing that escorts students through all the stages of the composing process
- editing and proofreading guidelines to help students check for several sentence-level problems likely to occur in that kind of writing
- a look at one writer at work showing some aspect of the process of writing the student essay in that chapter
- a trio of critical thinking activities designed to help students to reflect on and consolidate what they learned about writing and reading, and to consider the social dimensions of the genre of writing taught in that chapter

Part II. Critical Thinking Strategies collects in two separate chapters practical heuristic tools for invention and reading. The catalog of invention strategies includes clustering, looping, dramatizing, and questioning, while the catalog of reading strategies includes annotating, summarizing, exploring the significance of figurative language, evaluating the logic of an argument, and understanding the discourse of different disciplines.

Part III. Writing Strategies looks at a wide range of essential writers' strategies: paragraphing and coherence; logic and reasoning; and the familiar modes of presenting information, like narrating, defining, and classifying. Examples and exercises are almost all taken from contemporary nonfiction, and many exercises deal with reading selections appearing in Part I. This cross-referencing between Parts I and III facilitates teaching writing strategies in the context of purpose and audience.

Part IV. Research Strategies discusses both field and library research and includes thorough guidelines for using and documenting sources, with detailed examples of the MLA and APA documentation styles. The part concludes with a sample student research paper.

Part V. Writing for Assessment covers essay examinations, showing students how to analyze different kinds of exam questions and offering strategies for writing answers, and portfolios, helping students assemble a respresentative sample of their writing.

The Handbook is a complete reference guide with exercises covering sentence structure, usage, style, punctuation, mechanics, and common ESL problems. We have tried here to maintain a descriptive, rather than prescriptive, point of view. Instead of merely listing rules for using punctuation, for instance, we look at the many ways punctuation marks actually are used in contemporary nonfiction and then provide examples from the work of professional writers.

Proven Features

What has made *The St. Martin's Guide to Writing* such an effective teaching tool are several proven features: the practical guides to writing, the systematic integration of reading and writing, and activities to promote group discussion and inquiry.

Practical Guides to Writing. We do not merely talk about the composing process; rather, we offer practical, flexible guides that escort students through the entire process, from invention through revision and self-evaluation. Thus, this book is more than just a rhetoric that students will refer to occasionally. It is a guidebook that will help them to write. Commonsensical and easy to follow, these writing guides teach students to assess a rhetorical situation, identify the kinds of information they will need, ask probing questions and find answers, and organize their writing to achieve their purpose.

Systematic Integration of Reading and Writing. Because we see a close relationship between the abilities to read critically and to write intelligently, *The St. Martin's Guide* combines reading instruction with writing instruction. Each chapter in Part I introduces one kind of discourse, which students are led to consider both as readers and as writers. Readings are followed by questions that make students aware of how they as readers respond and at the same time help them understand the decisions writers make. Students are then challenged to apply these insights to their own writing as they imagine their prospective readers, set goals, and write and revise their drafts.

Activities to Promote Group Discussion and Inquiry. At the start of each of the writing chapters is an exercise For Group Inquiry that invites students to try out some of the thinking and planning they'll be doing for the kind of writing covered in that chapter. Then, following each reading comes a question For Discussion, designed to provoke thoughtful response about the social and political dimensions of the reading. In the Guide to Writing is another exercise For Group Inquiry that gets students to discuss their work in progress with one another and an opportunity for students to read and comment on each others' drafts. Finally, a new discussion activity invites students to explore the social dimensions of the genre they've been learning to write. All of these materials have been class-tested, and all include questions and prompts to guide students to work productively together.

New to This Edition

We have tried in this new edition to continue the tradition of innovation by turning current theory and research into practical classroom activities—with a minimum of jargon. Chief among these new features are a set of critical thinking activities concluding each Part I chapter, practical guidelines for editing in each writing guide, a catalog of critical reading strategies, a chapter on assembling a portfolio, and a section in the Handbook on editing common ESL problems.

Thinking Critically about What You've Learned. Each Part I chapter now concludes with three metacognitive activities to help students become aware of what they have learned about the process of writing, about the influence of reading on writing, and about the social and political dimensions of the genres they have learned to write. These activities are based on research showing that reflecting on what they have learned helps students deepen their understanding and remember better.

Editing Guidelines. Based on linguistic research identifying the most common sentence-level problems in each kind of writing taught in Part I, these guidelines help students recognize and edit their own sentence problems.

A Catalog of Critical Reading Strategies. Designed for easy reference, a new Chapter 12 offers a variety of proven reading strategies, including annotating, contextualizing, looking for patterns of opposition, reflecting on challenges to your beliefs and values, evaluating the logic of an argument, and understanding the discourse of various disciplines. These materials have been extensively class-tested.

A Chapter on Assembling a Portfolio. If you use portfolio evaluation in your course or just want students to learn to evaluate their own writing and learning, Chapter 24 has practical advice on how to use the resources of *The St. Martin's Guide* to assemble a portfolio and write a probing self-evaluation.

Editing Common ESL Problems. A new section of the Handbook is designed for students who speak English as a second language. Here they will find help with articles, adjective order, verbs, and other common ESL troublespots.

Ancillaries

Several innovative ancillaries accompany the *Guide*.

The Great American Bologna Festival and other student essays, Second Edition, edited by Paul Sladky (Augusta College), is a collection of essays written by students across the nation using *The St. Martin's Guide*. The ten chapters in the book correspond with those in Part I of the *Guide*. The book includes forms for you or your students to submit their writing for publication in future editions.

The St. Martin's Manual for Writing in the Disciplines, by Richard Bullock (Wright State University), is a handy reference for faculty, with ideas for using writing in courses across the curriculum. Among the topics covered are designing assignments that get students writing, using informal writing activities to help students learn, assigning portfolios, and responding to student writing.

The Instructor's Resource Manual has been greatly expanded from earlier editions and now includes a catalog of helpful advice for new instructors (by Alison M. Warriner, Sacred Heart University); guidelines on common teaching practices such as assigning journals and setting up group activities; guidelines on responding to and evaluating student writing (by Charles Cooper, formerly available as a separate booklet); suggested course plans; detailed chapter plans; an annotated bibliography in composition and rhetoric; and a selection of background readings.

Writer's Prologue, customized for *The St. Martin's Guide*, is an innovative software program for invention and drafting, peer editing, and revision. Adapted from the award-winning Daedalus System, this program is specifically designed to complement the writing guides found in the text. Available in IBM (0-312-10718-8) or Macintosh (0-312-10717-X) versions.

The St. Martin's Pocket Guide to Library Research and Documenting Sources provides information in a concise format on MLA, APA, Note-and-Bibliography, and CBE documentation styles.

The Guide to Documenting Sources Hotline is a pop-up software program based on *The St. Martin's Pocket Guide to Library Research and Documenting Sources*. Compatible with most word-processing programs, the *Hotline* is an online reference tool that uses multiple menus to give students immediate access to specific documentation styles while they are writing.

MicroGrade: A Teacher's Gradebook is an easy-to-use new software program for tracking grades and producing progress reports. It can be used on any computer system.

Upon adoption of *The St. Martin's Guide to Writing*, instructors are authorized to make copies of the *Hotline* and the customized *Writer's Prologue* for their students. If instructors prefer, they may order copies of the software for students to purchase through the bookstore.

ACKNOWLEDGMENTS

We owe an enormous debt to all the rhetoricians and composition specialists whose theory, research, and pedagogy have informed *The St. Martin's Guide to Writing*. We fear we would add reams to an already long book if we were to name everyone to whom we are indebted, however; suffice it to say that we have been eclectic in our borrowing.

We also must acknowledge immeasurable lessons learned from all the writers, professional and student alike, whose work we analyzed and whose writing we used in this and earlier editions.

So many instructors and students have contributed ideas and criticism over the years. We want especially to thank the staff, instructors, and students in the Third College Writing Program at the University of California at San Diego, where from 1979 until 1991 we developed and revised the *Guide*. We are still benefiting from the astute insights of Peg Syverson, Kate Gardner, and Kristin Hawkinson. Others who have made special contributions to this edition are Steven Axelrod, Jeremiah Axelrod, Kathryn O'Rourke, Stephanie Kay, and Jim Drake.

Many instructors across the nation have helped us to improve the book. For responding to a detailed questionnaire about the third edition, we thank Martin Achatz, Northern Michigan University; James Alexander, University of Wisconsin Center—Marshfield; Carol Alves, Rollins College; Marlene Anderson, California State University—San Bernardino; Bill Anderson, Southwest State University; Diana Badur, Black Hawk College; Barbara Bailey, Victor Valley College; Kay Baker, Ricks College; Jerry Baker, Cococino County Community College; James Barcus, Baylor University; Elizabeth Bookser Barkley, College of Mount St. Joseph; Larry Barkley, Mt. San Jacinto College—Menifee Valley; Anne Baron, Erie Community College; Claudia Basha, Victor Valley College; Charles Bauerlein, West Chester University; Charles Beiter, Waynesburg College; Dinah Benson, University of Colorado—Colorado Springs; Edwin Booher, Lincoln Land Community College; Douglas Bouzo, Southern Utah University; Ladson Bright, Cape Fear Community College; J. Brown; Michael Bryant, Drake University; JoAnn Buck, Guilford Technical Community College; Susan Bullard, Cedar Valley College; Phyllis Bunnell, Our Lady of the Lake University; Carlos Camargo, University of California—Berkeley; Beth Camp, Linn-Benton Community College; James Campbell, Lynchburg College; C.W. Campbell, Monroe Community College; Carol Cinclair, Brookhaven College; Ted Ciuba, Merced College; Jane Cocalis, Xavier University; Michael Connell, Kirkwood Community College; Philip Coots, Ashland Community College; Boyd

Creasman, West Virginia Wesleyan College; Mary Cross, Oakton Community College; Carol Cunningham, Bakersfield College; Richard Cunningham, Framingham State College; Elizabeth Curtin, Salisbury State University; Joan Curtin, DePaul University; Margaret Deeprez, Katharine Gibbs School; Michelle Dega, Boise State University; Ann Deprey, University of Wisconsin—Green Bay; Mary Devane, SUNY at Albany; Linda DiDesidero, Northwestern; Patricia Dolan, University of Wisconsin—Parkside; Ann Dowling, Cape Fear Community College; Martha Drummond, University of Wisconsin—Platteville; Timothy Duzynski, Kirkwood Community College; William Dynes, University of Indianapolis; Dina Elenbogen; Diane Ferrara, Bellevue College; Laurence Firebek, Diablo Valley College; Sheryl Fontaine, California State University—Fullerton; Marlene Fortney, University of Findlay; Carmen Freiberg, Morningside College; Elizabeth Gardner, Millersville University; Tom Gaston, Purdue University; John Gazda, Penn Valley Community College; Marjorie George, University of Texas—San Antonio; Randall Gloege, Eastern Montana College; Leslie Goerner, Utica College; Peggy Goodwin, Brevard College; Kathleen Gould, University of North Carolina—Wilmington; Albert Griffith, Our Lady of the Lake University; Loren Gruber, Northwest Missouri State University; Mark Halperin, Central Washington University; Kylie Hansen, Washington University; Harry Harder, University of Wisconsin—Eau Claire; Lee Harding, Mississippi College; Barbara Harris, University of Rhode Island; Jane Healey, Mercer University; Sarah Henderson, University of Portland; Patricia Henshaw, Sacramento City College; John Hofland, Dordt College; Leigh Holmes, Cameron University; Katherine Homan, UWC—Marinette; William Hope, Jefferson Technical College; Patricia Huhn, Trinidad State Junior College; Katie E. Hupp, Creighton College; Charles Jenkins, Chaffey College; Phyllis Johnson, Roberts Wesleyan College; Donna Johnson, Elmhurst College; C. Johnson, Virginia Wesleyan College; David Johnson, Northwestern College; Mary Joseph, Lander University; Raelyn Joyce, Kalamazoo Valley Community College; Mimi Kairschner, Moorpark College; John Kearney, Lebanon Valley College; Tom Kemme, Bellarmine College; Trudy Kennedy, Crafton Hills College; Christina Kennedy, Castleton State College; Nancy Kersell, Northern Kentucky University; Cynthia Kimball, University of Idaho & SUNY Buffalo; James Knickerbocker, Clarion University; Keith Kroll, Kalamazoo Valley Community College; Joan Kuzma Costello, Inver Hills Community College; Bill Lamb, Johnson County Community College; Rob Lamm, Arkansas State University; E. C. Lange, Northern Kentucky University; Jan LaVille, Des Moines Area Community College; Darby Lewes, Loyola University; Jian-Ahong Lin, Regis University; Paul Lizotte, Rivier College; Leona Maxwell, Northampton Community College; Bill McCarron, East Texas State University; Marcia McDonald, Belmont University; Paul McNaney, Elmira College; Mike Meeker, Winona State University; Richard Mezo, University of Guam; Donna Michels, St. Xavier University; Michael Miller, Longview

Community College; James Mims, Utah State University; Jim Moody, South Suburban College; Sharon Morrow; Robin Mosher, Kansas State University; Vicki Moss, Fashion Institute of Technology; Shirley Myers, West Valley & De Anza Community Colleges; Sheryl Mylan, University of Houston—Downtown; Carol Newell, Northern Virginia Community College; Karl Nicholas, Western Carolina University; Edward Norwood, California University of Pennsylvania; Lee Nott, Community College of Allegheny County; Kathleen Olds, Erie Community College; James Papworth, Ricks College; Marian O'Brien Paul, Metropolitan Community College; Diana Pavlac, College of the Ozarks; Trudy Peralta, Cerritos College; Robbie Pinter, Belmont University; Elizabeth Pittenger, Florida International University; John Schelling Pollock, Cabrillo College; Lynne Priogen, James Sprunt Community College; D. Ramphal, Brunswick Community College; Libby Rankin, University of North Dakota; Danny Rendleman, University of Michigan—Flint; Linda Riddell, San Bernardino Valley College; Judas Riley, University of Guam; Fredric Rissover, St. Louis Community College—Meramec; Chris Roberts, Clark State Community College; Margaret Roman, College of St. Elizabeth; Connie Rothwell, University of North Carolina—Charlotte; Peter Schiff, Northern Kentucky University; Mary Scott; Carolyn Scott, Simpson College; Larry Severeid, College of Eastern Utah; Virginia Shabatay, Palomar College; Nancy Shankle, Abilene Christian University; Judith Showalter, Miami University; James Simmons, University of North Dakota—Lake Region; Dianna Sims, Cochise College; Martha Sledge, Mississippi College; David Smit, Kansas State University; Jo Smith, Northwestern State University of Louisiana; Stephen Spencer, Wilmington College; David Surowitz, Marshall University; Joanna Tardoni, Western Wyoming Community College; Stephen Thomas, Maysville Community College; Dora Tippens, McHenry County College; Bill Toth, Western New Mexico University; Tramble Turner, Penn State University—Ogontz; John Van Rys, Dordt College; Norma Van Rheenen, Western Michigan University; Kathleen Walsh, Central Oregon Community College; Winifred Wasden, Northwest College; David Wickham, Mountain View College; R. J. Willey, Oakland Community College; James Wilson, University of New Mexico; Carol Wilson, Mission College; Leonard Winograd, Community College of Denver; Michelle Wolkomir, North Carolina State University; Sarah Wood, Murray State University; Linda Woodson, The University of Texas—San Antonio.

For reviewing new readings and critiquing the new metacognitive activities, we thank James Barcus, Baylor University; Richard Bullock, Wright State University; Beverly Chin, University of Montana; Amy Kurata, Kapiolani Community College; David Mair, University of Oklahoma; Michael Miller, Longview Community College; Steve Rayshich, Westmoreland County Community College; Meena Sachdeva, Kapiolani Community College; Peter Schiff, Northern Kentucky University; Lucy Schultz, University of Cincinnati; Nancy Shankle, Abilene Christian University; Paul Sladky, Augusta College;

Alison Warriner, Sacred Heart University; James Wilson, University of New Mexico.

We particularly want to express our enduring gratitude to Marilyn Moller and to her family for putting up with the long hours and interrupted vacations. There is simply no better editor than Marilyn. We are enormously grateful for the grace and intelligence of Mark Gallaher's editing as well as the patience and endurance of Denise Quirk's management of the book and all its ancillaries. We thank Denise as well for her astute revision of the chapters on research. We want to thank Kristin Bowen for her work on the Bologna book and Steven Kutz for all his help. To everyone at St. Martin's Press, we want to convey our deepest appreciation.

The St. Martin's Guide to Writing is enriched also by the work of several people who have written materials to accompany the book. We want to thank Richard Bullock for contributing *The St. Martin's Manual for Writing in the Disciplines: A Guide for Faculty,* Paul Sladky for editing the second edition of *The Great American Bologna Festival and other student essays,* Alison Warriner for composing the new opening section of the *Instructor's Resource Manual,* and Kristin Hawkinson for helping update other sections of the manual. We are especially grateful to the student authors for allowing us to reprint their work in *The Great American Bologna Festival* and in *The St. Martin's Guide.*

Rise wishes to thank her husband Steven for his enduring love, and to dedicate this edition with love to her mother Edna Borenstein, who always told her just to do the best she could—and had faith that she would. Charles wants to thank his wife Mary Anne, who has begun to suspect that adding to the family a successful textbook, with its demands, crises, and rewards, may be a bit like adopting a child. Mary Anne has never lost interest, and she has helped out immeasurably.

A Brief Contents

PART FOUR

Research Strategies

PART FIVE

Writing for Assessment

Handbook

Contents

BASIC FEATURES OF EXPLANATORY ESSAYS, 186

A Well-focused Subject / A Main Point or Thesis / An Appeal to Readers' Interests / A Logical Plan / Clear Definitions / Appropriate Writing Strategies / Careful Use of Sources

GUIDE TO WRITING, 189

THE WRITING ASSIGNMENT, 189

INVENTION AND RESEARCH, 190

Finding a Concept / Exploring the Concept / Focusing on One Aspect of the Concept / Researching Your Subject / Testing Your Choice / For Group Inquiry / Establishing a Main Point / Considering Explanatory Strategies

PLANNING AND DRAFTING, 193

Seeing What You Have / Setting Goals / Outlining / Drafting

GETTING CRITICAL COMMENTS, 195

Reading with a Critical Eye

REVISING AND EDITING, 197

Identifying Problems / Solving the Problems / Editing and Proofreading

A WRITER AT WORK, 202

USING SOURCES, 202

THINKING CRITICALLY ABOUT WHAT YOU'VE LEARNED, 204

Reflecting on Your Writing / Reviewing What You Learned from Reading / Considering the Social Dimensions of Concept Explanations

6 *Taking a Position*   *210*

Writing in Your Other Courses / For Group Inquiry

PURPOSE AND AUDIENCE, 230

BASIC FEATURES OF POSITION PAPERS, 231

A Well-defined Issue / A Clear Position / A Convincing Argument / A Reasonable Tone

GUIDE TO WRITING, 234

THE WRITING ASSIGNMENT, 234

INVENTION AND RESEARCH, 234

Choosing an Issue / Exploring the Issue / Considering Your Purpose and

PART TWO

Critical Thinking Strategies

PART THREE

Writing Strategies

PART FIVE

Writing for Assessment

Handbook

Editing for Problems of Style   *704*

FOURTH EDITION

The St. Martin's Guide to Writing

Why is writing important? Is there a connection between writing and thinking? Can writing be learned? What does reading have to do with learning to write? How can I learn to write more effectively and efficiently? These are some of the questions you may be asking as you begin this writing course. Read on—for *The St. Martin's Guide to Writing* offers some answers for these and other questions you may have.

WHY WRITING IS IMPORTANT

Writing has wide-ranging implications for the way we think and learn, as well as for our chances of success, our personal development, and our relations with other people.

Writing Influences the Way People Think

First, writing encourages us to be organized, logical, even creative in our thinking. Moreover, it urges us to ask questions, to look critically at what others have to say as well as what we ourselves think.

The grammatical and textual conventions of writing impose a certain kind of order on our thinking. To write comprehensible sentences and paragraphs, we need to put words in a certain order: follow subjects with verbs, coordinate parallel ideas, subordinate the particular to the general. And from different kinds of writing, we learn different ways of developing our thoughts: reflecting critically on our own behavior in autobiography; distinguishing fact from opinion in concept explanations; making judgments based on evidence and the dialectic between opposing points of view in position papers. Further, we learn to analyze and evaluate ideas and to synthesize what we learn from others and experience firsthand. In all these ways, writing fosters habits of critical inquiry.

> Writing keeps me from believing everything I read.   –Gloria Steinem

> Those who are learning to compose and arrange their sentences with accuracy and order are learning, at the same time, to think with accuracy and order.
>
> –Hugh Blair

Writing Contributes to the Way We Learn

When we take notes in class or as we read, writing helps us sort information and highlight what is important. Taking notes helps us remember what we are learning and yields a written record to review later. Outlining or summarizing provides an overview of a new subject and also fosters close analysis of it. Annotating as we read, with underlining and marginal comments, involves us in conversation—even debate—with other writers. Thus, writing helps us learn effectively and think critically.

And because we as writers are always composing new meanings, writing helps us find and establish our own knowledge and ideas. It allows us to bring together and connect new and old ideas: as we discover and understand new concepts, writing helps us relate them to other ideas. Thus, writing helps us test, clarify, and extend our understanding of the world.

> I write to understand as much as to be understood.   –Elie Wiesel

> The mere process of writing is one of the most powerful tools we have for clarifying our own thinking. I am never as clear about any matter as when I have just finished writing about it.   –James Van Allen

Writing Promotes Success in College and on the Job

Because writing encourages us to think critically and helps us learn, it also makes a significant contribution to academic and professional success. Students whose writing is logically organized, well-supported, and inventive usually do well in courses throughout the curriculum. Getting a job also depends partially on writing a persuasive application letter, and for many positions advancement requires facility in writing memos, letters, reports, and proposals.

> The aim of school is to produce citizens who are able to communicate with each other, to defend points of view, and to criticize. . . . Writing is not just another subject. There is a symbiotic relationship between writing and thinking.
> –Albert Shanker

Writing Fosters Personal Development

Through writing, we learn to reflect deeply on our personal experience and examine critically our most basic assumptions; thus, we come eventually to understand ourselves better. Moreover, becoming an author confers authority. It gives us the confidence to assert our own opinions, even in situations when others are likely to disagree.

> Writing is the act of saying *I*, of imposing oneself upon other people, of saying *listen to me, see it my way, change your mind.*   –Joan Didion

> Writing has been for a long time my major tool for self-instruction and self-development.   –Toni Cade Bambara

Writing Connects
Us to the World

As writing contributes to the way we think, it also impells us to communicate our thoughts and feelings, to take part in the conversations around us. The impulse to write can be as urgent as the need to share an experience with a friend, to question an argument in a book, or to respond to a provocative comment in class discussion.

As writers, we speak out for many different reasons: to entertain, to let readers know what we think or how we feel, to influence readers' decisions, actions, or beliefs. We may even confront readers, presenting them with a critical view of their attitudes and behavior; in this sense, writing can be a powerful political tool, especially for those who are generally silenced or marginalized.

> Writing is a struggle against silence.   –Carlos Fuentes
>
> Writing is a political instrument . . . a way to describe and control [your] circumstances.   –James Baldwin

EXERCISE 1.1

Reflect on the role writing has played in your education and personal life. Maybe you can recall a time—writing for yourself or for a school assignment—when writing enabled you to think in a way that surprised you. What kind of writing were you doing and what did you discover? Or think of an occasion when you experienced great success with a school assignment. How did this come about and what did you achieve? Or perhaps once you urgently needed to communicate with someone—in anger, love, hope, jealousy, disagreement—and writing seemed the best way to do it. Describe this occasion. What brought it about, what did you say, and what was the response? Write a brief essay, giving specific examples of how writing has affected your life.

HOW WRITING IS LEARNED

Writing is important. But can it be learned? This is a crucial question because writing has for centuries been veiled in mystery. Many people think of writing as magical or the result of natural talent. They assume "real" writers can dash off a perfect draft in one sitting with minimal effort. They believe that if you don't write brilliantly from the start, you'll never learn to write well. However, research shows that these assumptions are wrong, writing can be learned: that in fact, while some people may seem to have a gift for writing, virtually anyone can learn to write confidently enough to handle the writing required in college and on the job.

I believe in miracles in every area of life *except* writing.   –Isaac Bashevis Singer

Learning to write well takes time and much effort, but it can be done.

–Margaret Mead.

As you learn to write, you need to know three things:

how written texts work

how the writing process works

how to think critically about your learning

These three kinds of learning are interdependent: your development as a writer depends on your knowing all three and understanding this interdependence. Written texts are not all alike. Because they differ, they require different writing processes to produce different kinds of products. In this way, process and product are inextricably related, but in complex ways because the social situations calling for writing are so various. As you write in different situations, you need to reflect on what you are doing and learning. Such reflection reinforces and extends your learning.

How Written Texts Work

How a text works is a function of what it's for—its purpose and audience. Some texts—position papers, for example—try to convince readers to take the writer's point of view seriously. Other kinds of texts serve different purposes: an autobiographical essay conveys the significance of a particular event in the writer's life; a proposal urges readers to take certain actions to solve a problem; an explanation informs readers about something they don't know. Kinds of texts, then, can be categorized by their purposes and audiences. These categories are called writing *genres*.

Each genre has its own distinctive formal features and content. Autobiographical event essays, for example, are narrative in form and include descriptive detail and an indication of the event's significance. In contrast, proposals are argumentative in form, giving reasons why readers should adopt the proposed solution.

Although there's a lot of variation from one text to another within the same genre (no two autobiographies, for example, are exactly the same) texts in a genre nonetheless follow a general pattern. This textual patterning allows for a certain amount of predictability, without which communication would be difficult, if not impossible. Language—whether spoken or written—is a system of social interaction. Everyone who speaks the same language learns to recognize certain patterns—what particular words mean when used in different contexts, how words should be ordered to make sentences comprehensible, how sentences can be related to one another to make coherent paragraphs and essays, and so forth. These language patterns make communication possible.

To learn to read and write, we have to become familiar with the patterns or conventions of written texts. As readers, we develop expectations that enable us to anticipate where a text is going so that we can make sense of it as we read. Similarly, as writers we learn how to order and present our thoughts in language patterns that readers can recognize and follow. If you are writing a position paper, for example, you need to know that readers expect claims to be supported by relevant reasons and evidence.

Working within a genre does not mean, however, that writing must be formulaic or mechanical. Each genre has basic features but these are not a formula; rather, they provide broad frameworks within which writers are free to create. Most writers, in fact, find that working in a framework allows them to be more creative, not less. Some even blur the boundaries between genres. Innovations like these lead to change.

Change, as well as predictability, is built into the language system. Ultimately, effective texts must reflect changing social contexts, bringing together many competing interests and creating new forms of expression for those who have traditionally been silent.

> To write as a complete Caribbean woman, or man for that matter, demands of us retracing the African part of ourselves. It means finding the art forms of our ancestors and speaking in the *patois* forbidden us. It means also, I think, mixing in the forms taught us by the oppressor, undermining his language and co-opting his style, and turning it to our purpose.   –Michelle Cliff

How We Learn to Write Texts That Work.   To learn the conventions of a particular genre, you need to read examples of the genre. At the same time, you should also practice writing in the genre.

> Read, read, read. . . . Just like a carpenter who works as an apprentice and studies the master. Read!   –William Faulkner

Reading is crucial. As you read examples of a genre, you begin to recognize the predictable patterns as well as the possibilities for innovation. This knowledge is stored in memory and used both when you read and when you write in the genre.

Experienced writers read and learn from positive examples as well as negative ones. Sometimes, they focus on a particular problem—how to write realistic-sounding dialogue, for example. They don't look for answers in a single model, but sample many texts to see how different writers work with this feature of the genre. This is not imitation, but education. Like artists and craftsmen of all kinds, writers have always learned from other writers.

> I went back to the good nature books that I had read. And I analyzed them. I wrote outlines of whole books—outlines of chapters—so that I could see their structure. And I copied down their transitional sentences or their main sentences

or their closing sentences or their lead sentences. I especially paid attention to how these writers made transitions between paragraphs and scenes.

–Annie Dillard

EXERCISE 1.2

We've said that to learn to write in a particular genre, you need to read texts in that genre. To test this idea, make two lists: (1) the genres you've read [*variety or type*] recently (such as explanations of how to do something, stories, autobiographies, reports of current events, opinion pieces, reviews evaluating something); and (2) the genres you've written in and out of school. Based on your experience, does it help to have read something in the genre you are trying to write? Why, or why not? *yes; gives a pattern, giving new ideas to write about!*

How the Writing Process Works

Have you ever tried the dangerous method of writing? You begin by writing the first word of the introduction and write straight through to the last word of the conclusion. No planning or trying out ideas before writing; no adding, cutting, or revising as you write; no help from friends or teachers; no second drafts or second thoughts.

Desperate students, the night before a paper is due, may try the dangerous method. But it isn't a very smart way to write. All writers need to develop a process that will help them think critically about their subject and master the genre. They need to make writing a true process of discovery.

I don't see writing as a communication of something already discovered, as "truths" already known. Rather, I see writing as a job of experiment. It's like any discovery job; you don't know what's going to happen until you try it.

–William Stafford

recursive

Research on how writers write shows that the writing process is recursive, rather than linear. Instead of going from one word to the next, from introduction straight through to conclusion, the experience of writing is more like taking a path up a hill full of switchbacks, making you feel you're covering old ground when you're really rising to a new level.

linear- involving measurement in only one dimension; composed of or involving lines

Few writers begin with a complete understanding of their subject. Most use writing as a process of learning, recording ideas and information they've collected, exploring connections and implications, letting the writing lead them to greater understanding. As they develop their ideas and plan their draft, writers set goals for their writing: goals for the whole essay (to confront readers or inspire them, for example) and goals for particular passages (to make a sentence emphatic or include details in a paragraph). While writing, they often pause to reread what they've written to see whether they are satisfactorily fulfilling their goals. Rereading may lead to further invention and problem solving, to rewording or reorganizing, or even to reconsidering some goals. This continual shifting of attention is what makes the process

recursive. Invention doesn't stop when drafting begins; it continues throughout the process. Most writers plan and revise their plans; they draft and revise
their drafts; they write and read what they've written, then write some more.
Even when they have a final draft, most writers reread it one more time—
proofreading to edit for clarity, grammar, and spelling.

> You are always going back and forth between the outline and the writing, bring-
> ing them closer together, or just throwing out the outline and making a new
> one.   –Annie Dillard

Experienced writers depend on the writing process to lead them to new
ideas and insights. Many writers claim that they write in order to discover
what they think.

> How do I know what I think until I see what I say.   –E. M. Forster

Seasoned writers don't wait for inspiration. They work at their writing,
knowing it takes time and perseverence. The hard work comes in thinking
things out. Writers all have promising ideas, but until they've developed them
in writing, they can't know if their ideas make sense or lead anywhere.

> Don't think and then write it down. Think on paper.   –Harvey Kemelman

Once immersed in invention—figuring out what they want to say about
the subject, contemplating what readers already think about it, and so forth—
most writers find that they continue the process even when away from their
desks. Taking a walk, having a conversation, even dreaming can help the mind
see connections or solve problems that had proved frustrating earlier.

> I never quite know when I'm not writing.   –James Thurber

Like most creative activities, writing is a form of problem-solving. As they
work on a draft, most writers continually discover and try to solve writing
problems—how to bring a scene to life, how to handle objections, whether
to begin with this point or that. The more a writer knows about the subject
and genre, the better he or she can anticipate and solve problems. Experienced writers develop a repertoire of invention and writing strategies for solving problems they are likely to encounter. These are the tools of the trade.

> Writing is probably like a scientist thinking about some scientific problem, or an
> engineer about an engineering problem.   –Doris Lessing
>
> You have to work problems out for yourself on paper. Put the stuff down and
> read it–to see if it works.   –Joyce Cary

Although many writers do much of their work alone, writing does not
have to be a solitary activity. Most writers share their ideas as well as their
writing, actively seeking constructive critical comments from friends and col-

leagues. Playwrights, poets, and novelists attend writers' workshops, where other writers can read their drafts and offer suggestions for revising. Engineers, business executives, scientists, and government workers do much of their writing collaboratively, in teams.

> For excellence, the presence of others is always required.   –Hannah Arendt

> I like working collaboratively from time to time. I like fusing ideas into one vision. I like seeing that vision come to life with other people who know exactly what it took to get there.   –Amy Tan

EXERCISE 1.3

> Writing is like jumping into a freezing lake and slowly coming to the surface.
> –A student

> To me, writing is a horseback ride into heaven and hell and back. I am grateful if I can crawl back alive.   –Thomas Sanchez

How would you describe your own writing process? Think of a simile (writing is like _____) or a metaphor (writing is _____) that best expresses your view of writing. Compare your similes or metaphors with your classmates'. What do they suggest about your feelings toward writing?

How We Learn a Writing Process That Works.   As a student learning to write, you need to develop a writing process that is flexible and yet provides structure, doesn't oversimplify the process but doesn't overwhelm you either, helps you learn about your subject and about writing the kind of essay you're attempting. What you need are the Guides to Writing in Part I of this book. These guides suggest what you need to think about for each different writing situation. The first few times you write in a new genre, you can rely on these guidelines. Until you've become familiar with the basic features and strategies of each genre, these guidelines provide a scaffolding to support your work.

When engaging in any new and complex activity—driving, playing an instrument, skiing, or writing—we have to learn procedures or routines. These basically break down the activity into a series of stages or steps. In learning to play tennis, for example, you can isolate lobbing from volleying, or work on your backhand or serve. Similarly, in writing about an autobiographical event, you might first recall what happened, then fill in details of the scene or reflect on the event's significance. At each point you focus your attention on one problem or issue at a time. Dividing the process in this way makes a complex writing task manageable without oversimplifying it.

> You know when you think about writing a book, you think it is overwhelming. But, actually, you break it down into tiny little tasks any moron could do.
> –Annie Dillard

EXERCISE 1.4

Describe how you normally write. How much time do you spend thinking and making notes before writing a draft? What kinds of things do you do to help with invention—read what others have written, talk with friends, do freewriting, cluster your ideas, or whatever? How many drafts do you usually write? Do you share your drafts with friends or teachers to get their critical comments? What do you do when you revise a draft—change the wording, rearrange parts, cut or add whole sections? Do you proofread for clarity, grammar, and spelling? If so, at what point in the process?

How to
Think Critically
about Your
Learning

Research on learning makes it clear that thinking about your learning helps you remember what you've learned. It also helps you continue learning by bringing to mind what you've forgotten or didn't realize you knew.

Learning to write is like learning a foreign language. As young children, we are immersed in spoken language and acquire it naturally, almost effortlessly. In contrast, learning to write requires conscious effort. As beginners, we need to think about what we're doing—what verb tense to use, whether to use slang or more formal words, whether to concede a point or try to refute it, and so on.

As you practice different kinds, or genres, of writing, you will find that many of your decisions do not require conscious attention. You will be able to rely on strategies you know usually produce effective writing for you in that genre. But these strategies will not work in every case simply because every writing situation is unique. When you encounter a problem, you have to shift gears and deliberately seek a new way to solve the problem.

To find solutions, you have to bring to consciousness your knowledge of the genre and the writing process. Observations of writers at work show that experienced writers often reread what they have written to analyze and evaluate the approach they've taken to a writing problem. This reflection on what works and what does not helps writers anticipate and solve problems. It also helps them feel more competent and in charge of the process.

> Blot out, correct, insert, refine,
> Enlarge, diminish, interline,
> Be mindful, when invention fails,
> To scratch your head, and bite your nails.   —Jonathan Swift

How We Learn to Think Critically about Our Learning.   The exercises in this chapter are designed to help you begin thinking, writing, and talking with others about your writing experiences. As we've seen, such self-reflection is a key to learning to be a better writer. Each assignment chapter in Part I of this book concludes with a section, Thinking Critically about What You've Learned, that gives you an opportunity to look back and reflect on your own problem-solving process, the influence your reading of other texts in the genre has had on your own text, and what you've learned about the social dimensions of the genre, the ways that thinking and writing in the genre both reflect and are reflected by the society in which it is produced and consumed.

> I may remember some of the things that were said by the countless millions of words I've read, but finally what I've taken away . . . are habits of understanding, methods of reasoning, points of view, ranges of feeling . . . my mind is not merely mine, but is inhabited by a multitude of borrowed voices.   –William Gass

> To speak [or write] English is to think in that language, to adopt the ideology of the people whose language it is and to be 'inhabited' by their discourses.
>
> –Gloria Anzaldúa

EXERCISE 1.5

What do you hope to learn in this course? Write a brief account of your strengths and weaknesses as a writer. What specific improvements do you hope to make in your writing—in the texts you produce as well as the process you use?

USING THIS BOOK

This book is divided into several major sections.

Part I offers writing assignments for several important genres of nonfiction prose: autobiography, firsthand biography, profile, explanation, position paper, proposal, evaluation, causal analysis, and literary interpretation.

Parts II through V provide strategies for invention and critical reading, writing, and research. They also provide guidelines for writing research papers and using sources and for taking essay exams and assembling a portfolio.

Each writing assignment chapter in Part I provides readings from which you can learn how written texts of that kind work, and a Guide to Writing to lead you through the process of writing an essay of your own. In each chapter, you will also find a separate discussion of purpose and audience, and a summary of the basic features and strategies of the genre. At the end of each chapter, a section on Thinking Critically about What You've Learned will help you reflect on and consolidate your learning.

The *readings* in each chapter were written by professional writers as well as students using earlier editions of this book. They were selected to reflect a wide range of topics and voices. Reading these selections with a critical eye, you will see the many different ways writers use the genre.

Each reading selection is accompanied by questions and commentary to help you learn something about how written texts in the genre work. Following the reading are three groups of questions and some commentary: Questions *for discussion* invite you to explore with other students the social dimensions of the text; questions *for analysis* focus on key textual features and writing strategies; suggestions *for your own writing* offer topics you might write about; and the *commentary* points out additional features and strategies.

The *Guide to Writing* in each assignment chapter offers detailed guidelines for writing an essay in that genre, including help in invention and research, planning and drafting, getting critical comments, and revising and editing.

Invention and Research

Each guide begins with invention activities designed to help you find a topic, discover what you already know about it, consider your purpose and audience, research the topic further to see what others have written about it, and develop your ideas.

Invention is not something you can skip. It is the basic ongoing preoccupation of all writing. As writers, we cannot choose *whether* to invent; we can only decide *how*.

Invention can be especially productive when it is systematic—and when it is written down. Not only does it focus your attention on your purpose and audience, but it then helps you identify and solve problems. Exploratory writing can free you for awhile from the responsibility of composing coherent and grammatical prose and paragraphs and thus allow you to write more freely about your topic—turning writing into a mode of discovery.

Invention work may help you at several stages: while exploring your topic, while drafting, and while revising. The special advantage of the invention activities in each Part I chapter is that they focus on the issues of a particular kind of writing.

Use Writing to Explore Your Ideas. You can use writing to gather your thoughts and see where they lead. Simply try writing for five to ten minutes. The key to exploratory writing is to refrain from censoring yourself. Explore your ideas freely, letting one idea lead to another. Later you can reread what you've written and select the most promising ideas to develop.

Focus on One Issue at a Time. Explore your topic systematically by dividing it into its component parts and exploring them one at a time. For example, instead of trying to think of your whole argument, focus on one reason and the evidence you could use to support it or focus on how you might refute *disprove* one objection to your argument.

seep, filter

Give Your Ideas Time to Percolate. Begin the process well enough in advance of the deadline so that your thinking can develop fully. Spread your invention over several days, allowing your mind time to work on the topic.

Planning and Drafting

Once an initial period of invention is completed, you should review what you have learned about your topic and start to plan your essay. The Guides to Writing provide help from setting goals to organizing your ideas and information to achieve those goals. Planning requires you to put your ideas into a coherent, purposeful order appropriate to your readers; drafting challenges you to find the words that will be understandable and interesting for those readers. Invention continues as you draft, for you will make further discoveries about your topic as you work. But drafting requires you to shift your focus from generating new ideas and gathering further information to forging new and meaningful relations among your ideas and information.

As you begin your first draft, you should try to keep in mind a number of helpful and practical points, many of which have assisted professional writers as they begin drafting.

Choose the Best Time and Place.   You can write a draft any time and any place, as you probably already know. Writing gets done under the most surprising conditions. Drafting is likely to go smoothly, however, if you choose a time and place ideally suited for sustained and thoughtful work. The experience of writers (reported mainly in interviews) suggests that you need a place where you can concentrate for a few hours without repeated interruptions. Many writers find one place where they write best, and they return to that place whenever they have to write. Try to find such a place for yourself.

Make Revision Easy.   Write on only one side of the page. Leave wide margins. Write on every other line or triple-space your typing. Laying your draft out on the page this way invites changes, additions, cutting, and rearranging when you revise. If possible, compose on a word processor.

Set Reasonable Goals.   Divide the task into manageable bits. A goal of completing a long essay may be so intimidating that it keeps you from starting. Just aim for a small part of the essay—one section or paragraph—at a time.

Lower Your Expectations.   Be satisfied with less than perfect writing. Remember, you are working on a draft that you will revise. Approach the draft as an experiment or an exercise. Try things out. Follow digressions. Later, you can always go back and cross out a sentence or a section. And do not be critical about your writing; save the criticism until you've gotten some distance from your draft.

Do Easy Parts First.   Try not to agonize over the first sentence or paragraph. Just write. If you have trouble with the introduction, write an anecdote or example or assertion first, if that seems easier. If you have a lot of information, start with the part you understand best. If you get stuck at a difficult spot, skip over it and go on to an easier part. Just getting started can be difficult, but doing the simple parts first may ease this difficulty. If you put off getting started, your work will be rushed and late. Your ideas will not grow and change, and you will thus shut off your chances for important new insights about your topic. By starting late, you will increase your fear of writing; but by starting early with an easy part, you will find writing easier and more enjoyable. You will also do your best work.

Guess at Words, Spelling, Facts.   If you cannot think of just the right word, or if you have forgotten an important fact, just keep on drafting. You can search out the fact or find the elusive word later. If you cannot remember how to spell a word, guess and keep going. Later, you can look it up in a dictionary. Inexperienced writers lose large amounts of time puzzling over a word or spelling or trying to recall a specific fact. Sometimes they become completely blocked.

Write Quickly.   If you have reasonable goals, have not set your expectations too high, and are doing the easy parts first, then you should be able to draft quickly. Say what you want to say and move on. Review your notes, make a plan, and then put your notes aside. You can always refer to them later if you need an exact quote or fact. Now and then, of course, you will want to reread what you have written, but do not reread obsessively. Return to drafting new material as soon as possible. Avoid editing or revising during this stage. You need not have everything exactly right in the draft. If you want to delete a phrase or sentence, draw a line through it or use your word processor's strike-out function, in case you want to use the phrase or sentence later.

Take Short Breaks—and Reward Yourself!   Drafting can be hard work, and you may need to take a break to refresh yourself. But be careful not to wander off for too long or you may lose momentum. Set small goals and reward yourself regularly. That makes it easier to stay at the task of drafting.

Reading with a Critical Eye

After you have finished drafting your essay, you may want to show it to someone else for comments and advice on how to improve it. Experienced writers very often seek advice from others.

To evaluate someone else's draft, you need to read with a critical eye. You must be both positive and skeptical—positive in that you are trying to identify what is workable and promising in the draft, skeptical in that you need to question the writer's assumptions and decisions.

Here is some general advice on reading any draft critically.

Make a Record of Your Reading.   While talking over your impressions of a draft may be pleasurable and useful, you can be most helpful by putting your ideas on paper. When you write down your comments and suggestions—either on the draft or on another piece of paper—you leave a record that can be used later when it is time to revise.

Read First for an Overall Impression.   On first reading, try not to be distracted by errors of spelling, punctuation, or word choice. Look at big issues: clear focus, compelling presentation, forcefulness of argument, novelty and quality of ideas. What seems particularly good? What problems do you see? All you need to say is how the draft struck you initially: what you think it was trying to do and how well it did it. Write just a few sentences expressing your initial reaction.

Read Again to Analyze the Draft. This second reading focuses on individual parts of the draft, bringing to bear what you know about the genre and what you already know about the subject.

In reading the draft at this level, you must shift your attention from one aspect of the essay to another. Consider how well the opening paragraphs introduce the essay and prepare the reader to understand and accept it. Attend to subtle shifts in tone as well as more obvious writing strategies.

As you analyze, you are evaluating as well as describing, but a critical reading should not be merely an occasion for criticizing the draft. A good critical reader helps a writer see how each part works and how all the parts work together. By describing what you see, you help the writer see the draft more objectively, a perspective that is necessary for thoughtful revising.

Offer Advice, but Do Not Rewrite. As a critical reader, you may be tempted to rewrite the draft—to change a word here, correct an error there, add your ideas everywhere. Resist the impulse. Your role is to read carefully, to point out what you think is or is not working, to make suggestions and ask questions. Leave the revising to the writer.

In turn, the writer has a responsibility to listen to your comments but is under no obligation to do as you suggest. Then why go to all the trouble, you might ask. There are at least two reasons. First, when you read someone else's writing critically, you learn more about writing—about the decisions writers make, how a thoughtful reader reads, and the constraints of particular kinds of writing. Second, you play an instrumental role in constructing a text. As a critical reader, you embody for the writer the abstraction called "audience." By sharing your reaction and analysis with the writer, you complete the circuit of communication.

Revising

Even productive invention and smooth drafting rarely result in the essay a writer has imagined. Experienced writers are not surprised or disappointed when this happens, however. They expect to revise a draft—unless an imminent deadline precludes revising. They know that revising will move them closer to the essay they really want to write. Reading their drafts thoughtfully and critically—and perhaps reflecting on critical readings by others—they see many opportunities for improvement. They may notice misspelled words or garbled sentences; most important, however, they discover ways to delete, move, rephrase, and add material in order to say what they want to say more clearly and thoughtfully.

View the Draft Objectively.   To revise, you must first read your draft objectively, to see what it actually says instead of what you intended it to say. If you can, put the draft aside for a day or two. Getting another reader to describe the draft can also help you to view it more objectively.

Reconsider Your Purpose and Audience.   Ask yourself what you are trying to accomplish. Does your purpose still seem appropriate for these particular readers? How could you modify the essay to make it more effective? Consider each problem and possible solution in light of your overall writing strategy.

Revise in Stages.   Do not try to do everything at once. Begin by looking at the whole and then move to an analysis of the parts. Focus initially on identifying problems; consider possible solutions only after you have a general understanding of how the draft fails to achieve its purpose.

Look at Big Problems First.   Identify major problems that keep the draft from achieving its purpose. Does the essay have a clear focus, a compelling presentation, a consistent and appropriate tone? Are the ideas interesting and developed? Does the essay have all the features that readers will expect?

Focus Next on Clarity and Coherence.   Consider the beginning. How well does it prepare readers for the essay? Look at each section of the essay in turn. Do the paragraphs proceed in a logical order? Are there appropriate transitions to help readers follow from one point to the next? Are generalizations firmly and explicitly connected to specific details, examples, or supporting evidence?

Save Stylistic Changes and Grammatical Corrections for Last.   Do not focus on word choice or sentence structure until you are generally satisfied with what you have written. Then carefully consider your style and diction. Focus primarily on key terms to be sure they are appropriate and well defined.

Editing

Once you have finished revising, you then want to edit carefully to make sure that every word, phrase, and sentence is clear and correct. Using language and punctuation correctly is an essential part of good writing. Errors will distract readers and lessen your credibility as a writer.

Save editing until the end. Turn your attention to editing only *after* you have planned and worked out a revision. Too much editing too early in the writing process can limit, even block, invention and drafting.

Keep a List of Your Common Errors.   Note down grammatical and spelling errors you discover in your own writing. Most likely you'll soon recognize error patterns, things to check for as you edit your work.

Begin Proofreading with the Last Sentence.   To focus your attention on grammar and spelling, it may help to read backwards, beginning with the last sentence. Most writers get diverted thinking about what they are saying rather than how. Reading backwards makes it harder to pay attention to content, and thus easier to recognize writing problems.

Exchange Drafts with Another Student.   Because it is usually easier to see errors in someone else's writing than in your own, you might consider trading essays with a classmate and proofreading one another's writing.

Thinking Critically about What You've Learned

Each chapter in Part I concludes with a set of activities to help you think about what you've learned studying the genre in that chapter. There are three different activities: reflecting on your writing process to see how you solved problems writing that particular kind of essay; reviewing what you learned from reading essays of the type you were writing to see what specific influence your reading had on your writing; considering the social dimensions of the genre to explore how thinking and writing reflect and are reflected by the cultural context in which they are written.

If you are compiling a portfolio on your coursework to hand in at the end of the term, these reflections may help you assess your work.

Writing Activities

■ A scientist writes a book about a discovery she and several colleagues made, one that revolutionized scientific knowledge in her field. She tells the dramatic story of the race between her research team and a rival group at another university. Her team had nearly solved the problem when they heard a rumor that the other researchers had made a breakthrough. She confesses that she actually broke down and cried, imagining the Nobel Prize being awarded to her rivals. The rumor turned out to be false, and her team did indeed get credit for the discovery. She admits how jealous and frustrated she felt, commenting that scientists may strive for objectivity and disinterestedness but are really emotionally invested in their work and quite competitive.

■ In her autobiography, a black writer recalls her high school graduation from an all-black school in rural Arkansas in 1940. She writes about how very proud she felt until a white superintendent of schools made a condescending and insulting speech. Describing his speech and the self-hatred it inspired in her, she remembers thinking that she alone was suffering until she heard the restrained applause and recognized the proud defiance in everyone's eyes. Thus the incident, in many ways so grim, actually renewed her sense of pride.

■ Asked to recall a significant early childhood memory for a psychology class, a student writes about a fishing trip he took when he was nine. He reflects that the trip was signifi-cant because it was the first he ever took alone with his father and that it heralded a new stage in their relationship. He remembers wanting to go fishing but being afraid that he would do something wrong like getting seasick or losing the rod and disappointing his dad. He focuses the essay on one particular incident—his attempt to land a big fish. He writes that his first impulse was to panic and try to hand the rod to his father, but his dad insisted that he could handle it. During a struggle that seemed to last an hour but probably took only ten minutes, his dad sat beside him, offering advice and encouragement. Afterward, his dad said how proud he was and took his picture with the fish, a five-pound bass.

Remembering Events 2

■ A student in a sociology class studying friendship patterns writes a personal essay about the time in junior high when a girls' gang tried to enlist her. Though she didn't know any of the gang members, she guessed they wanted her because they heard she was taking karate lessons. She describes how frightened she was when they demanded to meet with her after school and then how relieved she felt after they decided she wasn't tough enough. As she writes about this incident, she is able to chuckle at her actions and feelings at the time.

Why do people write autobiographical stories? Perhaps out of nostalgia for the past, but perhaps as well to make sense of the past. When we write about significant events in our lives, we come to know ourselves better, bringing into focus what's truly important to us and clarifying our beliefs and values. We also examine the forces—within ourselves and in our social structures—that have shaped our lives and perspectives.

In addition, writing about our lives for others to read—and reading about other people's lives—can help us better understand one another. Often, we can see in other people's autobiography reflections of our own lives. Yet we also are reminded of the differences among us: reading autobiography teaches us to celebrate individuality. It also shows us how the material conditions of our lives—whether we are rich or poor, male or female, black or white, young or old—may affect how we think of ourselves as well as how we're treated by others.

Writing about our lives for others to read is not the same as writing for yourself. As a writer, you must remember that autobiography is public, not private. While it invites self-disclosure, writing autobiography need not be confessional. You get to choose how you want to represent yourself, to decide what aspect of your life to write about, what side of yourself to reveal. Your choice depends on the rhetorical situation in which you are writing: who you expect to read your story (your audience) and what you want them to learn about you from it (your purpose). We obviously are *not* exactly the same in every situation, and don't necessarily want others to respond to us in the same way all the time. Based on our purpose in writing to a particular audience, we make choices on how to present ourselves, sometimes taking risks and at other times playing it safe.

The scenarios that open this chapter suggest some of the complex rhetorical situations we encounter when writing about our experiences. The scientist in the first scenario, for example, reveals having feelings about her work that are not usually associated with the cool, disinterested practice of science. Making public this kind of personal disclosure may be risky because she knows that some readers will look down on her for "getting emotional"; they might even take her experience as proof that women are not fit to be scientists. We can only conjecture about why she decided to present herself this way: perhaps she wanted to challenge these attitudes and question assumptions about scientific objectivity, or maybe she just wanted to give nonscientists a behind-the-scenes glimpse into the competitive world of scientific research.

The point to remember is that based on their purpose and audience, all writers make choices about how they present themselves. Writing about personal experience involves fashioning a self in words much as a novelist constructs a character. As readers, we come to "know" the people we read about by the way they are described as well as by what they say and do.

As you work through this chapter, you will learn to present yourself purposefully by telling the story of your experience. You will learn to organize and pace the action to create dramatic tension; to describe scenes and people to make the story vivid and specific; to convey through words and images the event's significance to make the story meaningful.

Storytelling, you will discover, is an essential strategy in both academic and professional writing. Not only are some essays organized narratively like stories, but even essays organized topically often include the brief, "telling" stories we call anecdotes as illustrations for the main ideas.

Writing in Your Other Courses

In college, you may well have occasion to write about some of your personal experiences for your courses. Consider, for example, the following typical assignments:

- *For a psychology course:* Erik Erikson observed that "young people . . . are sometimes preoccupied with what they appear to be in the eyes of others as compared with what they feel they are." Test this idea against your own adolescent experience. Recount a single event when you cared tremendously about what your peers thought about you. How did their judgment influence your behavior and your sense of self?

- *For a sociology course:* Case studies of victimization have shown that victims tend to become distrustful and socially isolated. If you have had the unfortunate experience of being a victim, write briefly about what happened and how it has affected your social interactions.

- *For a political science course:* Voter apathy is known to be a widespread problem, but not much is known about the origins of voting behavior. Recall the first time you became interested in an election, and tell about the incident in some detail. Looking back on the incident, what did it teach you about the origins of your own voting behavior?

- *For a linguistics course:* Many linguists argue that grammar and word choice are social constructs, that "appropriateness" always depends on some context. Recall an occasion when you used language that others considered inappropriate or offensive. What did you say or write? How did you know your language had gone over prescribed boundaries? If you did it on purpose, explain why.

In this chapter, you will write about a significant event in your own life. But first you will read several examples of lively, engaging autobiographical stories that should give you ideas for writing about your own remembered event.

For Group Inquiry

The scenarios that open this chapter suggest some occasions for writing about events from one's life. Imagine that you have been asked to write about some childhood experience. Think of an event or incident that might "say something" about your life. It can be something startling, amusing, sad, exciting, whatever. The only requirement is for it to seem important to you now and for you to remember it well enough to tell about it.

Get together with two or three other students, and "try out" your stories on one another. You can be brief—three or four minutes each will do. After each story is told, go around the group for each member to say something about what the incident told (or suggested) about its author. Does everyone "hear" the same thing?

Then, as a group, discuss the rhetorical situation of telling about a remembered event by considering the following points:

■ Why did you choose the incident you did?

■ How did the audience—that is, the group—affect your choice?

■ What exactly did you want the others to learn from your story?

■ Are you surprised by what they said they learned about you?

■ What have you learned about telling autobiographical stories purposefully by working in a group that you might not have learned by working alone?

Readings

Annie Dillard won the Pulitzer prize for her very first book, *Pilgrim at Tinker Creek*. In that book, she describes herself as "no scientist," merely "a wanderer with a background in theology and a penchant for quirky facts." She has since written many other books, including collections of poetry, essays, and literary theory, as well as her autobiography, *An American Childhood*, from which this selection is taken.

In "Handed My Own Life," we see the early stirrings of Dillard's lifelong enthusiasm for learning and fascination with nature. As you read her story, think about why she wrote it. What do you think she wanted to tell readers about herself? What impression do you have of Annie Dillard from reading the story?

**HANDED MY
OWN LIFE**
ANNIE DILLARD

After I read *The Field Book of Ponds and Streams* several times, I longed for a   1
microscope. Everybody needed a microscope. Detectives used microscopes, both for
the FBI and at Scotland Yard. Although usually I had to save my tiny allowance for
things I wanted, that year for Christmas my parents gave me a microscope kit.

In a dark basement corner, on a white enamel table, I set up the microscope kit.   2
I supplied a chair, a lamp, a batch of jars, a candle, and a pile of library books. The
microscope kit supplied a blunt black three-speed microscope, a booklet, a scalpel,
a dropper, an ingenious device for cutting thin segments of fragile tissue, a pile of
clean slides and cover slips, and a dandy array of corked test tubes.

One of the test tubes contained "hay infusion." Hay infusion was a wee brown   3
chip of grass blade. You added water to it, and after a week it became a jungle in
a drop, full of one-celled animals. This did not work for me. All I saw in the microscope after a week was a wet chip of dried grass, much enlarged.

Another test tube contained "diatomaceous earth." This was, I believed, an ac-   4
tual pinch of the white cliffs of Dover. On my palm it was an airy, friable chalk. The
booklet said it was composed of the silicaceous bodies of diatoms—one-celled creatures that lived in, as it were, small glass jewelry boxes with fitted lids. Diatoms, I
read, come in a variety of transparent geometrical shapes. Broken and dead and dug
out of geological deposits, they made chalk, and a fine abrasive used in silver polish
and toothpaste. What I saw in the microscope must have been the fine abrasive—
grit enlarged. It was years before I saw a recognizable, whole diatom. The kit's
diatomaceous earth was a bust.

All that winter I played with the microscope. I prepared slides from things at   5
hand, as the books suggested. I looked at the transparent membrane inside an
onion's skin and saw the cells. I looked at a section of cork and saw the cells, and
at scrapings from the inside of my cheek, ditto. I looked at my blood and saw not
much; I looked at my urine and saw long iridescent crystals, for the drop had dried.

All this was very well, but I wanted to see the wildlife I had read about. I wanted   6
especially to see the famous amoeba, who had eluded me. He was supposed to live
in the hay infusion, but I hadn't found him there. He lived outside in warm ponds
and streams, too, but I lived in Pittsburgh, and it had been a cold winter.

Finally late that spring I saw an amoeba. The week before, I had gathered puddle   7
water from Frick Park; it had been festering in a jar in the basement. This June night
after dinner I figured I had waited long enough. In the basement at my microscope
table I spread a scummy drop of Frick Park puddle water on a slide, peeked in, and
lo, there was the famous amoeba. He was as blobby and grainy as his picture; I
would have known him anywhere.

Before I had watched him at all, I ran upstairs. My parents were still at table,   8
drinking coffee. They, too, could see the famous amoeba. I told them, bursting, that
he was all set up, that they should hurry before his water dried. It was the chance
of a lifetime.

Father had stretched out his long legs and was tilting back in his chair. Mother   9
sat with her knees crossed, in blue slacks, smoking a Chesterfield. The dessert dishes
were still on the table. My sisters were nowhere in evidence. It was a warm evening;
the big dining-room windows gave onto blooming rhododendrons.

Mother regarded me warmly. She gave me to understand that she was glad I   10
had found what I had been looking for, but that she and Father were happy to sit
with their coffee, and would not be coming down.

She did not say, but I understood at once, that they had their pursuits (coffee?) 11 and I had mine. She did not say, but I began to understand then, that you do what you do out of your private passion for the thing itself.

I had essentially been handed my own life. In subsequent years my parents would 12 praise my drawings and poems, and supply me with books, art supplies, and sports equipment, and listen to my troubles and enthusiasms, and supervise my hours, and discuss and inform, but they would not get involved with my detective work, nor hear about my reading, nor inquire about my homework or term papers or exams, nor visit the salamanders I caught, nor listen to me play the piano, nor attend my field hockey games, nor fuss over my insect collection with me, or my poetry collection or stamp collection or rock collection. My days and nights were my own to plan and fill.

When I left the dining room that evening and started down the dark basement 13 stairs, I had a life, I sat to my wonderful amoeba, and there he was, rolling his grains more slowly now, extending an arc of his edge for a foot and drawing himself along by that foot, and absorbing it again and rolling on. I gave him some more pond water.

I had hit pay dirt. For all I knew, there were paramecia, too, in that pond water, 14 or daphniae, or stentors, or any of the many other creatures I had read about and never seen: volvox, the spherical algal colony; euglena with its one red eye; the elusive, glassy diatom; hydra, rotifers, water bears, worms. Anything was possible. The sky was the limit.

For Discussion

Are you surprised by her parents' attitude or Dillard's reaction to it? Why, or why not? Why do you think Dillard makes the point that her parents continued to give her support and approval, while at the same time encouraging her to be independent? Recall your own experience of becoming independent from your parents or older mentors. What happened? How did you feel about it at the time? How do you feel about it now as you look back? Do you think that making this separation is really necessary? Discuss these questions with the students in your group.

Then think about your experience of collaborating with other students. How has the discussion helped you clarify and extend your thinking? Compare and contrast the experience of collaborating with peers to that of discussing your interests with parents or mentors, as Dillard tried to do.

For Analysis

1. Dillard's is a simple chronological narrative, but covers a long period, from Christmas to late spring. Outline the story, listing everything that happened during that stretch of time. Then, ask yourself why Dillard included it all: what role does each item on your list play in her story? Also notice how much space she devotes to each item. Given its relative importance, how much space would you give each item if you were rewriting the story?

2. Notice that the narrative leading up to the big discovery reports some things Dillard did routinely and some that happened only once. While she shows the one-time incidents in particular detail, for the recurring activities

she generalizes, summarizing what typically occurred. Mark on your outline which items are recurring and which are one-time occurrences.

3.   Writing about remembered events often features description of people and places. Look closely at the scene described in paragraphs 8–11. What dominant impression do you get of Dillard's parents from this description? Which words and phrases contribute most memorably to this impression?

For a discussion of dominant impression, see pp. 494–95.

4.   Here are some of the verbs Dillard uses in paragraph 7: *saw, had gathered, had been festering, figured, spread, was, would have known. Saw, figured, spread,* and *was* are simple past tense verbs. The other verbs are different. Without knowing their technical names, you can learn something important about writing about remembered events by examining these verbs closely. Skim the essay, underlining all the verbs that are not in the simple past tense. What do these different verb tenses allow Dillard to do as she tells her story?

For Your Own Writing

Think of some occasions when you recall learning something important or making a significant discovery. List them. Then, choose one occasion that you would be interested in writing about for readers who don't know you. What would you want them to learn about you from reading your essay?

Commentary

"Handed My Own Life" illustrates two basic features of writing about remembered events: a well-told story and an indication of its autobiographical significance. Good storytelling attracts readers' interest and makes us want to read on to find out what happened. Autobiographical significance gives a story its meaning. If the story didn't interest us, we wouldn't read it; if it didn't have significance, we would find it pointless.

Dillard attracts our interest immediately by presenting a self with which we can readily identify. Even if we've never wanted a microscope, we've all *longed for, needed, wanted* something as badly as she wants the microscope. We wonder what she'll do with it. Curiosity spurs our interest. Once she's on the track of the elusive amoeba, we wonder whether she'll find it.

In addition to arousing our curiosity, a story also has to have a point: it has to lead somewhere. What starts out as a simple story about a child's enthusiasm for a new toy takes a surprising turn. She not only discovers the amoeba, but also discovers something important about herself and her relationship with her parents. This discovery gives the event its significance. To be significant, an event needn't be earthshaking. Dillard's surely isn't. Her experience is significant because it taught her something she can generalize and apply to other situations: "that you do what you do out of your private passion for the thing itself" and not for the approval of others.

Notice that Dillard doesn't really tell us how she felt at the time of the incident, but only what she thought after some reflection. In paragraph 11, she writes that she "began to understand then," yet she doesn't say how long it took to understand fully what this event meant. Sometimes it takes a good deal of time and reflection before we gain understanding—and that is another reason why people write about remembered events. Writing gives us the opportunity to reflect on our experiences and, in hindsight, to figure out why they mean so much to us.

■   ■   ■

Tobias Wolff is probably best known for his short stories and for a novel, *The Barracks Thief*, for which he won the 1985 PEN/Faulkner award. "On Being a Real Westerner" comes from Wolff's autobiography, *A Boy's Life*, which was made into a movie in 1993. Reflecting on his writing process, Wolff has said that it is "part memory, part invention. I can no longer tell where one ends and the other begins. The very act of writing has transformed the original experience into another experience, more 'real' to me than what I started with."

The story Wolff tells here is based on an actual experience that occurred when he was ten years old. He and his mother had just moved west from Florida to Salt Lake City, followed by Roy, his divorced mother's boyfriend. "Roy was handsome," Wolff writes, "in the conventional way that appeals to boys. He had a tattoo. He'd been to war and kept a silence about it that was full of heroic implication." As you read, notice how Wolff's storytelling skills make this event come to life in the reader's imagination.

ON BEING A REAL WESTERNER
TOBIAS WOLFF

Just after Easter Roy gave me the Winchester .22 rifle I'd learned to shoot with. It was a light, pump-action, beautifully balanced piece with a walnut stock black from all its oilings. Roy had carried it when he was a boy and it was still as good as new. Better than new. The action was silky from long use, and the wood of a quality no longer to be found. **1**

The gift did not come as a surprise. Roy was stingy, and slow to take a hint, but I'd put him under siege. I had my heart set on that rifle. A weapon was the first condition of self-sufficiency, and of being a real Westerner, and of all acceptable employment—trapping, riding herd, soldiering, law enforcement, and outlawry. I needed that rifle, for itself and for the way it completed me when I held it. **2**

My mother said I couldn't have it. Absolutely not. Roy took the rifle back but promised me he'd bring her around. He could not imagine anyone refusing him anything and treated the refusals he did encounter as perverse and insincere. Normally mute, he became at these times a relentless whiner. He would follow my mother from room to room, emitting one ceaseless note of complaint that was pitched perfectly to jelly her nerves and bring her to a state where she would agree to anything to make it stop. **3**

After a few days of this my mother caved in. She said I could have the rifle if, and only if, I promised never to take it out or even touch it except when she and Roy were with me. Okay, I said. Sure. Naturally. But even then she wasn't satisfied. She plain didn't like the fact of me owning a rifle. Roy said he had owned several **4** rifles by the time he was my age, but this did not reassure her. She didn't think I could be trusted with it. Roy said now was the time to find out.

For a week or so I kept my promises. But now that the weather had turned warm   5
Roy was usually off somewhere and eventually, in the dead hours after school when I found myself alone in the apartment, I decided that there couldn't be any harm in taking the rifle out to clean it. Only to clean it, nothing more. I was sure it would be enough just to break it down, oil it, rub linseed into the stock, polish the octagonal barrel and then hold it up to the light to confirm the perfection of the bore. But it wasn't enough. From cleaning the rifle I went to marching around the apartment with it, and then to striking brave poses in front of the mirror. Roy had saved one of his army uniforms and I sometimes dressed up in this, together with martial-looking articles of hunting gear: fur trooper's hat, camouflage coat, boots that reached nearly to my knees.

The camouflage coat made me feel like a sniper, and before long I began to act   6
like one. I set up a nest on the couch by the front window. I drew the shades to darken the apartment, and took up my position. Nudging the shade aside with the rifle barrel, I followed people in my sights as they walked or drove along the street. At first I made shooting sounds—kyoo! kyoo! Then I started cocking the hammer and letting it snap down.

Roy stored his ammunition in a metal box he kept hidden in the closet. As with   7
everything else hidden in the apartment, I knew exactly where to find it. There was a layer of loose .22 rounds on the bottom of the box under shells of bigger caliber, dropped there by the handful the way men drop pennies on their dressers at night. I took some and put them in a hiding place of my own. With these I started loading up the rifle. Hammer cocked, a round in the chamber, finger resting lightly on the trigger, I drew a bead on whoever walked by—women pushing strollers, children, garbage collectors laughing and calling to each other, anyone—and as they passed under my window I sometimes had to bite my lip to keep from laughing in the ecstasy of my power over them, and at their absurd and innocent belief that they were safe.

But over time the innocence I laughed at began to irritate me. It was a peculiar   8
kind of irritation. I saw it years later in men I served with, and felt it myself, when unarmed Vietnamese civilians talked back to us while we were herding them around. Power can be enjoyed only when it is recognized and feared. Fearlessness in those without power is maddening to those who have it.

One afternoon I pulled the trigger. I had been aiming at two old people, a man   9
and a woman, who walked so slowly that by the time they turned the corner at the bottom of the hill my little store of self-control was exhausted. I had to shoot. I looked up and down the street. It was empty. Nothing moved but a pair of squirrels chasing each other back and forth on the telephone wires. I followed one in my sight. Finally it stopped for a moment and I fired. The squirrel dropped straight into the road. I pulled back into the shadows and waited for something to happen, sure that someone must have heard the shot or seen the squirrel fall. But the sound that was so loud to me probably seemed to our neighbors no more than the bang of a cupboard slammed shut. After a while I sneaked a glance into the street. The squirrel hadn't moved. It looked like a scarf someone had dropped.

When my mother got home from work I told her there was a dead squirrel in   10
the street. Like me, she was an animal lover. She took a cellophane bag off a loaf

of bread and we went outside and looked at the squirrel. "Poor little thing," she said. She stuck her hand in the wrapper and picked up the squirrel, then pulled the bag inside out away from her hand. We buried it behind our building under a cross made of popsicle sticks, and I blubbered the whole time.

I blubbered again in bed that night. At last I got out of bed and knelt down and did an imitation of somebody praying, and then I did an imitation of somebody receiving divine reassurance and inspiration. I stopped crying. I smiled to myself and forced a feeling of warmth into my chest. Then I climbed back in bed and looked up at the ceiling with a blissful expression until I went to sleep. 11

For several days I stayed away from the apartment at times when I knew I'd be alone there. 12

Though I avoided the apartment, I could not shake the idea that sooner or later I would get the rifle out again. All my images of myself as I wished to be were images of myself armed. Because I did not know who I was, any image of myself, no matter how grotesque, had power over me. This much I understand now. But the man can give no help to the boy, not in this matter nor in those that follow. The boy moves always out of reach. 13

For Discussion

Consider what this story seems to be saying about identity and role playing. Why do you think Wolff takes so much delight in dressing up as a soldier? What connection do you see between his playing soldier and his desire to be a "real Westerner"?

Why do you think soldiers and cowboys are idealized masculine roles in our society? What qualities of character do they represent? What are the feminine roles our society values most? If possible, consider these questions together with two or three other students, preferably including both men and women in the group.

How do you feel about these gender-related roles? Do they embody ideals that you hold for yourself? Looking back at the essay, do you think Wolff calls these stereotypical roles into question, or do you think he is basically uncritical of them?

For Analysis

1. What seems to be the significance of this story? What does Wolff learn from this particular incident? Where does he state the point most explicitly?

2. Successful narratives present a sequence of actions that build tension toward a high point or climax. This narrative is organized like a staircase, with each step up intensifying the suspense. To analyze this story's dramatic structure, first find the climax. Then, starting with the first paragraph, number each new step. What effect does this progression of steps have on you as one reader? Compare your response to that of your classmates. Did you all point to the same steps? If not, how can you account for the difference?

3. Look at the opening paragraphs. What purpose do they serve? If the essay opened instead with the second sentence of paragraph 5 ("In the dead hours after school . . .), what would be lost or gained?

4.   In paragraphs 7–13, Wolff describes his reactions at the time to what he was doing. Which of these remembered feelings and thoughts help you to understand what he was experiencing at the time? What impression do they give you of the young Wolff? Where do you see evidence of the adult writer's perspective? What does he seem to think about his younger self?

For Your
Own Writing

In this selection, Wolff describes experiencing what he calls the "ecstasy of my power" to inflict harm on others (paragraph 7). Can you recall any instances when you were in a position to exercise power over another person? What did you do? How did you feel? Think also of times when you were subject to someone else's power. How did you feel in that position? If you were to write about one of these instances, what ideas and feelings would you want to convey to your readers?

Commentary

This is a gripping story. One factor that makes it so dramatic is the topic. Putting a child together with a rifle immediately alerts readers to the possibility that something dreadful could happen. Thus the potential for suspense is great. But what makes the story so effective is Wolff's masterful use of two writing strategies: narration and description.

Good storytelling hinges on tension, usually on the reader's concern for the main character and anxiety about what will happen to him or her. If the tension slackens, if irrelevant details are introduced or the action meanders pointlessly, readers lose interest. Wolff instills tension in his narrative by pacing the action very carefully. He begins his story leisurely, summarizing his efforts to get Roy to give him the rifle and Roy's efforts to get Wolff's mother to let him have it. Once he gets the rifle, the pace picks up as the narrative moves with increasing speed from one incident to the next until finally the gun is fired and the squirrel drops.

Wolff uses another pacing technique when he gives a close-up of the action by showing concrete movements and gestures. In paragraph 7, for example, he builds suspense by focusing in on each minute action: "Hammer cocked, a round in the chamber, finger resting lightly on the trigger, I drew a bead on whoever walked by—women pushing strollers, children, garbage collectors laughing and calling to each other, anyone. . . ."

For more on specific narrative action, turn to pp. 482–86. For more on descriptive techniques, see Chapter 15.

This specific narrative action also contributes to the vividness of the writing. Wolff uses it together with the descriptive techniques of naming, detailing, and comparing to help readers visualize key parts of the scene. He carefully names important objects and their parts. For instance, it's not just any gun, but a Winchester .22. He adds many details (italicized in our example) to further describe the rifle: "It was a *light, pump-action, beautifully balanced* piece with a *walnut* stock *black* from all its oilings." Finally, he uses comparison in the form of metaphor and simile to further enliven his description: "the action was silky," the dead squirrel "looked like a scarf someone had dropped."

■   ■   ■

Audre Lorde (1934–1992) wrote more than a dozen books of fiction and nonfiction. She's probably best known as a poet, but she was also an inspiring teacher and political activist.

This selection, from her autobiography *Zami* (1982), recounts an event that occurred when Lorde was in the sixth grade at St. Catherine's School, where she was the only black child. Although she was born in New York, Lorde's parents were immigrants from the island of Grenada. Notice that Lorde uses some Grenadian dialect in recording her mother's speech, such as "what-the-france" (paragraph 5) and "among-you" (paragraph 7). As you read, think about why winning the election is so important to Lorde and why her mother tries to discourage her from running.

THE ELECTION
AUDRE LORDE

In the spring of the sixth grade, Sister Blanche announced that we were going 1 to hold elections for two class presidents, one boy and one girl. Anyone could run, she said, and we would vote on Friday of that week. The voting should be according to merit and effort and class spirit, she added, but the most important thing would be marks.

Of course, Ann Archdeacon was nominated immediately. She was not only the 2 most popular girl in the school, she was the prettiest. Ilene Crimmons was also nominated, her blonde curls and favored status with the Monsignor guaranteed that.

I lent Jim Moriarty ten cents, stolen from my father's pocket at lunchtime, so Jim 3 nominated me. A titter went through the class, but I ignored it. I was in seventh heaven. I knew I was the smartest girl in the class. I had to win.

That afternoon when my mother came home from the office, I told her about 4 the election, and how I was going to run, and win. She was furious.

"What in hell are you doing getting yourself involved with so much foolishness? 5 You don't have better sense in your head than that? What-the-france do you need with election? We send you to school to work, not to prance about with president-this election-that. Get down the rice, girl, and stop talking your foolishness." We started preparing the food.

"But I just might win, Mommy. Sister Blanche said it should go to the smartest 6 girl in the class." I wanted her to see how important it was to me.

"Don't bother me with that nonsense. I don't want to hear any more about it. 7 And don't come in here on Friday with a long face, and any 'I didn't win, Mommy,' because I don't want to hear that, either. Your father and I have enough trouble to keep among-you in school, never mind election."

I dropped the subject. 8

The week was a very long and exciting one for me. The only way I could get 9 attention from my classmates in the sixth grade was by having money, and thanks to carefully planned forays into my father's pants pockets every night that week, I made sure I had plenty. Every day at noon, I dashed across the street, gobbled down whatever food my mother had left for my lunch, and headed for the school-yard. . . .

I knew better than to say another word to my mother about the presidency, but 10 that week was filled with fantasies of how I would break the news to her on Friday when she came home.

"Oh, Mommy, by the way, can I stay later at school on Monday for a presidents' 11 meeting?" Or "Mother, would you please sign this note saying it is all right for me to accept the presidency?" Or maybe even, "Mother, could I have a little get-together here to celebrate the election?"

On Friday, I tied a ribbon around the steel barrette that held my unruly mass of 12 hair tightly at the nape of my neck. Elections were to be held in the afternoon, and when I got home for lunch, for the first time in my life, I was too excited to eat. I buried the can of Campbell's soup that my mother had left out for me way behind the other cans in the pantry and hoped she had not counted how many were left.

We filed out of the schoolyard and up the stairs to the sixth grade room. The 13 walls were still lined with bits of green from the recent St. Patrick's Day decorations. Sister Blanche passed out little pieces of blank paper for our ballots.

The first rude awakening came when she announced that the boy chosen would 14 be president, but the girl would only be vice-president. I thought this was monstrously unfair. Why not the other way around? Since we could not, as she explained, have two presidents, why not a girl president and a boy vice-president? It doesn't really matter, I said to myself. I can live with being vice-president.

I voted for myself. The ballots were collected and passed to the front of the room 15 and duly counted. James O'Connor won for the boys. Ann Archdeacon won for the girls. Ilene Crimmons came in second. I got four votes, one of which was mine. I was in shock. We all clapped for the winners, and Ann Archdeacon turned around in her seat and smiled her shit-eating smile at me. "Too bad you lost." I smiled back. I wanted to break her face off.

I was too much my mother's daughter to let anyone think it mattered. But I felt 16 I had been destroyed. How could this have happened? I was the smartest girl in the class. I had not been elected vice-president. It was as simple as that. But something was escaping me. Something was terribly wrong. It wasn't fair.

A sweet little girl named Helen Ramsey had decided it was her christian duty to 17 befriend me, and she had once lent me her sled during the winter. She lived next to the church, and after school, that day, she invited me to her house for a cup of cocoa. I ran away without answering, dashing across the street and into the safety of my house. I ran up the stairs, my bookbag banging against my legs. I pulled out the key pinned to my uniform pocket and unlocked the door to our apartment. The house was warm and dark and empty and quiet. I did not stop running until I got to my room at the front of the house, where I flung my books and my coat in a corner and collapsed upon my convertible couch-bed, shrieking with fury and disappointment. Finally, in the privacy of my room, I could shed the tears that had been burning my eyes for two hours, and I wept and wept.

I had wanted other things before that I had not gotten. So much so, that I had 18 come to believe if I really wanted something badly enough, the very act of my wanting it was an assurance that I would not get it. Was this what had happened with the election? Had I wanted it too much? Was this what my mother was always talking about? Why she had been so angry? Because wanting meant I would not get? But somehow this felt different. This was the first time that I had wanted something so badly, the getting of which I was sure I could control. The election was supposed to have gone to the smartest girl in the class, and I was clearly the smartest. That was something I had done, on my own, that should have guaranteed me the election. The smartest, not the most popular. That was me. But it hadn't happened. My mother had been right. I hadn't won the election. My mother had been right.

This thought hurt me almost as much as the loss of the election, and when I felt 19 it fully I shrieked with renewed vigor. I luxuriated in my grief in the empty house in a way I could never have done if anyone were home.

All the way up front and buried in my tears, kneeling with my face in the cush- 20 ions of my couch, I did not hear the key in the lock, nor the main door open. The first thing I knew, there was my mother standing in the doorway of my room, a frown of concern in her voice.

"What happened, what happened? What's wrong with you? What's this racket 21 going on here?"

I turned my wet face up to her from the couch. I wanted a little comfort in my 22 pain, and getting up, I started moving toward her.

"I lost the election, Mommy," I cried, forgetting her warnings. "I'm the smartest 23 girl in class, Sister Blanche says so, and they chose Ann Archdeacon instead!" The unfairness of it all flooded over me again and my voice cracked into fresh sobs.

Through my tears, I saw my mother's face stiffen with rage. Her eyebrows drew 24 together as her hand came up, still holding her handbag. I stopped in my tracks as her first blow caught me full on the side of my head. My mother was no weakling, and I backed away, my ears ringing. The whole world seemed to be going insane. It was only then I remembered our earlier conversations.

"See, the bird forgets, but the trap doesn't! I warned you! What you think you 25 doing coming into this house wailing about election? If I told you once I have told you a hundred times, don't chase yourself behind these people, haven't I? What kind of ninny raise up here to think those good-for-nothing white piss-jets would pass over some little jacabat girl to elect you anything?" Smack! "What did I say to you just now?" She cuffed me again, this time on my shoulders, as I huddled to escape her rain of furious blows, and the edges of her pocketbook.

"Sure enough, didn't I tell you not to come in here bringing down tears over 26 some worthless fool election?" Smack! "What the hell you think we send you to school for?" Smack! "Don't run yourself behind other people's business, you'll do better. Dry up, now, dry up!" Smack! She pulled me to my feet from where I had sunk back onto the couch.

"Is cry you want to cry? I'll give you something hard to cry on!" And she cuffed 27 me again, this time more lightly. "Now get yourself up from there and stop acting like some stupid fool, worrying yourself about these people's business that doesn't concern you. Get-the-france out of here and wipe up your face. Start acting like a human being!"

Pushing me ahead of her, my mother marched back through the parlor and into 28 the kitchen. "I come in here tired from the street and here you, acting like the world is ending. I thought sure enough some terrible thing happened to you, come to find out it's only election. Now help me put away this foodstuff."

I was relieved to hear her tone mollify, as I wiped my eyes. But I still gave her 29 heavy hands a wide berth.

"It's just that it's not fair, Mother. That's all I was crying about," I said, opening 30 the brown paper bags on the table. To admit I had been hurt would somehow put me in the wrong for feeling pain. "It wasn't the election I cared about so much really, just that it was all so unfair."

"Fair, fair, what's fair, you think? Is fair you want, look in god's face." My mother 31 was busily dropping onions into the bin. She paused, and turning around, held my puffy face up, her hand beneath my chin. Her eyes so sharp and furious before, now just looked tired and sad.

"Child, why you worry your head so much over fair or not fair? Just do what is 32 for you to do and let the rest take care of themselves." She smoothed straggles of hair back from my face, and I felt the anger gone from her fingers. "Look, you hair all mess-up behind from rolling around with foolishness. Go wash your face and hands and come help me dress this fish for supper."

For Discussion

As readers, we all tend to look at stories through the lens of our own experience. Our understanding and ability to judge an event are based largely on assumptions we have about people living in our society today. But the event portrayed in this selection took place more than twenty-five years ago, just after World War II. What can you infer from this story about the situation at that time for black people in America? Why does Lorde's mother say at the end, "Fair, fair, what's fair, you think? Is fair you want, look in god's face"?

Placing this event in the larger historical and social context leads us to consider what happened in political terms, as the story of an innocent child's first recognition that the world is not fair or just. How does seeing the story in this way lead you to understand the mother's response? How had she tried to protect her daughter from being hurt? How do you imagine she felt when she found her daughter alone in the darkened house, crying her heart out?

For Analysis

1. Look closely at the way Lorde develops her narrative. It begins with the announcement of the election and ends a week later. How much space does she devote to her electioneering during the week, to the election itself, and to what happened afterward? Compare Lorde's narrative to Dillard's and Wolff's. Notice how their narratives compress time at some points, covering extended periods in a few sentences. Also notice that, at some points, they use several paragraphs to cover something that occurred in a relatively short time. What conclusions can you draw from this analysis about the ways writers represent time in their stories?

2. Reread paragraphs 15–19, in which Lorde shows us what she did after losing the election. Notice that at some point we see her as if she were on a movie screen, smiling back at Ann Archdeacon, for example, and running upstairs with her bookbag banging against her legs. In addition to dramatizing her actions, Lorde also tells us what she was thinking. As you read, notice where she's showing action and where she's telling her thoughts. Bracket the passages where she's telling her thoughts so you can see more clearly the proportion of space Lorde devotes to each and how she intersperses telling with showing.

3.   The most dramatic part of the story comes in the end when her mother discovers her crying. Reread these paragraphs, looking closely at the way Lorde makes them dramatic. Explain how you think she does it.

4.   Relationships with parents often play an important role in autobiographical stories. Compare Lorde's relationship with her mother to the parent-child relationship in one of the other essays in this chapter: Dillard's relationship with her mother and father; Wolff's relationship with his mother; or Jean Brandt's relationship with her mother and father.

Speculate about why, in writing about the event, each author needed to also write about the parent-child relationship. In each case, how does the relationship contribute to the event's significance?

For Your
Own Writing

Can you think of a time when you had an emotional confrontation with another person? What was it about? Why do you think the emotions were so strong? If you were to write an autobiographical story about this event, how would you organize it? How would you decide how to present the confrontation? Would you dramatize it with direct dialogue? Would you paraphrase or summarize what was said?

Commentary

This story often has a powerful impact on readers because the feelings are expressed in such raw language and action. If you felt at ease reading Dillard's subdued story or on edge reading Wolff's intense narrative, reading this one may have come as a shock. You might wonder why Lorde chose to confront her readers in this way. To get some idea of Lorde's purpose, we might speculate about her assumptions, particularly about how her readers would be likely to react to the election results.

It's probable she assumed most readers would predict how the election was going to turn out. After all, there are only two alternatives: winning or losing. Think of stories like this that you've read or seen. Don't they typically end with disappointment? Unless they have resulted from serious internal or physical struggle so that victory is a surprise, happy endings are often regarded as sappy.

There are also other, more important, reasons for readers to expect Lorde to lose the election. Most readers have had experiences in life that have led them to be cynical, or at least wary. We know that school elections very often are not decided on the basis of merit but on popularity. Therefore, we are not surprised when Ann Archdeacon wins; after all, we are told straight off, she "was not only the most popular girl in the school, she was the prettiest." Knowing also that the young Lorde was new at the school and has to bribe someone to nominate her makes the results that much more predictable. Furthermore, we might guess that Lorde's status as the only black child in the school would also affect the election results.

Assuming that Lorde wanted her readers to predict the election would be lost, how do you think she expected most of them to react? Some might share the young Lorde's point of view and be angered by the election results. But because the results are so predictable, many readers might be more likely to share the mother's point of view and wonder why the young Lorde put herself in a position where she would most likely be disappointed and hurt. For these readers, the mother's fury might echo their own frustration and sense of powerlessness at the injustice in society.

For more on dialogue, see pp. 489–90.

Lorde conveys this fury dramatically, using dialogue for most of this part of the story. Dialogue gives a narrative immediacy, vividness, and drama. For contrast, notice that Lorde begins the selection by paraphrasing Sister Blanche's announcement about the upcoming election instead of quoting directly. Lorde chooses to paraphrase, to use her own words, because there is little drama in the announcement. What is most important is what the nun said, not how she said it. In portraying her mother's feelings and her own youthful reactions to them, however, Lorde must dramatize this significant part of her story by quoting directly. Paraphrasing or summarizing her mother's words would have created a very different impression.

■   ■   ■

Jean Brandt wrote this essay as a freshman. It tells about something she did when she was thirteen. Reflecting on how she felt at the time, Brandt writes: "I was afraid, embarrassed, worried, mad." As you read, look for places where these tumultuous and contradictory remembered feelings are expressed.

CALLING HOME
JEAN BRANDT

As we all piled into the car, I knew it was going to be a fabulous day. My grandmother was visiting for the holidays; and she and I, along with my older brother and sister, Louis and Susan, were setting off for a day of last-minute Christmas shopping. On the way to the mall, we sang Christmas carols, chattered, and laughed. With Christmas only two days away, we were caught up with holiday spirit. I felt lightheaded and full of joy. I loved shopping—especially at Christmas. 1

The shopping center was swarming with frantic last-minute shoppers like ourselves. We went first to the General Store, my favorite. It carried mostly knickknacks and other useless items which nobody needs but buys anyway. I was thirteen years old at the time, and things like buttons and calendars and posters would catch my fancy. This day was no different. The object of my desire was a 75-cent Snoopy button. Snoopy was the latest. If you owned anything with the Peanuts on it, you were "in." But since I was supposed to be shopping for gifts for other people and not myself, I couldn't decide what to do. I went in search of my sister for her opinion. I pushed my way through throngs of people to the back of the store where I found Susan. I asked her if she thought I should buy the button. She said it was cute and if I wanted it to go ahead and buy it. 2

When I got back to the Snoopy section, I took one look at the lines at the cash-   3
iers and knew I didn't want to wait thirty minutes to buy an item worth less than
one dollar. I walked back to the basket where I found the button and was about to
drop it when suddenly, instead, I took a quick glance around, assured myself no one
could see, and slipped the button into the pocket of my sweatshirt. I hesitated for
a moment, but once the item was in my pocket, there was no turning back. I had
never before stolen anything; but what was done was done. A few seconds later,
my sister appeared and asked, "So, did you decide to buy the button?"

"No, I guess not." I hoped my voice didn't quaver. As we headed for the en-   4
trance, my heart began to race. I just had to get out of that store. Only a few more
yards to go and I'd be safe. As we crossed the threshold, I heaved a sigh of relief.
I was home free. I thought about how sly I had been and I felt proud of my accomplishment.

An unexpected tap on my shoulder startled me. I whirled around to find a mid-   5
dle-aged man, dressed in street clothes, flashing some type of badge and politely
asking me to empty my pockets. Where did this man come from? How did he know?
I was so sure that no one had seen me! On the verge of panicking, I told myself
that all I had to do was give this man his button back, say I was sorry, and go on
my way. After all, it was only a 75-cent item.

Next thing I knew, he was talking about calling the police and having me arrested   6
and thrown in jail, as if he had just nabbed a professional thief instead of a terrified
kid. I couldn't believe what he was saying.

"Jean, what's going on?"   7

The sound of my sister's voice eased the pressure a bit. She always managed to   8
get me out of trouble. She would come through this time too.

"Excuse me. Are you a relative of this young girl?"   9

"Yes, I'm her sister. What's the problem?"   10

"Well, I just caught her shoplifting and I'm afraid I'll have to call the police."   11

"What did she take?"   12

"This button."   13

"A button? You are having a thirteen-year-old arrested for stealing a button?"   14

"I'm sorry, but she broke the law."   15

The man led us through the store and into an office, where we waited for the   16
police officers to arrive. Susan had found my grandmother and brother, who, still
shocked, didn't say a word. The thought of going to jail terrified me, not because
of jail itself, but because of the encounter with my parents afterward. Not more than
ten minutes later, two officers arrived and placed me under arrest. They said that I
was to be taken to the station alone. Then, they handcuffed me and led me out of
the store. I felt alone and scared. I had counted on my sister being with me, but
now I had to muster up the courage to face this ordeal all by myself.

As the officers led me through the mall, I sensed a hundred pairs of eyes staring   17
at me. My face flushed and I broke out in a sweat. Now everyone knew I was a
criminal. In their eyes I was a juvenile delinquent, and thank God the cops were
getting me off the streets. The worse part was thinking my grandmother might be
having the same thoughts. The humiliation at that moment was overwhelming. I felt
like Hester Prynne being put on public display for everyone to ridicule.

That short walk through the mall seemed to take hours. But once we reached   18
the squad car, time raced by. I was read my rights and questioned. We were at the

police station within minutes. Everything happened so fast I didn't have a chance to feel remorse for my crime. Instead, I viewed what was happening to me as if it were a movie. Being searched, although embarrassing, somehow seemed to be exciting. All the movies and television programs I had seen were actually coming to life. This is what it was really like. But why were criminals always portrayed as frightened and regretful? I was having fun. I thought I had nothing to fear—until I was allowed my one phone call. I was trembling as I dialed home. I didn't know what I was going to say to my parents, especially my mother.

"Hi, Dad, this is Jean." 19

"We've been waiting for you to call." 20

"Did Susie tell you what happened?" 21

"Yeah, but we haven't told your mother. I think you should tell her what you did and where you are." 22

"You mean she doesn't even know where I am?" 23

"No, I want you to explain it to her." 24

There was a pause as he called my mother to the phone. For the first time that night, I was close to tears. I wished I had never stolen that stupid pin. I wanted to give the phone to one of the officers because I was too ashamed to tell my mother the truth, but I had no choice. 25

"Jean, where are you?" 26

"I'm, umm, in jail." 27

"Why? What for?" 28

"Shoplifting." 29

"On no, Jean. Why? Why did you do it?" 30

"I don't know. No reason. I just did it." 31

"I don't understand. What did you take? Why did you do it? You had plenty of money with you." 32

"I know but I just did it. I can't explain why. Mom, I'm sorry." 33

"I'm afraid sorry isn't enough. I'm horribly <u>disappointed in you</u>." 34

Long after we got off the phone, while I sat in an empty jail cell, waiting for my parents to pick me up, I could still distinctly hear the disappointment and hurt in my mother's voice. I cried. The tears weren't for me but for her and the pain I had put her through. I felt like a terrible human being. I would rather have stayed in jail than confront my mom right then. I dreaded each passing minute that brought our encounter closer. When the officer came to release me, I hesitated, actually not wanting to leave. We went to the front desk, where I had to sign a form to retrieve my belongings. I saw my parents a few yards away and my heart raced. A large knot formed in my stomach. I fought back the tears. 35

Not a word was spoken as we walked to the car. Slowly, I sank into the back seat anticipating the scolding. Expecting harsh tones, I was relieved to hear almost the opposite from my father. 36

"I'm not going to punish you and I'll tell you why. Although I think what you did was wrong, I think what the police did was more wrong. There's no excuse for locking a thirteen-year-old behind bars. That doesn't mean I condone what you did, but I think you've been punished enough already." 37

As I looked from my father's eyes to my mother's, I knew this ordeal was over. Although it would never be forgotten, the incident was not mentioned again. 38

For Discussion

Brandt writes here about taking responsibility for her actions. Do you think she ultimately accepts responsibility for what she has done, or does she transfer some of the blame to others? If you have already read the essay in this chapter by Tobias Wolff, you might compare his story to Brandt's. Both of them break social rules: she gets caught, whereas he gets away with it.

Discuss what our society teaches us about breaking rules. Do some rules seem more bendable than others? Are some people treated differently than others for breaking the same rules? Why should accepting responsibility for what you have done change anything?

For Analysis

1.   Reread the essay, paying particular attention to Brandt's use of dialogue. What do you learn about her from what she says and how she says it? What do you learn about her relationship with her parents?

For more on descriptive strategies, turn to Chapter 15.

2.   Reread the essay, looking for examples of the descriptive strategies of naming, detailing, and comparing. How well does Brandt use these strategies? Give at least one example of each as support for your evaluation.

3.   The story begins and ends in a car, with the two car rides framing the story. Framing is a narrative device of echoing something from the beginning in the ending; what effect does this device have on your reading of the story?

4.   The Writer at Work section on pp. 57–63 includes some of Brandt's invention notes and her complete first draft. These materials show how her focus shifted gradually from the theft and subsequent arrest in her first draft to her emotional confrontation with her parents in the final revision, printed above.

Read over these materials, and comment on this shift in focus. Why do you think Brandt decided to stress her confrontation with her parents? Why do you think she decided, against the advice of the student who commented on her draft, to cut the scenes in the police car and station? Notice, in particular, that she left out of the final version the vivid image of herself hand-cuffed to the table (see p. 62, paragraph 5).

For more on sequencing narrative action, turn to pp. 482–86.

For Your
Own Writing

Can you think of a few occasions when you did something uncharacteristic? Perhaps you acted on impulse or took a chance you wouldn't ordinarily take. It doesn't have to be something reckless, dangerous, or illegal; it could be something quite harmless, even pleasant. Think of one occasion you might like to write about. What would you want your readers to recognize about you on the basis of reading your story?

Commentary

By letting us see her commit a crime and be arrested for it, Brandt makes a rather personal self-disclosure in this autobiographical story. Although readers are always interested in candid personal revelation, autobiographers have to decide for themselves just how personal they want their story to be. Making this decision yourself is especially important when you are writing for class. You certainly shouldn't feel compelled to disclose something you don't want to disclose.

We can see in her Writer at Work materials some of Brandt's decision process. She indicates in her invention writing that she had always been too "ashamed to tell anyone" about this particular event (p. 59). She seems to have decided to go ahead, in part, because she knows readers will recognize its significance. She also expects some readers to identify with her because they've done similar things. But her primary reason seems to be more personal. She finds that writing has helped her begin to come to terms with her many contradictory feelings about what she did and how she was treated. Without oversimplifying her feelings or fully understanding them, Brandt ultimately seems comfortable admitting what she did was wrong, while taking some pride in how she acted afterward.

As readers, we form our impressions of Brandt from what she does, but also from how she represents herself in her writing. Her revelation of remembered feelings and thoughts helps us see the experience from her point of view. We see, for example, the roller coaster of emotions she went through, her fear but also her exhilaration. She vividly conveys her panic at being caught, her terror at the prospect of going to jail, her feeling of being "alone and scared" on the way to the station, and her excitement when being searched.

While she claims in her invention writing no longer to feel angry at the manager or the police, she clearly satirizes the store manager. She portrays her experience with the police more ambiguously with an unusual emotional distance ("I viewed what happened to me as if it were a movie."), letting her father express righteous indignation instead of expressing it herself. She even omits from the final revision the first draft's disturbing image of her handcuffed to a table while being questioned by the police.

Perhaps the strongest emotions come out toward the end of the essay when she must confront her parents. Seeing herself reflected in their eyes seems to have been the most painful and memorable part of the experience. Maybe that is why she finally decided to write about this event: it gave her a way to replace that image with a more complex one that allows her to redeem some sense of pride.

PURPOSE AND AUDIENCE

Writers have various reasons for writing about their experiences. Reminiscing makes it possible to relive moments of pleasure and pain, but it also helps them to gain insight, to learn who they are now by examining who they used to be and the forces that shaped them. Reflecting on the past can lead to significant self-discovery.

Writing about personal experience is public, not private. The autobiographer writes to be read and is therefore as much concerned with self-presentation as with self-discovery. In this way, personal writing is necessarily persuasive, for all writers want to influence the way readers think of them. They present themselves to readers in the way they want to be perceived. The rest they keep hidden, though readers may read between the lines.

We read about others' experiences for much the same reason that we write about our own—to learn about how we live our lives: the decisions we face, the delights we share, and the fate that awaits us all. Reading autobiography can validate our sense of ourselves, particularly when we see our own experience reflected in another's life. Reading about others' lives can also challenge our complacency and help us appreciate other points of view. Not only can autobiography lead us to greater self-awareness by validating or challenging us, it can also enlarge our sympathies by awakening our humanity. When we read about others' lives, we are invited to empathize with another person's values and feelings and thus break the shell of our own isolation.

BASIC FEATURES OF ESSAYS ABOUT REMEMBERED EVENTS

Essays about remembered events share certain basic features: They turn actual experiences into meaningful stories and vividly present the scenes and people that are part of them. They seek to convey autobiographical significance by dramatizing the story and may also reflect on its meaning.

A Well-told Story

Writing about remembered events means first of all telling an interesting story. Whatever else the writer may attempt to do, he or she must shape the experience into a story that is entertaining and memorable. This is done primarily by building suspense. As readers, we may sense disaster, shudder in anticipation of a troubling disclosure, or look forward to a humorous turn of events. The important point is that the writer makes us want to know what will happen. We wonder whether Annie Dillard will ever find the elusive amoeba, if Tobias Wolff will shoot the rifle, how Audre Lorde will respond to the outcome of the election, and if Jean Brandt will get caught for shoplifting.

In addition to telling a suspenseful story, good writers work to create tension in their narratives. *Tension* draws readers into a story, making us nervous about what might happen. Three techniques for heightening tension are specific narrative action, sentence rhythm, and dialogue. Tension rises when Wolff shows specific narrative action, giving a detailed close-up of his play with the rifle. Sentence rhythm creates emphasis when Dillard repeats the same sentence pattern over and over again, making us wonder if anything will ever come of her search for the amoeba. And dialogue conveys the immediacy and drama of personal interactions, when Brandt re-creates her conversations with her parents. By drawing us into the action, these techniques contribute to our involvement in the story as readers. One moment we're distant observers, far from the action; the next, we're thrown right into it, with the participants.

For more on tension, narrative action, dialogue, and sentence rhythm, see pp. 482–91.

A Vivid Presentation of Significant Scenes and People

Scenes and people play an important role in most writing about remembered events. As in fiction, the scene provides a setting for the event. Instead of giving a generalized impression, skillful writers actually re-create the scene and let us hear the people. Vividness and specificity make the event—and the writing—memorable. Carefully selected details leave readers with some dominant impression of the whole tableau.

By moving in close, a writer can name specific objects in a scene: a table, a microscope, a blade of grass in the Dillard piece; a shopping center, some knickknacks, and a button in Brandt's essay. Good writers also provide details about the named objects. Dillard characterizes the table as "white enamel," the microscope as "blunt black three-speed," the blade of grass as "a wee brown chip." Brandt specifies that the shopping center was "swarming with frantic last-minute shoppers" and the coveted button was a "75-cent Snoopy button." Finally, simile and metaphor draw comparisons with other familiar things, helping readers to "see" the point and hence to better understand it. Brandt uses simile in her reference to *The Scarlet Letter* when she says she felt "like Hester Prynne being put on public display."

The descriptive strategies of naming, detailing, and comparing are discussed further on pp. 495–500.

For presenting important people, writers can choose from a variety of strategies, including physical description, action, and dialogue. They can give details of the person's appearance, as Dillard does for her mother: sitting "with her knees crossed, in blue slacks, smoking a Chesterfield." With a few carefully chosen details, writers can capture something of a person's mood.

Skilled writers show people in action. Wolff, for example, shows his mother's precise movements: "She took a cellophane bag off a loaf of bread and we went outside and looked at the squirrel. 'Poor little thing,' she said. She stuck her hand in the wrapper and picked up the squirrel, then pulled the bag inside out away from her hand."

Writers can also present people through dialogue, letting us infer from their own words what the people are like and how they feel about one another. Wolff's mother's words convey sympathy her son appears to lack. Lorde's mother reveals something about her own experience when she declares, "Fair, fair, what's fair, you think? Is fair you want, look in god's face." Brandt's mother seems disapproving when she says "sorry isn't enough" and that she's "horribly disappointed" in her daughter.

An Indication of the Significance

In essays about remembered events, we not only expect a well-told story with vivid details, but we also expect the story to have a point. Sometimes the meaning is merely implied, but often it is stated explicitly. There are two ways a writer can communicate this significance: by *showing* us that the event was important or by *telling* us directly what it meant. Most writers do both.

Showing is the heartbeat of an essay about a remembered event, for the event must be dramatized if readers are to appreciate its importance and understand the writer's feelings about it. Seeing the important scenes and people from the writer's point of view naturally leads readers to identify with the writer. Indeed, we can well imagine what that "unexpected tap on [the] shoulder" must have felt like for Brandt and how Dillard felt running upstairs to tell her parents about her great discovery.

Telling also contributes mightily to a reader's understanding, and so most writers explain something about the event's meaning and importance. They may tell us how they felt at the time, or how they feel now as they look back on the experience. Often writers do both, recalling their past feelings and thoughts and reflecting on the past from their present perspective. Wolff, for example, tells us some of his remembered feelings when he recalls feeling "like a sniper," and delighting in the "ecstasy" of power. He also tells us what he thinks about the experience in retrospect: "Because I did not know who I was, any image of myself, no matter how grotesque, had power over me. This much I understand now." What Dillard tells us is a combination of what she "began to understand" at the time and what she came to realize as she got older: "that you do what you do out of your private passion for the thing itself."

Telling is the main way that writers interpret the event for readers, but skillful writers are careful not to append these reflections artificially, like a moral tagged on to a fable. They also try not to oversimplify or moralize, for most readers are skeptical of writing that is sentimental or self-serving. Readers don't expect autobiographers to reveal everything, but they do expect them to be truthful in what they do disclose. We may not be able to identify with Wolff's compulsive need for a gun, but we have to admire his openness. Similarly while we may sympathize with Lorde's disappointment, we also recognize the reasons for her mother's anger.

Guide to Writing

THE WRITING ASSIGNMENT

Write an essay about a significant event in your life. Choose an event that will be engaging for readers and that will, at the same time, tell them something about you. Tell your story dramatically and vividly, giving a clear indication of its autobiographical significance.

INVENTION

The following invention activities are designed to help you choose an appropriate event, recall specific details, test your choice to be sure you can write about it successfully, and define its autobiographical significance.

Choosing an Event to Write About

Finding an event to write about requires some patience and reflection. Take time to sit quietly and let your mind go. Think of specific experiences you still remember well.

You might set a timer and brainstorm your lists on a computer with the monitor brightness turned all the way down. Enter as many possibilities as you can in ten minutes. Then, turn the brightness up, be sure all the items make sense, and print out a copy to make notes on.

Listing Events.　　List some events you might write about, even if you already have a promising event in mind. Taking a few minutes now to list additional possibilities may help you decide whether your initial idea is the one to pursue, and it gives you backups if you need them later. One way to search your memory is to think in terms of categories. Use the following categories and any others you can think of to get started in your search.

- Any "first," such as when you first realized you had a special skill, ambition, or problem; when you first felt needed or rejected; when you first became aware of some kind of altruism or injustice
- Any memorably difficult situation: when you had to make a tough choice, when someone you admired let you down (or you let someone else down), when you struggled to learn or understand something
- Any occasion when things did not turn out as expected: when you expected to be praised but were criticized, when you were convinced you would fail but succeeded
- Any incident that challenged your basic values or beliefs
- Any humorous event, one you still laugh about, perhaps one that seemed awkward or embarrassing at the time
- Any event that shaped you in a particular way, making you perhaps independent, proud, insecure, fearful, courageous, ambitious
- Any incident charged with strong emotions such as love, fear, anger, embarrassment, guilt, frustration, hurt, pride, happiness, joy

Focusing on key periods of time is another way to search your memory. Go back in five-year increments: one-to-five years ago, six-to-ten years ago, ten-to-fifteen, and so on. Try to recall an event from each period.

Choosing a Significant Event.　　Look over your list, and choose two or three promising events. These events can be common or unusual, humorous or serious, recent or distant, but consider them in light of these questions:

- Will I be able to tell what happened from beginning to end?
- Can I recall specific details about the action, scene, and people?

■ As a fragment of my life story, does this event reveal anything important about me?

■ Will I feel comfortable writing about it?

■ Will it arouse readers' curiosity and interest?

Decide on one event to write about. Not everything needs to be clear to you at this point, but choose an event you feel drawn to explore further, one you expect will make a good story and lead you to insights about yourself.

Sketching the Story

Having chosen a promising event in your life, begin by making a rough sketch of the story. During the next few days, you'll recall many details to fill in your sketch. For now, write informally for about five minutes or so, as if you were telling a friend what happened. If it's easier, make an outline using brief phrases to indicate what you and others did.

Finally, reread your sketch or outline, and put an asterisk (*) next to the high point or climax, the point you think the story is building toward.

Describing the Scene

Stories take place in one or more specific places or scenes, some of which may be described in detail. For example, Brandt's story has many different scenes including the shopping center, the General Store, the manager's office, and the police station—most of which are described with just a few vivid images. To create vivid images, you need to name the *outstanding features* in the scene and identify their specific *sensory details*. You can also create *similes* and *metaphors*. The following activities calling upon the different senses will help you recall and describe the scene or scenes in which the event took place.

Sights. Imagine each important scene in your story as if it were in a photograph or a movie. Put yourself in the picture and list the objects you "see" as you look around or walk through the scene (excluding people for the moment). Then choose a few memorable objects and write for a few minutes about each, trying to recall specific visual details: size, shape, color, texture. Think also in terms of simile (as when Wolff describes the dead squirrel as looking "like a scarf someone had dropped") and metaphor (as when Dillard describes the drop of water becoming "a jungle . . . full of one-celled animals).

Sounds. What sounds do you "hear" as you put yourself in the scene or scenes? Are there voices? animal sounds? horns honking? Is it quiet or noisy? Try simile and metaphor here too (remember Wolff comparing the sound of the rifle shot to "the bang of a cupboard slammed shut").

Smells, Tastes, Textures. As you picture each scene what do you smell? Is there any element you can taste? Study some of the objects in your picture, and

If you can, save these details of the scene and people on a word processor. Then, as you begin to draft later, you can call up the file on a second screen and easily transfer details you want to use in your draft.

describe some of the textures or surfaces of anything you can touch—are they soft or hard? smooth or rough?

Dominant Impression.   Now that you've imaginatively re-created the scene or scenes in which the event took place, write a sentence or two saying what dominant impression each should evoke. Should they seem homey? eerie? holiday-like? claustrophobic? Should every scene evoke the same mood?

Recalling Key People

Try to remember the significant people who played a role in the event—what they looked like, what they did, what they or you said.

Listing People.   List all the people who played more than a casual role. You may have only one or two people to list, or you may have several.

Describing Key People.   Choose the one or two people who made the event most significant for you. Take around five minutes to describe these people in writing—their appearance, their actions, and their significance in the event.

Re-creating Conversations.   Think about what was said: Can you recall any telling or unusual comments or choice of words? Do you remember any particular voices or accents? Try to reconstruct a real or imagined conversation between one or more of these persons and yourself. (Don't worry about accuracy; try to catch the spirit of the exchange. Unless the conversation was recorded, dialogue is bound to be imagined to some extent.) Set it up as a dialogue, as Jean Brandt does on pp. 57–58.

Finally, try to focus your thoughts about the key people in a sentence or two about your relationship with each of them and the role that he or she played in the event.

Testing Your Choice

Pause now to be sure you've chosen an event you will be able to write about successfully by asking yourself these questions:

- Am I still interested in this event? Do I feel drawn to explore its significance in my life and to tell others about it?
- Have I been able to recall enough details to describe it vividly?
- Do I recall enough about other people who were involved with this event?

If you cannot answer these questions affirmatively and confidently, you may want to find a different event to write about. If so, return to your original list of events for other possible subjects.

For Group Inquiry

You might find it useful to get together in a group with two or three other students and run your chosen events by one another. Assess the group's interest in the event you wish to write about, and invite their advice about whether it sounds promising. Does it seem likely to lead to an essay they would care to read? Your purpose is to decide whether you have chosen a good event to write about and thus to be able to proceed confidently to develop your essay.

Exploring the Significance

Following are some questions designed to help you better understand the meaning the event holds in your life.

Recalling Your Feelings at the Time.   Try to remember your feelings during the event and immediately thereafter. Spend about ten minutes writing about your response, using these questions to stimulate your memory:

- What was my first response to the event? What did I think? How did I feel? What did I do?
- How did I show my feelings?
- What did I want those present to think of me, and why?
- What did I think of myself at the time?
- Did I talk to anyone during or just after the event? What did I say?
- How long did these initial feelings last?
- What were the immediate consequences of the event for me personally?

Stop a moment to focus your thoughts. In two or three sentences try to articulate what your first response to the event seems to disclose about the event's original importance.

Exploring Your Present Perspective.   Next think about your present perspective on the event—your current feelings as well as any thoughts or insights you may have. Write for ten minutes about your present perspective, using these questions to get you started:

- Looking back, how do I feel about this event? Do I understand it differently now than I did then?
- What do my actions at the time of the event say about the kind of person I was then? In what ways am I different now? How would I respond to the same event if it occurred today?
- How would I summarize my current feelings? Are they settled, or do they still seem to be changing? Am I sure of my feelings about the event, or am I ambivalent?

If you have used a word processor to explore the event's significance, you might want to print out a copy of your reflections to read over and make notes on before trying to define the event's significance.

In two or three sentences explain what your present perspective reveals about you or about the event's importance in your life.

Defining the Significance.   In a sentence or two, state the significance of the event. What importance does it hold for you? What does it tell you about yourself? Then think about your readers and purpose. In another couple of sentences, explain why you've chosen to share this particular event. What, specifically, do you want your readers to think about you and the situation you were in?

PLANNING AND DRAFTING

The next activities are designed to help you to use your invention writing to set goals, to organize your narrative, and to write a first draft.

Seeing What You Have

It's a good idea at this point to print out a hard copy of what you have written on a word processor for easier reviewing.

You have now done a lot of thinking and writing about elements basic to an essay about a remembered event: your feelings, the autobiographical significance, specific sensory details, dialogue. Before going any further, reread everything you've written so far to see what you have. As you read through your invention materials, be on the lookout for surprising details or new insights. Watch for meaningful patterns and relationships. Highlight any such promising material by underlining or by making notes in the margin. Guided by the questions that follow, you should now be able to decide whether you have enough material to write an essay and whether you understand the autobiographical significance well enough.

- Will I be able to tell an interesting—possibly amusing or dramatic—story about my experience?
- Do I have enough descriptive details to re-create the scene and people vividly? What will be the dominant impression of my description and how will it reinforce the event's significance?
- Does the event still seem significant to me? Will my readers also find it meaningful?

If you do not see interesting details, connections, or patterns in your invention writing, you are not likely to write a good draft. Starting over is no fun, but there is no sense in starting to draft a composition if you do not feel confident about your topic.

If your invention writing looks thin but promising, there are many ways to fill it out. For example, try reshaping the story, adding new scenes, recalling additional sensory details, thinking more about your own reactions to the event, elaborating on significant people, or developing the specific historical or cultural context in which it took place.

Setting Goals

Before starting to draft, you should set goals to guide further invention and planning. Some of these goals concern the piece as a whole, such as holding readers' interest with a compelling story, satisfying their curiosity by maintaining a good pace in the narrative, or framing the story in a satisfying way. Other goals have to do with smaller issues, such as including memorable sensory details, creating vivid images, or making dialogue sound like real conversation. You will be making dozens of decisions—and solving dozens of problems—as you work your way through a draft; these decisions and solutions are determined by the goals you set.

Following are some questions that can help you set goals before you start drafting. You may also want to return to them as you work, to help keep your goals in focus.

Your Readers

- What do I want my readers to think of me and my experience? If I want them to see the event from my point of view, should I show them how I felt at the time, as Lorde does? Should I tell them what I thought, as Dillard does? Do I want to show them how my perspective has changed, as Brandt does?

- If my readers are likely to have had similar experiences, how can I convey the uniqueness of my experience or its special importance in my life? Should I tell them more about my background or the particular context of the event? Should I give them a glimpse, as Wolff does, of its impact years later?

- If my readers are *not* likely to have had similar experiences, how can I help them understand what happened and appreciate its importance? Should I reveal the social implications, as Lorde does, or show the cultural influences acting on me, as Wolff does?

- If my readers may be alarmed by my disclosures or may judge me harshly, can I do anything to get them to see my point of view? Should I try to get them to question their own preconceptions, as Wolff does with his observations about the "ecstasy of power"? Should I present my experience without apology or explanation, as Brandt does? Should I try to get my readers to identify with my social situation, as Lorde does?

The Beginning

- How shall I begin? What can I do in the opening sentences that will capture my readers' interest? Should I begin with the main event, integrating essential background information as I tell the story, as Lorde does? Should I establish the setting and situation right away, as Brandt does? Should I first present myself, as Dillard does, or should I provide the complete context for the event, as Wolff does? Or should I do something altogether different?

See Chapter 14 for information on structuring the narrative.

The Story

- What is the climax, or high point, of the story? For Wolff, it is shooting the squirrel. For Dillard, it first seems to be finding the amoeba, but it turns out that her second discovery—that she can be independent of her parents—is even more significant.

- How can I build tension and suspense leading to the climax? Can I show specific narrative action, as Wolff does? Should I use sentence rhythm, as Dillard does? Or dialogue, as Brandt and Lorde do?

- Should I tell the story chronologically? Would flashback or flashforward make the narrative more interesting?

- How can I use vivid descriptive detail to create a dominant impression that will reinforce the event's significance?

The Ending

- How should the essay end? Should I end reflecting on the meaning of the experience, like Dillard?

- If I want readers to think well of me, should I conclude with a philosophical statement, as Wolff does? Should I be satirical? Should I be self-critical and avoid smugness?

- If I want to leave readers with a sense of hope, can I find an image of harmony restored, as Lorde does, or an expression of optimism, as Dillard does? If I want to underscore the event's continuing significance in my life, can I show that the conflict was never fully resolved, as Brandt does?

- Should I frame the essay by echoing something from the beginning to give readers at least a superficial sense of closure, as Brandt does by setting the last scene, like the first, in the family car?

Outlining

Outlining on a word processor makes it particularly easy to experiment with different ways of sequencing your narrative.

An essay about a remembered event should be first of all a good story. The way you organize this story will depend on what happened, what significance it had for you, who your readers will be, and what impression you want to give them. As you draft and revise, you will discover the most appropriate organization for your story. For now, start to plan this organization by listing the main incidents in the order that they took place. Then list them in the order in which you think they should be presented in your story.

Drafting

If you can shift between screens, you might call up invention material on an alternate screen as you draft on the main screen, shifting back and forth to cut and paste invention material into your draft.

Start writing your essay, trying to maintain a focus on what took place in the event. Strive to paint a memorable picture of the scene and of any important people involved. Try also to describe the event in such a way as to say something about yourself and the event's significance in your life. If you feel stuck at any point in drafting the essay, try returning to the writing activities in the Invention section of this chapter. You may want to review the general planning and drafting advice given on pp. 12-14.

GETTING CRITICAL COMMENTS

Now is the time to try to get a good critical reading. All writers find it helpful to have someone else read and comment on their drafts, and your instructor may schedule such a reading as part of your coursework. Otherwise, you can ask a classmate, friend, or family member to read it over. If your campus has a writing center, you might ask a tutor there to comment on your draft. The guidelines in this section are designed to be used by *anyone*. (If you are unable to have someone else read over your draft, turn ahead to the revision section on pp. 52–56, which includes guidelines for reading your own draft with a critical eye.)

Your reader needs to know your intended audience and purpose. Briefly write out this information at the top of your draft:

Audience. Who are your readers?

Purpose. What do you want your readers to learn about you from reading about this event?

Reading with a Critical Eye

See Chapter 12 for a review of useful critical reading strategies.

Reading a draft critically means reading it more than once, first to get a general impression and then to analyze its basic features.

Reading for a First Impression.   Read first to enjoy the story and get a sense of its significance. As you read, try to notice any words or passages that contribute to your first impression, weak ones as well as strong ones.

After you've finished reading the draft, briefly give your impressions: How engaging is the story? Does the event seem truly significant? What in the draft do you think would especially interest the intended readers?

See pp. 41–43 to review the basic features.

Reading to Analyze.   Read then to focus on the basic features of writing about a remembered event.

Is the Story Told Well?

Identify the climax, and focus on how the narrative builds up to it. Note any places where the tension slackens and readers could lose interest in the outcome. Point to any sentences that seem boring or repetitious. Note any places where the story seems particularly vague or general.

Are Scenes and People Presented Vividly?

Indicate any scenes or people that seem nondescript or vague, that don't contribute to the dominant impression. Specify where dialogue rambles pointlessly, or where adding dialogue might help to dramatize a scene. Comment on the effectiveness of any similes or metaphors.

Is the Autobiographical Significance Clear?

Summarize the event's significance. What does it tell you about the author as an individual or about the cultural and economic forces that shaped the author's experience? Point to any places where the writer's remembered feelings and thoughts or present perspective could have been made clearer. Use an adjective or two (such as *thoughtful, self-deprecating, smug, sappy, vulnerable*) to describe your impression of the writer.

Is the Organization Effective?

Consider the *overall plan* for the essay, perhaps by outlining it briefly. Point to any places where the sequence of action isn't clear or where the narrative seems to meander pointlessly. Look to see if description or other information disrupts the flow of the narrative.

Look at the *beginning.* If it fails to draw you in or raises wrong expectations, say so. Point to another passage that might serve as a better opening.

Look at the *ending.* Indicate whether the resolution is too pat, overcomplicated, or unfocused. Point to any other passages that might work better as endings for the essay.

What Final Thoughts Do You Have?

What do you find most satisfying about this draft? Which parts need more work?

REVISING AND EDITING

This section will help you identify problems in your draft and revise and edit to solve them.

Identifying Problems

Even if your essay is saved to a computer file, reread from a hard copy, preferably draft quality. Onscreen or as letter-quality hard copy, a paper can look more "finished" than it really is. Add notes to yourself and quick revisions as you read through the draft.

To identify problems in your draft, you need to read it objectively, analyze its basic features, and study any comments you've received from others.

Getting an Overview.   Consider the draft as a whole, trying to see it objectively. It may help to do so in two steps:

Reread. If at all possible, put the draft aside for a day or two before rereading it. When you do, start by reconsidering your purpose. Then read the draft straight through, trying to see it as your intended readers will.

Outline. Make a scratch outline to get an overview of the essay's development. This outline can be sketchy—words and phrases instead of complete sentences—but it should identify the basic features as they appear.

Charting a Plan for Revision.   You may want to make a chart like the one below to keep track of any problems you need to solve. The left-hand column lists the basic features of writing about remembered events. As you analyze your draft and study any comments you've gotten from others, note the problems you want to solve in the right-hand column.

Basic Features   *Problems to Solve*

The story

Scenes and people

Autobiographical significance

Organization

Analyzing the Basic Features of Your Draft.   Turn now to the questions for analyzing a draft on pp. 51–52. Using these questions as guidelines, identify problems in your draft. Note things to solve on the preceding chart.

Studying Critical Comments.   Review any comments you've received from other readers, and add to the chart any points that *you* think needs attention. Try not to react too defensively to these comments; they simply show you how others respond to your draft. It's up to you to decide if and how you want to respond.

Solving the Problems

Having identified problems, you now need to figure out solutions and—most important of all—to carry them out. Basically, you have three ways of finding solutions: (1) review your invention and planning notes for additional information and ideas; (2) do further invention to answer questions you or your readers raised; and (3) look back at the readings in this chapter to see how other writers have solved similar problems.

Following are suggestions to get your started solving some of the problems common to writing about remembered events. For now, focus on solving those issues identified on your chart. Avoid tinkering with sentence-level problems at this time; that will come later when you edit.

The Story

Before revising on a word processor, copy your original draft to a second file. Then, should you change your mind about material you delete while revising, it will still be available to you.

- If the climax is hard to identify, look to find the high point of the narrative. Be sure that the story has a climax, that it leads somewhere and doesn't just go on without a destination.
- If the tension slackens where it should be building to the climax, try intensifying the pace—either by adding specific details about movements and gestures, varying the sentence rhythm, or substituting lively quoted dialogue for summarized dialogue.
- If some sentences are boring or repetitious, try varying them in terms of pattern and length. If they all begin with a subject, for instance, see if adding an introductory phrase to one helps. Or, if they are all approximately the same length, try combining some to vary rhythm.

Scenes and People

- If any scenes or people seem nondescript, try naming things more specifically and adding sensory details so that readers can see, touch, smell, taste, and hear aspects of the scene. Add similes and metaphors. Choose words that are concrete rather than abstract, specific rather than general.

- If any dialogue rambles pointlessly, liven it up with faster repartee or shorter, more pointed statements. Eliminate any unnecessary dialogue. Check the way it is introduced to see that it is not all in the form of "he said." Be more descriptive: "he cried out" or "she declared."

- If any description fails to contribute to the dominant impression, omit extraneous details or reconsider the impression you want to make.

Autobiographical Significance

- If the event's significance seems vague, look at the language you use to convey it. Ask yourself once again why the event stands out in your memory. What do you want readers to know about you from reading this essay?

- If the impression readers get of you is not the impression you wanted to make, look closely at the language you've used to express your feelings and thoughts. Consider whether you've projected a side of yourself you weren't aware of. If so, consider using this new insight to refocus what the story reveals about you.

- If your past or present feelings about the event do not come across clearly, review your invention writing or compose more expressive language—an image or metaphor perhaps—to show your feelings. Since feelings are often ambivalent and complicated, try to be expressive without oversimplifying.

Use your word processor's cut-and-paste or block-and-move functions to shift material around. Make sure that transitions are revised so that material fits in its new spot.

- If readers don't appreciate the event's uniqueness or special importance in your life, consider giving them more insight into your background or cultural heritage. Consider whether you want to confront readers' complacency or provincialism with strong language or shocking revelations.

Organization

- If the story is hard to follow, restructure it so that the action unfolds clearly. Fill in any gaps. Eliminate unnecessary digressions.

- If description or other information disrupts the flow of the narrative, try integrating it more smoothly by adding transitions. If that doesn't help, consider taking it out or moving it.

- If the beginning is weak, see if there's a better place to start. Review the draft and your notes for an image, a bit of dialogue, or a remembered feeling that might catch readers' attention or arouse their curiosity.

- If the ending doesn't work, see if there's a better place to end—a memorable image, perhaps, or a provocative assertion. Look to see if you can frame the essay by referring back to something in the beginning.

Editing and Proofreading

In working on your draft so far, you may have corrected some obvious errors, but grammar and style have not been a priority. Now is the time to check for errors in usage, punctuation, and mechanics, and also to consider matters of style.

Our research has identified several errors that often occur in writing of this kind. You should check your draft for three patterns in particular: missing commas after introductory elements, fused sentences, and misuse of past-perfect verbs.

When you use your word processor's spell-check function to aid in proofreading for spelling, keep in mind that it will not find all misspellings, particularly misused homonyms (such as there, their, and they're) and many proper nouns and specialized terms. Proofread these carefully yourself, using hard copy and a dictionary if necessary. Also proofread for words that should have been deleted when you edited a sentence.

Checking for Missing Commas after Introductory Elements.   Introductory elements in a sentence can be words, phrases, or clauses. A comma tells readers that the introductory information is ending and the main part of the sentence is about to begin. If there is no danger of misreading, you can omit the comma after single words or short phrases or clauses, but you'll never be wrong to include the comma. The best advice is always to follow introductory elements with a comma. Following are several examples of ways to edit introductory sentence elements taken from drafts done by college students using this book:

▶ As always,we would go to Domenico's Pizzeria.

▶ Through the nine-day run of the play,the acting just kept getting better and better.

▶ Knowing that the struggle was over,I felt through my jacket to find teabags and cookies the robber had taken from the kitchen.

▶ As I stepped out of the car,I knew something was wrong.

Checking for Fused Sentences.   Fused sentences occur when two independent clauses are joined with no punctuation or connecting word between them. When you write about a remembered event, you try to re-create a scene. In trying to re-create a scene, a writer might write a fused sentence like the following:

Sleet glazed the windshield the wipers were frozen stuck.

If you were telling a friend about this storm in person rather than in writing, you would pause briefly after the word *windshield*, and your intonation would fall noticeably. These cues would tell your listener unmistakably that one idea has ended (sleet glazed the windshield) and another one is beginning (the wipers were frozen stuck). Encountering these same words in printed text, however, readers need a punctuation mark to substitute for the missing spoken-language cues. There are several ways to edit fused sentences:

Make the clauses separate sentences.

▶ Sleet glazed the windshield. The wipers were frozen stuck.

Join the two clauses with a comma and *and, but, or, nor, for, so,* or *yet.*

▶ Sleet glazed the windshield , and the wipers were frozen stuck.

Join the two clauses with a semicolon.

▶ Sleet glazed the windshield; the wipers were frozen stuck.

Rewrite the sentence, subordinating one clause.

▶ ~~Sleet~~ As sleet glazed the windshield , the wipers ~~were~~ became frozen stuck.

Checking Your Use of the Past Perfect. Verb tenses indicate the time an action takes place. As a writer, you will in general use the present tense for actions occurring at the time you are writing (we *see*), the past tense for actions completed in the past (we *saw*), and the future tense for actions that will occur in the future (we *will see*).

When you write about a remembered event, you will often need to use various forms of the past tense: the past perfect to indicate an action that was completed at the time of another past action (she *had finished* her work when we saw her) and the past progressive to indicate a continuing action in the past (she *was finishing* her work).

One common problem in writing about a remembered event is the failure to use the past perfect when it is needed. For example:

▶ I had three people in the car, something my father had told me not to do on several occasions.

In the following sentence, the meaning is not clear without the past perfect:

▶ Coach Kernow told me I ~~ran~~ had run faster than ever before.

A Common ESL Problem. It is important to remember that the past perfect is formed with *had* followed by a past participle. Past participles usually end in *-ed, -d, -en, -n,* or *-t: worked, hoped, eaten, taken, bent.*

▶ Before Tania went to Moscow last year, she had not really ~~speak~~ spoken Russian.

A Writer at Work

FROM INVENTION TO DRAFT TO REVISION

This section looks at the writing process that Jean Brandt followed in composing her essay, "Calling Home." You will see some of her invention writing and her complete first draft, which you can then compare to the final draft, printed on pp. 36–38.

Invention

Brandt's invention produced about nine handwritten pages, but it took her only two hours, spread out over four days. Here is a selection of her invention writings. She began by choosing an event and then recalling specific sensory details of the scene and the other people involved. She writes two dialogues, one with her sister Sue and the other with her father. Following is the one with her sister.

Re-creating a Conversation

```
SUE: Jean, why did you do it?
ME: I don't know.  I guess I didn't want to wait in that
long line.  Sue, what am I going to tell Mom and Dad?
SUE: Don't worry about that yet, the detective might not
really call the police.
ME: I can't believe I was stupid enough to take it.
SUE: I know.  I've been there before.  Now when he comes
back try crying and act like you're really upset.  Tell
him how sorry you are and that it was the first time you
ever stole something but make sure you cry.  It got me
off the hook once.
ME: I don't think I can force myself to cry.  I'm not
really that upset.  I don't think the shock's worn off.
I'm more worried about Mom.
SUE: Who knows?  Maybe she won't have to find out.
ME: God, I hope not.  Hey, where's Louie and Grandma?
Grandma doesn't know about this, does she?
SUE: No, I sort of told Lou what was going on so he's
just taking Grandma around shopping.
ME: Isn't she wondering where we are?
SUE: I told him to tell her we would meet them in an
hour.
ME: How am I ever going to face her?  Mom and Dad might
possibly understand or at least get over it, but Grandma?
This is gonna kill her.
```

> SUE: Don't worry about that right now. Here comes the
> detective. Now try to look like you're sorry. Try to
> cry.

This dialogue helps Brandt recall an important conversation with her sister. Dialogues are an especially useful form of invention for they enable writers to remember their feelings and thoughts.

Brandt writes this dialogue quickly, trying to capture the language of excited talk, keeping the exchanges brief. She includes a version of this dialogue in her second draft but excludes it from her revision. The dialogue with her father does not appear in any of her drafts. Even though she eventually decides to feature other completely different conversations, these invention dialogues enable her to evaluate how various conversations would work in her essay.

Next, we see her first attempts to bring the autobiographical significance of the event into focus as she explores her remembered feelings and present perspective:

> Being arrested for shoplifting was significant because it
> changed some of my basic attitudes. Since that night
> I've never again considered stealing anything. This
> event would reveal how my attitude toward the law and
> other people has changed from disrespectful to very
> respectful.

Brandt begins by stating tentatively that the importance of the event was the lesson it taught her. Reading this statement might lead us to expect a moralistic story of how someone learned something the hard way. As we look at the subsequent invention activities and watch the draft develop, however, we will see how her focus shifts to her relations with other people.

Recalling Remembered Feelings

> I was scared, humiliated, and confused. I was ter-
> rified when I realized what was happening. I can still
> see the manager and his badge and remember what I felt
> when I knew who he was. I just couldn't believe it. I
> didn't want to run. I felt there wasn't anything I could
> do--I was afraid, embarrassed, worried, mad that it hap-
> pened. I didn't show my feelings at all. I tried to
> look very calm on the outside, but inside I was extremely
> nervous. The nervousness might have come through in my
> voice a little. I wanted the people around me to think I
> was tough and that I could handle the situation. I was
> really disappointed with myself. Getting arrested made
> me realize how wrong my actions were. I felt very

```
ashamed.  Afterward I had to talk to my father about it.
I didn't say much of anything except that I was wrong and
I was sorry.  The immediate consequence was being taken
to jail and then later having to call my parents and tell
them what happened.  I hated to call my parents.  That
was the hardest part.  I remember how much I dreaded
that.  My mom was really hurt.
```

Brandt's exploration of her first reaction is quite successful. Naming specific feelings, she focuses on the difference between what she felt and how she acted. She remembers her humiliation at being arrested as well as the terrible moment when she had to tell her parents. As we will see, this concern with her parents' reaction, more than her own humiliation, becomes the most important theme in her essay.

In exploring her first response to the event, Brandt writes quickly, noting down memories as they come to mind. Next, she rereads this first exploration and attempts to state briefly what the incident really reveals about her:

```
I think it reveals that I was not a hard-core criminal.
I was trying to live up to Robin Files's (supposedly my
best girlfriend) expectations, even though I actually
knew that what I was doing was wrong.
```

After longer pieces of exploratory writing, stopping to focus her thoughts like this helps Brandt see the point of what she has just written. Specifically, it helps her to connect diverse invention writings to her main concern: discovering the autobiographical significance of the event. Thus does she reflect on what her remembered feelings of the event reveal about the kind of person she was at the time: not a hard-core criminal. She identifies a friend, who will disappear from the writing after one brief mention. Next she looks at her present perspective on the event.

Exploring Present Perspective

```
At first I was ashamed to tell anyone that I had been ar-
rested.  It was as if I couldn't admit it myself.  Now
I'm glad it happened, because who knows where I'd be now
if I hadn't been caught.  I still don't tell many people
about it.  Never before have I written about it.  I think
my response was appropriate.  If I'd broken down and
cried, it wouldn't have helped me any, so it's better
that I reacted calmly.  My actions and responses show
that I was trying to be tough.  I thought that that was
the way to gain respectability.  If I were to get ar-
rested now (of course it wouldn't be for shoplifting), I
think I'd react the same way because it doesn't do any
```

```
good to get emotional.  My current feelings are ones of
appreciation.  I feel lucky because I was set straight
early.  Now I can look back on it and laugh, but at the
same time know how serious it was.  I am emotionally dis-
tant now because I can view the event objectively rather
than subjectively.  My feelings are settled now.  I don't
get upset thinking about it.  I don't feel angry at the
manager or the police.  I think I was more upset about my
parents than about what was happening to me.  After the
first part of it was over I mainly worried about what my
parents would think.
```

Writing about her present perspective confirms for Brandt that she feels comfortable enough to write for class about this event. Having achieved a degree of emotional distance, she no longer feels humiliated, silenced either by her embarrassment or her anger. Reassessing her reaction at the time, she is obviously pleased to recall that she did not lose control and show her true feelings. Staying calm, not getting emotional, looking tough—these are the personal qualities Brandt wants others to see in her. Exploring her present perspective seems to have led to a new, "respectable" self-image she can proudly display to her readers:

```
My present perspective shows that I'm a reasonable per-
son.  I can admit when I'm wrong and accept the punish-
ment that was due me.  I find that I can be concerned
about others even when I'm in trouble.
```

Next Brandt reflects on what she has written in order to articulate the autobiographical significance of the event.

Defining the Event's Autobiographical Significance

```
The event was important because it entirely changed one
aspect of my character.  I will be disclosing that I was
once a thief, and I think many of my readers will be
able to identify with my story, even though they won't
admit it.
```

After the first set of invention work, completed in about forty-five minutes on two separate days, Brandt is confident she has chosen an event with personal significance. She knows what she will be disclosing about herself and feels comfortable doing it. In her brief focusing statements she begins by moralizing ("my attitude . . . changed") and blaming others (Robin Files) but concludes by acknowledging what she did. She is now prepared to disclose it to readers ("I was once a thief"). Also, she thinks readers will like her story because she suspects many of them will recall doing something illegal and feeling guilty about it, even if they never got caught.

The First Draft

The day after completing the invention writing, Brandt reviews her invention and writes her first draft. It takes her about an hour.

Her draft is handwritten and contains few erasures or other changes, indicating that she writes steadily, probably letting the writing lead her where it will. She knows this will not be her only draft.

Before you read the first draft, reread the final draft, "Calling Home," in the Readings section of this chapter. Then as you read the first draft, consider what part it was to play in the total writing process.

It was two days before Christmas and my older sister and brother, my grandmother, and I were rushing around doing last-minute shopping. After going to a few stores we decided to go to Lakewood Center shopping mall. It was packed with other frantic shoppers like ourselves from one end to the other. The first store we went to (the first and last for me) was the General Store. The General Store is your typical gift shop. They mainly have the cutesy knick-knacks, posters, frames and that sort. The store is decorated to resemble an old-time western general store but the appearance doesn't quite come off. 1

We were all browsing around and I saw a basket of buttons so I went to see what the different ones were. One of the first ones I noticed was a Snoopy button. I'm not sure what it said on it, something funny I'm sure and besides I was in love with anything Snoopy when I was 13. I took it out of the basket and showed it to my sister and she said "Why don't you buy it?" I thought about it but the lines at the cashiers were outrageous and I didn't think it was worth it for a 75 cent item. Instead I figured just take it and I did. I thought I was so sly about it. I casually slipped it into my pocket and assumed I was home free since no one pounced on me. Everyone was ready to leave this shop so we made our way through the crowds to the entrance. 2

My grandmother and sister were ahead of my brother and I. They were almost to the entrance of May Co. and we were about 5 to 10 yards behind when I felt this tap on my shoulder. I turned around already terror struck, and this man was flashing some kind of badge in my face. It happened so fast I didn't know what was going on. Louie finally noticed I wasn't with him and came back for me. Jack explained I was being arrested for shoplifting and if my 3

parents were here then Louie should go find them. Louie
ran to get Susie and told her about it but kept it from
Grandma. By the time Sue got back to the General Store I
was in the back office and Jack was calling the police. I
was a little scared but not really. It was sort of exciting. My sister was telling me to try and cry but I
couldn't. About 20 minutes later two cops came and handcuffed me, led me through the mall outside to the police
car. I was kind of embarrassed when they took me through
the mall in front of all those people.

When they got me in the car they began questioning me,   4
while driving me to the police station. Questions just to
fill out the report--age, sex, address, color of eyes, etc.

Then when they were finished they began talking about   5
Jack and what a nuisance he was. I gathered that Jack had
every single person who shoplifted, no matter what their
age, arrested. The police were getting really fed up with
it because it was a nuisance for them to have to come way
out to the mall for something as petty as that. To hear
the police talk about my "crime" that way felt good because
it was like what I did wasn't really so bad. It made me
feel a bit relieved. When we walked into the station I remember the desk sergeant joking with the arresting officers
about "well we got another one of Jack's hardened criminals." Again, I felt my crime lacked any seriousness at
all. Next they handcuffed me to a table and questioned me
further and then I had to phone my mom. That was the
worst. I never was so humiliated in my life. Hearing the
disappointment in her voice was worse punishment than the
cops could ever give me.

This first draft establishes the main narrative line of events. About a third of
it is devoted to the store manager, an emphasis which disappears by the final
draft. What is to have prominence in the final draft—Brandt's feelings about
telling her parents and her conversations with them—appears here only in a
few lines at the very end. But its mention suggests its eventual importance,
and we are reminded of its prominence in Brandt's invention writing.

Brandt writes a second draft for another student to read critically. In this
draft, she includes dialogues with her sister and with the policemen. She also
provides more information about her actions as she considered buying the
Snoopy button and then decided to steal it instead. She includes visual details
of the manager's office. This draft is not much different in emphasis from the
first draft, however, still ending with a long section about the policemen and
the station. The parents are mentioned briefly only at the very end.

The reader tells Brandt how much he likes her story and admires her frankness. However, he does not encourage her to develop the dramatic possibilities in calling her parents and meeting them afterward. In fact, he encourages her to keep the dialogue with the policemen about the manager and to include what the manager said to the police.

Brandt's revision shows that she does not take her reader's advice. She reduces the role of the police officers, eliminating any dialogue with them. She greatly expands the role of her parents: the last third of the paper is now focused on her remembered feelings about calling them and seeing them afterward. In dramatic importance the phone call home now equals the arrest. Remembering Brandt's earliest invention writings, we can see that she was headed toward this conclusion all along . . . but she needed invention, three drafts, a critical reading, and about a week to get there.

Thinking Critically about What You've Learned

Now that you've worked extensively in autobiography—reading it, talking about it, writing it—you should take time to reflect on what you've learned: What problems did you have writing, and how did you solve them? What did you learn from reading about events in other people's lives that helped you write about a remembered event in your own life? Finally, you might stop to think critically about autobiography as a genre of writing: How does it influence the way we think about ourselves?

REFLECTING ON YOUR WRITING

To reflect on what you have learned about writing autobiography, first gather all of your writing—invention, planning notes, outlines, drafts, comments from other readers, revision plans, and final revision. Review these materials as you complete the following writing task.

- Identify *one* major problem you needed to solve as you wrote about a remembered event. Don't be concerned with sentence-level issues; concentrate on problems unique to autobiographical writing to discover how you wanted to present your experience. For example: Did you puzzle over how to present a particular scene or person? Was it difficult to structure the narrative so that it builds up to a climax? Did you find it hard (or uncomfortable) to convey the event's autobiographical significance?
- Determine how you came to recognize the problem. When did you first discover it? What called it to your attention? Did you notice it yourself, or did another reader point it out? Can you now see hints of it in your invention writing, your planning notes, or an earlier draft? If so, where specifically?

- Reflect next on how you went about solving the problem. Did you work on a particular passage, cut or add details, reorganize the essay? Did you reread one of the essays in the chapter to see how another writer handled similar material? Did you look back at the invention guidelines? Did you discuss the problem with another student, a tutor, or your instructor? If so, how did talking about it help, and how useful was the advice you got?

- Finally, write a page or so explaining to your instructor how you discovered and solved the problem. Be as specific as possible in re-constructing your efforts. Quote from your invention notes or early drafts, from readers' comments, from your revision plan, and from your final revision to show the various changes your writing underwent as you worked to solve the problem. Taking the time now to recall how you found and solved a particular writing prob-lem will help you become more competent and confident as a writer.

REVIEWING WHAT YOU LEARNED
FROM READING

Your own essay about a remembered event has no doubt been influ-enced by the essays you've read in this chapter. These readings may have helped you decide which of your own experiences would seem significant to your readers, or they may have given you ideas about how to evoke a vivid sense of place or how to convey your feelings about the event. Take time now to reflect on what you have learned from the selections in this chapter and to look for ways these readings have influenced your own writing.

- Reread the final revision of your essay; then look back at the se-lections you read before completing your own essay. Try to rec-ognize any specific influences. If you were impressed, for example, with the way one of the readings set a scene or used dialogue, dramatized the action or conveyed the autobiographical signifi-cance, look to see where you might have been striving for similar effects in your own essay. Look also for ideas you got from your reading: writing strategies you were inspired to try, specific details you were led to include, effects you sought to achieve.

- Write a page or so explaining to your instructor how the readings in this chapter influenced your essay. Do you find influence from a single selection or from several selections? Quote from the se-lections and your final revision to show how your essay was influ-enced by your reading of other essays in the same genre. Finally, if in reviewing the selections you have found something further you could do to improve your own essay, indicate briefly what you would change and which of the selections suggested the change.

CONSIDERING THE SOCIAL DIMENSIONS
OF AUTOBIOGRAPHY

"The unexamined life is not worth living," declared the Greek philosopher Socrates more than two thousand years ago, and few people would disagree today. One way to examine your life is by writing about events that have special significance for you. Contemplating this significance can lead you to recognize personal strengths and weaknesses and to clarify your beliefs and values.

At the same time, reading others' autobiographical writing can help forge connections among people. When we read about another person's life, we often see reflections of our own experience, enabling us to identify and empathize. Just as often, however, we are struck more by how different another's life is from ours, and we see that people can have radically different experiences, even within the same society. Think of the dramatic contrast between Audre Lorde's experience and Annie Dillard's, or between Dillard's and Tobias Wolff's. Reading their autobiographical essays makes us aware of how such factors as race, class, gender, age, health, region, and sexual orientation influence all our lives.

One way to understand Lorde's experience, for example, is to think about the legacy of racism: how it fosters anger and frustration, defeats hope and aspiration, and makes parents despair of protecting their children from hurt. Similarly, Wolff's experience gives us insight into how the American myth of the cowboy has defined manliness partly in terms of guns and power. Reading about such events in other people's lives may not completely bridge the divides that separate us, but it can help us better understand one another and the circumstances affecting our lives. Striving as readers and as writers to forge connections with other people is important, but so is recognizing the differences—welcome as well as unwelcome—that exist in our diverse society.

These ideas about autobiographical writing lead to some basic questions about how we understand ourselves and our relationships with others.

Autobiography and Self-Discovery. If autobiography leads to self-discovery, what do we mean by the "self"? Should we think of the self as our "true" essence or as the different roles we play in different situations? Put another way, does what you are define what you do or does what you do define who you are?

If we accept the idea of an essential self, autobiographical writing helps us in the search to discover who we truly are. Given this idea of the self, for example, we might see Tobias Wolff as searching to understand whether he is the kind of person who shoots squirrels or the kind of person who cries over dead animals. If, on the other hand, we accept the idea that the various roles we play are what create the self, then autobiographical writing allows us to reveal the many sides of our personality. This view of the self assumes that we are not the same to all people, but that we present different self-images to different people in different situations. Given this idea, we might see Wolff as presenting his sympathetic side to his mother, but keeping his aggressive, "manly" side secret from her.

Also recall Wolff's comment in the headnote prior to the reading: that autobiography for him is "part memory, part invention," that "the very act of writing has transformed the original experience into another experience more 'real' to me than what I started with." Here, he brings up another essential question about autobiography and self-discovery. How "true" is autobiography? Surely when we relate past experience through the distorting lens of memory, there are bound to be discrepancies between what we write and what "actually" happened. Moreover, in the interest of telling a good story—or presenting a particular image of themselves—autobiographers will almost inevitably edit or embellish the event in some way, whether consciously or not.

Ways of Interpreting Our Experience.   Beyond these questions of self-identity and autobiography lies the further question of how we interpret autobiography—whether psychologically, in terms of personal feelings, relationships, conflicts, and desires, or more publicly, in terms of the social, political, and cultural conditions within which we live. You can understand these different perspectives by applying them to the autobiographical selections in this chapter. Wolff's essay, for example, could be seen in psychological terms as a family drama, the story of an adolescent boy trying to assert his manhood. Or it could be seen in political terms as a critique of power and war. Brandt's essay could be interpreted psychologically, either in terms of her childish desire to have what she wants when she wants it or in terms of her conflict with her mother. It also could be interpreted politically, perhaps in terms of class, race, or gender: imagine how the arrest might have gone differently, for example, if Brandt were anything other than a young, white, middle-class woman.

For Discussion

Following are some questions that might spark thinking and discussion about the ways we represent our life experience in autobiographical essays. Note down your thoughts as you read them or discuss them in class. Then, write a page or so for your instructor exploring your own ideas and conclusions.

1. Many people believe that reading others' autobiographical essays opens our minds to a richer view of experience and a fuller understanding of people different from us: a different generation,

religion, ethnic group, gender, whatever. Recall one essay, either from this chapter or by one of your classmates, that strikes you as representing an experience quite different from your own.

How do you respond to this difference: Does it arouse your curiosity? Your compassion? Are you put off by the strangeness? Do you have contradictory feelings? What value, if any, do you see in reading about the lives of people different from you? As a writer, how do you feel about presenting your own life to readers who may be different from you?

2. What thoughts do you now have about autobiography and self-discovery. Do you think your own autobiographical writing reveals your single, essential, true self? Or does it show different aspects of your personality? When you were writing your essay about a remembered event, did you try to discover who you truly are? Were you aware of contradictions between how you acted at certain moments and how you like to think of yourself? Did you see yourself as playing different roles for different people?

Think about how you describe yourself in your invention notes and drafts. We can see from the Writer at Work that Brandt, for example, thought of herself in several different ways. Confronted by her mother's disapproval, Brandt writes in the final draft that she is a "terrible human being." But in her invention notes, she describes herself as basically a "reasonable" person who simply did something stupid.

Also think about how true or how fictional your story is. In what ways did you embellish memories, as Wolff says he did?

3. Consider how you've tended to interpret the essays you've read about significant events in other people's lives. Have you understood them primarily in personal, psychological terms? Or in social, possibly political terms? Or in some of both? In reading Annie Dillard's essay, for example, did you wonder why she was so intent on finding the amoeba? Did you see her behavior as obsessive or her need for approval as indicating low self-esteem? Or did you think of her essay more in social terms: perhaps, contrasting Dillard's privileged childhood to Lorde's or thinking about her parents' style of child-raising or whether they would have encouraged her scientific curiosity more if she had been a boy.

When you were writing about your own life, in what terms did you think about your experience? Did you see yourself as being motivated by certain needs or fears? Or did you see yourself as being influenced more by external forces? What do you think we gain or lose from these different ways of understanding experience?

■ Invited by a sports magazine to write an article about the person who most influenced him, a professional football player writes about his high school football coach. He admits that his coach had such a powerful influence that he still finds himself doing things to win his approval and admiration, even though he never was able to please him in high school. He relates several anecdotes to show how the coach deliberately tried to humiliate him: challenging him to an arm-wrestling match and laughing at him when he lost, and making him do so many pushups and run so many laps that he collapsed in exhaustion.

■ A novelist writes in her autobiography about an aunt who was notorious for lying. She describes some of her aunt's most fantastic lies and the hilarious trouble they caused. Most members of the family found the woman's behavior annoying and embarrassing, but the writer acknowledges having secretly sympathized with her. As she describes her aunt, the writer points out the resemblance between them: not only does she look like her aunt, but she too has a vivid imagination and likes to embellish reality.

■ For his political science class, a college junior writes a term paper about his internship as a campaign worker for an unsuccessful candidate. In one part of the paper he focuses on the candidate, whom he came to know and to admire. He describes the woman's energy and ambition, her broad understanding of issues and attention to detail. The student writes about the anger and bitterness he felt when she lost and his amazement that the candidate seemed genuinely philosophical about her defeat.

■ Upon learning that one of her former law professors is to be honored for service to the community, an attorney decides to write an article about him for her law school alumni magazine. She criticizes him for the hard treatment he gave her, the first black woman to attend the school, illustrating her point with a few anecdotes. But she also admits that she now realizes that although he often seemed unfair, he prepared her for the competitive world of law better than any of her other teachers did.

Remembering People 3

■ For a composition class, a student writes about an old friend who had once been like a sister to her. Along with anecdotes demonstrating how very close they were, she reconstructs a conversation they had that she's never forgotten. In it they talked about their hopes for the future, specifically about going away to college together and eventually opening a small business. But the friend got married instead, and they have since grown apart. Reflecting on her friend and on what happened to their friendship, the writer acknowledges feelings of loss and betrayal.

A s these scenarios suggest, the kind of biography you will be reading and writing in this chapter is firsthand biography, not the more formal researched biography of a widely known contemporary or historical figure. Firsthand biography describes someone who played a significant role in the writer's life. Like writing about remembered events, it is autobiographical. The aim is twofold: to portray the person vividly so that readers can imagine what he or she was like, and to show how the person was significant in your life.

Although your writing will reveal something about yourself and your relationship with the person, the focus should remain fixed on the person you are describing—physical appearance, mannerisms, way of speaking, typical behavior toward you and others, specific anecdotes illustrating character traits and giving insight into the nature of your relationship. You may, like the football player and the attorney, decide to write about someone who was once in a position of authority over you. Or you may, like the composition student, choose to describe a peer. The person you select may have been a passing acquaintance, like the unsuccessful candidate, or someone you knew for a long time, like the overly imaginative aunt. The possibilities are endless.

Writing about someone with whom you've had an important relationship invites you to consider the different roles others play in your life and to contemplate the complexity of personal relationships. Many of us have a tendency to oversimplify, to remember only the very best or the very worst. We may demonize those who have mistreated or frustrated us and idealize those who have helped or inspired us. Writing thoughtfully about another person may help you avoid thinking of others in terms of such caricature and stereotype. Searching your memory for descriptive details and illustrative anecdotes encourages you to portray others as complex individuals with both vulnerabilities and strengths. It can also lead you to acknowledge qualities you may have overlooked, see nuances you had not appreciated. Writing can even help you sort through and better understand your feelings, perhaps making you realize that they are less certain, more ambivalent, than you had previously thought.

Writing in Your Other Courses

Writing about other people and their significance in one's life is not a typical academic writing assignment, but you are likely to encounter it in one or more college courses nevertheless. Here are some assignments requiring this kind of writing:

- *For a theater workshop:* Write and perform a monologue portraying a significant person in your life. Rehearse and revise the monologue with another workshop member before presenting it in class.

- *For an education class:* Write about a teacher who was unusually effective, focusing on qualities that seem to have contributed to his or her effectiveness. To move beyond generalities, relate at least three specific occasions that show this teacher's effectiveness. What, exactly, did the teacher do, and how did she or he help you learn?

- *For a history class focusing on American ethnic groups:* Describe an older family member through whom you have best come to understand your ethnic roots. Relate two or three anecdotes that you think best represents what he or she taught you.

- *For a philosophy class:* What would constitute living a life according to Aristotle's Golden Mean? Describe a person you know who comes close to accomplishing this goal.

For Group Inquiry

The scenarios that open this chapter suggest some occasions for writing about people important in one's life. Imagine that you have been asked to write about someone who had a significant effect on your childhood. The person can be either another child or someone older, someone you still know or someone who long ago passed out of your life. The only requirements are that your relationship seems important to you now and that you remember the person well.

Get together with two or three other students. Allow around thirty minutes to work together—fifteen to discuss your subjects, and then fifteen to consider the rhetorical situation. Take two or three minutes each to describe your person, mentioning some unique characteristics and telling about something he or she once did. After presenting the person, ask the other members of the group for their impressions of him or her.

Then, as a group, consider the rhetorical situation of telling about a remembered person:

- What problems did you each encounter choosing and telling about someone? How did the audience—that is, the group—affect your choice?

- Did everyone in the group have the same impression of each subject? Were any of you surprised by any of the impressions?

- What did you each learn about yourself from telling about someone else?

Readings

Maya Angelou, a poet as well as an autobiographer, has also worked as an actress, singer, editor, professor, and administrator of the Southern Christian Leadership Conference. In 1993 she was honored by President Clinton when he asked her to write a poem for his inauguration. Her poem celebrated the ethnic diversity of the United States. She has said of her writing: "I speak to the black experience, but I am always talking about the human condition."

Angelou grew up during the 1930s in the small Arkansas town of Stamps, where she lived with her brother Bailey; her grandmother, the "Momma" mentioned in this selection; and her Uncle Willie. Momma and Willie operated a small grocery store. In this selection, from *I Know Why the Caged Bird Sings* (1970), Angelou writes about her memories of her uncle, from her perspective as an adult of forty. As you read, notice how she describes him and selects specific anecdotes to reveal their relationship.

UNCLE WILLIE
MAYA ANGELOU

When Bailey was six and I a year younger, we used to rattle off the times tables with the speed I was later to see Chinese children in San Francisco employ on their abacuses. Our summer-gray pot-bellied stove bloomed rosy red during winter, and became a severe disciplinarian threat if we were so foolish as to indulge in making mistakes. 1

Uncle Willie used to sit, like a giant black Z (he had been crippled as a child), and hear us testify to the Lafayette County Training Schools' abilities. His face pulled down on the left side, as if a pulley had been attached to his lower teeth, and his left hand was only a mite bigger than Bailey's, but on the second mistake or on the third hesitation his big overgrown right hand would catch one of us behind the collar, and in the same moment would thrust the culprit toward the dull red heater, which throbbed like a devil's toothache. We were never burned, although once I might have been when I was so terrified I tried to jump onto the stove to remove the possibility of its remaining a threat. Like most children, I thought if I could face the worst danger voluntarily, and *triumph*, I would forever have power over it. But in my case of sacrificial effort I was thwarted. Uncle Willie held tight to my dress and I only got close enough to smell the clean dry scent of hot iron. We learned the times tables without understanding their grand principle, simply because we had the capacity and no alternative. 2

The tragedy of lameness seems so unfair to children that they are embarrassed in its presence. And they, most recently off nature's mold, sense that they have only narrowly missed being another of her jokes. In relief at the narrow escape, they vent their emotions in impatience and criticism of the unlucky cripple. 3

Momma related times without end, and without any show of emotion, how Uncle Willie had been dropped when he was three years old by a woman who was minding him. She seemed to hold no rancor against the baby-sitter, nor for her just 4

God who allowed the accident. She felt it necessary to explain over and over again to those who knew the story by heart that he wasn't "born that way."

In our society, where two-legged, two-armed strong Black men were able at best   5 to eke out only the necessities of life, Uncle Willie, with his starched shirts, shined shoes and shelves full of food, was the whipping boy and butt of jokes of the underemployed and underpaid. Fate not only disabled him but laid a double-tiered barrier in his path. He was also proud and sensitive. Therefore he couldn't pretend that he wasn't crippled, nor could he deceive himself that people were not repelled by his defect.

Only once in all the years of trying not to watch him, I saw him pretend to himself   6 and others that he wasn't lame.

Coming home from school one day, I saw a dark car in our front yard. I rushed   7 in to find a strange man and woman (Uncle Willie said later they were school teachers from Little Rock) drinking Dr. Pepper in the cool of the Store. I sensed a wrongness around me, like an alarm clock that had gone off without being set.

I knew it couldn't be the strangers. Not frequently, but often enough, travelers   8 pulled off the main road to buy tobacco or soft drinks in the only Negro store in Stamps. When I looked at Uncle Willie, I knew what was pulling my mind's coattails. He was standing erect behind the counter, not leaning forward or resting on the small shelf that had been built for him. Erect. His eyes seemed to hold me with a mixture of threats and appeal.

I dutifully greeted the strangers and roamed my eyes around for his walking stick.   9 It was nowhere to be seen. He said, "Uh . . . this this . . . this . . . uh, my niece. She's . . . uh . . . just come from school." Then to the couple—"You know . . . how, uh, children are . . . th-th-these days . . . they play all d-d-day at school and c-c-can't wait to get home and pl-play some more."

The people smiled, very friendly.   10

He added, "Go on out and pl-play, Sister."   11

The lady laughed in a soft Arkansas voice and said, "Well, you know, Mr. John-   12 son, they say, you're only a child once. Have you children of your own?"

Uncle Willie looked at me with an impatience I hadn't seen in his face even when   13 he took thirty minutes to loop the laces over his high-topped shoes. "I . . . I thought I told you to go . . . go outside and play."

Before I left I saw him lean back on the shelves of Garret Snuff, Prince Albert   14 and Spark Plug chewing tobacco.

"No, ma'am . . . no ch-children and no wife." He tried a laugh. "I have an old   15 m-m-mother and my brother's t-two children to l-look after."

I didn't mind his using us to make himself look good. In fact, I would have pre-   16 tended to be his daughter if he wanted me to. Not only did I not feel any loyalty to my own father, I figured that if I had been Uncle Willie's child I would have received much better treatment.

The couple left after a few minutes, and from the back of the house I watched   17 the red car scare chickens, raise dust and disappear toward Magnolia.

Uncle Willie was making his own way down the long shadowed aisle between   18 the shelves and the counter—hand over hand, like a man climbing out of a dream. I stayed quiet and watched him lurch from one side, bumping to the other, until he reached the coal-oil tank. He put his hand behind that dark recess and took his cane in the strong fist and shifted his weight on the wooden support. He thought he had pulled it off.

I'll never know why it was important to him that the couple (he said later that he'd never seen them before) would take a picture of a whole Mr. Johnson back to Little Rock.   19

He must have tired of being crippled, as prisoners tire of penitentiary bars and the guilty tire of blame. The high-topped shoes and the cane, his uncontrollable muscles and thick tongue, and the looks he suffered of either contempt or pity had simply worn him out, and for one afternoon, one part of an afternoon, he wanted no part of them.   20

I understood and felt closer to him at that moment than ever before or since.   21

For Discussion

As Angelou says, Uncle Willie "couldn't pretend that he wasn't crippled, nor could he deceive himself that people were not repelled by his defect." Why are people often repelled by difference and disadvantage? How do we learn what to feel in the presence of people of unusual appearance or of different gender, ethnicity, or social class? Consider your earliest feelings about people who were different from you. How do you assess those feelings now? How do you manage your current encounters with difference or disadvantage?

For Analysis

1. Angelou lived with Uncle Willie for years. Here she singles out just two anecdotes to disclose something about their relationship; one in paragraph 2 and another in paragraphs 6–18. What does each illustrate about their relationship? What is the relation between the two anecdotes?

For more on specific narrative action, see pp. 487–89.

2. One way autobiographers present people memorably is through specific narrative action—showing a person moving or gesturing or in specific postures. Analyze the long anecdote in paragraphs 6–18, underlining each instance of specific narrative action. How do the actions contribute to this portrait of Uncle Willie?

For more on dialogue, see pp. 489–91.

3. What role does dialogue play in Angelou's essay? What do we learn about Uncle Willie from what he says and the way he says it?

4. Angelou tells us something about Uncle Willie in both paragraph 18 and paragraph 20, yet the two are quite different. What did she choose to do in each paragraph? How are the two paragraphs related?

For Your Own Writing

Consider writing a portrait of an adult outside your immediate family who has significantly influenced your life. You might write about a grandparent, aunt or uncle, teacher, or coach. How would you engage readers' interest and disclose the person's significance in your life? What details would you include? What anecdotes might you relate?

Commentary

We know that Uncle Willie was a very significant person in Angelou's life, yet she never tells us that directly. Instead, she shows us his significance through specific anecdotes, remembered feelings, and reflection. She might have begun the essay by stating her main point, announcing just how Uncle Willie was important to her. She chooses a much more engaging and effective strategy, however: she tells a story about how Uncle Willie forced her and her brother to memorize the multiplication tables. Learning about Uncle Willie's actions and her reactions at the time, we begin right away to understand their relationship.

This was not an easy relationship, but relationships with parents or guardians or mentors rarely are. We have mixed feelings about people we love, and autobiographers often explore these feelings frankly. Angelou shows us that Uncle Willie was proud, sensitive, and relatively prosperous. He and Momma provided a home for her, and he cared about her education. Yet Angelou is not at all sentimental about him. She admits that he sometimes scared her and that she did not always feel close to him. Had she been his child, she believed, he would have treated her better. Clearly he was not a perfect guardian, and she tells us so.

To learn about writing about remembered people, consider carefully how Angelou describes Uncle Willie. Notice how she describes his posture, face, hands; his shined high-top shoes, starched shirts, and cane. She describes objects in the scene with the same precision: the stove is "summer-gray" and in winter "rosy red." Uncle Willie leans back on shelves of "Garret Snuff, Prince Albert [smoking tobacco] and Spark Plug chewing tobacco." Coming home from school, Angelou finds not a couple from out of town drinking a soda, but schoolteachers from Little Rock drinking Dr. Pepper.

For more on naming and detailing, see pp. 495–98.

Throughout her essay Angelou relies on inventive similes and metaphors to present people, scenes, and feelings. Uncle Willie sits "like a giant black Z" and makes his way down the aisle "like a man climbing out of a dream." When Angelou enters the store, she senses something wrong, "like an alarm clock that had gone off without being set." These comparisons enable Angelou to understand her feelings more fully and to present them to us more concretely. Similes and metaphors are not mere decoration; they enable the reader to see with the writer's sensibility.

For more on simile and metaphor, see pp. 498–500.

■   ■   ■

Gerald **H**aslam is a professor of English at Sonoma State University in California known for his advocacy of western literature. He has published several short story collections, including *Okies: Selected Stories* (1973) and *Hawk Flights: Visions of the West* (1983). This essay, from *California Childhood* (1988), is about his great-grandmother. Notice how he relies on specific anecdotes and reconstructed conversations to present a subject from his childhood.

GRANDMA
GERALD HASLAM

''*Expectoran su sangre!*'' exclaimed Great-grandma when I showed her the small 1
horned toad I had removed from my breast pocket. I turned toward my mother, who
translated: ''They spit blood.''

''*De los ojos,*'' Grandma added. ''From their eyes,'' mother explained, herself 2
uncomfortable in the presence of the small beast.

I grinned, ''Awwwwww.'' 3

But my Great-grandmother did not smile. ''*Son muy toxicos,*''[1] she nodded with 4
finality. Mother moved back an involuntary step, her hands suddenly busy at her
breast. ''Put that thing down,'' she ordered.

''His name's John,'' I said. 5

''Put John down and not in your pocket, either,'' my mother nearly shouted. 6
''Those things are very poisonous. Didn't you understand what Grandma said?''

I shook my head. 7

''Well . . .'' mother looked from one of us to the other—spanning four gener- 8
ations of California, standing three feet apart—and said, of course you didn't. Please
take him back where you got him, and be careful. We'll all feel better when you
do.'' The tone of her voice told me that the discussion had ended, so I released the
little reptile where I'd captured him.

I later learned that my Great-grandmother—whom we simply called 9
''Grandma''—had been moving from house to house within the family, trying to find
a place she'd accept. She hated the city, and most of the aunts and uncles lived in
Los Angeles. Our house in Oildale was much closer to the open country where she'd
dwelled all her life. She had wanted to come to our place right away because she
had raised my mother from a baby when my own grandmother died. But the old
lady seemed unimpressed with Daddy, whom she called ''*ese gringo.*''

In truth, we had more room, and my dad made more money in the oil patch 10
than almost anyone else in the family. Since my mother was the closest to Grandma,
our place was the logical one for her, but Ese Gringo didn't see it that way, I guess,
at least not at first. Finally, after much debate, he relented.

In any case, one windy afternoon, my Uncle Manuel and Aunt Toni drove up and 11
deposited four-and-a-half feet of bewigged, bejeweled Spanish spitfire: a square,
pale face topped by a tightly-curled black wig that hid a bald head—her hair having
been lost to typhoid nearly sixty years before—her small white hands veined with
rivers of blue. She walked with a prancing bounce that made her appear half her
age, and she barked orders in Spanish from the moment she emerged from Manuel
and Toni's car. Later, just before they left, I heard Uncle Manuel tell my dad, ''Good
luck, Charlie. That old lady's dynamite.'' Daddy only grunted.

She had been with us only two days when I tried to impress her with my horned 12
toad. In fact, nothing I did seemed to impress her, and she referred to me as *el
malcriado,*[2] causing my mother to shake her head. Mom explained to me that
Grandma was just old and lonely for Grandpa and uncomfortable in town. Mom
told me that Grandma had lived over half a century in the country, away from the
noise, away from clutter, away from people. She refused to accompany my mother

[1]They're very poisonous.
[2]the brat

on shopping trips, or anywhere else. She even refused to climb into a car, and I wondered how Uncle Manuel had managed to load her up in order to bring her to us.

She disliked sidewalks and roads, dancing across them when she had to, then 13 appearing to wipe her feet on earth or grass. Things too civilized simply did not please her. A brother of hers had been killed in the great San Francisco earthquake and that had been the end of her tolerance of cities. Until my Great-grandfather died, they lived on a small rancho near Arroyo Cantua, north of Coalinga. Grandpa, who had come north from Sonora as a youth to work as a *vaquero*,[3] had bred horses and cattle, and cowboyed for other ranchers, scraping together enough of a living to raise eleven children.

He had been, until the time of his death, a lean, dark-skinned man with wide 14 shoulders, a large nose, and a sweeping handlebar mustache that was white when I knew him. His Indian blood darkened all his progeny so that not even I was as fair-skinned as my Great-grandmother, Ese Gringo for a father or not.

As it turned out, I didn't really understand very much about Grandma at all. She 15 was old, of course, yet in many ways my parents treated her as though she were younger than me, walking her to the bathroom at night and bringing her presents from the store. In other ways—drinking wine at dinner, for example—she was granted adult privileges. Even Daddy didn't drink wine except on special occasions. After Grandma moved in, though, he began to occasionally join her for a glass, sometimes even sitting with her on the porch for a premeal sip.

She held court on our front porch, often gazing toward the desert hills east of 16 us or across the street at kids playing on the lot. Occasionally, she would rise, cross the yard and sidewalk and street, skip over them, sometimes stumbling on the curb, and wipe her feet on the lot's sandy soil, then she would slowly circle the boundary between the open middle and the brushy sides, searching for something, it appeared. I never figured out what.

One afternoon I returned from school and saw Grandma perched on the porch 17 as usual, so I started to walk around the house to avoid her sharp, mostly incomprehensible, tongue. She had already spotted me. "*Venga aqui!*"[4] she ordered, and I understood.

I approached the porch and noticed that Grandma was vigorously chewing 18 something. She held a small white bag in one hand. Saying "*Qué deseas tomar?*"[5] she withdrew a large orange gumdrop from the bag and began slowly chewing it in her toothless mouth, smacking loudly as she did so. I stood below her for a moment trying to remember the word for candy. Then it came to me: "*Dulce*," I said.

Still chewing, Grandma replied, "*Mande?*"   19

Knowing she wanted a complete sentence, I again struggled, then came up with 20 "*Deseo dulce.*"

She measured me for a moment, before answering in nearly perfect English, 21 "Oh, so you wan' some candy. Go to the store an' buy some."

I don't know if it was the shock of hearing her speak English for the first time, 22 or the way she had denied me a piece of candy, but I suddenly felt tears warm my

[3]cowboy
[4]Come here!
[5]What do you want to take?

cheeks and I sprinted into the house and found Mom, who stood at the kitchen
sink. ''Grandma just talked English,'' I burst between light sobs.

''What's wrong?'' she asked as she reached out to stroke my head. 23

''Grandma can talk English,'' I repeated. 24

''Of course she can,'' Mom answered. ''What's wrong?'' 25

I wasn't sure what was wrong, but after considering, I told Mom that Grandma 26
had teased me. No sooner had I said that than the old woman appeared at the door
and hiked her skirt. Attached to one of her petticoats by safety pins were several
small tobacco sacks, the white cloth kind that closed with yellow drawstrings. She
carefully unhooked one and opened it, withdrawing a dollar, then handed the
money to me. ''*Para su dulce*,''[6] she said. Then, to my mother, she asked, ''Why
does he bawl like a motherless calf?''

''It's nothing,'' Mother replied. 27

''Do not weep, little one,'' the old lady comforted me, ''Jesus and the Virgin love 28
you.'' She smiled and patted my head. To my mother she said as though just realizing
it, ''Your baby?''

Somehow that day changed everything. I wasn't afraid of my great-grandmother 29
any longer and, once I began spending time with her on the porch, I realized that
my father had also begun directing increased attention to the old woman. Almost
every evening Ese Gringo was sharing wine with Grandma. They talked out there,
but I never did hear a real two-way conversation between them. Usually Grandma
rattled on and Daddy nodded. She'd chuckle and pat his hand and he might grin,
even grunt a word or two, before she'd begin talking again. Once I saw my mother
standing by the front window watching them together, a smile playing across her
face.

No more did I sneak around the house to avoid Grandma after school. Instead, 30
she waited for me and discussed my efforts in class gravely, telling mother that I was
a bright boy, ''*muy inteligente*,'' and that I should be sent to the nuns who would
train me. I would make a fine priest. When Ese Gringo heard that, he smiled and
said, ''He'd make a fair-to-middlin' Holy Roller preacher, too.'' Even Mom had to
chuckle, and my great-grandmother shook her finger at Ese Gringo. ''Oh you debil,
Sharlie!'' she cackled.

Frequently, I would accompany Grandma to the lot where she would explain that 31
no fodder could grow there. Poor pasture or not, the lot was at least unpaved, and
Grandma greeted even the tiniest new cactus or flowering weed with joy. ''Look
how beautiful,'' she would croon. ''In all this ugliness, it lives.'' Oildale was my home
and it didn't look especially ugly to me, so I could only grin and wonder.

Because she liked the lot and things that grew there, I showed her the horned 32
toad when I captured it a second time. I was determined to keep it, although I did
not discuss my plans with anyone. I also wanted to hear more about the bloody eyes,
so I thrust the small animal nearly into her face one afternoon. She did not flinch.
''*Ola señor sangre de ojos*,''[7] she said with a mischievous grin. ''*Qué tal?*''[8] It took
me a moment to catch on.

''You were kidding before,'' I accused. 33

[6]For your candy
[7]Hello mister bloody eyes
[8]What's up?

Why Grandma wanted the boy to return the toad to the lot

"Of course," she acknowledged, still grinning. 34

"But why?" 35

"Because the little beast belongs with his own kind in his own place, not in your 36 pocket. Give him his freedom, my son."

I had other plans for the horned toad, but I was clever enough not to cross 37 Grandma. "Yes, Ma'am," I replied. That night I placed the reptile in a flower bed cornered by a brick wall Ese Gringo had built the previous summer. It was a spot rich with insects for the toad to eat, and the little wall, only a foot high, must have seemed massive to so squat an animal.

Boy—could not figure out why a toad would leave the best environment for him to live in like Great-grandfather.

Nonetheless, the next morning when I searched for the horned toad it was gone. 38 I had no time to explore the yard for it, so I trudged off to school, my belly troubled. How could it have escaped? Classes meant little to me that day. I thought only of my lost pet—I had changed his name to Juan, the same as my Great-grandfather— and where I might find him.

building tense

I shortened my conversation with Grandma that afternoon so I could search for 39 Juan. "What do you seek?" the old woman asked me as I poked through flower beds beneath the porch. "Praying mantises," I improvised, and she merely nodded, surveying me. But I had eyes only for my lost pet, and I continued pushing through branches and brushing aside leaves. No luck.

Finally, I gave in and turned toward the lot. I found my horned toad nearly across 40 the street, crushed. It had been heading for the miniature desert and had almost made it when an automobile's tire had run over it. One notion immediately swept me: if I had left it on its lot, it would still be alive. I stood rooted there in the street, tears slicking my cheeks, and a car honked its horn as it passed, the driver shouting at me.

Grandma joined me, and stroked my back. "The poor little beast," was all she 41 said, then she bent slowly and scooped up what remained of the horned toad and led me out of the street. "We must return him to his own place," she explained, and we trooped, my eyes still clouded, toward the back of the vacant lot. Carefully, I dug a hole with a piece of wood. Grandma placed Juan in it and covered him. We said an Our Father and a Hail Mary, then Grandma walked me back to the house. "Your little Juan is safe with God, my son," she comforted. We kept the horned toad's death a secret, and we visited his small grave frequently.

Grandmother died
Grand-ma fell, broke hip

Grandma fell just before school ended and summer vacation began. As was her 42 habit, she had walked alone to the vacant lot but this time, on her way back, she tripped over the curb and broke her hip. That following week, when Daddy brought her home from the hospital, she seemed to have shrunken. She sat hunched in a wheelchair on the porch, gazing with faded eyes toward the hills or at the lot, speaking rarely. She still sipped wine every evening with Daddy and even I could tell how concerned he was about her. It got to where he'd look in on her before leaving for work every morning and again at night before turning in. And if Daddy was home, Grandma always wanted him to push her chair when she needed moving, calling, "Sharlie!" until he arrived.

I was tugged from sleep on the night she died by voices drumming through the 43 walls into darkness. I couldn't understand them, but was immediately frightened by the uncommon sounds of words in the night. I struggled from bed and walked into the living room just as Daddy closed the front door and a car pulled away.

Mom was sobbing softly on the couch and Daddy walked to her, stroked her   44
head, then noticed me. "Come here, son," he gently ordered.

I walked to him and, uncharacteristically, he put an arm around me. "What's   45
wrong?" I asked, near tears myself. Mom looked up, but before she could speak,
Daddy said, "Grandma died." Then he sighed heavily and stood there with his arms
around his weeping wife and son.

The next day my Uncle Manuel and Uncle Arnulfo, plus Aunt Chintia, arrived and   46
over food they discussed with my mother where Grandma should be interred. They
argued that it would be too expensive to transport her body home and, besides,
they could more easily visit her grave if she was buried in Bakersfield. "They have
such a nice, manicured grounds at Greenlawn," Aunt Chintia pointed out. Just when
it seemed they had agreed, I could remain silent no longer, "But Grandma has to
go home," I burst. "She has to! It's the only thing she really wanted. We can't leave
her in the city."

Uncle Arnulfo, who was on the edge, snapped to Mother that I belonged with   47
the other children, not interrupting adult conversation. Mom quietly agreed, but I
refused. My father walked into the room then. "What's wrong?" he asked.

"They're going to bury Grandma in Bakersfield, Daddy. Don't let 'em, please."   48

"Well, son . . ."   49

"When my horny toad got killed and she helped me to bury it, she said we had   50
to return him to his place."

"Your horny toad?" Mother asked.   51

"He got squished and me and Grandma buried him in the lot. She said we had   52
to take him back to his place. Honest she did."

No one spoke for a moment, then my father, Ese Gringo, who stood against the   53
sink, responded: "That's right . . ." he paused, then added, "We'll bury her." I saw
a weary smile cross my mother's face. "If she wanted to go back to the ranch then
that's where we have to take her," Daddy said.

I hugged him and he, right in front of everyone, hugged back.   54

No one argued. It seemed, suddenly, as though they had all wanted to do exactly   55
what I had begged for. Grown-ups baffled me. Late that week the entire family,
hundreds it seemed, gathered at the little Catholic church in Coalinga for mass, then
drove out to Arroyo Cantua and buried Grandma next to Grandpa. She rests there
today.

For Discussion

Haslam's family seems to have assumed that Grandma should live with one
of them (she "had been moving from house to house within the family, trying
to find a place she'd accept"). Discuss ways each of your families has accommodated older members. If elderly relatives have lived with your immediate
family, what role did they take? How did their presence influence your family?
What did you learn from this experience? What are your thoughts about the
care and housing of the elderly in our society?

For Analysis

1. What role does dialogue play in revealing the relationship between
Grandma and the young Haslam? Analyze each conversation between the
two of them, deciding what it contributes to the essay.

*For more on naming
and detailing, see
pp. 495–98.*

2.   Analyze how Haslam names things, gives details, and shows specific actions to present Grandma. Underline each use of these strategies, focusing on paragraphs 1–11 and 17–27. What do they add to the portrait?

3.   As in Maya Angelou's portrait of Uncle Willie, anecdotes play a central role in Haslam's portrait of Grandma. In the margin, mark off each anecdote. Then describe it briefly, and note what it tells us about Grandma.

4.   Study the way Haslam uses dashes in this essay. Underline each use of dashes, and consider what the enclosed material adds to each sentence. Is it the same kind of material in each case? If not, how does it differ? How else could the writer have punctuated these sentences?

For Your Own Writing

Recall some adults who influenced your early childhood and then, for whatever reason, passed out of your life. Consider neighbors, parents of friends, teachers, camp counselors, or relatives, for example. Choose one you could write about, and decide who your readers might be. How would you describe this person for those readers? What anecdotes would you present?

Commentary

Haslam's essay, like Angelou's, illustrates the importance of anecdotes in writing about people. Anecdotes are brief stories that usually include dialogue along with descriptive detail and narrative action. With anecdotes, writers can show rather than simply tell readers about the remembered person and their relationship. Anecdotes create vivid impressions. They can give readers a glimpse into the person's character, shed light on the writer's feelings about the person, or show how the relationship changed over time.

Haslam shows through a series of anecdotes how he came to know and love his great-grandmother. The opening anecdote, for example, makes her seem strange and forbidding. Not only is she very old and rigid in her ways, she also speaks a language he barely understands. Succeeding anecdotes show us different sides of the great-grandmother as the boy gets to know her better. We share his surprise when he discovers that she actually does speak English. We recognize her wisdom and kindness when she helps him cope with the horned toad's death. In both these cases, Haslam doesn't need to explain much: all he needs to do is show us what his great-grandmother was like through her actions and speech.

Dialogue usually plays an important part in anecdotes, presenting the person through his or her own words. But since writers recalling something that occurred in the distant past are unlikely to remember everything that was said, they often must invent dialogue. The key to good dialogue is that it captures the mood as well as the content of the conversation. It gives readers an impression of the person's character and how he or she relates to others, particularly to the writer. Written dialogues, unlike actual conversation, also tend to have fairly short exchanges. Seldom does one person hold forth at great length unless the writer wants to emphasize that particular character trait. Dialogue should not merely be filler, but should serve some purpose in portraying the person or revealing his or her significance.

Haslam's essay allows us to analyze closely a special kind of sentence relied on by nearly all contemporary professional writers, especially writers of autobiography: the cumulative sentence, in which phrases follow a main clause but do not modify a specific word in the clause. Here are examples from paragraphs 38–40:

> . . . so I trudged off to school, *my belly troubled.*
>
> I stood rooted there in the street, *tears slicking my cheeks,* . . .
>
> . . . and a car honked its horn as it passed, *the driver shouting at me.*

Autobiographers also often conclude a sentence with a word or phrase that modifies a specific word in a main clause. Here are two examples from paragraphs 39 and 40:

> . . . and she merely nodded, *surveying me.*
>
> I found my horned toad nearly across the street, *crushed.*

In the first sentence *surveying* modifies *she*, and in the second *crushed* modifies *horned toad*.

Sentences like these provide efficiency, rhythmic variety, compression of narrative action, and dramatic emphasis. They are more efficient simply because they save words. Imagining each cumulative element as a full sentence, you can readily see how at least one more word would be required. The sentences provide rhythmic variety by allowing a writer to avoid a string of predictable brief subject-plus-verb sentences (*I stood rooted there in the street. Tears slicked my cheeks. A car honked its horn as it passed. The driver shouted at me.*). Most important, such sentences compress action by linking two or more actions in the same clause, a device that provides greater immediacy (*car honked/driver shouting, she nodded/surveying me*); and they provide dramatic emphasis by holding off and singling out key elements (*crushed*).

■   ■   ■

Clyde **Edgerton,** a native of North Carolina, has been an Air Force pilot, teacher, and professional musician. He is also a prolific novelist. Among his recent books are *The Living, The Memory of Junior,* and *The Floatplane Notebooks.* This selection comes from *Family Portraits,* a collection of biographical essays edited by Carolyn Anthony. As you read Edgerton's portrait of his Uncle Bob, think about how he represents himself as a young boy. What do you learn about the young Edgerton's hopes and fears from reading this essay?

TIME TO GO, BOY
CLYDE EDGERTON

It is a Sunday morning, and he's coming to *visit*. He's driving through in his trac- 1
tor-trailer truck on the way to New York, from Florida, where he lives. He can stop
for only an hour or so. My mother, who is his sister, has reluctantly agreed that the
family may stay home from church for his visit.

It's 1949. I am a five-year-old boy, an only child. I live with my parents in a small 2
house in rural North Carolina.

His giant tractor-trailer truck is now parked a short way from my house, down 3
in front of the community store. I walk the distance with my parents, and there he
stands near the truck, talking, laughing, a toothpick in his mouth. Uncle Bob.

He sees me, picks me up, sets me on his shoulders, and starts walking around 4
the truck, talking to me. His undivided attention is mine. Uncle Bob's undivided attention will always be different from that of other adults, because it will exist in a
context of adventure. Here before me is a tractor-trailer truck: a dinosaur beast. And
it belongs to him. My blood kin. He, my Uncle Bob, drives it.

Now he is sitting with me, and only me, up in the cab. He has his hand on the 5
gearshift and is explaining how it works. He's doing this for me alone; only I am with
him. He talks to me about the inside of this cab *as if I were a grown man*. He pulls
back the curtain up behind the seat and there, right there in the cab, is a bed—
where the driver sleeps when he is away from home. The fact that someone could
be away from home, sleeping warmly and comfortably in the cab of a truck, is almost
more than I can imagine.

Back on the ground, he talks and laughs with a brother, sisters, in-laws. He has 6
narrow shoulders, but he's tall and sturdy. There's a tattoo on his forearm. He turns
and looks at me, while saying to my mother and father, "How about if I take the
boy on up to New York. He can sleep with me in the cab. I'll have him back in two
days."

My heart leaps up into the sky, where it loops, rolls, spins. 7

Mother and Father look at each other. 8

"We'll have to think about that," they say. 9

The conversation changes. I see something called New York in my mind—a 10
strange place with tall trees. I will ride in that giant truck and then at night I will
sleep up in that cab—in the bed behind the seat—far away from home, safe with
Uncle Bob.

I almost drown in a deep, sweet lake of anticipation. 11

He's preparing to leave. The conversation comes back to me and the trip. My 12
parents have decided.

I cannot go. 13

We hold to vague, yet powerful perceptions about certain long-past conversa- 14
tions, even after the exact words are forgotten. Hearing a tape recording of one of
those conversations probably would not change our perception—the feeling left by
the conversation—regardless of what the words really were. We would trust the
feeling over the words. Such a conversation took place after Uncle Bob drove off
without me that day in 1949. And during that conversation, someone said, "You
can't be sure about what Robert's hauling." In the air—and left with me forever—
was a feeling of lawlessness about the trip. Clearly my parents thought the trip
would be dangerous. I couldn't imagine how that might be so.

Years later, Uncle Bob told me something that explained, in part, my parents' 15 reluctance that day in 1949. Starting in 1941 he had hauled nontaxed whiskey up and down the East Coast in his truck. He was paid two dollars a mile. In 1944 he abruptly retired from that line of business, bought some land on Highway 301 just north of Ocala, Florida, put some money in the bank, built a store and home, and settled there with his fourth wife and his daughter. He was forty-eight. I was born that same year.

Uncle Bob stayed in the trucking business for a few more years, hauling fruit and **16** vegetables only. In the meantime, he turned his store and land into a combination café-bar-grocery store-service station-trailer park called Martin's Corner Trailer Park. Years before—I was not to learn why until I was grown—he had changed his name from Robert Ridley Warren to Walter Clarence Martin.

After settling down in Florida Uncle Bob wrote to my father, telling him that **17** some of the best quail hunting in the world was within driving distance of Martin's Corner. Uncle Bob owned several bird dogs and a jeep equipped for hunting. Yearly Christmas pilgrimages to Florida began—my parents and I visiting Uncle Bob and his family.

Soon I was old enough to go hunting with my father, Uncle Bob, and Uncle Bob's **18** hunting partner, Clarence Bethea. First, without a gun. Then, when I was twelve, with a gun. The traditions in my father's family—and in my mother's—were that a boy was allowed to start hunting with a shotgun at age twelve. I was no exception. The hunts, in a jeep and on foot through pine and scrub oak woods, with English pointer bird dogs, usually on a 25,000-acre ranch (posted) near Ocala, Florida, were the source of story after story I would tell to my friends in North Carolina as soon as I got home.

These hunting trips stand in my memory like gold. Two elements of the hunting **19** trip ritual, especially.

First, the way Uncle Bob woke me up in the mornings. I would have gone to **20** bed early the night before, excited, knowing that the next day would bring on the dogs, the jeep, shotguns, woods, the hunt. But night had to pass first. I would fall asleep, and then in the dark of the early morning I would feel through the covers a hand around my foot. I would awaken, move, lean up onto my elbows, and in the darkness hear Uncle Bob say, "Time to go, boy." That hold on my foot—gentle, patient, waiting for me to wake up—is something I often think of now when I wake before light. It seemed important to him not to jar me awake—to hold my foot as long as it took—before bringing me the best news in my world: "Time to go, boy."

The next part of the ritual is Uncle Bob cooking breakfast in the kitchen over in **21** the store—bacon, eggs, grits, and toast. He cracks an egg in the frying pan and begins singing, "I with I wath an apple, a-hanging in a tree, and every time my Thindy pathed, she'd take a bite of me." Then he says, "Come here, thun, take your thoothing thyrup." He is becoming his favorite uncle, Uncle Alfred, who died seventeen years before I was born, who always spoke with a lisp, and who was a family favorite. Uncle Bob cooks in silence for a minute, sings a bit, and then says again, "Come here, thun, take your thoothing thyrup." Silence. "Come here, you little thun of a bitch!—and take your *thoothing thyrup*!" Uncle Bob is Uncle Alfred, singing at breakfast, calling one of his children in to take their "soothing syrup." Then he laughs and says, "Ah, Lord, what a dandy he was. All them children, and when he whipped one, he'd whip them all—to be sure he got the right one. I do think about him often. He'd be coming in from the field, and he'd say, 'Muh [Nora, his wife],

Muh, put on the coffee.' And then that coffee would be just a perking up a storm. You'd hear it going *blu-lup, blu-lup*''—here Uncle Bob turns and looks at me and gets the sound just right, *blu-lup*—''and he'd pick up that pot of coffee and sip it right out of the spout. I seen him do it many a time. You might not believe that, but it's a fact. I seen him do it many a time.''

Uncle Bob might then tell another Uncle Alfred anecdote—all the while cooking   22 and serving breakfast—perhaps about Uncle Alfred and the red-eye (white light-ning), or maybe the one about Uncle Alfred and the fire poker, or Uncle Alfred and the revival meeting. The very same stories over and over and over. I got to know Uncle Alfred better than most of my living uncles.

I'm glad Uncle Bob was unconcerned with ''redundancy'' and told those stories   23 over and over. I never tired of them. They were about someone in my family, and thus also about me. In defining my family's history, Uncle Bob was defining me. Without him and his stories, I would be different than I am.

For Discussion

Edgerton remembers with delight his Uncle Bob's family stories, especially the stories about Uncle Alfred. Most families have a reservoir of stories that are told and retold. Think of one story you've heard repeated in your family and tell it to two of your classmates, who also will tell you theirs. Then, with all the members of your class, discuss the place of stories in a family's history. When are stories told, and what do they reveal? Do they function to create a family history or mythology? To help members of the family understand each other? To help individuals define themselves, as Edgerton claims?

For Analysis

1.   Angelou and Haslam use the past tense to write about a remembered person, but Edgerton opens his essay in the present tense. To understand Edgerton's technique, underline the verbs in the first three paragraphs of the essay. Reading on, you'll see that all of the verbs in the opening anecdote (through paragraph 13) are in the present tense. Why do you think Edgerton might have decided to use the present tense?

2.   Narrating events or anecdotes, writers may attempt to convey how they felt at the time. Reread the opening anecdote about Uncle Bob (paragraphs 1–13), and notice how Edgerton attempts to convey the feelings he remem-bers. For example, he reports remembered feelings directly: "My heart leaps up into the sky, where it loops, rolls, spins" (paragraph 7). He also relies on repetition: "He's doing this for me alone; only I am with him" (paragraph 5). Look for other examples of reported feelings and repetition. Then look for any other ways Edgerton conveys his feelings.

For more about narrative and descriptive techniques, see Chapters 14 and 15.

3.   In paragraph 21, we can observe the fabled storyteller, Uncle Bob, pre-senting a person who was important in his life. What strategies does Edgerton show Uncle Bob using? Can you find examples of specific narrative action, dialogue, naming and detailing, sensory language, metaphors or similes? How do Uncle Bob (and Edgerton) avoid sentimentalizing Uncle Alfred?

4.   A common problem when concluding essays about remembered people is the temptation to moralize (stating a simplistic judgment of the person) or

to sentimentalize the person (expressing feelings that seem false and exaggerated). Compare the way Edgerton concludes his essay to the way one or two other authors in this chapter conclude their essays. Do you think these writers avoid moralizing and sentimentalizing? If you think they do, how do they manage it? If you think they don't, point to examples of moralizing or sentimentalizing.

**For Your
Own Writing**

Edgerton writes fondly about "the hunting trip ritual." Was there anyone with whom you used to do something regularly? If so, what was it? Who took the lead—you or the other person? Think about what routinely happened, how you felt about it then, and how you feel about it now as you look back.

Commentary

For more on dialogue, see pp. 489–91.

As we've seen, anecdotes and dialogue are the stock-in-trade of firsthand biographers. Edgerton opens his essay with an anecdote showing what happened when he was five years old and his uncle offered to take him in his truck to New York. Notice that Edgerton doesn't report the entire conversation between his parents and Uncle Bob. He quotes only what interested him at the time: his uncle's offer and his parents' response that they'd have to think about it. He indicates that the conversation continued, but doesn't summarize it because it was not important to him. The anecdote concludes dramatically with the announcement of their decision: "I cannot go." Edgerton chooses to paraphrase their words, instead of quoting, perhaps in order to use the more dramatic personal pronoun "I" rather than the pronoun "he" that his parents would have used when speaking to his uncle or the pronoun "you" they would have used if they were speaking directly to the child.

In addition to anecdotes portraying one-time events, firsthand biographers also depict recurring activities. Edgerton, for example, concludes his essay by writing about the yearly hunting trips he took with Uncle Bob. In relating events that recurred many times, writers can use several different verb forms to indicate repeated or customary action: *would* ("I would fall asleep, and then . . . I would feel through the covers a hand around my foot"); *might* ("Uncle Bob might then tell another Uncle Alfred anecdote. . . ."); or the simple past tense ("It seemed important to him not to jar me awake. . . ."). Edgerton also uses the simple present tense ("He cracks an egg in the frying pan. . . .") and the present progressive tense ("He is becoming his favorite uncle, Uncle Alfred").

Another narrative technique worth noting in Edgerton's essay is his use of sentence rhythm. Writers vary the length of their sentences to alter the pace of the narrative and to emphasize certain actions. Notice, for example, that following the relatively longer sentences in the opening paragraph, the first two sentences in the second paragraph describing the writer as a boy are short and emphatic. The first of these has only two words ("It's 1949"), and the second is composed of a simple clause ("I am a five-year-old-boy") followed by a brief appositive phrase ("an only child") that communicates a great deal of information in three short words.

Not only does Edgerton purposefully vary the length of his sentences, he also uses incomplete sentences for artistic purposes. Two good examples appear near the end of the third and fourth paragraphs ("Uncle Bob" and "My blood kin"). Each consists only of a noun phrase, but treating these phrases as if they were complete sentences sets them apart, emphasizing young Edgerton's pride in identifying this impressive man driving a giant tractor-trailer truck as his uncle.

■   ■   ■

Jan Gray was a college freshman when she wrote the next selection, which portrays her father, a man toward whom she has ambivalent but mostly angry feelings. As you read, notice how Gray uses description to convey these feelings.

FATHER
JAN GRAY

My father's hands are grotesque. He suffers from psoriasis, a chronic skin disease   1
that covers his massive, thick hands with scaly, reddish patches that periodically flake off, sending tiny pieces of dead skin sailing to the ground. In addition, his fingers are permanently stained a dull yellow from years of chain smoking. The thought of those swollen, discolored, scaly hands touching me, whether it be out of love or anger, sends chills up my spine.

By nature, he is a disorderly, unkempt person. The numerous cigarette burns,   2
food stains, and ashes on his clothes show how little he cares about his appearance. He has a dreadful habit of running his hands through his greasy hair and scratching his scalp, causing dandruff to drift downward onto his bulky shoulders. He is grossly overweight, and his pullover shirts never quite cover his protruding paunch. When he eats, he shovels the food into his mouth as if he hasn't eaten for days, bread crumbs and food scraps settling in his untrimmed beard.

Last year, he abruptly left town. Naturally, his apartment was a shambles, and I   3
offered to clean it so that my mother wouldn't have to pay the cleaning fee. I arrived early in the morning anticipating a couple hours of vacuuming and dusting and scrubbing. The minute I opened the door, however, I realized my task was monumental: Old yellowed newspapers and magazines were strewn throughout the living room; moldy and rotten food covered the kitchen counter; cigarette butts and ashes were everywhere. The pungent aroma of stale beer seemed to fill the entire apartment.

As I made my way through the debris toward the bedroom, I tried to deny that   4
the man who lived here was my father. The bedroom was even worse than the front rooms, with cigarette burns in the carpet and empty bottles, dirty dishes, and smelly laundry scattered everywhere. Looking around his bedroom, I recalled an incident that had occurred only a few months before in my bedroom.

I was calling home to tell my mother I would be eating dinner at a girlfriend's   5
house. To my surprise, my father answered the phone. I was taken aback to hear

his voice because my parents had been divorced for some time and he was seldom
at our house. In fact, I didn't even see him very often.

"Hello?" he answered in his deep, scratchy voice.   6

"Oh, umm, hi Dad. Is Mom home?"   7

"What can I do for you?" he asked, sounding a bit too cheerful.   8

"Well, I just wanted to ask Mom if I could stay for dinner here."   9

"I don't think that's a very good idea, dear." I could sense an abrupt change in   10
the tone of his voice. "Your room is a mess, and if you're not home in ten minutes
to straighten it up, I'll really give you something to clean." Click.

Pedalling home as fast as I could, I had a distinct image of my enraged father.   11
I could see his face redden, his body begin to tremble slightly, and his hands gesture
nervously in the air. Though he was not prone to physical violence and always appeared calm on the outside, I knew he was really seething inside. The incessant motion of those hands was all too vivid to me as I neared home.

My heart was racing as I turned the knob to the front door and headed for   12
my bedroom. When I opened my bedroom door, I stopped in horror. The dresser
drawers were pulled out, and clothes were scattered across the floor. Everything on
top of the dresser—a perfume tray, a couple of baskets of hair clips and earrings,
and an assortment of pictures—had been strewn about. The dresser itself was tilted
on its side, supported by the bed frame. As I stepped in and closed the door behind
me, tears welled up in my eyes. I hated my father so much at that moment. Who
the hell did he think he was to waltz into my life every few months like this?

I was slowly piecing my room together when he knocked on the door. I choked   13
back the tears, wanting to show as little emotion as possible, and quietly murmured,
"Come in." He stood in the doorway, one hand leaning against the door jamb, a
cigarette dangling from the other, flicking ashes on the carpet, very smug in his handling of the situation.

"I want you to know I did this for your own good. I think it's time you started   14
taking a little responsibility around this house. Now, to show you there are no hard
feelings, I'll help you set the dresser back up." *hurt*

"No thank you," I said quietly, on the verge of tears again. "I'd rather do it   15
myself. Please, just leave me alone!" *disgusted*

He gave me one last look that seemed to say, "I offered. I'm the good guy. If   16
you refuse, that's your problem." Then he turned and walked away. I was stunned
at how he could be so violent one moment and so nonchalant the next.

As I sat in his bedroom reflecting on what he had done to my room, I felt the   17
utmost disgust for this man. There seemed to be no hope he would break his filthy
habits. I could come in and clean his room, but only he could clean up the mess he
had made of his life. But I felt pity for him, too. After all, he is my father—am I not
supposed to feel some responsibility for him and to love and honor him?

For Discussion   Jan Gray admits that her disgust for her father is mingled with pity. What is
there about parent-child relationships that results in these or other ambivalent
feelings? Why can we—at all times, in every situation—not simply love loving
parents and hate hateful parents? How can you account for the occasional
feelings of irritation, disappointment, disaffection, and distance that we all

have, even with the best of parents? How do you think you would represent this kind of ambivalence in writing about one of your parents?

For Analysis

1.   Gray opens the essay with two paragraphs of physical description naming and detailing certain features of her father's appearance as well as his characteristic habits. The first paragraph, for example, focuses on his hands. Underline the adjectives she uses to detail this particular physical feature. What is the dominant impression you get from these adjectives? What does the description in the second paragraph add to this initial impression?

*disorderly
unkempt person
spiteful
Controlling*

2.   How does Gray use dialogue to reveal her father's character? Notice her father's choice of words and her description of his tone and posture. What does the dialogue and description also reveal about Gray's relationship with her father? *anger*

3.   Look again at the way Gray describes the disorder in her father's apartment and her own room (paragraphs 3, 4, and 12). How does she make these scenes so vivid? What things does she name, and what details does she give? What seems to you the significance of these parallel scenes? How are they alike and different? *she recalls her father room & disgusting mess how could he do this to her.*

For more on naming and detailing, see pp 495–98.

For more on outlining, see pp. 432–35.

4.   The Writer at Work section on pp. 103–07 presents the first draft of this essay. Compare the two versions by making a scratch outline of the draft and the revision. What changes in organization did Gray make? Why do you think she made these changes, and what effect do they have? *The vacations does not prove her main point. excess face out*

For Your Own Writing

Imagine writing about someone with whom you had a serious conflict. How would you present this person? What overall impression of this person and of yourself would you like your readers to get from this essay?

Commentary

Like the other biographers in this chapter, Gray centers her essay around anecdotes taking place at different times and places. Instead of putting them in a simple chronological order beginning with the earliest, Gray embeds one anecdote within the other, using flashback to heighten the contrast between the two scenes. The last sentence of paragraph 4 provides a smooth transition into the flashback, and the opening phrase of paragraph 17 returns us to the time of the first anecdote.

Not only is the organization of this essay complex; so are the strong and complicated feelings Gray expresses. She obviously feels repulsed by her father's skin condition and habits, and his threatening phone conversation and "smug" destruction of her room make him come across as psychologically unstable and possibly dangerous, even though Gray specifically states that "he was not prone to physical violence." But, even though everything Gray tells and shows about her father is critical of him, she concludes the essay by expressing sympathy toward him. Some readers interpret her final sentence—a rhetorical question—as ironic, assuming that she could not possibly love and honor the man she has described. But Gray's own reflections on writing the essay acknowledge her ambivalence, feeings she has not—and may never—fully resolve. One reason we write about significant relationships is to work through such feelings. While we may not resolve our ambivalences, we can gain a greater understanding of why we feel as we do.

PURPOSE AND AUDIENCE

Writers of essays about remembered people generally have several purposes in mind. Perhaps the most prominent is better understanding the subject and his or her importance in the writer's life—analyzing and reaching conclusions about a significant personal relationship. Another purpose can be self-presentation, leading readers to see the writer in a particular way. Still another purpose can be entertaining readers with a vivid portrait of an unusual or engaging subject.

For several reasons, writing about remembered people requires careful attention to one's audience. Unless the writer uses vivid details so that readers can easily visualize the person, the portrait will seem flat and lifeless. The writer must also pace anecdotes to hold readers' attention. In addition, the writer hopes that no matter how unusual the subject, readers will see the person's significance in the writer's life.

BASIC FEATURES OF ESSAYS ABOUT REMEMBERED PEOPLE

Successful essays about remembered people offer a vivid portrait of their subject, give detailed presentations of anecdotes and scenes, and reveal the subject's significance to the writer.

A Vivid Portrait

At the center of an essay about a remembered person is a vivid portrait. Writers rely on dialogue and the full range of descriptive strategies—naming, detailing, comparing—to present a person to their readers.

In presenting Uncle Willie, Maya Angelou names many features of his appearance, singling out his posture, hands, face, and clothing. Through concrete visual details and comparisons, she helps us imagine his face "pulled down on the left side, as if a pulley had been attached to his lower teeth." She also helps us to see his specific movements as he makes his way down an aisle "hand over hand, like a man climbing out of a dream." Gerald Haslam portrays Grandma as "four-and-a-half feet of bewigged, bejeweled Spanish spitfire: a square, pale face topped by a tightly curled black wig . . . her small hands veined with rivers of blue."

For more on naming, detailing, and comparing, see pp. 495–500.

Besides presenting their subjects visually, autobiographers consistently let us hear their subjects speak so that we can infer what they are like. All the readings in this chapter include some dialogue. Angelou employs it to present a stuttering Uncle Willie, and Gray gives it prominence in the confrontation with her unpredictable, threatening father. Haslam reveals a bilingual, sharp-tongued Grandma; and Edgerton uses dialogue to show how his Uncle Bob entertained him with impersonations of Uncle Alfred. In addition to quoting, biographers also may summarize or paraphrase what they remember was said, as Edgerton does when he reports his parents' refusal to let him accompany his uncle in the truck to New York.

For more on dialogue, see pp. 489–91.

Detailed Anecdotes and Scenes

In portraying a significant relationship, a writer almost always needs to tell anecdotes and to describe the scenes in which they take place. Anecdotes—short, pointed stories about specific incidents—reveal the subject's character and dramatize the writer's relationship with him or her.

More than half of Angelou's portrait of Uncle Willie is taken up by anecdotes. In the first, Uncle Willie stops her just short of burning herself during her recitation of the multiplication tables. The second demonstrates the possibilities of an extended, dramatic anecdote in essays about remembered people. It begins (paragraph 6) with a general statement of what the anecdote will reveal: "Only once in all the years of trying not to watch him, I saw him pretend to himself and others that he wasn't lame." It ends (paragraph 20) with a return to this general idea: a conjecture about Uncle Willie's feelings about his lameness and his motives for deceiving the Little Rock couple. Within these "framing" elements, the anecdote includes tension, variation in pacing, specific narrative action, dialogue, and remembered feelings and present perspective. Angelou also describes parts of the scene in each anecdote. The stove warming the arithmetic lesson is a "dull red heater, which throbbed like a devil's toothache."

For more on these narrative strategies, see Chapter 14.

In addition to anecdotes depicting one-time incidents, biographers may also portray recurring activities. Edgerton concludes his essay by presenting what he calls the "hunting trip ritual." He describes the way his Uncle Bob typically woke him in the mornings and how he always entertained him with stories about Uncle Alfred while cooking breakfast. Not only does Edgerton give readers the flavor of Uncle Bob's repeated performances; he also remarks on the importance of these stories in his own life.

Indication of the Person's Significance

Portrait writers choose as their subjects people they consider significant—those they have loved or feared, those who have influenced them, those they have tried to impress—and they try to make clear exactly what that significance is. Whether or not they state this significance directly, they convey it through anecdotes, descriptions of recurring activities, vivid details—or all of these. For example, Haslam never tells us directly that he loved and revered Grandma, though he does say at one point, "I wasn't afraid of my great-grandmother any longer." Instead he shows us through anecdotes, recurring interactions with him and other family members, and Grandma's comments that she had earned his trust and that he had come to love her.

Angelou's relationship with Uncle Willie is highly ambivalent, like Gray's with her father. Neither tries to force a neat resolution, reducing deep and contradictory feelings to simple love or hate. They acknowledge ambivalence and accept it. In many portraits, in fact, the significance seems to lie in just this realization about the inevitable complexity of close relationships. Similarly, good writers avoid sentimentalizing the relationship, neither damning nor idealizing their subject. Gray comes close to damning her father, but stops just short of it by admitting her feelings of pity and responsibility. Angelou sympathizes with Uncle Willie's shame about his lameness and stuttering, but she does not present him as a long-suffering saint.

Guide to Writing

THE WRITING ASSIGNMENT

Write an essay about a person who has been important in your life. Strive to present a vivid portrait of this person, one that will let your readers see his or her character and the significance to you of the relationship.

INVENTION

The following activities will help you choose a subject, define his or her significance for you, characterize your relationship, and describe the person.

Choosing a Person to Write About

You might set a timer and brainstorm your list on a computer with the monitor brightness turned all the way down. Enter as many possibilities as you can in ten minutes. Then, turn the brightness up, be sure all the names make sense, and print out a copy to make notes on.

You may already have a person in mind. Even if you do, however, you will want to consider other people in order to choose the best possible subject. The following activities will help you make the choice.

Make a list of people you could write about, such as relatives, teachers, coaches, employers, friends, neighbors, and others. Make your list as complete as you can, including people you knew for a long time and those you knew briefly, people you knew long ago and those you knew recently, people you liked and those you disliked. Following are some categories of significant people that may give you ideas:

- Anyone who had authority over you or for whom you felt responsible
- Anyone who helped you in difficulty or made life difficult for you
- Anyone whose advice or actions influenced you
- Anyone who taught you something important about yourself

- Anyone who ever inspired strong emotions in you—admiration, envy, disapproval, fascination
- Anyone whose behavior or values led you to question your own
- Anyone who really surprised or disappointed you
- Anyone who cared for you or supported you

Look over your list of possible subjects and choose a person whom you can describe vividly, whose significance in your life you are eager to explore, and who interests you enough to interest your readers. You may find that your choice is easy to make, or you may have several subjects that seem equally attractive. Make the best decision you can for now. If the subject does not work out, you can try a different subject later.

Describing the Person

If you can, save these lists on a word processor. Then, as you begin to draft later, you can call up the file on a second screen and easily transfer details you want to use in your draft.

The following activities will help you recall specific information you can use to describe the person. If you complete them thoughtfully, you will have a wealth of remembered detail to draw on in drafting your essay. Even after you start drafting, these lists are a good place to capture fleeting memories that can be incorporated later as you need them.

Physical Features.   Try to visualize the person clearly. With this image in mind, list physical features you remember, putting one item on each line. Then describe each feature in words or brief phrases, such as "cheeks—round, bright red spots in middle." You might start at the top, with the person's hair and face, and work down to the feet. Or you might start with the person's general build, then move in close for specific details.

Next, think about the person's way of dressing, including jewelry, hats, or other accessories. List these items, including the purpose or occasion if necessary. Then describe the items in words or brief phrases.

Behavior.   Think about the way the person moved and acted and about his or her special interests or particular activities. Again, make a list as extensive as possible, considering the following points and putting one item on a line.

- Any specific gestures or habits you remember
- Activities or interests typical of the person
- Ways you recall him or her "in action": walking, running, driving a car, sitting at the kitchen table
- What you observed when the person expressed a mood or emotion. What expressions or actions showed you what the person was feeling?

Now go back and describe each item more fully in words or brief phrases if necessary.

Speech.   Think about times you observed the person in conversation. What can you remember about the way he or she speaks? List now:

- Any memorable phrases or expressions
- Tone of voice and the manner of speech
- The first thing you remember the person ever saying to you
- The most memorable thing you recall him or her saying

Reconstruct one or more brief conversations between the person and yourself or someone else. Set each conversation up as a dialogue, with each person's words starting a new line.

Anecdotes.   Can you recall any important events or incidents associated with your subject? Is he or she associated in your mind with a particular location, certain objects or activities, a particular time in your life, or another person? List these items, one per line.

Think of some anecdotes about specific incidents or events that stand out in your mind. Briefly list as many anecdotes as you can remember, one per line. Next to each one, put a number from 1 to 3, indicating how much that anecdote tells about the person or about your relationship to the person (1 = very telling, 2 = somewhat telling, 3 = not especially telling).

Choose one particularly telling anecdote from your list and write about it for ten minutes, describing what happened in a way that will interest a reader. Try to illuminate the person's character and make clear his or her significance to you. Give as much detail as you can remember, including dialogue if it is important to the anecdote.

Testing Your Choice

Now that you have chosen a person to write about and spent some time describing him or her, you should decide tentatively whether your choice is a good one. Write for no more than five minutes about the person, including any details, events, or ideas that come to mind. Your purpose is simply to discover whether memories begin flowing easily or not. If your initial memories seem promising, then you have probably made a good choice.

If at any point you lose confidence in your choice, however, return to your list to consider another subject.

For Group Inquiry

At this point you might find it useful to get together in a group with two or three other students and run your chosen topics by one another. Assess the group's interest in the person you wish to write about, and invite their advice about whether what you want to say about the person sounds promising. Your purpose is to determine whether you have chosen a good subject, someone you can describe vividly who played a significant role in your life.

Defining the
Person's
Significance

Now you should consider what significance the person has had in your life. The following activities can help you discover this significance and find a way to share it with your readers.

Recalling Remembered Feelings and Thoughts.   Call to mind your earliest memories of the person. Take about ten minutes to put your thoughts in writing, using the following questions to stimulate your memory:

If You Have Always Known This Person:

- What are my earliest memories of him or her?
- What was our relationship like initially?
- What did we do together? How did we talk to each other?
- In the early part of our relationship, how did we influence each other?

If You Met This Person at a Specific Time in Your Life:

- What do I remember about our first meeting—place, time, occasion, particular incidents, other people, words exchanged?
- Had I heard of this person before our first meeting? If so, what did I expect him or her to be like?
- What was my initial impression?
- How did I act when we met? What impression, if any, was I trying to make?
- Did I talk about the person to anyone after we met? What did I say?

Now stop to focus your thoughts. In a couple of sentences, indicate the person's importance to you early in your relationship.

Exploring Your Present Perspective.   Think about how you feel now in reflecting on your relationship with this person. Try to articulate your insights about his or her importance in your life. Take about ten minutes to put your thoughts on paper, using these questions as a guide:

- Would I have wanted the person to act differently toward me? How?
- How do I feel about the way I acted toward the person? Would I have behaved any differently had I known then what I know now? How?
- Looking back at our relationship, do I understand it any differently now than I did at the time?
- If my feelings toward the person were ambivalent, how would I describe them? What are my current feelings?

If you have used a word processor to explore the person's significance, you might want to print out a copy of your reflections to read over and make notes on before making your generalizations.

Now focus your thoughts about your present perspective. In two or three sentences, describe your present perspective on the person.

Generalizing.   Reflect on what you know about this person: analyze, explain, evaluate. Try to make as many general statements as you can about the person's values, attitudes, or conduct. Include anything you think might help readers understand him or her as a person.

PLANNING AND DRAFTING

This section will help you see what you have accomplished up to this point in your assignment, and determine what you need to explore more fully, as well as guide you in the next stages of the writing process.

Seeing What
You Have

You have now produced a lot of writing for this assignment: descriptions of the person's appearance and behavior, recollections of anecdotes and dialogue, analysis of his or her significance to you. Before going on to plan and draft your essay, reread what you have already written. Look for patterns: evidence of growth or deterioration, harmony or tension, consistency or contradiction in the person or in the relationship. See if you make any new discoveries or gain fresh insight. Jot your ideas in the margins, and underline or star any promising material. Then ask yourself the following questions:

It's a good idea at this point to print out a hard copy of what you have written on a word processor for easier reviewing.

- Do I remember enough specific details about the person? Will I be able to describe him or her vividly?
- Do I understand how the person was significant to me? Have I been able to state that significance clearly?
- Do my anecdotes and dialogues capture the person's character and portray our relationship effectively?
- Relationships tend to be complex. Will I be able to avoid sentimentality, oversimplifications, or stereotyping?

If your invention writing seems too general or superficial, or if it has not led you to a clear understanding of the significance the person holds in your life, then you may well have difficulty writing a coherent, developed draft. It may be that the person you have chosen is not a good subject after all. The person may not really be important enough to you; conversely, you may not yet have enough emotional distance to write about him or her. As frustrating as it is to start over, it is far better to do so now than later.

If your invention writing looks thin but promising, you may be able to fill it out by thinking more about your relationship with the person, probing your feelings more deeply, adding descriptive details, recalling other important anecdotes, reconstructing additional conversations.

Setting Goals

Before actually beginning to draft, most writers set goals for themselves: things to consider and problems to solve. These can include overall goals— keeping readers' interest, satisfying any curiosity about the person's significance, creating a vivid portrait of that person. Other goals involve smaller issues—selecting rich visual details, creating realistic dialogue, finding fresh images, connecting paragraphs to one another. All these goals, large and small, guide the decisions you will make as you draft and revise. Following are some questions that should help you in setting goals:

Your Readers

- Are my readers likely to know someone like this person? If so, how can I help them imagine this particular person?
- Will my readers be surprised by this person or by our relationship? Might they disapprove of either? If so, how can I break through their prejudices to get them to see the person as I do?
- How can I help readers see the significance this person has for me?

The Beginning

- How can the first sentence capture my readers' attention? Should I begin as Gray does, with an image of the person? With an anecdote, as Angelou, Haslam, and Edgerton do? Should I first present myself, or should I focus immediately on my subject?
- On what note should I open? What tone should I adopt—casual, distant, confiding, mournful, angry, sarcastic?
- Should I provide a context, as Edgerton and Gray do, or jump right into the action, as Angelou and Haslam do? Should I let readers *see* the person right away? Or should I *tell* them about him or her first?

Presenting the Person

- Which descriptive details best present the person?
- What direct statements should I make to characterize the person? What values, attitudes, conduct, or character traits should I emphasize?
- To help my readers understand my relationship with this person, what can I show them in our conversations and experience together?
- What insights or feelings do I need to discuss explicitly so my readers will see the person's significance in my life?

The Ending

- What do I want the ending to accomplish? Should it sum things up? Fix an image in readers' minds? Provide a sense of completion? Open up new possibilities?
- How shall I end? With reflection? With a statement of the person's significance? With speculation about my subject's feelings, as Angelou does? With the person's words? With an anecdote, as Haslam does?
- Shall I frame the essay by having the ending echo the beginning, as Haslam does?

Outlining

Outlining on a word processor makes it particularly easy to experiment with different ways of sequencing your anecdotes and main points.

After you have set goals for your draft, you might want to make a rough outline of your essay, indicating a tentative sequence for the main points you will cover. Note briefly how you plan to begin; list in order possible anecdotes, descriptions, conversations, or reflections; and note how you might end. As you draft, you may well diverge from your outline as you discover a better way to organize your essay.

Drafting

If you can shift between screens, you might call up invention material on an alternate screen as you draft on the main screen, shifting back and forth to cut and paste invention material into your draft.

Start drafting your essay, keeping in mind the goals you have set for it. As you write, try to describe your subject in a way that makes clear his or her importance in your life. If you get stuck while drafting, try exploring the problem using the writing activities in the invention section of this chapter. You may want to review the general drafting advice on pp. 12–14.

GETTING CRITICAL COMMENTS

Now is the time for your draft to get a good critical reading. Your instructor may arrange such a reading as part of your course work; otherwise, you can ask a classmate, friend, or family member to read it over. You could also seek comments from your campus writing center. The guidelines in this section can be used by *anyone* reviewing an essay about a remembered person. (If you are unable to have someone else read over your draft, turn ahead to the Revision section on pp. 99–102, where you'll find guidelines for reading your own draft critically.)

In order to provide focused, helpful comments, your reader must know your intended audience and purpose. Briefly write out this information at the top of your draft, answering the following questions:

Audience. Who are your readers? What assumptions do you have about how they'll react to your writing?

Purpose. What impression do you want readers to have of your subject? What do you want them to see about his or her significance in your life?

Reading with a Critical Eye

The following guidelines can be useful for approaching a draft with a well-focused, questioning eye.

Reading for a First Impression.   Begin by reading the draft straight through to get a general impression. Read for enjoyment, ignoring spelling, punctuation, and usage errors for now. Try to imagine the person and to understand his or her significance for the writer.

When you have finished this first quick reading, in just a few sentences give your overall impression. Summarize the person's significance as you understand it. If you have any insights about the person or the relationship that are not reflected in the draft, share your thoughts.

See pp. 89–91 to review the basic features.

Reading to Analyze.   Next, read to focus on the features basic to writing about a remembered person.

Is the Person Described Vividly?

Strong descriptive writing is specific and detailed. Note any places where you would like greater specificity or more detail. Point out any particularly effective descriptions as well as any that seem to contradict the overall impression the rest of the essay gives about the person.

Is there too much telling about the person's character and conduct through general statements rather than showing these through anecdotes, dialogue, and description? Point out vague or unnecessary statements as well as those that need illustration. Also indicate any statements that seem to be contradicted by anecdotes or dialogues. Point out any particularly revealing statements that help you understand the person's character or significance.

Are the Anecdotes Effective?

Review the anecdotes, noting any that are particularly effective in portraying the person or the relationship as well as any that seem unnecessary or confusing. Is each anecdote dramatic and well paced, or could any use more specific narrative action to show people moving, gesturing, talking? Is there anything else you think might be well illustrated by anecdote?

Then review the dialogues, pointing out any particularly effective ones as well as ones that sound artificial or stilted, that move too slowly, or that seem undramatic.

Is the Autobiographical Significance Clear?

What did you learn about the writer from reading this essay? Does the essay sentimentalize or demonize the person or the relationship? State the person's significance, and suggest ways of indicating this significance more precisely. Perhaps it is overstated, understated, or unclear. Assess whether all details and anecdotes contribute to showing the significance.

Is the Organization Effective?

Look at the *beginning*. Now that you have thought some about the essay, do you consider the beginning effective? Did it capture your interest and set up the right expectations? Point out any other passages that might make a better beginning, and explain why.

Look at the *ending*. Is it satisfying? Does it repeat what you already know? Does it oversimplify or reduce the meaning of the relationship to a platitude? Look to see if the essay might end at an earlier point. Does it frame the essay by referring back to the beginning—and if not, can you suggest a way it might? Try to suggest a different ending.

Consider the *overall plan*, perhaps by making a scratch outline. Decide whether the essay might be strengthened by shifting parts around, perhaps changing the order of anecdotes or moving the description of the person. Point out spots where your reading momentum slows.

What Final Thoughts Do You Have about This Draft?

What effect did the essay have on you personally? What cultural or psychological implications did it lead you to reflect on? What about the essay is most memorable? What most needs further work?

REVISING AND EDITING

Following are some guidelines to help you identify and solve problems as you revise your draft.

Identifying Problems

Even if your essay is saved to a computer file, reread from a hard copy, preferably draft quality. Onscreen or as letter-quality hard copy, a paper can look more "finished" then it really is. Add notes to yourself and quick revisions as you read through the draft.

To identify problems in your draft, you need to read it objectively, analyze its basic features, and study any comments you've received from others.

Getting an Overview.   Consider your draft as a whole, trying to see it with a critical eye. It may help to do so in two simple steps:

Reread. If at all possible, put the draft aside for a day or two before rereading it. When you do, start by reconsidering your purpose. Then read the draft straight through, trying to see it as your intended readers will.

Outline. Make a scratch outline to get an overview of the essay's development. This outline can be sketchy—words and phrases instead of complete sentences—but it should identify the basic features as they appear.

Charting a Plan for Revision.   A chart like the one below may help you keep track of any problems you need to solve. The left-hand column lists the basic features of writing about remembered people. As you analyze your draft and study any comments you've gotten from others, note the problems you want to solve in the right-hand column.

Basic Features	*Problems to Solve*
Presentation of the subject	
Anecdotes and scenes	
Autobiographical significance	
Organization	

Analyzing the Basic Features of Your Draft.   Turn now to the questions for analyzing a draft on p. 98 and above. Using them as guidelines, identify problems in your draft. Put anything you need to solve on the chart above.

Studying Critical Comments.   Review any comments you've received, referring to the draft on each point to see what led readers to make particular comments. Try not to react defensively. Ideally, these comments will help you see your draft for what it is (rather than what you hoped it would be) and identify specific problems.

Solving the Problems

Having identified problems in your draft, you now need to figure out solutions and—most important of all—to carry them out. Basically, you have three options: (1) review your invention and planning notes for material you can add to the draft; (2) do additional invention to answer specific questions you or other readers have; and (3) look back at the readings in this chapter to see how other writers have solved similar problems.

Following are suggestions on how you might respond to some of the problems common to writing about remembered people.

Presentation of the Subject

- If more visual detail is needed, try naming things more specifically and adding sensory detail to bring your subject to life. Choose concrete and specific words rather than abstract and general ones. Drawing comparisons, perhaps with similes and metaphors, can tell readers a good deal about your subject. Review your invention notes for details to add.

- Eliminate any details that seem irrelevant to the dominant impression you wish to give about your subject and your relationship.

- For additional dialogue, review your notes on your subject's speech patterns for memorable phrases or expressions. Try reconstructing a conversation between the two of you for words that might "say something" about your subject. Review the examples of dialogue in this chapter for ideas.

- Eliminate any dialogue that does not contribute to the dominant impression you want to give.

Anecdotes and Scenes

- If any of the anecdotes seem dull, try adding more specific narrative details to show movements and gestures.

- Eliminate any anecdotes that do not contribute to the point you're trying to make, or reconsider your point.

- If the essay could use more anecdotes, look over your notes for any incidents worth telling about. Think of incidents that might help to characterize your subject as well as the relationship between the two of you.

- If you need to elaborate on a scene, try naming specific objects and providing more sensory detail to help readers see, hear, smell, and otherwise experience the scene.

Before revising using a word processor, copy your original draft to a second file. Then, should you change your mind about material you delete while revising, it will still be available to you.

Autobiographical Significance

- To clarify the significance this person has had in your life, try to think of dialogue or anecdotes that might show readers more about your relationship. If any anecdotes or descriptive details seem irrelevant or contradictory, cut them or reconsider the significance. Look back to any notes you made on your feelings about your subject.

- If your portrait is too sentimental or demonizing, think again.

Organization

Use your word processor's cut-and-paste or block-and-move functions to shift material around. Make sure transitions are revised so material fits into its new spot.

- If the beginning is weak, see if there is a better place in your draft to begin. Look for engaging dialogue, or an intriguing anecdote, or a colorful description. Try to find something that will capture readers' attention.

- If the essay has any slow spots, perhaps you've described something too thoroughly or gotten sidetracked telling an anecdote. See if you can speed things along by eliminating some detail.

- If the ending is flat, review your draft to see if there's a better place to end. Or try ending with a question, to leave readers with something to ponder. See if there's something in your opening that could be referred to again in your ending, thus framing the essay.

Editing and Proofreading

When you use your word processor's spell-check function to aid in proofreading for spelling, keep in mind that it will not find all misspellings, particularly misused homonyms (such as there, their, *and* they're) *and many proper nouns and specialized terms. Proofread these carefully yourself, using hard copy and a dictionary if necessary. Also proofread for words that should have been deleted when you edited a sentence.*

Now is the time to check your draft for errors in style, usage, punctuation, and mechanics. Our research has identified several errors that frequently occur in writing about a remembered person: sentence fragments, missing hyphens in compound adjectives that precede nouns, and subject/pronoun repetition. Following are some guidelines to help you check and edit your draft for these common errors.

Checking for Sentence Fragments.   Sentence fragments are words punctuated as a sentence that lack some element necessary to a sentence, usually either a subject or a verb. Writing about a remembered person seems to invite sentence fragments such as the following:

> I felt sorry for Lucy. Not because of her weight problem but because of her own discomfort with herself.

The first five words are a sentence, containing a subject (*I*) and a verb (*felt*). The next fourteen words constitute a fragment; although they are punctuated like a sentence, beginning with a capital letter and ending with a period, they include neither a subject nor a verb. This kind of fragment seems to occur when writers try to present many specific details in order to help readers imagine the person. See how the following examples can be edited to attach the fragment to the sentence preceding it.

▶ I felt sorry for Lucy, Not because of her weight problem but because of her own discomfort with herself.

▶ Frank turned over the tarot cards one at a time, Each time telling me something about my future.

▶ There she stood at the door to our summer cabin, The spare, dimly lit space where we were to become closest friends and then bitter enemies.

Checking for Hyphens.   When you use compound adjectives that are not in a dictionary, you have to decide whether or not to use a hyphen. In general, you should hyphenate most compound adjectives that precede a noun but not those that follow a noun.

> Coach Brega was a feared but well-respected man.
> He was feared but well respected.

You may have used compound adjectives in the course of adding vivid detail in your writing about a remembered person. You should check your draft carefully to see that you've hyphenated compound adjectives correctly. Here are some more examples taken from student drafts of this kind of writing:

▶ The intruder turned out to be a fifteen year old runaway.

▶ One of my musician friends had a four channel mixing board.

▶ I bought a high powered Honda CRX.

A Note on Using Hyphens with Ethnic Designations.   Not everyone hyphenates compound adjectives that designate race or ethnicity. Some groups see a stigma in being labeled "hyphenated Americans" and prefer not to use hyphens with terms such as *African American* or *Italian American*, even when they're used as adjectives before a noun. In general, though, you won't be "wrong" to follow traditional practice by hyphenating such compound adjectives when they precede a noun:

> Asian-American literature / stories by Asian Americans

A Common ESL Problem.   Unlike some languages, English does not allow a subject to be repeated by a pronoun (*he, she, it, you, we, they*)

▶ My Great-Aunt Sonia she taught me to pick mushrooms.

▶ The person I miss the most from my country he is Luis Paulo.

▶ In Rio, the rivalry between Flamengo and Fluminense it is as strong as the one here between the Yankees and the Red Sox.

A Writer at Work

REVISING A DRAFT AFTER A CRITICAL READING

In this section we will look at the way Jan Gray's essay about her father evolved from draft to revision. Included here are her first draft and a written critique of it by one of her classmates. Read them, and then turn back to reread her final draft, "Father," printed earlier in this chapter.

The First Draft

Gray drafted her essay after spending a couple of hours on the invention and planning activities. She had no difficulty choosing a subject, since she had such strong feelings about and vivid memories of her father. She wrote the draft quickly in one sitting, not worrying about punctuation or usage. Though she wrote in pencil, her draft appears here typed and marked up with the pointings from the critical reading.

> My father is a large intelligent, overpowering man. 1
> He's well-respected in the food-processing trade for his
> clever but shrewd business tactics but I find his manipula-
> tive qualities a reflection of the maturity that he lacks.
> (For as long as I can remember he's always had to be in con-
> trol, decision-maker of the family and what he said was law.)
> There was no compromising with this man and for that reason
> I've always feared him.
>   When I was little and he used to still live with us, 2
> everytime he came home from work I avoided him as best I
> could. If he came in the kitchen I went in the livingroom
> and if he came into the livingroom I went upstairs to my
> bedroom just to avoid any confrontation.
>   Family trips were the worst. (There was nowhere to go, 3
> I was locked up with him in a camper or motel for 1 week, 2
> weeks or however long the vacation lasted.) I remember one
> trip in particular. It was the summer after my 12th Birth-
> day and the whole family (5 kids, 2 adults and one dog) were
> going to go "out west" for a month. (We travelled through
> Wyoming, North and South Dakota, Colorado and other neigh-
> boring states were on the agenda.) My father is the type
> who thinks he enjoys these family outings because as a loyal
> husband and father that's what he should do. Going to the
> state parks and the wilderness was more like a business trip
> than a vacation. He had made the agenda so no matter what
> we were to stick to it. That meant at every road sign like

Yellowstone Nat'l Park we had to stop, one or more of the
kids would get out stand by the sign and he'd take a picture
just so he could say we've been there. Get in and get out
as quick as possible was his motto to cover as much ground
in as little time as he could. I hated having to take
those pictures because it seemed so senseless--who cares
about the dumb signs anyway? But dad is a very impatient
man and any sign of non conformity was sure to put him in a
rage. Not a physical violence, no, my father never did get
violent but you always knew when he was boiling up inside.
I could sense it in the tone of his voice and the reddish
glaze that would cover his eyes. He would always stay very
calm yet he was ready to explode. He never physically hurt
anyone of us kids--sure we've all been spanked before but
only when we were younger. Although he constrained himself
from inflicting harm on people he didn't hold back from
damaging objects.

I remember one time I was calling my mother from a   4
girlfriend's house to ask if I could stay over for dinner
when my father unexpectedly answered the phone. "Hello?"
he said, in his usually gruffy manner.

"Oh, hi dad. Is Mom around?"   5

"What can I do for you?"   6

"Well, I just wanted to ask her if I could eat dinner   7
over here at Shana's."

"I don't think that's a very good idea. Your room is   8
a shambles and if your not home in 10 minutes I'm really
going to make a mess for you to clean up." Click.

I was in shock. I hadn't expected him to be there be-   9
cause at this time my parents were divorced but I knew he
was serious so I jumped on my bike and pedalled home as fast
as I could. I know I was there within ten minutes but apparently he didn't think so. I walked in the front door
and headed straight for my room. When I opened my bedroom
door I couldn't believe what I saw. My dresser drawers
were all pulled out and clothes strewn about the room, the
dresser was lying on its side and everything on top of the
dresser had been cast aside in a fit of anger. I closed my
door and tears began to well up in my eyes. I hated him so
much at the moment. All those years of fear suddenly
turned to anger and resentment. Who the hell was this man
to do this when he didn't even live in the house anymore?
I was slowly piecing my room back together when he knocked
on the door. I choked back the tears because I didn't want

him to know that his little outrage had gotten to me and
quietly said, "Come in."

    He opened the door and <u>stood in the doorway one arm</u>   10
<u>leaning on the door jamb and a cigarette with ashes falling</u>
<u>on the carpet dangling from his other hand.</u>

    "I want you to know I did this for your own good" He   11
said. "I think its time you started taking a little responsibility around this house. Now let me help you put
the dresser back up."

    "No thanks. I'd rather do it myself."   12

    "Aw, come on. Let's not have any hard feelings now."   13

    "Please, I said. I'd rather do it myself so would you   14
please leave me alone." By this time I was shaking and on
the verge of breaking out in tears. He gave me <u>one last</u>
<u>look that seemed to say, "I offered, I did the right thing,</u>
<u>I'm the good guy and she refused me so now it's her problem"</u>
<u>and he walked out.</u>

    I was so upset that he could be so violent one moment   15
and then turn around and patronize me by offering to help
clean up what he had done. That one incident revealed his
whole character to me.

    <u>My father is a spiteful, manipulative, condescending,</u>   16
<u>malicious man and from that day on I knew I would never un-</u>
<u>derstand him or want to.</u>

Gray opens her draft with a series of direct statements describing her father's
character and stating her feelings about him. The second paragraph illustrates
what we were told in the first. Paragraph 3 also serves as illustration, showing
her father's domination over the family and concluding with a physical description and a suggestion of his potential for violence.

    In paragraphs 4 to 15, Gray relates an anecdote. Though long, it is fast-
paced and dramatic. She uses dialogue to show us her father's character and
description to let us visualize the damage he did to her room. Then she ends
as she began—with a series of statements explicitly disclosing her feelings.

Critical Comments   A classmate named Tom Schwartz read Gray's draft. He first read it through
once and quickly wrote down his general impression. Following the critical
reading guide, Schwartz then reread the draft to analyze its features closely.
It took him a little more than half an hour to complete a full written critique,
which appears below. Each point corresponds to a step in Reading with a
Critical Eye earlier in this chapter.

    FIRST IMPRESSION: Your dad sure seems crazy. I can see
he's impossible to live with. Because he's your dad he's

naturally significant. You say you hate him and you call him a lot of names. But you also say he thought of himself as a loyal father. Was there anytime he was ok?

Is the Person Described Vividly?

I can't picture him. What did he look like? I like the description of your messed up room. I'd like even more detail, like what clothes were thrown around and where. Did he break anything when he tipped the dresser? Was the whole room a wreck or just the dresser? Oh yeah, the detail of his cigarette ashes falling on the carpet is great. He's the one who's making the mess, not you.

You make a lot of statements. Most need illustration. I don't get it about there being no compromising with him. What do you expect him to do? My dad is pretty strict too. But he doesn't wreck my room.

Are the Anecdotes Effective?

I don't get the vacation. Was it a birthday trip? Didn't you go to Yellowstone? Or did you just take pictures of signs? Sounds weird. The room anecdote is the best. It's really dramatic. The dialogue works as a frame I think. He had some nerve offering to help pick up the dresser. How smug and self-satisfied. Patronizing is right. Great anecdote.

Is the Organization Effective?

The beginning doesn't lead one to expect the room anecdote. The stuff about his business seems out of place. You're writing about your relationship with him not about his business. I don't have any suggestions.

The ending may be going too far now that I think of it. Also, even though you say you don't want to understand him, here you are writing about him. Maybe there's more to it than you're admitting. You could end with the paragraph before. The anecdote sure does reveal his character.

Is the Autobiographical Significance Clear?

I just said you might have more feelings than you're admitting. You certainly have every reason to hate him. You say he never really hit you. But he certainly was violent, like you said.

I'm not sure why you wrote about your dad. Maybe

```
you just feel strongly about him and need to figure him
out.  Maybe because he's colorful--unusual, unpredicta-
ble, not like other fathers, even divorced ones.  I think
he was a great choice for an essay. You disclose a lot of
unpleasant stuff about your family. You certainly seem
honest.
```

Final Thoughts

```
I guess it makes me feel lucky my dad and I get along.  I
don't know what I'd do if he was like your dad.  I still
wonder if your dad was all that bad.  He must have some
good sides.
```

This critique helped Gray a great deal in revising her draft. Reread her revision now to see what she changed; you will see that many of her changes were suggested by Schwartz.

In writing about what she learned from writing this essay, Gray remarked: "Tom's criticism helped me a lot. He warned me against making too many statements without illustrating them. He said I needed more showing and less telling. He also questioned the vacation anecdote. I guess it didn't have much of a point. And the incident with my room seemed to work so well I decided to add the part about my dad's apartment."

Gray realized that the heart of her essay was in the anecdote about her room. She also saw, from Schwartz's comments, that the opening paragraphs weren't working. Responding to his request for more physical description of her father, Gray returned to the invention activity in which she listed important details about the person's appearance. From this exploration, she came up with the detailed description of her father that now opens the essay. As she was describing her father, she remembered the incident of cleaning his apartment and decided to use the description of his filthy apartment to frame the description of her own ransacked room.

Perhaps Schwartz's greatest contribution, however, was to help Gray re-examine the real significance her father held in her life. Specifically, Schwartz made her realize that her feelings were more complicated than she let on in her first draft. In writing about what she learned, Gray concluded, "The feelings I wanted to express didn't come across. I had a hard time writing the paper because I held back on a lot of things. I'm pretty ambivalent in my feelings toward my father right now." Gray discovered she could disclose her feelings by showing her father, his room, and the confrontation over her room. Gray's portrait of her father turned out to be somewhat more sympathetic than her comments about him, expressing some ambivalence—pity as well as fury.

Thinking Critically about What You've Learned

You've spent considerable time by now reading and discussing essays about remembered people, as well as writing such an essay yourself, so it's a good point to reflect on what you've learned. What problems did you have as a writer, and how did you solve them? How did reading others' essays about remembered people influence your essay? Thinking critically, what sort of theorizing can you do about the social and cultural dimensions of this kind of writing?

REFLECTING ON YOUR WRITING

To reflect on what you have learned about writing an essay remembering a person, first, gather all of your writing—invention, planning notes, drafts, any critical comments from classmates and your instructor, revising notes and plans, and final revision. Review these materials as you complete the following writing task.

- Identify *one* writing problem you needed to solve as you wrote about a remembered person. Don't be concerned with sentence-level problems; concentrate on problems unique to developing an essay remembering a person. For example: Did you puzzle over how to create a vivid portrait, present revealing anecdotes and scenes? Was it difficult for you to probe the significance of the relationship?
- How did you recognize the problem? When did you first discover it? What called it to your attention? If you didn't become aware of the problem until someone else pointed it out to you, can you now see hints of it in your invention writings? If so, where specifically? When you first recognized the problem, how did you respond?
- Reflect on how you went about solving the problem. Did you work on the wording of a passage, cut or add details, or move paragraphs around? Did you reread one of the essays in this chapter to see how another writer handled the problem, or did you look back at the invention suggestions? If you talked about the writing problem with another student, a tutor, or your instructor, did talking about it help? How useful was the advice you got?
- Now, write a page or so telling your instructor about the problem and how you solved it. Be as specific as possible in reconstructing your efforts. Quote from your invention, draft, others' critical comments, your revision plan, or your revised essay to show the various changes your writing underwent as you tried to solve the problem. Taking time to explain how you identified a particular problem, how you went about solving it, and what you've learned from this writing experience can help you in solving future writing problems.

REVIEWING WHAT YOU LEARNED FROM READING

Your own essay has certainly been influenced to some extent by one or more of the essays remembering people you have read in this chapter, as well by classmates' essays that you've read. These other essays remembering people may have helped you choose which person to write about, they may have suggested how you could portray the person through anecdote and dialogue, they may have helped you see how to avoid sentimentalizing your relationship with the person, or they may have helped you in some other way. Take time now to reflect on what you have learned from the reading selections in this chapter and consider some ways your reading has influenced your writing.

- Reread the final revision of your essay; then look back at the selections you read before completing your essay. Do you see any specific influences? For example, if you were impressed with the way one of the readings avoided sentimentality, acknowledged ambivalent feelings, detailed a scene, or compared two people to reveal something important about one of them, look to see where you might have been striving for similar effects in your own writing. Also, look for ideas you got from your reading, writing strategies you were inspired to try, specific details you were led to include, effects you sought to achieve.

- Write a page or so explaining to your instructor how the readings in this chapter influenced your revised essay. Did one selection have a particularly strong influence, or were several selections influential in different ways? Quote from the selections and from your final revision to show how your essay was influenced by your reading of other essays remembering a person in this chapter. Finally, point out anything you have discovered you would now do to improve your own essay, based on reviewing the reading selections again.

CONSIDERING THE SOCIAL DIMENSIONS OF AUTOBIOGRAPHY

As a kind of autobiography, writing about remembered people shares with writing about remembered events (Chapter 2) the promise of self-knowledge. Reflecting on how a particular person influenced you in the past, either positively or negatively, can help you understand some of your current attitudes and feelings, beliefs and values. Similarly, looking back on a significant relationship may reveal how you typically respond in certain types of relationships, suggesting what you need and expect from other people. Moreover, because writing about significant people in your life requires that you look at yourself as a participant in a dynamic, reciprocal relationship, it invites you to acknowledge that you are not solely responsible for all of your achievements or all of your failings. It shows you how others have helped as well as hindered you, taught as well as thwarted you.

Empathy and Distance.   Because they focus on interpersonal relationships, essays about remembered people can also help you bridge the divide between yourself and others and encourage you to understand another's point of view. Maya Angelou, for example, writes about an incident that helped her understand Uncle Willie's deepest feelings. When she senses his vulnerability, she begins to see him not simply in terms of how he treats her but in terms of his own needs and frustrations, and her empathy allows her to feel closer to him. It does not, however, erase her other feelings of anger and resentment; in fact, what she realizes is that her feelings toward her uncle are more complicated than she had recognized. Because writing thoughtfully about others encourages a portrait that shows them as complex human beings rather than as simple stereotypes, writers often discover that their true feelings are, at least to some extent, ambivalent.

Yet, while essays remembering people can help you develop empathy, it is nonetheless true that, as with any autobiography, you are still writing primarily about yourself: you need, of course, to show what the person was like, but it is just as important to reveal the person's significance in your life. Moreover, however detailed and empathetic the portrait, it will always be partial and biased. You can only represent someone as *you* experienced and remember the person; you can never fully understand what another person thinks and feels or completely escape your own point of view.

Ways of Understanding Other People.   Aside from these issues of empathy and distance, our reading and writing of essays about remembered people is influenced by whether we tend to understand people psychologically, as acting out unconscious fears and desires, or socially, as embodying learned values and attitudes. For example, Maya Angelou's portrait of Uncle Willie could be interpreted psychologically in terms of a child's resentment of a father-surrogate or an adult's inability to show affection. But it could also be explained in terms of a larger social context. Uncle Willie's behavior toward Angelou and her brother might be connected to his position as an oppressed black man in the segregated South of the 1930s and 1940s. It might equally be connected to his position as a man with a marked physical disability in a society intolerant of physical difference. Depending on how you interpret people's behavior, you could see Uncle Willie's bullying either as a neurotic assertion of power or as an effort to stand tall.

Views of the Self.   Finally, if we assume that reading and writing about remembered people can contribute to self-discovery, we must consider how the "self" is defined and how it may be affected by significant relationships.

Many people think of the self as being formed early in life and remaining basically unchanged by later circumstances. If you accept this view, then you are likely to see people as fundamentally unaffected by personal relationships. Reading Jan Gray's essay, for example, you might see her as emotionally independent of her father, secure in her own sense of herself: she seems neither to need his praise nor to care about his criticism. Alternatively, you might think of the self as more fluid and variable, believing that the various roles we play in relationships constitute different aspects of the self and that the self changes as a result of interaction with significant people in our lives. Reading Gray's essay from this perspective could lead you to see her relationshp with her father as changing over time and Gray herself as different at different stages in the relationship. You might conclude that after her father wrecked her room, she was not the same person, that she was changed by the experience. You might speculate that seeing her father's pathetic apartment was a turning point that enabled her to distance herself from him emotionally, becoming less vulnerable and more comfortable with her anger.

For Discussion

Following are some questions for discussion about the way we understand relationships and represent them in essays remembering people. Note down your thoughts as you read through these questions or discuss them in class. Then, write a page or so for your instructor exploring your own ideas and conclusions.

1. We've said that writing about an important person from your past can help you understand some of your current attitudes, feelings, beliefs, and values. Test this assertion against your particular experience writing about a remembered person. What, if anything, did you learn about yourself as you are today from writing about someone important to you in the past?

    Then reflect on what your answer suggests about the nature of the self: Do you think of yourself as essentially the same as you were in the past or do you think of yourself as changed as a result of past relationships and experiences?

2. Think about your understanding of empathy and the role empathy plays in writing about remembered people. We've suggested that Maya Angelou's essay hinges on her developing empathy for her uncle. Do you agree with this analysis? Why, or why not?

    Do you see empathy as central to any other essay you read in this chapter? If so, explain its role. How great a role did empathy play in your own essay? What can you conclude about the place of empathy in writing about remembered people?

3. We've also suggested that empathizing with the remembered person does not erase other feelings but allows the writer to accept

ambivalent feelings and avoid stereotyping the person. Recall one or more examples of ambivalence in your own essay or in the other essays you read. In what ways do they suggest ambivalence? Do they help create a portrait that is not stereotyped?

4. How have you tended to interpret the essays in this chapter? Do you think of them primarily in psychological terms? Political and social terms? A little of both? In what terms do you interpret the relationship you wrote about? What do you think we gain or lose from each of these ways of understanding relationships between people?

5. Based on your reading of her essay, do you think Jan Gray changes as a result of her relationship with her father or do you see her as basically the same throughout? What in the essay makes you think as you do? Extend your analysis by rereading her first draft in the Writer at Work section and thinking about what it reveals of her childhood. Think about your own essay in the same terms. Does it reveal a single, unified self or one that is composed of different sides or that changes over the course of time?

What can you conclude about the impact of relationships on the self? Do relationships provide an opportunity for us to act out who we already are? Or do relationships change us by giving us different roles to play?

- A college student decides to profile a local radio station for the campus newspaper. In several visits to the station, she observes its inner workings and interviews the manager, technicians, and disc jockeys. Her profile shows how the disc jockeys, who make a living by being outrageous, are nonetheless engaged in very routine day-to-day work.

- A journalist assigned to write about a Nobel Prize–winning scientist decides to profile a day in her life. He spends a couple of days observing her at home and at work, and interviews colleagues, students, and family, as well as the scientist herself. Her daily life, he learns, is very much like that of other working mothers—a constant effort to balance the demands of her career against the needs of her family. He presents this theme in his essay by alternating details about the scientist's career with those about her daily life.

- A student in an art history class writes a profile of a local artist recently commissioned to paint outdoor murals for the city. The student visits the artist's studio and talks with him about the process of painting murals. The artist invites the student to spend the following day as part of a team of local art students and neighborhood volunteers working on the mural under the artist's direction. This firsthand experience helps the student describe the process of mural painting almost from an insider's point of view.

- A student in a sociology class profiles a controversial urban renewal project. After studying newspaper reports for the names of opponents and supporters of the project, she interviews several of them. Then she tours the site with the project manager. Her essay alternates description of the renovation with analysis of the controversy.

Writing Profiles   4

■ **For a writing workshop, a student profiles his college library's rare book room. In the essay, he narrates his adventure into this unfamiliar territory, whose existence he had hardly been aware of. Expecting shelf after shelf of leather-bound first editions, he is surprised to find manuscript drafts, letters, diaries, and dog-eared annotated books (including some cheap paperback editions) from famous authors' libraries.**

Magazines and newspapers are filled with profiles. Unlike conventional news stories, which report current events, profiles tell about people, places, and activities in our communities. Some profiles take us behind the scenes of familiar places, giving us a glimpse of their inner workings. Others introduce us to the exotic—peculiar hobbies, unusual professions, bizarre personalities. Still others probe the social, political, and moral significance of our institutions. At the heart of most profiles are vivid details and surprising insights that can capture readers' curiosity.

Because profiles share many features with autobiography, such as narrative, anecdote, description, and dialogue, you may use some of the strategies learned in writing about a remembered event (Chapter 2) or person (Chapter 3). Yet profiles differ significantly from autobiography. Whereas autobiography reflects on remembered personal experience, a profile synthesizes and presents newly acquired information. In writing a profile, you practice the field research methods of observing, interviewing, and note-taking commonly used by investigative reporters, social scientists, and naturalists. You also learn to analyze and synthesize the information you've collected.

The scope of the profile you write may be large or small, depending on your assignment and your subject. You could attend a single event such as a parade or a convention and write up your observations of the place, people, and activity. Or you might conduct an interview with a person who has an unusual hobby or occupation and write up a profile based on your interview notes. If you have the time to do more extensive research, you might write a full-blown profile based on several observations and interviews with various people.

Writing in Your Other Courses

Profiles are familiar forms of reading and writing assignments in various college courses. Here are some typical college profile assignments:

■ *For a business course:* Report on the organizational structure of a particular place of business, first visiting the business and interviewing employees at various levels.

■ *For an education course:* Observe a class where students are learning co-operatively, taking careful notes about what the teacher and students say and do. Based on what you know about cooperative learning principles, evaluate the teacher's effectiveness in applying them. Write a report on your conclusions, supported with specific details from your observations.

■ *For an anthropology course:* In "Deep Play: Notes on the Balinese Cock-fight," Clifford Geertz argues that the anthropologist, in order to acquire deep insights into a culture, should study everyday experiences as if they were printed texts. Geertz's own "close reading" of the Balinese cock-fight, for example, provides insights into Balinese status hierarchy and self-regard. Closely observe some instance of play or leisure in our culture and write an essay presenting your own "close reading" of this cultural text.

For Group Inquiry

The scenarios that open this chapter suggest some occasions for writing profiles. Imagine that you have been assigned to write a profile of a person, place, or activity on your campus or in your community. Think of subjects that you would like to know more about, and make a list of as many of them as you can. Consider local personalities (a flamboyant store owner, perhaps, or a distinguished teacher); places on campus (the student health center, an experimental laboratory); and activities in the community (a computer software company, a recycling center).

Get together with two or three other students, and read your lists to one another. Ask the others to tell you which item on your list is most interesting and to discuss with you briefly any questions they have about it. After you've all read your lists and gotten responses, discuss these questions:

■ Were you surprised by which item on your list the other members of the group found most interesting? Why?

■ Were you surprised by any of their questions about this subject? Why?

■ How would these questions influence your approach to the subject?

Readings

"Soup" is an unsigned profile that initially appeared in the "Talk of the Town" section of the *New Yorker* magazine (January 1989). The *New Yorker* regularly features brief, anonymous profiles like this one, whose subject is the fast-talking owner/chef of a takeout restaurant specializing in soup. As you read, notice the prominence given to dialogue.

SOUP
THE NEW YORKER

When Albert Yeganeh says "Soup is my lifeblood," he means it. And when he says "I am extremely hard to please," he means that, too. Working like a demon alchemist in a tiny storefront kitchen at 259-A West Fifty-fifth Street, Mr. Yeganeh creates anywhere from eight to seventeen soups every weekday. His concoctions are so popular that a wait of half an hour at the lunchtime peak is not uncommon, although there are strict rules for conduct in line. But more on that later.

"I am psychologically kind of a health freak," Mr. Yeganeh said the other day, in a lisping staccato of Armenian origin. "And I know that soup is the greatest meal in the world. It's very good for your digestive system. And I use only the best, the freshest ingredients. I am a perfectionist. When I make a clam soup, I use three different kinds of clams. Every other place uses canned clams. I'm called crazy. I am not crazy. People don't realize why I get so upset. It's because if the soup is not perfect and I'm still selling it, it's a torture. It's *my* soup, and that's why I'm so upset. First you clean and then you cook. I don't believe that ninety-nine per cent of the restaurants in New York know how to clean a tomato. I tell my crew to wash the parsley *eight* times. If they wash it five or six times, I scare them. I tell them they'll go to jail if there is sand in the parsley. One time, I found a mushroom on the floor, and I fired the guy who left it there." He spread his arms, and added, "This place is the only one like it in . . . in . . . the whole earth! One day, I hope to learn something from the other places, but so far I haven't. For example, the other day I went to a very fancy restaurant and had borscht. I had to send it back. It was *junk*. I could see all the chemicals in it. I never use chemicals. Last weekend, I had lobster bisque in Brooklyn, a very well-known place. It was *junk*. When I make a lobster bisque, I use a whole lobster. You know, I never advertise. I don't have to. All the big-shot chefs and the kings of the hotels come here to see what *I'm* doing."

As you approach Mr. Yeganeh's Soup Kitchen International from a distance, the first thing you notice about it is the awning, which proclaims "Homemade Hot, Cold, Diet Soups." The second thing you notice is an aroma so delicious that it makes you want to take a bite out of the air. The third thing you notice, in front of the kitchen, is an electric signboard that flashes, say, "Today's Soups . . . Chicken Vegetable . . . Mexican Beef Chili . . . Cream of Watercress . . . Italian Sausage . . . Clam Bisque . . . Beef Barley . . . Due to Cold Weather . . . For Most Efficient and Fastest Service the Line Must . . . Be Kept Moving . . . Please . . . Have Your Money . . . Ready . . . Pick the Soup of Your Choice . . . Move to Your Extreme . . . Left After Ordering."

"I am not prejudiced against color or religion," Mr. Yeganeh told us, and he jabbed an index finger at the flashing sign. "Whoever follows that I treat very well. My regular customers don't say anything. They are very intelligent and well educated. They know I'm just trying to move the line. The New York cop is very smart—he sees everything but says nothing. But the young girl who wants to stop and tell you how nice you look and hold everyone up—*yah*!" He made a guillotining motion with his hand. "I tell you, I hate to work with the public. They treat me like a slave. My philosophy is: The customer is always wrong and I'm always right. I raised my prices to try to get rid of some of these people, but it didn't work."

The other day, Mr. Yeganeh was dressed in chefs' whites with orange smears across his chest, which may have been some of the carrot soup cooking in a huge pot on a little stove in one corner. A three-foot-long handheld mixer from France sat on the sink, looking like an overgrown gardening tool. Mr. Yeganeh spoke to two young helpers in a twisted Armenian-Spanish barrage, then said to us, "I have no overhead, no trained waitresses, and I have the cashier here." He pointed to himself theatrically. Beside the doorway, a glass case with fresh green celery, red and yellow peppers, and purple eggplant was topped by five big gray soup urns. According to a piece of cardboard taped to the door, you can buy Mr. Yeganeh's soups in three sizes, costing from four to fifteen dollars. The order of any well-behaved customer is accompanied by little waxpaper packets of bread, fresh vegetables (such as scallions and radishes), fresh fruit (such as cherries or an orange), a chocolate mint, and a plastic spoon. No coffee, tea, or other drinks are served.

"I get my recipes from books and theories and my own taste," Mr. Yeganeh   6
said. "At home, I have several hundreds of books. When I do research, I find that I don't know anything. Like cabbage is a cancer fighter, and some fish is good for your heart but some is bad. Every day, I should have one sweet, one spicy, one cream, one vegetable soup—and they *must* change, they should always taste a little different." He added that he wasn't sure how extensive his repertoire was, but that it probably includes at least eighty soups, among them African peanut butter, Greek moussaka, hamburger, Reuben, B.L.T., asparagus and caviar, Japanese shrimp miso, chicken chili, Irish corned beef and cabbage, Swiss chocolate, French calf's brain, Korean beef ball, Italian shrimp and eggplant Parmesan, buffalo, ham and egg, short rib, Russian beef Stroganoff, turkey cacciatore, and Indian mulligatawny. "The chicken and the seafood are an addiction, and when I have French garlic soup I let people have only one small container each," he said. "The doctors and nurses love that one."

A lunch line of thirty people stretched down the block from Mr. Yeganeh's door-   7
way. Behind a construction worker was a man in expensive leather, who was in front of a woman in a fur hat. Few people spoke. Most had their money out and their orders ready.

At the front of the line, a woman in a brown coat couldn't decide which soup   8
to get and started to complain about the prices.

"You talk too much, dear," Mr. Yeganeh said, and motioned to her to move to   9
the left. "Next!"

"Just don't talk. Do what he says," a man huddled in a blue parka warned.   10

"He's downright rude," said a blond woman in a blue coat. "Even abusive. But   11
you can't deny it, his soup is the best."

For Discussion

Most people agree that the quality of American products and services has declined, particularly in relation to those in other industrialized countries, such as Japan, Sweden, or Germany. A popular book recently urged American business executives to *Search for Excellence*, claiming that profit will follow. Albert Yeganeh is a prime example of this philosophy.

Discuss your experiences as workers on the job and in school. How much do you care about the quality of your work? How have your work values been shaped by the situations in which you've worked? On the job, for example, what kinds of attitudes encourage—or discourage—high-quality work? In school, what has inspired you to do your best work? If you agree that the quality of American products and services is a problem, what do you think can or ought to be done about it?

For Analysis

1.   What do you learn about Yeganeh from what he says and how he says it? Instead of quoting him, the writer could have paraphrased the quoted material. (For example, at the beginning of paragraph 2, the writer might have written: "Mr. Yeganeh said that he believed soup to be good for the digestive system. He claimed that he always used only fresh ingredients in his soups.") What do the quotations add to the essay?

2.   Review the lengthy list in paragraph 6. How does this list add to what you know about Yeganeh and his restaurant? Why might the writer have chosen to list these particular soups?

For more about dominant impression, see pp. 494–95.

3.   In addition to profiling a person, this essay shows us his place of business. Reread the essay, underlining words and details that present the restaurant itself. What dominant impression does this language make?

4.   The only explicit opinion the writer expresses is in paragraph 3: "The second thing you notice is an aroma so delicious that it makes you want to take a bite out of the air." Nevertheless, most readers do form an opinion of Yeganeh and his restaurant. What opinion, if any, did you form? Review the essay to determine what might have led you to this judgment.

For Your
Own Writing

List several unusual people or places on campus or in your community that you could profile. Which of these would be most interesting to you? Why? What seems special about him, her, or it?

Commentary

"Soup" illustrates some of the problems writers face in organizing a profile. For activities, such as the surgical operation depicted in the following selection, the profile can basically follow a chronological organization from the beginning to the end of the event. For profiles of people and places, however, the writer imposes order by grouping bits of information and juxtaposing them in a way that seems to make sense. This kind of organization is called *analogical* or *topical,* as distinct from chronological.

"Soup" is a good example of topical organization. It begins by focusing on Yeganeh, thus letting readers know that what is special about the place is its eccentric owner. The focus remains on Yeganeh through the second paragraph, but the third takes us outside the restaurant and shows us what we would see and smell. In the fourth paragraph, the focus returns to Yeganeh, and paragraph 5 again shifts the focus—to a "behind the scenes" look at the soup kitchen. Although paragraphs 7–11 return to the exterior of the restaurant, the focus is now on the customers waiting in line.

Profiles reflect a writer's personal preferences for what's worth learning and writing about. Even so, writers, like the writer of "Soup," sometimes try to remain invisible. There is no "I" in "Soup," only "us" mentioned twice. This "us" in paragraphs 4 and 5 probably comes from the convention of the editorial "we" that some magazines and newspapers adopt, though the writer could have taken another writer along or perhaps just a friend. As you read the remaining essays, notice whether the writer seems visible or invisible. Depending on your subject and purpose, you can adopt either posture in your own profile essay.

■   ■   ■

David **Noonan,** the freelance journalist who wrote the following selection, started with a sure-fire subject, guaranteed to intrigue readers: a team of brain surgeons as they perform a complicated operation. His profile provides a direct look at something very few of us are likely ever to see—the human brain. He had to handle this subject with some delicacy, however, so as not to make readers uncomfortable with overly explicit description or excessive technical terminology. Think about your own responses as you read this piece, which was published in *Esquire* in 1983. Are you uneasy with any of the graphic detail or overwhelmed by the terminology?

INSIDE THE BRAIN
DAVID NOONAN

The patient lies naked and unconscious in the center of the cool, tiled room. His   1
head is shaved, his eyes and nose taped shut. His mouth bulges with the respirator that is breathing for him. Clear plastic tubes carry anesthetic into him and urine out of him. Belly up under the bright lights he looks large and helpless, exposed. He is not dreaming; he is too far under for that. The depth of his obliviousness is accentuated by the urgent activity going on all around him. Nurses and technicians move in and out of the room preparing the instruments of surgery. At his head, two doctors are discussing the approach they will use in the operation. As they talk they trace possible incisions across his scalp with their fingers.

It is a Monday morning. Directed by Dr. Stein, Abe Steinberger is going after a   2
large tumor compressing the brainstem, a case that he describes as "a textbook beauty." It is a rare operation, a suboccipital craniectomy, supracerebellar infratentorial approach. That is, into the back of the head and over the cerebellum, under the tentorium to the brainstem and the tumor. Stein has done the operation more than fifty times, more than any other surgeon in the United States.

Many neurosurgeons consider brainstem tumors of this type inoperable because   3
of their location and treat them instead with radiation. "It's where you live," says Steinberger. Breathing, heartbeat, and consciousness itself are some of the functions connected with this primary part of the brain. Literally and figuratively, it is the core of the organ, and operating on it is always very risky. . . .

The human skull was not designed for easy opening. It takes drills and saws and   4
simple force to breach it. It is a formidable container, and its thickness testifies to the value of its contents. Opening the skull is one of the first things apprentice brain surgeons get to do on their own. It is sometimes called cabinet work, and on this case Steinberger is being assisted in the opening by Bob Solomon.

The patient has been clamped into a sitting position. Before the first incision is   5
made he is rolled under the raised instrument table and he disappears beneath sterile green drapes and towels. The only part of him left exposed is the back of his head, which is orange from the sterilizing agent painted on it. Using a special marker,

Steinberger draws the pattern of the opening on the patient's head in blue. Then the first cut is made into the scalp, and a thin line of bright-red blood appears.

The operation takes place within what is called the sterile field, a small germfree 6 zone created and vigilantly patrolled by the scrub nurses. The sterile field extends out and around from the surgical opening and up over the instrument table. Once robed and gloved, the doctors are considered sterile from the neck to the waist and from the hands up the arms to just below the shoulders. The time the doctors must spend scrubbing their hands has been cut from ten minutes to five, but this obsessive routine is still the most striking of the doctor's preparations. Leaning over the trough-like stainless-steel sink with their masks in place and their arms lathered to the elbow, the surgeons carefully attend to each finger with the brush and work their way up each arm. It is the final pause, the last thing they do before they enter the operating room and go to work. Many at NI are markedly quiet while they scrub; they spend the familiar minutes running through the operation one more time. When they finish and their hands are too clean for anything but surgery they turn off the water with knee controls and back through the OR door, their dripping hands held high before them. They dry off with sterile towels, step into long-sleeved robes, and then plunge their hands down into their thin surgical gloves, which are held for them by the scrub nurse. The gloves snap as the nurse releases them around the doctors' wrists. Unnaturally smooth and defined, the gloved hands of the neurosurgeons are now ready; they can touch the living human brain.

"Drill the hell out of it," Steinberger says to Solomon. The scalp has been re- 7 tracted and the skull exposed. Solomon presses the large stainless-steel power drill against the bone and hits the trigger. The bit turns slowly, biting into the white skull. Shavings drop from the hole onto the drape and then to the floor. The drill stops automatically when it is through the bone. The hole is about a half inch in diameter. Solomon drills four holes in a diamond pattern. The skull at the back of the head is ridged and bumpy. There is a faint odor of burning bone.

The drilling is graphic and jarring. The drill and the head do not go together; 8 they collide and shock the eye. The tool is too big; its scale and shape are inappropriate to the delicate idea of neurosurgery. It should be hanging on the wall of a garage. After the power drill, a hand drill is used to refine the holes in the skull. It is a sterilized stainless-steel version of a handyman's tool. It is called a perforator, and as Solomon calmly turns it, more shavings hit the floor. Then, using powerful plierlike tools called Leksell rongeurs, the doctors proceed to bite away at the skull, snapping and crunching bone to turn the four small holes into a single opening about three inches in diameter. This is a *craniectomy*; the hole in the skull will always be there, protected by the many layers of scalp muscle at the back of the head. In a *craniotomy* a flap of bone is preserved to cover the opening in the skull.

After the scalp and the skull, the next layer protecting the brain is the dura. A 9 thin, tough, leathery membrane that encases the brain, the dura (derived from the Latin for *hard*) is dark pink, almost red. It is rich with blood vessels and nerves (when you have a headache, it's the dura that aches), and now it can be seen stretching across the expanse of the opening, pulsing lightly. The outline of the cerebellum bulging against the dura is clear. With a crease in the middle, the dura-sheathed cerebellum looks oddly like a tiny pair of buttocks. The resemblance prompts a moment's joking. "Her firm young cerebellum," somebody says. . . .

The dura is carefully opened and sewn back out of the way. An hour and fifteen 10 minutes after the drilling began, the brain is exposed.

The brain exposed. It happens every day on the tenth floor, three, four, and five 11
times a day, day after day, week in and week out, month after month. The brain
exposed. Light falls on its gleaming surface for the first time. It beats lightly, steadily.
It is pink and gray, the brain, and the cerebellar cortex is covered with tiny blood
vessels, in a web. In some openings you can see the curve of the brain, its roundness.
It does not look strong, it looks very soft, soft enough to push your finger through.
When you see it for the first time you almost expect sparks, tiny sparks arcing across
the surface, blinking lights, the crackle of an idea. You stare down at it and it gives
nothing back, reveals nothing, gives no hint of how it works. As soon as they see it
the doctors begin the search for landmarks. They start talking to each other, describing what they both can see, narrating the anatomy.

In the operating room the eyes bear much of the burden of communication. With 12
their surgical masks and caps in place, the doctors and nurses resort to exaggerated
stares and squints and flying eyebrows to emphasize what they are saying. After
more than two decades in the operating room, Dr. Stein has developed this talent
for nonverbal punctuation to a fine art. His clear blue eyes narrow now in concentration as he listens to Abe explain what he wants to do next. They discuss how to
go about retracting the cerebellum. "Okay, Abe," Stein says quietly. "Nice and easy
now."

The cerebellum (the word means *little brain*) is one of the most complicated parts 13
of the brain. It is involved in the processing of sensory information of all kinds as
well as balance and motor control, but in this case it is simply in the way. With the
dura gone the cerebellum bulges out of the back of the head; it can be seen from
across the room, protruding into space, striated and strange-looking.

When the cerebellum is retracted, the microscope is rolled into place and the 14
operation really begins. It is a two-man scope, with a cable running to a TV monitor
and a videotape machine. Sitting side by side, looking through the scope into the
head, Steinberger and Stein go looking for the tumor.

It is a long and tedious process, working your way into the center of the human 15
brain. The joke about the slip of the scalpel that wiped out fifteen years of piano
lessons is no joke. Every seen and unseen piece of tissue does something, has some
function, though it may well be a mystery to the surgeon. In order to spend hour
after hour at the microscope, manipulating their instruments in an area no bigger
than the inside of a juice can, neurosurgeons must develop an awesome capacity for
sustained concentration.

After two hours of talking their way through the glowing red geography of the 16
inner brain, Stein and Steinberger come upon the tumor. "Holy Toledo, look at
that," exclaims Steinberger. The tumor stands out from the tissue around it, purple
and mean-looking. It is the end of order in a very small, orderly place. It does not
belong. They pause a moment, and Abe gives a quick tour of the opening. "That's
tumor, that's the brainstem, and that's the third ventricle," he says. "And that over
there, that's memory."

A doctor from the pathology department shows up for a piece of the tumor. It 17
will be analyzed quickly while the operation is under way so the surgeons will know
what they are dealing with. The type of tumor plays an important part in decisions
about how much to take out, what risks to take in the attempt to get it all. A more
detailed tissue analysis will be made later.

It turns out to be a brainstem glioma, an invasive intrinsic tumor actually growing 18 up out of the brainstem. It is malignant. They get a lot of it but it will grow back. With radiation the patient could live fifteen years or even longer, and he will be told so. Abe Steinberger, in fact, will tell him. More than six hours after the first incision, the operation ends.

When the operation is over it is pointed out to Steinberger that he is the same 19 age as the patient. "Really?" he says. "It's funny, I always think of the patients as being older than me."

How they think of the patients is at the center of the residents' approach to 20 neurosurgery. It is a sensitive subject, and they have all given it a lot of thought. They know well the classic preconceived notion of the surgeon as a cold and arrogant technician. "You think like a surgeon" is a medical-school insult. Beyond that, the residents actually know a lot of surgeons, and though they say most of them don't fit the stereotype, they also say that there are some who really do bring it to life.

In many ways the mechanics of surgery itself create a distance between the sur- 21 geon and the patient. A man with a tumor is a case, a collection of symptoms. He is transformed into a series of X rays, CAT scans, and angiograms. He becomes his tumor, is even referred to by his affliction. "We've got a beautiful meningioma coming in tomorrow," a doctor will say. Once in the operating room the patient disappears beneath the drapes and is reduced to a small red hole. Though it is truly the ultimate intimacy, neurosurgery can be starkly impersonal.

"The goal of surgery is to get as busy as you can doing good cases and making 22 people *better* by operating on them," says Phil Cogen. "That automatically cuts down the time you spend with patients." Though this frustrates Cogen, who has dreams and nightmares about his patients "all the time," he also knows there is a high emotional price to pay for getting too close. "One of the things you learn to do as a surgeon in any field is disassociate yourself from the person you're operating on. I never looked under the drapes at the patient until my third year in neurosurgery, when it was too late to back out."

While Cogen prides himself on not having a "surgical personality," Abe Stein- 23 berger believes that his skills are best put to use in the operating room and doesn't worry too much about the problems of patient relations. "I sympathize with the patients," he says. "I feel very bad when they're sick and I feel great when they're better. But what I want to do is operate. I want to get in there and do it."

For Discussion

At the end of "Inside the Brain," Noonan raises the issue of coping with one's own feelings as well as with other people's feelings. "One of the things you learn to do as a surgeon in any field," Cogen says, "is disassociate yourself from the person you're operating on" (paragraph 22). Disassociating may be useful, but it also has costs—psychological and social. Psychologically, it denies feelings. It may become habitual, turning people into automatons. It leads to thinking of others as objects rather than people: " 'We've got a beautiful meningioma coming in tomorrow,' a doctor will say." Disassociating oneself from other's emotions and one's own may reflect a *fear* of feeling rather than serve as a practical strategy for dealing with feelings.

Think of a time when you felt the need to put aside your feelings in order to go on and do the thing in front of you. For example, has there ever been a time in school, or a sporting activity, or at work when you had to cut off your feelings in order to get something important done? Were you conscious at the time of what you were doing? What were the advantages and disadvantages of disassociating yourself from your feelings?

For Analysis

For a discussion of narrative pace, see pp. 487–91.

1.　The operation actually lasts six hours. To see how Noonan translates clock time into narrative time with its special qualities of pacing, tension, and drama, make a scratch outline of the essay. Where does the pace quicken and where does it slow? Which events receive the most and which the least narrative space in the essay? What advantages and disadvantages do you see in Noonan's narrative pacing and structure?

2.　Noonan quotes both Dr. Stein and Dr. Steinberger, letting us hear what they say during the operation (paragraphs 3, 7, 12, and 16). What do these quotations add to the essay? How might the essay have been different had Noonan paraphrased rather than quoted?

3.　Look at paragraphs 1 and 2. Either one could well have opened the essay. What would have been gained and what would have been lost if Noonan had begun his essay with paragraph 2?

4.　Mark Twain once wrote: "The difference between the *almost right* word and the *right* word is really a large matter—'tis the difference between the lightning bug and the lightning. After that, of course, that exceedingly important brick, the *exact* word. . . ." Reread Noonan's profile, noting any words that seem to you *right* or *exact*. Select two or three of these words and explain why you think Noonan chose them.

For Your Own Writing

If you were asked to profile a highly skilled specialist at work, what specialty would you choose? What kind of information would you need to write such a profile? Where would you get it?

Commentary

Some profiles, like Noonan's, require the writer to research the subject in order to understand it well. Although most of his information obviously comes from observing and interviewing, he must also have done some reading to familiarize himself with surgical terminology and procedures.

Just as important as the actual information a writer provides is the way he or she arranges and presents it. Information must be organized in a way appropriate to the audience as well as to the content itself. It must be both accessible to readers and focused on some main point or theme. Noonan focuses on the drama of the operation. He was clearly struck by the incongruity between the intimate action of probing a human brain and the impersonal way this probing was done. Profile writers often use such an incongruity as the theme of a profile.

Noonan uses narration to structure his profile. Instead of just telling us how brain surgery is done, he shows us the procedures firsthand. He presents us with an actual patient ("belly up under the bright lights"), and takes us through an actual operation—preparing the patient and the surgical instruments, drilling the skull, searching through the brain for the tumor.

One way Noonan creates tension and drama is by varying the pace of the narrative, slowing it here and quickening it there, closing in and moving back, telescoping or collapsing time as fits his purpose. Take a close look at the craniectomy (paragraphs 7–9) to see how Noonan varies the pace. He begins dramatically by quoting Dr. Steinberger ("Drill the hell out of it"), then sets the stage by telling us that the scalp has already been retracted and the skull exposed. With a series of active present-tense verbs and present participles, Noonan re-creates the actual drilling for us. But he only shows us the drilling of one hole; he summarizes the drilling of the other three. He also interrupts the narrative to reflect on his own thoughts and feelings. When he returns to narrating, we see Dr. Solomon calmly turning the perforator as "more shavings hit the floor" and hear the snapping and crunching of bone as an opening is made between the holes.

Not only does Noonan pace his narrative for dramatic effect, but he also paces the flow of information. Readers are willing to be informed by a profile, buy they are not prepared to find information presented as though they were reading an encyclopedia. By controlling the amount of information he presents, Noonan maintains a brisk pace that keeps his readers informed as well as entertained. He inserts bits of information into the narrative, as in paragraph 8 when he tells us that a hand drill is used after the power drill and how a craniotomy differs from a craniectomy. Sometimes the information takes only a second to read and is subordinated in a clause or a brief sentence. At other times, it seems to suspend the narrative altogether, as when Noonan explains the idea of a sterile field and describes the scrubbing-up process in paragraph 6.

Defining concisely and explaining clearly are essential to success in writing profiles. If you profile a technical or little-known specialty, you will need to define terms, tools, and procedures likely to be unfamiliar to your readers. However, the definitions and explanations must not divert readers' attention for too long a time from the details of a scene or the drama of an activity.

For a discussion of strategies of defining, see Chapter 16.

By examining Noonan's sentences closely, you can learn much that will help you in your own profile writing. For example, he occasionally opens sentences with modifying phrases called participial phrases:

> "*Using a special marker*, Steinberger draws the pattern of the opening on the patient's head in blue." (paragraph 5)

> "*Sitting side by side, looking through the scope into the head*, Steinberger and Stein go looking for the tumor." (paragraph 14)

> "*Once robed and gloved*, the doctors are considered sterile from the neck to the waist and from the hands up the arms to just below the shoulders." (paragraph 6)

"Directed by Dr. Stein, Abe Steinberger is going after a large tumor compressing the brain stem. . . ."* (paragraph 2)

As sentence openers, participial phrases are efficient and readable. They reduce the number of separate sentences needed, provide pleasing variety in sentence patterns, and are easy for readers to follow.

■   ■   ■

Catherine S. Manegold is a staff writer for the *New York Times*. She was formerly Southeast Asia Bureau Chief for the *Philadelphia Inquirer* and General Foreign Desk Editor at *Newsweek*. Her reporting has been nominated for the Pulitzer Prize four times, and she won the Overseas Press Award for her coverage of the 1991 Gulf War. This profile appeared in a 1993 *Times* series, "The Children of the Shadows," focusing on the struggle of poor urban children and teenagers.

SCHOOL SERVES NO PURPOSE
CATHERINE S. MANEGOLD

1   Crystal Rossi wears two streaks of bright magenta in her hair. They hang, stains of Kool-Aid, down her loose, long strands of blonde like a seventh grader's twist of punk: Don't come too close. Don't mess with me. Don't tell me what to do. I'm not like you.

2   At her Brooklyn public school, a kaleidoscope of teen-age rage, Crystal's teachers see a young girl with an attitude. They focus on her slouch, her Kool-Aid streaks, her grunge clothes and sullen anger and see all the signs of trouble. But those vivid slashes say the most, communicating a basic paradox of adolescence, the double-edged message: "bug off" and "LOOK AT ME."

3   This is the time, this tender age of 12, when every major decision on the treacherous road to adulthood looms. It is also the time, in the sixth and seventh grades, when some students start a long, slow fall away from school.

4   On the surface, Crystal hardly seems the sort of child who would stumble.

5   Her family is stable. Her stepfather works. Her mother takes care of the home. Her father lives just blocks away. Her school is typical, chaotic, underfinanced and overcrowded, but it is clean and relatively safe.

6   But in a competition between the street and schoolyard, the street seems to be winning.

7   "The classes are boring!" Crystal exploded one afternoon. "And the teachers are mean!" Her eyes downcast, she complained that too much class time was spent on discipline. "They are always yelling," she said. "I wish they would all just shut up."

8   Her face to the world is one of toughness. But in fact she is a child trying to navigate a difficult and often lonely road. In a whisper one day, her head cast down and fingers playing across a desk top, she admitted that she was often nervous.

9   "Sometimes I can't even sleep," she said. "I stay up all night, and then I'm too tired to get up in the morning."

10   She rarely allows herself to express such vulnerability. Instead, she tends toward bravado; in a rare moment of exuberance she tells her mother that she is a "leader"

who sets the pace in school. Her mother does not buy it. "No," her mother says as she shakes her head. "You are a follower."

Such deflations are consistent. What is absent is a quiet, steady voice of en- 11 couragement, a single figure to lead Crystal through the minefields of a childhood in Bensonhurst. Pressures abound, applied by teachers, parents and even friends, but Crystal seems without a touchstone to guide her and give her a sense of her potential.

At home, three other daughters occupy her mother's time and worry. Crystal's 12 sister, Colette, 15, is failing the ninth grade. Her halfsisters, Candice, 5, and Jovan, 2, demand attention and dominate family life, especially when their dad comes home and lifts them in a warm embrace. Crystal, lonely and lackluster, hides in plain sight.

Crystal says she wants to be a lawyer. But she has never actually met a lawyer 13 and is now flunking most of her classes. That career appeals because, she says, "you get to talk back to people" and "you make a lot of money."

Her teachers worry that she might not even make it to her high school gradu- 14 ation. They already see the signs. In class she ducks competition and is losing focus. Outside of school hers is a childhood of temptations and dangers: drugs, alcohol, gangs and older kids who linger on street corners wanting everything from sex to the coat off a 12-year-old's back.

There was a fleeting moment when Crystal's academic future seemed full of 15 promise. Her 34-year-old mother, Colleen Ficalora, said Crystal was once slated for a kindergarten for gifted students, "but she would have had to take a bus." Now, in the seventh grade at the Joseph B. Cavallaro Junior High School in Bensonhurst, Crystal is often restless, angry, and tuned out.

Mrs. Ficalora wants Crystal to break a family pattern. Not one of her own 14 16 brothers and sisters graduated from high school. Neither did she. Nor did Crystal's father or stepfather. If Crystal gets her diploma she will stand apart.

At school, some teachers are trying to help. But sitting in one class, a "resource 17 room" tailored to give troubled students individual attention, Crystal slumped on her desk. "We just sit there," she said later. "They are supposed to help you with stuff you don't understand. But I understand everything so I just sit there."

"Kids who study are all nerds," she said dismissively. "Who'd want to be like 18 that? Everybody makes fun of them."

But the kids make fun of one another for failing, too. 19

"Stooopid," Crystal taunted a friend in the resource room one morning. 20

"No, you're stupid, stupid," the girl retorted. 21

"No. You. You're stupid," Crystal shot back, her head resting on her desk top. 22

Most days, Crystal says, she is usually happy only at lunch, when she and her 23 friends bend over pizza and sandwiches "just talking." The time brings them to- gether, jostling and punching and trading stories of their day. Sometimes they vanish into a bathroom and plant thick lipstick kisses—perfect O's—on one another's fore- heads. Their mark of solidarity against a world too often hostile.

Of the 950 or so students at Cavallaro Junior High School on any given day, says 24 Rose P. Molinelli, the principal, 300 or more are at risk of everything from dropping out to doping up to slashing their wrists and watching their lives literally drain right out of them. One of the school's seventh-grade classes last year had five suicide attempts. This year has been quieter, but the threats remain.

"You can walk out this door any afternoon and get hurt," Mrs. Molinelli said as 25 she stooped on a busy stairwell to scoop up a bit of litter. Other pressures are subtler.

"The kids all know who is abused and who is having trouble at home and who 26
is in a gang," Mrs. Molinelli said. "They know who gets high. They know who gets
killed. It gets to them. I think all kids today are at risk. And parents are overwhelmed.
A lot of kids get lost."

Crystal glides through the environment as though untouched. When a fight 27
breaks out in the hall, she slips around the corner. But privately, she whispers about
the gangs, the kids who have been robbed or hurt or are threatened by bullies, and
of friends with "troubles" at home.

"I know a kid who just got shot," she said starkly. "He got shot and he is dead." 28

Classes run at or near their maximum of 30 children each, and teachers have to 29
struggle just to keep order, much less provide individual attention. Budget cuts have
whittled resources, and although Mrs. Molinelli says her teachers have come up with
creative ways to compensate for the shortages, she knows the children could use
more.

"We're on the edge," she said. "We're already on the edge and now they are 30
talking about more funding cuts. Right now, we've only got one guidance counselor
for 700 students. That's not enough."

Crystal's schedule includes one-on-one tutoring in a "rap class" where Cathy 31
Searao, a school drug counselor, spends time talking with troubled students partly
as a mentor and partly as a friend. Shrugging, embarrassed and monosyllabic, Crystal
says she likes the program because there "the teacher really talks to you." One afternoon Ms. Searao taught Crystal and a friend how to develop film. It was the one
moment in her school day when Crystal smiled. She shyly admits that she also enjoys
science and a dance program she goes to after school.

Mrs. Molinelli would like to see more individualized programs in the school. But 32
in the meantime, she fights cutbacks.

Crystal's mother wants more from the public school as well. "I feel like I try 33
my hardest," she said, "but I still need someone there education-wise who can back
me up."

In science, as a substitute teacher tried to teach the difference between fact and 34
opinion, Crystal spent her time, lipstick in one hand, a mirror in the other, tracing
steaks of red along her lips.

The toll of her inattention is already becoming all too clear. In the first semester, 35
Crystal passed every major class but science. But as the school year progressed, she
started drifting. In September Crystal made her way to class on time on every day
but one. In January she was late 12 days out of 20.

Her mother says it is a constant battle just to get Crystal up and out. As she and 36
her husband begin the day, the tone is set.

"I start trying to wake her up at 7 A.M.," Mrs. Ficalora said. "By 7:30, I am really 37
screaming."

Crystal's February report card included a 65 in social studies. She failed English, 38
math, science, foreign language and physical education. "We have already sent the
family an 'at risk' letter," said Diane Costaglioli, the assistant principal in charge of
the seventh grade. "She's on a decline."

At home, her mother tells her to do her homework but rarely checks, and her 39
stepfather, Louie Ficolara, an electrician at ABC, rarely asks about it. But together
they provide a raft of high-tech toys that keep Crystal occupied but unmotivated.

The basement room she shares with Colette has all the comforts—and distrac- 40 tions—of a fully equipped apartment. "Sometimes my mom punishes me by making me go to my room," Crystal said. "But that's O.K. We've got a television, a VCR, Nintendo, a radio, books, magazines, our own phone line, and a bunch of other stuff down there."

Upstairs, there are distractions, too. The television comes on just after Crystal 41 gets home at 3. It stays on well into the night.

Mrs. Ficalora complains that the family is not brought in to the school's daily 42 rhythms. "We don't even have to see the homework," she said. "So we don't know what they're dealing with."

Somehow, though, there has been a breakdown in communication. Last fall, 43 Crystal's school gave each student a homework planner that encouraged parents to be involved in each day's assignment. Crystal says she lost hers and her mother concedes that although she at times helps with homework, she usually is involved only at report-card time.

For Crystal, though, homework can seem almost quaint in a life that whirls 44 through a landscape full of real and perceived dangers. Outside school, her world stretches from glass-strewn lots where friends drink and smash bottles against brick walls to street corners where gang members pick fights. Her friends are an ethnic stew of Italian-Americans, Puerto Ricans, blacks, and immigrants—a multiracial bond that in coming years may well be tested.

So far, though, they face their fears together. Temptations and highs lurk every- 45 where. Though Crystal says she has not yet tried marijuana, LSD or crack, she talks about such drugs the way children used to talk of trolls and ice cream cones. Like most of her friends, she has already sampled alcohol and cigarettes. Other temptations await. "Everybody drinks," she said with a knowing shrug. "They drink and do acid in the park."

Crystal knows the varied routes to dropping out. But they do not scare her. 46 "They hang out," she said of the students who leave school. "They do weed. They drink. They do acid. Everybody knows what they are doing."

Sex looms, too. So far, boys don't seem to be her problem. Her mother prohibits 47 her from dating. But Crystal points out coolly, "When I'm out there you don't know where I am." Crystal's mother assumes that her 12-year-old can take care of herself. "I let her know that she has an independence," she said.

Yet just surviving is a constant struggle. Teachers, the police and parents say they 48 are often stunned by the casualness of the violence both inside and outside school. Hallways are full of a steady stream of students who sniffle that a friend has hit or kicked them. Students are called from class for fighting. Friends poke, trip and slap.

On the streets, fights start over nothing. Many boys link up with gangs. Crystal 49 lists their names, neighborhood by neighborhood, including two for girls, Bitches on a Mission, and the Five Million Hoodlums, to which some of her friends belong. "They can protect you," Crystal said somewhat admiringly. "They can keep you safe."

But it is toward her sister, Colette that Crystal most often turns for protection. 50 "She watches out for me," she said. "If somebody bothers me, she sends people after them."

Colette may be failing, but she has another quality that Crystal values far more 51 than grades. She is the one older person who always listens—and never punishes.

Still, anxiety pervades. "I'm always nervous," she said quietly one day at school, 52 her head cast down, her hands clasped tightly between her legs. "I get nervous over nothing. And then I'll get a really big headache."

One moment of ease comes in the minutes between school and life after school. 53 When the last bell rings, Crystal and her friends linger outside the building to remind one another that they care. Linking arms and passing gum and cigarettes around, they laugh and poke and share their secrets, their fears, their triumphs. Then they reach forward, one to the next, to kiss, almost somberly, and wish one another well.

For Discussion

In paragraph 11, Manegold reflects on Crystal's plight: "What is absent is a quiet, steady voice of encouragement, a single figure to lead Crystal through the minefields of a childhood in Bensonhurst. . . . Crystal seems without a touchstone to guide her and give her a sense of her potential."

Was there someone in your life during your late elementary and junior high school years who provided the kind of guidance Manegold believes Crystal is missing? If someone did serve as a guide for you, what did this person contribute to your "sense of potential"? Try to account for the social conditions that make it possible for a person to help a youngster in this way—resources of time, money, knowledge, materials, technology, and so forth. What do you think there is about Crystal's social world that prevents her from having this sort of help?

For Analysis

For more on these descriptive and narrative strategies, see Chapters 14 and 15.

1.   Manegold relies on diverse strategies to present Crystal to readers: detailing her visually, devising similes and metaphors, reporting what Crystal says, reporting what others say about her, and narrating her interactions with others. Find at least one example of each of these strategies, and label it in the margin. What do these diverse writer's strategies contribute to your dominant impression of Crystal?

2.   Manegold might have organized her profile around a single, typical day in Crystal's life, following her from early morning when she awakes to the end of the day when the television is finally turned off. Noonan ("Inside the Brain") uses this narrative pattern of organization by following one operation from beginning to end, even though he collected his information during several visits, interviews, and trips to the library to read about brain surgery. Like the author of "Soup," Manegold chooses to organize her information by topics that reveal various aspects of Crystal's life at home and at school. Imagine how the information in the profile could have been put together as a typical day in Crystal's life. Given Manegold's purpose, why do you think she chose a topical over a narrative organization?

3.   Manegold rarely tells us what to think about the people and events in her profile. Yet you probably were readily able to make inferences and judgments, particularly about the role other people play in Crystal's life. Think of one judgment you made about her mother or her girlfriends, for example, and trace in the text what led you to make that judgment. Annotate the text for relevant details.

4.   Writers would agree that it's not easy to conclude a profile effectively. Notice how after listing the certain dangers that Crystal faces, Manegold ends with the poignant scene of Crystal and her friends together, arms linked, kissing farewell. Compare this ending to the endings of "Inside the Brain" and "Soup." What do you think each of these endings attempts to accomplish?

**For Your
Own Writing**

Consider profiling a child or early adolescent who has overcome physical, emotional, or socioeconomic problems or achieved something notable by your community's standards. You might also consider profiling a talented child or early adolescent engaged in a sport; a musical, drama, or dance group; a creative writing or journalism project; a budding entrepreneurial enterprise; or volunteer work of some kind. You would want to observe the person in a variety of social interactions, in order to account for the contributions others make to the person's achievement. You may want to profile a person you know slightly, perhaps a child in a family you are acquainted with; but, since this is not an essay about a remembered person, you should probably not choose a member of your immediate family. You want to rely on fresh observations of someone who is something of a mystery to you at the beginning.

Commentary

A profile is a special kind of research project. It always involves visits to someone or someplace. It requires notes from observations and interviews, and it can include reading materials picked up at the place you are profiling. It can even lead to library research in order to gather information about the history and specialized aspects of a place or activity. Although Manegold seems not to have done any library research, she clearly visited the school several times, however, in order to follow Crystal around and to talk with her in different school settings. She interviewed several administrators and teachers. She also visited Crystal's home and spoke to her mother. We can easily imagine her arranging visits to the school and home, scheduling enough time on each visit to observe Crystal in different situations during and after school, taking notes as she watched and listened. Later, she must have reviewed her notes, adding details and impressions of what she had seen. These notes would have led her to think about what she wanted to discover on her next visit.

Manegold's research seems closer to that of the anonymous *New Yorker* author of "Soup" than to David Noonan's research for "Inside the Brain." Relying entirely on observations and interviews, the *New Yorker* writer includes extended quotations from Mr. Yeganeh and likely used a tape recorder, in addition to a notebook and pencil. By contrast, Noonan, though he includes much observational and interview material, relies to a noticeable extent on library research, where he picked up technical information about brain surgery. Manegold's research project is different from the other two in one important way: while their profiles focus on a single small location, hers ranges widely across a number of different scenes of the school and the neighborhood and encompasses Crystal's interactions with diverse individuals and groups.

Like the author of "Soup," Manegold offers few direct judgments or conclusions. Instead, she presents Crystal's life from several perspectives. When her people speak for themselves, we are able to make our own inferences about them, although Manegold does subtly guide our judgments by her language and by the information she decided to use from her many pages of notes. Still she leaves much for us to fill in. This "filling in" occurs, as in all our reading, as we combine what the text offers with our own memories and world knowledge. Not all profile writers leave us to make so many judgments and inferences. Brain Cable, in the next essay, and Noonan do more to guide our judgments.

■   ■   ■

Brain Cable wrote the following selection when he was a college freshman. Profiling a mortuary, Cable treats it with both seriousness and humor. He lets readers know his feelings as he presents information about the mortuary and the people working there. Notice in particular the way Cable uses his visit to the mortuary as an occasion to reflect on death.

THE LAST STOP
BRIAN CABLE

Let us endeavor so to live that when we come to die even the undertaker will be sorry.   –Mark Twain

Death is a subject largely ignored by the living. We don't discuss it much, not as children (when Grandpa dies, he is said to be "going away"), not as adults, not even as senior citizens. Throughout our lives, death remains intensely private. The death of a loved one can be very painful, partly because of the sense of loss, but also because someone else's mortality reminds us all too vividly of our own. 1

Thus did I notice more than a few people avert their eyes as they walked past the dusty-pink building that houses the Goodbody Mortuaries. It looked a bit like a church—tall, with gothic arches and stained glass—and somewhat like an apartment complex—low, with many windows stamped out of red brick. 2

It wasn't at all what I had expected. I thought it would be more like Forest Lawn, serene with lush green lawns and meticulously groomed gardens, a place set apart from the hustle of day-to-day life. Here instead was an odd pink structure set in the middle of a business district. On top of the Goodbody Mortuaries sign was a large electric clock. What the hell, I thought, mortuaries are concerned with time too. 3

I was apprehensive as I climbed the stone steps to the entrance. I feared rejection or, worse, an invitation to come and stay. The door was massive, yet it swung open easily on well-oiled hinges. "Come in," said the sign. "We're always open." Inside was a cool and quiet reception room. Curtains were drawn against the outside glare, cutting the light down to a soft glow. 4

I found the funeral director in the main lobby, adjacent to the reception room. Like most people, I had preconceptions about what an undertaker looked like. Mr. 5

Deaver fulfilled my expectations entirely. Tall and thin, he even had beady eyes and a bony face. A low, slanted forehead gave way to a beaked nose. His skin, scrubbed of all color, contrasted sharply with his jet black hair. He was wearing a starched white shirt, grey pants, and black shoes. Indeed, he looked like death on two legs.

He proved an amiable sort, however, and was easy to talk to. As funeral director, 6 Mr. Deaver ("call me Howard") was responsible for a wide range of services. Good- body Mortuaries, upon notification of someone's death, will remove the remains from the hospital or home. They then prepare the body for viewing, whereupon features distorted by illness or accident are restored to their natural condition. The body is embalmed and then placed in a casket selected by the family of the de- ceased. Services are held in one of three chapels at the mortuary, and afterward the casket is placed in a "visitation room," where family and friends can pay their last respects. Goodbody also makes arrangements for the purchase of a burial site and transports the body there for burial.

All this information Howard related in a well-practiced, professional manner. It 7 was obvious he was used to explaining the specifics of his profession. We sat alone in the lobby. His desk was bone clean, no pencils or paper, nothing—just a tele- phone. He did all his paperwork at home; as it turned out, he and his wife lived right upstairs. The phone rang. As he listened, he bit his lips and squeezed his adam's apple somewhat nervously.

"I think we'll be able to get him in by Friday. No, no, the family wants him 8 cremated."

His tone was that of a broker conferring on the Dow Jones. Directly behind him 9 was a sign announcing "Visa and Mastercharge Welcome Here." It was tacked to the wall, right next to a crucifix.

"Some people have the idea that we are bereavement specialists, that we can 10 handle the emotional problems which follow a death: Only a trained therapist can do that. We provide services for the dead, not counseling for the living."

Physical comfort was the one thing they did provide for the living. The lobby was 11 modestly but comfortably furnished. There were several couches, in colors ranging from earth brown to pastel blue, and a coffee table in front of each one. On one table lay some magazines and a vase of flowers. Another supported an aquarium. Paintings of pastoral scenes hung on every wall. The lobby looked more or less like that of an old hotel. Nothing seemed to match, but it had a homey, lived-in look.

"The last time the Goodbodies decorated was in '59, I believe. It still makes peo- 12 ple feel welcome."

And so "Goodbody" was not a name made up to attract customers, but the 13 owner's family name. The Goodbody family started the business way back in 1915. Today, they do over five hundred services a year.

"We're in *Ripley's Believe It or Not*, along with another funeral home whose 14 owners' names are Baggit and Sackit." Howard told me, without cracking a smile.

I followed him through an arched doorway into a chapel which smelled musty 15 and old. The only illumination came from sunlight filtered through a stained glass ceiling. Ahead of us lay a casket. I could see that it contained a man dressed in a black suit. Wooden benches ran on either side of an aisle that led to the body. I got no closer. From the red roses across the dead man's chest, it was apparent that services had already been held.

"It was a large service," remarked Howard. "Look at that casket—a beautiful 16 work of craftsmanship."

I guess it was. Death may be the great leveler, but one's coffin quickly reestab- 17
lishes one's status.

We passed into a bright, fluorescent-lit "display room." Inside were thirty coffins, 18
lids open, patiently awaiting inspection. Like new cars on the showroom floor, they
gleamed with high-glossy finishes.

"We have models for every price range."   19

Indeed, there was a wide variety. They came in all colors and various materials. 20
Some were little more than cloth-covered cardboard boxes, others were made of
wood, and a few were made of steel, copper, or bronze. Prices started at $400 and
averaged about $1,800. Howard motioned toward the center of the room: "The top
of the line."

This was a solid bronze casket, its seams electronically welded to resist corrosion. 21
Moisture-proof and air-tight, it could be hermetically sealed off from all outside
elements. Its handles were plated with 14kt. gold. The price: a cool $5,000.

A proper funeral remains a measure of respect for the deceased. But it is ex- 22
pensive. In the United States the amount spent annually on funerals is about two
billion dollars. Among ceremonial expenditures, funerals are second only to wed-
dings. As a result, practices are changing. Howard has been in this business for forty
years. He remembers a time when everyone was buried. Nowadays, with burials costing $2,000 a shot, people often opt instead for cremation—as Howard put it, "a
cheap, quick, and easy means of disposal." In some areas of the country, the cremation rate is now over 60 percent. Observing this trend, one might wonder whether
burials are becoming obsolete. Do burials serve an important role in society?

For Tim, Goodbody's licensed mortician, the answer is very definitely yes. Burials 23
will remain in common practice, according to the slender embalmer with the disarm-
ing smile, because they allow family and friends to view the deceased. Painful as it
may be, such an experience brings home the finality of death. "Something deep
within us demands a confrontation with death," Tim explained. "A last look assures
us that the person we loved is, indeed, gone forever."

Apparently, we also need to be assured that the body will be laid to rest in com- 24
fort and peace. The average casket, with its inner-spring mattress and pleated satin
lining, is surprisingly roomy and luxurious. Perhaps such an air of comfort makes it
easier for the family to give up their loved one. In addition, the burial site fixes the
deceased in the survivors' memory, like a new address. Cremation provides none of
these comforts.

Tim started out as a clerk in a funeral home, but then studied to become a mor- 25
tician. "It was a profession I could live with," he told me with a sly grin. Mortuary
science might be described as a cross between pre-med and cosmetology, with
courses in anatomy and embalming as well as in restorative art.

Tim let me see the preparation, or embalming, room, a white-walled chamber 26
about the size of an operating room. Against the wall was a large sink with elbow
taps and a draining board. In the center of the room stood a table with equipment
for preparing the arterial embalming fluid, which consists primarily of formaldehyde,
a preservative, and phenol, a disinfectant. This mixture sanitizes and also gives better
color to the skin. Facial features can then be "set" to achieve a restful expression.
Missing eyes, ears, and even noses can be replaced.

I asked Tim if his job ever depressed him. He bridled at the question: "No, it 27
doesn't depress me at all. I do what I can for people, and take satisfaction in enabling

relatives to see their loved ones as they were in life." He said that he felt people were becoming more aware of the public service his profession provides. Grade-school classes now visit funeral homes as often as they do police stations and museums. The mortician is no longer regarded as a minister of death.

Before leaving, I wanted to see a body up close. I thought I could be indifferent 28 after all I had seen and heard, but I wasn't sure. Cautiously, I reached out and touched the skin. It felt cold and firm, not unlike clay. As I walked out, I felt glad to have satisfied my curiosity about dead bodies, but all too happy to let someone else handle them.

For Discussion

"Death," Cable announces in the opening sentence, "is a subject largely ignored by the living. We don't discuss it much, not as children (when Grandpa dies, he is said to be 'going away'), not as adults, not even as senior citizens." Discuss the various ways that your families deal with death. Is the subject of death "largely ignored"?

For Analysis

1. How does the opening quotation from Mark Twain shape your expectations as a reader? Compare Cable's opening (the quotation and paragraphs 1 and 2) to the openings of the three previous profiles. What can you conclude about the opening strategies of these profile writers? Which opening do you find most effective, and why?

2. In this essay, Cable plays with two stereotypical preconceptions: the vulturelike undertaker (paragraphs 5 and 6) and the Forest Lawn–style funeral home (paragraph 3). How does the information presented in the rest of the profile confirm or deny these preconceptions?

3. Look again at paragraphs 18–21, where Cable describes the various caskets. What impression does this description give? How does it contrast with the preceding scene in the chapel (paragraph 15)?

4. Read over Cable's interview notes and the preliminary report he prepared from them on pp. 152–57. How has Cable integrated quotations from the interviews and sensory details from his observations into his essay. What does his choice of quotations reveal about his impression of Howard and Tim? What does his use of sensory details tell you about the effect the mortuary had on him? How do the quotations and sensory details shape your reaction to the essay?

For Your Own Writing

Think of a place or activity about which you have strong preconceptions, and imagine writing a profile about it. What would you choose to tell about? How might you use your preconceptions to capture readers' attention?

Commentary

Cable puts himself into the scene that he profiles. We accompany him on his tour of the mortuary, listen in on the interviews with Howard and Tim, and are made privy to his reflections—the feelings and thoughts he has about what he is seeing and hearing. In each of the other profiles in this chapter, the writer remains outside the scene, a more-or-less disembodied eye through which we see the people and place. Whereas the pronoun *I* is rare or non-existent in the other profiles, it is an essential part of Cable's rhetorical strategy. Similarly, he uses shared preconceptions to establish common ground with his readers, conveying the theme by contrasting these expectations with the discoveries he makes during his visits to the mortuary.

PURPOSE AND AUDIENCE

A profile writer's primary purpose is to inform readers. Whether profiling people (a restaurant owner, a junior high school student), places (a mortuary), or activities (brain surgery), the writer must meet readers' expectations of interesting material presented in a lively and entertaining manner. Although a reader might learn as much about brain surgery from an encyclopedia entry as from Noonan's profile, reading the profile is sure to be more enjoyable.

Readers of profiles expect to be surprised by such unusual subjects. If the subject is a familiar one, they expect it to be presented from an unusual perspective. When writing a profile, you will have an immediate advantage if your subject is a place, activity, or person that is likely to surprise and intrigue your readers. For example, the writer of "Soup" has the double advantage of both a colorful person and an unusual place. Even if your subject is very familiar, however, you can still delight your readers by presenting it in a way they had never before considered.

A profile writer has one further concern: to be sensitive to readers' knowledge of a subject. Since readers must imagine the subject profiled and understand the new information offered about it, the writer must take extreme care in assessing what readers are likely to have seen and to know. For a profile of a brain operation, the decisions of a writer whose readers have little medical expertise will be different from those of a writer whose readers are primarily doctors and nurses. Given Noonan's attention to detail, he is clearly writing for a general audience.

Profile writers must also consider whether readers know all the terms they want to use. Since profiles involve information, they inevitably require definitions and illustrations. For example, Noonan carefully defines many terms: *craniectomy*, *craniotomy*, *dura*, *cerebellum*, and so forth. However, he does not bother to define other technical terms like *angiogram* and *meningioma*. Since profile writers are not writing technical manuals or textbooks, they can choose to define only those terms necessary for readers to follow what is going on. Some concepts or activities will require extended illustrations, as when Noonan describes in detail what is involved in "opening the brain" or scrubbing up before entering the operating room.

For a discussion of sentence-definition strategies, see pp. 510–11.

BASIC FEATURES OF PROFILES

Successful profiles offer intriguing, well-focused subjects; center on a controlling theme; are presented vividly; and proceed at an informative, entertaining pace.

An Intriguing, Well-focused Subject

The subject of a profile is typically a specific person, place, or activity. In this chapter, the *New Yorker* writer shows us Albert Yeganeh, soup cook extraordinaire; Manegold shows us Crystal Rossi, a twelve-year-old struggling at school; Brain Cable describes a particular place, the Goodbody Mortuary; and David Noonan presents an activity, brain surgery. Although they focus on a person, place, or activity, all of these profiles contain all three elements: certain people performing a certain activity at a particular place.

Skilled profile writers make even the most mundane subjects interesting by presenting them in a new light. They may simply take a close look at a subject usually taken for granted, as Cable does when he examines a mortuary. Or they may surprise readers with a subject they had never thought of, as the *New Yorker* writer does in portraying a fanatical soup cook. Whatever they examine, they bring attention to the uniqueness of the subject, showing what is remarkable about it.

A Controlling Theme

Profiles nearly always center on a theme that reveals something surprising, either in the subject or in the writer's response to it. Noonan, for instance, points out a somewhat startling discrepancy between the impersonality of neurosurgery and the extraordinary intimacy of such an operation. The *New Yorker* writer contrasts Yeganeh's perfectionism with our preconceptions about fast-food restaurants. Cable's thematic focus is his personal realization about how Americans seem to capitalize on death almost as a way of coping with it. Manegold invites us to make inferences about what will happen to Crystal and who is responsible for her plight. This focus, or controlling theme, makes profiles something more than mere descriptive exercises or writeups of observations. Profiles interpret their subjects, revealing the writer's attitude and point of view. The theme provides the point, a reason for the writer to be writing to particular readers. Along with awareness of purpose and readers, this theme guides all the writer's decisions about how to organize and present the material.

A Vivid Presentation

Profiles particularize their subjects—one junior high school student's life, an actual surgical operation, a fast-talking restaurant owner, the Goodbody Mortuary—rather than generalize about them. Because profile writers are interested more in presenting individual cases than in making generalizations, they present their subjects vividly and in detail.

Successful profile writers master the writing strategies of description, often using sensory imagery and figurative language. The profiles in this chapter, for example, evoke the senses of sight (a "dusty-pink building" that "looked a bit like a church—tall, with gothic arches and stained glass—and somewhat like an apartment complex—low, with many windows stamped out of red brick"); touch ("a thin, tough, leathery membrane"); smell ("a faint odor of burning bone"); and hearing ("snapping and crunching bone"). Similes ("handheld mixer . . . looking like an overgrown gardening tool") and metaphors (kaleidoscope of teenage rage") also abound.

For more on using sensory description, see pp. 500–04.

Profile writers often describe people in graphic detail ("The patient lies naked and unconscious in the center of the cool, tiled room. His head is shaved, his eyes and nose taped shut. His mouth bulges with the respirator that is breathing for him."). They reveal personal habits and characteristic poses ("As he listened, he bit his lips and squeezed his adam's apple somewhat nervously."). They also use dialogue to suggest speakers' characters:

> He spread his arms and added, "This place is the only one like it in . . . in . . . the whole earth! One day, I hope to learn something from the other places, but so far I haven't."

Narration may be even more important, for it is used by many writers to organize their essays. Some profiles even read like stories, with tension and suspense building to a dramatic climax. Noonan's essay has two climaxes, first when the brain is exposed and second when the tumor is discovered. The climax of Cable's narrative occurs at the end when he touches a corpse. Both writers pace their narratives carefully to develop and sustain tension and drama.

The narrative strategies of conflict and pace are discussed on pp. 486–91.

An Informative, Entertaining Pace

Successful profile writers know that if they are to keep their readers' attention, they must entertain as well as inform. It is for this reason that they tell their stories dramatically and describe people and places vividly. They also pace the flow of information carefully.

Profiles present a great deal of factual detail about their subject. Noonan, for instance, tells us about the brain's parts (dura, cerebellum, brainstem), about surgical procedures (preparation of the patient, the difference between craniectomy and craniotomy), as well as about the attitudes of surgeons toward brain surgery. But this information is woven into the essay in bits and pieces—conveyed in dialogue, interspersed throughout the narrative, given in the description—rather than presented in one large chunk.

Parceling out information in this way increases the chances of comprehension: readers can master one part of the information before going on to the next. Perhaps even more important, such pacing injects a degree of surprise and thus makes readers curious to know what will come next. Varying the pacing of information may, in fact, help keep readers reading.

Guide to W...

THE WRITING ASSIG...

Write an essay about an in... place, or activity in your community. With the advice of y... you may have several options in
completing this assignment: a... event, place, or activity observed once or twice; a brief p... idual based on one or two
interviews; or a longer, more ful... file of a person, place, or
activity based on several observat... interviews. Observe your
subject closely, and then present wh... rned in a way that both
informs and entertains readers.

INVENTION AND RESEARCH

Preparing to write a profile involves several...
exploring your preconceptions of it, planning y...
liminary questions, and finding a theme or focus osing a subject,
osing some pre-
file.

**Choosing
a Subject**

When you choose a subject, you consider various po...
ising one, and check that particular subject's accessibi... lect a prom-

Listing Possibilities. You may already have a subject in mi...
But take a few minutes now to consider some other possi... profile.
more possibilities, the more confident you can be about you ts. The
Before you list possible subjects, consider realistically the...
available and the scope of the observing and interviewing you w have
accomplish. Whether you have a week to plan and write up one o e to
visit or interview or a month to develop a full profile will determ al
kinds of subjects will be appropriate for you. Consult with your inst t
you need help defining the scope of your writing project.

Following are several ideas you might use as starting points for you...
of subjects. Try to extend your list to ten or twelve possibilities. Consi...
every subject you can think of, even the unlikeliest. Consider unfamiliar su...
jects—people or places or activities you find fascinating or bizarre or perhaps
even forbidding. Take risks. People like to read about the unusual.

People

■ Anyone with an unusual job or hobby—a private detective, beekeeper,
classic-car owner, dog trainer

the year, labor organizer, pol-
radio personality

- A prominent local p~~~oach, distinguished teacher
itician, consumer a~~~vice or achievement
- A campus persona~~~olizes that of other people
- Someone recentl~~~
- Someone who~~~ning salon, body-building gym, health spa

Places ~~~ court, consumer fraud office

- A weight-r~~~ house, used-book store, antique shop, auction
- Small cla~~~ers' market
- A used-~~~ room, hospice, birthing center, psychiatric unit
hall, f~~~dest, biggest, or quickest restaurant in town
- A ho~~~ station, computer center, agricultural research facility,
- A ~~~faculty club, museum, newspaper office, health center
- T~~~paper, or magazine publisher; florist shop, nursery, or green-
~~~nshop; boatyard; automobile restorer or wrecking yard
- ~~~ng center; fire station; airport control tower; theater, opera, or
~~~ny office; refugee center; orphanage; convent or monastery

~~~citizens' volunteer program—voter registration, public television auc-
~~~ion, meals-on-wheels project
An unusual sports event—a marathon, frisbee tournament, chess match
- Folk dancing, roller skating, rock climbing, poetry reading

You might set a timer and brainstorm lists on a computer with the monitor brightness turned all the way down. Enter as many possibilities as you can in ten minutes. Then, turn the brightness up, be sure all the items make sense, and print out a copy to make notes on.

Making a Choice.   Look over your list and select a subject that you find personally fascinating, something you want to know more about. It should also be a subject that you think you can make interesting to readers.

If you choose a subject with which you are familiar, it is a good idea to study it in an unfamiliar setting. Let us say you are a rock climber and decide to profile rock climbing. Do not rely on your own knowledge and authority. Seek out other rock-climbing enthusiasts and even some critics of the sport to get a more objective view. When research is predictable for the writer, it will probably lead to dull and uninspired writing. Most writers report greatest satisfaction and best results when they profile unfamiliar activities.

Stop now to focus your thoughts. In a sentence or two, identify the subject you have chosen and explain why you think it is a good choice for you and for your readers.

Checking on Accessibility.   Having chosen a subject, make sure you will be able to observe it. Find out who might be able to give you information, and make

You might start a file on your disc that includes names, addresses, and phone numbers of people and places you need to contact.

some preliminary phone calls. Explain that you need information for a school research project. You will be surprised how helpful people can be when they have the time. If you are unable to contact knowledgeable people or get access to the place you need to observe, you may not be able to write on this subject. Therefore, try to make initial contact now.

For Group Inquiry

You might find it useful to get together in a group with two or three other students and run your chosen topics by one another. Assess the group's interest in the person, place, or activity you wish to write about, and invite their advice about whether it sounds promising. Does it seem likely to lead to a profile they would care to read? Your purpose is to decide whether you have chosen a good subject to write about and thus to be able to proceed confidently to develop your profile.

Exploring Your Preconceptions

Before you begin observing or interviewing, you should explore your initial thoughts and feelings about your subject. Take about ten minutes to write about your thoughts, using the following questions as a guide:

- What do I already know about this subject?
  How would I define or describe it?
  What are its chief qualities or parts?
  Do I associate anyone or anything with it?
  What is its purpose or function?
  How does it compare with other, similar subjects?
- What is my attitude toward this subject?
  Why do I consider this subject intriguing? What about it interests me?
  Do I like it? Respect it? Understand it?
- What do I expect to discover as I observe the subject?
  What would surprise me about it?
  Do I anticipate any troubling discoveries?
  Might I find anything amusing in it?
  Are there likely to be any notable incongruities—for example, between what the people are trying to do and what they are actually doing?
- How do my preconceptions compare with other people's?
  What makes my point of view unique?
  What attitudes about this subject do I share with other people?

Planning Your Project

Whatever the scope of your project—single observation, interview with follow-up, or repeated observations and interviews—you will want to get the most out of your time with your subject. Chapter 20 offers guidance in observing and interviewing, and will give you an idea of how much time will be required to plan, carry out, and write up an observation or interview.

Take time now to consult Chapter 20 and to write out a tentative research schedule. Figure out first the amount of time you have to complete your essay; then decide what visits you will need to make, whom you will need to interview, and what library work you might want to do. Estimate the time necessary for each. You might use a chart like the following one:

Keeping a schedule on discs allows for easy modification. As your plans change, you can print out a revised schedule.

Date	Time Needed	Purpose	Preparation
10/23	1 hour	observe	bring map and directions, pad of paper
10/25	1½ hours	library research	bring reference, notebook, change for copy machine
10/26	45 minutes	interview	read brochure and prepare questions
10/30	2 hours	observe and interview	prepare questions, confirm appointment, bring pad

Your plan will probably need to be modified once you actually begin work, but it is a good idea to keep some sort of schedule in writing.

If you are developing a full profile, your first goal is to get your bearings. Some writers begin by observing; others start with an interview. Many read up on the subject before doing anything else, to get a sense of its main elements. You may also want to read about other subjects similar to the one you have chosen. Save your notes.

Posing Some Preliminary Questions

Before launching your observations and interviews, try writing some questions for which you would like to find answers. These questions will provide orientation and focus for your visits. As you work, you will find answers to many of these questions. Add to this list as new questions occur to you, and delete any that come to seem irrelevant.

Each subject invites its own special questions, and every writer has his or her own particular concerns. Following are some questions one student posed for a profile of a campus rape-crisis center:

If you list questions on a computer, leave spaces between individual questions. When you print out a copy, you'll have room to write in answers as you interview and observe.

- Is rape a special problem on college campuses? On this campus? Why?
- Are most of the rapes on campus committed by unknown assailants? Or are they date rapes, committed by "friends"?
- Who provides information about the occurrence of rape on the campus, and how is this information made public?
- How is the center funded and operated?
- How well qualified are the people working in the center? What do they do? Do they counsel victims? Teach women how to defend themselves?
- How does the center publicize its services or contact rape victims to offer assistance? How many women actually use it?
- Do the police do anything to prevent rape on campus?

Finding a
Tentative Theme

When you have completed your visits, you must decide on a tentative theme for your profile. Begin by writing nonstop for about ten minutes, trying to answer as many of the following questions as are pertinent:

If you use a word processor to explore questions about your theme, print out a hard copy to review before trying to state your tentative theme.

■ What was the most important thing I learned? Why is it important?

■ If I could find out the answer to one more question, what would be the question? Why is this question so crucial?

■ Were there any incongruities, surprises, or contradictions? If so, what do they tell me about the subject?

■ What is the mood of the place? How do people seem to feel there?

■ What is most memorable about the people I observed and talked to?

■ What visual or other sensory impression is most memorable? What experiences can I associate with this sensory impression?

■ What is most striking about the activity I observed? What is likely to be most surprising or interesting to readers?

■ What about this subject says something larger about our lives and times?

■ What generalization or judgment do these personal reactions lead me to?

Take a few moments to reflect on what you have discovered. Then, in a sentence or two, state what now seems to you to be a promising theme or focus for your profile. What do you want readers to see as they read your profile? What do you want them to remember later about your subject?

PLANNING AND DRAFTING

As preparation for drafting, you need to review your invention or research notes to see what you have, set goals for yourself, and organize your profile.

Seeing What
You Have

You may now have a great deal of material—notes from visits, interviews, or reading; some idea of your preconceptions; a list of questions, perhaps with some answers. You should also have a tentative theme or focus. Read over your invention materials to see what you have. Your aim is to digest all the information you have gathered; to pick out the promising facts, details, anecdotes, and quotations; and to see how well your tentative theme focuses all the material you plan to include in the essay.

As you sort through your material, look at it in some of the following ways. They may help you clarify your theme or find an even better one.

It's a good idea at this point to print out a hard copy of what you have written on a word processor for easier reviewing.

■ Contrast your preconceptions with your findings.

■ Juxtapose your preliminary questions against answers you have found.

■ Compare what different people say about the subject.

■ Look for discrepancies between people's words and their behavior.

- Compare your reactions with those of the people directly involved.
- Consider the place's appearance in light of the activity that occurs there.
- Juxtapose bits of information, looking for contrasts or incongruities.
- Examine your subject as an anthropologist or archaeologist might, looking for artifacts that would explain its role in the society at large.

Setting Goals

The following questions will help to establish goals for your first draft. Consider each one briefly now, and return to them as necessary as you draft.

Your Readers

- Are my readers likely to be at all familiar with my subject? If not, what details do I need to provide to help them visualize it?
- If my readers are familiar with my subject, how can I present it to them in a new and engaging way? What information do I have that is likely to be new or entertaining to them?
- Is there anything I can say about this subject that will lead readers to reflect on their own lives and values?

The Beginning

The opening is especially important in a profile. Because readers are unlikely to have any particular reason to read a profile, the writer must arouse their curiosity and interest. The best beginnings are surprising and specific, the worst are abstract. Here are some strategies you might consider:

- Should I open with a striking image or vivid scene, as Noonan and Manegold do?
- Should I begin with a statement of the central theme?
- Should I start with an intriguing epigraph, as Cable does?
- Do I have an amazing fact that would catch readers' attention?
- Is there an anecdote that captures the essence of the subject?
- Should I open with a question, perhaps one answered in the essay?
- Do I have any dialogue that would serve as a good beginning, as in the *New Yorker* piece?

The General Organization

Profile writers basically use two methods of organizing their material: they arrange it either chronologically in a narrative or topically by grouping related materials.

If I Organize My Material Chronologically, as Noonan Does:

- How can I make the narrative dramatic and intense?
- What information should I integrate into the narrative?

- What information will require that I suspend the narrative to include? How can I minimize the disruption and resume the dramatic pace?
- What information should I quote and what should I summarize?
- How can I set the scene vividly?

If I Organize My Material Topically, as Manegold Does:

- What topics in my material best present the subject, inform readers, and yet hold their interest?
- How can I sequence the topics to bring out comparisons, similarities, contrasts, or incongruities in my material?
- What transitions will help readers make connections between topics?
- Where and how should I describe the subject so it will be vivid?

The Ending

- Should I try to frame the essay by repeating an image or phrase from the beginning or by completing an action begun earlier in the profile?
- Would it be good to end by restating the theme?
- Should I end with a telling image, anecdote, or bit of dialogue?

Outlining

If you plan to arrange your material chronologically, plot the key events on a timeline. Star the event you consider the high point or climax.

If you plan to arrange your material topically, by grouping related information, you might use clustering or outlining strategies to get a graphic view of the interconnections. Both these strategies will help you divide and group your information. After classifying your material, you might list the items in the order in which you plan to present them.

For more on clustering, see p. 431.

The following outlines illustrate the difference between chronological and topical organization. The first is a *chronological outline* of Noonan's profile on brain surgery:

the operating room and patient

the doctors

the operation (a preview)

the doctor's preparations for the operation

drilling through the skull

opening the dura

retracting the cerebellum

searching for the tumor

discovering the tumor

analyzing the tumor

the doctors' perspectives on brain surgery

If Noonan had wanted to emphasize the tremendous amount of knowledge and sophisticated technology that is involved in brain surgery, he might have chosen a *topical pattern* like the one below:

challenge of brain surgery as a specialty

who is attracted to it

special training required

a typical lecture to medical students by an experienced surgeon

the technology of brain surgery (perhaps through a tour of an operating room)

recent scientific breakthroughs in understanding brain disease

doctor's relations with their patients (the disassociation problem)

the rewards of a career in brain surgery

All of the material for this hypothetical topical essay, like the material in the actual chronological essay, would come from observations, interviews, and a little reading.

Outlining on a word processor makes it particularly easy to experiment with different ways of patterning and ordering your material.

The organization you choose will reflect the possibilities in your material and theme, your purpose, and your readers. At this point, your decision must be tentative. As you begin drafting, you will almost certainly discover new ways of organizing your material. Once you have a first draft, you and others may see ways to reorganize the material to achieve your purpose better with your particular readers.

Drafting

Start drafting your essay. By now, of course, you are not starting from scratch. If you have followed this guide, you will already have done a great deal of invention and planning. Some of this material may even fit right into your draft with little alteration.

Be careful not to get stuck trying to write the perfect beginning. Start anywhere. The time to perfect your beginning is at the revision stage.

If you can shift between screens, you might call up invention material on an alternate screen as you draft on the main screen, shifting back and forth to cut and paste invention material into your draft.

Once you are actually writing, try not to be interrupted. Should you find you need to make additional visits for further observations and interviews, do so after you have completed a first draft. You might look at the general advice on drafting on pp. 12–14.

GETTING CRITICAL COMMENTS

Now is the time for your draft to get a good critical reading. Your instructor may arrange such a reading as part of your course work; otherwise, you can ask a classmate, friend, or family member to read it over. If your campus has a writing center, you might ask a tutor there to read and comment on your draft. The guidelines that follow can be used by *anyone* reviewing a profile. (If you are unable to have someone else read over your draft, turn ahead to the Revision section on pp. 148–51, which provides guidelines for reading your own draft critically.)

In order to provide focused, helpful comments, readers must know your intended purpose and audience. Take time now to reconsider these two elements, jotting down the following information at the top of your draft.

> *Purpose.* What impression of your subject do you want to give readers?
>
> *Audience.* Who are your readers? What do you assume they already know about your subject? How have you planned to engage and hold their interest?

Reading with a Critical Eye

Reading a draft critically means reading it more than once, first to get a general impression and then to analyze its basic features.

Reading for a First Impression.　Read quickly through the draft first to get an overall impression. As you read, try to notice passages that contribute to your first impression. After you've finished reading the draft, note down your immediate reaction. What do you consider most interesting in the essay? State the theme, and indicate whether or not it is well focused. Is the profile adequately informative? Can you see any holes or gaps? Did it hold your interest?

See pp. 137–38 to review the basic features.

Reading to Analyze.　Read now to focus on the basic features of a profile.

Is the Subject Intriguing and Well-focused?

Indicate whether the profile contains enough details to identify the subject as a specific person, place, or event. Comment on the effectiveness of descriptive details used to show the subject's uniqueness. Point out any places where vague or general statements fail to hold your interest in the subject.

Is the Controlling Theme Clear?

Profiles must have a controlling theme, an angle or point that may be explicit (stated in the essay) or implicit (suggested by the details). Often, the theme involves some unexpected element or incongruity, either in the subject itself or in the writer's response to it. Identify what you think the theme may be; then look for information or description that may distract readers from it. Suggest ways to strengthen the thematic focus, perhaps through additional dialogue, visual details, or comparisons and contrasts.

Is the Presentation Vivid?

Profiles must present their subjects in specific details rather than general statements. Look at the description of objects, scenes, and people. Point out vivid and specific descriptions as well as places where readers would need further naming and detailing in order to imagine what the writer is talking about. Also point out any seemingly unnecessary or exaggerated description.

Consider the use of specific narrative action—moving, gesturing, talking.

Suggest ways to strengthen any sections of specific action, and point out any other places where it might be appropriate.

Is Information Presented in an Entertaining Way That Is Easy to Follow?

Profile readers expect to be informed as well as entertained, but they expect the information load to be manageable. Point out any places where you felt bogged down or overwhelmed with information or where information was not clearly presented or was inadequate. If necessary, look for ways to reduce or add information or to break up long blocks of information with description of scenes or people or narration of events.

Skim the essay for definitions, and indicate whether any seem unnecessary or unclear. Also point out any other terms that need defining.

Is the Organization Effective?

If the profile is organized chronologically, point out any places where the narrative seems to drag as well as any where it seems most dramatic and intense. Identify the climax or high point of the narrative.

If the profile is organized topically, look to see whether any topic presents too little or too much material and whether topics might be sequenced differently or connected more clearly.

Reread the *beginning*, and decide whether it is effective. Did it capture your attention? Is there any quotation, fact, or anecdote elsewhere in the draft that might make a better opening?

Look again at the *ending*. Indicate if it leaves you hanging, or seems too abrupt, or oversimplifies the material. Suggest another ending, possibly by moving a passage or quotation from elsewhere in the essay.

What Final Thoughts Do You Have?

What is the strongest part of this draft? What about the draft is most memorable? What in the draft is weak, most in need of further work?

REVISING AND EDITING

Following are some guidelines to help you identify problems in your own draft, and to revise and edit to solve them.

Identifying
Problems

To identify problems in your draft, you need to read it objectively, analyze its basic features, and study any comments you've received from others.

Getting an Overview.   Consider the draft as a whole, trying to see it objectively. It may help to do so in two steps:

Reread. If at all possible, put the draft aside for a day or two before rereading it. When you do, start by considering your purpose. Then read the draft straight through, looking mainly for its basic message.

Even if the draft of your essay is saved to a computer file, reread from a hard copy, preferably draft quality. On screen or as letter-quality hard copy, a paper can look more "finished" than it really is. Add notes to yourself and quick revisions as you read through the draft.

Outline. Make a scratch outline of the draft that identifies the stages of your presentation of your subject.

Charting a Plan for Revision.   A good way to start plotting out your revision course is with a two-column list like the one that follows. The left-hand column lists the basic features of profiles; the right-hand column lists any problems you or other readers identified with that feature.

Basic Features	*Problems to Solve*
Choice of subject	
Controlling theme	
Presentation of the subject	
Information flow	
Organization	

Analyzing Basic Features.   Turn now to the analysis questions on pp. 147–48. Analyze your draft following these guidelines, adding any specific problems to your chart of problems to solve.

Studying Critical Comments.   Review any comments you've received from other readers, and add to the chart any points that need attention. Try not to react too defensively to these comments; by letting you see how others respond to your draft, they provide invaluable information about both its possibilities and its problems.

Solving the Problems

Having identified problems in your draft, you now need to figure out solutions and to carry them out. Basically, you have three ways to turn: (1) review your observation or interview notes for other information and ideas; (2) do additional observations or interviews to answer questions you or other readers raised; and (3) look back at the readings in this chapter to see how other writers have solved similar problems. Following are some suggestions to get you started solving some of the problems common to profiles.

The Subject

- If the subject does not seem intriguing or remarkable, add specific descriptive details to help readers see why it is noteworthy.
- If any of your statements about your subject seem too general, revise them to focus on specific characteristics.

Controlling Theme

- If readers had difficulty describing the theme, clarify it. Try stating the theme more explicitly or eliminating any dialogue, description, anecdote, or factual detail that does not contribute to or that seems to contradict the point you are trying to make.

■ If your readers suggested focusing on something different, decide whether another theme would be more appropriate. If so, rework your draft to make the new theme clear.

Presentation of the Subject

■ If the subject does not seem vivid, add specific words and details so that readers can better imagine it. Look for places where you can include more sensory details—sights, sounds, smells, textures.

Information Flow

■ If readers felt bogged down by information at any point, move, condense, or eliminate some of it. Eliminate any unnecessary definitions.

■ If readers could not understand something, add more information or definitions. Make sure these fit smoothly into your essay and do not interrupt readers' attention to your main points.

Organization

For more on specific narrative action, see pp. 487–90.

Use your word processor's cut-and-paste or block-and-move functions to shift material around. Make sure transitions are revised so that material fits in its new spot.

■ If your essay is organized chronologically and seems to drag or ramble, find the climax, or high point, and try to heighten the suspense leading up to it. Add drama through specific narrative action, showing details of movements and gestures. Summarize activity to speed the story along.

■ If you organized topically and readers found the profile disorganized, try rearranging topics to see if another order makes more sense. Look at the outlines you have made to get ideas.

■ If the opening fails to engage readers' attention, consider alternatives. Think of questions you could open with, or look for an engaging image or dialogue later in the essay to move to the beginning. Go back to your observation or interview notes for other ideas.

■ If the ending seems weak, consider ending at an earlier point or moving something more striking to the end.

■ If at any point in your essay readers felt transitions between stages in the narrative or between topics were confusing or too abrupt, add appropriate phrasing or revise sentences to make transitions clearer or smoother.

Editing and Proofreading

In working on your draft up until now, you've probably not paid too much attention to matters of grammar and mechanics. Now, however, you should make time to check over your draft for errors in usage, punctuation, and mechanics. Our research has identified several errors that occur often in profiles. Two in particular are explained below.

Checking the Punctuation of Any Quotations. Because most profiles are based in part on interviews, you will almost certainly have quoted one or more people. When you quote someone's exact words, you enclose those words in quotation marks. There are clear conventions for punctuating quotations; check your draft for your use of the following specific punctuation marks.

All quotations should have quotation marks at the beginning and the end.

When you use your word processor's spell-check function to aid in proofreading for spelling, keep in mind that it will not find all misspellings, particularly misused homonyms (such as there, their, *and* they're*) and many proper nouns and specialized terms. Proofread these carefully yourself, using hard copy and a dictionary if necessary. Also proofread for words or phrases that should have been deleted when you edited a sentence.*

▶ "What exactly is civil litigation?" I asked.

Commas and periods go *inside* quotation marks.

▶ "I'm here to see Anna Post," I replied nervously.

▶ Tony explained, "Fraternity boys just wouldn't feel comfortable at the Chez Café."

Question marks and exclamation points go *inside* closing quotation marks if they are part of the quotation, *outside* if they are not.

▶ After a pause, the patient asked, "Where do I sign?"

▶ Willie insisted, "You can *too* learn to play Super Mario!"

▶ When was the last time someone you just ticketed said to you, "Thank you, Ms. Parking Officer, for doing a great job?"?

Use commas with signal phrases (*he said*, *she asked*, etc.) that accompany direct quotations.

▶ "This SOTA Cosmos turntable costs only $4,000," Jorge said.

▶ I asked, "So, where were these clothes from originally?"

A Common ESL Problem: Adjective Order. In trying to present the subject of your profile vividly and in detail, you have almost for certain included many descriptive adjectives. When you include more than one adjective in front of a noun, you may have difficulty sequencing them. For example, do you write "a large old ceramic pot" or "an old large ceramic pot"? Following is a chart showing the order in which adjectives are ordinarily arranged in front of a noun.

1. *Amount*: a/an, the, a few, six
2. *Evaluation*: good, beautiful, ugly, serious
3. *Size*: large, small, tremendous
4. *Shape, length*: round, long, short
5. *Age*: young, new, old
6. *Color*: red, black, green
7. *Origin*: Asian, Brazilian, German
8. *Material*: wood, cotton, gold
9. *Noun used as an adjective*: computer (as in *computer program*), cake (as in *cake pan*)
10. *The noun modified*

A Writer at Work

THE INTERVIEW NOTES AND WRITEUP

Most profile writers take notes when interviewing people. Later they may summarize their notes in a short writeup. In this section you will see some of the interview notes and a writeup Brain Cable prepared for his profile of a mortuary, printed earlier in this chapter.

Cable toured the mortuary and conducted two interviews—with the funeral director and the mortician. Before each interview he wrote out a few questions at the top of a sheet of paper and then divided it into two columns; he then used the left-hand column for descriptive details and personal impressions, the right-hand column for the information he got directly from the person he was interviewing. Below are Cable's notes and writeup for his interview with the funeral director, Howard Deaver.

Cable used the questions as a guide for the interview and then took brief notes during it. He did not concern himself too much with note-taking because he planned to spend a half-hour directly afterward to complete his notes. He kept his attention fixed on Deaver, trying to keep the interview comfortable and conversational and noting down just enough to jog his memory and to catch anything especially quotable. A typescript of Cable's interview notes follows.

The Interview

QUESTIONS

1. How do families of decreased view the mortuary business?
2. How is the concept of death approached?
3. How did you get into this business?

DESCRIPTIVE DETAILS &
PERSONAL IMPRESSIONS   INFORMATION

weird looking   "Call me Howard"
tall   How things work: Notification, pick
long fingers   up body at home or hospital, prepare
big ears   for viewing, restore distorted
low, sloping forehead   features--accident or illness,
Like stereotype--   embalm, casket--family selects,
skin colorless   chapel services (3 in bldg.),
                              visitation room--pay respects,
                              family & friends.

                              Can't answer questions about death--
                              "Not bereavement specialists. Don't

DESCRIPTIVE DETAILS & PERSONAL IMPRESSIONS	INFORMATION

DESCRIPTIVE DETAILS & PERSONAL IMPRESSIONS | INFORMATION

handle emotional problems. Only a trained therapist can do that."
"We provide services for dead, not counseling for the living." (great quote)
Concept of death has changed in last 40 yrs (how long he's been in the business)
Funeral cost $500-600, now $2000

plays with lips
blinks
plays with Adam's apple
desk empty--phone, no paper or pen

angry
disdainful of the Neptune Soc.

Phone call (interruption)
"I think we'll be able to get him in on Friday. No, no, the family wants him cremated."
Ask about Neptune Society--cremation
Cremation "Cheap, quick, easy means of disposal."
Recent phenomenon. Neptune Society --erroneous claim to be only one.
"We've offered them since the beginning. It's only now it's come into vogue."
Trend now back towards burial.
Cremation still popular in sophisticated areas
60% in Marin and Florida

Ask about paperwork--does it upstairs, lives there with wife Nancy

musty, old stained glass
sunlight filtered

Tour around (happy to show me around)
Chapel--Large service just done, Italian.

man in black suit
roses
wooden benches

"Not a religious institution--A business."
casket--"beautiful craftsmanship" --admires, expensive

```
DESCRIPTIVE DETAILS &
PERSONAL IMPRESSIONS      INFORMATION

contrast brightness       Display room--caskets about 30 of
fluorescent lights        them
plexiglass stands         Loves to talk about caskets
                          "models in every price range"
                          glossy (like cars in a showroom)
                          cardboard box, steel, copper, bronze
                          $400 up to $1800.  Top of line:
                          bronze, electronically welded, no
                          corrosion--$5000
```

Cable's notes include many descriptive details of Deaver as well as of various rooms in the mortuary. Though most entries are short and sketchy, much of the language finds its way into the essay. In describing Deaver, for example, Cable notes he fits the stereotype of the cadaverous undertaker, a fact Cable will make much of in his essay.

He puts quotation marks around Deaver's actual words, some of them complete sentences, others only fragments. We will see how he fills these quotes in when he writes up the interview. In only a few instances does he take down more than he can use. Even though profile writers want good quotes, they should not quote things they can better put in their own words. Direct quotation has a dual function in a profile—both to provide information and to capture the mood or character of the person speaking.

As you can see, Deaver was not able to answer Cable's questions about the families of the deceased and their attitudes toward death or mortuaries. The gap between the questions and Deaver's responses led Cable to recognize one of his own misperceptions about mortuaries—namely, that they serve the living by helping them adjust to the death of their loved ones. This misperception becomes an important theme of his essay.

After filling in his notes following the interview, Cable took some time to reflect on what he had learned. Here are some of his thoughts:

```
I was surprised how much Deaver looked like the undertak-
ers in scary movies.  Even though he couldn't answer any
of my questions, he was friendly enough.  It's obviously
a business for him (he loves to talk about caskets and to
point out all their features, like a car dealer kicking a
tire).  Best quote: "We offer services to the dead, not
counseling to the living."  I have to arrange an inter-
view with the mortician.
```

Writing up an account of the interview a short time afterward helped Cable to fill in more details and to reflect further on what he had learned.

His writeup shows him already beginning to organize the information he had gained from his interview with Deaver.

I. His physical appearance.

Tall, skinny with beady blue eyes embedded in his bony face. I was shocked to see him. He looked like the undertakers in scary movies. His skin was white and colorless, from lack of sunshine. He has a long nose and a low sloping forehead. He was wearing a clean white shirt. A most unusual man--have you ever seen those Ames Home Loan commercials? But he was friendly, and happy to talk to me. "Would I answer some questions? Sure."

II. What people want from a mortuary.

A. Well first of all, he couldn't answer my question as to how families cope with the loss of a loved one. "You'd have to talk to a psychologist about that," he said. He did tell me how the concept of death has changed over the last ten or so years.

B. He has been in the business for forty years. (forty years?!!?) One look at him and you'd be convinced he'd been there at least that long. He told me that in the old times everyone was buried. Embalmed, put in a casket, and paid final homage before being shipped underground forever and ever. Nowadays, many people choose to be cremated instead. Hence comes the success of the Neptune Society and those like it. They specialize in cremation. You can have your ashes dumped anywhere. "Not that we don't offer cremation services. We've offered them since the beginning," he added with a look of disdain. It's just that they've become so popular recently because they offer a "quick, easy, and efficient means of disposal." Cheap too --I think it is a reflection of a "no nonsense" society. The Neptune Society has become so successful because they claim to be the only ones to offer cremations as an alternative to expensive burial. "We've offered it all along. It's just only now come into vogue."

Sophisticated areas (I felt "progressive" would be more accurate) like Marin County have a cremation rate of over 60 percent. The phone rang. "Excuse me," he said. As he talked on the phone, I noticed now he played with his lips, pursing and squeezing them. He was blinking all the time too. Yet he wasn't a schitzo or anything like that. I meant to ask him how he got into this business, but I for-

got. I did find out his name and title. Mr. Deaver, general manager of Goodbody Mortuaries (no kidding, that's the
real name). He lived on the premises upstairs with his
wife. I doubt if he ever left the place.

III. It's a business!

Some people have the idea that mortuaries offer counseling and peace of mind--a place where everyone is sympathetic and ready to offer advice. "In some mortuaries,
this is true. But by and large this is a business. We offer services to the dead, not counseling to the living." I
too had expected to feel an awestruck respect for the dead
upon entering the building. I had also expected green
lawns, ponds with ducks, fountains, flowers, peacefulness--
you know, a "Forest Lawn" type deal. But it was only a
tall, Catholic-looking building. "Mortuaries do not sell
plots for burial," he was saying. "Cemeteries do that, after we embalm the body and select a casket. We're not a
religious institution." He seemed hung up on caskets--
though maybe he was just trying to impress upon me the differences between caskets. "Oh, they're very important. A
good casket is a sign of respect. Sometimes if the family
doesn't have enough money, we rent them a nice one. People
pay for what they get just like any other business." I
wonder when you have to return the casket you rent?

I wanted to take a look around. He was happy to give
me a tour. We visited several chapels and visiting rooms--
places where the deceased "lie in state" to be "visited" by
family and friends. I saw an old lady in a "fairly decent
casket," as Mr. Deaver called it. Again I was impressed by
the simple businesslike nature of it all. Oh yes, the
rooms were elaborately decorated, with lots of shrines and
stained glass, but these things were for the customers'
benefit. "Sometimes we have up to eight or nine corpses
here at one time, sometimes none. We have to have enough
rooms to accommodate." Simple enough, yet I never realized
how much (trouble?) people were after they died. So much
money, time, and effort go into their funerals.

As I prepared to leave, he gave me his card. He'd be
happy to see me again, or maybe I could talk to someone
else. I said I would arrange to call for an appointment
with the mortician. I shook his hand. His fingers were
long, and his skin was warm.

Writing up the interview thus helped Cable probe his subject more deeply. It also helped him to develop a witty voice for his essay. Cable's interview notes and writeup are quite informal; later he integrates these more formally into his full profile of the mortuary.

Thinking Critically about What You've Learned

Now that you've spent several days discussing profiles and writing one of your own, it's a good idea to spend some time reflecting on what you've learned about this genre. To do so, you should think first about your own writing process, discovering what you learned about solving a problem you encountered in writing your profile. Next, you'll review what you learned as a reader of profiles that helped you write your own. And, finally, we'll ask you to explore the social dimensions of profiles: in what ways do they influence our thinking about ourselves and the society we live in?

REFLECTING ON YOUR WRITING

To reflect on what you have learned about writing a profile, first gather all of your writing—invention, planning notes, drafts, any critical comments from classmates and your instructor, revising notes and plans, and final revision. Review these materials as you complete the following writing task.

■ Identify *one* writing problem you needed to solve as you worked on your profile. Don't be concerned with sentence-level problems; concentrate, instead, on problems unique to developing a profile. For example: Did you puzzle over how to organize your diverse observations into a coherent essay? Was it difficult to establish a controlling theme? Did you have any concerns about presenting the place and people vividly, pacing the flow of information, or any other aspect of the essay?

■ How did you recognize the writing problem? When did you first discover it? What called it to your attention? If you didn't become aware of the problem until someone else pointed it out to you, can you now see hints of it in your invention writings? If so, where specifically? When you first recognized the problem, how did you respond?

■ Reflect on how you went about solving the problem. Did you work on the wording of a passage, cut or add details about the place or people, or move paragraphs or sentences around? Did you reread one of the essays in this chapter to see how another writer handled the problem, or did you look back at the invention suggestions? If you talked about the problem with another student, a tutor, or your instructor, did talking about it help? How useful was the advice you got?

■ Now, write a page or so telling your instructor about the problem and how you solved it. Be as specific as possible in reconstructing your efforts. Quote from your invention, draft, others' critical comments, your revision plan, or your revised essay to show the various changes your writing underwent as you tried to solve the problem. When you've finished, consider how explaining what you've learned about solving this writing problem can help you solve future writing problems.

REVIEWING WHAT YOU LEARNED FROM READING

Your own essay has certainly been influenced to some extent by one or more of the profiles you have read in this chapter as well as by classmate's profiles you may have read. These other profiles may have helped you decide how to begin your essay or how to hold your readers' attention by alternating engaging visual details about the place with drier information about what goes on there. They may have suggested how you could reveal something about a person by quoting exactly what the person told you, or they may have offered examples of how to define specialized terms in a clear way. Take time now to reflect on what you have learned from the reading selections in this chapter and consider some ways your reading has influenced your writing.

■ Reread the final revision of your essay; then look back at the profiles you read before completing your own. Do you see any specific influences? For example, if you were impressed with the way one of the readings presented a place through concrete details, made an ordinary activity seem interesting, focused all of the materials around a compelling and unexpected theme, or reconstructed dialogue from interview notes, look to see where you might have been striving for similar effects in your own writing. Also, look for ideas you got from your reading, writing strategies you were inspired to try, specific details you were led to include, effects you sought to achieve.

■ Write a page or so explaining to your instructor how the readings in this chapter influenced your revised essay. Did one reading have a particularly strong influence, or were several readings influential in different ways? Quote from the readings and from your final revision to show how your essay was influenced by your reading of other profiles in this chapter. Finally, point out any ways you might improve your profile that you discovered in reviewing the other readings.

CONSIDERING THE SOCIAL DIMENSIONS OF PROFILES

Profiles offer some of the same pleasures as autobiographies, novels, and films—good stories, memorable characters, exotic places or familiar places viewed freshly, vivid images of people at work and play. They divert and entertain. They may even shock or fascinate. In addition, by intent and design, they offer information that we nearly always feel we can rely on. This special combination of diversion and information gives profiles a unique role to play among all the kinds of reading and writing available to us.

Like travel writing and natural history, profiles nearly always take us to a particular place, usually a place we've never been. For example, Cable provides many visual details of Goodbody Mortuary, with its gothic arches and stained glass, its hotel-like lobby with couches and coffee tables, aquarium, and pastoral paintings. The author of "Soup" describes Soup Kitchen International's appearance from the street so well that we could easily find it even if we did not know its number on West Fifty-fifth Street.

But the larger appeal of profiles is that they present real people most readers will never have a chance to meet. Often, profiles present people the writer admires—and assumes readers will admire—for their achievements, endurance, dedication, skill, or unselfishness. For example, we may find it easy to admire Mr. Yeganeh for his commanding knowledge of the world's soups and his devotion to quality, just as we may be in awe of Noonan's brain surgeons for their great skill and extraordinary concentration. Profiles also present less admirable people; these may occasionally be shown as cruel, greedy, or selfish, but, more often, they are people, such as Crystal, we can sympathize with because of their innocence or bad luck. The strongest profiles present us with neither saints, monsters, nor helpless victims, but rather with people of mixed motives, human failings, and some resources even in dire situations. Noonan, for example, invites us to admire the brain surgeons but also to question their lack of feeling for their patients, and Manegold's profile suggests that Crystal herself bears some responsibility for her disaffection from school.

Entertaining Readers versus Showing the Whole Picture. Entertaining and informing us by presenting unusual people in particular places, profiles broaden our view of the world. It is hard to imagine doing without them. We also have to recognize, however, that profiles may offer a more limited view of their subjects than they seem to. For example, a profile writer's impulse to entertain readers may lead to an exclusive focus on the dramatic, bizarre, colorful, or humorous aspects of a place or activity, ignoring equally important everyday, humdrum, ironic, or paradoxical aspects. Imagine a profile of a travel agent focusing on the free trips he or she enjoys as part of the job but ignoring the everyday demands of dealing with clients, the energy-draining precision required by computer-based airline reservation systems, and the numbing routine of addressing envelopes and mailing tickets to clients. Such a profile would provide a limited and distorted picture of a travel agent's work. While hardly distorted, Noonan's profile of a brain operation does skip over the more tedious parts of the procedure (the two-hour negotiation through the brain before the tumor is found, for example) as a way of keeping readers involved in the drama of the moment.

In addition, by focusing on the dramatic or glamorous aspects of a subject, profile writers tend to ignore economic or social consequences and to slight "supporting players." Profiling the highly praised chef in a trendy new restaurant, a writer might not ask whether the chef participates in the city's leftover-food-collection program for the homeless or find out who the kitchen workers and wait staff are, how the chef treats them, how much they are paid. Profiling the campus bookstore, a writer might become so entranced by the details of ordering books for hundreds of courses, shelving them so that they can be found easily, and selling them efficiently to hoards of students during the first week of a semester that he could forget to ask about textbook costs, pricing policies and profit margins, and payback on used textbooks. (Note that Noonan quotes only the surgeons; the nurses and other technicians involved in the brain operation remain anonymous. Neither do the costs of so elaborate a procedure—and who pays for it and profits from it—concern him.)

The Writer's Viewpoint.   While profiles may seem impartial and objective, they inevitably reflect the views of their writers. The choice of subject, the details observed, the questions asked, the ultimate focus and presentation—all these are influenced by the writer's interests and values, gender and ethnicity, and assumptions about social and political issues. We would expect a vegetarian to write a very different profile of a cattle ranch than would a writer who nearly always orders a hamburger or prime rib when eating out. Consequently, profiles should often be read critically, particularly because the writer's values are likely to be unstated. For example, we might question elements of Manegold's portrait of Crystal and her family: How might a writer close to Crystal's background present the girl and her world differently from the way this well-educated, well-traveled outsider does?

For Discussion

Following are some questions that can help you think critically about the benefits and pleasures as well as the potential distortions of profiles. As you read and, perhaps, discuss these questions in class, note down your thoughts and reactions. Then, write a page or so for your instructor presenting your own ideas about profiles and the way they shape our image of the world.

1. We've asserted that profiles broaden readers' view of life by providing knowledge about diverse people and places. Test that assertion against the profiles you have read while working on this assignment. Consider profiles published here as well as those written by your classmates, and choose one that broadened your view of life and one that did not. How would you explain your response to both of these profiles? Then think back to the subjects you considered for your profile. Did you intentionally choose a subject that would "broaden readers' view of life"? Explain what motivated your choice.

2. Many Americans seem preoccupied with entertainment and sports stars and with bizarre and sensational events, a fact that influences how profiles are written. Consider whether any of the profiles you've read have glamorized or sensationalized their subjects and ignored less colorful but centrally important everyday activities. Might this be a problem with your own profile?

3. Some critics of television blame this preoccupation with the bizarre and sensational for the decline in serious public debate over social and economic issues: often all that seems to be available is brief pronouncements during newscasts and talk-show shouting matches. Single out a profile you read that seems to have overlooked potential social or economic consequences of an activity, business, or institution. What, exactly, has been overlooked? Why do you think the writer did so?

4. In any of the profiles you've read, has a person of great achievement been presented as though he or she accomplished everything on his or her own? Who has been ignored? What has been left out? What do you think this reluctance to go behind the scenes and to see who's doing the dirty work suggests about peoples' interests and values? Why do you think Americans tend to see achievement as an individual effort and to overlook those who contributed?

5. Consider the attitudes, values, and views of the writers of this chapter's profiles. Are these attitudes obvious or hidden? How can you tell? How did your own assumptions, values, gender, and ethnicity influence your choice of a subject to profile, your approach to learning about it, and your attitudes toward it? Are your attitudes obvious or hidden? If obvious, how did you make them so, and did you feel as though you were taking a risk? If hidden, why did you think it best to keep your personal views out of sight?

■ A business reporter for a newspaper writes an article about *virtual reality*. She describes the lifelike, three-dimensional experience created by wearing gloves and video goggles wired to a computer. To help readers understand this new concept, she contrasts it with television. For investors, she describes which corporations have shown an interest in the commercial possibilities of virtual reality.

■ In a textbook for introductory linguistics, a college professor discusses *syntactic development*, tracing children's gradual control of sentences, from the earliest two-word sentences through all basic sentence patterns. After reviewing the research on syntactic development, he divides the information into stages of development and describes what children do within each stage, including brief transcripts of monologues and conversations to illustrate each stage of development. He also discusses the work of key researchers and cites their major publications. Because he is writing for beginning students of linguistics, he carefully defines all special linguistic terms.

■ For a presentation at the annual convention of the American Medical Association, an anesthesiologist writes a report on the "*awareness during surgery*" concept. He presents evidence that patients under anesthesia, as in hypnosis, can hear; and he also reviews research demonstrating that they can perceive and carry out instructions that speed their recovery. He describes briefly how he applies the concept in his own work: how he prepares patients before surgery, what he tells them under anesthesia, and how their recovery goes.

■ A high school math teacher writes an article for a journal read by other math teachers about the nature of *functions and graphs* and the learning and teaching of them. Pointing out that the organizing power of functions and graphs is increasingly recognized as important for math learning, he reviews recent research on the tasks required in learning functions and graphs and describes their algebraic, tabular, and graphic representations.

Explaining Concepts 5

■ As part of a group assignment, a ninth-grader at a summer biology camp in the Sierra Nevada reads about the condition of mammals at birth. She discovers the distinction between *altricial mammals* (born nude and helpless within a protective nest) and *precocial mammals* (born well formed with eyes open and ears erect). In her part of the group report, she develops this contrast point by point, giving many examples of specific mammals but focusing in detail on altricial mice and precocial porcupines. Domestic cats, she points out, are an intermediate example—born with some fur, but with eyes and ears closed.

Explanatory writing serves a limited but very important purpose: to inform readers. In general, it does not feature its writers' experiences or feelings, as autobiography (Chapters 2 and 3) does. Instead, successful explanatory writing confidently and efficiently presents information—the writing job, in fact, required most every day in virtually every profession. It may be based on firsthand observation (Chapter 4) but always moves beyond description of specific objects and scenes to explanation of general concepts and ideas. Since it deals almost exclusively with established information, explanatory writing tends not to argue for its points. It does not aspire to be more than it is: a way for readers to find out about a particular subject. Much of what we find in newspapers, encyclopedias, instruction manuals, reference books, and research reports is explanatory writing.

This chapter focuses on one important kind of explanatory writing. The readings all explain some concept—"love," "contingent workers," "individualism," and "schizophrenia." Learning to explain a concept is especially important to you as a college student: it will help you to read textbooks, which themselves exist to explain concepts; it will prepare you to write a common type of exam and assignment; and it will acquaint you with the basic strategies—definition, classification, comparison, process narration—common to all types of explanatory writing.

The term *concept* refers to a major idea or principle. Every field has its concepts: physics has "atom," psychiatry has "schizophrenia," literature has "irony," writing has "invention," music has "harmony," and mathematics has "probability." You can see from this brief list that concepts are central to the understanding of virtually every subject. Indeed, much of human knowledge is made possible by concepts. Our brains evolved to do conceptual work—to create concepts, communicate them, and use them to think.

Concept explanations often focus on a limited aspect of a concept, so as not to overwhelm readers with information or in order to acknowledge what readers may already know. In our culture, for example, whole books have been written about a universally familiar concept such as "love"; most readers have experienced it, read about it, and thought about it more than a little. Consequently, Anastasia Toufexis, who wrote the first essay in this chapter, knew that she had to offer readers either little-known or recently discovered information about love. She met this challenge, one you will inevitably face in researching and planning your essay, by focusing on recent discoveries about the body's neurochemical changes during the familiar phenomenon we call "love."

Above all, explanatory writing should be interesting. We read explanations either out of curiosity or out of necessity. But even when we are self-motivated, bad writing can turn us off. Explanatory writing goes wrong when the flow of new information is either too fast or too slow for its readers, when the information is over their heads or too far below, or when the writing is too abstract or just plain dull.

Writing in Your Other Courses

In your college courses you will frequently be asked to explain or apply concepts. Following are some typical assignments:

- *For a chemistry course:* In your own words, explain the "law of definite proportions" and show its importance to the field of chemistry.

- *For a government course:* Choose one emerging democracy in eastern Europe, research it, and report on its progress in establishing a democratic government. Consider carefully its present arrangements for "political parties," "majority rule," "minority rights," and "popular consent."

- *For an English course:* Many works of literature depict "scapegoat" figures. Select two written works and two films, and discuss how their authors and directors present the social conflicts that lead to the creation of scapegoats.

For Group Inquiry

Try explaining a familiar concept to two or three other students. Some possible concepts might include the following:

ambition	hypertext	maturity
creativity	interval training	community
friendship	job satisfaction	civil rights
success	photosynthesis	manifest destiny

Once you have chosen a concept, think about what others in the group are likely to know about it and how you can inform them about it in two or three minutes. Consider how you will define the concept and what other strategies you might use—description, comparison, and so on—to explain it in an interesting, memorable way.

In turn, explain your concepts. After each explanation, take turns telling the speaker one or two things you learned about the concept.

Once you have all explained your concepts, discuss as a group what you learned from the experience:

- What most surprised you about this activity?
- What was most satisfying and least satisfying about explaining your concept?
- What strategies did you find yourselves using to present your concepts?

Readings

Anastasia Toufexis, an associate editor at *Time* since 1978, has written major reports, including some best-selling cover stories, for nearly every section of the magazine: medicine, health and fitness, law, environment, education, science, and national and world news. Toufexis received her bachelor's degree in premedicine from Smith College in 1967 and spent several years reporting for medical and pharmaceutical magazines. She has won a number of awards for her work at *Time* and has lectured on newsmagazine journalism and science writing at Columbia University, the University of North Carolina, and the School of Visual Arts in New York. As you read, notice how Toufexis brings together a variety of sources of information to present a <u>neurochemical perspective on love</u>.

LOVE: THE RIGHT CHEMISTRY
ANASTASIA TOUFEXIS

Love is a romantic designation for a most ordinary biological—or, shall we say, chemical?—process. A lot of nonsense is talked and written about it.

—Greta Garbo to Melvyn Douglas in *Ninotchka*

O.K., let's cut out all this nonsense about <u>romantic love</u>. Let's bring some scientific precision to the party. Let's put l<u>ove</u> under a microscope.   1

When rigorous people with Ph.D.s after their names do that, what they see is   2 not some silly, senseless thing. No, their probe reveals that <u>love rests firmly on the foundations of evolution, biology and chemistry.</u> What seems on the surface to be irrational, intoxicated behavior is in fact part of nature's master strategy—a vital force that has helped humans survive, thrive and multiply through thousands of years. Says Michael Mills, a psychology professor at Loyola Marymount University in Los Angeles: "Love is our ancestors whispering in our ears."

It was on the plains of Africa about 4 million years ago, in the early days of the   3 <u>human species</u>, that the notion of <u>romantic love probably first began to blossom</u>— or at least that the first cascades of <u>neurochemicals</u> began flowing from the brain to the bloodstream to produce goofy grins and sweaty palms as men and women gazed deeply into each other's eyes. When mankind graduated from scuttling around on all fours to walking on two legs, this change made the whole person visible to fellow human beings for the first time. Sexual organs were in full display, as were other characteristics, from the color of eyes to the span of shoulders. As never before, each individual had a unique allure.

topic sent When the sparks flew, new ways of making love enabled sex to become a romantic encounter, not just a reproductive act. Although mounting mates from the rear was, and still is, the method favored among most animals, humans began to enjoy face-to-face couplings; both looks and personal attraction became a much greater part of the equation. 4

topic sent Romance served the evolutionary purpose of pulling males and females into long-term partnership, which was essential to child rearing. On open grasslands, one parent would have a hard—and dangerous—time handling a child while foraging for food. "If a woman was carrying the equivalent of a 20-lb. bowling ball in one arm and a pile of sticks in the other, it was ecologically critical to pair up with a mate to rear the young," explains anthropologist Helen Fisher, author of *Anatomy of Love*. 5

Comparison Western pairs to 4 years While Western culture holds fast to the idea that true love flames forever (the movie *Bram Stoker's Dracula* has the Count carrying the torch beyond the grave), nature apparently meant passions to sputter out in something like four years. Primitive pairs stayed together just "long enough to rear one child through infancy," says Fisher. Then each would find a new partner and start all over again. 6

head why itch to 7yr due to 2nd child born What Fisher calls the "four-year itch" shows up unmistakably in today's divorce statistics. In most of the 62 cultures she has studied, divorce rates peak around the fourth year of marriage. Additional youngsters help keep pairs together longer. If, say, a couple have another child three years after the first, as often occurs, then their union can be expected to last about four more years. That makes them ripe for the more familiar phenomenon portrayed in the Marilyn Monroe classic *The Seven-Year Itch*. 7

If, in nature's design, romantic love is not eternal, neither is it exclusive. Less than 5% of mammals form rigorously faithful pairs. From the earliest days, contends Fisher, the human pattern has been "monogamy with clandestine adultery." Occasional flings upped the chances that new combinations of genes would be passed on to the next generation. Men who sought new partners had more children. Contrary to common assumptions, women were just as likely to stray. "As long as prehistoric females were secretive about their extramarital affairs," argues Fisher, "they could garner extra resources, life insurance, better genes and more varied DNA for their biological futures. . . ." 8

Lovers often claim that they feel as if they are being swept away. They're not mistaken; they are literally flooded by chemicals, research suggests. A meeting of eyes, a touch of hands or a whiff of scent sets off a flood that starts in the brain and races along the nerves and through the blood. The results are familiar: flushed skin, sweaty palms, heavy breathing. If love looks suspiciously like stress, the reason is simple: the chemical pathways are identical. 9

Above all, there is the sheer euphoria of falling in love—a not-so-surprising reaction, considering that many of the substances swamping the newly smitten are chemical cousins of amphetamines. They include dopamine, norepinephrine and especially phenylethylamine (PEA). Cole Porter knew what he was talking about when 10 he wrote "I get a kick out of you." "Love is a natural high," observes Anthony Walsh, author of *The Science of Love: Understanding Love and Its Effects on Mind and Body.* "PEA gives you that silly smile that you flash at strangers. When we meet someone who is attractive to us, the whistle blows at the PEA factory."

But phenylethylamine highs don't last forever, a fact that lends support to ar- 11 guments that passionate romantic love is short-lived. As with any amphetamine, the body builds up a tolerance to PEA; thus it takes more and more of the substance to produce love's special kick. After two to three years, the body simply can't crank-up the needed amount of PEA. And chewing on chocolate doesn't help, despite popular belief. The candy is high in PEA, but it fails to boost the body's supply.

Fizzling chemicals spell the end of delirious passion; for many people that marks 12 the end of the liaison as well. It is particularly true for those whom Dr. Michael Lie- bowitz of the New York State Psychiatric Institute terms "attraction junkies." They crave the intoxication of falling in love so much that they move frantically from affair to affair just as soon as the first rush of infatuation fades.

Still, many romances clearly endure beyond the first years. What accounts for 13 that? Another set of chemicals, of course. The continued presence of a partner grad- ually steps up production in the brain of endorphins. Unlike the fizzy amphetamines, these are soothing substances. Natural pain-killers, they give lovers a sense of se- curity, peace and calm. "That is one reason why it feels so horrible when we're aban- doned or a lover dies," notes Fisher. "We don't have our daily hit of narcotics."

Researchers see a contrast between the heated infatuation induced by PEA, along 14 with other amphetamine-like chemicals, and the more intimate attachment fostered and prolonged by endorphins. "Early love is when you love the way the other person makes you feel," explains psychiatrist Mark Goulston of the University of California, Los Angeles. "Mature love is when you love the person as he or she is." It is the difference between passionate and compassionate love, observes Walsh, a psycho- biologist at Boise State University in Idaho. "It's Bon Jovi vs. Beethoven."

Oxytocin is another chemical that has recently been implicated in love. Produced 15 by the brain, it sensitizes nerves and stimulates muscle contraction. In women it helps uterine contractions during childbirth as well as production of breast milk, and seems to inspire mothers to nuzzle their infants. Scientists speculate that oxytocin might encourage similar cuddling between adult women and men. The versatile chemical may also enhance orgasms. In one study of men, oxytocin increased to three to five times its normal level during climax, and it may soar even higher in women.

Chemicals may help explain (at least to scientists) the feelings of passion and 16 compassion, but why do people tend to fall in love with one partner rather than a myriad of others? Once again, it's partly a function of evolution and biology. "Men are looking for maximal fertility in a mate," says Loyola Marymount's Mills. "That is in large part why females in the prime childbearing ages of 17 to 28 are so desir- able." Men can size up youth and vitality in a glance, and studies indeed show that men fall in love quite rapidly. Women tumble more slowly, to a large degree because their requirements are more complex; they need more time to check the guy out. "Age is not vital," notes Mills, "but the ability to provide security, father children, share resources and hold a high status in society are all key factors."

Still, that does not explain why the way Mary walks and laughs makes Bill dizzy 17 with desire while Marcia's gait and giggle leave him cold. "Nature has wired us for one special person," suggests Walsh, romantically. He rejects the idea that a woman

[handwritten margin note: Love rests firmly on the foundations of biology, evolution, & chemistry.]

or a man can be in love with two people at the same time. Each person carries in his or her mind a unique subliminal guide to the ideal partner, a ''love map,'' to borrow a term coined by sexologist John Money of Johns Hopkins University.

Drawn from the people and experiences of childhood, the map is a record of whatever we found enticing and exciting—or disturbing and disgusting. Small feet, curly hair. The way our mothers patted our head or how our fathers told a joke. A fireman's uniform, a doctor's stethoscope. All the information gathered while growing up is imprinted in the brain's circuitry by adolescence. Partners never meet each and every requirement, but a sufficient number of matches can light up the wires and signal, ''It's love.'' Not every partner will be like the last one, since lovers may have different combinations of the characteristics favored by the map. 18

[handwritten margin note: conclu.]

O.K., that's the scientific point of view. Satisfied? Probably not. To most peo- ple—with or without Ph.D.s—love will always be more than the sum of its natural parts. It's a commingling of body and soul, reality and imagination, poetry and phen- ylethylamine. In our deepest hearts, most of us harbor the hope that love will never fully yield up its secrets, that it will always elude our grasp. 19

[handwritten margin notes: uncertainty; chemical is part of love please; history repeats itself.]

It's quite natural to resist scientific explanations or analysis of love and other of life's mysteries that involve people's ideals and visions. Some readers will feel that Toufexis's essay takes all the romance out of love. Consider, however, what's to be gained by such explanations. What do you think motivates re- searchers to study love? Why does Toufexis seem to take special pleasure in reporting the results of these studies? And how do you respond? How, for example, do you respond to such controversial ideas as these:

> While Western culture holds fast to the idea that true love flames for- ever . . . , nature apparently meant passions to sputter out in something like four years. (paragraph 6)

> From the earliest days . . . the human pattern has been ''monogamy with clandestine adultery.'' (paragraph 8)

> Each person carries in his or her mind a unique subliminal guide to the ideal partner, a ''love map.'' . . . (paragraph 17)

1. At the beginning of this chapter, we make the following assertions about explanatory writing in general and concept explanation in particular:

- It seeks to inform readers about a specific subject.
- It presents information confidently and efficiently.
- It may attempt to engage readers' interests.
- It relies almost exclusively on established information.
- It does not feature its writers' experiences or feelings.
- It tends not to argue for its points.
- It usually focuses on one aspect of the concept.

Consider whether each of these assertions is true of Toufexis's essay.

2.   Concept explanations offer more than a collection of information. They make a point about the concept. What would you say is Toufexis's point? Where in the essay do you see evidence of this point?

3.   Consider Toufexis's assumptions about her readers. These assumptions are not stated in the essay, of course, but you may be able to infer them. What does she seem to assume about her readers' knowledge, beliefs, and feelings related to the concept of love? What parts of the essay suggest Toufexis's assumptions?

4.   To keep readers on track, writers of explanations offer prominent cues. One such cue is the transition sentence that opens a new paragraph, referring to information in the previous paragraph. To see how Toufexis relates information paragraph by paragraph, examine each opening sentence in paragraphs 7–15, underlining any parts that refer to the previous paragraph. Your underlining will show that these transitions work in a variety of ways. Choose three transitions that function in different ways and try to explain the differences.

For Your Own Writing

Like Toufexis, you could write an essay about love or romance, but with a different focus: on its history (How and when did it develop as an idea in the West?), its cultural characteristics (How is love regarded presently among different American ethnic groups or world cultures?), its excesses or extremes, its expression between parent and child, or the phases of falling in and out of love. Also consider writing about other concepts involving personal relationships, such as jealousy, co-dependency, idealization, stereotyping, or homophobia.

Commentary

Observing an important requirement of essays explaining concepts, Toufexis provides several different kinds of cues to keep readers on track. In addition to paragraph-opening transitions (see question 4 above), Toufexis carefully forecasts the topics and direction of her essay in her second paragraph: ". . . their probe reveals that love rests firmly on the foundations of evolution, biology, and chemistry." This forecast helps readers anticipate the types of scientific information Toufexis has selected for her special focus on love.

For more on cueing readers, see Chapter 13.

Besides offering frequent transitions and a forecast, Toufexis also frames her explanation. Writers create a frame when they relate the end of an essay to its beginning, providing readers a satisfying sense of closure. At both the beginning and end of her essay, Toufexis refers to science, scientists, and Ph.D.s. She also contrasts romantic feelings themselves with the scientific approach to understanding the neurochemistry of those feelings. Note, however, that she does not simply paraphrase what she said earlier. Instead, she "echoes" the beginning in a subtle way by returning to references, ideas, and key words or phrases the reader will remember.

You can feature all of these cues—transitions, forecasting, framing—in your essay explaining a concept. While forecasting and framing are optional, transitions are essential; without them, your readers will either stumble along resentfully or stop in confusion and irritation.

Concept explanations are based on authoritative, expert sources, on established material gleaned from reputable publications or interviews. Toufexis makes use of both these kinds of sources. She apparently arranged phone interviews with six different professors specializing in diverse academic disciplines: psychology, anthropology, psychiatry, and sexology. (She does not identify the discipline of one professor—Walsh, in paragraph 10—but from the title of his book we might guess that he is a biochemist.) We assume that she read at least parts of the two books she names in paragraphs 5 and 10, and perhaps she also read still other sources, which may have led her to some of the professors she interviewed.

What is obvious about Toufexis's use of sources is that she does not indicate precisely where she obtained all the information she includes. For example, she does not cite the source of the anthropological information in paragraphs 3–5, although a reader might guess that she summarized it from *Anatomy of Love,* cited at the end of paragraph 5. We cannot be certain whether the quote at the end of paragraph 5 comes from the book or from an interview with its author. These liberties in citing sources are acceptable in newspapers and magazines, including the leading ones educated readers count on to keep them up to date on developments in various fields. Experienced readers know that reporters, who write about surprisingly diverse topics as part of their jobs, rely entirely on sources for their articles and essays. They understand that Toufexis is not an expert on the neurochemistry of love; they accept her role as synthesizer and summarizer of authoritative sources.

Toufexis's role is much like your role when writing your essay for this chapter: relying on a variety of authoritative sources, you, too, will explain a concept to readers who know less about it than you do. However, you will want to cite your sources more precisely and fully than Toufexis does, because complete citation of sources is expected in all academic writing, both student and professorial. Veronica Murayama's essay in this chapter provides guidance, as does Chapter 22.

Part III covers these and other writing strategies in detail.

Also worth commenting on is Toufexis's use of some of the writing strategies that make concept explanations possible: narrating, classifying, and analyzing effects. Toufexis relies on narrative in paragraphs 3 and 4 to sketch out the evolution of romantic love. She uses past tense verbs common to narrative ("began," "gazed," "graduated") along with clauses and phrases indicating time ("when," "in the early days," "the first time," "as never before"). She uses classification to organize the information about chemicals in paragraphs 9–15, first setting up the classification in paragraph 9—which is also an example of internal forecasting—and then presenting information about three kinds of chemicals: phenylethylamines (paragraph 13), endorphins (paragraph 14), and oxytocin (paragraph 15). Toufexis analyzes effects in paragraphs 5–8, where she suggests the benefits of romantic love for human evolution.

■   ■   ■

Janice Castro, a graduate of the University of California at Berkeley, is an associate editor at *Time*, where she writes about politics and business. She has been at *Time* since 1973. Some of her major reports have been on the high cost of medical care, the crisis over drugs in the workplace, quality in American manufacturing, the state of the U.S. work force, and Japanese investment in the United States. She was a principal writer for *Time*'s 1992 special issue on women. In the 1993 selection that follows, Castro discusses changes in the way American companies do business, changes that rely on part-time and free-lance workers, a group Castro calls the "contingent" work force.

CONTINGENT WORKERS
JANICE CASTRO

1   The corporation that is now the largest private employer in America does not have any smokestacks or conveyor belts or trucks. There is no clanging of metal on metal, no rivets or plastic or steel. In one sense, it does not make anything. But then again, it is in the business of making almost everything.

2   Manpower Inc., with 560,000 workers, is the world's largest temporary employment agency. Every morning, its people scatter into the offices and factories of America, seeking a day's work for a day's pay. As General Motors (367,000 workers), IBM (330,500) and other industrial giants struggle to survive by shrinking their payrolls, Manpower, based in Milwaukee, Wisconsin, is booming along with other purveyors of temporary workers, providing the hands and the brainpower that other companies are no longer willing to call their own.

3   Even as its economy continues to recover, the U.S. is increasingly becoming a nation of part-timers and free-lancers, of temps and independent contractors. This "disposable" work force is the most important trend in business today, and it is fundamentally changing the relationship between Americans and their jobs. For companies large and small, the phenomenon provides a way to remain globally competitive while avoiding the vagaries of market cycles and the growing burdens imposed by employment rules, antidiscrimination laws, health-care costs, and pension plans. But for workers, it can mean an end to the security and sense of significance that came from being a loyal employee. One by one, the tangible and intangible bonds that once defined work in America are giving way.

4   Every day, 1.5 million temps are dispatched from agencies like Kelly Services and Manpower—nearly three times as many as 10 years ago. But they are only the most visible part of America's enormous new temporary work force. An additional 34 million people start their day as other types of "contingent" workers. Some are part-timers with some benefits. Others work by the hour, the day or the duration of a project, receiving only a paycheck without benefits of any kind. The rules of their employment vary widely and so do the attempts to label them. They are called short-timers, per-diem workers, leased employees, extra workers, supplementals, contrac-

way of talking / language   *outsourced?*

tors—or in IBM's ironic computer-generated parlance, "the peripherals." They are what you might expect: secretaries, security guards, salesclerks, assembly-line workers, analysts and CAD/CAM designers. But these days they are also what you'd never expect: doctors, high school principals, lawyers, bank officers, X-ray technicians, biochemists, engineers, managers—even chief executives.

Already, one in every three U.S. workers has joined these shadow brigades carrying out America's business. Their ranks are growing so quickly that they are expected to outnumber permanent full-time workers by the end of this decade. Companies keep chipping away at costs, stripping away benefits or substituting contingent employees for full-time workers. This year alone, U.S. employers are expected to use such tactics to cut the nation's $2.6 billion payroll costs as much as $800 million. And there is no evidence to suggest that such corporate behavior will change with improvement in the economy.   5

No institution is immune to the contingent solution. Imagine the surprise of a Los Angeles woman, seriously injured in an auto accident, when she recently asked a radiology technician at the hospital about a procedure. "Don't ask me," he snapped. "I'm just a temp." In Appleton, Wisconsin, the Aid Association for Lutherans is using temps to keep track of $3.6 million in relief funds for victims of Hurricane Andrew. The State of Maine uses temps as bailiffs and financial investigators. IBM, once the citadel of American job security, has traded 10% of its staff for "peripherals" so far. Says IBM administrative manager Lillian Davis, in words that would have been unimaginable from a Fortune 500 executive 20 years ago: "Now that we have stepped over that line, we have decided to use these people wherever we can."   6

The number of people employed full time by Fortune 500 companies has shrunk from 19% of the work force two decades ago to less than 10% today. Almost overnight, companies are shedding a system of mutual obligations and expectations built up since the Great Depression, a tradition of labor that said performance was rewarded, loyalty was valued and workers were a vital part of the enterprises they served. In this chilly new world of global competition, they are often viewed merely as expenses. Long-term commitments of all kinds are anathema to the modern corporation. For the growing ranks of contingent workers, that means no more pensions, health insurance or paid vacations. No more promises or promotions or costly training programs. No more lawsuits for wrongful termination or other such hassles for the boss. Says Secretary of Labor Robert Reich: "These workers are outside the traditional system of worker-management relationships. As the contingent work force grows—as many people find themselves working part time for many different employers—the social contract is beginning to fray."   7

As the underpinnings of mutual commitment crumble, time-honored notions of fairness are cast aside for millions of workers. Working temp or part time often means being treated as a second-class citizen by both employers and permanent staff. Says Michelle Lane, a former temp in Los Angeles: "You're just a fixture, a borrowed thing that doesn't belong there." Being a short-timer also can mean doing hazardous work without essential training, or putting up with sexual and racial harassment. Placement officers report client requests for "blond bombshells" or people without accents. Says an agency counselor: "One client called and asked us not to send any black people, and we didn't. We do whatever the clients want, whether it's right or not."   8

Workers have little choice but to cope with such treatment since most new job openings are the labor equivalent of uncommitted relationships. More than 90% of the 365,000 jobs created by U.S. companies last month were part-time positions taken by people who want to work full time. "The fill-ins are always desperate for full-time jobs," says one corporate personnel officer. "They always ask." Richard Belous, chief economist for the National Planning Association in Washington has studied the proliferation of tenuous jobs. "If there was a national fear index," he says, "it would be directly related to the growth of contingent work." 9

Once contingent workers appear in a company, they multiply rapidly, taking the places of permanent staff. Says Manpower chairman Mitchell Fromstein: "The U.S. is going from just-in-time manufacturing to just-in-time employment. The employer tells us, 'I want them delivered exactly when I want them, as many as I need, and when I don't need them, I don't want them here.' " Fromstein has built his business by meeting these demands. "Can I get people to work under these circumstances? Yeah. We're the ATMs of the job market." 10

In order to succeed in this new type of work, says Carvel Taylor, a Chicago industrial consultant, "you need to have an entrepreneurial spirit, definable skills and an ability to articulate and market them, but that is exactly what the bulk of the population holed up inside bureaucratic organizations doesn't have, and why they are scared to death." Already the temping phenomenon is producing two vastly different classes of untethered workers: the mercenary work force at the top of the skills ladder, who thrive; and the rest, many of whom, unable to attract fat contract fees, must struggle to survive. 11

The flexible life of a consultant or contract worker does indeed work well for a relatively small class of people like doctors, engineers, accountants and financial planners, who can expect to do well by providing highly compensated services to a variety of employers. David Hill, 65, a former chief information systems officer for General Motors, has joined with 17 other onetime auto-industry executives (median salary before leaving their jobs: $300,000) to form a top-of-the-line international consulting group. "In the future," says Hill, "loyalty and devotion are going to be not to a Hughes or Boeing or even an industry, but to a particular profession or skill. It takes a high level of education to succeed in such a free-flowing environment. We are going to be moving from job to job in the same way that migrant workers used to move from crop to crop." 12

Many professionals like the freedom of such a life. John Andrews, 42, a Los Angeles antitrust attorney, remembers working seven weeks without a day off as a young lawyer. He prefers temping at law firms. Says he: "There's no security anymore. Partnerships fold up overnight. Besides, I never had a rat-race mentality, and being a lawyer is the ultimate rat-race job. I like to travel. My car is paid for. I don't own a house. I'm not into mowing grass." 13

But most American workers do better with the comfort and security of a stable job. Sheldon Joseph was a Chicago advertising executive until he was laid off in 1989. Now he temps for $10 an hour in a community job-training program. Says the 56-year-old Joseph: "I was used to working in the corporate environment and giving my total loyalty to the company. I feel like Rip Van Winkle. You wake up and the world is all changed. The message from industry is, 'We don't want your loyalty. We want your work.' What happened to the dream?" 14

[Employers defend their new labor practices as plain and simple survival tactics.] 15
American companies are evolving from huge, mass-production manufacturers that
once dominated markets to a new species of hub-and-network enterprises built for
flexibility in a brutally competitive world. The buzz phrase at many companies is "ac-
cordion management"—the ability to expand or contract one's work force virtually
at will to suit business conditions.

[Boardroom discussions now focus on what are called "core competencies"—   16
those operations at the heart of a business—and on how to shed the rest of the
functions to subcontractors or nonstaff workers.] Managers divide their employees
into a permanent cadre of "core workers," which keeps on shrinking, and the contingent workers, who can be brought in at a moment's notice. Most large employers
are not even certain at any given time how many of these helpers are working for
them—nor do they usually care. Says a manager: "We don't count them. They're
not here long enough to matter." Some analysts wonder whether America's celebrated rise in productivity per worker (2.8% last year) is all it seems to be, since so
many of those invisible hands are not being counted. So profound is the change that
the word core has evolved a new meaning, as in "she's core," meaning that she is
important and distinctive because she is not part of the contingent work force.

Indeed managers these days can hire virtually any kind of temp they want. Need   17
an extra lawyer or paralegal for a week or so? Try Lawsmiths in San Francisco or
Project Professionals in Santa Monica, California. Need a loan officer? Bank Temps
in Denver can help. Engineers? Sysdyne outside Minneapolis, Minnesota. CAD/CAM
operators? You don't even need to buy the equipment: in Oakland, California, Western Temporary Services has its own CAD/CAM business, serving such clients as the
U.S. Navy, the Air Force, Chevron, Exxon and United Technologies. Doctors and
nurses? A firm called Interim in Fort Lauderdale, Florida, can provide them anywhere
in the country. Need to rent a tough boss to clean up a bad situation? Call IMCOR,
a Connecticut-based firm that boasts a roster of senior executives expert at turna-
rounds. Says IMCOR chairman John Thompson: "Services like ours are going to continue to flourish when businesses change so rapidly that it's in no one's interest to
make commitments. Moving on to the next place where you're needed is going to
be the way it is. We will all be free-lancers."

For now, most citizens will have to scramble to adapt to the new age of the   18
disposable worker. Says Robert Schaen, a former comptroller of Chicago-based
Ameritech who now runs his own children's publishing business: "The days of the
mammoth corporations are coming to an end. People are going to have to create
their own lives, their own careers and their own successes. Some people may go
kicking and screaming into the new world, but there is only one message there:
You're now in business for yourself."

For Discussion

Castro reports on a surprising change in the employment conditions of American workers. As recently as ten to fifteen years ago, most workers held full-
time jobs with health care coverage, paid vacations, and pension plans. Many
had virtual job security, continuing on the same job for thirty or forty years,
until retirement. Now one-third of American workers are contingent, and
Castro predicts that they will outnumber permanent, full-time workers by

2000. What might this change mean for you personally? How could it influence your hopes for the future?

For more on definition, see Chapter 16.

For Analysis

1.   Although Castro provides a lot of information about the contingent worker phenomenon, we can be confident she selected the information from much more than was available to her. Given her selection and arrangement, what seems to be the point she wants to make with all the information she provides? Where in the essay do you find evidence of this point?

2.   Writers of essays explaining concepts nearly always find themselves devising careful definitions for the central concept and other key terms. In paragraph 4, Castro tentatively defines "contingent workers." How does she go about constructing this definition? What is included in it? How satisfactory do you find this initial definition of the concept?

3.   It is likely that you found Castro's essay understandable on first reading and needed only occasionally to reread a sentence or brief section in order to clarify meaning. Reread the essay, making a list of any features that seem to you to contribute to its readability.

4.   For explanatory writing to win readers' confidence, it must seem authoritative, its writer at least a temporary expert on some small part of a subject. Review both the Toufexis and Castro essays, listing qualities that make them seem authoritative and trustworthy. Do both invite your trust in similar ways? Are they equally successful in winning your trust?

For Your Own Writing

Consider writing about the contingent worker concept but with a focus different from Castro's. For example, you could focus on the debate between labor and business over contingent work (sorting out the issues and reporting what you learn, but not taking a side yourself), the history of contingent or part-time work in America, or changes brought about in the lives of those who have had to give up full-time jobs and take up contingent work. Or you could write about some other concept central to current discussions of work, such as career path, glass ceiling, burnout, networking, mentoring, management styles, or collective bargaining.

Commentary

Castro makes good use of a variety of sources. As a business reporter, she has access to published materials and computer data sources that provide the many facts and statistics she includes about corporations and employment trends. Since she has written about contingent workers and related topics before, she has developed a store of information. In addition, she apparently interviewed fourteen different people for this new report, and it may be that some of her facts and statistics come from these interviews. Following her magazine's convention for citing sources, she names her interviewees but does not identify other sources of information, perhaps because she knows her readers will accept it as well established. She seems to assume that readers will accept her statistics about American business just as they accept baseball scores and weather reports.

Writers face a special challenge in planning and organizing essays explaining concepts. First, they gather a lot of information about a concept. Then they must find a focus that will be suitable for their readers and the constraints of the assignment or publication. For example, Castro focuses on the ironies, causes, and effects of the increase in contingent workers. Finally, writers must select only the information that will illustrate the point they want to make and then find a way to organize the information so that readers can make sense of the text without too much uncertainty or frustration. Let's consider Castro's plan. Here is a scratch outline of her essay, with paragraph numbers indicated parenthetically:

Ironic opening: Manpower employs more than G.M. (1–2)

Increase in part-time and free-lance employment represents a fundamental change. (3)

Contingent workers are tentatively defined. (4)

The number of contingents is growing and not likely to decline when the economy improves. (5)

All kinds of institutions and businesses are relying on contingents. (6)

Mutual obligations between employer and employee are being shed. (7)

Contingents are second-class citizens. (8, 9)

Demand for contingents is increasing. (10)

Some contingents find success. (11–13)

But most Americans still prefer a secure job. (14)

Employers have a number of arguments for relying on contingents. (15)

Employers distinguish sharply between core and contingent employees. (16)

Some contingents are highly specialized. (17)

Workers will have to adapt to this change. (18)

At the beginning, Castro contextualizes and defines the concept (paragraphs 1–4). She then reports on the nature of contingent work (5–10) and its mixed impact on employees (11–14). Finally, she presents employers' views (15–17) and concludes that workers seem to have no choice but to adapt to the changed nature of employment (18). Given Castro's purpose and readers, her plan seems sensible, and most readers will find it easy to follow.

Finally, there are special kinds of sentence structures that enable writers to present information effectively. For example, Castro relies on appositives and parenthetical explanations that efficiently combine into one sentence information that might otherwise require two sentences:

IBM, *once the citadel of American job security*, has traded 10% of its staff for "peripherals" so far. (paragraph 6)

> Says Michelle Lane, *a former temp in Los Angeles:* "You're just a fixture, a borrowed thing that doesn't belong there." (paragraph 8)
>
> As General Motors (*367,000 workers*), IBM (*330,500*), and other industrial giants struggle to survive. . . . (paragraph 2)

Further efficiency can be gained in explanatory writing by combining information into series or lists:

> . . . . avoiding the vagaries of market cycles and the growing burden imposed by *employment rules, antidiscrimination laws, health-care costs, and pension plans.* (paragraph 3)
>
> They are called *short-timers, per-diem workers, leased employees, extra workers, supplementals, contractors*—or in IBM's ironic computer-generated parlance,—"*the peripherals.*" (paragraph 4)
>
> They are what you might expect: *secretaries, security guards, salesclerks, assembly-line workers, analysts, and* CAD/CAM *designers.* (paragraph 4)

Items in a series or list must be grammatically parallel. Lists can be set up by a colon, as in the third example.

■   ■   ■

The authors of the next essay are sociologists. Robert N. Bellah, the author of several books, including *The New Religious Consciousness*, teaches at the University of California at Berkeley; his colleagues teach at other American universities. This selection comes from their book, *Habits of the Heart: Individualism and Commitment in American Life* (1985). As you read it, notice how they define American individualism by first describing the mythic version, in cowboy and detective fiction, and then contrasting it with a real version, in Abraham Lincoln. What seems to be the point of this contrast?

AMERICAN INDIVIDUALISM

ROBERT N. BELLAH
RICHARD MADSEN
WILLIAM M. SULLIVAN
ANN SWIDLER
STEPHEN M. TIPTON

A deep and continuing theme in American literature is the hero who must leave 1 society, alone or with one or a few others, in order to realize the moral good in the wilderness, at sea, or on the margins of settled society. Sometimes the withdrawal involves a contribution to society, as in James Fenimore Cooper's *The Deerslayer.* Sometimes the new marginal community realizes ethical ends impossible in the larger society, as in the interracial harmony between Huckleberry Finn and Jim. Sometimes the flight from society is simply mad and ends in general disaster, as in *Moby Dick.* When it is not in and through society but in flight from it that the good is to be realized, as in the case of Melville's Ahab, the line between ethical heroism and madness vanishes, and the destructive potentiality of a completely asocial individualism is revealed.

America is also the inventor of that most mythic individual hero, the cowboy, 2 who again and again saves a society he can never completely fit into. The cowboy has a special talent—he can shoot straighter and faster than other men—and a special sense of justice. But these characteristics make him so unique that he can never fully belong to society. His destiny is to defend society without ever really joining it. He rides off alone into the sunset like Shane, or like the Lone Ranger moves on accompanied only by his Indian companion. But the cowboy's importance is not that he is isolated or antisocial. Rather, his significance lies in his unique, individual virtue and special skill and it is because of those qualities that society needs and welcomes him. Shane, after all, starts as a real outsider, but ends up with the gratitude of the community and the love of a woman and a boy. And while the Lone Ranger never settles down and marries the local schoolteacher, he always leaves with the affection and gratitude of the people he has helped. It is as if the myth says you can be a truly good person, worthy of admiration and love, only if you resist fully joining the group. But sometimes the tension leads to an irreparable break. Will Kane, the hero of *High Noon*, abandoned by the cowardly townspeople, saves them from an unrestrained killer, but then throws his sheriff's badge in the dust and goes off into the desert with his bride. One is left wondering where they will go, for there is no longer any link with any town.

The connection of moral courage and lonely individualism is even tighter for that   3
other, more modern American hero, the hard-boiled detective. From Sam Spade to Serpico, the detective is a loner. He is often unsuccessful in conventional terms, working out of a shabby office where the phone never rings. Wily, tough, smart, he is nonetheless unappreciated. But his marginality is also his strength. When a bit of business finally comes their way, Philip Marlowe, Lew Archer, and Travis McGee are tenacious. They pursue justice and help the unprotected even when it threatens to unravel the fabric of society itself. Indeed, what is remarkable about the American detective story is less its hero than its image of crime. When the detective begins his quest, it appears to be an isolated incident. But as it develops, the case turns out to be linked to the powerful and privileged of the community. Society, particularly "high society," is corrupt to the core. It is this boring into the center of society to find it rotten that constitutes the fundamental drama of the American detective story. It is not a personal but a social mystery that the detective must unravel.

To seek justice in a corrupt society, the American detective must be tough, and   4
above all, he must be a loner. He lives outside the normal bourgeois pattern of career and family. As his investigations begin to lead him beyond the initial crime to the glamorous and powerful center of the society, its leaders make attempts to buy off the detective, to corrupt him with money, power, or sex. This counterpoint to the gradual unravelling of the crime is the battle the detective wages for his own integrity, in the end rejecting the money of the powerful and spurning (sometimes jailing or killing) the beautiful woman who has tried to seduce him. The hard-boiled detective, who may long for love and success, for a place in society, is finally driven to stand alone, resisting the blandishments of society, to pursue a lonely crusade for justice. Sometimes, as in the film *Chinatown*, corruption is so powerful and so total that the honest detective no longer has a place to stand and the message is one of unrelieved cynicism.

Both the cowboy and the hard-boiled detective tell us something important   5
about American individualism. The cowboy, like the detective, can be valuable to society only because he is a completely autonomous individual who stands outside it. To serve society, one must be able to stand alone, not needing others, not depending on their judgment, and not submitting to their wishes. Yet this individualism

is not selfishness. Indeed, it is a kind of heroic selflessness. One accepts the necessity of remaining alone in order to serve the values of the group. And this obligation to aloneness is an important key to the American moral imagination. Yet it is part of the profound ambiguity of the mythology of American individualism that its moral heroism is always just a step away from despair. For an Ahab, and occasionally for a cowboy or a detective, there is no return to society, no moral redemption. The hero's lonely quest for moral excellence ends in absolute nihilism.

If we may turn from the mythical heroes of fiction to a mythic, but historically 6 real, hero, Abraham Lincoln, we may begin to see what is necessary if the nihilistic alternative is to be avoided. In many respects, Lincoln conforms perfectly to the archetype of the lonely, individualistic hero. He was a self-made man, never comfortable with the eastern upper classes. His dual moral commitment to the preservation of the Union and the belief that "all men are created equal" roused the hostility of abolitionists and Southern sympathizers alike. In the war years, he was more and more isolated, misunderstood by Congress and cabinet, and unhappy at home. In the face of almost universal mistrust, he nonetheless completed his self-appointed task of bringing the nation through its most devastating war, preaching reconciliation as he did so, only to be brought down by an assassin's bullet. What saved Lincoln from nihilism was the larger whole for which he felt it was important to live and worthwhile to die. No one understood better the meaning of the Republic and of the freedom and equality that it only very imperfectly embodies. But it was not only civic republicanism that gave his life value. Reinhold Niebuhr has said that Lincoln's biblical understanding of the Civil War was deeper than that of any contemporary theologian. The great symbols of death and rebirth that Lincoln invoked to give meaning to the sacrifice of those who died at Gettysburg, in a war he knew to be senseless and evil, came to redeem his own senseless death at the hand of an assassin. It is through his identification with a community and a tradition that Lincoln became the deeply and typically American individual that he was.

Notes

1. On individualism in nineteenth-century American literature see D. H. Lawrence, *Studies in Classic American Literature* (1923; Garden City, N.Y.: Doubleday, Anchor Books, 1951). On the image of the cowboy see Will Wright, *Sixguns and Society: A Structural Study of the Western* (Berkeley and Los Angeles: University of California Press, 1975). On cowboys and detectives see John G. Cawelti, *Adventure, Mystery, and Romance: Formula Stories as Art and Popular Culture* (Chicago: University of Chicago Press, 1976).

2. On the hero's avoidance of women and society see Leslie Fieldler, *Love and Death in the American Novel* (New York: Stein and Day, 1966), and Ann Swidler, "Love and Adulthood in American Culture," in *Themes of Work and Love in Adulthood*, ed. Neil J. Smelser and Erik H. Erikson (Cambridge, Mass.: Harvard University Press, 1980), pp. 120–47.

3. The best book on Lincoln's meaning for American public life is Harry V. Jaffa, *Crisis of the House Divided: An Interpretation of the Lincoln-Douglas Debates* (Garden City, N.Y.: Doubleday, 1959). Reinhold Niebuhr's remarks appear in his essay "The Religion of Abraham Lincoln," in *Lincoln and the Gettysburg Address*, ed. Allan Nevins (Urbana, Ill.: University of Illinois Press, 1964), p. 72.

For Discussion

The authors feel that too many Americans hold a concept of individualism that values isolation, and that leads potentially to despair and nihilism, the belief that all values are meaningless and that existence is senseless. They advocate an alternative to nihilism that values commitment to community and tradition. Why do so many Americans seem to feel an "obligation to aloneness"? Do you think that Americans undervalue community and tradition? Why do you think so? How much commitment do you feel to a community or tradition? To the United States as a community of citizens?

For Analysis

1.   Unlike the Castro essay, this one does not offer any initial definition of the concept. Instead, working from various examples of fictional and real heroes, it gradually builds a definition of "American individualism." Trace this incremental definition—keeping in mind that it includes both mythical and real individualism—by underlining general statements, phrases or sentences, that contribute to it. You might begin with "must leave society" in paragraph 1. Then summarize these statements in order to understand the concept of "American individualism."

2.   What do you take to be the point of this essay's explanation about American individualism?

3.   Analyze the examples in paragraphs 2 and 3. In paragraph 2, what does each example contribute? How are the examples presented differently in paragraphs 2 and 3? Why do you think the authors use so many examples (three cowboys and five detectives)? Given the essay's point, what advantages do you see in the author's use of examples?

4.   Make a scratch outline of the plan this essay follows. Then examine the first sentence in each paragraph closely to see how it cues readers to the plan. Specifically, how does each sentence connect previous information with what follows and also reiterate the subject of the essay?

See the scratch outline of Castro's article on p. 176 for an example.

For Your
Own Writing

Bellah and his coauthors find examples in movies of the concept of "mythic individualism." Think of movies you've seen—recent ones as well as older ones. What ideas do they represent? For example:

1. What do war films suggest about concepts like masculinity, heroism, patriotism, or male bonding?
2. What do teen films suggest about the generation gap, adolescent rebelliousness, or community?
3. What do romantic comedies suggest about gender roles, friendship and marriage, or sexual politics?

To write about a concept in one of these types of films, view at least two films, taking careful notes on how the concept is revealed.

Commentary

This selection illustrates the importance of comparison and contrast in explaining concepts. In the opening paragraph, destructive Ahab is contrasted with ethical Huck Finn and Jim. In the second paragraph, Shane and the Lone Ranger are contrasted with Will Kane. Paragraphs 2, 3, and 4 compare detectives and cowboys, and paragraph 5 interprets and summarizes this comparison. Finally, paragraph 6 contrasts Ahab and the most asocial cowboys and detectives with Abraham Lincoln. We might call Bellah's basic strategy definition by contrast.

For more about comparison and contrast, see Chapter 18.

The essay also makes use of another strategy often found with comparison and contrast: classification. It is easy to imagine the authors considering several cowboys for paragraph 2. The three they chose seem representative of three different kinds of cowboy heroes; that is, they created a three-part classification based on this difference and then assigned to each part a cowboy most readers would recognize. Classifying enables writers to reorganize information in ways that contribute to their main point.

For more on classifying, see Chapter 17.

The authors of this piece do not cite any specific sources, but an appendix to the book the selection comes from lists the many articles and books that provide the research base for it.

■ ■ ■

Veronica Murayama wrote this essay as a college freshman. In it she defines a psychiatric concept, the debilitating mental illness called schizophrenia. Since this illness has been exhaustively studied and so much has been written about it, Murayama had to find a manageable focus for her essay. As you read, consider how she made this choice. Notice, too, how she seeks to engage your interest in the concept.

SCHIZOPHRENIA: WHAT IT LOOKS LIKE, HOW IT FEELS
VERONICA MURAYAMA

*Some mental illnesses, like depression, are more common than schizophrenia, but few are more severe. A schizophrenic has delusions and hallucinations, behaves in bizarre ways, talks incoherently, expresses little feeling or else feelings inappropriate to the situation, and is incapable of normal social interactions. Because these symptoms are so severe, about half the hospitalized mentally ill in America are schizophrenics. Only 1 percent of Americans (between 2 and 3 million) are schizophrenic, and yet they occupy about one-fourth of the available beds in our hospitals ("Schizophrenic," 1987, p. 1533). Up to 40 percent of the homeless may be schizophrenic (King, 1989, p. 97).   1

Schizophrenia has been recognized for centuries, and as early as the seventeenth century its main symptoms, course of development, and outcome were described. The term "schizophrenia," first used in 1908, refers to the disconnection or splitting of the mind that seems basic to all the various forms of the disease. It strikes both men and women, usually during adolescence or early adulthood, and is found all over the world. Treatment may include chemotherapy, electroconvulsive therapy, psychotherapy, and counseling. Hospitalization is ordinarily required, but usually not for more than a few months. It seems that about a third of patients recover completely and the rest can eventually have "a reasonable life adjustment," but some effect of the illness nearly always remains, most commonly lack of feeling and re-   2 duced drive or ambition ("Schizophrenic," 1987, pp. 1533, 1537–1539). Schizophrenia hits adolescents especially hard, and the effect on their families can be disastrous.

Though much is known about schizophrenia and treatment is reasonably effective, specialists still argue about its causes. For example, various researchers blame an unsatisfactory family life in which one or both parents suffer from some form of mental illness (Lidz, 1973), some combination of genetic inheritance and family life ("Schizophrenic," 1987, p. 1534; "Schizophrenia," 1987, p. 192), or "an early developmental neuropathological process" that results in reduced size of certain brain areas (Suddath, Cristison, Torrey, Casanova, & Weinberger, 1990, p. 793). What is known and agreed on, however, is what schizophrenia looks like to an observer and what it feels like to a sufferer, and these are what I want to focus on in this essay. I have always believed that when people have knowledge about any type of human suffering, they are more likely to be sympathetic with the sufferer. Schizophrenic symptoms are not attractive, but they are easy to understand. The medical manuals classify them approximately as follows: bizarre delusions, prominent hallucinations, confusion about identity, unconnected speech, inappropriate affect, disturbances in psychomotor behavior, impaired interpersonal functioning, and reduced drive.

Schizophrenics themselves experience the disease to a large extent as delusional thinking. For example, one woman said, "If I see a phone, I can talk on it without picking it up, immediately, anywhere in the world. But I don't abuse it. I'm authorized by AT&T. In the Yukon. And RCA" (Shane, 1987). It is common for schizophrenics to have delusions that they are being persecuted—that people are spying on them, spreading false stories about them, or planning to harm them. Events, objects, or people may be given special threatening significance, as when a patient believes a television commentator is making fun of him. Other delusions are very likely: "the belief or experience that one's thoughts, as they occur, are broadcast from one's head to the external world so that others can hear them; that thoughts that are not one's own are inserted into one's mind; that thoughts have been removed from one's head; or that one's feelings, impulses, thoughts, or actions are not one's own, but are imposed by some external force" ("Schizophrenia," 1987, p. 188). Sometimes delusions are grandiose, as when a patient thinks that he is the Messiah and will save the world or that she is the center of a conspiracy. A woman patient wrote, "I want a revolution, a great uprising to spread over the entire world and overthrow the whole social order. . . . Not for the love of adventure! No, no! Call it unsatisfied urge to action, if you like, indomitable ambition" (cited in Lidz, 1973, p. 134).

Related to delusions are hallucinations, which are very common in schizophrenics. Usually they hear voices coming from inside or outside the head, making insulting remarks, commenting on behavior, or giving commands that can sometimes be dangerous to others. Sometimes they hear sounds like humming, whistling, or machinery.

These false ideas and imaginary sensations leave schizophrenics confused about their identities. Feeling ruled by forces outside themselves, they lack normal feelings of individuality and uniqueness. One patient wrote, "I look at my arms and they aren't mine. They move without my direction. Somebody else moves them. . . . I have no control. I don't live in me. The outside and I are all the same" (cited in Mendel, 1974, p. 111).

Besides revealing their delusions and hallucinations, schizophrenics' speech is of-   7
ten rambling and unconnected. It may shift rapidly from one topic to another that
is seemingly completely unrelated or only loosely related, and the speaker does not
show any awareness of the lack of connection. One patient, a man, said, "I have
always believed in the good of mankind but I know I am not a woman because I
have an Adam's apple" ("Schizophrenic," 1987). Sometimes the topics are so unrelated that the patient's speech becomes incoherent and incomprehensible. Even
when it is connected, schizophrenic speech can sometimes contain very little information because it is vague, abstract, or repetitive.

Schizophrenics also present themselves in recognizable ways, referred to as "in-   8
appropriate affect." Their voices are often monotonous and their faces expression-
less. They may express little if any emotion, and their emotional responses do not
seem varied. On the other hand, their responses may seem completely inappropriate
to the situation, or there may be unpredictable outbursts of anger.

Another visible feature of schizophrenia is disturbed psychomotor behavior. The   9
most severely ill may move around very little or sit rigidly and resist being moved.
Here is what one patient felt: "When I was acting so stiff and wasn't talking I had
the feeling that if I moved the whole world might collapse. . . . I don't know why,
but I seemed like I was the center of everything and everything depended on my not
moving" (cited in Mendel, 1974, p. 108). Patients may take up strange postures or
engage in rocking or pacing. At the other extreme, they may move excitedly and
apparently purposelessly. Unfortunately, violent behavior is possible as well. One
manual points out that "grotesque violence, with self-mutilation (often of sexual organs) or murderous attacks, may occur. Matricide [killing one's mother], the rarest
form of murder, is most often perpetrated by schizophrenics, as is filicide [killing
one's brother or sister]. . . . The risk of suicide is increased in all stages of schizophrenic illness" ("Schizophrenic," 1987, p. 1535). One woman patient wrote,
"Death is the greatest happiness in life, if not the only one. Without hope of the
end, life would be unendurable" (cited in Mendel, 1974, p. 137).

Even if violence does not occur, it is not surprising that the speech and behavioral   10
symptoms I have described are almost invariably accompanied by—and contribute
to—impaired interpersonal functioning. Once schizophrenics become obsessed with
delusions, hallucinations, and illogical ideas, they are often too distracted and centered on themselves to interact with other people. Such patients are notable for their
emotional detachment even from family members or friends they were previously
close to. They also withdraw from all other social interactions, dropping out of school
or leaving jobs. They simply cannot face the outside world. Some schizophrenics behave quite differently, however, at least during some phases of the illness. They
"cling to other people, intrude upon strangers, and fail to recognize that excessive
closeness makes people uncomfortable and likely to pull away" ("Schizophrenia,"
1987, p. 189).

Along with social impairment comes loss of drive or ambition. Schizophrenics   11
typically have difficulty in initiating actions, making decisions, or following through
with plans, and their work and other responsibilities often suffer severely as a result.

It is important to know that doctors, counselors, and psychoanalysts do not easily   12
label someone schizophrenic. They do not do so unless many of the symptoms I have
described are present and unmistakable. Since depression has some of the same
symptoms as schizophrenia and the treatment of the two is quite different, doctors

have to be especially careful not to confuse them. We have come a long way from the time when schizophrenics were considered dangerous lunatics and were locked away without treatment, sometimes for life. Doctors now recognize the illness and can counsel both patients and families and prescribe drugs that have proven effective. The problem today is that so many of the homeless are believed to be schizophrenic, and it seems unlikely that many of them ever receive treatment.

References

King, K. (1989, November). Lost brother. *Life*, pp. 94–98.

Lidz, Theodore. (1973). *The origin and treatment of schizophrenic disorders*. New York: Basic.

Mendel, W. M. (1974). A phenomenological theory of schizophrenia. In A. Burton, J. Lopez-Ibor, & W. M. Mendel, *Schizophrenia as a life style* (pp. 106–155). New York: Springer.

Schizophrenia. (1987). *Diagnostic and statistical manual of mental disorders* (3rd. ed.) (pp. 187–198). Washington, DC: American Psychiatric Association.

Schizophrenic disorders. (1987). *The Merck manual of diagnosis and therapy* (15th ed). (pp. 1532–1539). Rahway, NJ: Merck and Company.

Shane, S. (1987, July 28). Relatives bear demoralizing task of patient care. [Baltimore] *Sun*, p. 14.

Suddath, R. L., Cristison, G. W., Torrey, E. F., Casanova, M. F., & Weinberger, D. R. (1990). Anatomical abnormalities in the brains of monozygotic twins discordant for schizophrenia. *The New England Journal of Medicine*, 322, 791–793.

For Discussion

Murayama's essay demonstrates that schizophrenia is a diagnosable medical problem. It is only one of many mental illnesses, perhaps the most widespread being depression, which afflicts 15 percent of Americans. People with mental illness need help because their suffering is acute and the costs to their families and to society are great, yet mental health funds are often the first to be cut in times of budget constraints. How would you explain the neglect of mental health resources? What community resources for the mentally ill are you aware of?

For Analysis

1. How, in paragraph 1, does Murayama seek to engage readers' interest in her topic? Compare her strategy with Toufexis's and Castro's. In what ways do their beginnings seem appropriate or inappropriate for their subject?

2. How does Murayama frame her essay? (Framing means referring at the end to something mentioned at the beginning.) Compare her frame with Toufexis's. What advantages do you see in framing an explanatory essay?

3. Examine the list of references at the end of the essay. What generalizations can you make about the sources? How does Murayama cite her sources within the essay? Where does she quote directly, and to what effect?

4. Do you find this essay's organization logical and easy to follow? Support your answer with specific examples from the essay.

Turn to pp. 202–04 to see how Murayama surveyed sources and found a focus of her essay.

5.   In the Writer at Work at the end of this chapter you will find all of the sources for paragraph 9. With the help of the Commentary below, analyze the relation between Murayama's paragraph and the sources. What conclusions can you reach about her use of sources? Notice where she quotes, paraphrases, or summarizes. How might you have used the sources differently?

**For Your
Own Writing**

You might want to consider writing an essay that would let you learn about another type of mental illness, such as hypochondriasis, mood disorders, bipolarism, phobic behaviors, or autism. The two manuals Murayama cites catalog many such illnesses. Like her, you would also want to look for current research and popular articles on your topic.

Commentary

Not only does Murayama try in her introduction to engage readers' interest in her topic, but she also provides an extended context for her focus on the symptoms of schizophrenia. Assuming her readers know little about her topic, she provides a broad orientation, giving information about its history, causes, and treatment. She does not extend this context too far, however; at the end of paragraph 3 she announces her focus.

   This announcement also forecasts the plan of the essay. A forecast identifies the main topics or ideas in an essay, usually in the sequence in which they will be discussed. The list of schizophrenic symptoms Murayama gives lays out her topics and their sequence and also identifies the key terms she will rely on throughout the essay. Readers seeking information benefit from such an obvious cue because it enables them to predict what is coming.

   It is also worth noting some of the ways Murayama incorporates quoted material into her own sentences. In some cases, she uses a dialogue cue, like *he said*, or *she wrote*:

> One patient, *a man, said,* "I have always believed in the good of mankind. . . ." (paragraph 4)

> One *woman patient wrote,* "Death is the greatest happiness in life. . . ." (paragraph 8)

In other cases, she uses a colon:

> Here is what one patient felt: "When I was acting so stiff and wasn't talking. . . ." (paragraph 8)

She uses a noun clause with *that*:

For more on quoting sources, see pp. 595–97.

> One manual points out *that* "grotesque violence . . . may occur." (paragraph 8)

PURPOSE AND AUDIENCE

Though it often seeks to engage readers' interests, explanatory writing gives prominence to the facts about its subject. It aims at readers' intellects rather than their imaginations, determined to instruct rather than entertain or argue.

To set out to teach readers about a concept is no small undertaking. To succeed, you must know the concept so well that you can explain it simply, without jargon or other confusing language. You must be authoritative without showing off or talking down. You also know your readers or imagine them as clearly as possible. Primarily, you must estimate what they already know about the concept in order to decide which facts will be truly new to them. You will want to define unfamiliar words and pace the information carefully so that your readers are neither bored nor overwhelmed.

This assignment requires a confident purposefulness, a willingness to cast yourself in the role of expert, that may not come naturally to you in this stage of your development as a writer. Students are most often asked to explain things in writing to readers who know more than they do—their instructors. When you plan and draft this essay, however, you will be aiming at readers who know less—maybe much less—than you do about the concept you are explaining. Like Toufexis and Castro, you could write for a general audience of adults who regularly read a newspaper and subscribe to a few magazines. Even though some of them may be more widely educated than you, you can readily and confidently assume the role of expert after a couple of hours of library research, your purpose being to deepen these readers' understanding of a concept they may already be familiar with. You could also write for upper-elementary or secondary-school students, introducing them to a completely unfamiliar concept, or to your classmates, demonstrating to them that a concept in an academic discipline they find forbidding can actually be made not only understandable but also interesting. Even if your instructor asks you to consider your reader to be him or her alone, you can assume your instructor is willing to be informed about nearly any concept you choose, except for concepts central to his or her academic specialty.

You've spent many years in school reading explanations of concepts: your textbooks in every subject have been full of concept explanations. Now, instead of receiving these explanations, you'll be delivering one. To succeed, you'll have to accept your role of expert and the more passive position of your readers. Your readers expect you to be confident, authoritative, and very well informed; they expect that your information is accurate and that you haven't excluded anything essential to their understanding. Your role and your readers' inability to challenge your information put you in a particularly powerful position as a writer.

BASIC FEATURES OF EXPLANATORY ESSAYS

Essays explaining concepts display certain basic features: a well-focused subject, a point or thesis, an appeal to readers' interests, a logical plan, clear definitions, writing strategies appropriate to the essay's point and to the kind of information it presents, and careful use of sources.

A Well-focused Subject	The primary purpose for explaining a concept is to inform readers, but writers of explanatory essays cannot possibly hope to say everything there is to say about a concept, nor would they want to. Instead, they must make choices about what to include, what to emphasize, and what to omit. Most writers focus on one aspect of the concept. Veronica Murayama, for example, focuses on the symptoms of schizophrenia.
A Main Point or Thesis	In explaining a concept, all writers make some point about the concept. The point, or thesis, asserts something significant or interesting about the concept. For example, Murayama makes the point in her essay that the more readers know about mental illness, the more likely they are to be understanding of those who suffer from it.
An Appeal to Readers' Interests	In explaining concepts, good writers usually try to appeal directly to their readers' interests. They may put this appeal right at the beginning, as Toufexis does by being blunt ("Let's cut out all this nonsense about romantic love.") and challenging ("Let's put love under a microscope.") or as Castro does by setting up an ironic contrast between Manpower and General Motors. Bellah and his colleagues refer to fictional cowboys and detectives that readers can be expected to recognize.
A Logical Plan	Explanations must follow a clear path to keep readers on track. For organizing explanations and cueing readers, experienced writers rely on many strategies. They divide the information in such a way that it supports the main point and then alert readers to these divisions with forecasting statements, topic sentences, transitions, and summaries. In addition, they may try to frame the essay for readers by relating the ending to the beginning. We have seen these features repeatedly in the readings in this chapter. For example, Toufexis frames her essay with references to Ph.D.s, she forecasts the three sciences from which she has gleaned her information about the neurochemistry of love, and nearly all of her paragraphs begin with a transition sentence.
	Good writers never forget that readers need clear signals. Because the writer already knows the information and is aware of how it is organized, it can be difficult to see it the way someone reading the essay for the first time would. That is precisely how it must be seen, however, to be sure that the essay includes all the signals the reader will need.
For more on cueing readers, see Chapter 13.	
Clear Definitions	Essays explaining concepts depend on clear definitions. In order to relate information clearly, a writer must be sensitive to the readers' knowledge; any terms that are likely to be unfamiliar or misunderstood must be explicitly defined, as Toufexis defines "attraction junkies" (paragraph 12) and "endorphins" (paragraph 13). In a sense, all the readings in this chapter are extended definitions of concepts, and all the authors offer relatively concise, clear definitions of their concepts at some point in their essays. Castro ten-

See Chapter 16 for
further discussion of
definitions.

tatively defines "contingent worker" early in her essay. Bellah stresses the paradox in the definition of American individualism: "One accepts the necessity of remaining alone in order to serve the values of the group."

Appropriate Writing Strategies

Many writing strategies are useful for presenting information. The strategies a writer uses are determined by the point he or she wishes to make and the kind of information available to work with. Following are some of the writing strategies that are particularly useful in explaining concepts.

For more about
classification and division,
see Chapter 17.

Classification and Division.   One way of presenting information is to sort it into groups and discuss them one by one. Murayama, for example, uses the classification of schizophrenic symptoms found in medical manuals as a way of organizing her description of the disease. She lists the symptoms at the end of paragraph 3 and then discusses each one in turn. Bellah and his colleagues take the concept of the hero and use division two different ways. First, they discuss two types of heroes: the cowboy and the detective. Then they divide heroes another way: fictional heroes and historically real heroes.

For further illustration of
these narrative strategies,
see Chapter 14.

Process Narration.   Many concepts involve processes that unfold over time, like the geologic scale, or over both time and space, like bird migration, which could be illustrated by telling a story of a typical bird's migration between Canada and Mexico. Process narration involves some of the basic storytelling strategies required in autobiography or fiction: narrative time signals, summarizing action, and transitions showing temporal relationship. For example, Toufexis briefly narrates the development of romantic attraction (paragraphs 3–4).

For more about
comparison and contrast,
see Chapter 18.

Comparison and Contrast.   This strategy is especially useful for explaining concepts because it helps readers to understand something new by showing how it is similar to or different from things they already know. Castro contrasts Manpower and General Motors and core and contingent workers. Murayama contrasts schizophrenics who withdraw from others with those who cling and intrude. The Bellah selection relies on several comparisons and contrasts: in the opening paragraph the authors contrast fictional protagonists (Deerslayer, Huck and Jim, Ahab) prominent in American literature; in paragraphs 2 and 3, they compare two types of "mythic individual hero," the cowboy and the detective; and in the final paragraph they contrast the mythic hero with a real hero, Abraham Lincoln.

Cause and Effect.   Still another useful strategy for explaining a concept may be to report its causes or effects. Toufexis explains the evolutionary benefits of romantic love and Castro describes throughout her essay the effects of contingent employment on workers and the workplace. Bellah and colleagues report other scholars' speculations about the nihilistic results of the lonely mythic hero's quest. (The authors' notes indicate they are reporting speculations other than their own.)

Notice that authors of explanatory writing either report established causes or effects of the subject or report others' speculated causes or effects. They usually do not speculate about possible causes or effects themselves.

Careful Use of Sources

Explaining concepts nearly always draws on information from many different sources. Writers often draw on their own experience and observation, but they almost always do additional research into what others have said about their subject. Referring to sources, particularly to expert ones, always lends authority to an explanation.

How writers treat sources depends on the writing situation. Certain situations, such as college assignments or scholarly papers, have prescribed rules for citing and documenting sources. Students and scholars are expected to cite their sources formally because their readers judge their writing in part by what they've read and how they've used their reading. In Chapter 22, two different ways of citing sources are presented: the Modern Language Association (MLA) style, used chiefly in the humanities, and the American Psychological Association (APA) style, used by many social and natural scientists. Both of these styles call for parenthetical citations within the essay that are keyed to a list of works cited at the end. Ask your instructor which style you should follow.

On more informal writing occasions—newspaper and magazine articles, for example—readers do not expect writers to include page references or publication information, but they do expect them to identify their sources in some way; this is often done casually within the text of the article.

For more on reading sources with a critical eye, see pp. 589–92.

See pp. 595–600 for helpful advice on paraphrasing, summarizing, and quoting.

Sources should be used with the greatest care. Since you nearly always find more sources on a concept than you can use, you must evaluate them carefully, choosing those that are the most reputable and current and that provide the best support for the point you want to make about the concept. For example, Murayama examined twelve sources before deciding to focus on the symptoms of schizophrenia. Consequently, she set aside those sources concerned with the history, causes, or treatment of schizophrenia.

Experienced writers make judicious decisions about when to paraphrase, summarize, or quote their sources. They take special care to integrate quotations smoothly into their own texts, deliberately varying the way they do it.

Guide to Writing

THE WRITING ASSIGNMENT

Write an essay that explains a concept. Choose a concept that interests you and that you want to study further. Consider carefully what your readers already know about it and how your essay might add to what they know.

INVENTION AND RESEARCH

The following guidelines will help you to find a concept, understand it fully, select a focus appropriate for your readers, research the focus in depth, and devise strategies for presenting what you've discovered in a way that will be truly informative for your particular readers.

Finding a Concept

Even if you already have a concept in mind, completing the following notes will help you to be certain of your choice.

Listing Concepts.   List as many concepts as you can. The longer your list, the more likely you are to find just the right concept to write about. And should your first choice not work out, you will have a ready list of alternatives. Include concepts you already know something about as well as some you know only slightly and would like to research further.

Consider first the concepts in the suggestions For Your Own Writing on pp. 169, 175, 180, and 185.

You might set a timer and brainstorm your lists on a computer with the monitor brightness turned all the way down. Enter as many possibilities as you can in ten minutes. Then, turn the brightness up, be sure all the concepts make sense, and print out a copy to make notes on.

Your courses provide many concepts you will want to consider. Following are typical concepts from several academic and other subjects. Your class notes or textbooks will suggest many others.

- *Literature:* hero, antihero, picaresque, the absurd, pastoral, realism
- *Philosophy:* existentialism, nihilism, logical positivism, determinism
- *Business management:* autonomous work group, quality circle, cybernetic control system, management by objectives, zero-based budgeting
- *Psychology:* Hawthorne effect, assimilation/accommodation, social cognition, moratorium, intelligence, divergent/convergent thinking, operant conditioning, short-term memory, tip-of-the-tongue phenomenon
- *Government:* majority rule, minority rights, federalism, popular consent, exclusionary rule, political party, political machine, interest group, political action committee
- *Biology:* photosynthesis, morphogenesis, ecosystem, electron transport, plasmolysis, phagocytosis, homozygosity, diffusion
- *Art:* cubism, Dadaism, surrealism, expressionism
- *Math:* Mobius transformation, boundedness, null space, eigenvalue, factoring, Rolle's theorem, continuity, derivative, indefinite integral
- *Physical sciences:* matter, mass, weight, energy, atomic theory, law of definite proportions, osmotic pressure, first law of thermodynamics, entropy
- *Public health:* alcoholism, winter depression, contraception, lead poisoning, prenatal care
- *Environmental studies:* acid rain, recycling, ozone depletion
- *Sports:* squeeze play, hit and run (baseball); power play (hockey); nickel defense, wishbone offense (football); serve and volley offense (tennis); setup (volleyball); pick and roll, inside game (basketball)

Choosing a Concept.   Now look over your list and select one concept to explore. Pick a concept that interests you, one you feel eager to learn more about. Consider also whether it might interest others. You may know very little about the concept now, but the guidelines that follow will help you research it and to understand it fully.

Exploring the Concept

Discovering What You Already Know.   Start with what you know. Take a few minutes to write out whatever you know about the concept you have chosen and why you find it interesting and worth knowing about. Write quickly, without planning or organizing. Feel free to write in phrases or lists as well as in sentences. You might also want to make drawings or charts. Ask questions.

Gathering Information.   Check any materials you already have at hand that explain your concept. If you are considering a concept from one of your academic courses, you will find an explanation in your textbook or lecture notes. You may also find useful material in your lecture notes.

To acquire a comprehensive, up-to-date understanding of your concept and to write authoritatively about it, you will also need to know how experts besides your textbook writer and instructor define and illustrate the concept, and to learn about current research or perspectives. For this information you can go to the library. Consider this first visit to the library an opportunity to orient yourself to what is available on your concept. You can look for ways to focus your research during a follow-up library visit.

Chapter 21 provides a search strategy and specific sources for pursuing your concept.

Consulting an Expert.   Is there someone very knowledgeable about your concept who might be helpful? If you are writing about a concept related to a subject you are studying, one of your instructors might be someone to consult. Not only could an expert answer questions, but he or she might also direct you to important or influential articles or books.

Focusing on One Aspect of the Concept

Once you have done some research on your concept, you need to choose a focus for your essay. Since more is known about most concepts than you can include in an essay and since concepts can be approached from so many perspectives—history, definition, significance, recent research—you must have a focus in order to produce a worthwhile piece of writing. Murayama, for example, focuses her essay about schizophrenia on its symptoms. By limiting your essay, you can avoid a common mistake: trying to explain superficially and hurriedly everything that is known about a concept.

Analyzing Your Readers.   To help you decide on a focus, identify and analyze your readers, because the focus must reflect both your special interest in the concept and what you think is likely to be your readers' knowledge of and interest in it. Even if you are writing only for your instructor, you must be aware of his or her knowledge of your concept.

Take around ten minutes to describe your readers in writing. Think carefully about the following questions as you write:

- Who are my readers? How diverse a group are they?
- In what kind of publication might my essay appear?
- How much are my readers likely to know about this concept?
- Why might they want to learn about this concept?
- What aspects might be especially informative and interesting to them?
- How can I engage and hold their interest?

Choosing a Focus. With your interests and your readers' interests in mind, choose a focus and write a few sentences justifying its appropriateness.

Researching Your Subject

Return to the library to select relevant material from what you surveyed on your first visit. In addition, seek out new material. Keep a careful record of all promising sources, including essential information for citing these sources. Check with your instructor about whether you should follow the Modern Language Association (MLA) or the American Psychological Association (APA) style of ackowledging sources. In this chapter, the Murayama essay follows APA style.

For MLA and APA guidelines, see pp. 602–12.

Consider photocopying the promising sources most relevant to your focus. Doing so may save you return trips to the library if your essay takes an unpredictable turn or if you need more on a particular point.

Testing Your Choice

Pause now to test whether you have chosen a workable concept and focused it appropriately. As painful as it may be to consider, starting fresh with a new concept would be better than continuing with an unworkable one. The following questions can help you test your choice:

- Do I still have a strong personal interest in my concept?
- Have I discovered a focus for writing about this concept?
- Have I located enough information for an essay with such a focus?
- Will readers have interest in this aspect of my subject? Do I see possibilities for engaging and holding their interest in it?

If you cannot answer all of these questions affirmatively, you should consider refocusing your subject or selecting another concept to write about.

For Group Inquiry

At this point it might be a good idea to get some response to your subject. Get together in a group with two or three other students. One by one, announce your concepts and intended readers, and then explain what in particular you plan to focus on and what your main point will be. Ask the group whether your plan sounds interesting for your intended readers. Get them to help you consider what these readers are likely to know about your concept, what new information about it might be especially interesting and informative for them, and how you might begin your essay to engage their interest.

Establishing a Main Point

Besides a focus, which limits your topic, your essay needs a main point or thesis. The point in an essay explaining a concept can be stated or implied. You'll recall that Castro's implied point seems to be that increasing use of contingent workers will create a fundamental change in Americans' standard of living and that Murayama's stated point is that knowledge about mental illness makes people more sympathetic with sufferers.

Probing the Significance of Your Concept.   Begin by reviewing your invention notes and research materials. With your own interest and your readers' expectations in mind, write for several minutes, answering these questions:

- What makes this aspect of this concept interesting to me?
- What is most important about it?
- What is most surprising or unusual in the information?
- Why should my readers bother to read about it?
- What significance might it have for their lives?

Stating a Point.   When you have finished writing, read over what you have written, and write one or two sentences that sum up the point you want to get across to your readers.

Considering Explanatory Strategies

If possible, work on a word processor so you can save your writing to establish a main point and to consider explanatory strategies. Then, as you begin to draft later, you can call up the file on a second screen and easily transfer details you want to use in your draft.

Before you move on to plan and draft your essay, consider some possible ways of presenting the information you have. Following are some questions that can help you to determine which writing strategies might prove useful. Answer each one with a sentence or two.

- What terms are used to name the concept, and what do they mean? (definition, Chapter 16)
- How is it like or unlike related concepts? (comparison and contrast, Chapter 18)
- How can an explanation of this concept be divided into parts? (classification and division, Chapter 17)
- How does this concept happen or how do you do it? (process narration, Chapter 14)
- What are its known causes or effects? (cause and effect, Chapter 9)

PLANNING AND DRAFTING

Here are some guidelines to help you to get the most out of your invention notes, to determine specific goals for your essay, and to write a first draft.

Seeing What You Have

It's a good idea at this point to print out a hard copy of what you have written on a word processor for easier reviewing.

Reread everything you have written so far. This is a critically important time for reflection and evaluation. Before beginning the actual draft, you must decide whether your subject is worthwhile and whether you have sufficient information for a successful essay.

It may help as you read to annotate your invention writings. Look for details that will support your point and appeal to your readers. Underline or circle key words, phrases, or sentences; make marginal notes. Your goal here is to identify the important elements in what you have written so far.

Be realistic. If at this point your notes do not look promising, you may want to refocus your concept or select a different concept to write about. If your notes seem thin but promising, you should probably do further research to find more information before continuing.

Setting Goals

Successful writers are always looking beyond the next sentence to larger goals. Indeed, the next sentence is easier to write if you keep larger goals in mind. The following questions can help you set these goals. Consider each one now and then return to them as necessary while you write.

Your Readers

- How much are my readers likely to know about this concept? How can I build on their knowledge?
- What new information can I present to them?
- How much information will be enough and how much will be too much?
- How can I organize my essay so that my readers can follow it easily?
- What tone would be most appropriate? Would an informal tone like Toufexis's or a formal one like Bellah's be more appropriate?

The Beginning

- How shall I begin? Should I open with a provocative statement, as Toufexis does? Should I begin with a general statement about the concept, as Bellah and Murayama do? With a surprising or ironical fact as Castro does? With a question? What kind of opening would be most likely to capture my readers' attention?
- Should I assert my point immediately, or should I first set the context?
- How can I best forecast the plan my explanation will follow? Should I offer a detailed forecast? Or is a brief description sufficient?

The Ending

- How shall I end? Should I restate my point?
- Should I relate the ending to the beginning, as Toufexis does, so as to frame the essay?

Writing Strategies

- To what extent do I need to define my terms? Can I rely on brief sentence definitions or will I need to write extended definitions?
- Should I include any tables, charts, or graphs?
- Do I need to include any particular examples?
- Can comparisons or contrasts help readers understand the information?
- Should I include any anecdotes?
- Do I need to explain any processes or describe any historical events?

Outlining

See pp. 432–35 for more on outlining.

Outlining on a word processor makes it particularly easy to experiment with different ways of ordering information and using transitions.

Give some thought now to organization. Many writers find it helpful to outline their material before actually beginning to write. Whatever outlining you do before you begin drafting, consider it only tentative. Never be a slave to an outline. As you draft, you will usually see some ways to improve on your original plan. Be ready to revise your outline, to shift parts around, to drop or add parts. Consider the following questions as you plan:

- How should I divide the information?
- What order will best serve my purpose and point?
- What kinds of transitions will I need between the main parts of my essay?

Drafting

If you can shift between screens, you might call up invention material on an alternate screen as you draft on the main screen, shifting back and forth to cut and paste invention material into your draft.

Begin drafting your essay, keeping your main point in mind. Remember also the needs and expectations of your readers; organize and define and explain with them in mind. Work to increase their understanding of your concept. You may want to review the drafting advice on pp. 12–14.

GETTING CRITICAL COMMENTS

Now is the time to try to get a good critical reading. All writers find it helpful to have someone else read and comment on their drafts, and your instructor may schedule such a reading as part of your coursework. If not, you can ask a classmate, friend, or family member to read it over. If your campus has a writing center, you might ask a tutor there to read and comment on your draft. The guidelines that follow are designed to be used by *anyone* reviewing an explanatory essay. (If you are unable to have someone else read over your draft, turn ahead to the Revision section on pp. 197–201, which gives guidelines for reading your own draft with a critical eye.)

In order to provide focused, helpful comments, your reader must know your intended audience and purpose. Briefly write out this information at the top of your draft:

Audience. Who are your readers?

Purpose. What do you want to tell your readers about the concept?

Reading with a
Critical Eye

Reading a draft critically means reading it more than once, first to get a general impression and then to analyze its basic features.

See Chapter 12 for a review of useful critical reading strategies.

Reading for a First Impression.   Read first to get a sense of the concept and its significance. As you read, try to notice any words or passages that contribute to your first impression, weak ones as well as strong ones. After you've finished reading the draft, briefly give your impressions. Is the concept well focused and clearly explained? Did you find the essay informative and easy to read? What in the draft do you think would especially interest the intended readers?

See pp. 186–89 to review the basic features.

Reading to Analyze.   Now reread to focus on the basic features of writing an explanatory essay.

Is the Concept Appropriately Focused?

What aspect of the concept does the essay focus on? Given the concept, does the focus seem too broad or too narrow? Can you think of another focus that would make the essay more successful?

Is the Point Well Made?

Identify the point the essay makes about the concept. Is it stated directly or implied? If the essay doesn't seem to make a point (stated or implied), can you think of one that would declare the significance of the information?

Is the Content Appropriate for Its Intended Readers?

Does it tell them all they are likely to want to know about this concept? Can you suggest additional information that should be included? What questions about the concept that readers are likely to have are not answered? Is there information that seems superfluous? Will the information seem predictable or bland?

Is the Organization Effective?

Look at the way the essay is organized, outlining it briefly. Is the information logically divided? If not, suggest a better way to divide it. Also consider the order—can you suggest a better way of sequencing the information?

Look at the *beginning*. Will it pull intended readers into the essay and make them want to continue? Does it adequately forecast the direction of the essay? If possible, suggest a better way to begin.

Find the obvious *transitions* in the draft. Are they helpful? If not, try to improve one or two of them. Look for additional places where transitions would be helpful.

Look at the *ending*. Is it effective? Does it frame the essay by referring back to something at the beginning? Should it? If you can, suggest a better way to end. Imagine someone with limited time reading this essay. This reader wants—and needs—to proceed at an even, quick pace, with as little effort as possible. Where might this draft slow a reader down?

Are Definitions Clear?

Examine the definitions. Are any likely to be unclear to readers? Point out any terms that may need to be defined for the intended readers.

Are Writing Strategies Appropriately Used?

Besides definition, what writing strategies are used and how effective are they? Examine each recognizable use of process narration, comparison and contrast, cause and effect, or classification and division, and identify any that seem unclear, incomplete, or otherwise ineffective. Can you think of ways to improve these? Are there other places where a strategy would enable readers to comprehend the concept more fully?

Are Sources Carefully Used?

If sources have been used, begin by reviewing the list of sources cited. Given the purpose, readers, and focus of the essay, does the list seem balanced and are the selections appropriate? Try to suggest concerns or questions readers knowledgeable about the concept might raise. Then consider the use of sources within the text of the essay. Should there be more (or fewer) source citations? Where? Are there places where summary or paraphrase would be preferable to quoted material or vice versa? Note any places where quoted material is awkwardly inserted into the text and recommend ways to smooth them out.

What Final Thought Do You Have?

Which part needs the most work? What do you think the intended readers will find most informative or memorable?

REVISING AND EDITING

This section will help you to identify problems in your draft and to revise and edit to solve them.

Identifying Problems

Even if your essay is saved to a computer file, reread from a hard copy, preferably draft quality. Onscreen or as letter-quality hard copy, a paper can look more "finished" than it really is. Add notes to yourself and quick revisions as you read through the draft.

To identify problems in your draft, you need to get an overview of it, analyze its basic features, and study any comments from other readers.

Getting an Overview.   First consider the draft as a whole, trying to see it objectively. It may help to do so in two steps:

Reread. If possible, put the draft aside for a day or two before rereading it. When you go back to it, start by reconsidering your audience and purpose. Then read the draft straight through, trying to see it as your intended readers will.

Outline. Make a scratch outline to get an overview of the essay's development. This outline can be sketchy—words and phrases instead of complete sentences—but it should identify the main ideas as they appear.

Charting a Plan for Revision.   You may want to make a chart like the following one to keep track of any problems you need to solve. The left-hand column lists the basic features of explanatory writing. As you analyze your draft and study any comments you've gotten from others, note the problems you want to solve in the right-hand column.

Basic Features   *Problems to Solve*

Concept Focus

Main Point

Appeal to Readers

Organization

Definitions

Writing Strategies

Sources

Analyzing the Basic Features of Your Draft.   Turn now to the questions for analyzing a draft on pp. 196–97. Using these as guidelines, identify problems in your draft. Note anything you need to solve on the preceding chart.

Studying Critical Comments.   Review any comments you've received from other readers, and add to the chart any points that need attention. Try not to react too defensively to these comments; by letting you see how others respond to your draft, they provide invaluable information about how you might improve it.

Solving the Problems

Before revising using a word processor, copy your original draft to a second file. Then, should you change your mind about material you delete while revising, it will still be available to you.

Having identified problems, you now need to figure out solutions and to carry them out. Basically, you have three ways of finding solutions: (1) review your invention and planning notes and sources for additional information and ideas; (2) do further invention or research to answer questions your readers raised; and (3) look back at the readings in this chapter to see how other writers have solved similar problems.

Following are suggestions to get you started solving some of the problems common to explanatory essays. For now, focus on solving those issues identified on your chart. Avoid tinkering with sentence-level problems; that will come later when you edit.

The Focus

■ If the focus is too broad, consider limiting it further so you can treat it in more depth. If readers were less than interested in the aspect you focused on, consider focusing on some other aspect of the concept.

■ If the focus is too narrow, you may have isolated too minor an aspect. Go back to your invention and look for other larger or more significant aspects.

The Point

- If the point is not obvious, make it clear somewhere in the essay.
- If the point lacks significance, reconsider the importance or implications of your material. Review your sources for suggestions of significance. Consider what readers would find surprising or important in your material.

Appeal to Readers

- If the content seems incomplete, review your invention writing and sources for further information to satisfy your readers' needs or answer their concerns and questions.
- If any of the content seems superfluous, eliminate it.
- If the content seems predictable or bland, search for novel or surprising information to add.

Organization

Use your word processor's cut and paste or block-and-move functions to shift material around. Make sure that transitions are revised so that material fits in its new spot.

- If the essay does not unfold logically and smoothly, reorganize it so that it is easy to follow. Try constructing an alternative outline. Add transitions or summaries to help keep readers on track.
- If the beginning is weak, try making your focus and point obvious immediately, forecasting the plan of your essay, or opening with an unusual piece of information that would catch readers' interest.
- If the ending is inconclusive, consider restating your point there or moving important information to the end. Try summarizing highlights of the essay or framing it by referring back to something in the beginning. Or you might reflect on the future of the concept or assert its usefulness.

Definitions

- If your concept is not clearly defined, add a concise definition early in your essay, or consider adding a brief midpoint or concluding summary that defines the concept. Remove any information that blurs readers' understanding of the concept.
- If other key terms are inadequately defined, supply clear definitions, searching your sources or checking a dictionary if necessary.

Writing Strategies

- If the content seems thin or the definition of the concept blurred, consider whether any other writing strategies would improve the presentation.
- Try comparing or contrasting the concept with a related one, preferably one more familiar to readers.
- Consider ways to divide or classify the information that would make it easier to understand or provide an interesting perspective on the topic.

- Try explaining its known causes or effects.
- See whether adding examples will enliven or clarify your explanation.
- Tell more about how the concept works.

Use of Sources

- If sources are inadequate, return to the library to find additional ones. Consider dropping weak or less reliable sources. Ensure that your sources cover your focus in a comprehensive, balanced way.
- If you rely too much either on quoting or on summarizing and paraphrasing, change some of your quotations to summaries or paraphrases, or vice versa.
- If quoted material is not smoothly integrated into your own text, revise to make it so.
- If there are discrepancies in your in-text citations or list of sources, check citation styles in Chapter 22. Be sure that all of the citations exactly follow the style you are using.

Editing and Proofreading

Thus far you have not worried much about grammar or style. Now, however, you need to take the time to check for errors in usage, punctuation, and mechanics—and also to consider matters of style. Research has identified several errors that are especially common in writing that explains concepts; following are some brief guidelines that can help you check and edit your draft for these errors.

When you use your word processor's spell check function to aid in proofreading for spelling, keep in mind that it will not find all misspellings, particularly misused homonyms (such as there, their, and they're), typos that are themselves words (such as fro for for), and many proper nouns and specialized terms. Proofread these carefully yourself, using hard copy and a dictionary if necessary. Also proofread for words that should have been deleted when you edited a sentence.

Checking the Punctuation of Adjective Clauses.   Adjective clauses include both a subject and a verb and give information about a noun or pronoun. They often begin with *who*, *which*, or *that*. Here is an example from Veronica Murayama:

It is common for schizophrenics to have delusions that they are being persecuted.

(adjective clause)

Because adjective clauses add information about the nouns they follow—defining, illustrating, or explaining—they can be useful in writing that explains a concept. The challenge in punctuating an adjective clause is knowing whether to include a comma. First you have to decide whether or not the clause is essential to the meaning of the sentence. Clauses that are essential to the meaning of a sentence should not be set off with a comma; clauses that are not essential to the meaning must be set off with a comma. Here are two examples from Murayama:

ESSENTIAL   It is common for schizophrenics to have delusions that they are being persecuted.

NONESSENTIAL   Related to delusions are hallucinations, which are very common in schizophrenics.

In the first sentence, the adjective clause defines and limits the word *delusions*. If the clause were removed, the meaning of the sentence would change and would be overly general, to say simply that schizophrenics commonly have delusions. In fact, the statement is that they have a certain kind of delusions, "delusions that they are being persecuted." The adjective clause is thus essential to the meaning of the sentence and is not set off with a comma.

In the second sentence, the adjective clause gives information that is not essential to the sentence. Taking away the adjective clause ("which are very common in schizophrenics") in no way changes the meaning of the sentence. As a nonessential element, the clause is set off from the sentence with a comma.

To decide whether an adjective clause is essential or nonessential, mentally delete the clause. If taking out the clause changes the meaning of the sentence or makes it unclear, the clause is probably essential and should not be set off with commas. If the meaning of the sentence does not change enormously, the clause is probably nonessential and should be set off with commas.

▶ Postpartum neurosis,which can last for two weeks or longer,can adversely affect a mother's ability to care for her infant.

▶ The early stage starts with memory loss,which usually results in forgetting recent life events.

▶ Seasonal affective disorders are mood disturbances/that occur with a change of season.

▶ The coaches,/who do the recruiting should be disciplined.

Adjective clauses following proper nouns always require commas.

▶ Nanotechnologists defer to K. Eric Drexler,who speculates imaginatively about the uses of nonmachines.

Checking for Commas around Interrupting Phrases.   Writing that explains a concept calls on a writer to supply a great deal of information. Much of this information will be added in phrases that interrupt the flow of a sentence. Words that interrupt are usually set off with commas. Be especially careful with interrupting phrases that fall in the middle of a sentence: such phrases must be set off with two commas, one at the beginning and one at the end:

▶ People on the West Coast, especially in Los Angeles,have always been receptive to new ideas.

▶ Alzheimer's disease,named after the German neuropathologist Alois Alzheimer, is a chronic degenerative illness.

▶ These examples,though simple, present equations in terms of tangible objects.

A Writer at Work

USING SOURCES

This section describes how Veronica Murayama searched for sources and integrated them into one part of her essay on schizophrenia, which appears on pp. 181–84.

Finding Sources

Following directions in the Invention and Research section of this chapter, Murayama went to the library to see what she could find readily on schizophrenia. She wanted a quick orientation to the concept so that she could decide on a focus for her essay and for further research. This initial search led her right away to two books and four current articles:

> *Schizophrenia as a Life Style*, 1974
> *The Origin and Treatment of Schizophrenic Disorders*, 1973
> "Drug Gains FDA Approval," *Science News*
> "Drugs among Young Schizophrenics," *Science News*
> "Seeking Source of Schizophrenia," *USA Today*
> "Relatives Bear Demoralizing Task of Patient Care," [Baltimore] *Sun*

She read the articles, skimmed the books, and then talked to a reference librarian. When Murayama explained the assignment—emphasizing her need for an overview—and showed the materials she had already collected, the librarian recommended that she check two basic references on mental illness, the first relied on by medical doctors, the second by psychotherapists and other mental health counselors:

> *The Merck Manual of Diagnosis and Therapy*
> *Diagnostic and Statistical Manual of Mental Disorders*

After reading closely the materials on schizophrenia in these two sources, she decided that given the information in all her sources she had enough material on these topics:

> the history of the description and treatment of schizophrenia
> its effects on families of schizophrenics
> the current debate about its causes
> the current preferred treatment of it
> current research on it
> its symptoms

She was drawn both to the debate about causes and to symptoms, but when she discussed these alternatives with a small group in her writing class, she recognized that the others, like herself before she began her research, knew so little about schizophrenia that they would be most engaged and informed by a description of the illness itself—what it looks like to a therapist diagnosing it and what it feels like to a patient experiencing it.

When she met with her instructor, he pointed out that she should seek out recent reports in a respected medical journal such as *The New England Journal of Medicine*. In that journal she found the research report demonstrating that certain areas of schizophrenics' brains appear to be smaller than the same areas in brains of those not suffering from the illness. This interesting research finding appears as one clause in paragraph 3 in her essay.

Now she returned to the library and reread the sources that provided information about the symptoms of schizophrenia. The basic information she needed was in the two reference manuals. Her quotes from patients came mainly from one of the books, *Schizophrenia as a Life Style*. She did not use or cite the *Science News* and *USA Today* articles.

Murayama's search for sources was far from comprehensive, but it was certainly adequate for a brief essay. She wisely stopped searching when she felt she had the information she needed. It turned out that she used only a small part of her information on symptoms.

Integrating Sources

Two paragraphs from Murayama's essay illustrate a sound strategy for integrating sources into your essay, relying on them fully—as you nearly always must do in explanatory writing—and yet making them your own. Here is paragraph 10 from Murayama's essay (the sentences are numbered for ease of reference):

(1) Even if violence does not occur, it is not surprising that the speech and behavioral symptoms I have described are almost always accompanied by—and contribute to—impaired interpersonal functioning. (2) Once schizophrenics become obsessed with delusions, hallucinations, and illogical ideas, they are often too distracted and centered on themselves to interact with other people. (3) Such patients are notable for their emotional detachment even from family members or friends they were previously close to. (4) They also withdraw from all other social interactions, dropping out of school or leaving jobs. (5) They simply cannot face the outside world. (6) Some schizophrenics behave quite differently, however, at least during some phases of the illness. (7) They "cling to other people, intrude upon strangers, and fail to recognize that excessive closeness makes other people uncomfortable and likely to pull away" ("Schizophrenia," 1987, p. 189). (8) Along with social impairment comes loss of drive or ambition. (9) Schizophrenics typically have difficulty in initiating actions, making decisions, or following through with plans, and their work and other responsibilities often suffer severely as a result.

All of the information in Murayama's paragraph comes from the following brief sections of the *Diagnostic and Statistical Manual of Mental Disorders*.

Volition. The characteristic disturbances in volition are most readily observed in the residual phase. There is nearly always some disturbance in self-initiated, goal-directed activity, which may grossly impair work or other role functioning. This may take the form of inadequate interest, drive, or ability to follow a course of action to its logical conclusion. Marked ambivalence regarding alternative courses of action can lead to near-cessation of goal-directed activity.

Impaired interpersonal functioning and relationship to the external world. Difficulty in interpersonal relationships is almost invariably present. Often this takes the form of social withdrawal and emotional detachment. When the person is severely preoccupied with egocentric and illogical ideas and fantasies and distorts or excludes the external world, the condition has been referred to as "autism." Some with the disorder, during a phase of the illness, cling to other people, intrude upon strangers, and fail to recognize that excessive closeness makes other people uncomfortable and likely to pull away.

Comparing the source and Murayama's paragraph 10, we can see that her first sentence introduces the name of the symptom, which she borrows in part from the symptom name in the source. Sentence 2 paraphrases the source. Sentences 3–5 are her own elaborations of the material in the source basically giving concrete examples of the more abstract discussion in the original source. Sentence 6 again paraphrases the source. Then, finally, she quotes the source. Following the quotation, in sentences 8 and 9 she summarizes the information in the source paragraph labeled *Volition.*

Thinking Critically about What You've Learned

At this point you have considerable experience with essays explaining concepts—reading them, talking about them, even writing one of your own. Now is a good time to reflect on the act of reading and writing concept essays and to think critically about how explanations of concepts influence the way we think about ourselves and our culture.

REFLECTING ON YOUR WRITING

Take time now to reflect on what you have learned about writing an essay explaining a concept. First, gather all of your writing—invention, planning notes, drafts, any critical comments from classmates and your instructor, revising notes and plans, and final revision. Review these materials closely before you complete the following writing task.

- Identify *one* writing problem you needed to solve as you worked to explain the concept in your essay. Don't be concerned with sentence-level problems; concentrate instead on problems unique to developing a concept explanation. For example: Did you puzzle over how to focus your explanation? Did you worry about how to appeal to your readers' interests, identify and define the terms your readers would need explained, or clearly forecast the main ideas without boring readers? Did you have trouble integrating sources smoothly?

- How did you recognize the writing problem? When did you first discover it? What called it to your attention? If you didn't become aware of the problem until someone else pointed it out to you, can you now see hints of it in your invention writings? If so, where specifically? How did you respond when you first recognized the problem?

- How did you go about solving the problem? Did you work on the wording of a particular passage, cut or add information, move paragraphs or sentences around, add transitions or forecasting statements, use any different writing strategies? Did you reread one of the essays in this chapter to see how another writer handled the problem or look back at the invention suggestions? If you talked about the writing problem with another student, a tutor, or your instructor, did talking about it help? How useful was the advice you got?

- Now, write a page or so telling your instructor about the problem and how you solved it. Be as specific as possible in reconstructing your efforts, quoting from your invention, your draft, others' critical comments, your revision plan, or your revised essay to show the various changes your writing underwent as you tried to solve the problem. Thinking in detail now about how you identified a particular problem, how you went about solving it, and how what you've learned from this experience can help you in solving future writing problems you encounter.

REVIEWING WHAT YOU LEARNED FROM READING

To some extent your own essay has been influenced by other concept explanations you have read in this chapter and by your classmates' essays. For example, your reading may have helped you choose a topic or realize you needed to do research. A reading may have suggested how to structure your essay or how to use a strategy like classification to put your concept into a larger context. Take time now to reflect on what you have learned about concept explanations from the readings in this chapter and acknowledge some influences they have had on your own writing.

- Reread the final revision of your essay; then look back at the selections you read before completing your essay. Name any specific influences. For example, if you were impressed by the way one of the readings described the origins or originators of the concept, organized the information, or connected to readers' knowledge through analogy or comparison, look in your revised essay to see where you were striving for similar effects with your own writing. Also, look for ideas you got from your reading, writing strategies you were inspired to try, specific details you were led to include, effects you sought to achieve.

■ Write a page or so explaining to your instructor how the readings in this chapter influenced your revised essay. Did one reading have an especially strong influence, or were several readings influential in different ways? Quote from the selections and from your final revision to show how your essay explaining a concept was influenced by your reading of other concept explanations in this chapter. Finally, briefly explain any further improvements you would make in your essay based on your review of the chapter's readings.

CONSIDERING THE SOCIAL DIMENSIONS OF CONCEPT EXPLANATIONS

"Knowledge is power," as the saying goes, and concepts are the building blocks of knowledge, essential to its creation and acquisition. We use concepts to name and organize ideas and information in areas as diverse as snowboarding and psychiatry. Academic disciplines and most of the professions are heavily concept-based, enabling newcomers to be introduced efficiently, if abstractly, to the basic knowledge they need to begin to work in a field.

Knowledge and Authority.   As you have learned from your reading, research, and writing for this chapter, writers explaining concepts present knowledge as established and uncontested. They presume to be unbiased, objective, and disinterested, and they assume readers will not doubt or challenge the truth or value of the knowledge they present. This stance encourages readers to feel confident about the validity of the explanation.

In spite of this confident assertiveness, however, explanatory writing should not always be accepted at face value. Textbooks and reference materials, in particular, often represent a limited view of what counts as knowledge in an academic discipline, leaving out certain sources of information and kinds of knowledge. Psychological and sociological concepts about human nature and social interaction, for example, may disregard the "common sense" of personal experience and devalue the creative imaginings of novelists and poets. Thus, textbooks should be read critically, questioningly, with the reader's full participation as an active thinker.

The Power of Authority.   At the same time, however, we recognize that concept explanations involve power relations: the writer establishes what is to count as knowledge about a subject and how that knowledge is to be used; the reader, at least in the beginning of studying a subject, is powerless to judge the accuracy and completeness of the information or to discern the writer's motives or ideology. The writer's decisions about what to include and exclude remain hidden, so that readers of an introductory psychology textbook, for example, will simply not know that it does not include discussion of recent research suggesting that cognitive development involves major changes in brain physiology. The reader is not invited to question the writer's choices but rather is placed in the passive position of recipient.

You probably recognize this feeling from reading textbooks in subjects you've never studied before. Student readers of textbooks generally accept the role of passive recipient. They work solely to memorize and understand terms and their definitions because they expect to be tested on what they can repeat back from memory or on how they can apply concepts to demonstrate their understanding. Seldom do students in introductory courses question their textbooks or think critically about the concepts being presented. Ironically, research shows we learn and remember best when we think critically about and question a text.

For Discussion

Following are some questions that can help you think critically about the role of concept explanations, focusing on those found in textbooks because your most direct experience with concept explanations at this point is probably in your academic work. As you read through and, perhaps, discuss these questions in class, note down your thoughts and reactions. Then, write a page or so for your instructor presenting your own thoughts about the function of concept explanations in your life and in our society and culture.

1. We've said concept explanations make their knowledge seem to be true. How do they typically do this? Give a few examples from the readings in this chapter and from this or another textbook to illustrate. What can you say about your own attempt to sound authoritative in explaining your concept?
2. We've also said that concept explanations present established knowledge. How do you think knowledge gets established in an academic field such as biology, psychology, or history?
3. Do you think concept explanations should present *only* established knowledge? What if a few experts in a field question some of the concepts in one of your textbooks? Should their questions be included? Given your reasons for reading the textbook and the goals of the textbook writer, what do you think would be gained or lost if such questions were included?

4. Is it true in your experience that teachers, especially in introductory courses, expect students basically to memorize concepts presented in textbooks? As we've mentioned, learning research suggests that we learn best when we think critically about and question a text. Identify one assumption or assertion you've found in this chapter, either in the reading selections or in the text discussion, that you could question. What do you think such questioning can contribute to your learning?

5. How does your thinking about the preceding questions help you interpret the aphorism at the beginning of this section: "Knowledge is power"?

■ For a sociology class, a student writes a term paper on surrogate mothering. She first learned about the subject from television news but feels that she needs more information in order to write a paper on it. In the library, she finds several newspaper and magazine articles that help her better understand the pros and cons of the issue. In her paper, she argues that surrogate mothering is bad socially and politically because it exploits poor women by creating a class of breeders to serve the rich.

■ A college journalism student writes an editorial for the campus newspaper condemning the practice of hazing fraternity pledges. He acknowledges that most hazing is harmless but argues that hazing can get out of hand and even be lethal. He refers specifically to two inci-dents reported in the national news in which students died as a result of hazing. In one case, the student died of alcohol poisoning after drinking too much liquor; in the other, the student had a heart attack after running the track many times. To show that the potential for similar tragedy exists on his own campus, the writer recounts hazing anecdotes told to him by several students. He con-cludes with a plea to the frater-nities on campus to curtail their hazing practices before someone gets seriously hurt or killed.

■ After reading that a local judge has banned the sale of a recording by a popular rap group on the grounds that its lyrics are obscene, a concerned citizen writes a letter to the editor of her local newspaper. The writer points out that according to the standards set by the U.S. Supreme Court in a 1973 case, something can be declared obscene only if it is "patently offensive; appeals to the prurient interest; and lacks serious literary, artistic, political, or scientific value." Although she acknowledges that some listeners may be offended by its sexually explicit lyrics, the writer argues that the recording does have artistic value and therefore should not be censored.

■ For a political science class, a student is assigned to write an essay either supporting or op-posing the right of public employees to strike. Having no strong opinion on the issue herself, she discusses it with her mother, a nurse in a county hospital, and her uncle, a fire fighter. Her mother feels that public employees like hospital workers and teachers should have the right to strike, but that police officers and fire fighters should not because public safety would be endan-gered. Her uncle disagrees,

Taking a Position 6

arguing that allowing hospital workers to strike would jeopardize public safety as much as allowing fire fighters to strike. He insists that the central issue is not public safety, but individual rights. In her essay, the student supports the right of public employees to strike but argues that a system of arbitration should be used where a strike might jeopardize public safety.

■ A committee made up of business and community leaders investigates the issue of regulating urban growth. They prepare a report for the City Council in which they explain the controversy, summarize the arguments for and against regulation, and argue their own opinion that growth should be unregulated. The reasons they give for their conclusion are that supply and demand will regulate development without governmental interference, that landowners should be permitted to sell their property to the highest bidder, and that developers are guided by the needs of the market and thus serve the people.

Taking a position is the first of four chapters on argumentative writing. When you take a position, your aim is not primarily to express yourself, as in Chapters 2 and 3. Nor is it basically to inform readers, as in Chapters 4 and 5. Your primary aim is to persuade readers to adopt your position. Or when persuasion is not possible—when fundamental interests and values are irreconcilable—you try to make the best possible case for your position and assertively refute objections.

Although we may feel very strongly about our opinions, there is seldom a simple right or wrong answer in controversies. Opinions depend to some extent on facts, but they also depend on less objective factors like values and principles. To be convincing, an argument must not only present logical reasons backed by solid evidence, but must also be based on shared values and assumptions. The opening scenario on the issue of censoring rap music provides a good example, for its argument rests on establishing the importance of a basic American value—freedom of artistic expression—and on demonstrating that the album does in fact have artistic merit.

Writing a persuasive position paper is intellectually challenging. It requires you to look critically at your own thinking and to understand others' points of view. You must separate opinion from fact, reason logically, marshal supporting evidence, and recognize the values and beliefs underlying your own and others' opinions.

The most convincing arguments, you will see, appeal to readers in several ways. They appeal to logic by making a sound, well-reasoned, and well-supported argument. They appeal to emotion by making the reader share the writer's concern about the issue. They appeal to the reader's ethical sense by establishing the writer's credibility and by basing the argument on a common set of values and principles.

As citizens in a democracy, we have a special duty to inform ourselves about current issues, to weigh thoughtfully the pros and cons of these issues, and to participate in the public debate over them. Some current issues we might be expected to take a position on include whether explicit sexual education and condom distribution to prevent AIDS should take place in public schools, whether taxes should be raised to build more housing for the homeless, whether experiments on animals should be banned. In your future occupations, you may have many occasions to take a position. Educators argue over admissions standards and course requirements; business executives debate marketing strategies and investment decisions; health care providers argue over treatment options and hospital policies.

| Writing in Your Other Courses | In your college courses, you will frequently be asked to take positions and support them with appropriate evidence. Consider, for instance, some typical assignments: |

- *For an American history course*: Does the Monroe Doctrine justify the American invasions of Grenada and Panama?
- *For an economics course*: David M. Gordon claims in "Class and the Economics of Crime" that "ghetto crime is committed by people responding quite reasonably to the structure of economic opportunities available to them." Write an essay agreeing or disagreeing with this statement.
- *For a sociology course*: "Organized crime is inevitable as long as drug use is illegal." Drawing on course readings, agree or disagree with this position.
- *For a health sciences course*: Summarize the debate over aerial malathion spraying to control the Mediterranean fruit fly and take a position, arguing for or against it. Make clear your reasons for taking one side or the other.

For Group Inquiry

Get together with another student, and choose an issue that has two clearly opposing positions. You don't have to be authorities on the issue, but you should be familiar with some of the arguments that are usually raised on each side. Then decide which of you will argue which side. The side you take doesn't have to be the one you prefer; in fact, taking the opposing position can help you think through your own.

Spend five minutes alone considering the various reasons you could put forth in support of your position. Choose the single best reason and develop a brief argument to convince the other person why this reason should change his or her mind. Then, take twenty minutes to debate the issue. For each side, follow three steps: one person argues for his or her claim, the other person refutes that claim, and finally the first responds to the refutation.

After the debate, spend some time discussing this argument process by considering the following questions:

- On what basis did you each choose the reason you put forth?

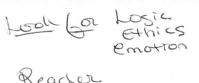 

Reader

- Knowing now how it can be refuted, would you still choose the same reason? Would you argue for it any differently?
- How did the other person's refutation or argument alter your view of the issue or your understanding of him or her?

Readings

Donella H. Meadows is a professor of environmental studies at Dartmouth College and has written several books, including *The Global Citizen* (1991) and *Beyond the Limits: Confronting Global Collapse, Envisioning a Sustainable Future* (1992). Here, Meadows addresses the question of whether radio and television talk shows foster democracy, an issue that came to the fore during the 1992 Presidential campaign after Ross Perot launched his candidacy on *Larry King Live* and promised, if elected, to hold "electronic town meetings" to debate solutions for the nation's problems. (The town meeting is a New England institution dating from colonial times.)

Before reading the essay, reflect on the talk shows you have seen on television or heard on radio, such as those moderated by Rush Limbaugh, Oprah Winfrey, or Geraldo Rivera. Do you usually think of these shows as contributing to the national debate on important issues? Why, or why not?

RUSH AND LARRY, COAST TO COAST: THIS IS NOT DEMOCRACY IN ACTION
DONELLA H. MEADOWS

I'm a talk-show junkie. I'd rather listen to real folks stumbling to express their own thoughts than to polished puppets reading what others have written. I tune into Larry, Rush and the folks who call in, to keep myself awake, chuckling, thinking and every now and then yelling in outrage. 1

One item of talk I hear is about the power of talk shows. They are restoring democracy, it is said, to a nation that has concentrated too much power within one narrow East Coast Beltway. Just by venting our opinions into a national satellite feed, you and I can scuttle a congressional pay raise, elevate a wise-cracking Texan to a presidential candidacy or bring down a potential attorney general because she hired an illegal alien.[1] 2

We don't need Ross Perot to create an electronic town meeting, they say. It's already going on, coast-to-coast, on multiple channels, 24 hours a day. 3

Now, much as I like the talk shows, I'm also from New England, and I can say that there's a big difference between the Rush Limbaugh show and a town meeting. And much as I like town meetings, they are not as effectively democratic as they could be. 4

[1]Washington, D.C., is the area within the "East Coast Beltway," Ross Perot is the "wise-cracking Texan," and Zoë Baird is the "potential attorney general" whose candidacy was withdrawn when it was discovered that she had hired an illegal alien to care for her children.

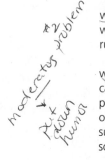

One problem with both call-in shows and town meetings is that they're not rep-   5
resentative. Only those who take the trouble, and don't have to go to work, and
aren't busy with the kids can participate. Even within that set, the loudest mouths
and most made-up minds dominate the air time. At town meetings, you can see the
shy folks, the ones who have trouble sounding off in public, leaning against the back
wall or bending over their knitting. On talk radio, those people are invisible, but
they're there. It's a mistake to think that the blowhards who call in speak for the
nation.

A second problem is that, as we know well from town meetings, the power isn't   6
with the people, it's with the moderator. He or she establishes the rules, decides
who to call on, changes the subject, cuts people off. In talk radio, there is only one
rule: Break for the commercial on time.

Some call-in moderators are neutral and courteous. Then there's Rush Limbaugh,   7
who is funny and pompous and a scapegoater and hatemonger. His popularity could
cause you to draw some terrible conclusions about the state of mind of the American
people. It helps to remember that Bill Cosby is popular, too. I heard an interview the
other day with a psychologist who was hired by Cosby to go over each script to be
sure it contained no "put-down" humor—no joke made at the expense of any person or group. Limbaugh's show is pure put-down humor.

The purpose of the commercial media is not to foster democracy, of course; it's   8
to entertain in order to attract attention in order to sell. Therefore, talk shows have
a fast pace. They flip from topic to topic. There is time to spout off, but no time for
serious debate. Talk shows can only transmit knee-jerk responses to hot-button
items. They can deal with Zoë Baird's child-care arrangements, but they seem un-
interested in Ron Brown's links to corporations and foreign governments. They have
plenty to say about gays in the military, but they can't fathom Yugoslavia. They get
exercised about Congress bouncing checks worth a few thousand dollars, while billions of dollars slide away into the S&L disaster.[2]

The talk shows not only miss the biggest, most profound issues; they can be   9
breeding grounds for careening falsehoods. One man tells Larry King that a cellular
phone gave his wife brain cancer, causing a national panic before there's a shred of
evidence. Rush Limbaugh pronounces the greenhouse effect a fiction made up by
commie-pinko environmentalists, and decades of good science are swept away.

Even if everyone could participate, even if the moderators were fair and respon-   10
sible, even if the pace were deliberate enough to have a real conversation, there
would be a final problem with democracy by talk radio. We are not very good at
talking to one another. We are better at coming back with one-liners than at listening with open minds. We have few public role models showing us how to demand
and judge evidence, how to weigh conflicting opinions, how to deal with uncertainty
and complication.

What I hear every day on talk radio is America's lack of education—and I don't   11
mean lack of college degrees. I mean lack of the basic art of democracy, the ability
to seek the great truths that can come only by synthesizing the small truths possessed by each of us.

[2]Zoë Baird is the candidate for attorney general referred to earlier, while Ron Brown is former
head of the Democratic party and current secretary of commerce. Gays in the military, the war
in Yugoslavia, Congress bouncing checks, and the S&L (savings and loan) problem were all
newsworthy events at the time the article was written.

The world is richly varied and wildly complicated. Each person experiences only 12
a piece of it. To make any sense of the world, to make the right decisions as a nation,
we need many points of view—east and west, rich and poor, male and female, liberal and conservative, urban and rural, black and white, yes, even straight and gay.
Democracy wins out over any government dominated by just one point of view, because only democracy has at least the potential of seeing the world complete and
whole.

That's why talk shows and town meetings are good things. They will be even 13
better when they let all voices be heard with respect, with inquiry, and with dedication to finding the truth, rather than ridiculing the opposition.

For Discussion

In paragraph 10, Meadows makes a series of assertions about Americans: "We
are not very good at talking to one another. We are better at coming back
with one-liners than at listening with open minds. We have few public role
models showing us how to demand and judge evidence, how to weigh conflicting opinions, how to deal with uncertainty and complication."

Recall the last occasion when you argued with someone over a controversial issue. What was the issue? How do you think Meadows would describe
the argument—as basically an exchange of one-liners or as an open-minded
exchange of views? How would you describe it?

Do you agree with Meadows's assumption that we should listen to one
another with open minds? What if you think the other person's position is
morally objectionable? It's one opinion

For Analysis

1. Notice that in the opening paragraph Meadows describes herself as a
"talk-show junkie." Skim the essay, noting in the margin other places where
Meadows represents herself to readers. What adjectives would best describe
the image of Meadows you get from reading this essay? How does this image
affect your willingness to be convinced by her argument? 12th paragy.

2. Meadows, like most writers of position papers, tries to convince readers
by using logic. In paragraphs 4–5, for example, she argues that talk shows
are "not as effectively democratic as they could be" because, like town meetings, they are not "representative." She assumes that for something to be
considered democratic, it must be representative.

To examine the logic of her argument, ask yourself the following questions: First, do you agree that if something is not representative, it cannot be
considered democratic? Second, do you agree with her that call-in talk shows
are not representative? Third, if you accept the first assumption as well as the
second, then must you also accept Meadows's conclusion that talk shows are
not democratic? Why, or why not?

3. In paragraph 3, Meadows reports a common belief that the electronic
town meeting already exists in the form of the talk show. Then, she spends
three paragraphs comparing town meetings and talk shows. Why do you think

For more on comparison and contrast, see Chapter 17.

she uses the strategy of comparison and contrast to try to make her argument more convincing? How convincing do you find this part of her argument?

4.   The primary kind of evidence Meadows uses to support her argument is example. Skim the essay and put brackets around each example; then, explain briefly how these examples contribute to her argument.

For Your Own Writing

Consider any other controversial issues you can think of that involve the media—television, radio, film, music video, or recording. For example, should individuals be able to sell videotapes they've copied from commercial broadcasts? Should prime-time television programs be permitted to show nudity? Should movies that represent conflict between different nationalities or American ethnic groups be monitored to prevent stereotyping? Should store owners be prohibited from selling "R-rated" recordings to people under eighteen?

Select one issue on which you have a position. What assumptions have led you to choose this issue? How might you, like Meadows, construct an argument based on some of your assumptions? Which of your assumptions do you think readers who take an opposing position might respond to positively?

Commentary

Writers taking a position on a controversial issue develop an argumentative strategy based on what they assume readers already think and feel about the issue and what they want readers to think and feel. Meadows assumes that her readers have been misinformed about the value of talk shows. Her aim is to set them right. She wants to convince readers that talk shows neither substitute for nor foster democratic debate. She also wants to educate readers about what she calls "the basic art of democracy."

For a detailed discussion of counterarguing, see pp. 550–52.

Meadows's argumentative strategy, then, is to counterargue or refute the popular opinion that talk shows are "restoring democracy." The following scratch outline shows how refutation organizes the essay:

identifies herself as liking talk shows (1)

reports the opposing position: talk shows are "restoring democracy" (2–3)

states her own position: talk shows are "not as effectively democratic as they could be" (4)

reason 1: "they're not representative" (5)

reason 2: they give moderators the power; "power isn't with the people" as it should be in a democracy (6–7)

reason 3: because their purpose is to entertain and sell products, they allow "no time for serious debate" and therefore breed falsehood (9–10)

reason 4: participants "lack the basic art of democracy" (10–12)

restates her position: talk shows would be better if they practiced the art of democracy (13)

For more on making claims, see pp. 534–38. For more about thesis statements, see pp. 466–67.

Notice that Meadows begins her refutation by trying to establish her credibility with readers as someone who likes talk shows. Using phrases like *it is said* and *they say*, Meadows indicates that the position she's refuting is popular. In paragraph 4, she makes her disagreement explicit by assertively stating her position, or claim, which is also the thesis of her essay. Then, she systematically gives reasons (in paragraphs 5–12) why the popular opinion is wrong, and concludes by restating her own position.

For more on cues and transitions, see pp. 476–81.

This plan is simple and straightforward. Because she wants to make it easy for readers to follow her argument, Meadows provides clear cues and transitions. For example, the word "Now" (paragraph 4) signals her disagreement with the popular view, and the phrases "One problem" and "A second problem" announce her first two reasons in paragraphs 5–6. She doesn't go on in this vein, presumably because she doesn't want to bore readers by numbering every point, but she does provide a summary of her points at the beginning of paragraph 10: "Even if everyone could participate, even if the moderators were fair and responsible, even if the pace were deliberate enough to have a real conversation, there would be a final problem with democracy by talk radio. We are not very good talking to one another." This summary also serves as a transition to her last and most important point about the art of democracy.

For more on the use of definition, see Chapter 16.

Meadows concludes by defining the art of democracy, as she sees it. *Democracy* is the key term in this debate. Readers' acceptance or rejection of Meadows's argument depends largely on what they think is appropriate democratic debate. Meadows argues that talking loudly, having one's mind already made up, scapegoating, hatemongering, putting others down, spouting off, giving knee-jerk responses, and so on, do not foster democracy. Instead, she argues that democracy requires a different set of behaviors such as listening with an open mind, demanding and judging evidence, dealing with uncertainty and complication, seeking the great truths by synthesizing the partial truths. If she can convince readers to accept her definition of what is and is not democratic speech, Meadows assumes they will also accept her position on talk shows.

■   ■   ■

William K. Kilpatrick teaches education at Boston College and frequently lectures to parents and teachers. In the following essay, he summarizes the basic argument of his most recent book, *Why Johnny Can't Tell Right from Wrong: Moral Illiteracy and the Case for Character Education* (1992).

To demonstrate that there is a moral crisis in America today, Kilpatrick opens his essay with a vivid anecdote. In the book, he also cites grim statistics to give readers a sense of the problem's scope:

> An estimated 525,000 attacks, shakedowns, and robberies occur in the public high schools each month. Each year nearly three million crimes are committed on or near school property—16,000 per school day. About 135,000 students

students

carry guns to school daily; one fifth of all students report carrying a weapon of some type. Twenty-one percent of all secondary school students avoid using the rest room out of fear of being harmed or intimidated.

Before reading the essay, reflect on your own high school experience. Did you feel endangered? Do you think there was a widespread lack of morality among the students in your school? What moral values were you taught in school?

CHILDREN MUST BE TAUGHT TO TELL RIGHT FROM WRONG

WILLIAM K. KILPATRICK

1   In Cambridge, Mass., a 15-year-old is accused of murdering a college student during a mugging, then bragging to his two high school-age accomplices that the knife went all the way through the body.

2   After the boy's arraignment, some of his classmates cried. Not for the loss of a promising life, but for the high bail that had been placed on their friend. When a reporter asked one of them what the appropriate punishment for murder should be, he responded, "counseling." Said another, a girl, "What's the big bleepin' deal? People die all the time. So what?"

3   Many of today's young people have a difficult time seeing any moral dimension to their actions. There are a number of reasons why that's true, but none more prominent than a failed system of education that eschews teaching children the traditional moral values that bind Americans together as a society and a culture. That failed approach, called "decision-making," was introduced in schools 25 years ago. It tells children to decide for themselves what is right and what is wrong. It replaced "character education." Character education didn't ask children to reinvent the moral wheel; instead, it encouraged them to practice habits of courage, justice and self-control.

4   In the 1940s, when a character education approach prevailed, teachers worried about students chewing gum; today they worry about robbery and rape.

5   Decision-making curriculums pose thorny ethical dilemmas to students, leaving them with the impression that all morality is problematic and that all questions of right and wrong are in dispute. Youngsters are forced to question values and virtues they've never acquired in the first place or upon which they have only a tenuous hold. The Polyannaish assumption behind this method is that students will arrive at good moral conclusions if only they are given the chance. But the actual result is moral confusion.

6   For example, a recent national study of 1,700 sixth- to ninth-graders revealed that a majority of boys considered rape to be acceptable under certain conditions. Astoundingly, many of the girls agreed.

7   This kind of moral illiteracy is further encouraged by values-education programs that are little more than courses in self-esteem. These programs are based on the questionable assumption that a child who feels good about himself or herself won't want to do anything wrong. But it is just as reasonable to make an opposite assumption: namely, that a child who has uncritical self-regard will conclude that he or she can't do anything bad.

8   Such naive self-acceptance results in large part from the non-directive, non-judgmental, as-long-as-you-feel-comfortable-with-your-choices mentality that has pervaded public education for the last two and one-half decades. Many of today's

drug education, sex education and values-education courses are based on the same 1960s philosophy that helped fuel the explosion in teen drug use and sexual activity in the first place.

Meanwhile, while educators are still fiddling with outdated "feel-good" approaches, New York, Washington, and Los Angeles are burning. Youngsters are leaving school believing that matters of right and wrong are always merely subjective. If you pass a stranger on the street and decide to murder him because you need money—if it feels right—you go with that feeling. Clearly, murder is not taught in our schools, but such a conclusion—just about any conclusion—can be reached and justified using the decision-making method. 9

It is time to consign the fads of "decision-making" and "non-judgmentalism" to the ash heap of failed policies, and return to a proved method. Character education provides a much more realistic approach to moral formation. It is build on an understanding that we learn morality not by debating it but by practicing it. 10

What's the lesson for schools? That they need to get back in the habit of encouraging good habits of behavior. Schools also need to re-learn the importance of example and imitation in forming character. We become good people not by inventing our own values but by finding the best examples—from life, from literature, from history—and trying to follow them. 11

Teaching right from wrong has as much bearing on a culture's survival as teaching reading, writing or science, and there exists a great wealth of knowledge about how to do it. Teachers do have the right—and the duty—to teach basic morality. If they can find the courage to again shoulder that responsibility, teen-age boys would soon come to realize that rape is wrong under any circumstance, and a misguided young woman might begin to understand why the murder of a young man is indeed a big deal. 12

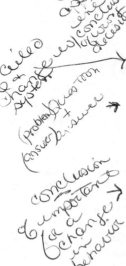

For Discussion

To get a better understanding of the decision-making exercises Kilpatrick criticizes, choose *one* of the following exercises and discuss it with a couple of classmates:

1. Imagine a ship is sinking, and there is not enough room for everyone on the lifeboat. You must decide who will live and who will drown. On what basis do you decide?

2. Imagine you're with a friend in a store. Unbeknown to you, your friend steals something. Your friend gets away, but you are stopped by the store manager who demands that you reveal your friend's name and address. How do you decide what to do?

After doing the exercise, take a few minutes to discuss its value: What does it teach about morality? Do you agree with Kilpatrick's criticism of such exercises? Why, or why not?

For Analysis

For an example of a scratch outline see p. 240 in this chapter.

1. To analyze Kilpatrick's argumentative strategy, begin by making a scratch outline of the essay. Then, briefly explain his strategy.

2. Given your analysis of Kilpatrick's argumentative strategy, how effective is the opening anecdote? What does it try to accomplish? How could the

For a survey of argumentative strategies, see Chapter 19.

"decision-making" or "non-judgmentalism" approach be used to explain the behavior Kilpatrick reports in this anecdote?

3.   Writers of position papers often argue indirectly by the way they name key terms. In paragraphs 7–10, for example, Kilpatrick uses the term "non-judgmentalism" instead of "choice" or "values clarification," the terms generally used by proponents of the approach. Why do you think he uses "non-judgmentalism"? What do the different terms imply? Why do you think he also refers to it as a "feel-good" approach?

4.   Look closely at the way Kilpatrick concludes his argument. He could have ended with paragraph 11. Why do you think he includes paragraph 12? Given his argumentative strategy, what purpose does this final paragraph serve?

For Your Own Writing

Think of a controversial moral issue on which you have an opinion. Here are a few possibilities: shoplifting, plagiarism, date rape, doctor-assisted suicide. On what values or principles would you base your argument?

Commentary

Anecdotes are discussed on pp. 542–43; comparison and contrast is covered in Chapter 18, and causal analysis in Chapter 17.

Position papers may use a range of different writing strategies to present their reasons and evidence. Kilpatrick begins his essay with an anecdote to illustrate what he means by moral illiteracy. Through comparison and contrast, he shows how character education differs from decision-making and non-judgmentalism. Finally, he analyzes cause and effect to argue that the decision-making and non-judgmentalism approaches cause moral confusion rather than clarification.

It is also worth noting the way Kilpatrick makes his writing flow smoothly from one sentence to another. For example, in paragraph 2 pronouns or repeated words link each sentence to the preceding one. In the second sentence, the pronoun *that* in the phrase "why that's true" refers back to the point made in the first sentence. Similarly, the third sentence begins with the phrase "That failed approach," again using the pronoun *that* and also repeating the word "failed"" from sentence two. Sentences four and five both begin with the pronoun *it*, referring back to the "failed approach," and sentence six opens by repeating the name of the alternative approach that ended the preceding sentence. This kind of cohesive chaining helps readers follow the thread of the argument and is particularly useful when a complicated argument is compressed into a small space.

See pp. 476–79 for more on such cohesive devices.

As we pointed out in the headnote, this selection summarizes the basic argument of Kilpatrick's recent book. Unlike his article, the book refers to many other books, articles, and research studies—a total of thirty-one pages of citations. Writers of extensively researched position papers often write brief articles for newspapers and magazines summarizing their arguments. In so doing, they—like Kilpatrick—generally follow the conventions of newspaper writing and do not cite their sources. Writing a position paper for a college

*See Chapters 21 and
22 for information
about finding and
acknowledging sources.*
class, on the other hand, you will be expected to follow the conventions of academic writing and cite your sources. The final two essays in this chapter illustrate academic citation.

■   ■   ■

Amitai Etzioni, a professor at George Washington University, has written many books and articles and is founding editor of the new journal *Responsive Community*. The following position paper on hate speech was excerpted from his most recent book, *The Spirit of Community: Rights, Responsibilities, and the Communitarian Agenda* (1993).

Communitarianism is a movement Etzioni and others established to supplant traditional political positions, such as conservatism and liberalism, that they believe needlessly polarize debate and oversimplify the complex issues Americans face. Communitarianism seeks to change the tenor of public debate, to make it less contentious and more productive. Etzioni proposes in his book that Americans draw up a new social contract based on the idea that while we have rights as individuals, we also have responsibilities to serve the common good.

On the issue of hate speech, Etzioni tries to turn the debate away from legal rights to civic responsibilities because he thinks that "rights talk polarizes debate." What rights and responsibilities do you think of in regard to speech?

**UNIVERSITIES
SHOULD
EDUCATE, NOT
REGULATE**
AMITAI ETZIONI

In 1986, before some people concerned with racist, sexist, and homophobic speech sought to curb free speech on, of all places, university campuses, Wayne Dick, a student at Yale, displayed a satiric poster (Schumacher, "Anti-Gay" 1). It was entitled "Bestiality Awareness Days (BAD) Week" and was intended to satirize "GLAD Week"—Gay and Lesbian Awareness Days—an annual event at Yale. On the poster, Dick included the thinly veiled names of several gay faculty members and students. One of the students, Pat Santana (referred to in the poster as Professor Pet Satanna), argued that he had been "slandered" by the poster, which he deemed "visual harassment" (qtd. in Blank). Dick defended himself by saying that homosexuality is "immoral," and that "although homosexuality might be considered normal now, not all people consider it normal" (qtd. in Schumacher, "Anti-Gay" 6).

After a contentious hearing, Dick was put on probation for two years for harassing and intimidating Santana and other gays and lesbians. His defenders, however, continued to argue that he was well within his right of free speech. The executive director of the Connecticut Civil Liberties Union, William Olds, protested that the student was disciplined "for what appears to be an exercise in free expression" (qtd. in Barnes). Others noted that Yale's undergraduate regulations read, in part: "Even when some members of the University community fail to meet their social and ethical responsibilities, the paramount obligation of the university is to protect their right to free expression" (Schumacher, "Student").

Those who favored Dick's punishment, though, argued that one should not wantonly hurt others. An alumna of Yale, Carrie Costello, a founder of the Ad Hoc Com-

1

2

3

mittee Against Defamation, explained that "we stand very strongly for free speech, but that does not include the right to harass or intimidate, or the right to slander individuals" (qtd. in Schumacher, "Anti-Gay" 6).

Others countered that once we limit speech because it hurts some people, soon   4 much speech, especially that of dissenting voices, would be banned. This would violate a main idea behind the First Amendment: to protect especially well the right to speech of those who provoke someone else's ire. After all, it is hardly necessary to protect speech that is endearing, evokes wide favor, or is conformist. In the same vein, Yale's president, Benno C. Schmidt, Jr., stated that the university should accord "paramount value" to "freedom of expression, even to expression that is distasteful or silly" (qtd. in Conti and Rothschild). Others argued, in effect, "Sticks and stones may break my bones, but words will never harm me"—that people should be mature enough to be able to handle verbal slurs.

Other universities faced the same basic question: What is the proper balance   5 between the right to free speech and the need to sustain community? Should our commitment to allow people to speak freely permit those who spout hate to set one group apart from others? How can we respect the right to free speech and at the same time reduce the tension that breaks community into groups seething with hatred for one another?

By 1992 more than 130 American universities had enacted so-called speech   6 codes—codes that define what may or may not be said on campus and how prohibited speech will be punished (Barker). Among them are Emory, Trinity, Tufts, the University of Connecticut, the University of Pennsylvania, the University of North Carolina at Chapel Hill, and Stanford.

At the University of Pennsylvania, students may be punished for "behavior, verbal   7 or physical, that stigmatizes or victimizes individuals" and "creates an intimidating or offensive environment" ("Colleges"). (A Penn professor commented sarcastically: "Penn is a tolerant and diverse community, and if you do not agree with its particular notions of tolerance and diversity, it gladly will reeducate you" [qtd. in Kors].) Tufts forbids slurs or insults in classrooms or dormitories but allows them in the student newspaper, on the campus radio station, and in public lectures. The University of Connecticut was much less tolerant: students could have been expelled from class for using "derogatory names, inappropriately directed laughter, inconsiderate jokes, and conspicuous exclusion [of a classmate] from conversation" ("Colleges").

At the University of Wisconsin, a student would violate the school's code if "he   8 or she intentionally made demeaning remarks to an individual based on that person's ethnicity, such as name calling, racial slurs, or 'jokes'; and . . . his or her purpose in uttering the remarks was to make the educational environment hostile for the person to whom the demeaning remark was addressed . . ." (Chapter UWS 17.06(2)(a)2.(c)1).

Communitarians like me hold that legal restrictions on free speech are not only   9 very difficult to delineate, but are ineffectual to boot. At best they may curb public expressions of racial, ethnic, and gender hatred, but they do not get at the root causes. The *Los Angeles Times* editorialized: "Speech codes don't attack the racism and other attitudinal baggage that students bring with them to college. Codes suppress the words without exploring and combating the lazy and irrational thinking that spawns prejudice based on ethnicity, religion, or sex" ("Fighting Intolerance"). The ACLU's president, Nadine Strossen, similarly argues that speech codes "are doing nothing to stop racism and bigotry. For university administrators, they are a cheap solution to a complex problem" (qtd. in Savage).

Those who are concerned about hateful expressions need to seek deeper and 10 more educational remedies. One place to start is to draw a distinction between what you have a right to say and what is civil and Communitarian speech.

This is more or less where the issue was left in recent public debates about 11 speech codes—at a rather unsatisfactory place, from a Communitarian viewpoint. True, the right of free speech has been rather well protected. One may even view the debate about speech codes as a kind of grand social reinoculation, reinforcing in the body politic the antibody against constricting free speech. By arguing vigorously about the issue, the merits of free speech, the values that sustain it were stressed again and again, which is fine as far as it goes. But by and large little was done to deal with the underlying pain and injury to those who are the subjects of verbal abuse that led them to demand curbs on hate speech to begin with. *Speech was attended to, but not community.* If we say that hate is undesirable but we cannot lay a glove on those who instigate it, we are resigning ourselves to a society that will be ever more divided and hostile. There is good reason for concern.

A comprehensive study of universities found that although intolerance was ram- 12 pant, the universities engaged in "a culture of denial"—either resisting suggestions to deal with the problem or responding with a few ill-conceived, limited countermeasures (People 6). Fifty-seven percent of the colleges studied reported that intolerance posed a problem on their campuses. But the majority also reported that they had no programs or limited ones to deal with it.

Franklyn S. Haiman, a Northwestern University professor of communications, 13 concludes in an article in defense of unrestricted speech:

> The roots of group hatred stretch far beyond the reach of our educational institutions. . . . They are interwoven with problems of economic wealth and poverty, of political power and powerlessness, of psychological insecurity and fear. They will not be solved by writing laws and rules against racist speech. (30)

This basically amounts to saying to minorities who are distressed by streams of verbal abuse, verbal harassment, and psychological hounding: "Tough s———. *It is* good for the First Amendment!" We can do better. We ought to do more. . . .

We should inform people who spout prejudice and spread hate that we consider 14 them to be bigoted, uncivilized boors, people whose company we shun. "Sure," we may tell them, "you have a right to say most anything you want, but using this right in certain ways is not morally appropriate or socially acceptable." If enough of us make that clear, they are likely to put their First Amendment rights to better use than insulting others. At least the victims of slurs will know that the community does not share the hate and prejudice expressed by some and that the community *is* offended by them.

There are a whole slew of other educational tools: debates and assemblies, 15 courses on the sources and dynamics of prejudice, and one-on-one and small-group interracial dinners. . . .

Others report that peer counseling can be quite effective in dealing with sexual 16 harassment (People 20). Trained student volunteers work with other students across the campus as peer educators, leading information and discussion sessions. Of course, regular, professional counselors are required, too, but the combination of students and professionals can be positive and productive.

In short, universities are supposed to educate. If faculties cannot reach most students and show them the evils of hatred, prejudice, and discrimination, they need additional training themselves. They ought not to be given the easy way out of their responsibilities by regulating the expression of hate while leaving the hate itself unscathed. Hate is an ugly and unwholesome human expression all by itself; and it is particularly detrimental to building and sustaining the mutual support and commitment to shared undertakings on which community thrives.   17

Works Cited

Barker, Mayerene. "University Divided over Proposal for Speech Codes." *Los Angeles Times* 16 May 1991: B3.

Barnes, Patricia G. "Yale Chided for Disciplining Student Who Mocked Homosexuals." *New Haven Register* 7 Aug. 1986: 1.

Blank, Stephanie. " 'BAD Week' Flyer Angers Students." *Yale Daily News* 16 Apr. 1986: 3.

"Colleges Take Two Basic Approaches in Adopting Anti-Harassment Plans." *Chronicle of Higher Education* 4 Oct. 1989: A38.

Conti, Sam, and Richard Rothschild. "Schmidt, Others Address Dick Case." *Yale Daily News* 3 Oct. 1986: 1.

"Fighting Intolerance with Intolerant Speech Codes." Editorial. *Los Angeles Times* 13 May 1991: B4.

Haiman, Franklyn S. "The Remedy Is More Speech." *American Prospect* 6 (Summer 1991): 30–35.

Kors, Alan Charles. "It's Speech, Not Sex, the Dean Bans Now." *Wall Street Journal* 12 Oct. 1989: A16.

People for the American Way. *Hate in the Ivory Tower: A Survey of Intolerance on College Campuses and Academia's Response.* Washington, DC: People for the American Way, 1991.

Savage, David G. "Forbidden Words on Campus." *Los Angeles Times* 12 Feb. 1991: A17.

Schumacher, Richard. "Anti-Gay Poster Sparks Free Speech Controversy." *Yale Daily News* 3 Sept. 1986: 1, 6.

---. "Student Demands Rehearing." *Yale Daily News* 10 Sept. 1986: 1.

University of Wisconsin. *University of Wisconsin System Administrative Code.* Aug. 1989.

For Discussion

Do you think campuses like your own should have rules against "hate speech"? Why, or why not? Perhaps the key to any argument on this issue is how one defines hate speech. How does Etzioni define it? How would you define it?

For Analysis

1. Etzioni and Kilpatrick both begin their arguments with anecdotes. Given that each has his own purpose, audience, and argumentative strategy, evaluate how well this choice of opening works in the two essays.

2.   Notice that paragraph 5 consists only of questions. These might be "rhetorical" questions that the writer intends to answer or they might be real questions for readers to think about and answer for themselves. Which do you think they are, and how do they fit into Etzioni's argumentative strategy?

3.   Paragraphs 6–8 describe codes designed by different universities to regulate hate speech. Why do you think Etzioni describes these codes? What do these paragraphs add to his argument?

4.   In the headnote, we pointed out that Communitarianism seeks to shift the focus of public debate from legal rights to civic responsibilities. If Etzioni doesn't argue against hate speech on the basis of rights, on what basis does he argue in this essay? How does he try to convince readers that this is the proper basis for deciding the issue? How convincing do you find this argument to be?

For Your Own Writing

In debating social issues, people often disagree over competing rights. On the issue of whether metal detectors should be installed on high-school campuses, for example, some people oppose metal detectors because they invade the right to privacy, while others support them because they protect the right to safety. Think of another social issue. What are the competing rights? If you were to take a position on this issue, what right would you argue for? What would you say?

Commentary

In this essay, Etzioni speaks as a Communitarian. For example, he begins paragraph 9 with the self-identification "Communitarians like me. . . . " In paragraph 11, he expresses what he calls "a Communitarian viewpoint." He even refers, in paragraph 10, to what he calls "Communitarian speech," which he distinguishes from "what you have a right to say." All these references to Communitarianism remind us that this position paper is from the book that sets forth the Communitarian agenda. Etzioni's purpose in writing this essay, therefore, is twofold: to argue his position on hate speech and to illustrate a Communitarian approach to a troubling public issue.

Assuming that Etzioni is using this essay to show how a Commuitarian thinks about such issues, why does he cite so many outside references and quote others so frequently? One possible answer is that he wants to reassure readers that he is trustworthy. In relating the incident at Yale, for example, Etzioni relies on several different sources, suggesting that his reporting is unbiased. Similarly, he refers to several different university speech codes, quoting from a variety of them, to prove his assertion that hate speech has become a serious issue on many university campuses. Finally, he quotes authorities—the *Los Angeles Times*, the president of the ACLU—to demonstrate that other thoughtful people have come to the same conclusion he has.

All of these citations contribute to the impression Etzioni is trying to make on readers. He knows that if readers think of him as credible and unbiased

For more on using authorities, see pp. 541–42.

and if they see him as one of many thoughtful people who take a similar position, they are more likely to be swayed by his argument. His effort to establish himself as trustworthy also goes along with his Communitarian desire to avoid contentiousness. Etzioni's style of argument is consistent with what he is arguing for: the replacement of hate with a community spirit of "mutual support and commitment." You might contrast Etzioni's effort to transcend conflict with Meadows's and Kilpatrick's more contentious styles of argumentation.

■　　■　　■

Jessica Statsky wrote the following essay about children's competitive sports for her freshman composition course. Before reading, recall your own experiences as an elementary school child playing competitive sports, either in or out of school. If you weren't actively involved yourself, did you know anyone who was? Looking back, do you think that winning was unduly emphasized? What value was placed on having a good time? On learning to get along with others? On developing athletic skills and confidence?

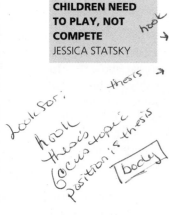

CHILDREN NEED TO PLAY, NOT COMPETE

JESSICA STATSKY

hook

Look for:
hook
thesis
thesis
topic
focus
Position is thesis
thesis →
body

Over the past three decades organized sports for children have increased dra- 1 matically in the United States. And though many adults regard Little League Baseball and Peewee Football as a basic part of childhood, the games are not always joyous ones. When overzealous parents and coaches impose adult standards on children's sports, the result can be activities that are neither satisfying nor beneficial to children.

I'm concerned about all organized sports activities for children between the ages 2 of six and twelve. The damage I see results from noncontact as well as contact sports, from sports organized locally as well as those organized nationally. Highly organized competitive sports such as Peewee Football and Little League Baseball are too often played to adult standards, which are developmentally inappropriate for children and can be both physically and psychologically harmful. Furthermore, because they eliminate many children from organized sports before they are ready to compete, they are actually counterproductive for developing either future players or fans. Finally, because they emphasize competition and winning, they unfortunately provide occasions for some parents and coaches to place their own fantasies and needs ahead of children's welfare.

One readily understandable danger of overly competitive sports is that they en- 3 tice children into physical actions that are bad for growing bodies. For example, a twelve-year-old trying to throw a curve ball may put abnormal strain on developing arm and shoulder muscles, sometimes resulting in lifelong injuries (Koppett 294). Contact sports like football can be even more hazardous. Thomas Tutko, a psychology professor at San Jose State University and coauthor of the book *Winning is Everything and Other American Myths*, said: "I am strongly opposed to young kids playing tackle football. It is not the right stage of development for them to be taught to crash into other kids. Kids under the age of fourteen are not by nature physical. Their main concern is self-preservation. They don't want to meet head on and slam into each other. But tackle football absolutely requires that they try to hit each other as hard as they can. And it is too traumatic for kids" (qtd. in Tosches A1).

As Tutko indicates, even when children are not injured, fear of being hurt detracts from their enjoyment of the sport. One mother of an eight-year-old Peewee Football player explained, "The kids get so scared. They get hit once and they don't want anything to do with football anymore. They'll sit on the bench and pretend their leg hurts . . . " (qtd. in Tosches A32). Some children are driven to even more desperate measures. For example, in one Peewee Football game a reporter watched the following scene as a player took himself out of the game:

> "Coach, my tummy hurts. I can't play," he said. The coach told the player to get back onto the field. "There's nothing wrong with your stomach," he said. When the coach turned his head the seven-year-old stuck a finger down his throat and made himself vomit. When the coach turned back, the boy pointed to the ground and told him, "Yes there is, coach. See?" (Tosches A1).

Besides physical hazards and anxieties, competitive sports pose psychological dangers for children. Martin Rablovsky, a former sports editor for the *New York Times*, said that in all his years of watching young children play organized sports, he noticed very few of them smiling. "I've seen children enjoying a spontaneous pre-practice scrimmage become somber and serious when the coach's whistle blows," Rablovsky said. "The spirit of play suddenly disappears, and sport becomes joblike" (qtd. in Coakley 94). The primary goal of a professional athlete—winning—is not appropriate for children. Their goals should be having fun, learning, and being with friends. Although winning does add to the fun, too many adults lose sight of what matters and make winning the most important goal. Several studies have shown that when children are asked whether they would rather be warming the bench on a winning team or playing regularly on a losing team, about 90 percent choose the latter (Smith, Smith, and Smoll 11).

Winning and losing may be an inevitable part of adult life, but they should not be part of childhood. Too much competition too early in life can affect a child's development. Children are easily influenced, and when they sense that their competence and worth are based on their ability to live up to their parents' and coaches' high expectations—and on their ability to win—they can become discouraged and depressed. According to Dr. Glyn C. Roberts, a professor of kinesiology at the Institute of Child Behavior and Development at the University of Illinois, 80 to 90 percent of children who play competitive sports at a young age drop out by sixteen (Kutner).

This statistic illustrates another reason I oppose competitive sports for children: because they are so highly selective, very few children get to participate. Far too soon a few children are singled out for their athletic promise, while many others, who may be on the verge of developing the necessary strength and ability, are screened out and discouraged from trying out again. Like adults, children fear failure, and so even those with good physical skills may stay away because they lack self-confidence. Consequently, teams lose many promising players who with some encouragement and experience might have become stars. The problem is that many parent-sponsored, out-of-school programs give more importance to having a winning team than to developing children's physical skills and self-esteem.

Indeed, it is no secret that too often scorekeeping, league standings, and the drive to win bring out the worst in adults who are more absorbed in living out their own fantasies than in enhancing the quality of the experience for children (Smith, Smith, and Smoll 9). Recent newspaper articles on children's sports contain plenty of horror stories. *Los Angeles Times* reporter Rich Tosches, for example, tells the story of a brawl among seventy-five parents following a Peewee Football game. As a result of the brawl, which began when a parent from one team confronted a player from the other team, the teams are now thinking of hiring security guards for future games. Another example is provided by a *Times* editorial about a Little League manager who intimidated the opposing team by setting fire to one of their team's jerseys on the pitching mound before the game began. As the editorial writer commented, the manager showed his young team that "intimidation could substitute for playing well" ("Bad News").

Although not all parents or coaches behave so inappropriately, the seriousness   9
of the problem is illustrated by the fact that Adelphi University in Garden City, New York, offers a sports psychology workshop for Little League coaches, designed to balance their "animal instincts" with educational theory in hopes of reducing the "screaming and hollering," in the words of Harold Weisman, manager of sixteen Little Leagues in New York City. In a three-and-one-half hour Sunday morning work-shop, coaches learn how to make practices more fun, treat injuries, deal with irate parents, and be "more sensitive to their young players' fears, emotional frailties, and need for recognition" (Schmitt). Little League is to be credited with recognizing the need for such workshops.

Some parents would no doubt argue that children can't start too soon preparing   10
to live in a competitive free-market economy. After all, secondary schools and col-leges require students to compete for grades, and college admission is extremely competitive. And it is perfectly obvious how important competitive skills are in find-ing a job. Yet the ability to cooperate is also important for success in life. Before children are psychologically ready for competition, maybe we should emphasize co-operation and individual performance in team sports rather than winning.

Many people are ready for such an emphasis. In 1988 one New York Little   11
League official who had attended the Adelphi workshop tried to ban scoring from six-to-eight-year-olds' games—but parents wouldn't support him (Schmitt). An in-novative children's sports program in New York City, City-Sports-For-Kids, empha-sizes fitness, self-esteem, and sportsmanship. In this program's basketball games, every member on a team plays at least two of six eight-minute periods. The basket is seven feet from the floor, rather than ten feet, and a player can score a point just by hitting the rim (Bloch). I believe this kind of local program should replace overly competitive programs like Peewee Football and Little League Baseball.

Authorities have clearly documented the excesses and dangers of many com-   12
petitive sports programs for children. It would seem that few children benefit from these programs and that those who do would benefit even more from programs emphasizing fitness, cooperation, sportsmanship, and individual performance. Thir-teen- and fourteen-year-olds may be eager for competition, but few younger chil-dren are. These younger children deserve sports programs designed specifically for *their* needs and abilities.

Works Cited

Bloch, Gordon B. "Thrill of Victory Is Secondary to Fun." *New York Times* 2 Apr. 1990, late ed.:C12.

"The Bad News Pyromaniacs?" Editorial. *Los Angeles Times* 16 June 1990:B6.

Coakley, Jay J. *Sport in Society: Issues and Controversies.* St. Louis: Mosby, 1982.

Koppett, Leonard, *Sports Illusion, Sports Reality.* New York: Houghton, 1981.

Kutner, Lawrence, "Athletics, through a Child's Eyes. *New York Times* 23 Mar. 1989, late ed.:C8.

Schmitt, Eric. "Psychologists Take Seat on Little League Bench." *New York Times* 14 Mar. 1989, late ed.:B2.

Smith, Nathan, Ronald Smith, and Frank Smoll. *Kidsports: A Survival Guide for Parents.* New York: Addison-Wesley, 1983.

Tosches, Rich. "Peewee Football: Is It Time to Blow the Whistle?" *Los Angeles Times* 3 Dec. 1988: A1 +.

For Discussion

Statsky makes the point that whereas competition is highly valued in our culture, cooperation tends to be downplayed. In what ways does our society encourage competition? How is cooperation encouraged? Does the educational system, in your experience, encourage one more than the other? Which of the two seems to be valued most highly in advertising, television, and movies? Who do you think benefits most from this cultural preference? Who loses?

For Analysis

For discussion and illustration of these cueing devices, see Chapter 12.

1.   Make a scratch outline of Statsky's argument. Then evaluate her organization. Put brackets around the cueing devices—statements forecasting what is to come, summaries of what has just been said, topic sentences, and transitions—she uses to help readers stay on track. Point to any places where you lose track or get confused.

2.   Statsky's argumentative strategy includes showing that she and her readers share the same values. Point to a passage where you feel she is trying to build a bridge of shared values between herself and her readers. How does this appeal affect your response to this passage and to the whole essay?

3.   Skim the essay, noting each time Statsky quotes authorities. What do you think is the cumulative effect of quoting so many different people? Choose the quotation that you find most effective, and explain why.

4.   Reread the conclusion. What is Statsky trying to accomplish by ending the essay this way? How well do you think her conclusion works?

5.   Read the Writer at Work discussion on pp. 247–48. Notice in her analysis of purpose and audience how Statsky describes the readers she intends to address and her proposed argumentative strategy. Review the revised essay to see whether she kept to this plan or modified it in some way.

For Your Own Writing

Make a list of issues related to childhood and adolescence. (Should elementary and secondary schools be on a year-round schedule? Should children have the right to "divorce" their parents? Should adolescents who commit serious crimes be tried as adults?) Then choose an issue that you think you could write about. What position do you think you would take? Why?

Writers of position papers must be especially careful not to define the issue too broadly or to overstate their position. Statsky defines her issue by identifying several parameters such as age, geography, school affiliation, and type of sport. She restricts the subject by both age and school affiliation, limiting it to children between the ages of six and twelve (paragraph 2), and to "parent-sponsored out-of-school" sports (paragraph 7). On the other hand, she allows for sports organized nationally as well as locally and for all kinds of sports, noncontact as well as contact. Finally, to ensure that her readers know the kind of organized, competitive team sports she's talking about, Statsky gives two familiar examples: Peewee Football and Little League Baseball.

Statsky also qualifies her thesis by avoiding absolute or unconditional language. In the opening paragraph, for example, she uses the words *not always* to soften her assertion: "These games are *not always* joyous ones." Similarly, in the next sentence, instead of saying "the result is" she allows for other possibilities by saying "the result *can be*." Such minor adjustments in word choice can have an important effect on readers because they make Statsky's position seem reasonable, without making her seem indecisive. Indeed, Statsky presents her argument confidently and assertively.

PURPOSE AND AUDIENCE

In writing a paper that takes a position on a controversial issue, you may have a variety of purposes. First and foremost, you will write to express your opinion. But you will do more than simply state what you think; you will also present an argument explaining and justifying your point of view. Although your position paper will nearly always be written for others to read, writing can also lead you to clarify your own thinking. Anticipating other's views—accepting the points you consider well taken and refuting those with which you disagree—will help you develop your understanding of the issue and confidence in your own point of view.

In addition to expressing an opinion, most position papers are intended to influence other people's thinking on important issues. Assuming that logical argument will prevail over prejudice, you try to change readers' minds by presenting compelling reasons supported by solid evidence, and by pointing out flaws in other's reasoning. You seek common ground in shared interests, values, and principles. You may show that you are reasonable by moderating your own views and urging others to compromise as well, in order to reach a consensus of opinion.

When agreement seems beyond reach, however, it is highly unlikely that you will be able to change readers' minds with a single essay, no matter how well written it is. Most writers addressing an audience so opposed to their position are satisfied if they can simply win their readers' respect for their different point of view. Often, however, all that can be done is to sharpen the differences. Position papers written in these circumstances tend to be more contentious than compromising.

Purpose and audience are thus closely linked when you write a position paper. In defining your purpose and developing an effective argumentative strategy, you need also to define your readers clearly: where they stand on the issue—whether they oppose your position, are undecided, or basically agree with you—and also how they think about the issue—for example, whether they see it as a moral issue, an issue of civil liberties, or an issue that affects them personally.

BASIC FEATURES OF POSITION PAPERS

Position papers generally share the following basic features: a well-defined issue, a clear position, a convincing argument, and an appropriate tone.

A Well-defined Issue

Position papers concern controversial issues, matters on which people disagree. The issue may arise from a particular occasion or be part of an ongoing debate. In either case, the writer must clearly explain the issue.

Donella Meadows can assume that virtually all of her readers will be familiar with the issue on which she focuses, because it involves the popular media. Nevertheless, she reminds them that many people equate call-in talk shows with informed democratic debate, a view with which she disagrees.

In contrast, William K. Kilpatrick cannot assume that his readers will be familiar with the "decision-making" approach adopted by educators over the last twenty-five years as a primary way of presenting ethics in the classroom. Therefore, in order to argue against it, he must define the approach and describe in some detail what he sees as its consequences.

In addition to establishing that the issue exists, a writer needs to define it for the writing purpose. Defining an issue means saying what kind of issue it is. For instance, Amitai Etzioni defines the issue of hate speech in terms of what is "civil," rather than in terms of the right to free expression as many of his readers will. Meadows suggests that the level of public discussion and debate in the United States, as evidenced by call-in talk shows, is an issue of fundamental importance to a democratic society. Kilpatrick defines the issue of how values should be taught not in the narrow terms of educational methodology but broadly, in terms of the effect the method has on society as a whole. Sometimes, defining the issue also involves marking its boundaries. Jessica Statsky, for example, limits the organized team sports she is talking about to those sponsored by parents outside schools for children of certain ages.

A Clear Position

In addition to defining the issue, the essay should also clearly indicate the writer's position. Writers may qualify their claims to accommodate strong opposing arguments, but they should avoid vagueness or indecision.

Very often writers declare their position in a thesis statement early in the essay. The advantage of this strategy is that it lets the audience know right away where the writer stands. Statsky states her thesis explicitly in the opening paragraph and sets forth her reasons at the end of the second paragraph. Meadows states her thesis in paragraph 4, after a brief introduction that defines the viewpoint with which she disagrees; Kilpatrick states his thesis in paragraph 3, after giving a graphic example of the consequences of the "failed approach" he argues against.

For more about making claims, see pp. 534–38. For more about the thesis statement, see pp. 466–68.

The thesis may also appear later in the essay. Postponing the thesis is particularly appropriate when the writer wants to weigh the pros and cons before announcing his or her position. Etzioni does this, agreeing first with arguments against any limit on free expression but ultimately criticizing people who hold that position for ignoring the pain and humiliation suffered by victims of hate speech; not until the final three paragraphs does he present his own position in detail.

A Convincing Argument

A position paper cannot merely assert a writer's views. To convince readers, writers must provide sound reasoning and solid evidence in support of their claims. They must also anticipate possible opposing arguments and either accommodate or refute them.

Sound Reasoning and Solid Evidence. To be sure that readers will be able to follow an argument, the main points supporting a claim should be not only stated clearly but also explained and fully developed. For example, in arguing that call-in talk shows do not represent true democratic debate, Meadows points out that, like town meetings, they are dominated by "the loudest mouths and most made-up minds," so they can never be truly representative; that "the power isn't with the people, it's with the moderator," who actually controls the terms of the debate; that commercial considerations mean the only issues discussed are those that can be defined in the very simplest terms. Moreover, she argues, such talk shows have little value in terms of public discussion because the participants are more interested in "ridiculing the opposition" than in "finding the truth." Readers may or may not be convinced by this argument, but by explaining and developing it fully, Meadows makes sure that they understand her reasoning.

For guidance on finding published sources, see Chapter 21.

A writer can cite various kinds of evidence in support of a position, including anecdotes, authorities, and statistics.

Anecdotes are used to bolster and to illustrate an argument. Kilpatrick cites an outrageous example of teenage violence and moral indifference as a graphic illustration of his argument.

Testimony from authorities—people especially knowledgeable about the issue—also enhances the credibility of an argument. Statsky cites many authorities, including professors, reporters, physicians, coaches, and parents. As most writer do, she identifies these authorities by giving their credentials.

For more on these and other kinds of evidence, see pp. 538–46.

Statistics are another common kind of evidence. Statsky cites statistics to demonstrate that a very high proportion of children—between 80 and 90 percent—drop out of organized sports by the time they enter their teens. She wisely indicates the source of these statistics, a professor at the University of Illinois, because knowledgeable readers tend to be skeptical of statistics that are not attributed to a source.

Counterarguing. In addition to presenting reasons and evidence, a writer may also need to acknowledge opposing points of view and often to accommodate or refute them. Accommodating an opposing argument basically involves admitting that it has validity and qualifying one's own view to account for it. Refuting an opposing argument means trying to show how it is wrong.

Etzioni offers a good example of a writer accommodating other viewpoints: while stating explicitly that he sees no value in legal restrictions on free speech, he also shows that he is sympathetic to the victims of hate speech and their proponents, many of whom advocate such restrictions. Further, he offers an alternative approach to dealing with hate speech that he believes can eliminate it more effectively than can legal restrictions.

For a discussion of anticipating opposing arguments, see pp. 550–52.

Statsky, on the other hand, explicitly acknowledges and then refutes the argument that competitive sports are good for young children because they need to learn to live in a competitive world. First, she suggests, young people will have time to learn competitive skills as teenagers when they are more ready to compete; and second, the ability to cooperate is equally important for success and can be fostered by team sports in which winning isn't the primary goal.

An Appropriate Tone

Position papers often concern highly controversial issues about which writers—and readers—feel very strongly. The challenge for writers, therefore, is to find a tone that adequately expresses their feelings without shutting down communication altogether. Ideally, writers gain readers' confidence and respect both by the way they reason and by the language they use.

Meadows, for example, writes quite informally and colloquially; she establishes a bond with readers who enjoy call-in talk shows by saying that she herself is a "talk-show junkie," before going on to suggest the limitations of such broadcasts.

Kilpatrick assumes a more passionate tone; he is clearly angered by what he sees as "a failed system of education that eschews teaching children the traditional moral values that bind Americans together as a society and a culture," and even readers who disagree with his position are likely to respect his concern. Some readers may react negatively, however, to buzzwords such as *traditional moral values*. As terms associated with particular ideologies, buzzwords (*imperialist, secular humanism,* and *politically correct* are other examples) can establish common ground with sympathetic readers, but they cannot be counted on to convince those who are not already sympathetic. In fact, they may serve primarily to widen the differences between the writer's position and opposing positions.

Etzioni and Statsky strike a tone that is more formal than Meadows's and more restrained than Kilpatrick's. Such a tone is common to much academic argument.

Guide to Writing

THE WRITING ASSIGNMENT

Write a position paper on a controversial issue. Examine the issue critically, take a position, and develop a reasoned argument in support of your position.

INVENTION AND RESEARCH

At this point you need to choose and explore an issue, consider your purpose and audience, formulate your thesis, test your choice, develop your reasoning, and anticipate readers' concerns.

Choosing an Issue

You might set a timer and brainstorm your list on a computer with the monitor brightness turned all the way down. Enter as many possibilities as you can in ten minutes. Then, turn the brightness up, be sure all the items make sense, and print out a copy to make notes on.

Writing a position paper offers an opportunity to think deeply about an important issue. Following are some activities that can help you choose a promising issue and that may suggest ways to begin thinking about it.

Listing Issues.   Begin by making a list of issues you might write about. Put them in the form of questions, like the following examples. Make the list as long as you can. Include both issues on which you already have ideas and ones you do not know much about but would like to explore further.

- Should drug testing be required in sports and industry?
- Should school boards be able to ban books from school libraries?
- Should the primary purpose of a college education be job preparation?
- Should parents of teenagers have to give permission for their children to get contraceptives or abortions?
- Should schools attempt to teach spiritual and moral values?
- Should undercover police officers be permitted to pose as high school students in order to identify sellers and users of drugs?
- Should extended training in music performance or art making (drawing, painting, sculpting) be required of all high school students?
- Should college admission be based solely on academic achievement?

- Since fraternity hazing practices have caused injuries and even deaths, should fraternities be banned from college campuses?
- Should women serve in combat positions in the military?
- Should public schools require students to perform community service as a condition of graduation?

Choosing an Intriguing Issue. Select an issue from your list that seems especially interesting, one that you would like to know more about. It should be an issue about which people disagree.

Your choice may be influenced by whether you have time for research or whether your instructor requires it. You would have to research issues like affirmative action programs fairly extensively before you could adequately define a position and argue it well. Such issues, which have been debated for years and written about repeatedly, make excellent topics for extended research projects. Other issues, like whether warning labels should be put on potentially offensive recordings, may be approached more confidently from personal experience and limited research. Still other topics may be more suitable if your time is limited or your instructor wants you to argue a position without doing research, topics like separate college organizations for African-American, Asian, and Latino students or special academic assistance for athletes. One possibility is to write on an issue currently affecting your community or college. You could define and explore fully issues like these with classmates or friends; and, with care, you could identify a wide range of opposing arguments.

Exploring the Issue

To understand the issue and the rhetorical situation, you will need to define the issue, examine the pros and cons, and decide on your position.

Defining the Issue. To begin thinking about the issue, write for about five minutes explaining how you understand it. If you feel strongly about the issue, briefly state why, but don't present your argument at this time. Focus on defining what you think the issue is. Who cares about it, and why? How does the issue affect different people? What's at stake? What kind of issue is it—personal, political, economic, moral? Describe its features, scope, and history.

Refer to Chapter 20 for advice on interviewing an expert or surveying opinion and to Chapter 21 for guidelines on doing library research.

Doing Research. If you do not know very much about the issue or the various views on it, do some research before continuing. You can gather information by talking to others or by reading what others have written.

If you do not have time for research but do not feel confident that you know enough about your topic to write a thoughtful essay, you should consider another subject, one about which you are better informed. Return to your list of possible issues and start over again.

On p. 586 is a list of sources representing particular viewpoints.

Jessica Statsky's pro/con chart appears on pp. 247–48.

Set up your word processor to create parallel columns if you wish to save your pro/con chart to a computer file.

Determining the Pros and Cons.   Begin by dividing a page into two columns. Write the word *Pro* at the top of the left-hand column and *Con* at the top of the right-hand column. Then, in the appropriate column, list the reasons on each side of the issue. You do not have to find a con reason for every pro, and vice versa. Try to be as thorough as you can now, even if you find later that you need to do research.

Deciding on a Tentative Position.   Once you have examined the pros and cons of an issue, state the position you now take on it. This is a tentative position, liable to change as you develop your ideas and learn more about the issue.

Considering Your Purpose and Audience

Now that you've taken a tentative position, you are ready to consider your purpose and audience. Write a couple of paragraphs, identifying your readers, clarifying your purpose, and developing an argumentative strategy. Consider the following questions:

- What do I expect my readers to think and feel about the issue?
- What basic values or assumptions about the issue do we share? What fundamental differences in worldview or experience keeps us from agreeing?
- What kinds of evidence about this issue—facts, expert opinion, firsthand experience, and so on—are they likely to find convincing?
- Given the answers to the previous questions, what argumentative strategy should I adopt?

Consider several different ways of appealing to your readers. By considering various strategies now, you prepare yourself to make thoughtful decisions later.

Stating Your Thesis

Write a sentence or two stating your thesis. Choose your words carefully. Try to make your position clear and assertive, stated neither too timidly nor bombastically.

You will have ample opportunity to revise your thesis as you learn more about the issue and develop your argument. Stating it now, even tentatively, will help you to focus the rest of your invention and planning.

Testing Your Choice

This is a good time to evaluate whether or not you should proceed with this particular issue. To make this decision, ask yourself the following questions:

- Does this topic really interest me? Have I begun to understand the issue and to formulate my own view?
- Do I know enough about it now to plan and write my essay, or can I learn what I need to know in the time I have remaining?
- Is the topic manageable within my time and space limits?

■ Do I have a good sense of how others view this issue and how I might address my readers?

As you explore the issue further and develop your argument, you will want to reconsider these questions. If at any point you decide that you cannot answer them affirmatively, you may want to choose a different issue.

For Group Inquiry

You might find it useful at this point to get together with two or three other students and run your chosen topics by one another. Assess the group's interest in the issue you've chosen to write about, and invite their advice about whether it sounds promising. Does it seem likely to lead to a paper they would care to read? Your purpose is to decide whether you have chosen a good issue to write about and thus can proceed confidently to develop your ideas.

Developing Your Reasoning

To construct a convincing argument, you should list reasons for your position, choose the strongest ones, and develop them fully.

If you saved your pro/con chart to a computer file, you might copy your "pro" column to a new document to develop your reasons and your "con" column to a second document to consider readers' concerns.

Listing Reasons.   Review your pro/con chart and then write down every plausible reason you could give to convince readers that *your* position on this issue should be taken seriously. It might help to think of your reasons as *because* or *that* clauses attached to your thesis statement. For example, "My position is X because . . . " or "A reason I think X is that. . . . "

Choosing the Strongest Reasons.   Review your list with your readers in mind. Put a check by the reasons that would carry the most weight with them and are most important to you. If none of your reasons seems very strong, you might need to reconsider your position, do some more research, or even pick another topic.

If you can, save your reasons and your readers' concerns on a word processor. Then, as you begin to draft later, you can call up the file on a second screen and easily transfer specific ideas you want to use in your draft.

Developing Your Best Reasons.   Take your strongest reasons and write for five minutes on each one, explaining it to your readers and providing evidence to support it. You may discover that you need some specific information. Do not stop to locate it now; just make a note about what you need and continue writing. If you decide not to include some of these reasons, you may not need the information after all. Later, before drafting or even when revising your draft, you will be able to follow up and locate any information you still need.

Anticipating Readers' Concerns

This section will help you to anticipate readers' concerns and to decide which ones you will accommodate and which you will refute.

Listing Opposing Arguments.   Begin by listing all the opposing arguments and objections to your argument you can think of. You will almost certainly have discovered some in the process of exploring the pros and cons, and researching the issue. It might also help to write out an imaginary conversation with someone who disagrees with you on the issue.

Accommodating Legitimate Concerns.   Review your list of opposing arguments and objections to your argument, and decide which of them you think you should change your argument to accommodate. Write a few sentences for each one indicating how you will have to qualify your thesis, or change your argument. Also, briefly explain why you are conceding this point.

Refuting Illegitimate Concerns.   Review the list to find opposing arguments and objections to your argument that you can refute. For each one, write for five minutes developing your refutation. Try to explain why you do not find the arguments convincing. They may be irrelevant, only partially true, or not true at all. They may be fallacious: a "straw man" or "*ad hominem*" argument, for example. Or they may simply be based on a totally different and irreconcilable set of assumptions about the rights and responsibilities of individuals and society, for example.

See pp. 552–53 for more on logical fallacies.

If you need to check facts or find some other information, make a note to do so later. It will be most efficient at this point simply to list the points you need to check and to save the research until a later time.

Restating Your Thesis

Now that you have developed your argument, you may want to reformulate your thesis. Consider whether you should change your language to qualify or limit your claim.

PLANNING AND DRAFTING

Before you begin drafting your essay, take some time to review your notes and see what you have, to set goals for your essay, to prepare an outline, and to draft your position paper.

Seeing What You Have

It's a good idea at this point to print out a hard copy of what you have written on a word processor for easier reviewing.

If you have completed all the invention work, you will have accumulated several pages of notes. Review these carefully to see what you might use in your draft. Mark passages that seem especially promising, that show conviction, have vivid writing, contain pointed examples, demonstrate strong reasoning. Note places where you reach out to readers, share their concerns and values, acknowledge their feelings, and modify your own views to accommodate theirs.

If your invention notes are skimpy, you may not have given enough thought to the issue or know enough at this time to write a convincing essay about it. You have several alternatives. You can do more invention and research. You can go on to write a draft, hoping that you will get more ideas as you write. Or you can go back and choose a new topic.

For more on general invention activities, see pp. 430–41.

Setting Goals

Experienced writers set overall goals for themselves before drafting their essays. They decide what they will try to achieve and how they will go about it. To help you set realistic goals, consider the following questions now. You may also find it helpful to return to some of these questions as you outline and draft your essay.

Your Purpose and Audience

- What can I realistically hope to accomplish by addressing these particular readers? Are they deeply committed to their opinions? Should I try, as Meadows does, to make readers see that their view is mistaken? Should I try to change readers' way of thinking about the issue, as Etzioni does?

- Can I address readers' special concerns, acknowledge the legitimacy of their feelings, or define the issue in terms that appeal to common values and assumptions? Shall I appeal, as Kilpatrick does, to readers' sense of moral outrage? Can I demonstrate, as Etzioni does, that I am aware of the civil issues involved?

- Can I draw on any common experiences that relate to this issue? Could I share my own experience, as Meadows does?

The Beginning

- How can I engage readers' attention immediately? Should I begin with a shocking anecdote, as Kilpatrick does, or a surprising example, like Etzioni? Should I use a rhetorical question or startling statistics to draw readers into the argument?

- How much do I need to explain about the controversy and define the terms before proceeding with my argument? Should I summarize both sides, as Etzioni does? Should I limit the issue, as Statsky does?

Your Argument

- If I have more than one reason, how should I order the reasons? From strongest to weakest? From the most to the least predictable? From simplest to most complex? Can I sequence them logically, so that one leads inevitably to the next?

- Which objections to my argument and opposing arguments should I mention, if any? Shall I acknowledge and refute them all, as Meadows does? Shall I focus, as Statsky does, on two? What would I gain from conceding something? What would I lose?

The Ending

- How can I conclude my argument effectively? Should I repeat my thesis, as Statsky does? Shall I look to the future, as Meadows does, or urge readers to take action, as Kilpatrick does?

- Can I end on a note of agreement by reminding readers of the common concerns and values we share?

Outlining

Outlining on a word processor makes it easy to experiment with different ways of ordering reasons, evidence, opposing arguments, and refutations.

Some position papers include everything—an extended definition of the issue, an elaborate argument with multiple reasons and evidence, and several opposing arguments, some of which are accommodated while others are refuted. Your essay may not be so complicated, but you will still have to decide how to arrange the different parts. Once you have considered strategies for beginning and ending your essay and determined how you might order your reasons, consider the organization carefully and prepare a tentative outline.

Here is how Statsky organized her position paper on children's competitive sports:

identifies issue, states thesis, and gives reasons

explains and supports reason 1—competing at too early an age is developmentally inappropriate and may be harmful physically

explains and supports reason 2—competing at too early an age also may be harmful psychologically

refutes opposing argument—that children need to learn to live in a competitive world—by arguing that childhood is just the training period, not the real thing

explains and supports reason 3—because competitive sports are so selective, very few children participate and reap the potential benefits

explains and supports reason 4—parents and coaches sometimes use children's sports to act out their own fantasies in ways harmful to the children

refutes opposing argument—that children need to learn to live in a competitive world—by arguing that cooperation ought to be emphasized because it is as important to society as is competition

concludes by reasserting the position and framing the essay

However you choose to arrange your essay, making an outline before drafting will help you to get started. An outline presents a route, neither the only one nor necessarily the best, but one that will get you going in the right direction.

Drafting

If you can shift between screens, you might call up invention material on an alternate screen as you draft on the main screen, shifting back and forth to cut and paste invention material into your draft.

With an outline and goals as your guide, begin drafting your essay. As you draft, remember the importance of audience in a position paper. Keep your audience in mind by writing to a particular (real or imaginary) reader, thinking of your writing as a transcript of what you would say to this person. Also keep in mind your purpose in addressing this particular reader. Remember that establishing common ground depends on acknowledging the intelligence, experience, values, and concerns of your readers.

Use your outline to guide your drafting, but do not worry if you diverge from your original plan. Writing sometimes has a logic of its own that carries the writer along. As you pick up momentum, you may leave the outline behind. If you get stuck, refer to it again. You might want to review the general advice on drafting on pp. 12–14.

GETTING CRITICAL COMMENTS

Now is the time for your draft to get a good critical reading. Your instructor may arrange such a reading as part of your course work; otherwise, you can ask a classmate, friend, or family member to read it over. If your school has a writing center, you might ask a tutor there to read and comment on your draft. The guidelines in this section are designed to be used by *anyone* reviewing a position paper. (If you are unable to have someone else review your draft, turn ahead to the Revision section on pp. 243–46 for help reading your own draft with a critical eye.)

In order to provide focused, helpful comments, your reader must know your intended purpose and audience. Briefly write out this information at the top of your draft.

Audience. To whom are you directing your argument? What do you assume they already know and think about this issue?

Purpose. What effect can you reasonably expect your argument to have on these particular readers? If they are unlikely to adopt your position, what do you want them to know about the issue?

Reading with a Critical Eye

Reading a draft critically means reading it more than once, first to get a general impression and then to analyze its basic features.

See Chapter 12 for a review of critical reading strategies.

Reading for a First Impression. Read the essay through quickly to get a sense of its argument. Then, write a few sentences describing your initial reaction. Did you understand the writer's position? Indicate whether the argument bolstered your own opinion, made you reconsider or defend your own position, or made you think seriously about the issue for the first time. What did you find most convincing in the essay? Least convincing?

See pp. 231–34 to review the basic features.

Reading to Analyze. Read now to evaluate the argument, focusing on basic features of writing a position paper.

Is the Issue Well-defined?

Check to see how the issue is defined. Indicate if there is enough information to understand the issue and why it is important. What questions still need to be answered? Determine whether the issue, as it is stated, is even arguable. For example, does it seem to be a question of fact or is it basically a matter of faith—and therefore not worth arguing about?

Is the Thesis Clear?

Find the clearest statement of the thesis, and write it down or underline it. Given the writer's description of the readers and purpose, how appropriate are the terms of the thesis? Indicate if you think the thesis should be qualified.

Is the Argument Supported by Convincing Reasons and Evidence?

Find the reasons given to support the thesis, and number them in the margin: Reason 1, Reason 2, and so on. Then consider each reason in turn, looking at how it is explained and supported. Point to any reasons that need to be explained more clearly or supported more convincingly. Have any important reasons been left out or any weak ones overemphasized? Note any supporting evidence that seems weak as well as places where more evidence is needed.

See pp. 552–53 for more on logical fallacies and faulty reasoning.

Look for faulty reasoning. Note any sweeping generalizations (broad statements asserted without support). Indicate if the issue has been oversimplified or if either/or reasoning (unfairly limiting the argument to only two alternatives) is being used.

How Are Objections and Opposing Arguments Handled?

Look for places where other positions on this issue are mentioned, and specifically places where objections are acknowledged and opposing arguments entertained. Note any areas of potential agreement that could be emphasized and any concessions that need to be made. Check for any attempts to refute arguments, and suggest, if you can, how the refutation could be strengthened.

Again, look for faulty reasoning. Point out any personal attacks on opponents rather than on their reasoning. Have only the weakest objections or opposing arguments been acknowledged, thus misrepresenting the opposition?

Is the Tone Appropriate?

What words would you use to describe the tone of this essay—bitter, or sarcastic, for example? Given the writer's description of the purpose and audience, how appropriate does this tone seem to you? Point to places in the essay where you could suggest word changes that might make the tone more effective.

Is the Organization Effective?

Look at the beginning and ending to evaluate their effectiveness and, if necessary, suggest how they might be made stronger. In particular, note whether the beginning gives a preview of the argument or whether one is needed. Review the sequence in which the reasons and any opposing arguments are presented to see if they should be reordered. Check to see if any evidence is misplaced. Point to effective uses of transitions, summaries, and topic sentences and places where they could be added.

What Final Thoughts Do You Have?

What is the strongest part of the argument? What is the weakest part, most in need of further work?

REVISING AND EDITING

This section will help you identify problems in your draft and then to revise and edit to solve the problems.

Identifying
Problems

To discover problems in your draft, you need to read it objectively, analyze its basic features, and study any comments you've received from others.

Getting an Overview.   Consider the draft as a whole, trying to see it objectively. It may help to do so in two steps:

Reread. If at all possible, put the draft aside for a day or two before rereading it. When you do, start by reconsidering your purpose. Then read the draft straight through, trying to see it as your intended readers will.

Outline. Quickly outline the draft to see where the issue is defined, the position is stated, each reason is explained and supported, and any opposing arguments are refuted.

Even if your essay is saved to a computer file, reread from a hard copy, preferably draft quality. Onscreen or as letter-quality hard copy, a paper can look more "finished" than it really is. Add notes to yourself and revisions as you read through the draft.

Charting a Plan for Revision.   You may want to use a chart like the one that follows to keep track of the work you need to do as you revise. The left-hand column lists the basic features of position papers; as you analyze your draft and study any comments from other readers, use the right-hand column for noting any problems to solve.

Basic Features	*Problems to Solve*
Definition of the Issue	
Thesis Statement	
Reasons and Evidence	
Counterarguments	
Tone	
Organization	

Analyzing the Basic Features of Your Draft.   Turn now to the questions for analyzing a draft on pp. 241–42. Following these guidelines, note the specific problems you need to solve on the chart above.

Studying Critical Comments.   Review any comments you've gotten from other readers, and add to the chart any that you intend to act on. Try not to react defensively to these comments; by letting you see how other readers respond to your draft, they provide invaluable information about how you might improve it.

Solving the Problems

Having identified problems in your draft, you now need to figure out solutions and—most important of all—to carry them out. Following are some suggestions on how you might respond to some of the problems common to writing position papers.

Definition of the Issue

Before revising using a word processor, copy your original draft to a second file. Then, should you change your mind about material you delete while revising, it will still be available to you.

- If the essay does not provide enough information about the issue for a reader to understand it, add more. Consider adding examples, quoting authorities, or simply explaining the issue further.
- If the issue might strike readers as unimportant, state explicitly why you think it is important and why, in your view, they should think so too. Try to think of an anecdote that would demonstrate its importance.

Thesis Statement

- If readers might not find or recognize your thesis, you may need to rewrite your thesis statement to make it clearer. If your thesis is implied but not directly expressed, consider stating it explicitly so as to avoid misunderstanding.
- If your thesis is not appropriately qualified to account for exceptions or strong objections to your argument, modify it by limiting its scope.

Reasons and Evidence

- If readers might have difficulty separating your reasons, announce them more explicitly.
- If any of your reasons seem vague or weak, either delete them or explain them more fully. Consider telling an anecdote or making a comparison or contrast to show how this reason relates to the others.
- If your evidence seems weak or scanty, review your invention notes or do some more research to gather additional facts, statistics, or quotations from authorities.
- If you use any sweeping generalizations, try to be more specific and to support your assertions with evidence and examples.
- If you have oversimplified the argument, for example by using either/or reasoning, add some qualifying language that shows you are aware of the issue's true complexity.

Counterarguing

- If you can make any concessions to opposing views, consider doing so. Try to find common ground with readers by acknowledging the legitimacy of their concerns. Show readers where you share their values, interests, and assumptions.
- If your refutation of an objection seems unconvincing, try to strengthen it. Avoid attacking your opponents. Instead, provide solid evidence—

known authorities, facts and statistics from reputable sources—to convince readers that you can argue objectively.

■ If you have ignored strong, opposing arguments, take account of them. If you cannot refute them, you might have to acknowledge their legitimacy.

Tone

■ If the tone seems inappropriate, consider altering your language. Think some more about your feelings and your purpose and audience. You may need to express your strong feelings about the issue more directly or indicate why you feel as you do. If you expect readers to dismiss your concerns, you might try a more combative or confrontational style—forcefully refuting their arguments. If you are trying to build a bridge of shared concerns, consider personalizing your writing by using "I" or a personal anecdote.

Organization

See Chapter 13 for advice about cueing readers so they can follow your argument.

■ If the beginning seems weak or dull, consider opening with a striking anecdote or surprising quotation.

■ If readers might have trouble following your argument, consider adding a brief forecast of your main points at the beginning of your essay.

■ If the reasons and refutations are not logically arranged, reorder them. Consider announcing each reason and refutation more explicitly.

When you use your word processor's cut-and-paste or block-and-move functions to shift material around, make sure that transitions are revised so that material fits in its new spot.

■ If any evidence does not closely follow the point it is intended to support, move it.

■ If the ending seems weak or vague, search your invention notes for a strong quotation or add language that will reach out to readers.

Editing and Proofreading

Thus far you have not worried much about grammar or style. Now, however, you need to take the time to check for errors in usage, punctuation, and mechanics—and also to consider matters of style. Research has identified several errors that are especially common in writing that explains concepts; following are some brief guidelines that can help you check and edit your draft for these errors.

When you use your word processor's spell check function to aid in proofreading for spelling, keep in mind that it will not find all misspellings, particularly misused homonyms (such as there, their, and they're), typos that are themselves words (such as fro for for), and many proper

Checking for Commas before Coordinating Conjunctions That Link Independent Clauses. An independent clause is a group of words that can stand alone as a complete sentence. Writers often join two or more such clauses with coordinating conjunctions (*and, but, for, or, nor, so,* or *yet*) in order to link related ideas in one sentence. Look at one example from Jessica Statsky's essay:

Winning and losing may be an inevitable part of adult life, but they should not be part of childhood.

nouns and specialized terms. Proofread these carefully yourself, using hard copy and a dictionary if necessary. Also proofread for words that should have been deleted when you edited a sentence.

In this sentence, Statsky links two ideas: (1) that winning and losing may be part of adult life, and (2) that they should not be part of childhood. Writing that takes a position often joins ideas in this way, as writers set forth evidence or examples in support of their claims.

When joining independent clauses in this way, you should use a comma before the coordinating conjunction so that readers easily see where one idea stops and the other starts.

▶ The new immigration laws will bring in more skilled people,but their presence will take jobs away from other Americans.

▶ Sexually transmitted diseases are widespread, and many students are sexually active.

Do not use a comma, however, when the coordinating conjunction joins words that are not independent clauses.

▶ Newspaper reporters have visited pharmacies/and observed pharmacists selling steroids illegally.

▶ We need people with special talents/and diverse skills to make the United States a stronger nation.

Checking the Punctuation of Conjunctive Adverbs.　The reasoning required in taking a position seems to invite the use of conjunctive adverbs (*consequently, furthermore, however, moreover, therefore, thus,* etc.) to connect sentences and clauses. Conjunctive adverbs that open a sentence should be followed by a comma.

▶ Consequently,many local governments have banned smoking.

▶ Therefore,talented nurses will leave the profession because of poor working conditions and low salaries.

If a conjunctive adverb joins two independent clauses, it must be preceded by a semicolon and followed by a comma.

▶ The recent vote on increasing student fees produced a disappointing turnout; moreover,the presence of campaign literature on ballot tables violated voting procedures.

▶ Children watching television recognize violence but not its intention; thus,they become desensitized to violence.

Conjunctive adverbs that fall in the middle of an independent clause are set off with commas.

▶ Due to trade restrictions, however, sales of Japanese cars did not surpass sales of domestic cars.

A Common ESL Problem.   Because the distinctions in meaning among some common conjunctive adverbs are subtle, nonnative speakers often have difficulty using them accurately. The difference between *however* and *nevertheless*, for example, is small; each is used to introduce statements that contrast with what precedes it. *Nevertheless* emphasizes the contrast, whereas *however* softens it. You should check usage of such terms in an English dictionary rather than a bilingual one. *The American Heritage Dictionary of the English Language* has special usage notes to help distinguish frequently confused words.

A Writer at Work

EXPLORING THE ISSUE

Jessica Statsky, whose revised essay appears on pp. 226–29, began exploring her chosen issue by making a pro/con chart. Since she opposes competitive sports programs for young children, the items on the Con side of the chart identify the reasons supporting her position, while the items on the Pro side anticipate the reasons of those who support such programs. At the bottom of each column she briefly identifies the groups of people who would likely hold opposing views on the issue.

PRO	CON
--competition teaches the child how to succeed in later life	--teaches the child to be vengeful, burns the child out
--when a child is allowed to feel the thrill of winning, he or she experiences a boost in self-esteem	--causes the child depression when he or she loses and does not please the parents and/or coach
--allows children to prove to themselves and others their capabilities	--takes away the spontaneous fun of sports and free playing
--gives the child an incentive to excel	--causes children unnecessary physical strain (not good for growing kids to be overworking their bodies in stressful and unusual ways)

```
              PRO                        CON
People supporting this      --instills characteristics
position would include        and values that are based
coaches and parents who       on negative attitudes
favor discipline and value  --when major stress is
competition.                  placed on winning, the
                              development of each
                              child's potential is made
                              less important
                            --parents and coaches
                              indulge their own crazy
                              ideas about winning and
                              ignore best interests of
                              children

                            People supporting this
                            position might include
                            sports psychologists, some
                            doctors who treat injured
                            children, and parents who
                            want to protect their
                            children from too much
                            stress and competition.
                            Many sports reporters who
                            have covered Little League
                            or Peewee Football also
                            seem to support this
                            position
```

Library research was essential for Statsky's project. She was surprised to find a number of books devoted to children's sports and pleased to locate several articles readily in indexes to the *New York Times* and the *Los Angeles Times*. Surveying and selecting research furthered her understanding of the purpose and audience for her essay. Here is what she wrote in her notes on considering purpose and audience:

```
I think I will write mainly to parents who are consider-
ing letting their children get involved in competitive
sports and to those whose children are already on teams
and who don't know about the possible dangers. Parents
who are really into competition and winning probably
couldn't be swayed by my arguments anyway. I don't know
how to reach coaches (but aren't they parents?) or league
organizers. I'll tell parents some horror stories and
```

also present solid evidence from psychologists that competitive sports can really harm children under the age of
twelve. I think you'll be impressed with this scientific
evidence.

    I share with parents one important value: the best
interests of children. Competition really works against
children's best interests. Maybe parents' magazines
(don't know of any specific ones) publish essays like
mine.

Thinking Critically about What You've Learned

Now that you've read and discussed several essays taking a position
and written one of your own, it's a good time to think critically about
what you've learned. What problems did you encounter as you were
writing and how did you solve them? How did the position papers you
read influence your own writing? How do position papers in general
reflect cultural attitudes about public debate and controversy?

REFLECTING ON YOUR WRITING

To reflect on what you've learned about writing an essay taking a position, first gather all of your writing—invention, planning notes,
drafts and critical comments, revision plan and final revision. Review
these as you complete the following writing task.

- Identify one writing problem you encountered as you worked on
  the essay. Don't be concerned with general writing problems; focus on a problem that specifically involves planning and writing a
  position paper. For example: Did you puzzle over how to convince
  your readers that the issue is important? Did you have trouble asserting your position forcefully while acknowledging other points
  of view? Was it difficult to refute any objection readers might
  raise?
- At what stage in the process did you first recognize the problem?
  Was it, for example, when you were thinking about your readers'
  attitudes, trying to decide how to sequence your ideas, or getting
  critical comments on a draft? What called the problem to your attention? If you didn't become aware of it until rather late in the
  process, can you now see hints of it in your invention writings or
  early drafting? If so, where specifically?
- Reflect on how you tried to solve the problem. Did you try to reword, reorganize, or simply cut the part that was problematic? Did
  you reread your invention writing? Did you need to do more invention or research? Did you seek advice from a classmate or your
  instructor?

■ Now, write a page or so explaining what the problem was, how you discovered it, and how you went about solving it. Be specific by quoting from your invention writing, drafts, others' critical comments, your own revision plan, and your final revision. Show the various changes your writing and thinking underwent. If you're still uncertain about your solution, say so. The point is not to prove that you've solved the problem but to show what you've learned about solving problems as you write.

REVIEWING WHAT YOU LEARNED
FROM READING

The position papers you've read have almost certainly influenced the one you wrote. For example, selections in this chapter may have helped you decide that you needed to do some library research before you could argue responsibly for your position, that you could use personal anecdote as part of your supporting evidence, or that you should try to anticipate readers' objections and questions. Take time now to reflect on the possible influences your reading has had on your thinking and writing.

■ Review the readings in this chapter as well as the final draft of your own essay. Did any of the position papers in the chapter (or by your classmates) influence your choice of topic or argumentative strategy? For example, consider whether any reading influenced how you decided to use authorities, refute objections, or establish common ground. In deciding what tone to adopt—whether to be contentious or accommodating to different points of view— did you think of how others you respect debate this kind of issue? Consider also debates you've seen recently in newspapers and magazines or heard on television or radio. How have these examples of arguing influenced your writing?

■ Write a page or so explaining to your instructor how your writing has been influenced by others. You may focus on a single influence or discuss how you used different models to develop your own style of taking a position. Give examples comparing what you did in your essay and what you've seen others do.

CONSIDERING THE SOCIAL DIMENSIONS
OF POSITION PAPERS

Taking positions on important social and political issues is essential in a democracy. Doing so gives each of us a voice. Instead of remaining silent and on the margins, we can enter the ongoing debate. We can affect others, perhaps convincing them to change their minds or at least to take a different point of view seriously. Airing our differences also allows us to live together in relative peace. Instead of brawling with each other at school board meetings, in legislative halls, on street corners, or in the classroom, we argue. Voices may be raised in anger and frustration, differences may seem insurmountable, but at least no one is physically hurt and, with luck, common ground can be found.

Presenting an argument that takes account of opposing viewpoints also influences the way we think, encouraging us to consider issues rationally, to find reasons for our own opinions and to understand the reasons behind opposing opinions. Finding such reasons involves examining our assumptions—the fundamental ideas we have about how things are or should be—as well as the assumptions of others (which may be the same as our own or very different). Thinking rationally also requires us to find evidence that grounds our opinions in something other than belief—in facts that can be verified, in the authority of experts, in experiences with which others can identify. Finally, thinking rationally requires us to look seriously at objections to our argument. Knowing we must defend our position, we are presumably more likely to take positions that are defensible. Ideally, then, writing position papers fosters the kind of reasonable debate that enables a diverse society like ours to hold together.

Yet, while this rational way of arguing about controversial social issues is highly valued in our society, questions have been raised in recent years concerning its presumed objectivity, its power to exclude people, and its suppression of dissent.

The Illusion of Objectivity. As a society, we value reasoned argument, in part, because we think it enables us to transcend personal bias and narrow self-interest—in other words, to be objective. Recently, however, it has been argued that objectivity itself is only an illusion, that it is impossible to escape one's history and culture to achieve some mythical, purely "objective" stance. Race, nationality, class, gender, religion, region, schooling, access to the media—all these influence who we are and what we believe. Everything we learn and know, as well as *how* we learn and know, derives from individual experience and perception. Consequently, according to this viewpoint, the fact that we are able to give objective-*sounding* reasons for our opinions doesn't guarantee they are unbiased or even reasonable: what appears to be rational thought may be merely rationalization, a way of justifying fundamentally intuitive personal convictions. In other words, supporting a position with a "well-reasoned" argument may simply be a game we play to trick others—and often ourselves—into believing that we are open-minded and our opinions rational.

Exclusion from Power. A second critique of the kind of argumentation we've presented in this chapter is that, by valuing it so highly, our society privileges one mode of thinking and presenting ideas over all others. Since skill at rational argument is essential to success in college and access to most of the professions that confer status, money, and power in our society, those whose educational options, cultural traditions, or perhaps even natural ability keep them from mastering logical argumentation are clearly at a disadvantage. Even when they possess other important creative or technical abilities, they may well be excluded from the corridors of power because they cannot participate in rational debate.

Suppressing Dissent. Finally, some critics argue that our society privileges reasoned argument over other modes of discourse in dealing with social issues in order to control dissent. Instead of expressing what may be legitimate outrage and inciting public concern through passionate language, dissenters are urged to be dispassionate and reasonable. They may even be encouraged to reach common ground with those whose views they find repugnant for the sake of peaceful compromise. While it may help to prevent violent confrontation, this emphasis on reasoned argument may also prevent an honest and open exchange of differences. In the end, this way of arguing may serve to maintain the status quo by silencing the more radical voices within the community.

For Discussion

Following are some questions to help you consider the social dimensions of taking a position. As you read and, perhaps, discuss these questions in class, note down your thoughts and reactions. Then, write a page or so for your instructor presenting your ideas about the role writing that takes a position plays in our society.

1. We've said that reasoned position-taking is dominant in our society. Nevertheless, television and radio talk shows like "The Rush Limbaugh Program" and "Crossfire" seem to have replaced calm, reasoned debate with a more contentious, in-your-face style of argumentation. Why do you think this kind of argument is so popular nowadays? How do you respond to Donella Meadows's point that such shows should not be confused with true democratic debate?

2. One critique of reasoned argument is that it pretends to be more objective than it actually is, that the reasons position takers give are really justifications for their personal opinions. How would you respond to this criticism? Do you think reasoned argument should try to be objective? When you were writing your own position paper, were you trying to be objective? Which of your reasons would you now identify as objective-sounding, chosen because you thought your readers would find it convincing, not because you really believed it?

3. We've said that mastering logical argumentation is necessary for success in school, business, and the professions. Why do you think this might be so? How would you respond to the criticism that be

ing required to master this kind of thinking and writing is exclusionary and therefore unfair? Do you believe yourself to be adept at logical thinking?

4. As a writer and reader of position papers, do you think having to take into account opposing points of view encourages people to moderate their views? In writing your own essay, how did you handle opposing views? How much did having to consider them help you clarify or sharpen differences between your position and opposing positions? Did considering opposing views lead you to modify your own?

5. Position papers, of course, differ from actual debate in that the writer represents the opposing views: those who hold these views cannot speak for themselves. When you were planning your own essay and trying to anticipate other points of view, how did you represent what others think? Did you use their words or your own? What difference might it make whose words are used? When you were deciding how to present other views, did you choose the more or less extreme versions? Consider your reasons for making this choice and what difference it might make.

6. Do you think the emphasis on reasoned argument in our society discourages dissent? Might more passionate approaches to social issues be more effective? For example, suppose that Jessica Statsky's argument against competitive children's sports had instead taken the form of a satiric, highly unflattering portrait of the kinds of parents and coaches who push children to compete too early. Do you think that such alternative ways of expressing opinions on social issues are sometimes appropriate? If not, why not? If so, how would you justify them?

■ A college professor writing for a national magazine proposes that since a college education now costs so much, students be given the option of earning a college degree by examination, rather than through attendance and course completion. He gives three reasons readers should take his proposal seriously: it would save resources, contribute to social mobility, and free unconventional students to pursue self-education. Anticipating two of his readers' likely objections, he argues that students should be given the choice of doing without the social interaction and personal development college provides and that an inexpensive screening exam could be devised to identify applicants who seemed unlikely to succeed on the final degree exam. Anticipating readers' predictable reservations that one exam could really assess all that could be learned in four years of college, he outlines a month-long exam testing both general knowledge and competence in a major field and involving written, oral, and practical components. He proposes charging $3,000.00 for the degree exam.

■ For a political science class, a student analyzes the question of presidential terms of office. Citing examples from recent history, she argues that presidents spend the first year of each term getting organized and the fourth year either running for reelection or weakened by their status as a lame duck. Consequently, they are fully productive for only half of their four-year terms.

She proposes limiting presidents to one six-year term, claiming that this change would remedy the problem by giving presidents four or five years to put their programs into effect. She acknowledges that it could make presidents less responsive to the public will, but insists that the system of legislative checks and balances would make that problem unlikely.

■ A newspaper columnist writes about the problem of controlling the spread of AIDS. Since symptoms may take years to appear, she notes, people infected with the AIDS virus unwittingly pass it on to their sexual partners. She discusses three solutions that have been proposed: having only one sexual partner, engaging in safer sexual practices, or notifying and testing the sexual partners of those found to have the disease. She argues that the first solution would solve the problem but may not be feasible, and that the second would not work because safer sexual practices are not absolutely reliable. In support of the third solution—tracing of sexual partners—she argues that tracing has worked to control other diseases and that it should help overcome a major obstacle in controlling AIDS—the widespread but false assumption that heterosexuals are not really at risk.

■ Several students in the predentistry program at a large state university realize how uncertain they are about requirements, procedures, and strategies for applying to dental school. One of them writes a proposal to the head of the program suggesting the need for a handbook for predentistry students. To dramatize that a problem exists and is considered serious by students, he points out the declining rate of admission

Proposing Solutions 7

to dental schools of students in the program and includes an informal survey of current enrollees. He mentions other programs that provide such a pamphlet. Realizing that few faculty members would take time for such a project, he proposes that students do the actual writing and handle the printing and distribution; two faculty members would serve simply as advisers. He asks that the publication costs be borne by the predentistry program, however, pointing out that students would donate their time.

■ A college student who works at a pizzeria notices certain problems caused by rapid turnover of employees. Newcomers often misplace things, forget procedures for cleaning up, and interrupt other employees to ask for help operating the espresso machine. Since the company offers cash awards for ideas for improving procedures or service, the student writes a letter to the owners suggesting ways to reduce these problems. Knowing that rapid turnover is inevitable, she concentrates on procedures for orienting and training new staff.

Proposals serve an important role in a democracy, informing citizens about problems affecting their well-being and also suggesting actions that could be taken to remedy these problems. As the examples to the left demonstrate, people write proposals every day in business, government, education, and the professions. Proposals are a basic ingredient of the world's work.

As a special form of argument, proposals have much in common with position papers, described in Chapter 6. Both analyze a subject and take a definite stand on it. Both give reasons and evidence and acknowledge readers' likely objections or questions. Proposals, however, go further: they urge readers to support a particular policy or take specific action. They argue for a proposed solution to a problem, succeeding or failing by the strength of that argument.

In most disciplines and professions, problem solving is a basic way of thinking. For example, scientists use the scientific method, a systematic form of problem solving; political scientists and sociologists propose solutions to troubling political and social problems; engineers regularly employ problem-solving techniques in building bridges, automobiles, or computers; attorneys find legal precedents to solve their clients' problems; teachers continually make decisions about how to help students with learning problems; counselors devote themselves to helping clients solve personal problems; business owners or managers daily solve problems large and small.

Problem solving depends on a questioning attitude. In addition, it demands imagination and creativity. To solve a problem, you need to see it anew, to look at it from new angles and in new contexts.

Since a proposal tries to convince readers that its way of defining and solving the problem makes sense, proposal writers must be sensitive to readers' needs and expectations. As you plan and draft a proposal, you will want to determine whether your readers are aware of the problem and whether they recognize its seriousness, and you will want to consider their views of any other solutions. Knowing what your readers know, their assumptions and biases, the kinds of arguments likely to appeal to them is a central part of proposal writing.

Writing in Your
Other Courses

As the opening writing scenarios illustrate, college students find occasions both in class and at work to propose solutions to problems. Below are some further examples of college assignments calling for problem-solving skills:

■ *For an economics class:* The *maquiladora* industry along the U.S.-Mexican border provides foreign exchange for Mexico and low-paying jobs for half a million Mexicans, as well as profits for American manufacturers. Yet this innovative binational arrangement has created serious problems on the Mexican side of the border: inadequate housing, health care, and public services; on-the-job injuries; and environmental damage. Study one of these problems, research it, and propose a solution. Address your proposal to the mayor of Nogales, Tijuana, or Juarez.

■ *For a business class:* Take the case of a corporation wishing to install a workstation network but unwilling as yet to give up its mainframe computers. Propose a solution to this problem. Research the possibilities of mainframe-workstation integration, explain the problem carefully, and argue convincingly for your solution. Address your proposal to the CEO of the corporation.

■ *For a biology class:* Apply the principle of circadian rhythm to the problem of jet lag. Explain circadian rhythm, define jet lag in light of it, and speculate about how knowledge of it might help reduce the effects of jet lag. It might help to think of yourself as writing an article for the travel section of a newspaper.

For Group Inquiry

You can readily experience the complexities and possibilities involved in proposing solutions by thinking through a specific problem and trying to come up with a feasible proposal. With two or three other students, form a group and select someone to take notes during your discussion.

■ First, identify two or three problems within your college or community, and select one that you all recognize and agree needs to be solved.

■ Next, consider possible solutions to this problem, and identify one solution that you can all support.

■ Finally, decide on an individual or group who has authority to take action on your proposed solution, and figure out how you would go about convincing this audience (1) that the problem is serious and must be solved and (2) that your proposed solution is feasible and should be supported. Consider carefully what questions this audience might have about your proposal and what objections might be raised.

Before the group separates, reflect on your efforts at proposing a solution to a problem. What surprised or pleased you? What difficulties did you encounter?

Readings

William L. Kibler has earned degrees from the University of Florida and Texas A & M University, where he is presently associate director of the Department of Student Affairs. His many publications on academic integrity include a 1987 coauthored book, *Academic Integrity and Student Development: Legal Issues and Policy Perspectives.* The following proposal appeared in the *Chronicle of Higher Education,* a weekly source of news and opinion read primarily by college administrators and faculty. Kibler's proposal grows out of his belief that cheating in college is not simply another kind of misbehavior to be punished when students are caught at it, but rather a larger moral problem to be addressed by the whole campus in terms of students' personal integrity.

Though Kibler aims his essay at administrators and faculty, he also envisions a central role for students in promoting academic integrity. As you read, notice the role he assigns students, as well as the proposed consequences if they are caught cheating. Would Kibler's proposal reduce cheating?

A COMPREHEN-SIVE PLAN FOR PROMOTING ACADEMIC INTEGRITY
WILLIAM L. KIBLER

Research suggests that students on most, if not all, campuses cheat on their course work and tests. Donald McCabe, associate professor of management at Rutgers University, recently conducted a survey in which 67 percent of the students responding, who attended 31 highly selective colleges and universities, admitted to cheating in college. It is difficult to document whether the problem is increasing, but most experts agree that it is a serious issue affecting all segments of higher education. 1

Cheating, of course, is not a new problem, either in higher education or in society at large. But part of the reason that cheating remains a problem in colleges and universities may be that institutions are treating it as a behavioral aberration rather than as a moral issue. When cheating is discovered, most institutions address only the misbehavior, without requiring the student to confront the moral issues involved in deciding to cheat to achieve a goal. By failing to address those underlying issues, colleges are missing the chance to discuss the importance of integrity. 2

College administrators seem unsure about how to approach the problem. I discovered last year, after conducting a national study of nearly 200 colleges and universities, that on many campuses little is being done to prevent or deal effectively with cheating. Following is a summary of some of the disturbing results of the research:

■ *Unavailability of data.* Nearly one-half of the institutions surveyed could not report the number of cases of cheating handled on their campuses over the previous three academic years, because they had not kept track.

■ *Lack of honor codes.* Only 27 percent of the institutions had honor codes. Fewer than half of those institutions had implemented the elements to make them "working honor codes," such as requiring students to sign a pledge stating they would not cheat, mandating that students report offenders, and administering un-proctored exams. When many institutions abandoned their honor codes because of concerns about their effectiveness, they also abandoned the chance to offer a com-munitywide statement on the importance of integrity and why dishonesty would not be tolerated.

■ *Inadequate involvement of faculty members and students*. Only two-thirds of the institutions reported that their faculty members were involved in developing and enforcing standards, and only one-third said that any students were involved.

■ *Lack of coordination*. Two-thirds of the institutions reported that no office or person was responsible for coordinating efforts to prevent cheating or to promote academic integrity.

■ *Lack of training*. Fewer than half of the institutions offered any kind of training to faculty members or teaching assistants on how to deal with academic dishonesty. Almost 70 percent of the people responsible for determining sanctions for cheating had no training in student development, making it unlikely that the developmental level of the student—such as his or her decision-making skills or ability to relate moral reasoning and behavior—were considered or that sanctions such as a required educational seminar were used.

■ *Lack of educational programs*. Only 3 percent (just six institutions) required students who were caught cheating to participate in some educational program de-signed to help them reconsider their behavior. The most prevalent sanctions were just to fail the student on the assignment or in the course.

Unfortunately, there is no quick fix, no single or simple solution to the problem of student cheating. Adopting an honor code and widely publicizing it is not enough. Institutions must adopt a comprehensive approach involving the entire institution—students, faculty members, and administrators.   4

The solution I propose, based on my recent research, is built on the concept that the most effective way to prevent cheating is to actively promote academic integrity, while at the same time effectively confronting those who do cheat. Confronting cheating should include sanctions that respond to the behavior as well as educational programs or seminars that address developmental issues.   5

The first step is for institutions to establish an ethos that promotes academic integrity, one that defines it and holds it up as something to be revered. Such an ethos can be created with the help of an honor code, code of conduct, or other strong, clear statements about what the institution expects from its students, exactly how cheaters will be punished, and why cheating actually hurts, rather than helps, students. Students must understand that integrity is valuable and that if their grades are not based on honest accomplishment, they may mislead employers and others. If they also cheat in their careers and are discovered, they could damage any pro-fessional reputation they've developed.   6

After setting out its standards, the institution then must use all the tools it has to communicate its position on academic integrity and its intention not to tolerate dishonesty: direct correspondence to faculty members and students; mandated dis-cussions about cheating during orientation meetings for students and faculty mem-bers, as well as during individual classes at the beginning of semesters; printed ma-terial such as handbooks; and the campus news media.   7

Faculty members are the most critical element in insuring the success of any cam-puswide effort to promote academic integrity. They should reflect, communicate,   8 and enforce the institution's values. They also should be involved in developing and implementing whatever system the institution creates; their participation will give them a sense of personal commitment to, and ownership of, the system.

Many faculty members refuse to address the problem of academic dishonesty, 9 feeling the rules are too complicated and the procedures for enforcing them too time-consuming. Others try to minimize the problem for fear that it may reflect badly on their ability to teach. Young faculty members, in particular, may ignore cheating because it might reveal that they lack the skills or experience to avert it. Still others do not like to report cheating because they do not want to be branded as "zealots" or "troublemakers" by colleagues or students. The institution must help train faculty members in ways to prevent cheating and in how to create a classroom atmosphere in which honesty is clearly the expected standard.

It also is essential that students be involved in developing and carrying out sys- 10 tems to promote academic integrity. Failure to involve students creates an "us versus them" atmosphere, which tends to promote cheating. Students can serve on honor or disciplinary boards and on review committees that assess how well an institution's process for assuring academic integrity is working.

Finally, an institution must coordinate its efforts to insure that all the elements 11 of its system are implemented. One office should be responsible for monitoring relevant data, assessing the effectiveness of policies and procedures, coordinating communication efforts, and coordinating training programs on academic dishonesty and ways to prevent it.

Besides acting to create an ethos of academic integrity, institutions must develop 12 policies that deal effectively with students who still choose to cheat. Those policies should include:

■ Appropriate sanctions. These might include a notation concerning academic dishonesty on a transcript, required counseling, and required attendance at a class or seminar on academic integrity.

■ A required educational program for offenders. Such a program should include discussion of what cheating is and why it is unacceptable. It should also include education in moral development, to help students understand the relationship between moral reasoning and behavior. By using discussions, case studies, and role-playing exercises, students can be helped in responding to ethical dilemmas. Finally, the program or seminar should include training in academic skills to help students gain confidence in their abilities to succeed in the classroom without cheating.

■ Testing policies that emphasize prevention of cheating. These could include procedures that protect the security of tests before they are administered, proctoring services, assigned seating and use of different versions of the same test during exams, and guidelines for making writing assignments that limit opportunities for plagiarism.

■ Methods of reporting cheating that are unintimidating—for example, that allow the person reporting cheating to remain anonymous.

Faculty members and administrators can no longer ignore their responsibilities to 13 promote academic integrity. They must help students develop the values they need to deal effectively with the moral and ethical dilemmas facing them. Clearly communicating an institution's expectations for academic honesty is an important way to foster students' development. Frequent discussions about integrity provide the opportunity for academics to communicate the value they place on integrity relative to other values such as achievement and competition. When cheating does occur, campus procedures should make students confront the ethical implications of their behavior, expose them to discussion of moral reasoning, and help them understand that effective learning depends on honesty, respect, rigor, and fairness.

For Discussion

Kibler assumes that students cheat in college because they either don't know the rules or don't respect them. For him, cheating is a moral issue, a simple question of right and wrong: students cheat because they lack moral integrity or because they have not reached a stage of moral development to recognize that cheating represents such a lack of integrity. Kibler does acknowledge, however, that certain teaching practices may contribute to the problem. Do you think any of the following may contribute to cheating in college: large class sizes; the way courses are organized, exams given, and papers assigned; the way teachers teach—the kind of inspiration and enthusiasm they offer students and the kind of help they give with challenging assignments?

How might your teachers make it less tempting or easy to cheat? Also, would a clearly established and strictly enforced honor code discourage cheating? Why, or why not?

For Analysis

1. At the beginning of this chapter we make the following assertions about writing that proposes solutions:

- It analyzes a problem and takes a definite stand on it.
- It strives to see the problem in new ways, looking at it from new angles and in new contexts.
- It gives reasons why readers should support a proposed solution.
- It anticipates that readers may prefer solutions other than the one being proposed.
- It anticipates readers' questions and reservations about the solution being proposed.

Consider whether each of these assertions is true of Kibler's essay.

2. Reread paragraphs 1–3 to see how Kibler presents the problem. What resources and strategies does he use to demonstrate that the problem exists and is serious?

3. In arguing for his solution, beginning at paragraph 5, Kibler is careful to help his readers follow his argument from one point to the next. Look at the first sentences in paragraphs 5–13, and underline the word or phrase that connects each paragraph explicitly to the one before it. What cues does Kibler employ to keep readers on track?

For more on cues, see Chapter 13.

4. Writers proposing solutions to problems usually try to anticipate readers' questions, objections, and reservations. Kibler does so briefly in paragraph 9. What specific objections does he anticipate? Does he seem sympathetic or dismissive toward faculty concerns?

For Your
Own Writing

Consider writing about a problem in your high school, college, or community. List two or three problems you would like to see solved, and then focus on one of them in order to consider what would be involved in writing about it. To whom would you address your proposal to solve this problem, hoping this individual or group would take your proposed solution seriously and even lead the effort to implement it? Consider how you would present the problem and describe your solution. What reasons would you give to support your solution? How would you anticipate readers' questions, reservations, or outright objections?

Commentary

Think of essays proposing solutions as having two basic parts: presenting a problem and proposing a solution for it. A scratch outline of Kibler's essay reveals this basic two-part plan:

Problem (paragraphs 1–3)

cheating widespread, considered a serious issue (1)

colleges fail to treat cheating as a moral problem (2)

little is being done to stop cheating—colleges usually don't know how much cheating is going on, few schools have honor codes, faculty and students not involved, there is no coordinated effort and no training for faculty or programs for students caught cheating (3)

Solution (paragraphs 4–13)

a comprehensive approach to cheating is required (4)

promote academic integrity, punish cheating (5)

establish an ethos (6)

communicate the position on academic integrity (7)

get faculty involved, offer training (8, 9)

get students involved (10)

coordinate all efforts (11)

develop policies to reduce cheating and deal with cheaters—sanctions, programs, test security, methods for reporting cheating (12)

recap (13)

This scratch outline also helps us understand Kibler's argumentative strategy. He begins by demonstrating the seriousness of the problem: 67 percent of students cheat, and no college is immune; colleges seem confused about the problem and unsure what to do. It is easy to imagine that with this opening strategy Kibler would get the attention of conscientious college administrators. From the beginning he tries to redefine the problem as moral, not behavioral. The success of his argument for his solution depends on his readers' willingness to accept this redefinition. Here he takes a big risk. And he takes an additional risk in announcing that the problem has "no quick fix," that it will require a comprehensive, campus-wide effort to implement his proposed solution. Even the faculty will have to become involved. Since some busy administrators prefer quick fixes and shrink from attempting to divert faculty from their teaching and research, they might just stop reading at this point. We can assume that Kibler believes they will keep reading, though, because of the way he has redefined the problem—as a moral problem rooted in the issue of academic integrity. What president or dean would not wish for greater academic integrity in his or her college?

Kibler is then extremely careful to reassure readers that a complex campus-wide effort can be achieved with a step-by-step approach. First, the college must establish an "ethos that promotes academic integrity." ("Ethos" refers to a widely held belief, in this case that cheating is immoral.) Then, certain faculty and students must devise an honor code and educate everyone about it, and a coordinator must ensure that everything works as planned. Finally, policies will be announced that explain the ramifications for students who violate the campus ethos and honor code.

The key to his argumentative strategy seems to be devoting considerable space—well over half the essay—to explaining how his demanding solution may be implemented. In order not to be viewed as only a complainer or moralizer and lose credibility with his readers he must show authoritatively the pragmatic actions that can be undertaken to reduce cheating.

His authority is further enhanced by the fact that he has not only read the research on this problem but conducted research himself, surveying 200 colleges. You, too, may find that research is essential to the success of your proposal. For example, if you propose a solution to a college or community problem, you may need to interview several people to learn more about the problem and to discover likely questions or reservations they have about your proposed solution. Interviewing people involved makes sense: you want them to accept your definiton of the problem, approve your solution, and work energetically to see that it is implemented.

■   ■   ■

Mickey Kaus, a graduate of Harvard University and Harvard Law School, has been writing about public policy issues for fifteen years. He has worked at *Newsweek* and is now a senior editor for the *New Republic*, a national weekly magazine of news and opinion. His recent book, *The End of Equality*, argues for greater civility (considerateness, politeness) in public life. In the following proposal, Kaus considers the problem of verbal harassment of women by men in public places. Beginning by rejecting another solution proposed by a feminist law professor, Kaus sets up the problem as a conflict between an individual's right to free speech (a man's right to make vulgar comments about a passing woman's appearance) and the need for civility in the "public sphere," when people are moving around their communities, shopping, working, or at leisure. The question seems to be whether the First Amendment to the Constitution permits restraints on speech in certain situations. (Passed in 1791 as part of the Bill of Rights, the amendment says, "Congress shall make no law . . . abridging the freedom of speech. . . .") Some writers on this issue take the position that speech should rarely if ever be restricted, while others take the position that speech may be restricted under certain circumstances.

As you read, notice the way Kaus considers and rejects other proposed solutions to public verbal harassment before he proposes his own solution.

STREET HASSLE
MICKEY KAUS

The latest issue of the prestigious *Harvard Law Review* features a sixty-page ar- 1
ticle by Northwestern law professor Cynthia Grant Bowman on the "street harassment" of women. Bowman argues that "wolf-whistles, sucking noises and catcalls" directed at women in public places—as well as comments that "range from 'Hello, baby' to vulgar suggestions and outright threats"—are part of a "spectrum of means by which men objectify women and assert coercive power over them." She wants to make these things illegal, or at least subject the harassers to civil lawsuits.

Bowman would seem to offer conservative curmudgeons their fattest target 2
since a liberal judge in New York ruled that beggars had a constitutional right to panhandle in the subways. Her article amply displays many of the annoying aspects of "feminist jurisprudence." There is, first, the tendency to exaggerate the harm done by male misbehavior. "[A]ny incident of harassment, no matter how 'harmless,' " is held to reinforce fear of rape "by demonstrating that any man may choose to invade a woman's personal space, physically or psychologically. . . ." Bowman also implies that men cannot understand what it feels like for a woman to be sexually taunted. In keeping with this assumption, she cites *The Washington Post*'s Courtland Milloy as "one woman" who has eloquently recounted the evils of harassment. Last time I checked, Milloy was a man. And Bowman ignores the possibility that a "reasonable woman" might ever *want* men to hit on her.

Take it away, Rush Limbaugh. Or, rather, take it away, TNR.[1] A couple of weeks 3
ago this magazine ran a Notebook item dismissing Bowman's article with the observation that "in a free country, being maddened is a hazard of existence."

Sometimes, though, it's too easy to be a curmudgeon. Compare Bowman's ar- 4
guments with those in that New York subway panhandling case. In the latter, conservatives insisted on preserving order in public spaces, at the expense of a borderline First Amendment claim. Is the case against "street harassment" all that different? One would expect those who most loudly lament the loss of civility and public order to be the most sympathetic to Bowman's complaint. Certainly *Public Interest*-type[2] conservatives such as James Q. Wilson, who argues for "the priority of the good over personal rights," should understand that beggars aren't the only people whose assertion of "rights" can threaten the common sphere of living. Mr. Wilson, meet Ms. Bowman.

---

[1]TNR refers to the *New Republic*, the magazine in which this essay originally appeared.
[2]The *Public Interest* is a conservative political journal.

After reading Bowman's article, I conducted an unscientific survey of female acquaintances, asking if they were in fact bothered by "street harassment." None were as distressed as Bowman is. But almost all said they were regularly harassed, at least on the "hey, baby" level. And while some claimed to enjoy the milder forms of hassling (e.g., the whistles), most said they often changed their routes in order to avoid public spaces where they thought they would be taunted.

For all her foolishness, Bowman has pointed up a severe violation of civility, one that seems to diminish public life for a large portion of the American population. The problem is what to do about it. The pursuit of civility in public spaces is a peculiarly difficult enterprise for Americans accustomed to framing legal issues in terms of conflicting rights. Quite simply, it is impossible to describe the civil ordering of the public sphere in terms of "rights," or at least in terms of the absolute speech-like rights we're used to. I'm walking down the street talking to a friend. A stranger walks up and begins to harangue me. I turn my back. He keeps haranguing. I have a "right" to be there. He has a "right" to be there too. We both have "rights." But something has to give.

Worse, the question of whether we want to restrain the haranguer inevitably hinges on the content of his expression. It makes a difference if he says, "Hello, baby," or "[F—ing] bitch." It even makes a difference if he's funny or trite. The required judgment is almost aesthetic.

It won't do to simply note, with liberal communitarians[3] such as William Galston, that "there is a gap between rights and rightness that cannot be closed without a richer moral vocabulary . . . that invokes principles of decency [and] duty." That's true. But how do we get ourselves a public sphere that reflects this decency, when we no longer have a culture that takes care of the problem automatically?

At least three approaches seem to be available. First, re-education. Amitai Etzioni, in his forthcoming book, *The Spirit of Community*, despairs of any attempt to put a "notch" in the First Amendment to allow the prohibition of offensive speech. Instead, he suggests, why not require offenders "to attend classes that will teach them civility?" This may make some sense in a university setting (which is the context of Etzioni's discussion). As a remedy for "street harassment," it seems pathetically inadequate. Even if we could send harassers to the moral equivalent of traffic school, it would probably provoke more ridicule than re-education. There's something creepy about the idea of state-sponsored re-education classes, anyway.

Second, as Bowman suggests, we might give "targets" of street harassment the right to sue for civil damages, perhaps for "intentional infliction of emotional distress." Yet this seems a recipe for disastrous litigiousness. Do we really want every woman who feels "dissed" to be able to require a judge to determine the "reasonableness" of the dissing?

The third, and least unsatisfactory, approach is to delegate the required semiaesthetic judgments to the police by making "street harassment" a misdemeanor, just as other sorts of public disturbances are misdemeanors. Litigiousness would be avoided by having a third party (a cop) decide on the spot whether civility had been violated. Pennsylvania already has a law penalizing anyone who intentionally "engages in a course of conduct or repeatedly commits acts which alarm or seriously annoy" another person "and which serve no legitimate purpose." The trouble, as

[3]For more on communitarianism, see the Amitai Etzioni headnote on p. 221.

Bowman notes, is that this sort of ordinance typically applies only to those who repeatedly harass a single person, not to those who harass a series of passers-by. But this defect can be easily remedied. If it's not a violation of the First Amendment to arrest a man who calls one pedestrian a ''bitch'' fifteen times, why is it a violation to arrest him if he says it once to fifteen different pedestrians?

Few police departments would actually arrest any but the most egregious violators, of course—though female police officers might have interestingly different priorities in this regard. But the law would at least give cops a basis for telling offenders to ''move along.'' Most importantly, the law might also stimulate the cultural change that everybody, including Bowman, agrees is the only real solution to the problem. Until then, her argument will be hard to dismiss.   12

For Discussion

Consider the times when, in public, strangers have said something to you that felt like an intrusion or harassment. Perhaps someone asked you for money, threatened you, intimidated you, or just wanted to talk. Make a list of these occasions, and discuss which ones seem to be clear instances of Constitutionally protected speech and which ones communities might enact laws against that would not be overturned on legal appeal.

For Analysis

See pp. 274–75 in this chapter for an example of a scratch outline.

1.   Make a scratch outline of Kaus's essay. Given his purpose and readers, what advantages do you see in his plan?

2.   Using your scratch outline as a guide, think about Kaus's argumentative strategy in presenting the problem to be solved. What do you think he is trying to accomplish with his readers in paragraphs 1–8? How does he use Bowman, Limbaugh (a politically conservative talk-show host), Wilson, and Galston to prepare readers for his solution?

3.   Since many of Kaus's readers—male and female—are feminists, he risks alienating them if he seems to be treating Bowman unfairly. Do you think he treats her unfairly? Review paragraphs 1–2, 5–6, and 10–12 for evidence to support your conclusion.

See Chapter 13 for a discussion of cues.

4.   When Kaus presents three alternative solutions in paragraphs 9–11, he provides obvious cues—a forecast and transitions—to keep readers on track. Underline these cues and describe briefly how they guide the reader.

For Your Own Writing

What social problems—of national importance or of interest in your own community—concern you? List some, and choose one you might write about. How would you define and present the problem? What solution would you propose, and what alternative solutions might you evaluate?

Commentary

Kaus's essay illustrates the importance in some proposals of anticipating and evaluating alternative solutions, a special strategy of counterargument. Kaus anticipates two alternative solutions to the problem of street hassles: Etzioni's proposal to re-educate people who are uncivil (paragraph 9) and one of Bowman's proposals, to allow victims to sue (paragraph 10). Kaus might have

See pp. 546–52 for more
on anticipating reader's
concerns.

acknowledged these alternatives, merely mentioning them to let readers know he was aware of them; or he could have accommodated them, integrating parts of all of them into his own proposed solution. Instead, he refutes them, calling Etzioni's solution "pathetically inadequate" and Bowman's "a recipe for disastrous litigiousness."

Like Kibler, Kaus carried out some research to learn more about the problem to be solved, in his case talking casually to a few female friends. He uses what he learns to challenge what he considers to be Bowman's exaggerations but also to acknowledge that even the milder street hassles cause women to avoid certain public spaces.

Kaus's essay also illustrates an interesting dilemma faced by many writers who propose solutions to problems: recognizing that the real solution is out of reach, they propose instead an interim or partial solution. For example, in his last paragraph, Kaus acknowledges that the only lasting solution to street hassles is "cultural change;" and yet he unapologetically argues for the only change that he thinks is possible at the moment, a law making street hassling a misdemeanor, like running a stop sign. When you plan your essay proposing a solution, you, too, may face the dilemma of proposing an interim solution that can be put into effect immediately or arguing for a much more far-reaching solution that would be much harder to implement.

■   ■   ■

Adam Paul Weisman wrote the next selection in 1987 for the *New Republic*, a national news and opinion magazine. It proposes a solution to the problem of teenage pregnancy. As you read, ask yourself how Weisman's admission that his solution is not original—that it has already been tried—affects your reaction to it.

**BIRTH CONTROL
IN THE SCHOOLS**
ADAM PAUL
WEISMAN

Should contraceptives be distributed to teenagers in public schools? A research panel of the National Academy of Sciences spent two years studying adolescent pregnancy in America, and decided they should. Its 1986 report, *Risking the Future*, prompted a new wave of angry debate about how to reduce the high rate of teenage pregnancy in the United States.   1

No one disputes the severity of the problem. Teen pregnancy ruins young lives and perpetuates a tragic cycle of poverty. According to the Alan Guttmacher Institute, the rate of pregnancy among American women aged 15 to 19 was almost ten percent in 1981. That far outstrips the next closest industrialized nation, England, where the rate is less than 5 percent. Guttmacher estimates that more than 80 percent of teenage pregnancies in the United States are unintended and unwanted. Every year about four in 100 women aged 15 to 19 have an abortion. But those looking for ways to reduce these statistics have divided into two distinct camps: one favoring contraception, the other, sexual abstinence.   2

The contraception advocates point out that a majority of teenagers have already   3 rejected abstinence. In 1986, 57 percent of 17-year-olds say they have had sex. This camp believes that schools, as a central location in young peoples' lives, are a good place to make contraceptives available. Three recent studies (by the National Academy of Sciences, the Guttmacher Institute, and the Children's Defense Fund) have taken this view, while also calling for programs geared toward postponing adolescent sexual involvement and including parents in school sex education classes.

The abstinence advocates believe the answer lies in inculcating values based on   4
a clear understanding that sex is simply wrong for teenagers. They say that moral lessons are best taught by parents in the home, but that schools should continue the job by teaching a chaste morality. Secretary of Education William Bennett[1] has been the most outspoken proponent of this view. Exposing students to "mechanical" means of pregnancy prevention, he says, encourages "children who do not have sexual intimacy on their minds to . . . be mindful of it."

Bennett concedes that "birth control clinics in schools may prevent some births."   5
And indeed, whatever the drawbacks, the contraception advocates have one strong advantage in this debate: their approach works. The only rigorous study of a pregnancy prevention program for urban teenagers was conducted in Baltimore from 1982 to 1983 by researchers from Johns Hopkins Medical School. The Hopkins-run birth-control clinic, located across the street from one school and nearby another, reduced the pregnancy rate in the schools it served by 30 percent while pregnancy rates in control schools soared 58 percent.

"Why did this program work?" asks Dr. Laurie Zabin, the program's director, in   6
her report on the experiment. "Access to high-quality, free services was probably crucial to its success. Professional counseling, education, and open communications were, no doubt, also important. All these factors appear to have created an atmosphere that allowed teenagers to translate their attitude into constructive preventive behavior." And what of those students who were virgins? According to Zabin, that group of girls (not very large) delayed initiation of sexual activity an average of seven months longer than those in the control groups, strong evidence that awareness of contraception is not directly linked to promiscuity.

But the existing school-based clinics that distribute or arrange for birth control   7
are not just rooms plastered with Planned Parenthood posters where contraceptives are handed out. They are full-service health clinics that came into existence to provide young people with comprehensive health care. Public health officials, including many who have doubts about distributing contraceptives in schools, agree that in many places, particularly the inner city, health care for adolescents is inadequate. The school–based clinic, like the school lunch program, seeks to make all students healthy enough to get the most out of education.

This is not to say that school-based clinics don't do a lot in the way of contra-   8
ception. According to Douglas Kirby, director of research for the Center for Population Options, a group that advocates and monitors school-based clinics, 15 percent to 20 percent of visits to clinics are for family planning. The majority are for general health care. Twenty-eight percent of the clinics actually dispense contraceptives or other prescription drugs. About half of the clinics write prescriptions that are filled off-campus; the rest diagnose and counsel teens before making referrals to outside health agencies.

[1]William Bennett was Secretary of Education during most of the Reagan administration.

The clinics also seem to help reduce unintended pregnancies. In St. Paul 33 per- 9
cent of girls made use of the clinic's contraceptive services, and birth rates dropped
by 50 percent. Thanks to the clinic's counseling, four out of five of the girls who did
have children stayed in school, and only 1.4 percent of them had another pregnancy
before graduation. Nationally, about 17 percent of teenage mothers become preg-
nant again within a year.

Bennett argues that distributing birth control is "not what school is for," and 10
that doing so represents "an abdication of moral authority." Many educators have
similar concerns. They fear that communities and government are trying to dump
another social problem—like drug counseling and AIDS education—on the schools
when they could better be handled in the home. Diane Ravitch, an adjunct professor
of history and education at Teachers College in New York, says, "Schools are increasingly being pushed to be social service centers, and they don't do that well."

Yet clearly schools do more than teach students the three R's. Schools are where 11
many teenagers learn to drive, weld, and cook. And numerous surveys reveal that
over 80 percent of parents think it is a proper place for their children to learn about
sex. Dr. Stephen Joseph, health commissioner for New York City, explains that if it
weren't for the involvement of schools, the United States never could have achieved
100 percent immunization rates, a worthy goal that "wasn't perceived as the role
of the school either at that time."

If the pressing health crisis were non-sexual in nature—tuberculosis, for exam- 12
ple—it's hard to believe that educators such as Bennett wouldn't be the first to volunteer schools as a locus for a solution. And of course, if the problem of teen pregnancy is one that the schools shouldn't be expected to deal with, that would exclude
any program of anti-sex indoctrination as well as the distribution of contraceptives.
Putting such indoctrination into the curriculum is, arguably, more intrusive on the
schools' basic function than the existence of a birth control or general health clinic.
Bennett's speeches rule out the very real possibility that schools could prosecute a
moral agenda and *also* support a clinic.

Despite the success of Zabin's off-campus model, there is a good reason school- 13
based clinics receive such wide support in the health services community: teenagers
are notoriously lazy. As Cheryl Hayes, director of the NAS study explains, "If teenagers have to wait in the rain for a bus to take them to a clinic, there is a good
chance they will never make it to the clinic." If the goal is providing health care and
family planning services to teenagers, it is unlikely that anything will work as well as
locating those services where most teenagers are: at school.

Of course the real question that excites people isn't whether teenagers should 14
get birth control at school, but whether they should get it at all. There is no hard
evidence linking exposure to contraception with promiscuity, and it is unlikely any
teenager who watches prime-time television is less than "mindful" (as Bennett puts
it) of sexual intimacy. Although Bennett has dismissed the recommendations of *Risking the Future* as "stupid," the opponents of making contraception available to teenagers have yet to offer an effective alternative. As for the "parental authority" that
birth control availability is said to undermine, a 1986 Planned Parenthood survey of
1,000 teenagers revealed that 31 percent of parents discuss neither sex nor birth
control with their children. The failure of parental authority is manifest in the almost
900,000 unintended teenage pregnancies in 1983. *Risking the Future* only makes
that failure painfully clear.

For Discussion

How do you react to Weisman's proposal that school-based health clinics be permitted to distribute birth-control information and contraceptives? Do you think it is appropriate for schools to play such a role? What advantages or dangers do you see?

For Analysis

1.   How does Weisman set the stage for his argument in the title and the first two paragraphs? What advantages or disadvantages do you see in his opening? Compare Weisman's opening paragraphs to the two opening paragraphs in Kibler's essay and the three opening paragraphs in Kaus's essay. What can you conclude about strategies for opening essays proposing solutions to problems?

2.   Weisman at first appears to be a neutral reporter rather than an advocate for a particular solution. Is this tone maintained consistently throughout the essay? Point to passages where the same tone is evident or where a different tone emerges. How does the neutral reporter's tone serve Weisman's overall argumentative strategy?

3.   In paragraph 5, Weisman cites the example of the Johns Hopkins University birth-control clinic. How does he use this example to support his argument? How effective is the example?

4.   How does Weisman present the advantages of his solution so that they will appeal to supporters of the abstinence solution? What common values and concerns does he call upon?

For Your
Own Writing

Teenagers are part of the problem in this proposal, but they can also play a positive role in solving social problems. For example, high school students can teach illiterate adults to read or refurbish playgrounds and parks. Think of a problem that teenagers might be able to help solve. If you were to propose a solution to this problem, how would you explain the problem? How would you go about convincing other students that they should participate?

Commentary

Instead of developing an original proposal, like Kibler, Weisman advocates a solution others have proposed, researched, and argued for. His essay illustrates a strategy that is often important in proposals: acknowledging an alternative solution, evaluating that alternative, and refuting it.

After establishing the problem, Weisman introduces the two solutions that have been proposed: encouraging teenagers to abstain from sexual activity and providing birth-control information to them. To demonstrate his fairness, Weisman presents the abstinence solution objectively, even sympathetically. He accepts the legitimacy of this proposed solution and objects only on the grounds that it does not work.

The fact that Weisman's proposed solution does appear to work is the cornerstone of his argument. He uses Secretary Bennett's own words to argue that the contraception solution works in at least some cases, then cites the

Johns Hopkins study as the centerpiece of his argument. Furthermore, by noting that birth-control counseling "delayed initiation of sexual activity" for some of the teenagers, he makes a forceful appeal to those in favor of abstinence.

Not only does Weisman support his solution with reasons and evidence, but he also anticipates and refutes a major objection to it. This objection, that schools should not be used to solve social and moral problems, he refutes in two ways. First, he reasons that the problem of teenage pregnancy is a health crisis and that there is ample precedent for dealing with such problems through the schools. This argument appeals to humanitarian concerns, but is unlikely to convince those who consider teenage pregnancy a moral issue. To those readers, he offers a second argument: if birth-control information is excluded from the schools, then "any program of anti-sex indoctrination" must also be excluded. In other words, the argument against school-based birth-control clinics could also be made against teaching sexual abstinence. Both are forms of sex education.

For more on anticipating readers' concerns, see pp. 546–52.

Weisman's argumentative strategy in this proposal is to show that he understands and respects the values of those who advocate an alternative solution and that he shares their desire to remedy the problem. He appeals to them on practical grounds, arguing that his solution will get the job done.

■   ■   ■

Patrick O'Malley wrote the following essay when he was a college freshman. In it, he proposes that college professors give students frequent brief examinations in addition to the usual midterm and final exams. After discussing with his instructor his unusual rhetorical situation—a freshman advising professors—he decided to revise the essay into the form of an open letter to professors on his campus, a letter that might appear in the campus newspaper.

O'Malley's essay may strike you as unusually authoritative. This air of authority is due in large part to what O'Malley learned about the possibilities and problems of frequent exams as he interviewed two professors (his writing instructor and the writing program director) and talked with several students. As you read, notice particularly how he is able to anticipate professors' likely objections to his proposals and their preferred solutions to the problem he identifies.

**MORE TESTING,
MORE LEARNING**
PATRICK O'MALLEY

It's late at night. The final's tomorrow. You got a C on the midterm, so this one   1
will make or break you. Will it be like the midterm? Did you study enough? Did you study the right things? It's too late to drop the course. So what happens if you fail? No time to worry about that now—you've got a ton of notes to go over.

Although this last-minute anxiety about midterm and final exams is only too fa-   2
miliar to most college students, many professors may not realize how such major,

infrequent, high-stakes exams work against the best interests of students both psychologically and intellectually. They cause unnecessary amounts of stress, placing too much importance on one or two days in the students' entire term, judging ability on a single or dual performance. They don't encourage frequent study, and they fail to inspire students' best performance. If professors gave additional brief exams at frequent intervals, students would be spurred to study more regularly, learn more, worry less, and perform better on midterms, finals, and other papers and projects.

Ideally, a professor would give an in-class test or quiz after each unit, chapter, or focus of study, depending on the type of class and course material. A physics class might require a test on concepts after every chapter covered, while a history class could necessitate quizzes covering certain time periods or major events. These exams should be given weekly, or at least twice monthly. Whenever possible, they should consist of two or three essay questions rather than many multiple-choice or short-answer questions. To preserve class time for lecture and discussion, exams should take no more than 15 or 20 minutes.

The main reason why professors should give frequent exams is that when they do, and when they provide feedback to students on how well they are doing, students learn more in the course and perform better on major exams, projects, and papers. It makes sense that in a challenging course containing a great deal of material, students will learn more of it and put it to better use if they have to apply or "practice" it frequently on exams, which also helps them find out how much they are learning and what they need to go over again. A recent Harvard study notes students' "strong preference for frequent evaluation in a course." Harvard students feel they learn least in courses that have "only a midterm and a final exam, with no other personal evaluation." They believe they learn most in courses with "many opportunities to see how they are doing" (Light, 1990, p.32). In a review of a number of studies of student learning, Frederiksen (1984) reports that students who take weekly quizzes achieve higher scores on final exams than students who take only a midterm exam and that testing increases retention of material tested.

Another, closely related argument in favor of multiple exams is that they encourage students to improve their study habits. Greater frequency in test taking means greater frequency in studying for tests. Students prone to cramming will be required—or at least strongly motivated—to open their textbooks and notebooks more often, making them less likely to resort to long, kamikaze nights of studying for major exams. Since there is so much to be learned in the typical course, it makes sense that frequent, careful study and review are highly beneficial. But students need motivation to study regularly, and nothing works like an exam. If students had frequent exams in all their courses, they would have to schedule study time each week and gradually would develop a habit of frequent study. It might be argued that students are adults who have to learn how to manage their own lives, but learning history or physics is more complicated than learning to drive a car or balance a checkbook. Students need coaching and practice in learning. The right way to learn new material needs to become a habit, and I believe that frequent exams are key to developing good habits of study and learning. The Harvard study concludes that "tying regular evaluation to good course organization enables students to plan their work more than a few days in advance. If quizzes and homework are scheduled on specific days, students plan their work to capitalize on them" (Light, 1990, p.33).

By encouraging regular study habits, frequent exams would also decrease anxiety by reducing the procrastination that produces anxiety. Students would benefit psychologically if they were not subjected to the emotional ups and downs caused by major exams, when after being virtually worry-free for weeks they are suddenly ready to check into the psychiatric ward. Researchers at the University of Vermont found a strong relationship between procrastination, anxiety, and achievement. Students who regularly put off studying for exams had continuing high anxiety and lower grades than students who procrastinated less. The researchers found that even "low" procrastinators did not study regularly and recommended that professors give frequent assignments and exams to reduce procrastination and increase achievement (Rothblum, Solomon, & Murakami, 1986, pp. 393, 394).

Research supports my proposed solution to the problems I have described. Common sense as well as my experience and that of many of my friends support it. Why, then, do so few professors give frequent brief exams? Some believe that such exams take up too much of the limited class time available to cover the material in the course. Most courses meet 150 minutes a week—three times a week for 50 minutes each time. A 20-minute weekly exam might take 30 minutes to administer, and that is one-fifth of each week's class time. From the student's perspective, however, this time is well spent. Better learning and greater confidence about the course seem a good tradeoff for another 30 minutes of lecture. Moreover, time lost to lecturing or discussion could easily be made up in students' learning on their own through careful regular study for the weekly exams. If weekly exams still seem too time-consuming to some professors, their frequency could be reduced to every other week or their length to 5 or 10 minutes. In courses where multiple-choice exams are appropriate, several questions take only a few minutes to answer.   7

Another objection professors have to frequent exams is that they take too much time to read and grade. In a 20-minute essay exam a well-prepared student can easily write two pages. A relatively small class of 30 students might then produce 60 pages, no small amount of material to read each week. A large class of 100 or more students would produce an insurmountable pile of material. There are a number of responses to this objection. Again, professors could give exams every other week or make them very short. Instead of reading them closely they could skim them quickly to see whether students understand an idea or can apply it to an unfamiliar problem; and instead of numerical or letter grades they could give a plus, check, or minus. Exams could be collected and responded to only every third or fourth week. Professors who have readers or teaching assistants could rely on them to grade or check exams. And the scantron machine is always available for instant grading of multiple-choice exams. Finally, frequent exams could be given *in place of* a midterm exam or out-of-class essay assignment.   8

Since frequent exams seem to some professors to create too many problems, however, it is reasonable to consider alternative ways to achieve the same goals. One alternative solution is to implement a program that would improve study skills. While such a program might teach students how to study for exams, it cannot prevent procrastination or reduce "large test anxiety" by a substantial amount. One research team studying anxiety and test performance found that study skills training was "not effective in reducing anxiety or improving performance" (Dendato & Diener, 1986, p. 134). This team, which also reviewed other research that reached the same conclusion, did find that a combination of "cognitive/relaxation therapy" and study skills training was effective. This possible solution seems complicated, however, not to   9 mention time-consuming and expensive. It seems much easier and more effective to change the cause of the bad habit rather than treat the habit itself. That is, it would make more sense to solve the problem at its root: the method of learning and evaluation.

Still another solution might be to provide frequent study questions for students 10 to answer. These would no doubt be helpful in focusing students' time studying, but students would probably not actually write out the answers unless they were required to. To get students to complete the questions in a timely way, professors would have to collect and check the answers. In that case, however, they might as well devote the time to grading an exam. Even if it asks the same questions, a scheduled exam is preferable to a set of study questions because it takes far less time to write in class, compared to the time students would devote to responding to questions at home. In-class exams also ensure that each student produces his or her own work.

Another possible solution would be to help students prepare for midterm and 11 final exams by providing sets of questions from which the exam questions will be selected or announcing possible exam topics at the beginning of the course. This solution would have the advantage of reducing students' anxiety about learning every fact in the textbook, and it would clarify the course goals, but it would not motivate students to study carefully each new unit, concept, or text chapter in the course. I see this as a way of complementing frequent exams, not as substituting for them.

From the evidence and from my talks with professors and students, I see fre- 12 quent, brief in-class exams as the only way to improve students' study habits and learning, reducing their anxiety and procrastination, and increase their satisfaction with college. These exams are not a panacea, but only more parking spaces and a winning football team would do as much to improve college life. Professors can't do much about parking or football, but they can give more frequent exams. Campus administrators should get behind this effort, and professors should get together to consider giving exams more frequently. It would make a difference.

References

Light, R. J. (1990). *Explorations with students and faculty about teaching, learning, and student life.* Cambridge, MA: Harvard University Graduate School of Education and Kennedy School of Government.

Frederiksen, N. (1984). The real test bias: Influences of testing on teaching and learning. *American Psychologist, 39,* 193–202.

Rothblum, E. D., Solomon, L., & Murakami, J. (1986). Affective, cognitive, and behavioral differences between high and low procrastinators. *Journal of Counseling Psychology, 33,* 387–394.

Dendato, K. M., & Diener, D. (1986). Effectiveness of cognitive/relaxation therapy and study-skills training in reducing self-reported anxiety and improving the academic performance of text-anxious students. *Journal of Counseling Psychology, 33,* 131–135.

For Discussion   O'Malley advocates frequent brief exams as a solution to the problems of midterm and finals anxiety, poor study habits, and disappointing exam performance. What do you think of his proposal in light of your own experience? Which of your high school or college courses have included frequent exams? Did they offer the benefits O'Malley claims? Did you learn more because of them? Did courses without frequent exams produce the problems he identifies?

For Analysis

1.   Reread paragraph 3 carefully to discover how O'Malley defines and qualifies the solution. Underline key words and phrases that indicate what kind of exams he advocates. For his purpose and readers, does he adequately qualify the solution? Does anything seem unnecessary? Should anything be added? Does each key term hold up usefully throughout the essay?

For a discussion of forecasting statements, see pp. 467–68.

2.   In paragraph 2, how does O'Malley forecast the plan of his essay? Does the forecast predict the order of main parts? What else, if anything, might he have included in the forecast?

3.   Reread paragraphs 4–6 and underline the most direct statements of the reasons O'Malley gives in support of his proposal. Why do you think he makes these reasons so easy to notice? What role do they play in the proposal?

4.   Compare how O'Malley and Weisman, the author of the previous selection, acknowledge alternative solutions and establish shared values with their readers. What role do these two strategies play in the overall argumentative strategy of each essay? How successfully does each writer manage the two strategies?

5.   Turn to the Writer at Work discussion on pp. 293–95. Compare the last paragraph in the section of O'Malley's draft with paragraph 4 in his revision, and list specific changes he made from draft to revision. Knowing his purpose and readers, what advantages do you see in his changes?

For Your Own Writing

Consider writing about a problem you have encountered in learning something new, either in or out of school. What problem would you select, and to whom would you propose a solution to it? What solution would you propose, and how might you convince these readers to take action on it?

Commentary

O'Malley's essay demonstrates the importance of taking readers seriously. Not only did he interview both those who would carry out his proposal (professors) and those who would benefit from it (students), but he featured in his essay what he had learned in these interviews. Paragraphs 7–11 directly acknowledge professors' objections, their questions, and the alternative solutions they would probably prefer. If at all possible, it is good to interview possible readers and thus to find out their likely objections, questions, and preferred solutions.

O'Malley's plan is also worth noting:

opening: a scenario to introduce the problem

presentation of the problem and introduction of the solution details of the solution

reason 1: to support the solution: improved learning and performance

reason 2: improved study habits

reason 3: decreased procrastination and anxiety

accommodate objection 1: class time is limited

accommodate objection 2: too much work

refute alternative solution 1: offer study skills training

refute alternative solution 2: provide study questions

accommodate alternative solution 3: provide sample exam questions

closing: reiterate the proposed solution and advise briefly about first steps in implementing it

The essay seems to follow an appropriate order for O'Malley's purpose and readers. It is especially easy to follow because of explicit cues to readers: forecasts (previews of what is coming next), paragraph breaks, transitions, and summaries. Most important, the plan is logical and convincing. It is not the only possible plan—the alternative solutions might have been acknowledged before O'Malley argues for his solution, for example—but it is a very effective plan. This orderly plan developed over several days of invention, drafting, and revising.

PURPOSE AND AUDIENCE

More than any other kind of writing, proposals depend on the writer to anticipate readers' needs and concerns—because most proposals are calls to action. They attempt not only to convince readers but also to inspire them, to persuade them to support or to put into effect the proposed solution. What your particular readers know about the problem and what they are capable of doing to solve it determine how you address them.

Readers of proposals are often unaware of the problem. In this case, your task is clear: present them with facts that will convince them of its existence. These facts may include statistics, testimony from witnesses or experts, and examples. You can also speculate about the cause of the problem and describe its ill effects.

Sometimes readers recognize the existence of a problem but fail to take it seriously. When this is so, you may need to connect the problem closely to readers' own concerns. For instance, you might show how much they have in common with those directly affected by it, or how it affects them indirectly. However you appeal to readers, you must do more than alert them to the problem; you must also make them care about it. You want to touch readers emotionally as well as intellectually.

There will be occasions when readers are concerned about the problem but assume that someone else is taking care of it and that they need not become personally involved. Faced with this situation, you might want to demonstrate that those they thought were taking care of the problem have failed. Another assumption readers might make is that a solution they supported in the past has already solved the problem. You might point out that the original solution has proved unworkable or that new solutions have become available through changed circumstances or improved technology. Your aim is to rekindle these readers' interest in the problem.

Perhaps the most satisfying proposals are addressed to those who can take immediate action to remedy the problem. Your chances of writing such a proposal are good if you choose a problem faced by a group to which you belong. You not only have a firsthand understanding of the problem but also have a good idea what solution other members of the group will support. (You might informally survey some of them before you submit your proposal in order to test your definition of the problem and your proposed solution.) When you address readers who are in a position to take action, you obviously want to assure them that it is wise to do so. You must demonstrate that the solution is feasible, that it can be implemented, and that it will work.

BASIC FEATURES OF PROPOSALS

Effective proposals include the following features: a well-defined problem, a feasible solution, a convincing argument, and a reasonable tone.

A Well-defined
Problem

A proposal is written to offer a solution to a problem. Before presenting the solution, a proposal writer must be sure that readers know what the problem is. Both William L. Kibler and Patrick O'Malley, for example, spend their first three paragraphs defining the problem. All the writers in this chapter state the problem explicitly. Adam Paul Weisman identifies it directly as teenage pregnancy. Kibler asserts that too many college students cheat and colleges are doing too little to discourage it, and Mickey Kaus offers evidence from informal research among female friends to suggest the extent of public harassment of women. O'Malley points to several specific problems caused by "major, infrequent, high-stakes exams."

Stating the problem is not enough, however: the writer may have to establish that it indeed exists and is serious enough to need solving. Sometimes a writer can assume that readers will recognize the problem. For example, Weisman can safely assume that all readers will be aware of the high rate of teenage pregnancy and will acknowledge its seriousness, even though they disagree about a solution. At other times readers may not be aware of the problem. O'Malley, for example, explicitly says that many professors do not realize the harmful effects of infrequent exams.

In addition to stating the problem and establishing its existence and seriousness, a proposal writer may need to analyze the problem: its causes and its consequences, its history and past efforts of dealing with it. This information not only helps readers understand the problem, but it may also provide grounds for the proposed solution. When Weisman points out that most teenagers have had sex, for instance, he is preparing readers for his argument that offering contraceptives is a better way to reduce unwanted teenage pregnancies than preaching abstinence.

A Proposed Solution

Once the problem is established, the writer must present and argue for a particular solution, which constitutes the thesis of the proposal. Weisman states his thesis thus: "Whatever the drawbacks, the contraception advocates have one strong advantage in this debate: their approach works." In the same way, O'Malley asserts, "If professors gave additional brief exams at frequent intervals, students would be spurred. . . ."

A Convincing Argument

The main purpose of a proposal is to convince readers that the writer's solution is the best way of solving the problem. Proposal writers argue for their solutions by trying to demonstrate all of the following:

that the proposed solution will solve the problem

that it is a feasible way of solving the problem

that it stands up against anticipated questions and objections

that it is better than other ways of solving the problem

Arguing That the Proposed Solution Will Solve the Problem. A writer must give reasons and evidence to show that the proposed solution will indeed solve the problem. To this purpose, Weisman cites the Johns Hopkins study as evidence that the program he proposes will work, and Kibler argues that only a comprehensive program promoting academic integrity will reduce cheating.

Arguing That the Proposed Solution Is Feasible. In arguing that the proposal is feasible, the writer must demonstrate how it can be implemented. The easier it seems to implement, the more likely it is to win readers' support. Therefore, writers generally set out the steps required to put the proposal into practice, an especially important strategy when the solution might seem difficult, time-consuming, or expensive to enact.

All the writers in this chapter, except Kaus, offer specific suggestions for implementing their proposals. Weisman points to an actual instance in which his proposal has been effectively implemented. Kibler devotes most of the space in his essay to detailing step by step how college administrators could launch a program promoting academic integrity. O'Malley offers professors several specific ways to give their students frequent, brief exams.

Anticipating Reservations and Objections.   An important part of arguing for a proposal is to anticipate objections or reservations readers may have about the proposed solution. Weisman anticipates the objection that schools should not be used as "social service centers." He attempts to refute it by arguing that schools have provided health-related services in the past and that if birth-control information is banned from the schools, then teaching sexual abstinence must also be banned. O'Malley understands that professors will object to the time required to give and grade frequent exams but outlines several ways to reduce the time.

For illustrations of other ways to anticipate reader's reservations and objections, see pp. 546–52.

Considering and Rejecting Alternative Solutions.   Finally, the writer has to convince readers that his or her solution is preferable to other possible solutions. This is done by examining the other possibilities and demonstrating what is wrong with them. Weisman considers the proposal that teenagers be encouraged to abstain from sexual activity. O'Malley considers study skills training, study questions, and sample exam questions as alternatives to frequent exams.

The best way to reject an alternative solution is simply to demonstrate that it does not work, as Weisman tries to do. Another way is to show that the alternative solves only part of the problem. This is O'Malley's strategy in rejecting the idea of sample exam questions.

A Reasonable Tone

Regardless of the proposal or the argument made on its behalf, proposal writers must adopt a reasonable tone. The objective is to advance an argument without "having" an argument. That is, writers must try to avoid taking an adversarial or quarrelsome stance with their readers. The aim is to bridge any gap that may exist between writer and readers, not widen it.

Writers can build such a bridge of shared concerns by showing respect for their readers and treating their concerns seriously. They discuss objections as an attempt to lay to rest any doubts readers may have. They consider alternative solutions as a way of showing they have explored every possibility in order to find the best possible solution.

Most important, they usually do not attack those raising objections or offering other solutions by questioning their intelligence or goodwill. Kibler, Weisman, and O'Malley go out of their way to show respect for those who might question their proposed solutions or who advocate competing solutions. In contrast, while Kaus acknowledges that legal scholar Bowman has identified a serious problem in men's street hassling of women, he refers to her article as "annoying" and accuses her of "foolishness." Yet, ultimately, his own solution incorporates elements of her proposal to make street harassment illegal rather than "protected" speech. Whatever his motive, his essay illustrates that writers proposing solutions do occasionally become contentious, perhaps when their purpose is more to assert a position on the issue raised by the problem than to enlist particular readers' support for a specific solution. When readers can be addressed who can take action to solve a problem, however, respect for the readers and a reasonable tone throughout are more likely to bring success.

Guide to Writing

THE WRITING ASSIGNMENT

Write an essay proposing a solution to a problem. Choose a problem faced by a community or group to which you belong, and address your proposal either to one or more members of the group or to an outsider who might help solve the problem.

INVENTION AND RESEARCH

As you prepare to write a proposal, you will need to choose a problem you can write about, identify your prospective readers, find a tentative solution to it, and develop reasons for adopting your proposal rather than an alternative.

Choosing a Problem

One possible problem you could write about may come to mind immediately. Even so, you will want to think about various problems before settling on a topic. The following exercise is a good way to get started.

You might set a timer and brainstorm your lists on a computer, listing down under each heading. If you can work on separate screens, head one "College" and the other "Neighborhood." Enter as many possibilities as you can in ten minutes. Then, print out a copy to make notes on.

Considering Problems in Various Communities.   Divide a piece of paper into two columns. In the left-hand column list all communities, groups, or organizations to which you belong. Include as many communities as possible: college, neighborhood, hometown, cultural or ethnic groups. Also include groups you participate in: sports, musical, work, religious, political, support, hobby, and so on. In the right-hand column list any problems that exist within each group. Here's how a chart might begin:

Community	*Problem*
Your College	poor advising or orientation
	shortage of practice rooms in music building
	no financial aid for part-time students
	lack of facilities for handicapped students

Community   *Problem*

Your Neighborhood   need for traffic light at dangerous
                                               intersection

                                               unsupervised children getting into
                                               trouble

Choose one problem from your list that you consider especially important. It should be one that seems solvable, though you need not know the exact solution now; and it should concern others in the group. It should of course be a problem you can explore in detail—and one you are willing to discuss in writing.

Proposing to solve a problem in a group or community to which you belong gives you one inestimably important advantage: you can write as an expert, an insider. You know about the history of the problem, have felt the urgency to solve it, and perhaps have already thought of possible solutions. Equally important, you will know precisely to whom to address the proposal, and you can interview others in the group to get their views of the problem and to understand how they might resist your solution. You will be in a position of knowledge and authority—from which comes confident, convincing writing. Local problems are not at all unimportant just because they lack national scope.

Should you want to propose a solution for a large national social problem, concentrate on one with which you have direct experience and for which you can suggest a detailed plan of action. Even better, focus on unique local aspects of the problem. For example, if you would like to propose a solution to the problem of lack of affordable child care for children of college students or working parents, you have a great advantage if you are a parent who has experienced the frustration of finding professional, affordable child care. Moreover, it may well be that even though such a problem is national in scope, it can *only* be solved campus by campus, business by business, neighborhood by neighborhood.

Analyzing and Defining the Problem

You need now to analyze the problem carefully and then to try to define it. Keep in mind that you will have to be able to demonstrate to readers that the problem exists and is serious and that you have a more than casual understanding of its causes and consequences. If you find that you cannot do so, you will want to select some other problem to write about.

If you can, save these responses on a word processor. Then, as you begin to draft later, you can call up the file on a second screen and easily transfer details you want to use in your draft.

Analyzing.   Start by writing a few sentences in response to these questions:

- Does the problem really exist? How can I tell?
- What caused this problem? Can I identify any immediate causes? any deeper causes? Is the problem caused by a flaw in the system, a lack of resources, individual misconduct or incompetence? How can I tell?

■   What is the history of the problem?

■   What are the bad effects of the problem? How is it hurting members of
    the community or group? What goals of the group are endangered by the
    existence of this problem? Does it raise any moral or ethical questions?

■   Who in the community or group is affected by the problem? Be as specific
    as possible: Who is seriously affected? minimally affected? unaffected?
    Does anyone benefit from its existence?

■   What similar problems exist in this same community or group? How can
    I distinguish my problem from these?

Defining.   Write a definition of the problem, being as specific as possible.
Identify who or what seems responsible for it, and give one recent example.

**Identifying Your
Readers**

Whom do you wish to address—everyone in the community or group, a
committee, an individual, an outsider? You want to address the person or
group who can take action to implement the solution you propose. In a few
sentences, describe your readers, stating your reason for directing your proposal to them. Then take ten minutes to write about these readers:

■   How informed are they likely to be about the problem? Have they shown
    any awareness of it?

■   Why would this problem be important to them? Why would they care
    about solving it?

■   Have they supported any other proposals to solve the problem? If so, what
    do their proposals have in common with mine?

■   Do they ally themselves with any group that might cause them to favor
    or reject my proposal? Do we share any values or attitudes that could
    bring us together to solve the problem?

■   How have they responded to other problems? Do their past reactions
    suggest anything about how they may respond to my proposal?

**Finding a
Tentative Solution**

Solving problems takes time. Apparent solutions often turn out to be impossible. After all, a solution has to be both workable and acceptable to the
community or group involved. Consequently, you should strive to come up
with several possible solutions whose advantages and disadvantages can be
weighed. Keep in mind that the most imaginative solutions sometimes occur
only after you've struggled with a number of other possibilities.

   Look back at the way you defined the problem and described your readers.
Then, with these in mind, list as many possible solutions as you can think of.
For ideas, reflect on the following problem-solving questions:

*Using a word processor,
you might create a
separate file for solutions
or add them to your
definition file.*

■   What solutions to this problem have already been tried?

■   What solutions have been proposed for related problems? Might they
    solve this problem as well?

- Is a solution required that would disband or change the community or group in some way?
- What solution might eliminate some of the causes of the problem?
- What solution would eliminate any of the bad effects of the problem?
- Maybe the problem is too big to be solved all at once. Try dividing it into several parts. What solutions might solve these parts?
- If a series of solutions is required, which should come first? second?
- What solution would ultimately solve the problem?
- What might be a daring solution? What would be the most conservative solution, acceptable to nearly everyone in the community or group?

Give yourself enough time to let your ideas percolate, continuing to add to your list of possible solutions and to consider the advantages and disadvantages of each one in light of your prospective readers. If possible, discuss your solutions with members of the community or group who can help you consider advantages and disadvantages of the possible solutions.

Choosing the Most Promising Solution.   In a sentence or two, state what you would consider the best possible way of solving the problem.

Determining Specific Steps.   Write down the steps necessary to carry out your solution. This list will provide an early test of whether your solution can, in fact, be implemented.

Defending Your Solution

Proposals have to be feasible—that is, they must be both reasonable and practical. Imagine that one of your readers opposes your proposed solution and confronts you with the following statements. Write several sentences refuting each one.

- It won't really solve the problem.
- I'm comfortable with things as they are.
- We can't afford it.
- It will take too long.
- People won't do it.
- Too few people will benefit.
- I don't even see how to get started on your solution.
- It's already been tried, with unsatisfactory results.
- You're making this proposal because it will benefit you personally.

Answering these questions should help you prepare responses to possible objections. If you feel you need a better idea of how others are likely to feel about your proposal, talk to a few people involved with the problem. The more you know about your readers' concerns, the better you will be able to anticipate reservations they may offer or alternative solutions they might prefer.

Testing Your Choice

Now examine the problem and your chosen solution to see whether they will result in a strong proposal. Start by asking the following questions:

- Is this a significant problem? Do other people in the community or group really care about it, or can they be persuaded to care?
- Will my solution really solve the problem? Can it be implemented?
- Can I answer objections from enough people in the community or group to win support for my solution?

As you plan and draft your proposal, you will probably want to consider these questions again. If at any point you decide that you cannot answer them affirmatively and confidently, you may want to find another solution or even to write about some other problem.

For Group Inquiry

Now might be a good time to get together with two or three other students and run your chosen topics by one another. Assess their awareness of the problem, and "try out" your solution on them. Are they convinced that it is a possible solution? a good solution? What objections or reservations do they offer? What alternative solutions do they suggest? Does the problem you have chosen still seem important, and your solution feasible?

Offering Reasons for Your Proposal

To make a convincing case for your proposed solution, you will need to offer your readers good reasons for adopting your proposal.

You might create a separate computer file for reasons, or add them to an earlier file.

Listing Reasons.   Write down every plausible reason you could give that might persuade readers to accept your proposal. These reasons should answer readers' key question: "Why is this the best solution?"

Choosing the Strongest Reasons.   Keeping your readers in mind, look over your list and put an asterisk next to the strongest reasons. If you do not consider two or three of your reasons strong, you may anticipate difficulty developing a strong proposal and should reconsider your topic.

Developing Your Strongest Reasons.   Now look at these strongest reasons and explain briefly why you think each one will be effective with your particular readers. Then take around five minutes to write about each reason, developing your argument on its behalf.

Considering Alternative Solutions

Even if your readers are likely to consider your proposal reasonable, they will probably want to compare your proposed solution with other possible solutions. List alternative solutions that might be offered, and consider the advantages and disadvantages of each one next to your solution. You might find it helpful to chart the information as follows:

Possible Solutions	Advantages	Disadvantages
My solution		
Alternative solution 1		
Alternative solution 2		

Doing Research

For guidelines on library research, see Chapter 21.

Thus far you have relied largely upon your own knowledge and instincts for solving the problem. You may now feel that you need to do some library research to learn more about the causes of the problem, perhaps, or to find more technical information about implementing the solution. If you are proposing a solution to a problem about which others have written, you will probably want to find out how they have defined it and what solutions they have proposed. You may need to acknowledge these solutions in your essay, either accommodating or refuting them. Now is a good time—before beginning to draft—to get any additional information you need.

PLANNING AND DRAFTING

To help you plan your essay and begin drafting, review what you have done so far, set some specific goals for yourself, and prepare an outline.

Seeing What You Have

It's a good idea at this point to print out a hard copy of what you have written on a word processor for easier reviewing.

Reread your invention notes, asking yourself whether you have a good topic—an interesting problem with a feasible solution. If at this point you are doubtful about the significance of the problem or the success of your proposed solution, you might want to look for a new topic. If you are unsure about these basic points, you cannot expect to produce a persuasive draft.

   If your invention material seems thin but promising, however, you may be able to strengthen it with additional invention writing. Consider the following questions:

- Could I make a stronger case for the seriousness of the problem?
- Could I find more reasons for readers to support my solution?
- Are there any other ways of refuting attractive alternative solutions or troubling questions about my own proposed solution?

Setting Goals

Before beginning to draft, think seriously about the overall goals of your proposal. Not only will the draft be easier to write once you have clear goals, but it will almost surely be more convincing.

   Following are some goal-setting questions to consider now. You may find it useful to return to them while drafting, for they are designed to help you focus on exactly what you want to accomplish with this proposal.

Your Readers

- What do my readers already know about this problem?
- Are they likely to welcome my solution or resist it?
- Can I anticipate any specific reservations or objections they may have?
- How can I gain readers' enthusiastic support? How can I get them to help implement the solution?
- What kind of tone would be most appropriate? How can I present myself so that I seem both reasonable and authoritative?

The Beginning

- How can I immediately engage my readers' interest? Should I open with a dramatic scenario, like O'Malley? With statistics that highlight the seriousness of the problem, like Kibler? By quoting an authority on the problem, like Kaus? With a question, like Weisman?
- What information should I give first?

Defining the Problem

- How much do I need to say about the problem's causes or history?
- How can I show the seriousness of the problem? Should I use statistics, like Kibler and Weisman? Stress negative consequences, like O'Malley?
- Is it an urgent problem? How can I emphasize this? Should I redefine the problem, like Kibler?
- How much space should I devote to defining the problem? Only a little space, like O'Malley, or much space, like Kibler?

Proposing a Solution

- How can I present my solution so that it looks like the best way to proceed? Should I show how to implement it in stages, like Kibler? Focus on reasons to support it, like O'Malley?
- How can I make the solution seem easy to implement? Or should I acknowledge that the solution may be difficult to implement and argue that it will be worth the effort?

Anticipating Objections

- Should I mention every possible objection to my proposed solution? How might I choose among them?
- Has anyone raised these objections? Should I name the person?
- Should I accommodate certain objections?
- What specific reasons can I give for refuting each objection? How can I support these reasons?
- How can I refute the objections without seeming to attack anyone?

Rejecting Alternative Solutions

- How many alternative solutions do I need to mention? Which ones should I discuss?
- Should I indicate where these alternatives come from? Like Kaus, should I name those who proposed them?
- What reasons should I give for rejecting the alternative solutions? Like O'Malley, can I offer any evidence in support of my reasons?
- How can I reject these other solutions without seeming to criticize their proponents? Both Weisman and O'Malley succeed at this.

The Ending

- How should I conclude? Should I end by restating the problem and summarizing the solution, as Kibler does? By arguing that the solution is workable and might bring about cultural change, as Kaus does? By arguing that some readers' preferred solution is sure to fail, as Weisman does? Or simply by summarizing my solution and its advantages, as does O'Malley?
- Is there something special about the problem itself I should remind readers of at the end?
- Should I end with an inspiring call to action or a scenario suggesting the consequences of a failure to solve the problem?
- Would a shift to humor or satire be an effective way to end?

Outlining

Outlining on a word processor makes it particularly easy to experiment with different ways of planning your essay.

After setting goals for your proposal, you will be ready to make a working outline. The basic outline for a proposal is quite simple:

the problem
the solution
the reasons for accepting the solution

This simple plan is nearly always complicated by other factors, however. In outlining your material you must take into consideration many other details, such as whether readers already recognize the problem, how much agreement exists on the need to solve the problem, how many alternative solutions are available, how much attention must be given to the other solutions, and how many objections should be expected.

Here is a possible outline for a proposal where readers may not understand the problem fully and other solutions have been proposed:

presentation of the problem
  its existence
  its seriousness
  its causes
consequences of failing to solve the problem

description of the proposed solution

list of steps for implementing the solution

discussion of reasons to support the solution
  acknowledgment of objections
  accommodation or refutation of objections

See pp. 274–75 for another sample outline.

consideration of alternative solutions and their disadvantages

restatement of the proposed solution and its advantages

Your outline will of course reflect your own writing situation. As you develop it, think about what your readers know and feel, and about your own writing goals. Once you have a working outline, you should not hesitate to change it as necessary while writing. For instance, you might find it more effective to hold back on presenting your own solution until you have dismissed other possible solutions. Or you might find a better way to order the reasons for adopting your proposal. The purpose of an outline is to identify the basic features of your proposal and help you organize them effectively, not to lock you into a particular structure.

Most of the information you will need to develop each feature can be found in your invention writing and research notes. How much space you devote to each feature is determined by the topic, not the outline. Do not assume that each entry on your outline must be given one paragraph—in the preceding example, each of the reasons for supporting the solution may require a paragraph, but you might also present the reasons, objections, and refutations all in one paragraph.

Drafting

If you can shift between screens, you might call up invention material on an alternate screen as you draft on the main screen, shifting back and forth to cut and paste invention material into your draft.

After reviewing your outline, start drafting the proposal. Let the outline help you write, but don't hesitate to change it if you find that drafting takes you in an unexpected direction. If you get stuck in drafting, return to the invention activities earlier in this chapter. As you draft, keep in mind the two main goals of proposal writing: (1) to establish that a problem exists that is serious enough to require a solution; and (2) to demonstrate that your proposed solution is feasible and is the best possible alternative. You might want to review the general advice on drafting on pp. 12–14.

GETTING CRITICAL COMMENTS

At this point your draft would benefit from a good critical reading. All writers find it helpful to have someone else read and comment on their drafts, and your instructor may schedule such a reading as part of your coursework. Otherwise, you can ask a classmate, friend, or family member to read it over. If your campus has a writing center, you might ask a tutor there to read and comment on your draft. In this section are guidelines designed to be used by *anyone* reviewing an essay proposing a solution to a problem. (If you are unable to get someone else to review your draft, turn to the Revision section on pp. 289–93 where you will find guidelines for approaching your own draft with a critical eye.)

To provide focused, helpful comments, your reader must know your intended audience and purpose. At the top of your draft, write out the following information:

Audience. Who are your readers?

Purpose. What do you hope will happen as a result of your proposal?

Reading with a Critical Eye

Reading a draft critically means reading it more than once, first to get a general impression and then to analyze its basic features.

Reading for a First Impression.   Read first to get a basic understanding of the problem and the proposed solution to it. As you read, try to notice any words or passages that contribute either favorably or unfavorably to your impression. After reading the draft, briefly write out your impressions. How convincing do you think the essay will be for its particular readers? What do you notice about the way the problem is presented and the solution argued for?

See pp. 276–79 to review the basic features.

Reading to Analyze.   Now read to focus on the basic features of proposal writing. Consider the following questions:

How Well Is the Problem Defined?

Decide whether the problem is stated clearly. Is enough information given about its causes and consequences? What more might be done to establish its seriousness? Is there more readers might need or wish to know about it?

How Clearly Is the Solution Presented?

Restate the solution. Is it clear? How could its presentation be strengthened? Are steps for implementation laid out? If not, might readers expect or require them? Does the solution seem practical? If not, why?

How Convincing Is the Argument for the Solution?

Look at the reasons and evidence offered to support this solution. Are they sufficient? Which are most and least convincing? Why?

Consider the treatment of objections to the proposed solution. What reasons and evidence refuting objections seem most convincing? Which seem least convincing? Why? Are there other objections or reservations that need to be acknowledged?

Are alternative solutions discussed and either accommodated or refuted? What are the most convincing reasons given against any other solutions? Which are least convincing, and why?

How Appropriate Is the Tone?

Is the proposal advanced in a reasonable tone, one that argues forcefully yet finds some common ground with readers who may advocate alternative solutions? Are such solutions accommodated or rejected without a personal attack on those who propose them?

How Effective Is the Organization?

Evaluate the *overall plan* of the proposal, perhaps by outlining it briefly. Would any parts be more effective earlier or later? Look closely at the ordering of the argument for the solution—the presentation of the reasons and the accommodation or refutation of objections and alternative solutions. How might the sequence be revised to strengthen the argument? Point to any gaps in the argument.

Is the *beginning* engaging? If not, how might it be revised to capture the readers' attention? Does it adequately forecast the main ideas and the plan of the proposal? Can you think of other ways to begin?

Evaluate the *ending*. Does it frame the proposal by echoing or referring to something at the beginning? If not, how might it do so? Does the ending convey a sense of urgency? Can you think of a stronger way to conclude?

What Final Thoughts Do You Have?

What is the strongest part of this proposal? What part most needs more work?

REVISING AND EDITING

This section will help you to identify problems in your draft and to revise and edit to solve them.

Identifying Problems

To identify problems in your draft, you need to read it objectively, analyze its basic features, and study any comments you've received from others.

Getting an Overview.   Consider the draft as a whole, trying to see it objectively. It may help to do so in two steps:

Reread. If at all possible, put the draft aside for a day or two before rereading it. When you reread, start by reconsidering your audience and purpose. Then read the draft straight through, trying to see it as your intended readers will.

Even if your essay is saved to a computer file, reread from a hard copy, preferably draft quality. Onscreen or as letter-quality hard copy, a paper can look more "finished" than it really is. Add notes to yourself and quick revisions as you read through the draft.

Outline. Make a scratch outline to get an overview of the essay's development. This outline can be sketchy—words and phrases instead of complete sentences—but it should identify the basic features as they appear.

Charting a Plan for Revision.   Use the following chart to keep track of any problems you need to solve. The left-hand column lists the basic features of proposals. As you analyze your draft and study any comments from others, note in the right-hand column the problems you want to solve.

Basic Features   *Problems to Solve*

Definition of the problem

Presentation of the solution

Argument for the solution

Acknowledgement of alternative
solutions

Tone

Organization

Analyzing the Basic Features of Your Draft.   Turn now to the questions for
analyzing a draft on pp. 288–89. Using these as guidelines, identify problems
in your draft. Note anything you need to solve on the chart above.

Studying Critical Comments.   Review any comments you've received from
other readers, and add to the chart any points that need attention. Try not
to react too defensively to these comments; by letting you see how others
respond to your draft, they provide invaluable information about how you
might improve it.

Solving the Problems

Before revising using a word processor, copy your original draft to a second file. Then, should you change your mind about material you delete while revising, it will still be available to you.

Having identified problems, you now need to find solutions and to carry them
out. You have three ways of finding solutions: (1) review your invention notes
for additional information and ideas; (2) do further invention to answer questions your readers raised; and (3) look back at the readings in this chapter to
see how other writers have solved similar problems.

Following are suggestions to get you started on solving some of the problems common to writing proposals. For now, focus on solving those problems
identified on your chart. Avoid tinkering with sentence-level problems; that
will come later, when you edit.

Definition of the Problem

■   If the problem is not clearly defined, consider sketching out its history,
     including past attempts to deal with it, discussing its causes and conse-
     quences more fully, dramatizing its seriousness more vividly, or compar-
     ing it to other problems readers may be familiar with.

Presentation of the Solution

■   If the solution is not adequately described, try outlining the steps or
     phases in its implementation. Help readers see how easy the first step will
     be, or acknowledge the difficulty of the first step.

Argument for the Solution

■   If the argument seems weak, try to think of more reasons why readers
     should support your proposal.

- If your refutation of any objection or reservation seems unconvincing, consider accommodating it by modifying your proposal.
- If you have left out any likely objections readers will have to the solution, acknowledge them and either accommodate or refute them.
- If you neglected to mention alternative solutions some readers are likely to prefer, do so now. Consider whether you want to accommodate or reject these alternatives. For each one, try to acknowledge its good points but argue that it is not so good a solution as your own. You may, in fact, want to strengthen your own solution by incorporating into it some of the good points from alternatives.

Tone

- If your tone seems too adversarial, revise to acknowledge your readers' fears, biases, and expectations.

Organization

Use your word processor's cut-and-paste or block-and-move functions to shift material around. Make sure that transitions are revised so that material fits in its new spot.

- If the argument or the essay is hard to follow, find a better sequence for the major parts. Try to put reasons supporting your solution in a more convincing order—leading up to the strongest one rather than putting it first, perhaps. Shift refutation of objections or alternative solutions so that they do not interrupt the main argument. Add explicit cues to keep the reader on track: previews of what is coming, transitional phrases and sentences, brief summaries of points just made.

For more on cues, see Chapter 13.

- If the beginning is weak, is there a better place to start? Would an anecdote or an example of the problem engage readers more quickly?
- If the ending doesn't work, consider framing your proposal by mentioning something from the beginning of your essay, or ending with a call for action that expresses the urgency of implementing your solution.

Editing and Proofreading

You've probably worried little thus far about matters of grammar and style. Now, however, is the time to check for errors in usage, punctuation, and mechanics, and also to consider matters of style.

When you use your word processor's spell check function to aid in proofreading for spelling, keep in mind that it will not find all misspellings, particularly misused homonyms (such as there, their, and they're), typos that are themselves words (such as fro for for), and many proper nouns and specialized

Checking for Ambiguous Use of *This* and *That*. One common error many of us make is to use *this* and *that* vaguely, to refer to other words or ideas. Such usage can confuse readers if it's not absolutely clear what exactly is being referred to. In writing a proposal, you must frequently refer to the problem and the solution, and you'll often use pronouns to avoid the monotony or wordiness of repeatedly referring to them by name. Check your draft carefully for ambiguous use of *this* or *that*. Often the easiest way to edit such usage is to add a specific noun after *this* or *that*, as Patrick O'Malley did in the following example from his essay in this chapter:

terms. Proofread these carefully yourself, using hard copy and a dictionary if necessary. Also proofread for words that should have been deleted when you edited a sentence.

Another possible solution would be to help students prepare for midterm and final exams by providing sets of questions from which the exam questions will be selected or announcing possible exam topics at the beginning of the course. This solution would have the advantage of reducing students' anxiety about learning every fact in the textbook. . . .

O'Malley avoids an ambiguous *this* in the second sentence by repeating the noun *solution*. (He might also have written *this preparation*.) Following are some other sentences from proposals shown as they might be edited to avoid ambiguity:

▶ A reasonable fee increase of about forty dollars a year would not be resisted by students. This _∧ would pay for the needed dormitory remodeling. *(fee increase)*

▶ Compared to other large California cities, San Diego has the weakest programs for conserving water. This _∧ and our decreasing access to Colorado River water give us reason to worry. *(neglect)*

▶ Compared to other proposed solutions to this problem, that is clearly the most feasible. *(one)*

Checking for Sentences That Lack an Agent.　Part of proposing a solution to a problem is to indicate who exactly should take action to solve the problem. Such action-takers are called "agents." An agent is one who can act. Look at one of O'Malley's sentences, for example:

To get students to complete the questions in a timely way, professors would have to collect and check the answers.

In this sentence, *professors* are the agents. They certainly have the authority to assign and collect study questions, and they would need to take this action in order for this solution to be successfully implemented. Had O'Malley instead written "the answers would have to be collected and checked," the sentence would lack an agent. Naming an agent helps make his argument convincing, demonstrating to readers that O'Malley has thought through one of the key parts of any proposal: who is going to take action.

Following are sentences from student proposals that illustrate how you can edit agentless sentences:

▶ ~~A survey could be planned~~ to find out more about students' problems scheduling the courses they need. *(Your staff should plan a survey)*

▶ Extending the deadline to mid-quarter ~~would make sense~~. *(It would make sense for the registrar to extend)*

Sometimes it is appropriate to write agentless sentences, however. Study the following examples from O'Malley's essay:

These exams should be given weekly, or at least twice monthly.

Exams could be collected and responded to only every third or fourth week.

Still another solution might be to provide frequent study questions for students to answer.

These sentences are all fine without naming explicit agents because it is clear from the larger context who will perform the action. In each case, it is obvious that the action will be carried out by a teacher.

A Writer at Work

STRENGTHENING THE ARGUMENT

This section focuses on Patrick O'Malley's successful efforts to strengthen the argument for his proposed solution in his essay "More Testing, More Learning." Read first the three paragraphs below from his draft. Then compare these with paragraphs 4–6 in his revision on pp. 270–75. As you read, take notes on differences you observe between draft and revision.

The predominant reason why students perform better with multiple exams is that they improve their study habits. Greater regularity in test taking means greater regularity in studying for tests. Students prone to cramming will be forced to open their textbooks more often, keeping them away from long, "kamikaze" nights of studying. Regularity prepares them for the "real world" where you rarely take on large tasks at long intervals. Several tests also improve study habits by reducing procrastination. An article about procrastination from the <u>Journal of Counseling Psychology</u> reports that "students view exams as difficult, important, and anxiety provoking." These symptoms of anxiety leading to procrastination could be solved if individual test importance was lessened, reducing the stress associated with the perceived burden.

With multiple exams, this anxiety decrease will free students to perform better. Several, less important tests may appear as less of an obstacle, allowing the students to worry less, leaving them free to concentrate on their work without any emotional hindrances. It is proven that "the performance of test-anxious subjects varies inversely with evaluation stress." It would also

be to the psychological benefit of students if they were
not subjected to the emotional ups and downs of large exams where they are virtually worry-free one moment and
ready to check into the psychiatric ward the next.

　　Lastly, with multiple exams, students can learn how
to perform better on future tests in the class. Regular
testing allows them to "practice" the information they
learned, thereby improving future test scores. In just
two exams, they are not able to learn the instructor's
personal examination style, and are not given the chance
to adapt their study habits to it. The American Psychologist concludes: "It is possible to influence teaching
and learning by changing the type of tests."

One difference you may have noted between the draft and revision paragraphs is the sequencing of specific reasons why readers should accept the
solution and take action on it. Whereas the draft moves in three paragraphs
from improving study habits to decreasing anxiety to performing better on
future tests, the revision moves from learning more and performing better
on major exams to improving study habits to decreasing anxiety. The reason
for the change was that a response from a classmate and a conference with
his instructor helped O'Malley to see that the most convincing reason to his
readers—professors—would probably be the improved quality of students'
learning, not their habits and feelings. As he continued thinking about his
argument and discovering further relevant research, he shifted his emphasis
from the psychological to the intellectual benefits of frequent exams.

　　You may also have noticed that each paragraph of the revision is better
focused. The psychological benefits (reduced anxiety as a result of less procrastination) are now discussed mainly in a single paragraph (the third),
whereas in the draft they were mixed in with the intellectual benefits in the
first two paragraphs. O'Malley also tried to use more precise language: for
example, he changed "future tests" to "major exams, projects, and papers."

　　Another change you may have noticed is that all of the quoted research
material in the draft has been replaced in the revision. Extending his library
research for evidence to support his reasons, O'Malley discovered the very
useful Harvard report. As his argument found a more logical sequence, more
precise terms, and fuller elaboration, he saw different ways to use the research
studies he had turned up initially and quoted in the draft.

　　A final difference is that in the revision O'Malley argues his reasons more
effectively. Consider the paragraphs on improved study habits. In the draft
paragraph O'Malley shifts abruptly from study habits to procrastination to
anxiety. Except for study habits, none of these topics is developed; and the
quotation adds nothing to what he has already said. By contrast, the revision
paragraph focuses strictly on study habits. O'Malley keeps the best sentences

from the draft for the beginning of the revised paragraph, but he adds several new sentences attempting to convince readers of the soundness of his argument that frequent exams change students' study habits. These sentences anticipate a possible objection ("It might be argued . . . "), note a contrast between complex academic learning and familiar survival skills, and assert claims about the special requirements of regular academic study. The quotation from the Harvard report supports rather than merely repeats O'Malley's claims, and it effectively concludes the paragraph.

Thinking Critically about What You've Learned

By this point, you have had considerable experience with proposals—reading them, talking about them, and writing one. Now, then, is a good time to think about what you've learned about this genre. First, we'll ask you to reflect on your own writing process, discovering what you learned about solving problems you encountered in writing a proposal. Then, you will review how reading other proposals influenced your own. Finally, you'll have a chance to explore from a critical perspective the role proposals play in shaping our society and our lives.

REFLECTING ON YOUR WRITING

To reflect on what you have learned about writing an essay proposing a solution, first, gather all of your writing—invention, planning notes, drafts, any critical comments from classmates and your instructor, revising notes and plans, and final revision. Review these materials and refer to them as you complete the following writing task.

- Identify *one* writing problem you needed to solve as you worked on your proposal essay. Don't be concerned with sentence-level problems; concentrate, instead, on problems unique to developing a proposal essay. For example: Did you puzzle over how to convince readers that your proposed solution would actually solve the problem you identified? Did you find it difficult to outline the steps required to implement the solution? Did you have trouble coming up with alternative solutions your readers might favor?
- How did you recognize the writing problem? When did you first discover it? What called it to your attention? If you didn't become aware of the problem until someone else pointed it out to you, can you now see hints of it in your invention writings? If so, where specifically? When you first recognized the problem, how did you respond?
- Reflect on how you went about solving the problem. Did you work on the wording of a passage, cut or add details about the problem

or solution, or move paragraphs or sentences around? Did you re-read one of the essays in this chapter to see how another writer handled the problem, or did you look back at the invention suggestions? If you have talked about the writing problem with another student, a tutor, or your instructor, did talking about it help? How useful was the advice you got?

■ Now, write a page or two telling your instructor about the problem and how you solved it. Be as specific as possible in reconstructing your efforts. Quote from your invention, draft, others' critical comments, your revision plan, or your revised essay to show the various changes your writing underwent as you tried to solve the problem. Taking time to explain how you identified a particular problem, how you went about solving it, and what you've learned from this writing experience can help you in solving future writing problems.

REVIEWING WHAT YOU LEARNED FROM READING

Your own essay has certainly been influenced to some extent by one or more of the proposals you have read in this chapter, as well as by classmates' essays you may have read. These other proposals may, for example, have helped you decide how to show your readers the seriousness of the problem you focused on, or they may have suggested how you could convince readers that your proposed solution deserves their support and that they should ignore alternative solutions. Take time now to reflect on what you have learned from the readings in this chapter and consider some ways your reading has influenced your writing.

■ Reread the final revision of your essay; then look back at the selections you read before completing your essay. Do you see any specific influences? For example, if you were impressed with the way one of the readings defined the problem, built a bridge of shared concerns with readers, detailed the steps in implementing the solution, argued against an alternative solution, or demonstrated that the solution would not cost too much, look to see where you might have been striving for similar effects in your own writing. Also, look for ideas you got from your reading, writing strategies you were inspired to try, specific details you were led to include, effects you sought to achieve.

■ Write a page or so explaining to your instructor how the readings in this chapter influenced your revised essay. Did one selection have a particularly strong influence, or were several selections influential in different ways? Quote from the selections and from your final revision to show how your proposal essay was influenced by your reading of other proposals in this chapter. Finally, point out any ways you've discovered to improve your revised essay still further as you've reviewed the readings in this chapter.

CONSIDERING THE SOCIAL DIMENSIONS OF PROPOSALS TO SOLVE PROBLEMS

Proposals to solve problems are the workhorses of our society. Business, education, and government especially depend on proposals to decide where to direct resources and energy. Proposals enable us as individuals and as a society to make things better. We probably value this kind of thinking and writing because it makes us feel effective. It convinces us that difficulties can be overcome, that we can make practical, material changes that will improve our lives and the lives of others. We tell ourselves that with a little time, hard work, and ingenuity, we *can* make a difference. And this attitude has produced many positive changes in our culture—improvements in civil rights, in gender equality, in business and applied sciences as diverse as bridge building and environmental protection. Even so, thorny problems persist in the very areas where the most gains have been accomplished.

Who Defines the Problem? First, proposing solutions shapes our thinking about some aspect of our own and others' lives by labeling it a "problem." Yet those most directly affected by the solution may not even accept this definition and least want to see any change. Most men who harass women on the street, for example, do not see their behavior as a "problem," yet they would, if Kaus's proposal became reality, feel its most negative effect in the form of misdemeanor citations. Similarly, not all students regard not being tested often enough as a "problem," but O'Malley's "solution" would affect them nonetheless.

This question of definition becomes particularly difficult when a relatively powerless constituency in our society—the homeless, illegal immigrants, unwed teenage mothers—is designated a "problem" by politicians, and others in the mainstream. Writers (and readers) of proposals must tread carefully in such circumstances. For example, many politicians and citizens consider immigration from Mexico a problem; we hear arguments that immigrants take American jobs and sometimes require expensive social services like schooling and medical care. In Southern California, Arizona, and Texas, however, many farmers and business owners rely on legal and illegal immigrant workers to keep costs of production low, and studies have shown that workers pay more in taxes on their wages than they absorb in social services. Immigrants themselves view their migration not as a problem but as an opportunity, for which they may take considerable risks in getting across the border. Those who agree there is a problem advocate solutions that range from building high fences and training more attack dogs to strengthening the Mexican economy so that jobs will be available to the Mexican people.

The Frustrations of Effecting Real Change. No matter how well-researched and well-argued, many proposals are simply never carried out. The head of a personnel department might spend weeks drawing up a persuasive and feasible proposal for establishing a company day care center, only to have upper management decide not to commit the necessary resources. A team of educators and social scientists might work several years researching and writing a comprehensive book-length proposal for dealing with the nation's drastic illiteracy rate, but never see their solutions carried out because of lack of co-ordination among the country's various educational institutions and governing bodies. In fact, it might be argued that the most successful proposals often operate on the smallest scale. That is, for example, a proposal suggesting ways for a single community to increase literacy rates would probably have a better chance for implementation and ultimate success than would the more far-reaching national proposal. (Yet, this is not to rule out the value of the national proposal, on which the local proposal might, in fact, be based.)

Further, in choosing among competing alternative proposals, decision-makers—who usually hold the power of the purse strings and necessarily represent a fairly conservative position—often go for the one that is cheapest, most expedient, and least disruptive. They may also choose small, incremental changes over more fundamental, radical solutions. While sometimes the best choice, such immediately feasible solutions may also merely patch over a problem, failing to solve it structurally. They may even inadvertently maintain the status quo by throwing the dog a bone—giving those who want change something to chew on, but not really relieving their hunger. Worse, they can cause people to give up all attempts to resolve a problem after superficial treatments fail.

For Discussion. Following are some questions that can help you think critically about the role of essays proposing solutions. As you read and, perhaps, discuss these questions in class, note down your responses. Then, write a page or so for your instructor presenting your thoughts about the social dimensions of proposal-writing.

1. Some believe that Americans value solving problems because it makes them feel effective and progressive. It could be argued, however, that Americans tend to avoid problems. What do you think?

2. Consider whether the proposals you've read attempt fundamental or superficial change. For which proposals is this an easy question to answer and for which is it a hard question? What about your own proposal? If you find it more difficult than you thought to

answer this question, or if you and your classmates disagree, how can you account for this difficulty and disagreement?

3. How specifically would the proposals you've read and written actually make things better? Whose interests would be served by these solutions? Who would be affected without their own stated interests being served?

4. Because proposal writing invites writers to select problems that are solvable, they might inadvertently attempt to solve a minor problem that's actually only a small part of a major problem. Do any of these proposals—including yours—reveal this misdirection? If so, which ones, and what do you think is the major problem in each case? Do you think the minor problem is worth solving as a first step toward solving the major problem, or is it perhaps an unfortunate diversion?

5. How do the proposals you've read and written challenge the status quo? If they do, what is the status quo they challenge, and just how do they challenge it? What road blocks might deter these challenges? Might they be more successfully carried out on a local scale?

6. Do any of these proposals try to improve the status of a group that is not particularly powerful? If so, what would you guess might be the motives of the proposal writer? What evidence is there that the writer is a member of this group or has consulted members of the group? What gives the writer authority to speak for them?

7. Many commentators argue that we shouldn't try to solve fundamental social problems by "throwing money at them." Do you think this is legitimate criticism of most proposals to solve such problems? Or is this a manipulative justification for allowing the rich and powerful to maintain the status quo? What else, besides money, is required to solve serious social problems? Where are these other "resources" to come from?

In an article about the upcoming Rose Bowl game, a reporter for the *Los Angeles Times* evaluates the two competing teams, who represent the Pacific Ten and Big Ten conferences. She predicts victory for the Pacific Ten team, contending that it has a better-balanced offense as well as more depth and experience at each position. As support for her prediction, the reporter names several specific players and mentions some key plays from earlier games. To refute the likely objection that the Pacific Ten team won fewer games during the regular season, she argues that it played a much tougher schedule than the Big Ten team.

The president of a large computer corporation writes a letter recommending one of his employees for an upper-level management position at another company. He praises her judgment, energy, and interpersonal skills, mentioning several incidents as support for his claims. He describes in detail her contributions to several specific projects.

A *Skiing* reporter writes an article evaluating two popular makes of slalom skis. He assumes his audience to be made up of experienced downhill skiers who may not have actually done any slalom racing. Focusing on design, he argues that one make is superior to the other. He cites specific differences in waist width, sidecut radius, camber, and shovel stiffness as support for his judgment.

In a column syndicated to college newspapers, a writer reviews two newly revised paperback thesauri. Both are selling well in college bookstores. The reporter compares the two on the basis of size, price, and usefulness. Usefulness leads to further comparisons of format and specific sample entries. She concludes by recommending one thesaurus over the other.

A staff member of a politically liberal public policy group writes an article evaluating a conservative state senator whom her group opposes on most issues. After researching the senator's legislative activities and voting record, she decides to base her evaluation on three areas: the senator's responsibility in carrying out legislative duties, his voting record in support of public programs, and his willingness to educate the voters on important issues. These areas provide adequate support for her negative judgment: the senator is often absent for important votes, he votes consistently against antipoverty bills, and he makes little effort to provide his constituents with news about important issues. She documents each of these reasons—and all the others in her article—with specific evidence gathered in her research. At several points in the paper she contrasts the senator's activities and voting record with those of other state senators.

We all make judgments. Many times each day we make evaluations, usually spontaneously, in response to events, people, things. In everyday conversation we often share our evaluations. Rarely do we think out a reasoned, detailed argument for our evaluations, although we constantly give reasons for our opinions in a casual way. By contrast, we expect judgments stated in writing to be authoritative and persuasive, with a planned, coherent, reasoned argument. We expect that the writer will use appropriate standards of evaluation, and that the judgment will be supported with reasons, evidence, and examples.

If your college has a system of student course evaluations, you will regularly evaluate your instructors. On the job, you will be evaluated and may eventually evaluate others for promotions, awards, or new jobs. You may also be asked to evaluate various plans and proposals, and your success at these important writing tasks may in large part determine your career success. In a more fundamental way, studying and writing evaluations contributes to your intellectual development, teaching you to define the standards for any judgments you are called upon to make and then to develop a reasoned argument with evidence to support your evaluation.

Your purpose in writing evaluations is to convince readers that you have made an informed judgment. You may want to convince them that a particular movie is worth seeing, a research report seriously flawed, a competitor's product brilliantly innovative, an applicant for a position not the person to hire. In these and innumerable other writing situations in college and on the job, you must establish your authority and credibility in order to win the trust of your readers. You do that essentially by basing your judgment on sound reasoning and solid evidence. This evidence comes from a thorough analysis of your subject, an analysis that ensures a detailed and comprehensive understanding.

Writing in Your
Other Courses

Evaluation is basic to thinking and learning—and thus to writing. It underlies all types of argument, forming with cause-and-effect analysis the basic building blocks of argument. As a college student, you may be asked to evaluate books, artworks, scientific discoveries, or current events, as these typical assignments suggest:

- *For a film studies course*: Of the genres we've studied this semester, I've selected action films as the basis for your final exam. In the library, at either 2:00 or 8:00 p.m. on December 6, you can view *The Sugerland Express* (Steven Spielberg, 1974). You may want to see the film twice. Take notes to prepare for the following essay exam: explain how the film belongs to the action genre and evaluate it as an example of the genre, comparing it to other action films screened and discussed in class.

- *For an astronomy course*: Which of two theories—the big bang theory or the pulsating universe theory—better explains the origin of the universe?

- *For a political science course*: Evaluate the two major presidential candidates' performances during one of their scheduled televised debates. If possible, record the debate so that you can analyze it closely and quote the candidates directly. Make a file of newspaper and magazine clippings on the debate, along with reports of polls taken before and after it. Take notes on the post-debate television commentary. Use this material to support your judgment of who won the debate.

- *For a twentieth-century American history course*: Review one of several published studies of the Vietnam War. Your review should describe the approach taken in the book and evaluate both the accuracy of its facts and the quality of its interpretation.

For Group Inquiry

Assume that you have been asked to review some form of popular entertainment. Get together with two or three other students and choose a type of entertainment you all know fairly well: country-western music, horror movies, music videos, magic acts, or any other kind of entertainment. Then discuss what standards should be used in reviewing this type of entertainment. For example, the standards for reviewing a movie might include the movie's entertainment value (if it's a comedy, is it funny?), the quality of its ideas (if it's about relationships, is it insightful?), and its technical qualities (such as acting, direction, cinematography). Try to agree on the two or three most important standards. Then reflect on what you have learned about the role of such standards in making evaluations:

- Which standards did you agree about readily, and which created disagreement in the group?
- How can you account for these differences?
- Where do you suppose your standards came from?
- How do you think experts decide on theirs?

Readings

David **Ansen** wrote the following review of a controversial 1989 movie, *Do the Right Thing*, for *Newsweek* magazine. *Newsweek*, along with other magazines and television talk shows, ran special features on the movie and its producer-director-writer, Spike Lee.

If you have not seen *Do the Right Thing*, you might want to rent the video, but seeing the movie is not essential, since reviews are written primarily for readers who are trying to decide whether or not to see a particular film. As you read this review, consider whether you would decide to see *Do the Right Thing* on the basis of what Ansen says about it.

SEARING, NERVY AND VERY HONEST
DAVID ANSEN

Somewhere near the midpoint in Spike Lee's "Do the Right Thing"—as the summer heat in Bedford-Stuyvesant reaches the boiling point—there occurs an astonishing outpouring of racial invective, five short soliloquies of ethnic slurs directed straight at the camera. A black man insults Italians. An Italian defames blacks. A Puerto Rican castigates Koreans. A white cop rips into Puerto Ricans. A Korean slanders Jews. At which point Lee cuts to the neighborhood radio deejay, Mister Señor Love Daddy, screaming into his mike "Time Out!" . . . 1

Nigger, dago, kike, spic. There they are, America's dirtiest words, hurled across the screen in Lee's nervy, complex, unsettling movie. The sequence makes you catch your breath, but you also laugh as you laughed when Lenny Bruce or Richard Pryor touched a raw nerve of publicly unspoken experience. And Lee's rude comic impulse is the same as theirs: unless we air these noxious fumes, and acknowledge just how dire the racial situation has become, this great unmelted pot might well explode. 2

When white filmmakers deal with race (from Stanley Kramer's "The Defiant Ones" to Alan Parker's "Mississippi Burning"), no matter how fine their intentions, they tend to speak in inflated, self-righteous tones, and they always come down to Hollywood's favorite dialectic, bad guys versus good guys. They allow the audience to sit comfortably on the side of the angels. In "Do the Right Thing," Lee blows away the pieties and the easy answers. He prefers abrasion and ambiguity to comfort and tidiness. As a black filmmaker, he's too close to the subject—and too much the artist—to oversimplify the issues. The beauty of "Do the Right Thing" is that all the characters, from the broadest cartoons to the most developed, are given their humanity and their due. 3

At the end of the story there is violence, police brutality, a riot. Sal's pizzeria, a white-run business that has existed peacefully in the black community for 25 years, suddenly becomes the target of pent-up rage. The owner, Sal (Danny Aiello, who's never been better), is no ogre—he's a sympathetic figure, a peacemaker who's arguably an unconscious racist. His son Pino (John Turturro), on the other hand, is blatantly antiblack, the closest to a villain the movie gets. Lee isn't saying the violence is inevitable, or even just. But we see how it comes to pass, a combination of heat, irritation, insensitivity, stubbornness and centuries of systematic oppression. 4

Lee trusts his audience: he doesn't need to stack the deck. You can feel he's 5
working out his own ambivalence on screen. His rich portrait of the Bed-Stuy community is both affectionate and critical. Take the character of Buggin' Out (Giancarlo
Esposito). He's the most militant black in the movie, but Lee shows his rage as misplaced and foolish. His attempt to boycott Sal's because there are no pictures of
blacks on the walls—only Italian-Americans—is greeted by most with derision. When
Mother Sister (Ruby Dee), the block's wise old watchdog, sees Sal's go up in flames
we're startled by her exhilaration at the violence. But moments later she's wailing in
despair at the destruction. It's one of the movie's points that we are all nursing wildly
contradictory impulses: our heads and hearts aren't always in sync. This is no cop-
out, it's unusually honest reporting.

"Do the Right Thing" is a kind of compacted epic played out in jazzy, dissonant 6
scenes that dance in and out of realism. Lee's deliberately discordant style didn't jell
in "School Daze," an ambitious but turgid look at the divisions in a black college.
Here the clashing styles add up and pay off. You leave this movie stunned, challenged and drained. To accuse Lee of irresponsibility—of inciting violence—is to be
blind to the movie he has made. The two quotes that end the film—Martin Luther
King's eloquent antiviolent testament and Malcolm X's acknowledgment that violence in self-defense may be necessary—are the logical culmination of Lee's method.
There can be no simple, tidy closure. Not now. Not yet. Lee's conscience-pricking
movie is bracing and necessary: it's the funkiest and most informed view of racism
an American filmmaker has given us.

For Discussion

Ansen refers to the two quotations that appear at the end of *Do the Right
Thing*. The first, by Martin Luther King, Jr., asserts that violence is always to
be avoided, whereas the second, by Malcolm X, counters that violence may
sometimes be necessary. Reflecting on your own experience, consider
whether violence is ever justifiable. Can you recall an occasion when you used
violence or were tempted to? What did you think the use or the show of force
would accomplish in this particular situation? What alternatives did you have?
In general, why do you think people resort to violence? In what ways does
American culture encourage or discourage violence?

For Analysis

1.   At the beginning of this chapter, we make the following assertions about
writing that evaluates:

- It makes a judgment.
- It tries to convince readers that the judgment is reasonable.
- It bases its judgment on standards appropriate to its subject.
- It strives to show that it fully understands its subjects.
- It gives reasons for its judgment.
- It supports its reasons with evidence and examples.

Consider whether each of these assertions is true of Ansen's review.

2.   Ansen uses the writing strategy of comparing and contrasting at two
different points in the essay. Find these passages. Which of the two strate-

For a discussion of comparison and contrast, see Chapter 18.

gies—comparison or contrast—is being used in each case? What does each accomplish in this essay?

3. In paragraph 6 Ansen refers to an objection by others that *Do the Right Thing* incites people to violence. On what grounds does he refute this criticism? In your view, how effective is his refutation? What advantages or disadvantages do you see in placing this refutation in the last paragraph?

4. To influence readers' decision whether or not to see a movie, a reviewer needs to gain readers' confidence. Has Ansen won your confidence? If so, how? If not, why not?

For Your Own Writing

If you were to review a movie, which one would you choose? What would be your basic judgment of this movie? What reasons would you give to convince your readers to support your judgment? Are there any criticisms of the movie that you would need to respond to in your review? If so, how would you handle them?

Commentary

This essay is typical of most movie reviews in that it primarily addresses readers who have heard about the movie and are trying to decide whether or not to see it. What these readers want to know is whether the film is worth their time and money. Ansen answers this question for *Do the Right Thing* with a thumbs up, but he knows that a good review must do more than simply assert a judgment. It must also give reasons for that judgment and cite evidence from the movie to support these reasons.

A scratch outline will help us understand his argumentative strategy:

a shockingly frank scene from the movie, immediately illustrating Ansen's title (1)

response to this scene, interpretation of it (2)

Lee's refusal to oversimplify (3)

final scene and its key characters (4)

point of the final scene (4)

Lee's trust in his audience to tolerate ambivalence and contradiction (5)

comparison to Lee's previous film (6)

refutation of the objection that Lee is irresponsible, explicit judgment of the film (6)

Ansen's title—"Searing, Nervy, and Very Honest"—lets us know immediately what he thinks about the film. This judgment is echoed in paragraph 2 in slightly different terms: "nervy, complex, unsettling." Although Ansen doesn't state explicitly, "I like this film," readers can readily see that he is praising *Do the Right Thing* and on what grounds.

His reasons for admiring the film center on the way it represents the current racial situation in America. Ansen argues that Spike Lee departs from the safe route most other filmmakers have taken when dealing with racial tensions. Instead of oversimplifying the situation, he says, Lee portrays relations between blacks and whites in all their disturbing complexity. Instead of leaving viewers feeling complacent and self-satisfied, Lee challenges them to reflect on their own values and actions.

Because Ansen knows that most moviegoers won't like being challenged, he must convince his readers that *Do the Right Thing* unsettles viewers for a good reason, and that we should admire Lee for being "nervy" and "honest." This is the essence of his argumentative strategy. Ansen carries through this strategy by trying to convince his readers that "honest reporting" is especially important in this case, airing the "noxious fumes" of racial hatred and thus helping us to realize "how dire the racial situation has become." He even goes so far as to suggest that this film might possibly help to prevent an explosion of violence.

This idea that a movie attempting to portray reality should do so honestly, without oversimplifying or giving easy answers to the difficult questions it poses, is Ansen's primary basis for judging the film. Writers do not always have to justify the basis for their judgments, as Ansen does here. If they think that their judgment will not be readily understood or accepted by their readers, however, they must develop an argumentative strategy like Ansen's that establishes the basis for judgment.

Finally, Ansen offers evidence from the movie to support his argument. In arguing that *Do the Right Thing* doesn't oversimplify, for example, he shows that Sal is portrayed sympathetically, even though he's "arguably an unconscious racist," while the militant Buggin' Out is shown to be "foolish." And to illustrate the film's "nerviness," he summarizes a sequence of scenes in which members of different ethnic groups mouth ethnic slurs.

Concrete details and examples drawn from the movie give a review credibility, helping readers both to understand and to accept the writer's argument. They also give readers a taste of the movie so that they can make their own judgments about whether it seems interesting and worth seeing. To achieve this degree of specificity, the reviewer probably has to see the film more than once and almost certainly has to take notes during or immediately after it. When you plan your own evaluation essay, make sure that you will have the opportunity to do this kind of intensive note taking, whether you review a film or some other subject.

■   ■   ■

Barbara Ehrenreich is the author of seven books, including a critique of the 1980s, *The Worst Years of Our Lives: Irreverent Notes from a Decade of Greed* (1989), and a study of the middle class, *Fear of Falling* (1989). Her essays appear regularly in the *American Scholar*, the *Atlantic*, and the *New Republic*, where this selection originally appeared in April 1990. In it she reviews the situation comedy *Roseanne*, starring Roseanne Barr.[1] As you read, notice how she includes numerous specific details and examples from different episodes of the show.

THE WRETCHED
OF THE HEARTH
BARBARA
EHRENREICH

"Roseanne" the sitcom, which was inspired by Barr the standup comic, is a radical departure simply for featuring blue-collar Americans—and for depicting them as something other than half-witted greasers and low-life louts. The working class does not usually get much of a role in the American entertainment spectacle. In the seventies mumbling, muscular blue-collar males (*Rocky, The Deer Hunter, Saturday Night Fever*) enjoyed a brief modishness on the screen, while Archie Bunker, the consummate blue-collar bigot, raved away on the tube. But even these grossly stereotyped images vanished in the eighties, as the spectacle narrowed in on the brie-and-chardonnay class. Other than "Roseanne," I can find only one sitcom that deals consistently with the sub-yuppie condition: "Married . . . with children," a relentlessly nasty portrayal of a shoe salesman and his cognitively disabled family members. There may even be others, but sociological zeal has not sufficed to get me past the opening sequences of "Major Dad," "Full House" or "Doogie Howser." [1]

Not that "Roseanne" is free of class stereotyping. The Connors must bear part of the psychic burden imposed on all working-class people by their economic and occupational betters. . . . They indulge in a manic physicality that would be unthinkable among the more controlled and genteel Huxtables. They maintain a traditional, low-fiber diet of white bread and macaroni. They are not above a fart joke. [2]

Still, in "Roseanne" I am willing to forgive the stereotypes as markers designed to remind us of where we are: in the home of a construction worker and his minimum-wage wife. Without the reminders, we might not be aware of how thoroughly the deeper prejudices of the professional class are being challenged. Roseanne's fictional husband Dan (played by the irresistibly cuddly John Goodman) drinks domestic beer and dedicates Sundays to football; but far from being a Bunkeresque boor, he looks to this feminist like the fabled "sensitive man" we have all been pining for. He treats his rotund wife like a sex goddess. He picks up on small cues signaling emotional distress. He helps with homework. And when Roseanne works overtime, he cooks, cleans, and rides herd on the kids without any of the piteous whining we have come to expect from upscale males in their rare, and lavishly documented, encounters with soiled Pampers. [3]

Roseanne Connor has her own way of defying the stereotypes. Variously employed as a fast-food operative, a factory worker, a bartender, and a telephone salesperson, her real dream is to be a writer. When her twelve-year-old daughter Darlene (brilliantly played by Sara Gilbert) balks at a poetry-writing assignment, Roseanne gives her a little talking-to involving Sylvia Plath:[2] "She inspired quite a few women, including *moi*." In another episode, a middle-aged friend thanks Roseanne for inspiring her to dump her chauvinist husband and go to college. We have come a long way from the ditherhing, cowering Edith Bunker. [4]

---

[1] Now, Roseanne Arnold.
[2] American poet and novelist (1932-63).

Most of the time the Connors do the usual sitcom things. They have the little 5
domestic misunderstandings that can be patched up in twenty-four minutes with
wisecracks and a round of hugs. But "Roseanne" carries working-class verisimilitude
into a new and previously taboo dimension—the workplace. In the world of employment, Roseanne knows exactly where she stands: "All the good power jobs are
taken. Vanna turns the letters. Leona's got hotels. Margaret's running England . . .
'Course she's not doing a very good job. . . .''

The class conflict continues on other fronts. In one episode, Roseanne arrives late 6
for an appointment with Darlene's history teacher, because she has been forced to
work overtime at Wellman. The teacher, who is leaning against her desk stretching
her quadriceps when Roseanne arrives, wants to postpone the appointment because
she has a date to play squash. When Roseanne insists, the teacher tells her that
Darlene has been barking in class, "like a dog." This she follows with some psy-
chobabble—on emotional problems and dysfunctional families—that would leave
most mothers, whatever their social class, clutched with guilt. Not Roseanne, who
calmly informs the yuppie snit that, in the Connor household, everybody barks like
dogs.

It is Barr's narrow-eyed cynicism about the family, even more than her class con- 7
sciousness, that gives "Roseanne" its special frisson. Archie Bunker got our attention
by telling us that we (blacks, Jews, "ethnics," WASPS, etc.) don't really like each other.
Barr's message is that even within the family we don't much like each other. We
love each other (who else do we have?); but The Family, with its impacted emotions,
its lopsided division of labor, and its ancient system of age-graded humiliations, just
doesn't work. Or rather, it doesn't work unless the contradictions are smoothed out
with irony and the hostilities are periodically blown off as humor. Coming from mom,
rather than from a jaded teenager or a bystander dad, this is scary news indeed. . . .

On the one hand, she presents the family as a zone of intimacy and support, 8
well worth defending against the forces of capitalism, which drive both mothers and
fathers out of the home, scratching around for paychecks. On the other hand, the
family is hardly a haven, especially of its grown-up females. It is marred from within
by—among other things—the patriarchal division of leisure, which makes dad and
the kids the "consumers" of mom's cooking, cleaning, nurturing, and (increasingly)
her earnings. Mom's job is to keep the whole thing together—to see that the mort-
gage payments are made, to fend off the viperish teenagers, to find the missing
green sock—but mom is no longer interested in being a human sacrifice on the altar
of "pro-family values." She's been down to the feminist bookstore; she's been reading Sylvia Plath.

This is a bleak and radical vision. Not given to didacticism, Barr offers no pro- 9
grammatic ways out. Surely, we are led to conclude, pay equity would help, along
with child care, and so on. But Barr leaves us hankering for a quality of change that
goes beyond mere reform: for a world in which even the lowliest among us—the
hash-slinger, the sock-finder, the factory hand—will be recognized as the poet she
truly is.

For Discussion

Some people consider America a classless country, but Ehrenreich sees definite class divisions within our society. She specifically identifies a working or
blue-collar class and a professional or yuppie class. How difficult do you think

it is for people to move from a lower class into a higher class? In other words, to what extent is the "American dream" really possible? If you think moving up is largely a myth, why do so many people continue to believe in it? Do you ever feel you want to move up? Do you have a plan for doing so?

For Analysis

For more on thesis statements, see pp. 466–67.

1.   What is Ehrenreich's judgment of *Roseanne*? Find the passage that you think is the most explicit statement of her thesis. On what basis does she make this judgment?

2.   Skim the essay, noting where Ehrenreich relates Roseanne to other television programs and films. What part does comparison and contrast play in her overall argumentative strategy?

3.   In providing evidence from the *Roseanne* series, Ehrenreich refers both to specific episodes and to elements that occur throughout the series. Skim her essay, marking references to specific episodes with a line in the margin and general references to the series with a double line. If she is evaluating the series as a whole, why do you think she refers to specific episodes? What does each kind of reference contribute to her review?

4.   Ehrenreich has some fun with this essay. Reread it, noting any passages where her writing seems especially witty. How does her use of humor influence your willingness to accept her judgment?

For Your Own Writing

Ehrenreich evaluates a television series, not just a single program. If you were assigned to evaluate a series of something—such as the *Star Wars* or *Jaws* movies, Rembrandt's or Van Gogh's self-portraits, the *Lord of the Rings* books, or a television series—what would you choose? Whatever you were to choose, you would need to examine closely several items in the series, taking notes for evidence to support your judgment.

Commentary

A great temptation for writers evaluating a subject they feel strongly about is to give it unqualified praise or blame. Few things, however, are all good or all bad, and readers are likely to see such a characterization as either/or thinking—a logical fallacy, or error in reasoning, that weakens an argument partly by undermining the writer's credibility. Ehrenreich is enthusiastic about *Roseanne* but tempers her praise in paragraph 2, where she points out that the program is not "free of class stereotyping."

Also notable is the way Ehrenreich makes her writing readable by careful use of topic sentences. Topic sentences announce the topic of the paragraph they introduce, but they may also connect the paragraph to preceding ones. Paragraph 2, for example, begins with a sentence that refers explicitly to class stereotyping, the central idea of the first paragraph. The opening sentence of paragraph 7 makes a similarly helpful connection, summarizing the central point of the first six paragraphs and identifying the main topic of the next few paragraphs.

For more on strategies for coherence, see pp. 476–79.

Two stylistic features also deserve mention: the use of the colon and repetition of sentence openings. Ehrenreich uses the colon for a variety of purposes. Sometimes it introduces an example: "Other than 'Roseanne,' I can find only one sitcom that deals consistently with the sub-yuppie condition: 'Married . . . with children,' . . .'" (paragraph 1). At other times it specifies or defines: "Still, in 'Roseanne,' I am willing to forgive the stereotypes as markers designed to remind us of where we are: in the home of a construction worker and his minimum-wage wife" (paragraph 3). And at still other times it introduces a quotation: "Roseanne gives her a little talking-to involving Sylvia Plath: 'She inspired quite a few women, including *moi*.' "

Ehrenreich repeats sentence openings to strengthen the bonds between sentences, to create a pleasing rhythm, and to emphasize the material that is repeated. The last three sentences in paragraph 2, for example, open with a "*they* + verb" construction. In paragraph 3, Ehrenreich uses a "*he* + verb" pattern in three consecutive sentences but then varies it by beginning the next sentence with a prepositional phrase followed by the expected pattern.

■   ■   ■

Kevin Stewart wrote this essay in his freshman composition course. It evaluates Tobias Wolff's remembered event essay, "On Being a Real Westerner," in Chapter 2 of this book and reveals Stewart's reasons for valuing it. As you read, notice the way Stewart provides evidence to support his argument both by citing many details in the selection and by relating his personal experience.

AN EVALUATION OF TOBIAS WOLFF'S "ON BEING A REAL WESTERNER"
KEVIN STEWART

Tobias Wolff's "On Being a Real Westerner" was a pleasure to read, and the story's tension built quickly. On rereading, I had time to admire Wolff's strategies of narrative action and detailing of the scene and people. On reflection, I was able to relate the story to my personal experience, and to appreciate the way Wolff expressed the significance of the event for his life. 1

This selection is unquestionably a "good read." It is not a simple story, because it reveals a lot and shows a range of emotions, but it is very easy to read. In the opening paragraph Wolff describes how he got a rifle from his stepfather Roy over the objections of his mother. Once we get to the main event in paragraph 5, the story moves quickly. The young Wolff's dressing up in combat and hunting gear and following people in the rifle sights of the unloaded gun seem harmless and even comical, but my response to the story changes abruptly at the beginning of paragraph 7 with the mention of live ammunition: "Roy stored his ammunition in a metal box he kept hidden in the closet." The tension and the possibility for disaster increase in paragraph 8, with mention of Wolff's irritation, and then become nearly unbearable with the opening of paragraph 9, "One afternoon I pulled the trigger," an action which the next sentence immediately suggests will be directed at one of the two old people Wolff says he was aiming at on the street. We must bear this suspense until the old people round a corner and the boy gets the two squirrels in the 2 rifle sights. That offers some relief from the tension, but in the back of my mind I kept thinking that maybe this is the beginning of a shooting spree in which several people will be killed.

While the tension contributes powerfully to my engagement with the story, the   3 careful focus of the scene and action also contributes. The scene is the apartment and specifically the living room, including what the boy can see of the street from the window. Wolff doesn't digress to describe the view or to tell us what people were wearing or whether the squirrels were gray or brown or black. Instead, Wolff keeps the focus on his actions and feelings. Only once does Wolff break the forward movement, and that is in paragraph 8 where he reflects briefly on the connection of this childhood event to his experience years later in the Vietnam War.

Still another thing that adds to my interest in the story and increases the tension   4 for me as a reader is the narrative action, Wolff's specific movements and gestures and those of other actors in the scene that help me imagine what is going on. As I've said, some of the boy's actions seem to me comical and some seem terrifying. For example, he marches around the apartment, "striking brave poses in front of the mirror" and sets up a "nest" on the couch, assuming his "position," like a sniper in a Sarajevo apartment building. Then, ominously, we see him "nudging the shade aside" and "cocking the hammer and letting it snap down." In the climactic para- graph 9, we learn that he has been "aiming at two old people" who "walked so slowly." We see the squirrels "chasing each other back and forth on the telephone wires." Wolff tells us he fired, and the squirrel "dropped straight into the road." These specific actions greatly increase my interest in the story because they each give me a strong visual image, almost as real to me as the memory of observing actions like these or seeing a film of them.

Besides enjoying this selection as a "good read," I admire the way it details ob-   5 jects and participants in the scene. The first paragraph provides examples of naming objects and detailing them. The objects of attention are the rifle (or "piece"), its action, and its stock. The rifle is detailed as follows: "light, pump-action, beautifully balanced," "better than new." The action is detailed as "silky from long use," and the stock as "walnut," "black from all its oilings," "the wood of a quality no longer to be found." These details help me understand Wolff's intense interest in the rifle, his deep desire to own it, and his great pleasure in having it for himself. In paragraph 5, the details provide a different impression, a comic or perhaps even pathetic one, based on the boy's attempts to dress up like a real Westerner. Wolff goes beyond mentioning that he dressed up in hunting gear to provide specific details: "fur troop- er's hat, camouflage coat, boots that reached nearly to my knees."

Another reason I especially liked the story was that it reminded me of the few   6 times I hunted with a weapon. One fall when I was thirteen, my uncle took me twice to hunt doves. He lent me one of his small-gauge shotguns, and we walked along ranch roads looking for doves. In nearly treeless western Oklahoma, doves perch on telephone or electrical lines. Practicing good sportsmanship, we would shoot only when they flew. I never killed a dove because they were so fast. They would leave a line at top speed within a second and would be out of range usually before I could aim and fire. I never hit anything in many tries, but my uncle managed to kill two or three doves both times we went out. Except for frustration over my bad aim and timing, I really enjoyed the two hunting trips, and the doves tasted delicious when my aunt baked them. But I never asked to go again, and I never owned a shotgun.

When I was ten, though, I did make a kill with my own weapon. Like most of my friends, I owned a BB gun. I bought it with money saved from earnings from my newspaper route. We shot at cans, as well as lizards, horned toads, and birds. We rarely killed or injured any of these creatures, but one time when I was on my own, pinging discarded cans and watching for toads and birds, I spotted a yellow and black oriole. I shot at it without even aiming carefully. To my surprise, it fell out of the mesquite tree, like Wolff's squirrel dropping from the telephone line. I remember the feelings of guilt and regret I experienced when I picked up this bird. I had noticed orioles migrating through our town, but I had never seen one up close. It was larger and more beautiful than I imagined. I buried it and never told anyone about it, but I thought about it many times afterward and never forgot the emotion I felt.

Finally, I liked Wolff's recollection of this boyhood event because the significance 7 was easy to grasp. I know that significance can be implied, but I prefer that the writer actually state the significance of the event. Wolff declares the significance of the event at the beginning and end, framing the story, and also right in the middle. At the beginning he makes clear why, from his adult perspective, the rifle was important to him as a boy: "[I]t completed me when I held it." He also says, "A weapon was the first condition . . . of being a real Westerner," and he very much wanted to be that sort of person. At the end, he returns to this idea of what the rifle did for him. He says that he could only imagine himself armed because "any image of myself, no matter how grotesque, had power over me." He makes the point that these are not insights he had at the time of the event but rather reflections from his present perspective as an adult. It's not surprising that these powerful images of himself with a rifle would remind Wolff of his later experiences in Vietnam. In paragraph 8, Wolff reflects on the dangers and limits of power: "Power can be enjoyed only when it is recognized and feared. Fearlessness in those without power is maddening to those who have it." Wolff seems to conclude that the power that comes from carrying a gun is fragile, uncertain, and temporary.

I haven't yet read much autobiography, but it's hard for me to imagine a more 8 successful story of a remembered event than Wolff's. We get a dramatic engaging story filled with many vivid details. Probably anyone who has ever fired a pistol, rifle, or shotgun can relate some personal experience to that of Wolff's. We know that the event is significant in Wolff's life because he tells us so, but beyond that we recognize that the event reveals something important about the images and myths that attract young American men. Wolff seems to have gained insights into who he was, who he became in Vietnam, and who he is now. Yet he stops short of moralizing, and he doesn't allow sentimentality to creep into his remembered feelings and present perspective.

For Discussion

Stewart seems to believe that writing about personal experience should avoid sentimentality—expression of trite or predictable feeling or excessive, indulgent expression of feeling. Think about a time when you've related personal experiences to people you've known well. Think also about personal experiences you've especially enjoyed hearing other people tell. What part do remembered and present feelings play in those stories? Consider also the kinds of movies, television dramas, and novels you enjoy. Do these feature or avoid obvious emotions or overstated expression of feelings? From these reflections, what can you conclude about the role of expressed emotion or feeling in everyday stories and popular culture?

For Analysis

1.   Notice in the opening paragraph that Stewart forecasts his reasoning and his plan. Skim the essay to confirm that each reason mentioned here is in fact argued in the essay and in just the sequence Stewart forecasts. Also notice whether any other writers in this chapter used forecasting in the opening paragraph. What advantages or disadvantages do you see in forecasting an evaluation?

For more on forecasting, see pp. 467–68.

2.   Stewart uses different types of reasons to justify his evaluation. Categorize the reasons by type, and identify each type with a brief phrase. Do you find any type inappropriate? If so, why? Do you find one type more convincing than another? If so, explain briefly.

3.   Stewart gives readers cues to each stage of his essay. To examine his cues, underline the first sentence in each paragraph, beginning with paragraph 2. Notice first which cues signal a new reason and which signal further parts of the argument for the same reason. Then examine each cue, noticing whether it refers to what has come before, what is to come next, or both. Pick two or three paragraph transition cues that seem particularly effective to you and explain how they do their work.

For more on transitional cues, see pp. 479–81.

4.   Review paragraphs 3, 5, and 6, underlining each separate piece of evidence from the Wolff selection. Then, given Stewart's purpose in each paragraph, decide which is the most effectively argued. What is there about the amount, type, and appropriateness of the evidence that encouraged you to single out this paragraph as best-argued?

For Your Own Writing

Like Stewart, you could evaluate an essay in any Part I chapter of this book. To review possible bases for your evaluation, you would want to reread carefully the Commentary following each reading in the chapter and the Purpose and Audience and Basic Features sections that follow the readings. The Guide to Writing in this chapter provides further help with this writing possibility.

You might also consider evaluating a short story, novel, or poem.

Commentary

Encouraged to evaluate a reading in any Part I chapter for which his class had written an essay, Stewart readily chose Chapter 2: Remembering Events because he believed he had written his best essay for that chapter. Since the selection from Tobias Wolff's autobiography was easily his favorite reading, he was drawn to finding out more about why he liked it so much in order to make a case for readers that it is an outstanding example of its genre.

Stewart felt that he was in a particularly authoritative position to evaluate Wolff's piece: he had not only read the other selections in the chapter, broadening his understanding of the possibilities of narrating a remembered event, but also written one of his own, giving him an insider's view of how the genre worked. Moreover, he had written about and discussed the Thinking about Your Writing activities at the end of the chapter.

To review and consolidate what he had learned, Stewart reread the four selections in the chapter, the Commentaries following each, and the Basic Features discussion. He was not constrained by the Commentary following the Wolff selection; in fact, he goes well beyond it. Nor did he attempt to evaluate the selection from all possible perspectives offered by the resources in the chapter. Rather, he justifies his evaluation with reasons particularly appropriate for the Wolff selection: engagement with a well-told story, detailing of objects and participants in the scene, relation to personal experience, and explicit statement of significance.

Stewart does not compare or contrast the Wolff selection with others in the chapter because his writing situation did not invite it. The selections are meant to illustrate various approaches and strategies for writing a readable, memorable remembered event essay. Therefore, Stewart could not plausibly argue that the Wolff selection is the "best" in the chapter. Instead, he argues that it is an outstanding example of its genre, giving appropriate reasons to support his judgment.

■   ■   ■

Jason Thornton wrote this essay as a college freshman in 1987. With his classmates in mind as readers, Thornton evaluates a then newly released album, *Document*, by the rock group REM. As you read, notice the many references he makes to other albums and groups.

DOCUMENTING DOCUMENT
JASON THORNTON

Joshua Tree may well become the best-remembered rock album of 1987. Certainly it is one of the best-selling and one of the most talked-about LPs of the year. But the biggest isn't always the best, and the one album released this year that truly surpasses U2's epic is REM's masterpiece, *Document*. Although REM—"America's most successful fringe band," according to rock critic David Fricke—is often overshadowed by bigger, more pop-oriented groups, this four-man band from Athens, Georgia, has a large cult following. Its first release, 1981's *Murmur*, was recently voted one of the top 100 albums of the past 20 years by *Rolling Stone* rock critics. REM makes music like no one else, incorporating a large range of sounds from punk to country-Western, from Aerosmith-like hard rock to folkish melodies, to a style not unlike Andy Warhol's art rock band, the Velvet Underground. Many bands try to incorporate as many sound styles as REM, but no one does it as well. 1

The music on *Document*, like that on REM's *Life's Rich Pageant*, is more catchy and more pop-oriented than the group's older albums like *Reckoning* or this year's strange B-side compilation, *Dead Letter Office*. REM's songs have become more vivid, forceful, and straightforward. The group had a hand (along with Scott Litt) in producing *Document*, and they show they can handle this task as well as they handle 2 their instruments. They also show they can bring more life and energy to their vinyl sound than their past producers could. Singer Michael Stipe's stinging, haunting lyrics are more prominent than on past REM LPs, creating a wonderful verbal richness and bringing forth powerfully suggestive images.

REM has always been a band of contrasts and paradoxes. *Murmur* sounded like 3. folk music, a style that generally uses acoustic instruments, except that REM used electric guitars. By all rights, the music of its past five albums would be ideal for keyboards or synthesizers, but REM rarely uses a single keyboard track. Instead, it relies on the simple trio of Peter Buck's wide range of guitar playing; Mike Mills's rough bass lines; and Bill Berry's droning, occasionally militant drums. Despite the simple methods, REM forges complex songs through a mixture of melodies, simple chords, numerous rhythms, and staggering vocal harmonies. Once together, this mixture forms a swirly, moody track that manages not to sound muddy, bogged down, or inconsistent. Sometimes with REM the finest points seem to be the roughest edges: each feedback whine from the guitar amp and rough vocal from Stipe seems well planned and strategically placed.

Often REM shows its originality in the sharp contrast between bitter lyrics and 4 upbeat music. In *Document*'s "Disturbance at the Heron House," for example, the band plays a catchy, cheerful sixties-influenced tune as Stipe describes a democracy gone mad by way of mob rule:

> They gathered up the cages
> The cages and courageous
> The followers of chaos
> Out of control.

Throughout the song Berry pounds out a foot-stomping drum beat that keeps the rhythm while Stipe sings about a "stampede at the monument"—a symbol of a large mass of people assaulting their government.

One of the best traits of *Document* is the constant theme of social and political 5 protest. The album opens with "Finest Worksong," a riveting rock anthem in which Stipe sings, "The time to rise/Has been engaged/We're better/Best to rearrange," a call for an uprising by the lower classes of society. As the song progresses, Stipe continues to discuss the faults of society until he finally comes to a conclusion on what he feels is the basis of America's social and economic difficulties: "What we want/What we need,/Has been confused." Greed is expressed as a single three-line concept, as Buck's guitars, sounding almost like heavy metal, carry the song along with Mills's and Berry's rhythms.

In "Exhuming McCarthy," with its sleazy bass line and trumpeting horn playing 6 by guest musician Steve Berlin, REM recalls an embarrassing event in American political history, Senator Joseph McCarthy's Communist "witchhunts" of the 1950s. Stipe sings about McCarthy's belief that he was able to spot and slay the Communist dragon in society: "Enemy sighted, enemy met/I'm addressing the real politic." "Exhuming McCarthy" starts off with a strange typewriter sound, contains an actual taped voice from a McCarthy hearing mixed into the guitar solo, and ends with an superbly harmonized double vocal, where two tracks of Stipe's voice sing drastically different things yet blend together wonderfully.

There have been a few criticisms of the album. Although most of REM's lyrics 7 tend to be abstract, the ones in "Fireplace" go too far. The song is made up of confusing extracts from a speech by Mother Ann Lee, an eighteenth-century leader of the Shaker religious sect, and its mixture of slow rock and waltz rhythms struggle to carry these lyrics along. "Strange," originally performed by the British band Wire, seems out of place on a REM album, with its lyrical style different from Stipe's norm; but Buck, Mills, and Berry still manage to create a reasonably decent version of the song. Another *Document* song, "It's the End of the World As We Know It (And I Feel Fine)," has been considered by many to be only an imitation of Bob Dylan's "Subterranean Homesick Blues."

REM makes up for these shortcomings, however, on other songs such as the   8 album's ballads. No REM album would be complete without a few ballads like *Document's* strange but appealing "Oddfellows Local 151." In this song Stipe creates a character more typical of John Steinbeck than of a modern rock star: a small-town storyteller who has taken to drinking but still manages to impress his fellow towns-people with his tales and "wisdom."

The most important song on this album, however, is "The One I Love," REM's   9 finest song to date. "The One I Love" starts off as a melancholy, regretful love song relying on lyrics such as

> This one goes out to the one I love,
> This one goes out to the one I left behind,
> A simple prop to occupy my time.

Slowly, the song goes beyond the simple boy/girl relationships of most love songs and introduces the complex problem of the effect on a relationship of distance and time away from a loved one. In the end, "The One I Love" becomes an expression of the pain and guilt one feels because of unfaithfulness to a loved one.

> This one goes out to the one I love,
> This one goes out to the one I left behind,
> Another prop has occupied my time,

"The One I Love" and the other songs on *Document* constitute the best REM   10 album yet and one of the best LPs of the year. With its upbeat tunes mixed with contrasting lyrics, its themes of social and political protest, and its touching ballads, REM shows that it deserves to be classified in the same league with some of the top bands around today, such as U2. *Document* may not end up getting as much air play as *Joshua Tree*, and it may not sell as many copies; but artistically it equals or betters the other album, breaking through the boundaries of conventional song-writing and record making, taking rock music to a plateau never before achieved.

For Discussion

Thornton says that one of *Document's* best traits is the "constant theme of social and political protest." Although he doesn't claim that every song should have a political message, he does seem to be saying that social protest is an important basis for judging rock music in general. What other rock songs from the late 1980s and the 1990s deal with America's social and economic difficulties? Make a list of recent songs of this kind and discuss Thornton's association of rock with social protest. Why do you think he associates the two? Do you?

For Analysis

1. Reread the opening and closing paragraphs to see how Thornton frames the essay by referring at the end to something from the beginning. What advantages or disadvantages do you see in this strategy?

2. In paragraph 1, Thornton quotes a rock critic and refers to a *Rolling Stone* list of top albums. How does this evidence contribute to his argument?

3. Throughout the essay Thornton quotes song lyrics. Reread the essay, stopping to consider how well each quotation works. Note particularly what he says about the lyrics. How does he introduce them? Does he seem to assume his readers will already know the songs he's quoting? How much does he explain? Are there any places where you have difficulty figuring out the point he's trying to make? Why?

4. In paragraph 7 Thornton discusses the album's shortcomings. What advantages or disadvantages do you see in his including this negative criticism in an otherwise positive review? Also, why do you think he places this passage where he does? Where else might he have put it?

5. Turn to the Writer at Work section on pp. 331–33, where Thornton charts his reasons and evidence and attempts to justify his reasons before drafting the essay. In what ways does his attempted justification allow him to test the appropriateness and contribution of each reason and to discover how they might work together to make a convincing argument?

For Your
Own Writing

What recording, music video, or live performance would you wish to evaluate? On what basis would you judge it?

Commentary

The process of evaluating is essentially comparative because judgments are based on comparison with other things of the same kind. To assert the importance of *Document*, Thornton compares it with the best-selling album of the year, U2's *Joshua Tree*. He also compares *Document* with earlier REM albums to show how the group has matured, pointing out that its recent music is "more catchy and pop-oriented" and the lyrics are "more vivid, forceful, and straightforward."

Comparison is not used only to praise *Document*. Thornton also identifies two songs that are weak in comparison with the other songs on the album: "Strange," originally performed by another group, and "It's the End of the World As We Know It (And I Feel Fine)," widely considered an imitation of a Bob Dylan song.

These comparisons show that Thornton knows a lot about the kind of music he's evaluating, and they also help to support his judgment of the album.

PURPOSE AND AUDIENCE

When you evaluate something, you seek to influence readers' judgments and possibly also their actions. Your primary aim is to convince readers that your judgment is well informed and reasonable, and therefore that they can feel confident in making decisions based on it. Good readers don't simply accept reviewers' judgments, however, especially on subjects of importance. More likely, they read reviews to learn more about a subject so that they can make an informed choice themselves. Consequently, most readers care less about the forcefulness with which you assert your judgment than about the reasons and evidence you cite to support it.

Effective writers develop an argumentative strategy designed for their particular readers. Your argumentative strategy determines every writing decision you make, from what you reveal about the subject to the way you construct your argument—which reasons you use, whether you justify the basis for your reasoning, how much and what kinds of evidence you cite.

You may want to acknowledge directly your readers' knowledge of the subject, perhaps revealing that you understand how they might judge it differently. You might even let readers know that you have anticipated their objections to your argument. In responding to objections, reservations, or different judgments, you could agree to disagree on certain points but seek to find common grounds for judgment on others.

BASIC FEATURES OF EVALUATIONS

Evaluations generally include the following basic features: a clearly defined subject, a clear and well-balanced judgment of the subject, and a convincing argument for this judgment. They often also include pointed comparisons between the subject and other things of the same kind.

A Clearly
Defined Subject

The subject being evaluated should be clearly identified, usually with some description. David Ansen names the movie he's reviewing in the opening sentence. Kevin Stewart gives us the author and title of the autobiographical selection he is evaluating. Barbara Ehrenreich names her subject and also provides some descriptive details, identifying it as a "sitcom" inspired by Roseanne Barr "the stand-up comic" and "featuring blue-collar Americans."

In general, evaluations provide only enough information to give readers a context for the judgment. Movie and book reviews may include more information than other kinds of evaluations because reviewers assume readers will be unfamiliar with the subject and are reading, in part, to learn more about it. Readers of movie reviews, for example, want to know who the actors and director are, where the movie takes place, and generally what happens in it. Ansen therefore explains that *Do the Right Thing* takes place "as the summer heat in Bedford-Stuyvesant reaches the boiling point" and identifies some of the actors and the characters they play, telling us, for instance, that Ruby Dee is Mother Sister, "the block's wise old watchdog."

For a recently released movie, the writer must decide how much of the plot to reveal. Here reviewers must walk a fine line—trying not to spoil the suspense while explaining how well or how poorly the suspense is managed. When reviewing a movie everyone is talking about, like *Do the Right Thing*, reviewers are released from this constraint, for they can assume that most readers are already familiar with the general plot outline and mostly want to know the reviewer's opinion of the film. Ansen does not bother keeping from readers the outcome of the plot: he talks about police brutality and the destruction of Sal's pizzeria.

A Clear,
Balanced
Judgment

Evaluation essays are focused around a judgment—an assertion that something is good or bad or that it is better or worse than something of the same kind. This judgment is the thesis, or main point, of the essay. Usually the judgment is clearly stated in various ways throughout the essay and reasserted at the end. For example, Thornton claims in his opening paragraph that *Document* is a "masterpiece" and concludes by saying that it "equals or betters [*Joshua Tree*], breaking through the boundaries of conventional songwriting and record making, taking rock music to a plateau never before achieved."

Although readers expect a definitive judgment, they also appreciate a balanced one that acknowledges both good and bad points of the subject. Ehrenreich, for instance, praises *Roseanne* for representing blue-collar Americans more realistically than other programs have, but also acknowledges that the show is not free of class stereotyping.

A Convincing
Argument

An evaluation cannot merely state its judgment but must argue for it. To be convincing, an evaluative argument must give reasons for the judgment. Stewart, for example, admires Tobias Wolff's "On Being a Real Westerner" because it is engaging, readable, and vividly written; it reminds Stewart of personal experiences; and it declares its significance. Ansen praises Spike Lee's *Do the Right Thing* primarily for the realistic and challenging way it presents race relations in America.

In addition to giving reasons, writers of evaluations must support their judgments with evidence. The kinds of evidence used vary according to the subjects. All of the essays in this chapter rely primarily on textual evidence— describing, quoting, paraphrasing, and summarizing aspects of the movie, television program, essay, or album: Ansen, for example, paraphrases an exchange of insults; Ehrenreich summarizes some typical actions of Roseanne's television husband; Thornton quotes song lyrics; and Stewart mentions details of plot and action. In addition, some use other kinds of evidence. Thornton refers to authorities: a rock critic and *Rolling Stone*. Stewart narrates two personal experiences.

Sometimes reviewers anticipate and respond to readers' objections or questions. They may accommodate these objections by making concessions, as Thornton does when he acknowledges that some of REM's lyrics are too abstract. Or they may refute them, as Ansen does when he claims that "to accuse Lee of irresponsibility—of inciting violence—is to be blind to the movie he has made."

Pointed Comparisons

Comparisons are not a requirement of evaluative writing, but they are often useful. One good way to assess something, after all, is to set it next to another of its kind. If you are evaluating a movie, for instance, you naturally judge it relative to other movies of the same kind. You can compare it with other movies, looking at similarities; or you can contrast it, looking at differences.

All of the writers in this chapter, except Stewart, use comparisons or contrasts. Thornton's evaluation of *Document* centers on a comparison and contrast with the more successful, better-known *Joshua Tree*. Ansen contrasts *Do the Right Thing* with other movies dealing with race relations, and Ehrenreich contrasts *Roseanne* with movies and television sitcoms featuring working-class characters and with *The Cosby Show's* portrait of genteel family life.

Guide to Writing

THE WRITING ASSIGNMENT

Choose a subject to evaluate. Write an essay assessing your subject addressed to a particular group of readers, giving them all of the background information, reasons, and evidence they will need to accept your evaluation. Your principal aim is to convince these readers that your judgment of this subject is informed and reasonable.

INVENTION AND RESEARCH

At this point you need to choose a subject, evaluate it closely, analyze your readers, and develop an argument to support your evaluation.

Choosing a Subject

You may already have something in mind to evaluate. Even so, consider some other possibilities to be sure you're making the best choice.

Listing Possible Subjects.   List anything you would be interested in evaluating, trying to think of at least one subject in each of the following categories.

- *Media*: a television program, magazine, or newspaper

You might set a timer and brainstorm your list on a computer with the brightness turned all the way down. Enter as many possibilities as you can in ten minutes. Then, turn the brightness up, be sure all the items make sense, and print out a copy to make notes on.

■ *Arts*: a movie, recording, performance, or work of art

■ *Written works*: a poem, short story, novel, essay, or one of the readings in this book

■ *Education*: a school, program, teacher, or textbook

■ *Government*: a government department or official; a proposed or existing law; a candidate for public office

■ *Campus*: a class, department, library, or sports team

■ *Leisure*: an amusement park, museum, restaurant, or resort

Making a Choice.   Review your list, and choose the subject that seems most promising. Look for a subject that you could evaluate with authority—something you already know well or could examine closely. Consider whether you know the standards by which people ordinarily evaluate something of this kind.

Exploring Your Subject

Before going much further, you need to make a tentative judgment and to ascertain what you already know about the subject and what additional information you may need.

Considering Your Present Judgment.   Although your opinion about your subject may change as you think and write about it in more detail, for now, set down your current opinion as clearly as you can. In a sentence or two, simply state your judgment. Don't explain why you're making this judgment; just say what it is.

Considering What You Think and Know about Your Subject.   Write for around ten minutes about your feelings and knowledge about your subject, considering these questions for guidance:

■ How certain am I of my judgment? Do I have any doubts? Why do I feel the way I do?

■ Do I like (or dislike) everything about my subject, or only certain parts?

■ Are there any similar things I should consider (other restaurants or movies, for example)?

■ Is there anything I will need to do right away in order to evaluate this subject authoritatively? If I need to do any research, can I get the information I need?

Analyzing Your Readers

You will be trying to convince particular readers to consider your evaluation seriously, perhaps even to take some action as a result—to see a certain television series, for instance, or take a specific class. Consequently, you must analyze these readers carefully, considering what they are likely to know and think about your subject. Take ten minutes to analyze your readers in writing. Use these questions to stimulate your analysis:

- Who are my readers? What values and attitudes do we share that might enable me to gain their trust?
- What are they likely to know and think about my subject?
- What other subjects of the same type might they be familiar with? How are they likely to judge these other subjects?
- What about my judgment might surprise them? On what basis might they disagree with me?

Developing an Argumentative Strategy

Once you have some sense of who your readers will be, you can begin to think about your argumentative strategy. Basically, an argumentative strategy is a plan for how to accomplish a particular purpose with specific readers. For an evaluation, your purpose will be to convince your readers to accept your judgment about the subject; your argumentative strategy would be to present reasons for your judgment and to show evidence to support those reasons. The reasons you give should be appropriate to the subject and must be selected with your readers' sensibilities in mind.

It might help you in working out your argumentative strategy to keep track of your reasons and evidence on a chart. Simply divide a piece of paper into two vertical columns, labeling the first *Reasons* and the second *Evidence*. Putting all your material on such a chart will help you to see at a glance where your argument is strong and where you need to give it more thought or collect more evidence.

A completed chart of this sort is shown on pp. 331–32.

List the Reasons for Your Judgment.　Consider the reasons for your judgment: Why do you like or dislike the film or restaurant or whatever you are evaluating? To identify your reasons, try completing the following statement:

_____ is a good/bad _____ because _____.

Jason Thornton, for example, might have begun to state his reasons for liking the REM album *Document* as follows:

If you can, list these reasons and evidence on a word processor. Then, as you begin to draft later, you can call up the file on a second screen and easily transfer details you want to use in your draft.

> <u>Document</u> is a good <u>rock album</u> because <u>its lyrics are easy to relate to</u>.

Put down all the reasons you can think of for your judgment about your subject, and then look over your list to decide which ones would be the most convincing for your particular readers. Imagine you were evaluating the new Walt Disney hotel designed by Michael Graves, for instance. If your readers were professional architects, you would probably look for architectural reasons; that it is the most architecturally distinctive hotel at Walt Disney World, for instance. If, however, your readers were school children, you'd surely focus on some other reasons: that it is the only hotel filled with familiar Disney characters, perhaps.

Finding Evidence.　When you have listed as many reasons as you can, look to find evidence to illustrate each reason. Evidence comes in many forms: de-

If you have generated a list of reasons on a computer, you can easily add supporting evidence following each reason.

scriptive details, quotations, statistics, authoritative testimony, anything that supports a reason. Most, if not all, evidence in evaluations of the type you will write comes from the thing being evaluated. For that reason, it is important for you to examine your subject closely even if you are already quite familiar with it—resee the movie, revisit the restaurant, reread the novel. As you do so, enter evidence next to the relevant reason in your reasons and evidence chart. Thornton, for example, quotes specific lyrics as evidence of easy-to-relate-to lyrics. Evidence for the architectural distinctiveness of Michael Graves's Disney hotel might be that other well-respected architects have praised it; for the hotel's featuring Disney characters everywhere, that it has Mickey Mouse doorknobs and Dumbo lampposts. You will probably find that the amount of evidence you can show for each reason will vary. Some reasons will have only one piece of evidence, while others may have many.

Justifying Your Reasons. If your readers are likely to be surprised by some of your reasons, object to any of them, or expect you to use reasons other than the ones you've chosen, you will need to justify them. Consider them individually and as a set. Begin by writing about each one, explaining why it is appropriate for evaluating this kind of subject. Then write about the set, explaining why you've chosen to use these reasons and not others that readers might expect you to use.

Drawing Comparisons. It is a good idea to get some sense of how your subject compares. Doing this will help you to recognize strengths and weaknesses in your subject, and may lead you to material you can use in your essay. In comparing the REM album with one by U2, for instance, Jason Thornton compares his subject, which he thinks readers may not be completely familiar with, to another similar subject, one they are more likely to know.

Testing Your Choice

Pause now to decide whether you have the makings of a convincing argument. Ask yourself the following questions:

- Do I know enough about my subject to evaluate it fully?
- Do I care enough about this subject to want to convince readers to accept my opinion about it?
- Are my reasons for thinking what I do about my subject strong ones? Are they reasons that will appeal to my readers?
- Do I have adequate evidence to convince readers that my reasons have a basis? Will I be able to check out my subject closely again if I need additional evidence?

For Group Inquiry

At this point it might be helpful to get together in a group with two or three other students. Announce your subject and intended readers, state your judgment, and give the reasons for your judgment. Then ask the group whether these seem to be convincing reasons. Can they suggest any other reasons that might strengthen your argument? This kind of feedback can help you to know whether your reasoning is likely to seem to readers a strong justification for your judgment.

PLANNING AND DRAFTING

The following will help you review your invention writings to see what you have so far, to establish goals for your evaluation, and to make a tentative outline to guide you as you draft.

Seeing What You Have

It's a good idea at this point to print out a hard copy of what you have written on a word processor for easier reviewing.

By now you have done considerable thinking and writing about your evaluation. You have explored many aspects of your subject, analyzed your readers, and developed an argumentative strategy. Take some time now to reread your invention notes thoughtfully, highlighting anything you think you will be able to use in the draft and noting connections between ideas. Also keep an eye out for problems you may have overlooked earlier, and consider how you might deal with them. For example, look for places where your evidence is thin or contradictory or your reasoning weak.

Setting Goals

Before you begin drafting, think seriously about the overall goals of your evaluation. Having clear goals will make the draft not only easier to write but almost surely more focused as well, and therefore more convincing.

Following are some questions designed to help you focus on what exactly you want to accomplish with this evaluation. You may find it useful to return to them while you are drafting.

Your Readers

- What do I want my readers to think about the subject as a result of reading my essay? Do I want to show them how it succeeds, as all of the writers in this chapter do, or how it fails?
- Should I assume, as Ansen does, that my readers are likely to have read other evaluations of the subject? Or should I assume, as Thornton does, that I am introducing them to it?
- How can I gain my readers' trust? Should I show them how familiar I am with comparable subjects? Should I indicate any special knowledge I have?
- What tone should I take? Should I be witty like Ehrenreich, serious like Ansen and Stewart, enthusiastic like Thornton?

Presentation of the Subject

- Should I place the subject historically, as Thornton and Ehrenreich try to do?

- If the subject has a plot, how much of it should I tell?
- How can I capture the flavor of my subject? Can I cite notable details, as Ansen and Stewart do, or refer to some typical incidents, as Ehrenreich does?

Your Argument

- How should I state my judgment? Should I make it a comparative judgment, as Thornton and Ansen do? Should I put it up front, as Thornton does, or wait a bit, like Ansen, until I've provided a context?
- How can I show that my judgment is fair and well balanced? Can I refer to specific weaknesses without taking away from the larger strengths, as Thornton does?
- How can I support my reasons? Can I find textual evidence to quote or paraphrase, as Stewart does? Can I call upon authorities, as Thornton does?
- What facts, statistics, or other evidence could I use?

The Beginning and the Ending

- Should I open by stating my judgment, as Ehrenreich and Stewart do? By comparing my subject with one more familiar to readers, as Thornton does? By describing the subject, as Ansen does?
- How should I conclude? Should I try to frame the essay by echoing something from the opening, or from another part of the essay, as Thornton does? Should I conclude by restating my judgment, as Ansen does?

Outlining

Evaluations may be organized in various ways. The important thing is to include all essential parts: a presentation of the subject, a judgment of some kind, and reasons and evidence to support the judgment. In addition, you will want to arrange your reasons in some logical order: from most obvious to least obvious, most general to most technical, least convincing to most convincing, least important to most important.

For readers already familiar with the topic, your outline might look like this:

Outlining on a word processor makes it particularly easy to experiment with different ways of organizing your essay.

presentation of the subject

judgment

reason 1
   evidence

reason 2
   evidence

reason 3
   evidence, with a comparison

consideration of an opposing judgment

conclusion

For readers unfamiliar with the topic, you will need to begin with some description of your subject, including perhaps some background discussion and definition of terms.

There are many other possible organizations. Whichever you choose, remember that an outline should serve only as a guide. It can help you to organize your invention materials and provide a sense of direction as you start drafting, but you should feel free to depart from it if you see a better way of developing your argumentative strategy.

Drafting

Before you begin to draft your evaluation, reread all your notes and, if possible, take a last look at your subject. If you are evaluating a published work (such as a poem, story, novel), reread it. If you are writing about a movie, see it again. Your subject must be completely fresh in your mind.

If you can shift between screens, you might call up invention material on an alternate screen as you draft on the main screen, shifting back and forth to cut and paste invention material into your draft.

Start drafting, focusing on your readers and how you can convince them to share your judgment of the subject. If you run into trouble, reconsider each element in your evaluation. Perhaps you should think of better reasons or add more evidence to support the reasons you give. You may need to take another look at your criteria. If you really get stuck, turn back to the invention activities in this chapter to see if you can fill out your material. You might want to review the general advice about drafting on pp. 12–14.

GETTING CRITICAL COMMENTS

All writers find it helpful to have someone else read their drafts and give them critical comments. Your instructor may arrange such a reading as part of your coursework; if not, you can ask a classmate, friend, or family member to read your draft. If your college has a writing center, you might ask a tutor there to read and comment on your draft. Following are guidelines designed to be used by *anyone* reviewing an evaluation essay. (If you cannot get someone else to read your draft, turn to the Revision section on pp. 327–31, which includes guidelines for reading your own draft with a critical eye.)

In order to provide helpful comments, your reader must know your intended audience and purpose. Briefly write out this information at the top of your draft:

Audience. Who are your readers?

Purpose. What do you want your readers to think about your subject from reading this essay?

Reading with a Critical Eye

Reading a draft critically means reading it more than once, first to get a general impression and then to analyze its basic features.

See chapter 12 for a review of critical reading strategies.

Reading for a First Impression.   Read first to understand the essay's judgment. As you read, try to notice any words or passages that contribute, either favorably or unfavorably, to your first impression. After you've finished reading the draft, briefly write down your impressions. What is the essay's judgment? How convincing do you think the argument will be for the intended readers?

See pp. 318–20 to review the basic features.

Reading to Analyze.   Read the draft again, this time focusing on the basic features of an evaluation.

Is the Subject Clearly Presented?

Check to see how the subject is described. Is there anything else the intended readers might be curious about or might need to know? Point to any details that seem unnecessary or redundant.

Is the Judgment Clear and Balanced?

Is the judgment about the subject stated explicitly enough? Is it clear? Check to see that there is a balanced appraisal, acknowledging how the subject succeeds as well as fails.

Is the Argument Convincing?

Do the reasons given for the judgment seem relevant? Is sufficient evidence given for each reason? Is the argument convincing?

Are Any Comparisons Pointed and Appropriate?

Look at any comparisons or contrasts between the subject and other things of the same kind. What do they contribute to the evaluation? Are there too many comparisons? Are there places where comparisons might be added?

Is the Organization Effective?

Note any places where the essay seems disorganized or confusing. Are there topic sentences at the beginning of paragraphs? Would adding some make the essay easier to read? Consider whether any reasons ought to be reordered.

Look at the *beginning*. Is it engaging? If not, can you see any other passages in the draft that might be more interesting? Does it provide sufficient background information?

Look at the *ending*. Does it leave you thinking about the subject? Point to any passage elsewhere in the draft that might work as a conclusion.

What Final Thoughts Do You Have?

What is the strongest part of the argument? What is the weakest part, most in need of further work?

REVISING AND EDITING

This section will help you identify problems in your draft and revise and edit to solve them.

**Identifying
Problems**

To identify problems in your draft, you need to read it objectively, analyze its basic features, and study any comments you've gotten from others.

Even if your essay is saved to a computer file, reread from a hard copy, preferably draft quality. Onscreen or as letter-quality hard copy, a paper can look more "finished" than it really is. Add notes to yourself and quick revisions as you read through the draft.

Getting an Overview.   Consider the draft as a whole, trying to judge it objectively. It may help to do so in two steps:

Reread. If possible, put the draft aside for a day or two before rereading it. When you do, start by reconsidering your audience and purpose. Then read the draft straight through, trying to see it as your intended readers will.

Outline. Make a scratch outline to get an overview of the essay's development. This outline can be sketchy—words and phrases instead of complete sentences—but it should identify the basic features as they appear.

Charting a Plan for Revision.   You can use the following chart to keep track of any problems you need to solve. The left-hand column lists the basic features of evaluative writing. In the right-hand column, note the problems you want to solve.

Basic Features	*Problems to Solve*
The subject	
The judgment	
The argument	
Comparisons	
Organization	

Analyzing the Basic Features of Your Draft.   Turn now to the questions for analyzing a draft on p. 327. Using these questions as guidelines, identify problems in your draft. Note anything you need to solve on the chart above.

Studying Critical Comments.   Review any comments you've received from other readers, and add to the chart any points that need attention. Try not to react too defensively to these comments: by letting you see how others respond to your draft, they provide invaluable information about how you might improve it.

**Solving
the Problems**

Having identified problems, you now need to figure out solutions and to carry them out. Basically, you have three ways of finding solutions: (1) review your invention and planning notes for information and ideas to add to the draft; (2) do further invention and research to answer questions your readers raised; and (3) look back at the readings in this chapter to see how other writers have solved similar problems.

Before revising using a word processor, copy your original draft to a second file. Then, should you change your mind about material you delete while revising, it will still be available.

    Following are suggestions to get you started on solving some of the problems common to evaluative writing. For now, focus on solving those issues identified on your chart. Try not to worry about sentence-level problems at this time; that will come later when you edit.

The Subject

- If the subject is not clear, name it explicitly and describe it in specific detail. Try to anticipate and answer your intended readers' questions.
- If the subject is presented in too much detail, cut extraneous and repetitive details. If your subject has a plot, try to sketch it without telling the whole story.

The Judgment

- If the judgment is vague or ambiguous, restate it so that there can be no confusion about your evaluation.
- If the judgment seems too one-sided, try balancing your praise or criticism. Note something worth praising or a possible weakness.

The Argument

- If any reasons seem inappropriate or vague, try to clarify them. Review your invention writing, looking for material to strengthen your reasons. Or you may need to explore your reasons further. Consider whether any of the reasons should be combined or separated.
- If the evidence is thin, review your invention writing and reexamine the subject for additional evidence.

Comparisons

- If any comparisons or contrasts seem pointless or inappropriate, eliminate them.
- If there are too many comparisons, consider dropping some.
- If you don't compare or contrast your subject with anything else, try to do so and see whether it strengthens your argument.

Organization

Use your word processor's cut-and-paste or block-and-move functions to shift material around. Make sure that transitions are revised so that material fits in its new spot.

- If the essay seems disorganized or confusing, you may need to add transitions, summaries, or topic sentences. You may also need to do some major restructuring, such as moving your presentation of the subject or reordering your reasons.
- If the beginning is weak, see if there's a better place to start. Review your notes for an interesting quotation, image, or scene to open with.
- If the ending doesn't work, see if you can frame the essay by echoing a point made earlier.

Editing and Proofreading

When you use your word processor's spell check function to aid in proofreading for spelling, keep in mind that it will not find all misspellings, particularly misused homonyms (such as there, their, and they're,) typos that are themselves words (such as fro for for), and many proper nouns and specialized terms. Proofread these carefully yourself, using hard copy and a dictionary if necessary. Also proofread for words that should have been deleted when you edited a sentence.

Now is the time to check your draft for errors in usage, punctuation, and mechanics—and to consider matters of style. Following are guidelines to check for two errors that often occur in evaluations.

Checking Comparisons.   Whenever you evaluate something, you inevitably make comparisons. You might want to show that a new recording is inferior to an earlier one, that one film is stronger than another, that this café is better than that one. You should make a point of checking to see that all comparisons in your writing are complete, logical, and clear.

Editing to Make Comparisons Complete

▶ Jazz is as good, if not better than, Morrison's other novels.
  [insert: as]

▶ I liked the Lispector story because it's so different.
  [insert: from anything I've ever read.]

Editing to Make Comparisons Logical

▶ Chris Rock's Pookie is more serious than any role he's played.
  [insert: other]

▶ Ohio State's offense played much better than ~~Michigan.~~
  [insert: Michigan's did.]

Check also to see that you say *different from* instead of *different than.*

▶ Carrying herself with a confident and brisk stride, Katherine Parker seems different ~~than~~ the other women in the office.
  [insert: from]

▶ Films like *Internal Affairs* that glorify violence for its own sake are different ~~than~~ films like *New Jack City* that use violence to make a moral point.
  [insert: from]

Combining Sentences.   When you evaluate something, you generally present your subject in some detail—defining it, describing it, placing it in some context. Close analysis of many evaluations written by students using this book revealed that writers often give such details almost one by one, in separate sentences. Combining closely related sentences can make your writing more readable, helping readers see how ideas relate. See how Kevin Stewart combined two closely related sentences in his essay.

▶ In paragraph 5, the details provide a different impression. ~~It is~~ a comic or perhaps even pathetic impression. ~~This impression comes from~~ the boy's attempts to dress up like a real Westerner.
  [insert: based on]

From three separate sentences, Stewart combined details about the "different impression" into one sentence. He did so using two common strategies for sentence-combining: an appositive phrase (a noun phrase that renames the noun or pronoun that immediately precedes it: "a comic or perhaps even pathetic one") and a verbal phrase (phrases with verb forms that function as adjectives, adverbs, or nouns: "based on the boy's attempts to dress up like a real Westerner").

Using Appositive Phrases to Combine Sentences

▶ "Something Pacific" was created by Nam June Paik, ~~He is~~ a Korean artist who is considered a founder of video art.

▶ One of Dylan's songs ridiculed the John Birch Society. ~~This song was called~~ "Talkin' John Birch Paranoid Blues."

Using Verbal Phrases to Combine Sentences

▶ Batman's life-saving ropes sprung from his wristbands and belt buckle, ~~They car-ried~~ *carrying* Vicki Vale and him out of peril.

▶ The coffee bar flanks the bookshelves, ~~It entices~~ *enticing* readers to relax with a book.

A Writer at Work

PLANNING AN ARGUMENTATIVE STRATEGY

In developing an evaluative essay, a writer must decide what reasons will be most convincing to readers. In this section, we will see how Jason Thornton, the writer of "Documenting *Document*," charted his reasons and evidence and then explored ways of justifying the reasons for particular readers. Following is a chart he made to consider the reasons and evidence for his essay.

REASONS	EVIDENCE
1. lyrics are easy to relate to	"Finest Worksong"
2. lyrics are literary, intellectual	"Oddfellows Local 151" "Exhuming McCarthy"
3. haunting lyrics	"The One I Love"
4. catchy, poplike music	"Heron House" song
5. <u>Document</u> shows REM's great versatility, freshness, originality	mixes hard rock, folk, punk, country-western with electric guitars

REASONS	EVIDENCE
6. lyrics work well with music	"Disturbance at the Heron House" combines bitter lyrics and upbeat music
7. <u>Document</u> well produced	REM had a hand in album's production

After charting out his plans, Thornton considered which reasons he should use in the essay. He then attempted to justify his reasons to gauge the strength of his argumentative strategy. Following is his writtten analysis of the reasons, first individually and then as a set.

<u>Justifying Reasons</u> Much of the song's strength comes from the quality of its lyrics. Thus, this must be an important basis for evaluating an album. How easily you can relate to a song's lyrics can greatly affect how much you like the song. Why do alienated teenagers listen to heavy metal? Because the music reflects aspects of their lives. People enjoy music that reveals something of themselves.

I should be able to demonstrate how easy REM's lyrics are for most listeners to relate to because they are so abstract and "open." Their abstractness allows different interpretations, though it can be confusing. Mentioning this potential weakness might make me seem like a fair judge. My review would seem more objective, less one-sided. It might also be good to say something about the Americanism of the lyrics--one more reason we can relate to them! Also, by showing how literary and intellectual REM's lyrics can be, I might be able to convince readers that these songs are well thought-out and fairly artistic.

The music is, without a doubt, the most important reason why a person would buy an album. Therefore, I have to convince readers that REM's music is both original and accessible. People like variety and newness, but many folks shy away from the radically different. Thus, it will be important that I focus on the familiar appeal of the music on <u>Document</u>. So I should comment on the pop-oriented, catchy aspects of these songs, mentioning also their diversity of style. Even though it's an artistic record, <u>Document</u> can be enjoyed in mainstream pop/rock terms

Production, although often ignored, is also important. If an album isn't recorded or mixed well, it won't sound good and this could distract from the music's other merits. I need to make readers aware that <u>Document</u> is well produced. I might want to compare its production to that of U2's <u>Joshua Tree</u>.

   And style is important. Listeners judge an album or group on what kind of music it has. Convincing readers of REM's diversity and style will be important. Plus, REM's way of combining many styles--like working folk with a typical rock assortment of guitars, bass, and drums would show a freshness and originality in the band's approach.

   Finally, how well the songs are written must be included. I need to show how certain lyrics work with the music. Also, I might want to mention songs that have been criticized as imitative.

   I've read numerous record reviews, and I think that these reasons are not unusual. It seems that they all come down to listener enjoyment. Other points could be used to evaluate the band's performance, such as musicianship or the conventionality of chord progressions, but these reasons are used more often to evaluate jazz, classical, or even art-rock. They would be out of place here. Many of the reasons I'm citing overlap, but that's because they're all related. It might be best to evaluate <u>Document</u> on a song-by-song basis, using specific songs as examples of specific points.

   I think I'll try to combine all the negative criticism in one paragraph and maybe put it somewhere in the middle, to break up all the praise.

As he drafted the essay and again as he revised it, Thornton returned to the chart and this exploratory writing for ideas.

Thinking Critically about What You've Learned

Having read and discussed several essays that make evaluations as well as having written such an essay yourself, you're in a good position now to think critically about what you've learned. What problems did you encounter as you were writing, and how did you solve them? How did the essays you read influence your own writing? How do written evaluations and reviews reflect and influence social and cultural attitudes?

REFLECTING ON YOUR WRITING

Begin by gathering your invention and planning notes, drafts and critical comments, revision plan, and final revision. Review these as you complete the following writing task.

- Identify *one* significant writing problem you encountered while writing the essay. Don't be concerned with sentence-level problems; focus on a problem specific to writing an evaluation. For example: Did you have trouble deciding how much information to include in presenting your subject? Did your judgment come across as vague or as too one-sided? Was it difficult to come up with clear reasons for your judgment or enough evidence to support those reasons?

- How did you first recognize this problem? Was it, for example, when you were thinking about how to state your judgment, trying to decide on your argumentative strategy, determining your organizational plan, or getting critical comments on a draft? What called the problem to your attention? Looking back, do you see signs of it in your early invention work? If so, where specifically?

- Reflect on how you attempted to solve the problem. If it arose during invention, did you go back to look at your subject again (rereading an essay, for example, or rescreening a movie)? Did you look for other related subjects with which to compare the subject of your evaluation? If it arose during drafting, did you do further invention to solve the problem—listing more reasons for your judgment, for example? Did you rethink your presentation of the subject? If you noticed the problem as you were revising, did you reword, reorganize, add new material, or simply cut the part that was problematic? Did you review your invention notes or return again to your subject for further evidence to support your judgment?

- Now, write a page or so explaining to your instructor what the problem was, how you discovered it, and how you went about solving it. Be specific by quoting from your invention writing, drafts, others' critical comments, your own revision plan, and your final revision. Show the various changes your writing and thinking underwent. If you're still uncertain about your solution, say so. The point is not to prove that you've solved the problem but to show what you've learned about solving problems in the process of writing.

REVIEWING WHAT YOU LEARNED
FROM READING

You've read several evaluative essays in this chapter and also possibly one or more drafts of evaluative essays written by classmates. Your reading of these essays probably influenced in one way or another the evaluative essay you wrote.

■ To reflect on the possible influence your reading may have had on your own thinking and writing, review the readings in this chapter as well as your own essay. Consider whether any of the essays in the chapter or by your classmates influenced your choice of subject or the way you organized your essay. Look for ideas you got from your reading or writing strategies you were inspired to try. For example, did one of the essays suggest a way for you to open or close your evaluation, balance your judgment by qualifying it in some way, or introduce evidence to support your judgment?

■ Write a page or so explaining to your instructor how your writing has been influenced by others. You may focus on a single influence or discuss what you learned from parts of different essays. Give examples, showing how you've built on what you've seen other writers do. You might also point out anything you'd now change in your essay, based on this review of the other readings.

CONSIDERING THE SOCIAL DIMENSIONS OF WRITING THAT MAKES EVALUATIONS

Making evaluations plays an important role in all occupations and professions. Manufacturers and assembly-line workers must continually evaluate their processes and products, asking questions about the quality of materials from outside suppliers, the efficiency of particular manufacturing processes, and the quality of the goods produced in terms of a company's own standards and in relation to competitors' products. Instructors evaluate developments in their academic specialities, deciding when a discovery, idea, or principle has become well enough established to include in their curricula. In the classroom, they continually evaluate how well students understand demonstrations and lectures, and ultimately they judge each student's achievement, usually assigning it a letter or number grade. Doctors and researchers on the staff of the federal Food and Drug Administration monitor the quality of the country's food production and evaluate the accuracy of advertising claims made by food manufacturers. Staff members also review studies of the benefits and side effects of drugs in order to decide when they can safely be prescribed by doctors. And, of course, consumers rely heavily on evaluations, such as those by the highly respected Consumer's Union, which provides frequent, independent evaluations of a wide range of consumer products. Its monthly magazine, *Consumer Reports*, is credited, for example, with encouraging the trend toward purchases of Japanese, Swedish, and German cars by arguing that, at least until very recently, they outperformed American cars.

A special kind of evaluation, which has been the focus of this chapter, is the media or arts review—judgments about the quality of movies, television programs and series, musical performances, books, and so forth. We rely on such evaluations to help us decide what movies or performances to see, what books to buy, what exhibits to attend. They confirm or challenge our attraction to a particular television series or musical group. The best media reviewers develop impressive expertise. They come to be trusted by readers to set standards for movies, musical recordings, novels, works of art. They educate readers, helping shape their judgment and discrimination, building their confidence in recognizing a clumsy, passable, or outstanding work or performance. At their best, reviewers counterbalance advertising: instead of enticing us to see every movie that comes to town, they help us choose among all the advertised movies. A trusted media or arts reviewer for a local newspaper can come to influence a community's values, building a local consensus, for example, about what constitutes a successful musical performance and encouraging tolerance or even appreciation for new kinds of music.

Elevating and Rejecting. As helpful as media and arts reviewers may be, however, the social influence they exert should also be viewed critically. For example, because they must be judgmental, praising some movies and damning, ignoring, or dismissing others, film reviewers inevitably foster an attitude of elevating and rejecting, conferring value on some movies, directors, or even types of movies and devaluing the rest. This attitude of elevating and rejecting may be adopted by viewers as well, particularly those who are least confident of their judgments and who rely on reviewers to make judgments for them. They may judge too quickly, without trusting their own experience and without taking time to reflect on the possible value of something unexpected or offbeat. Ehrenreich admits readily that she wants to elevate *Roseanne* to the status of very best sitcom dealing with blue-collar or working-class Americans and to reject *Major Dad* and others in this category. It is hard to imagine, given her distaste for *Married with Children*, that she would ever review it, even to pan it.

Excluding and Silencing. By deciding what to review and what to ignore, media and arts reviewers determine what receives public attention and what remains invisible, and their decisions may often be based to a large extent on economic factors: Which review is likely to sell more newspapers or bring in more advertising? (In this sense, reviewers are part of a larger publicity apparatus; indeed, in our age of giant media conglomerates, a movie or music reviewer in a national magazine may well work for the same parent company that provided the film or the recording being reviewed—a situation that may not lead to the most objective viewpoint.) Local theater or musical groups without money to advertise their performances may get a brief listing in the newspaper; but unless they are occasionally reviewed, they will be unlikely to attract enough ticket buyers to survive (and the less mainstream their offerings, the less likely they are to be reviewed). Similarly, a new artist is simply not as likely to be reviewed widely as is a more established one.

For a long time, this sort of prejudice against the new and different kept many women and ethnic minority writers in America from being appreciated by reviewers—both in the universities and in the media—thus preventing them from earning a living by their work and effectively silencing their voices. This situation has changed in some ways—Ansen, for example, seems to want to ensure that Spike Lee's films are not excluded from movie theaters and that Lee is not silenced even though *Do the Right Thing* might be criticized for inflaming social tensions—but reviewers still have great power to determine what is a "successful" work of art and what isn't.

Hidden Assumptions of Evaluators. Since successful reviewers exude confidence and expertise, it is easy to overlook the fact that media and arts reviews reflect a reviewer's personal preferences, values, and ideology. Even the most fair-minded reviewer writes from the perspective of a particular religion, gender, age, social class, and sexual orientation. Consider the possibility that Stewart evaluated Tobias Wolff's autobiographical excerpt so favorably because they are both white males of the same social class and have both handled guns in the West. Consider, too, that Stewart might not have singled out this selection for evaluation if he had not been able to connect it to his personal experience.

Experienced reviewers are also very likely to be aware of insider issues and conflicts on which they take a position. For example, a writer who is known by others in the publishing business to be extremely helpful in advising younger writers and generous in his or her reviews of their work may have his or her own work favorably reviewed based as much on personality as on the work's quality. Similarly, a rock critic's knowledge that a group was experiencing strong internal conflict during the production of a recording might well influence his or her evaluation of that recording.

For Discussion

Following are some questions that can help you think critically about the role of writing that makes evaluations, particularly media and arts reviews. As you read and, perhaps, discuss these questions in class, note down your responses. Then, write a page or so for your instructor presenting your thoughts about the social dimensions of reviews.

1. We've said that media and arts reviewers make an important social contribution. Reread Kevin Stewart's and Jason Thornton's essays, thinking about what they offer readers. Also think about what you

tried to offer in your essay. How is it possible to say that essays like yours and the others in this chapter make a social contribution?

2. To what extent do you rely on reviews in the magazines and news-papers you read (including your college newspaper) and in tele-vision news or entertainment shows that offer reviews? Do they influence what you decide to read or watch? usually? sometimes? Never? Do you read only those reviews that evaluate something you have already seen or heard? If possible, read again or recall a review that influenced you in some way and explain this influence. How, in general, have reviews contributed to the way you make judgments? Have they made you more confident, more tentative, or what? Try to give a specific example.

3. Would you say you are quick to judge movies, novels, television series, or musical recordings; or do you tend to be more tentative, waiting until you've heard or seen a performance again and have time to think about it? How did you go about deciding how to evaluate the subject of your essay?

4. Reflect on how your gender, age, social class, religion, and political perspective influenced the subject you chose to evaluate and your evaluation of it. Then take one other essay in the chapter and con-sider the same influences. You will have to infer some influences, since you don't have a lot of information about the authors. What can you conclude about the way reviewers' personal perspectives influence their reviewing?

■ In a popular magazine, a psychologist speculates about the causes of a phenomenon known to many parents: kids love Nintendo. She considers several possible causes for this phenomenon—the influence of television, the power of advertising—but concludes that the primary reason children like to play Nintendo is that it fills certain psychological needs. One such need is to escape from everyday reality, where the demands are many and often contradictory. Playing Nintendo, children know what is expected of them. This need for an ordered universe suggests a related and even more important need that Nintendo may satisfy: the need for mastery. Nintendo offers the child the opportunity for mastery. Unlike many other challenging games, Nintendo can be mastered in the privacy of one's own room, away from the judging eyes of peers, parents, and teachers. In addition, the child doesn't have to begin with much mastery to get satisfaction from playing. Games like the very popular *Super Mario* allow children to develop their skills incrementally, building their confidence and skill at the same time.

■ For a popular magazine, two anthropologists write an article in which they speculate about the causes for the universal phenomenon of the "afternoon lull," the period of reduced energy after the midday meal. Referring to research studies, they reject the possibility that the lull is caused either by the biochemical effects of eating or by a change in body temperature. They also reject the possibility that the lull is due to laziness or a desire for diversion. They argue instead that it is caused by a biological rhythm established during early human evolution in the tropics, where heat peaks in the early afternoon.

■ For a university social-policy institute, a survey researcher reports a steady 22-year decline in the percentage of college freshmen who say they plan to major in physical sciences or mathematics. He demonstrates the trend in a single table reporting survey results for the years 1966–1988. The researcher speculates that deteriorating math instruction in schools and the lure of computer science are sustaining the trend but that a significant underlying cause is materialism—students' interest in making money quickly rather than in developing their minds for careers that have a slower payoff.

Speculating about Causes 9

We all quite naturally attempt to explain causes. Because we assume everything has a cause, we predictably ask "Why?" when we notice something new or unusual or puzzling.

Many things can be fully and satisfactorily explained. When children ask "Why is the sky blue in the day and black at night?" parents can provide an answer. But there are other questions we can answer only tentatively: Why did the United States become involved in Vietnam? Why do minority groups in American society continue to suffer discrimination? Questions such as these often have only plausible, not definitive, explanations because we cannot design a scientific experiment to identify the actual cause conclusively. The decline in SAT scores, for example, has been attributed to the rise in television viewing among children. Though this cause is plausible, we cannot know for certain that it is actually responsible for the drop in scores.

Much of what we want to know about can never be known definitively and unarguably, but can only be speculated about on the basis of the best available evidence and experience. Writing that speculates about causes plays an important role in academic and professional life, as the scenarios that open this chapter suggest. Government specialists analyze the causes of unemployment or homelessness to design policies intended to solve social problems. Business executives study the reasons for increases in sales or declines in worker productivity. Educators look at why some teaching techniques work and others do not or how family problems affect students' performance in school.

This chapter presents several essays arguing for the causes of some phenomenon or trend. A phenomenon is something notable about the human condition or social order—fear of failure, for example, or racial discrimination. A trend is a significant change extending over some period of time, generally months or years. It can be identified by an increase or decrease—for example, a rise in the rate of births of babies with AIDS or a decline in the number of applicants to law school.

When you speculate about causes, you first need to describe your subject and then to propose some causes and argue for one or more as the best available explanation. You do not have to prove that your explanation is right, but you must attempt to <u>convince readers</u> that it is plausible.

This chapter is designed to introduce you to one of the more common and important writing situations you will meet in college. Speculating about why things are the way they are or why things change will help you develop your powers of creativity as you speculate about possible causes, your powers of judgment as you weigh these possibilities and choose the most plausible ones, and your powers of reasoning as you devise an argumentative strategy to present your speculations to your readers.

Writing in Your Other Courses

As a student, you too face assignments that ask you to speculate about and evaluate causes, such as the following:

- *For an American history course:* When Japanese-Americans were forcibly moved to "relocation camps" during World War II, the government officially cited the danger that they would prove disloyal to the United States in its war with Japan. Some historians, however, have argued that racial prejudice and economic jealousy played a large part in the government's decision. On the basis of the assigned readings on this topic, how important do you think these unofficial reasons were?

- *For a political science course:* During 1989 Communist governments crumbled almost without resistance in the Soviet Union and much of eastern Europe, while in China the government succeeded in crushing a movement toward a more open political system. From what you have learned about the characteristics of Communist rule in the Soviet bloc and in China, why do you think the movements against the party succeeded in one case and not the other?

- *For a literature course:* Why does Huck Finn "light out for the Territory" at the novel's end? Defend your answer with evidence from the book.

- *For a biology course:* Why is AIDS concentrated among homosexuals in this country but among heterosexuals in Africa? In your answer, consider differences in such factors as sexual practices and attitudes and general standards of health and medical care.

For Group Inquiry

Get together with two or three other students and make a list of a dozen or so trends—such as the decline in voting in the United States or the increasing popularity of Mexican food—whose causes you are interested in speculating about. Choose one trend that interests all of you, and spend ten or fifteen minutes discussing its likely causes and the importance of each.

When you've finished, take a few more minutes to reflect on the process you've been engaged in.

- Where did your ideas about causes come from—reading, television, your own imagination?

- How did you decide which causes were more important than others?
- Do you recall other occasions when you tried to analyze the causes of something? How did you go about it?

Readings

Stephen King is America's best-known writer of horror fiction. In the following essay, written for *Playboy*, King speculates about the popular appeal of horror movies. Before you begin reading, think about your own attitude toward horror films. Do you enjoy them? "Crave" them? Dislike them? Or are you indifferent?

As you read, notice how assertively King presents his assumptions about people, such as the ones in the opening sentence. How does he try to get you to accept these assumptions? Is he successful?

[handwritten margin notes: "What is Stephen King saying in paragraph?" and "assumes everyone is in some way mentally ill."]

**WHY WE CRAVE
HORROR MOVIES**
STEPHEN KING

I think that we're all mentally ill; those of us outside the asylums only hide it a   1
little better—and maybe not all that much better, after all. We've all known people
who talk to themselves, people who sometimes squinch their faces into horrible
grimaces when they believe no one is watching, people who have some hysterical
fear—of snakes, the dark, the tight place, the long drop . . . and, of course, those
final worms and grubs that are waiting so patiently underground. *[handwritten: "insane to surface"]*

When we pay our four or five bucks and seat ourselves at tenth-row center in   2
a theater showing a horror movie, we are daring the nightmare.

Why? Some of the reasons are simple and obvious. To show that we can, that   3
we are not afraid, that we can ride this roller coaster. Which is not to say that a
really good horror movie may not surprise a scream out of us at some point, the
way we may scream when the roller coaster twists through a complete 360 or plows
through a lake at the bottom of the drop. And horror movies, like roller coasters,
have always been the special province of the young; by the time one turns 40 or
50, one's appetite for double twists or 360-degree loops may be considerably
depleted. *[handwritten: "exhausted"]*

We also go to re-establish our feelings of essential normality; the horror movie   4
is innately conservative, even reactionary. Freda Jackson as the horrible melting
woman in *Die, Monster, Die!* confirms for us that no matter how far we may be
removed from the beauty of a Robert Redford or a Diana Ross, we are still light-
years from true ugliness.

And we go to have fun.   5

Ah, but this is where the ground starts to slope away, isn't it? Because this is a   6
very peculiar sort of fun, indeed. The fun comes from seeing others menaced—
sometimes killed. One critic has suggested that if pro football has become the voy-

[handwritten margin notes alongside paragraphs 3–6: "physical feelings / expressions / unconscious / older", "knowledge", "reality", "key word", "brings back to think that his assumption is right", "try convincing", "threaten", "inborn / opposes change"]

eur's version of combat, then the horror film has become the modern version of the public lynching.

It is true that the mythic, "fairy-tale" horror film intends to take away the shades of gray. . . . It urges us to put away our more civilized and adult penchant for analysis and to become children again, seeing things in pure blacks and whites. It may be that horror movies provide psychic relief on this level because this invitation to lapse into simplicity, irrationality, and even outright madness is extended so rarely. We are told we may allow our emotions a free rein . . . or no rein at all. **7**

If we are all insane, then sanity becomes a matter of degree. If your insanity leads you to carve up women like Jack the Ripper or the Cleveland Torso Murderer, we clap you away in the funny farm (but neither of those two amateur-night surgeons was ever caught, heh-heh-heh); if, on the other hand, your insanity leads you only to talk to yourself when you're under stress or to pick your nose on your morning bus, then you are left alone to go about your business . . . though it is doubtful that you will ever be invited to the best parties. **8**

The potential lyncher is in almost all of us (excluding saints, past and present; but then, most saints have been crazy in their own ways), and every now and then, he has to be let loose to scream and roll around in the grass. Our emotions and our fears form their own body, and we recognize that it demands its own exercise to maintain proper muscle tone. Certain of these emotional muscles are accepted—even exalted—in civilized society; they are, of course, the emotions that tend to maintain the status quo of civilization itself. Love, friendship, loyalty, kindness—these are all the emotions that we applaud, emotions that have been immortalized in the couplets of Hallmark cards and in the verses (I don't dare call it poetry) of Leonard Nimoy. **9**

When we exhibit these emotions, society showers us with positive reinforcement; we learn this even before we get out of diapers. When, as children, we hug our rotten little puke of a sister and give her a kiss, all the aunts and uncles smile and twit and cry, "Isn't he the sweetest little thing?" Such coveted treats as chocolate-covered graham crackers often follow. But if we deliberately slam the rotten little puke of a sister's fingers in the door, sanctions follow—angry remonstrance from parents, aunts, and uncles; instead of a chocolate-covered graham cracker, a spanking. **10**

But anticivilization emotions don't go away, and they demand periodic exercise. We have such "sick" jokes as, "What's the difference between a truckload of bowling balls and a truckload of dead babies?" (You can't unload a truckload of bowling balls with a pitchfork . . . a joke, by the way, that I heard originally from a ten-year-old.) Such a joke may surprise a laugh or a grin out of us even as we recoil, a possibility that confirms the thesis: If we share a brotherhood of man, then we also share an insanity of man. None of which is intended as a defense of either the sick joke or insanity but merely as an explanation of why the best horror films, like the best fairy tales, manage to be reactionary, anarchistic, and revolutionary all at the same time. **11**

The mythic horror movie, like the sick joke, has a dirty job to do. It deliberately appeals to all that is worst in us. It is morbidity unchained, our most base instincts let free, our nastiest fantasies realized . . . and it all happens, fittingly enough, in the dark. For those reasons, good liberals often shy away from horror films. For myself, I like to see the most aggressive of them—*Dawn of the Dead*, for instance—as lifting **12**

(handwritten marginal notes:)

Which we so rarely get to release.

horror movie allows us to let our emotions wordlessly in

execute

different degrees of insanity / start w/ being sane to insanity / (religious) / Baker

What's socially acceptable and not acceptable

Society's reward / treatment

We cannot change all

horror movies are here to stay but controversial

The good shy away. bad appealing / find amusement

opening the subconcious + feeding for reaction.

a trap door in the civilized forebrain and throwing a basket of raw meat to the hungry alligators swimming around in that subterranean river benath.

Why bother? Because it keeps them from getting out, man. It keeps them down   13
there and me up here. It was Lennon and McCartney who said that all you need is
love, and I would agree with that.

As long as you keep the gators fed.   14

horror movies may keep the insanity in perspective in that it is far fetched

For Discussion

"The potential lyncher is in almost all of us," says Stephen King, "and every now and then, he has to be let loose to scream and roll around in the grass." King seems to say that horror films perform a social function by allowing us to exercise (or possibly exorcise) our least civilized emotions. How do you react to this idea? What value do horror movies have for you? What do you think about the social value of horror films—or of some other kind of film? It might help to think in terms of a specific film you've seen recently.

For Analysis

1.   A successful argument often depends on a careful definition of a key term. Which term does King define? What significance does the definition have for King's argument? How convincing do you find his definition?

2.   Why do you think King begins as he does? Given his argument and his particular readers, what advantage do you see in this beginning?

Scratch outlines are discussed on pp. 432–35; transitions, on pp. 479–81.

3.   Causal arguments must be carefully planned in order to lead readers through the speculations. To discover King's plan, make a scratch outline of the selection. Then, to follow one way he keeps readers on track, analyze the transitions at the beginning of each paragraph. Begin by underlining the word or phrase that makes the exact connection with the previous paragraph.

Turn to pp. 530–32 for a discussion of analogy.

4.   How effective do you find the analogy in paragraph 3? Consider carefully the ways in which horror movies and roller coaster rides are similar, and dissimilar. Can you think of another analogy that would work?

For Your Own Writing

Think of some phenomenon of popular culture that interests you. Speculate about its causes. For instance, have you ever wondered why romance novels are so popular? Police shows and soap operas? Survivalist war games? Singles bars? Computer hacking? How would you present the phenomenon to your readers and develop an argument for its causes?

Commentary

To understand King's argument, it may help to distinguish between obvious and hidden causes. King begins with a cause that seems obvious but is still worth mentioning: we go to horror films because we want to prove that we can sit through them, just as we ride roller coasters to show ourselves and others that we have the courage to do it (paragraph 3). This cause seems plausible, though not at all surprising. We can assume that King mentions it right away because he assumes readers will be thinking of it. It enables him both to connect to a very common experience of his readers and to set an obvious cause aside in order to move on to the not-so-obvious causes, which are the heart of his argument.

King next entertains a very different cause: we go to horror movies "to re-establish our feelings of essential normality." This cause is much less predictable than the first. It may even be somewhat puzzling, and King might have argued it further. He asserts that horror movies are conservative and gives one illustration about the ugliness of their characters. However plausible this cause, it does move us from obvious causes toward the one hidden (unexpected, unlikely, risky) cause that King is to argue at length—we "crave" horror movies (not just attend them casually) in order to manage our uncivilized emotions of fear, violence, and aggression.

We may not accept King's psychology or find this hidden cause convincingly argued, but we are almost certainly interested in the argument itself, perhaps intrigued, maybe even shocked by either the idea or the examples. Whatever our reaction, King has not bored us with causes so obvious that we could have predicted all of them before reading the selection. In your own causal analysis essay, your first goal will be to speculate creatively about your subject so that you can come up with at least one not-so-obvious cause. Like King, you may want to place this cause last, after discussing other more obvious causes, and to argue for it at length and with ingenuity.

Experienced writers let their readers know that they are taking into account their values and beliefs as well as anticipating their objections and questions. We see this strategy in the way King attempts to get us to accept his striking assertions about our basic nature: "we're all mentally ill" (paragraph 1), "the potential lyncher is in almost all of us" (paragraph 9), and "anticivilization emotions . . . demand periodic exercise" (paragraph 11). Knowing these are debatable assertions, King defines his terms and qualifies them in a way that will enable most readers to consider his argument seriously, instead of rejecting it irritably. For example, he defines the disguised insanity in all of us in terms of all too familiar private habits and personal fears. Later he reminds us that sick jokes, which nearly all readers have told or laughed at from time to time, reveal our "anticivilization emotions." At the end of paragraph 11, he says, to paraphrase: "Look, I know you may be resisting my argument; but if I acknowledge that we share a brotherhood of man, then I think you should be able to acknowledge that we share an insanity of man, as I have been arguing. I'm not trying to encourage sick jokes or excuse aggression and violence but only to explain why we crave horror movies." This kind of direct acknowledgment of readers' points of view increases a writer's credibility and results in a more convincing argument.

For more about acknowledging readers' concerns, see pp. 547–48.

Befitting his subject, King's tone is tough but engaging. We know what his thesis is and where he is going with the argument. Whether or not we are convinced, we can admire this thoughtfulness and craft.

■   ■   ■

K. C. **Cole** began her writing career as a reporter and editor and has written several books on education, science, and women's issues: *Facets of Light* (1980), *Between the Lines* (1982), and *Sympathetic Vibrations: Physics as a Way of Life* (1984). In the following essay, written for the *New York Times* in 1981, she seeks to explain why so few women go into science. Like Stephen King, she speculates about the causes of a familiar phenomenon.

Before you begin reading, give some thought to her topic. Why don't more women become scientists, mathematicians, or engineers? Reflect on your own experience: Did you like or dislike science in high school? How would you explain your feelings?

**WHY THERE ARE
SO FEW WOMEN
IN SCIENCE**
K. C. COLE

1   I know few other women who do what I do. What I do is write about science, mainly physics. And to do that, I spend a lot of time reading about science, talking to scientists and struggling to understand physics. In fact, most of the women (and men) I know think me quite queer for actually liking physics. "How can you write about that stuff?" they ask, always somewhat askance. "I could never understand that in a million years." Or more simply, "I hate science."

2   I didn't realize what an odd creature a woman interested in physics was until a few years ago when a science magazine sent me to Johns Hopkins University in Baltimore for a conference on an electrical phenomenon known as the Hall effect. We sat in a huge lecture hall and listened as physicists talked about things engineers didn't understand, and engineers talked about things physicists didn't understand. What *I* didn't understand was why, out of several hundred young students of physics and engineering in the room, less than a handful were women.

3   Sometime later, I found myself at the California Institute of Technology reporting on the search for the origins of the universe. I interviewed physicist after physicist, man after man. I asked one young administrator why none of the physicists were women. And he answered: "I don't know, but I suppose it must be something innate. My seven-year-old daughter doesn't seem to be much interested in science."

4   It was with that experience fresh in my mind that I attended a conference in Cambridge, Mass., on science literacy, or rather the worrisome lack of it in this country today. We three women—a science teacher, a young chemist and myself—sat surrounded by a company of august men. The chemist, I think, first tentatively raised the issue of science illiteracy in women. It seemed like an obvious point. After all, everyone had agreed over and over again that scientific knowledge these days was a key factor in economic power. But as soon as she made the point, it became clear that we women had committed a grievous social error. Our genders were suddenly showing; we had interrupted the serious talk with a subject unforgivably silly.

5   For the first time, I stopped being puzzled about why there weren't any women in science and began to be angry. Because if science is a search for answers to fundamental questions then it hardly seems frivolous to find out why women are excluded. Never mind the economic consequences.

6   A lot of the reasons women are excluded are spelled out by the Massachusetts

Institute of Technology experimental physicist Vera Kistiakowsky in a recent article in *Physics Today* called ''Women in Physics: Unnecessary, Injurious and Out of Place?'' The title was taken from a nineteenth-century essay written in opposition to the appointment of a female mathematician to a professorship at the University of Stockholm. ''As decidedly as two and two make four,'' a woman in mathematics is a ''monstrosity,'' concluded the writer of the essay.

Dr. Kistiakowsky went on to discuss the factors that make women in science today, if not monstrosities, at least oddities. Contrary to much popular opinion, one of those is *not* an innate difference in the scientific ability of boys and girls. But early conditioning does play a stubborn and subtle role. A recent *Nova* program, ''The Pinks and the Blues,'' documented how girls and boys are treated differently from birth—the boys always encouraged in more physical kinds of play, more active explorations of their environments. Sheila Tobias, in her book, *Math Anxiety*, showed how the games boys play help them to develop an intuitive understanding of speed, motion, and mass. 7

The main sorting out of the girls from the boys in science seems to happen in junior high school. As a friend who teaches in a science museum said, ''By the time we get to electricity, the boys already have had some experience with it. But it's unfamiliar to the girls.'' Science books draw on boys' experiences. ''The examples are all about throwing a baseball at such and such a speed,'' said my stepdaughter, who barely escaped being a science drop-out. 8

The most obvious reason there are not many more women in science is that women are discriminated against as a class, in promotions, salaries and hirings, a conclusion reached by a recent analysis by the National Academy of Sciences. 9

Finally, said Dr. Kistiakowsky, women are simply made to feel out of place in science. Her conclusion was supported by a Ford Foundation study by Lynn H. Fox on the problems of women in mathematics. When students were asked to choose among six reasons accounting for girls' lack of interest in math, the girls rated this statement second: ''Men do not want girls in the mathematical occupations.'' 10

A friend of mine remembers winning a Bronxwide mathematics competition in the second grade. Her friends—both boys and girls—warned her that she shouldn't be good at math: ''You'll never find a boy who likes you.'' My friend continued nevertheless to excel in math and science, won many awards during her years at Bronx High School of Science, and then earned a full scholarship to Harvard. After one year of Harvard science, she decided to major in English. 11

When I asked her why, she mentioned what she called the ''macho mores'' of science. ''It would have been O.K. if I'd had someone to talk to,'' she said. ''But the rules of comportment were such that you never admitted you didn't understand. I later realized that even the boys didn't get everything clearly right away. You had to stick with it until it had time to sink in. But for the boys, there was a payoff in suffering through the hard times, and a kind of punishment—a shame—if they didn't. For the girls it was O.K. not to get it, and the only payoff for sticking it out was that you'd be considered a freak.'' 12

Science is undeniably hard. Often, it can seem quite boring. It is unfortunately too often presented as laws to be memorized instead of mysteries to be explored. It is too often kept a secret that science, like art, takes a well-developed esthetic sense. Women aren't the only ones who say, ''I hate science.'' 13

That's why everyone who goes into science needs a little help from friends. For 14 the past ten years, I have been getting more than a little help from a friend who is a physicist. But my stepdaughter—who earned the highest grades ever recorded in her California high school on the math Scholastic Aptitude Test—flunked calculus in her first year at Harvard. When my friend the physicist heard about it, he said, "Harvard should be ashamed of itself."

What he meant was that she needed that little extra encouragement that makes 15 all the difference. Instead, she got that little extra discouragement that makes all the difference.

"In the first place, all the math teachers are men," she explained. "In the second 16 place, when I met a boy I liked and told him I was taking chemistry, he immediately said, 'Oh, you're one of those science types.' In the third place, it's just a kind of a social thing. The math clubs are full of boys and you don't feel comfortable joining."

In other words, she was made to feel unnecessary, injurious and out of place.   17

A few months ago, I accompanied a male colleague from the science museum 18 where I sometimes work to a lunch of the history of science faculty at the University of California. I was the only woman there, and my presence for the most part was obviously and rudely ignored. I was so surprised and hurt by this that I made an extra effort to speak knowledgeably and well. At the end of the lunch, one of the professors turned to me in all seriousness and said: "Well, K.C., what do the women think of Carl Sagan?" I replied that I had no idea what "the women" thought about anything. But now I know what I should have said: I should have told him that his comment was unnecessary, injurious and out of place.

For Discussion

Does your own experience in math and science support or contradict Cole's argument? How much math and science did you take in high school? Are girls in the 1990s still made to feel out of place in these courses? If you believe they are, can you think of any causes in addition to the ones Cole presents? Were there certain math and science courses that girls were more likely to take or enjoy? If so, what do you think are the reasons?

For Analysis

1.   Cole writes for educated newspaper readers. Does she seem to be writing primarily to men or to women or to both equally? What do you think is her purpose? Point to specific evidence in the essay to support your answer.

2.   In paragraphs 1–5, how does Cole present the phenomenon she speculates about? Given her readers and purpose, what advantages or disadvantages do you see in her beginning?

3.   Unlike King, Cole relies on published sources as support for her argument. Review the essay to identify all these sources, and then decide what each contributes to the essay.

4.   Cole also makes effective use of her own personal experiences. List each example that she mentions from this source and note briefly what it contributes to her argument. What can you conclude about the role of personal experience in arguments speculating about causes?

For Your
Own Writing

Consider some well-recognized social or educational problem you might write about for a specific group of readers—discriminatory university hiring practices, cheating on exams, diminishing aid for the poor. Choose a topic, and consider its causes. What plausible causes can you think of now, without doing any research? Which of these causes would be obvious to these readers? Which might surprise them?

Commentary

Whereas Stephen King relies solely on his own inventive speculations to explain why we crave horror movies, K. C. Cole relies on others' speculations, primarily those of physicist Vera Kistiakowsky, to explain why there are so few women in science. Cole goes well beyond reporting Kistiakowsky's proposed causes, however. Primarily, she evaluates them against her own experience. For example, after she reports Kistiakowsky's claim that girls are "sorted out" of science in junior high, Cole mentions two specific examples, one of a friend, the other of her stepdaughter. And after she notes Kistiakowsky's argument that girls are made to feel out of place in science, Cole recalls a friend who excelled in science through high school but majored in English in college because of the "macho mores" in her college science courses.

From her wide experience of discrimination against women in science, Cole could have relied entirely on her own speculations for the causes that make up her argument. Instead, she relies on Kistiakowski, whose book may even have inspired Cole to write the essay. Cole's strategy is not at all unusual for a writer of such an essay. In writing to speculate about causes, you too may want to research causes others have proposed to explain your subject. When you do so, you must explicitly evaluate each cause, not only acknowledging its source but also then refuting it or, like Cole, accommodating it—acknowledging its validity and incorporating it into your own argument.

For more about refuting and accommodating alternative causes, see pp. 546–52.

Though Cole mentions several sources, she does not give formal citations for them: newspaper writing rarely cites sources formally. She does, however, identify her sources—Kistiakowsky's "recent article" in *Physics Today*, a "recent" *Nova* program—so that readers could easily track them down. Your instructor may expect you to cite your sources formally, as does the writer of the final selection in this chapter. If so, Chapter 22 provides guidance.

The commentary following King's essay distinguishes between obvious and hidden causes. Cole's essay demonstrates other classifications of causes that are important in causal analysis. In her argument, differences in early conditioning of boys and girls are a *remote* or *background* cause: since she discounts innate or genetic differences, conditioning through experience seems the earliest possible cause for women's absence from science. Such conditioning seems a *sufficient* cause, since it is so difficult to overcome. It is not, however, a *necessary* cause, since other causes Cole mentions would be sufficient to reduce the number of women in science. With early conditioning as a plausible remote cause, the remaining causes in Cole's list—sorting in junior high, discrimination, the peripheral status of women science majors in college, and lack of encouragement—seem plausible *immediate* causes—things that cause individual women to abandon science at a particular point. They are also *perpetuating* causes, helping to maintain or strengthen an aversion to science that has already begun.

Your own essay will be much more thoughtful and convincing if you can analyze the causes you are considering to determine whether they could be considered remote, immediate, sufficient, necessary, or perpetuating causes of the subject. You probably will not want to use these labels in the essay, but such an analysis can help you understand how convincing your causes are and how they are related to one another. For instance, if a cause is immediate or perpetuating, you will want to ask yourself what other causes might lie behind it, because these might be more important and influential.

■   ■   ■

Victor Fuchs, a professor of economics at Stanford, has for many years been a research associate at the National Bureau of Economic Research. This selection is from his book *How We Live: An Economic Perspective on Americans from Birth to Death* (1983). Here he speculates about the causes of a trend. As you begin reading, notice the care with which Fuchs documents the existence of the trend.

The tone of Fuchs's essay is more serious than that of King's. Fuchs does not let his personality show. His essay is not only impersonal, it is dryly factual; it seems to move slowly, but such slowness is actually a tribute to the rigor of Fuchs's careful reasoning and attention to detail.

As you read, pay attention to both the causes Fuchs rejects and the ones he proposes to explain the increase in suicides among young people.

SUICIDE AMONG YOUNG PEOPLE
VICTOR FUCHS

Although the vigor and vitality of most young people are the envy of their elders, a significant range of serious health problems are present at ages 15–24, including venereal disease, alcoholism, and drug abuse. Moreover, a large number of adolescents and youth are making themselves vulnerable to future health problems through cigarette smoking, poor diet, and inadequate exercise (Institute of Medicine 1978). One of the most disturbing trends is rising mortality among youth at a time when death rates at all other ages are declining rapidly. Male death rates at ages 15–19 and 20–24 were 12 percent *higher* in 1977 than in 1960, while mortality at other ages *declined* an average of 12 percent. A large differential in mortality trends by age is also evident for women. The deaths of young people take a tremendous emotional toll and are also particularly costly because these men and women are at the threshold of productive lives during which they and society could realize a return on the investment that has been made in them. 1

The principal reason for the divergent trends in mortality by age is the increase in self-destructive behavior by young men and women (see the tabulation below). 2

Among young men, suicide and motor vehicle accidents now account for half of all deaths, and among women for well over 40 percent. More youth die from suicide alone than from cancer, cardiovascular disease, diabetes, pneumonia, and influenza combined. The rising death rate from homicide also contributes to the rising death rate among the young. Homocide rates have approximately doubled at most ages, but because it is a relatively more important cause of death among the young, this doubling has had more of an impact on their overall rate. The high homicide rate among nonwhite men is particularly shocking, averaging about 50 per year per hundred thousand at ages 15–19 and over 100 per hundred thousand at ages 20–24. These rates imply that almost one out of every 100 black youths who turn 15 becomes a homicide victim before the age of 25! Apart from violent deaths, the trends in mortality of young men and women have been as favorable as at older ages.

	Percent change in age-sex-specific death rates, 1960 to 1977	
	Ages 15–24	Ages 25 and over
Suicide	145	6
Motor vehicle accidents	25	−15
Homicide	113	83
All other causes	−22	−21

Why did suicide rates among young people increase so rapidly in the 1960s and 1970s? It is much easier to rule out answers to this question than to find ones that will withstand critical examination. For instance, it is highly unlikely that the trend is a result of differences in the reporting of suicides, although reporting practices do vary considerably over time and in different areas. Changes in reporting, however, would affect the suicide rate at all ages, and there was no comparable increase at other stages of life. The emotional trauma of the Vietnam War was felt more keenly by young people and this may have contributed to the increase in suicides, but there are two problems with this explanation. First, after the war ended the suicide rate among young people kept on rising, rather than falling back to prewar levels (see Figure 9.1). Second, suicide rates at ages 15–24 in Canada and Sweden have been rising as rapidly and are as high as in the United States. Neither country was much affected by the Vietnam War. 3

Suicides have been blamed on deteriorating economic conditions, but Figure 9.1 shows that the rate has been rising in good times as well as bad; the long-term trend is much stronger than any response to business cycle fluctuations. Furthermore, the suicide level is slightly higher among white than nonwhite youth and the rate of increase has been as rapid for whites as for nonwhites, despite the large race differentials in youth employment. One of the more mischievous arguments currently in vogue is that the problems of children and youth are the result of high unemployment and that their solution lies in better macroeconomic policies. Of course low unemployment is better than high, and price stability is preferable to inflation, but anyone who believes that the increases in suicides among youth, births to unwed mothers, juvenile crime, and one-parent homes are primarily the result of macroeconomic conditions is ignoring readily available evidence. All these problems were 4

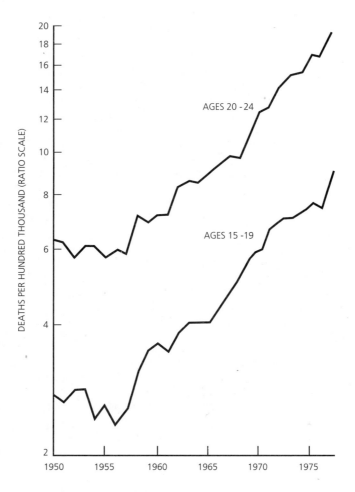

Figure 9.1.
Suicide rates among
youth, 1950–1977
Sources: U.S. Bureau of the
Census, *Vital Statistics of the
United States*, 1950–1977;
idem, *Current Population Reports*, series P-25, nos. 310,
519, 721, and 870.

increasing particularly rapidly during the second half of the 1960s, when the unemployment rate averaged 3.8 percent and economic growth was extremely rapid.

Some mental health experts attribute the increases in suicides among the young 5
to the rapid changes in the American family. A study at Bellevue Hospital in New
York City of 102 teenagers who attempted suicide showed that only one-third of
them lived with both parents (*Newsweek*, August 28, 1978, p. 74). Parents may be
failing to provide enough structure and security for children either because they are
not present or because they are preoccupied with their own lives and careers, or
simply because they are too permissive. In a review of psychosocial literature on adolescence, Elder (1975) concludes: Adolescents who fail to receive guidance, affection, and concern from parents—whether by parental inattention or absence—are
likely to rely heavily on peers for emotional gratification, advice, and companionship,
to anticipate a relatively unrewarding future, and to engage in antisocial activities"
(italics added). On the other hand, some experts contend that too many demands

and the setting of unrealistic standards by parents also predispose young people toward suicide.

Some evidence of a relation between family background and suicide appears in 6 a long-term longitudinal study of fifty thousand male students of Harvard University and the University of Pennsylvania that compared the characteristics of 381 men who eventually committed suicide with a set of living control subjects randomly chosen from the same school and year as the suicides (Paffenbarger, King, and Wing 1969). One of the strongest results was a positive relation between suicide and loss of father. At the time of the original interview (average age 18) the future suicides were more likely than the controls to have a deceased father (12.4 percent versus 8.1 percent) or to have parents who had separated (12.6 percent versus 8.9 percent). The difference in paternal loss through death or separation was statistically significant at a high level of confidence. The future suicides also differed from the control by having a larger percentage of fathers who were college-educated (69.1 percent versus 56.6 percent) and who were professionals (48.8 percent versus 38.4 percent). Loss of mother did not differ between the suicides and the controls.

It must be emphasized that the rapid increase in suicide rates among youth is 7 unique to that age group—there is nothing comparable at other ages. By contrast, the doubling of death rates from homicide at young ages reflects a general increase in violent crime that has affected all age groups, although not in exactly equal degree.

For some problems, such as the sharp increase in suicides, no simple or even 8 moderately complex public policy solution is in the offing. Young people may be succumbing to what Abraham Maslow (1959) forecast as the ultimate disease of our time—"valuelessness." The rise in suicides and other self-destructive behavior such as motor vehicle accidents and drug abuse may be the result of weakening family structures and the absence of fathers, as suggested by the study of Harvard University and University of Pennsylvania students. We can't be sure of the cause, but if it's along the lines suggested above, the challenge to public policy is staggering.

References

Elder, Glen H., Jr. 1975. Adolescence in the life cycle: An introduction. In *Adolescence in the life cycle: Psychological change and social context*, ed. Sigmund E. Dragastin and Glen H. Elder, Jr. New York: Halsted-Wiley.

Institute of Medicine. 1978. *Adolescent behavior and health*. Washington, D.C.: National Academy of Sciences.

Maslow, Abraham H. 1959. *New knowledge in human values*. New York: Harper and Brothers.

Paffenberger, Ralph S. Jr.; Stanley H. King; and Alvin L. Wing. 1969. Characteristics in youth that predispose to suicide and accidental death in later life. *American Journal of Public Health* 59 (June): 900–908.

For Discussion

"The rise in suicides and other self-destructive behavior" among young people, Fuchs suggests, "may be the result of weakening family structures and the absence of fathers." How convincing do you find this explanation? Among young people you know, to what extent does behavior like reckless driving and alcohol or drug abuse seem related to parental neglect or absence?

If you've ever done something you consider self-destructive, what speculations would you have now about why you did it?

For Analysis

1. How does Fuchs demonstrate that there is a trend of increased suicide
among young people? What role do the table and figure play? Has he convinced you that the trend actually exists?

2. What causes does Fuchs propose to explain the increasing number of
suicides among young people? Analyze his proposed causes in terms of the
categories introduced earlier: obvious, hidden, precipitating, perpetuating,
necessary, and sufficient. (You may want to review the discussion of these
categories in the Commentary following the King and Cole essays.)

3. What kind of evidence does Fuchs offer for his proposed causes? How
convincing do you find his argument?

4. In "ruling out answers" to his question at the beginning of paragraph
3, Fuchs rejects alternatives to his own proposed causes. List the alternative
causes he rejects in paragraphs 3 and 4. In paragraph 7, Fuchs reiterates his
objections to an alternative cause he had discussed earlier. Why do you think
he does this? Why do you think he devotes so much space to considering
alternatives that he then rejects?

5. How does Fuchs conclude his essay? Does he frame it by repeating some
element from the beginning? How successful do you find his ending?

For Your
Own Writing

Imagine that you've been asked to write about some recent trend as an example of "how we live" (to borrow the title of the book from which this
essay was taken). What trends have caught your attention? Choose one. How
would you demonstrate the increase or decrease that constitutes the trend?
What causes come immediately to mind?

Commentary

Fuchs's essay is easy to read because it follows a simple plan:

    beginning
        context for suicide trend
        demonstration of suicide trend
    consideration and rejection of alternative causes
    argument for proposed causes
        parental failure
        loss of father
    reiteration of why the most likely alternative cause should be rejected
    ending

Essays speculating about the causes of trends nearly always begin by demonstrating the existence of the trend and then move on to the causes. The
challenge in planning such an essay is in ordering the causes to make the most

convincing argument. Another decision that must be made is where to take up alternative causes.

Writing about trends involving people and groups usually demands the kind of careful arguments Fuchs presents. It is the sort of argumentative writing we rely on for help in making social-policy decisions when there is no unarguable scientific evidence to tell us what to do. Such analysis helps us to consider plausible arguments, decide which is the best one, and then decide what to do.

Fuchs's essay provides causal analysis typical of the social sciences. You will encounter such analysis often in the texts you will be required to read as a college student as well as in the social or political analysis found on the editorial pages of newspapers and magazines. You may very well be asked to write a causal analysis yourself, either as an essay exam or as a term paper.

Chapter 22 provides detailed information on using each style.

The source citation style in Fuchs's essay and the following essay by Kim Dartnell is the style favored in the social sciences, that of the American Psychological Association. The style favored in the humanities, that of the Modern Language Association, is used in the Statsky essay in Chapter 7.

■   ■   ■

Kim **Dartnell** looks at the plight of homeless women in the following essay, written when she was a college freshman. Like Fuchs's essay, it illustrates how a writer can use library research to document a trend and try to determine its causes.

Before reading the essay, recall what you know about the homeless in America and homeless women in particular. What reasons can you think of for Americans to find themselves without homes?

WHERE WILL THEY SLEEP TONIGHT?
KIM DARTNELL

On January 21, 1982, in New York City, Rebecca Smith froze to death, after living for five months in a cardboard box. Rebecca was one of a family of thirteen children from a rural town in Virginia. After graduating from high school as the valedictorian of her class and giving birth to a daughter, she spent ten years in mental institutions, where she underwent involuntary shock treatment for schizophrenia. It was when she was released to her sister's custody that Rebecca began wandering the streets of New York, living from day to day. Many social workers tried unsuccessfully to persuade her to go into a city shelter, and she died only a few hours before she was scheduled to be placed in protective custody. (Hombs and Snyder, 1982, p. 56).

Rebecca Smith's story is all too typical of those of the increasing number of homeless women in America. Vagrant men have always been a noticeable problem in American cities, and their numbers have increased in the 1980s. Vagrancy among women is a relatively new problem of any size, however. In 1979, New York City had one public shelter for homeless women. By 1983 it had four. Los Angeles has recently increased the number of beds available to women in its skid-row shelters

(Stoner, 1983, p. 571). Even smaller communities have noticed an increase in homeless women. It is impossible to know their number or the extent of their increase in the 1980s, but everyone who has studied the problem agrees that it is serious and that it is getting worse (Hombs and Snyder, 1982, p.10; Stoner, 1984, p. 3).

Who are these women? Over half of all homeless women are under the age of   3
forty. Forty-four percent are black, forty percent white. The statistics for homeless men are about the same (Stoner, 1983, p. 570). These women are almost always unemployed and poorly educated, unlike Rebecca Smith, and few are homeless by choice. An expert in the field has written, "Homeless women do not choose their circumstances. They are victims of forces over which they have lost control." The women try in various ways to cope with their dangerous lifestyle. To avoid notice, especially by the police, some have one set of nice clothes that they wash often. They shower in shelters or YWCA's and try to keep their hairstyle close to the latest fashions. An extreme is the small number of women who actually sleep sitting up on park benches to avoid wrinkling their clothes. On the other end of the spectrum are the more noticeable "bag ladies," who purposely maintain an offensive appearance and body odor to protect themselves from rape or robbery (Stoner, 1983, pp. 568, 569).

Why has there been such an increase in the number of vagrant American   4
women? There are several causes of this trend. For one thing, more and more women are leaving their families because of rape, incest, and other forms of abuse. To take one example, the Christian Housing Facility, a private organization in Orange County, California, that provides food, shelter, and counseling to victims of abuse, sheltered 1,536 people in 1981, a 300-percent increase from the year before (Stoner, 1983, p. 573). It is unclear whether such increases are due to an actual increase of abuse in American families, or whether they result from the fact that it is more socially acceptable for a woman to be on her own today. Another factor is that government social programs for battered women have been severely cut back, leaving victims of abuse no choice but to leave home.

Evictions and illegal lockouts force some women onto the streets. Social welfare   5
cutbacks, unemployment, and desertion all result in a loss of income. Once a woman cannot pay her rent, she is likely to be evicted, often without notice.

Another problem is a lack of inexpensive housing. Of today's homeless women,   6
over fifty percent lived in single rooms before they became vagrants. Many of the buildings containing single-room or other cheap apartments have been torn down to make way for more profitable use of the land or renovated into more expensive housing. Hotels are being offered new tax incentives that make it economically unfeasible to maintain inexpensive single rooms. This is obviously a serious problem, one that sends many women out onto the streets every year.

Alcoholism has been cited as a major reason for the increase in the number of   7
homeless women. I don't feel this is a major contributing factor, however. First, there hasn't been a significant general increase in alcoholism to parallel the rise in homeless women; second, alcoholism occurs at all levels of financial status, from the executive to the homeless. Rather, I would suggest that alcoholism is usually a result of homelessness rather than the cause.

Probably the biggest single factor in the rising number of homeless women is   8
the deinstitutionalization of the mentally ill. One study estimated that ninety percent of all vagrant women may be mentally ill (Stoner, 1983, p. 567), as was the case

with Rebecca Smith. The last few years have seen an avalanche of mental patients released from institutions. Between 1955 and 1980 the number of patients in mental institutions dropped by 75 percent, from about 560,000 to about 140,000. There are several reasons for this decline. New psychotonic drugs can now "cure" patients with mild disturbances. Expanded legal rights for patients lead to early release from asylums. Government-funded services such as Medicare allow some patients to be released into nursing or boarding homes. The problem is that many of these women have not really known any life outside the hospital and suddenly find themselves thrust out into an unreceptive world, simply because they present no threat to society or are "unresponsive to treatment." Very few of them are ever referred to community mental health centers, as deinstitutionalization policies assumed. Instead, many go straight out on the streets. Others may live with family or in some other inexpensive housing at first, but sooner or later they are likely to end up in the streets as well.

Although deinstitutionalization seems to have been the biggest factor in the in- 9
crease in vagrant women, there is some evidence that the main cause is economic. Unemployment hit 10.1 percent in 1982, the highest it has been since 1940. Yet that same year saw $2.35 billion cut from food-stamp programs. Reductions in another federal welfare program, Aid to Families with Dependent Children (AFDC), hit women particularly hard because four out of five AFDC families are headed by women, two thirds of whom have not graduated from high school (Hombs and Snyder, 1982). Together with inflation, unemployment, and loss of other welfare benefits, these cuts have effectively forced many women into homelessness and can be expected to continue to do so at a greater rate in the years to come.

The United States may be one of the world's most prosperous nations, but for 10
Rebecca Smith and others like her, the American Dream is far from being fulfilled.

References

Hombs, M. E., & Snyder, M. (1982). *Homelessness in America.* Washington, DC: Community for Creative Non-Violence.

Stoner, M. R. (1983). The plight of homeless women. *Social Service Review, 57,* 565–581.

Stoner, M. R. (1984). An analysis of public and private sector provisions for homeless people. *The Urban and Social Change Review, 17,* 2–10.

For Discussion

What is your first response to Dartnell's essay? How frequently do you encounter homeless people, and how do you respond to them? Why do you think our society allows people to remain homeless?

For Analysis

1. What is Dartnell's purpose in this essay? What does she seem to assume about her readers?

2. In paragraphs 3 and 7, Dartnell rejects two alternative causes that are frequently used to explain why women are homeless. How does she construct her refutations? How convincing do you find them? Why do you think Dartnell makes a point of refuting these particular arguments?

3.   Write out a brief outline of this essay. How does Dartnell order her proposed causes? What advantages or disadvantages do you see in this order?

4.   How does Dartnell begin and end her essay? How effective is this way of beginning and ending a causal argument?

5.   Now that you have completed a comprehensive analysis of Dartnell's essay, how convincing do you find her explanation for the increasing number of homeless women? If you find it convincing, how would you explain its effectiveness? If it is not convincing, how could it be improved?

For Your Own Writing

Think of a troubling social trend you might write about. How would you demonstrate its existence, and what causes would you propose to explain it?

Commentary

Dartnell's essay illustrates how important a small amount of research can be for an essay explaining the causes of a social trend. She uses only three sources, all located on one visit to the library, which provide adequate documentation for both the trend and her proposed causes. Her sources include two essays she found in social science journals and a book on the general topic of homelessness in America. Dartnell depends on these sources for her evidence—statistics and the particular case of Rebecca Smith. She also uses the authority of her sources to bolster her argument, quoting from Stoner in paragraph 3, for example, to persuade readers that they should not blame homeless women for their plight but rather see them as victims.

For more about these and other kinds of evidence, see pp. 538–46.

PURPOSE AND AUDIENCE

The chief purpose of an essay speculating about causes is to convince readers that the proposed causes are plausible. You must, thus, construct a coherent, logical, authoritative argument that readers will take seriously. Sometimes, like King and Cole, you may want readers to look at a phenomenon or trend in a new way, to go beyond obvious or familiar explanations. At other times, you may, like Dartnell, hope to influence policy decisions regarding a social problem. There may even be occasions when you believe your readers are so unmoveable that you can only hope to sharpen your differences, challenging or refuting their ideas.

Your audience will also affect your purpose. If you think your readers are only mildly curious about the subject, you might write partly to stimulate their interest. If you expect they will be strongly opposed to your speculations or very skeptical of them, you could try to show that you understand their point of view. If you believe the distance between you and them to be un-bridgeable, you could even accentuate your differences, explaining why you think their views are implausible.

BASIC FEATURES OF ESSAYS SPECULATING ABOUT CAUSES

Essays that explain causes typically include two basic features: a presentation of the subject and a convincing causal argument.

A Presentation of the Subject

First, it is necessary to identify the subject, sometimes quite extensively, depending on what the writer thinks the readers know or need to know. Writers sometimes devote a large portion of the essay to the subject—describing it with specific details and examples, establishing that it actually exists (or existed) with facts, statistics, and statements by authorities.

In writing about a phenomenon he knows will be familiar to his readers, Stephen King simply asserts in his title the popular fascination with horror movies. If he had been concerned that his readers might not accept this assertion, he could have cited statistics to demonstrate the popularity of horror movies. In the original essay from which this selection was excerpted, King also describes a number of particular examples of the genre in all of their gory detail. Because we all know what horror movies are—whether we've seen or studiously avoided them—we do not need such detailed description to understand his analysis of why some people, at least, "crave" this type of film. But such details can still be useful for engaging readers' interest in the subject or impressing them with its importance.

In contrast, K. C. Cole starts by describing in detail the phenomenon whose causes she speculates about—the small number of women in science. Knowing that readers are unlikely to have firsthand experience of professional science, Cole takes us to three scientific conferences to show us how few women are present.

In an essay about a trend, a writer must always demonstrate that the trend exists. Notice how Victor Fuchs very carefully documents the increase in youth suicides, presenting figures to show the sharp increase in suicides since 1960 as well as other statistics. In the same way, Kim Dartnell uses well-documented statistics to demonstrate that the number of homeless women is increasing. Because her subject is likely to be personally unfamiliar to some readers, she also describes some typical homeless women and presents an example, the case of an individual woman.

In some cases the writer may have to show that the subject is in fact a trend—an established, significant change—as opposed to a fad, which is only a short-term, superficial change. For example, a new form of exercise might become a fad if many people try it out for a few months. But this brief popularity would not make it a trend. It might, however, be considered part of a trend—a general increase in health-consciousness, for example.

It may also be necessary to provide other details about a trend. When did it start? Is it completed or continuing? Is it decelerating or accelerating? Where is the source for these details? Is it authoritative? A thorough presentation of the trend may have to answer all these questions.

A Convincing
Causal Argument

At the heart of an essay that analyzes the causes of something is the causal argument itself—presentation of the causes, presentation of evidence in support of each cause, and anticipation of objections and alternative causes. Causal arguments are tricky. Effects have a way of being mistaken for causes. Causes proposed as sufficient to explain a phenomenon may not be necessary to explain it. A proposed cause may turn out to have originated only after a trend started. Since skeptical readers are quick to spot these reasoning errors, writers must take care in constructing their argument.

In proposing causes, writers need to be very sensitive to their readers. First, they must present their causes in a logical order that will be easy to follow. Thus Dartnell, writing for nonexperts, begins with an immediate and concrete cause (abuse) and concludes with a background and perpetuating cause (economics). To hold readers' interest, writers must also not emphasize causes readers would consider obvious or predictable.

Writers must marshal evidence for each cause they propose. They may use statistics, factual cases and examples, and anecdotes. Fuchs gives statistics (paragraphs 5 and 6) to support his argument about the most likely cause of the increase in suicide among young people. Similarly, Dartnell offers statistical evidence of the economic forces behind female homelessness. She also includes a factual case; the opening narrative about a particular homeless woman. Cole includes several examples and anecdotes—concrete, one-time incidents—as evidence of the causes she proposes for the scarcity of women in science.

For more about argumentative evidence, see pp. 538–46.

Most important, writers must anticipate readers' possible objections to and questions about the proposed causes, showing they have considered (and rejected) any other possible causes. Cole twice acknowledges that many men find science unpleasant or mystifying for the same reasons women do. Fuchs emphatically rejects several alternative causes before proposing his own explanation of the increase in youth suicides. Dartnell refutes the objection that many homeless women choose their condition, and she not only shows evidence that alcoholism is not a cause of increased homelessness, but goes on to suggest that it is usually an effect instead.

Guide to Writing

THE WRITING ASSIGNMENT

Think of some important or intriguing phenomenon or trend, and explain why it has occurred. Describe your subject, demonstrate its existence if necessary, and propose possible causes for it. Your purpose is to convince your readers that the proposed causes are plausible.

INVENTION AND RESEARCH

Following are some activities to help you find a subject, explore what you know about it, and do any necessary research.

Finding a Subject

Consider both phenomena and trends as possible subjects. A *phenomenon* is something notable about the human condition or the social order—some people's fear of speaking to a group, for example, or opposition to gun-control legislation. A *trend* is a significant change extending over many months or years. It can be identified by some sort of increase or decrease—a rise in the birthrate, a decline in test scores.

Some subjects can be approached as either phenomena or trends. For example, you could, like Fuchs, speculate about the causes of the increasing suicide rate among young people, or you could simply speculate about the causes of such suicides, ignoring that their numbers are increasing.

You might set a timer and brainstorm your lists on a computer with the monitor brightness turned all the way down. Try to enter as many possibilities as you can in ten minutes. Then, turn the brightness up, make sure all the items are clear to you, and print out a copy to make notes on.

Listing Phenomena.   First list any current phenomena you might want to write about. Following are some possibilities to consider. Start with some of them, and see if they bring to mind other topics of interest to you.

- The workplace—satisfaction or dissatisfaction with a job, white-collar crime, discrimination against women, reliance on part-time help, loyalty to a company, respect or lack of respect for a supervisor
- College—a noisy library, a shortage of parking, an instructor's skill or popularity, cheating, a successful or unsuccessful class or course, a feeling or lack of community
- Personal life—competitiveness, idealism, creativity, popularity, jealousy, laziness, workaholics, contentiousness, rage
- Politics and government—hostility to politicians, low voter turnout, political action committee (PAC) influence, high cost of running for public office, negative campaigning
- Environment—failure to reduce pollution, the garbage crisis, difficulty of starting and maintaining recycling programs, concern about food safety
- Life stages—the "terrible twos," teenage alienation or rebellion, midlife crisis, abrupt career changes
- Popularity of current musical styles or other art forms
- Continuing influence or popularity of a book, movie, actor, novelist, social activist, athlete, politician, religious leader, television program

Listing Trends.   List all the trends you can think of, from the past as well as the present. Consider trends you have studied and can research as well as those you know firsthand. Try to think of trends you would like to understand better and be sure that the possibilities you list are trends, not fads. To start, consider the following possibilities:

- Shifting patterns in education—increasing interest in computer science or in teaching as a career, increase in home schooling, increase in community college enrollments, declining numbers of math and science majors, increase in number of black students attending black colleges
- Changes in patterns of leisure or entertainment—increasing consumption of fast food, declining interest in a particular style of music, increase in competitive cycling, increase or decrease in a magazine's circulation
- Shifts in religious practices—decreasing support for television evangelists, increasing incidence of women ministers or rabbis, increasing interest in Asian religions, increased membership in fundamentalist churches
- New patterns of political behavior—increase in conservatism or liberalism, a growing desire for isolationism from world affairs, developing power of minorities and women
- Societal changes—increases in the number of women working, unmarried teenagers having babies, single-parent households, telecommunicating
- Changes in politics or world affairs—spreading influence of capitalism, increasing terrorist activity, increasing numbers of women elected to political office, growing ethnic conflicts
- Changes in economic conditions—increase in low-paying service jobs, increasing cost of medical care, decline in standard of living
- Completed artistic movements or historical trends—impressionism, pop art, the struggle for female suffrage, industrialization

Choosing a Subject.   Now look over your list and pick one subject to write about. You may or may not already have some ideas about why this phenomenon or trend occurred. As you analyze it in some detail, you will have the opportunity to consider possible causes and to decide which ones are the most important.

Of the two types of subjects, a trend may be more challenging because you nearly always must do research to demonstrate that it actually exists, that something has been increasing or decreasing over an extended period of time. (Usually one or two references will be adequate.) Since a trend begins at a specific point, you must take care that the causes you propose as the sources of the trend actually precede its onset. You may also need to differentiate between causes that launched the trend and those that perpetuate it.

Stop now to focus your thoughts. In one or two sentences, describe the subject you have decided to analyze.

Exploring What You Know about Your Subject

Do some thinking now about the subject you have chosen to analyze. Consider what you know about it, figure out why you are interested in it, decide where you might find more information about it. Write for around ten minutes, noting everything you know about the subject.

Considering Causes

Think now about what might have caused your subject, listing possible causes and then analyzing the most promising.

If you can, save your work exploring and considering causes on a word processor. Then, as you begin to draft later, you can call up the file on a second screen and easily transfer details you want to use in your draft.

Listing Possible Causes.   Write down all the things you can think of that might have caused your subject, considering each of the following:

- immediate causes (those responsible for making the phenomenon or trend begin when it did)
- remote, background causes (those from the more distant past)
- perpetuating causes (those that may have contributed to sustaining or continuing the phenomenon or trend)
- obvious causes
- hidden causes

Selecting the Most Promising Causes.   Review your list and select five or six "promising" causes, ones that seem to you to provide a plausible explanation of your subject. Since you will next need to analyze these causes, it might be helpful to list them in table form. On a piece of paper, list the causes in a column on the left, leaving five or six lines between each cause.

See pp. 376–77 for an example of such a table.

Analyzing Promising Causes.   Next to each potential cause on the table, explain why you think it is real and important. Consider each of the following questions as you analyze the causes:

- Is it a necessary cause? Without it, could the subject have occurred?
- Is it a sufficient cause? Could it alone have caused this subject?
- Would this cause affect everybody the same way?
- Would this cause always lead to phenomena or trends like this?
- If the subject is a trend, do you know of any statistical evidence that this cause increases or decreases in correlation with the trend?
- Can you think of any particular anecdotes or examples that demonstrate the cause's importance?
- Have any authorities suggested it is an important cause?
- Is it actually a result of the subject rather than a cause?
- Is it a remote cause or an immediate cause?
- Is it a perpetuating cause?
- Is it an obvious cause or a hidden cause?

Researching Your Subject

In exploring your subject, you may have found that you already know enough to describe or define it adequately for your readers. Should you need to know more, consult library sources or a faculty or community expert.

If you are speculating about the causes of a *trend*, you will also need to do some research to confirm that it actually is a trend and not just a phenomenon or fad. To do so you will need to find factual, and probably statistical, evidence of an increase or decrease over time—and also of the date when this change began. (Recall that Fuchs uses a graph to show the increase in youth suicides and that Dartnell provides statistical evidence that the number of homeless women is increasing.) If you are unable to confirm the trend, you will need to select another that you can confirm.

On pp. 588–89 is a list of sources especially useful for researching trends.

Testing Your Choice

Once you have explored your subject, considered its possible causes, confirmed its existence, and described it in some detail, take some time to review your material and decide whether your subject is workable. Does the subject still interest you? Are the causes you've come up with not simply obvious ones? Would you like to research it further? If your subject does not seem promising, return to your list of possible subjects to select another.

For Group Inquiry

One good way of testing your subject is with a group of two or three other students. In turn, name your subjects and then ask group members what causes come to their minds. Then name the causes you have in mind and discuss whether the other members of the group accept these as likely causes. Find out what, if anything, they already know about your subject. Feedback of this kind can help you to know what objections to expect from readers; it can also help you to uncover some other possible causes.

Researching Causes

Some causal arguments can be made fully and convincingly on the basis of your own knowledge and intuition. In fact, you may have to rely on your own ideas to explain very recent phenomena or new, emerging trends. Most subjects, however, will already have been noticed by others, and you will want to learn what they have said about the causes. Doing research can be helpful in several ways: (1) to confirm or challenge your own ideas, (2) to suggest other acceptable causes, (3) to provide evidence of causes, (4) to identify other causes your readers may find plausible, and (5) to help you see some of the reservations readers may have about the causes you suggest.

As you discover causes others have proposed, add the most interesting or plausible ones to your table. Analyze these as you did your own proposed causes. In your essay, you may want to accommodate them—integrate them fully or partially into your own argument—or refute them.

As you gather evidence about causes, remember to record information for acknowledging your sources.

For guidelines on acknowledging sources, see pp. 602–12.

Considering Your Readers

Because you will be trying to make a convincing case for some particular readers, you should know as much as possible about your prospective readers. Only after you have analyzed your readers can you confidently decide how to present these causes in your essay—which to emphasize, which will require the most convincing evidence, which will be obvious. Take a few minutes to answer the following questions:

- Who are my readers? (Describe them briefly.)
- What do they know about my subject, and how much proof of its existence or defining or describing of it might they require?
- What attitudes might they have about my subject? Do they care about it? Are they indifferent to it? Might they derive or understand it differently from me?
- Will they be in agreement with my argument already? Skeptical but convinceable? Resistant and perhaps even antagonistic?
- What causes would they be most likely to think of?
- Which of my possible causes might they be skeptical of, and why?
- What else do I know about my readers?

Developing Your Argument

Again, saving your preliminary arguments on a word processor may help you draft your essay more efficiently.

Once you have figured out your expectations of your readers, review your table of causes and analyses and make a list of all the causes that you believe contribute significantly to your subject. Make a separate list of any other causes for which you have evidence. When you write your essay, you may wish to mention these minor causes to show that you have considered a wide range of possibilities. To try out your arguments, write about each of the significant causes for around five minutes, summing up all the evidence you have found. Develop your argument with your readers in mind; remember that you must convince them that your causes are reasonable ones.

Anticipating and Refuting Objections

You should expect readers to evaluate your essay critically, considering your reasons and evidence carefully before accepting your explanation. It would be wise, therefore, to account for any possible objections they could raise. Consider the two most likely objections and figure out ways to refute them. Write out a few sentences to prepare your refutation.

Refuting Alternative Causes

As they read your essay, your readers may think of other causes that seem more plausible to them than your causes. Try to think of two or three such causes now—perhaps ones you analyzed earlier—and write a few sentences about each one explaining why you did not consider it or want specifically to reject it. Why are these causes less plausible than your own? Why might readers prefer the causes they think of?

PLANNING AND DRAFTING

You should now review what you have learned about your topic and start to plan your first draft by setting goals and making an outline.

Seeing What
You Have

Pause now to reflect on your notes. Reread everything carefully in order to decide whether you can really prove that your subject exists (or existed) and can offer a convincing explanation of its causes.

Setting Goals

Before you begin your draft, you should consider some specific goals for your essay. Not only will the draft be easier to write once you have established goals, but it is likely to be more convincing.

It's a good idea at this point to print out a hard copy of what you have written on a word processor for easier reviewing.

Following are questions to help you set goals. You may find it useful to return to them while you are drafting, for they are designed to help you to focus on specific elements of an essay speculating about causes.

Your Readers

- What are my readers likely to know about the subject?
- How can I interest them in understanding its causes?
- How can I present myself so that my readers will consider me informed and authoritative?

The Beginning

- What opening would make readers take this subject seriously and really want to think about what caused it? Should I personalize it? Should I begin with a case, as Dartnell does, or by citing statistics, as Fuchs does?

Presentation of the Subject

- Do I need to demonstrate that my subject really exists? If I am analyzing a trend, do I need to demonstrate that it is not just a fad? How much and what kind of evidence do I need for these points?

The Causal Argument

- How many causes should I propose? Should I mention or give evidence for minor causes?
- How can I present my proposed causes in the most effective order? Should I arrange them from most important to least important or vice versa? From most obvious to least obvious or vice versa? From immediate to remote or vice versa?
- Do I need to make other distinctions among causes, such as between a cause that starts a trend and one that keeps it going or between sufficient and necessary causes?
- How much and what kind of evidence do I need to offer to make each cause plausible to readers? Are any causes so obvious that evidence is unnecessary? Does any cause require evidence to prove that it existed before the phenomenon or trend began?
- How can I refute readers' objections to my proposed causes?
- How can I refute alternative causes readers might propose?

The Ending

■ How should I end my essay? Should I frame it by referring back to the beginning? Do I need to summarize my causes? Should I conclude with a conjecture about larger implications, as Fuchs does?

Outlining

Outlining on a word processor makes it particularly easy to experiment with different ways of ordering the four parts of a causal analysis.

A causal analysis may contain as many as four basic parts: (1) a presentation of the subject; (2) a presentation of proposed causes and evidence for them; (3) a consideration of readers' objections, questions, or reservations; and (4) a consideration and refutation of alternative causes. These parts can be organized in various ways. If your readers are not likely to think of any causes other than the ones you are proposing, you could begin with a statement describing the subject and indicating its importance or interest. Then state your first proposed cause and elaborate on the evidence that it has contributed to the subject and the reasons that likely objections are unconvincing. Follow the same pattern for any other causes you propose. Your conclusion could then refer to—and explain—the lack of other explanations for your subject.

> presentation of the subject
> first proposed cause with evidence and refutation of objections, if any
> second proposed cause with evidence and refutation of objections, if any
> (etc.)
> conclusion

If you need to account for alternative causes likely to occur to readers, you could discuss them first and give your reasons for rejecting them before offering your own proposed causes. Many writers save their own causes for last, hoping readers will remember them best.

> presentation of the subject
> alternative causes and reasons for rejecting them
> proposed causes with evidence and refutation of objections, if any
> conclusion

Another option is to put your own causes first followed by alternatives. This is a good way to show the relative likelihood of your causes over the others. You might then end with a restatement of your causes.

> presentation of the subject
> proposed causes with evidence and refutation of objections, if any
> alternative causes compared with your causes
> concluding restatement of proposed cause

There are of course many other possible ways to organize a causal analysis, but these outlines should help you to start planning your own essay.

Drafting

Begin drafting your essay, keeping in mind the following tips on writing an essay of causal analysis:

■ Remember that in writing about causes you are dealing with probabilities rather than certainties; therefore, you should generally not try to claim you have the final, conclusive answer but only that your explanation is plausible. Qualify your statements and acknowledge opposing views.

If you can shift between screens, you might call up invention material on an alternate screen as you draft on the main screen, shifting back and forth to cut-and-paste invention material into your draft.

■ Try to enliven your writing and to appeal to your readers' interests and concerns. Causal analysis is potentially rather dry.

■ Remember that your outline is just a plan. Writers often make major discoveries and reorganize as they draft. Be flexible. If you find your writing taking an interesting, unexpected turn, follow it to see where it leads. You will have an opportunity to look at it critically later.

■ If you run into a problem as you draft, see whether any of the invention activities earlier in this chapter will help. If, for instance, you are having difficulty making the subject seem important or interesting, you could analyze your readers further, find a way to personalize the subject with a quotation or an anecdote, or look for some attention-getting statistical evidence.

■ If you are having difficulty refuting objections or alternative causes, try composing a dialogue between yourself and an imaginary reader who does not agree with you.

You may now want to review the general advice on drafting given on pp. 12–14.

■ If you find you need more information, you might want to interview an expert, survey a group, or do further library research.

GETTING CRITICAL COMMENTS

At this point your draft should get a good critical reading. All writers find it helpful to have someone else read their drafts and give them critical comments. Your instructor may arrange such a reading as part of your coursework; otherwise, you can ask a classmate, friend, or family member to read it over. If your campus has a writing center, you might ask a tutor there to read and comment on your draft. (If you are unable to have someone else read over your draft, turn ahead to the Revision section on pp. 371–75, which gives guidelines for reading your own draft with a critical eye.)

In order to provide focused, helpful comments, your reader must know your intended audience and purpose. Briefly write out this information at the top of your draft:

Audience. Who are your readers? What do you assume they already know and think about your subject and its causes? Do you expect them to be receptive, skeptical, resistant, antagonistic?

Purpose. What do you hope to accomplish with your readers?

Reading with a
Critical Eye

Reading a draft critically means reading it more than once, first to get a general impression and then to analyze its basic features. Following are guidelines designed to be used by anyone reviewing an essay speculating about causes.

See Chapter 12 for a review of critical reading strategies.

Reading for a First Impression. Read the essay straight through. As you read, try to notice any words or passages that contribute to your first impression, weak ones as well as strong ones.

After you've finished reading the draft, write a few sentences giving your impressions. Did the essay hold your interest? What most surprised you? What did you like best? Did you find the causal argument convincing?

See pp. 360–61 to review the basic features.

Reading to Analyze. Now read to focus on the basic features of writing an essay speculating about causes.

Is the Subject Presented Well?

How well does the draft present the phenomenon or trend? Does it give enough information to make readers understand and care about the subject? Does it establish that the subject actually exists? If the subject is a trend, does it demonstrate a significant increase or decrease over time? Where might additional details, examples, facts, or statistics help?

Are the Causes and Evidence Convincing?

Look first at the proposed causes and list them. Do there seem to be too many? Too few? Do any seem either too obvious (not worth mentioning) or too obscure (remote in time or overly complicated)? Note any causes that seem merely to have been the immediate trigger of the subject or to have kept it going rather than starting it, or that are not sufficient in themselves to result in the subject. Are the limitations of these causes mentioned? If not, do they need to be?

Next, examine the evidence for each cause—anecdotes, facts, statistics, reference to authorities, and so on. Which evidence is most convincing? Which seems unconvincing? Where would more evidence or a different kind strengthen the argument? Might readers expect additional evidence that a cause existed before the phenomenon or trend began?

Check for errors in reasoning. Does the argument mistakenly assume that just because something occurred before the beginning of the phenomenon or trend, it was therefore a cause? Are any of the proposed causes of the subject actually effects of it instead?

Are Possible Objections and Questions Acknowledged Adequately?

Look for places where readers' possible objections to or questions about the proposed causes are acknowledged. How well are they handled? Should any of them be taken more seriously? Can you see other ways of either accommodating or refuting objections? Do any of the refutations attack or ridicule the persons raising the objections? What other questions or objections might readers raise?

Are Alternative Causes Acknowledged Adequately?

If causes proposed by others are acknowledged, are they presented fairly? Is it clear why they have been rejected? Do the refutations of them seem convincing? Do any of the refutations attack or ridicule the persons proposing the causes? Can you think of other plausible causes?

Is the Organization Effective?

Given the expected readers, are the causes presented in an effective order? Can you think of a better order?

Reread the *beginning*. Will it engage the readers? Imagine at least one other way to open. Look for sections of the essay that could be moved to the beginning—an intriguing anecdote, for instance, or a surprising statistic.

Study the *ending*. Does the essay conclude decisively and memorably? Think of an alternative ending. Could something be moved to the end?

What Final Thoughts Do You Have?

What is this draft's strongest part? What about it is most memorable? What is weak, most in need of further work?

REVISING AND EDITING

This section will help you to identify problems in your draft and to revise and edit to solve them.

Identifying Problems

To identify problems in your draft, you need to get an objective overview of it, analyze its basic features in detail, and assess any critical comments on it by other readers.

Even if your essay is saved to a computer file, reread from a hard copy, preferably draft quality. Onscreen or as letter-quality hard copy, a paper can look more "finished" than it really is. Add notes to yourself and quick revisions as you read through the draft.

Getting an Overview.   Begin by considering your draft as a whole, trying to see it as objectively as you can. The following steps will help you do this:

Reread. If at all possible, put the draft aside for a day or two before rereading it. When you go back to it, start by reconsidering your audience and purpose. Then read the draft straight through, trying to see it as your intended readers will.

Outline. Make a scratch outline of the draft to chart its development. Words and phrases will do as long as they identify the subject and any important details, the proposed causes, and any objections you hope to respond to and alternative causes you intend to refute.

Charting a Plan for Revision.   Once you have an overview of your draft, use the following chart to keep track of specific problems you need to solve. The left column lists the basic features of essays speculating about causes. As you analyze your draft and study any comments you've gotten from others, use the right column to note any problems with each feature.

Basic Features   *Problems to Solve*

Presentation of the subject

Presentation of causes and evidence

Response to possible objections and questions

Response to alternative causes

Organization

Analyzing the Basic Features of Your Draft.   Turn now to the questions for analyzing a draft on pp. 370–71. Using these questions as guidelines, identify problems in your draft, noting specific points on the chart above.

Studying Critical Comments.   Now review any comments you've received from other readers. Try not to react defensively to these comments. Rather, look at them as information that can help you improve your draft. Add to the chart any problems readers have identified.

Solving the Problems

You now need to figure out solutions to the problems in your draft and to carry them out. Basically, you have three ways of finding solutions: (1) review your invention and planning notes for other information and ideas; (2) do additional invention or research; and (3) look back at the readings in this chapter to see how other writers have solved similar problems. Following are suggestions to get you started on addressing some of the problems common to writing that speculates about causes.

Before revising using a word processor, copy your original draft to a second file. Then, should you change your mind about material you delete while revising, it will still be available to you.

Presentation of the Subject

■ If your subject is less than clear or its existence is not clearly established, you may need to discuss it in greater detail. Consider adding anecdotes, statistics, citations from authorities, or other details. If your subject is a trend, be sure you show evidence of a significant increase or decrease over an extended period.

Presentation of Causes and Evidence

■ If you've proposed what seem like too many causes, clarify the role each one plays: is it obvious? hidden? sufficient? necessary? immediate, remote, or perpetuating? (You need not use these labels.) In addition, you may need to emphasize one or two causes or delete some that seem too obvious, too obscure, or relatively minor.

- If you've proposed what seem like too few causes for a complex subject, try to think of other possible causes, especially hidden or remote ones. Do further research if necessary.
- If your evidence is skimpy or weak, look for more or stronger evidence.
- If you've made errors in reasoning, correct them. For example, if you cannot argue convincingly that a proposed cause not only occurred before the phenomenon or trend began but also contributed to it, you will have to delete that cause or at least present it more tentatively. If you have confused a cause with an effect, clarify their relationship.

Response to Possible Objections and Questions

- If any refutations of objections to your proposed causes don't seem convincing, try to provide stronger evidence. If you cannot do so, you may have to accommodate the objections.
- If any refutations attack or ridicule people, revise to focus on the objections.
- If readers have raised questions about your argument, you may need to provide more information about your subject or more evidence for proposed causes.
- If readers have made any additional objections to your argument, consider whether you need to accommodate or refute them. That is, can you acknowledge their validity and incorporate them into your own argument, or can you give reasons and evidence why they are wrong?

Response to Alternative Causes

- If any refutations of alternative causes don't seem convincing, try to provide stronger evidence, or consider accommodating the alternative causes.
- If any refutations attack or ridicule people, revise to focus on specific alternative causes which you believe to be implausible.
- If readers have suggested any causes you had not considered, decide whether they are plausible and should be integrated into your argument. If they seem implausible, decide whether to mention and refute them.

Organization

Use your word processor's cut-and-paste or block-and-move functions to shift material around. Make sure that transitions are revised so that material fits in its new spot.

- If your readers found the argument disorganized or hard to follow, consider reordering it by arranging the causes in order of increasing rather than decreasing importance, grouping related causes together, or moving the refutations of alternative causes to precede your own causes. Your plan may be more understandable if you forecast it at the beginning. Provide summaries, transitions, and other cues for readers.
- If the beginning is dull, try opening with a surprising fact or engaging anecdote or by emphasizing your subject's puzzling nature.

■ If the ending is weak, try to make it more emphatic or interesting, perhaps by restating your main cause or causes, framing (referring to something mentioned at the beginning), or inviting readers to speculate further.

Editing and Proofreading

At this point you should focus attention on matters of grammar and style. Check carefully for errors in usage, punctuation, and mechanics, and consider also any ways you might edit your writing style to suit your purpose and audience. Research into writing of this kind has revealed several errors in mechanics and usage that are especially likely to occur. Following are guidelines designed to help you check and edit your draft for these errors.

When you use your word processor's spell check function to aid in proofreading for spelling, keep in mind that it will not find all misspellings, particularly misused homonyms (such as there, their, and they're), typos that are themselves words (such as fro for for), and many proper nouns and specialized terms. Proofread these carefully yourself, using hard copy and a dictionary if necessary. Also proofread for words that should have been deleted when you edited a sentence.

Checking Your Use of Numbers.   Speculating about causes very frequently calls for you to use numbers. Whether to indicate the scope of a phenomenon or to cite the increase or decrease of a trend, writing that speculates about causes often cites dates, percentages, fractions, and other numbers. Look, for example, at these excerpts from Kim Dartnell's essay:

> In 1979, New York City had one public shelter for homeless women. In 1983, it had four.

> Between 1955 and 1980, the number of patients in mental institutions dropped by 75 percent, from about 560,000 to 140,000.

Dartnell spells out numbers that can be written as one or two words but uses figures for numbers that require more than two words. She uses figures for dates and percentages.

Conventions for presenting numbers in writing are easy to follow. Here are some sentences from student papers written using this chapter, each edited to demonstrate conventional ways of using numbers in academic writing.

Spelling Out Numbers and Fractions of One or Two Words

▶ According to the World Health Organization, as many as ~~1~~ ^one person in every ~~50~~ ^fifty may be infected with HIV.

▶ Maybe ~~2/3~~ ^two-thirds of the smoke from a cigarette is released into the air.

Using Figures for Numbers and Fractions of More Than Two Words

▶ That year the Japanese automobile industry produced only ~~four thousand eight hundred thirty-seven~~ ^4,837 vehicles, mostly trucks and motorbikes.

▶ This study shows that Americans spend an average of ~~five-and-one-third~~ ^5 1/3 hours a day watching television.

Writing Percentages and Dates with Figures

▶ Comparing 1980 to 1960, we can see that time spent viewing television increased ~~twenty-eight~~ ^28 percent.

Spelling Out Numbers That Begin a Sentence

    Thirty
▶ ~~30~~ percent of commercial real estate in Washington, D.C., is owned by
      ∧
foreigners.

Checking for "Reason Is Because" Constructions.   Speculating about causes calls upon you to show evidence and reasons to support your speculation. Analysis of many papers written for this chapter revealed many sentences constructed around a "reason is because" pattern. For example: "The reason we lost the war is because troop morale was down." This sentence is redundant: since *because* means "for the reason that," the sentence says essentially that "the reason we lost the war is for the reason that troop morale was down." If you find this pattern in your writing, there are two easy ways to edit out the redundancy:

REDUNDANT   The reason we lost the war is because troop morale was down.
CLEAR   The reason we lost the war is that troop morale was down.
CLEAR   We lost the war because troop morale was down.

                                                                      that
▶ Her research suggests that one reason women attend women's colleges is ~~because~~
                                                                       ∧
they want to avoid certain social pressures.

                Older
▶ ~~A reason older~~ Americans watch so much television ~~is~~ because they tend to be
sedentary.   ∧

A Writer at Work

ANALYZING CAUSES

For a writer planning an essay explaining causes, the most important part of invention and research is analyzing the causes. Because the causes are the heart of the argument, it takes rigorous analysis of each cause during the invention stage to compose a convincing argument.

    Here we will look at the table of causes and analyses that Kim Dartnell developed for her essay on homeless women. (The revised version of her essay appears on pp. 356–59.)

    Dartnell began this invention activity intending to write about the trend of homelessness in general, without considering men and women separately. Only after she had started to do some research did she realize that not only were there an increasing number of homeless women but that there had been several recent reports on the subject.

    She began her analysis before going to the library, entering the first four causes on her table and completing a partial analysis. After she decided to focus on women, she added the other causes and completed the analysis.

TABLE OF CAUSES AND ANALYSES

Causes	Analyses
1. unemployment	Necessary cause for this trend. Could be sufficient, would affect everybody the same way, causes loss of income. Immediate cause that has grown in importance recently.
2. inflation	Relates to unemployment--as such, may be necessary but not sufficient by itself, especially affects unemployed and poor. Perpetuating, immediate, hidden cause.
3. alcoholism	Not necessary, not sufficient. Common conception is all homeless are drunks. Refute this cause since alcohol use hasn't risen in proportion to homelessness. Alcoholism is found at all levels of society, and so can't say that it causes homelessness. May be a result of unemployment or homelessness. No one really knows what causes alcoholism--or what it causes.
4. cutbacks in welfare	Necessary cause, could be sufficient. Affects women especially, causes loss of income, homelessness. Immediate cause--with no money, people forced to beg or move in with others.
5. abuse	There's always been abuse. Neither necessary nor sufficient. Affects women and children more. Research shows it's risen in proportion to homelessness (Stoner).
6. release from institutions	Many women being released from mental institutions. Necessary, may be sufficient. Immediate cause for the mentally ill. May be coupled with economic problems. Rebecca Smith is a good example. Evidence shows this is increasing as homelessness increases. Couldn't be a result. Perpetuates the trend. (Use Stoner, Hombs and Snyder data.)

| 7. evictions | Necessary and sufficient cause, due to economic reasons. Immediate cause. Affects females more, but also affects men. As evictions increase, more homeless. Perpetuating cause. |
| 8. lack of housing | Necessary and sufficient, but related to economic reasons. Cheap housing is harder to find due to redevelopment and gentrification. Renovation affects those already without housing more. Could mention Rebecca Smith. Perpetuating cause. |

Once she had analyzed all these possible causes, Dartnell could decide how to use them to make the most convincing explanation. She had to decide which causes to emphasize, which ones to combine, which ones to omit, and how to order the causes to produce the most effective argument. Last, she had to try to find any potential objections to her arguments, which she would then have to answer. As it happened, she decided to use all of these causes except for alcoholism, which she would mention and refute.

She begins her essay with a discussion of abuse, thinking it was the one cause of homelessness that most affects women. She then discusses evictions and housing, treating each of these causes in a separate paragraph. Next she mentions—and refutes—alcoholism as a cause. Only then does she develop the cause for which she had the most evidence—deinstitutionalization. Finally, she combines several causes—unemployment, inflation, welfare cutbacks—into one paragraph on economic causes.

Certainly these causes might be presented in a different order—deinstitutionalization might be effectively placed either first or last, for example—but Dartnell's plan serves her topic well. By covering her topic so comprehensively and discussing it in a clear, logically organized manner, she presents a convincing argument.

Thinking Critically about What You've Learned

By now you've worked extensively with causal speculation about phenomena and trends—reading it, talking about it, writing it. You can continue to learn about causal speculation by taking time to reflect on your experiences and attitudes. What problems did you encounter? How did the essays in this chapter influence your work? What ideas do you have about the role causal speculation plays in the way we think about ourselves and the world around us?

REFLECTING ON YOUR WRITING

In order to reflect on what you have learned about writing essays speculating about causes, first, gather all of your writing—invention, planning notes, drafts, any critical comments from classmates and your instructor, revising notes and plans, and final revision. Review these and refer to them as you complete the following writing task.

■ Identify *one* problem you needed to solve as you worked on your essay. Don't be concerned with sentence-level problems; concentrate instead on problems unique to developing an essay speculating about causes. For example: Did you puzzle over how to present your subject in a way that would interest your readers? Did you have trouble demonstrating that a trend exists? Was it difficult to decide on a logical sequence for presenting causes? Did you worry about the need to evaluate alternative causes?

■ How did you recognize the problem? When did you first discover it? What called it to your attention? If you didn't become aware of the problem until someone else pointed it out to you, can you now see hints of it in your invention writings? If so, where specifically? When you first recognized the problem, how did you respond?

■ Reflect also on how you went about solving the problem. Did you work on the wording of a passage, cut or add causes or counter-arguments, conduct further research, move paragraphs or sentences around? Did you reread one of the essays in this chapter to see how another writer handled the problem, or did you look back at the invention suggestions? If you talked about the problem with another student, a tutor, or your instructor, did talking about it help? How useful was the advice you got?

■ Now, write a page or so telling your instructor about the problem and how you solved it. Be as specific as possible in reconstructing your efforts. Quote from your invention, draft, others' critical comments, your revision plan, or your revised essay to show the various changes your writing underwent as you tried to solve the problem. Taking time to explain how you identified a particular problem, how you went about solving it, and what you've learned from this experience can help you in solving future writing problems.

REVIEWING WHAT YOU LEARNED
FROM READING

Your own essay has certainly been influenced to some extent by one or more of the essays in this chapter and by any essays you read by classmates. These other essays may have helped you decide on an appropriate subject, or helped you recognize the importance of discovering both immediate and background causes of your trend or phenomenon. They may have suggested ways to bring up alternative causes in relation to your own preferred ones or demonstrated how to argue against a prominent alternative cause likely to be favored by your readers. Take time now to reflect on what you have learned about causal speculation from the readings in this chapter and consider how they may have influenced your own writing.

- Reread the final revision of your essay; then look back at the selections you read before completing your essay. Do you see any specific influences? For example, if you were impressed with the way one of the readings established its trend, presented causes in a logical order, used personal experience and observation to support a cause, argued convincingly against an alternative cause, or addressed readers in a considerate tone, look to see where you may have been striving for similar effects in your own writing. Also, look for ideas you got from your reading, writing strategies you were inspired to try, specific details you were led to include, effects you sought to achieve.

- Write a page or so explaining to your instructor how the readings in this chapter influenced your revised essay. Did one selection have a particularly strong influence, or were several selections influential in different ways? Quote from the readings and from your final revision to show how your causal explanation was influenced by your reading of other causal essays. Finally, point out anything you would now improve in your essay based on your review of this chapter's selections.

CONSIDERING THE SOCIAL DIMENSIONS OF CAUSAL SPECULATION

Persuasive writing, as we have defined it in this text, deals with probabilities and possibilities, not with certainties. Causal speculation is persuasive writing *par excellence* because it confronts aspects of social life that we do not yet understand and may never fully understand. If we lacked this great social resource, we would feel helpless in the face of threatening social problems. They would seem like random acts of a chaotic universe. Instead, when confronted with the alarming evidence that the teenage suicide rate is high, and even increasing, we can start speculating about why so many teenagers are ending their own lives. We can evaluate competing causes and decide which are the most plausible. Finally, we can take action, feeling reassured that our knowledge is sound, even though speculative and likely to change over time. Useful as it is, however, causal speculation poses problems for unwary readers and writers.

The Power of Authority.   First, if we are not careful, we may be deluded into thinking that what seems to be the best current explanation for the causes of a trend or phenomenon is the *only* explanation. If we are inattentive, we may forget that speculating about causes tends to give greater voice to certain interests and to minimize or silence others. Some analyses, particularly those of "experts" such as economists and demographers, often are granted more authority than analyses favored by parents, teachers, community and religious leaders, or indeed those most directly affected. Fuchs, for example, interviewed no parents of children who committed suicide, and Dartnell apparently talked to no homeless women directly.

In addition, readers too often forget that causal reasoning is always shaped by the analyst's ideology—the set of beliefs, values, and attitudes that determines a person's worldview. For example, Stephen King—a horror writer himself—has a real interest in establishing the horror genre as a legitimate literary and cinematic form; it is not surprising, then, that he would emphasize psychological benefits as a basis for the popularity of horror movies rather than something more negative. Kim Dartnell is clearly sympathetic to the plight of homeless women; a less sympathetic analyst might come up with a completely different explanation for the causes of their homelessness.

Even the way we define a phenomenon or trend can color our explanation of its causes. For example, following the original acquittal of the police officers accused of beating motorist Rodney King in Los Angeles during the spring of 1992, many people took to the streets, starting fires and looting. Whereas some observers called these events a "riot," others more sympathetically called it an "uprising." These two terms reflect opposite ways of understanding what happened, pointing to entirely different sets of possible causes. A great deal is at stake when society must decide whether the causes were linked to frustration with racism and unequal justice, on the one hand, or to lack of an adequate police "presence" and respect for the law, on the other hand.

Causes and Blame.   An even tougher problem is that causal explanations sometimes become exercises in assigning blame. K. C. Cole comes close to this when she suggests that male scientists tend to make professional science inhospitable to women. Worse, causal explanation may even be used to blame those who are adversely affected by the conditions they supposedly have caused. In the past, for example, a woman's "provocative" clothing could actually be cited in court as a cause (and possible justification) for her being raped. Similarly, the homeless are sometimes blamed for causing their own plight. In cases like these, causal explanation often becomes a way to avoid confronting our social responsibility and allows us to put off working toward solving serious social problems.

For Discussion

The following questions can help you think critically about the role of causal speculation in our society, focusing on the readings by Fuchs and Dartnell. Review these two readings. Then, as you read through and, perhaps, discuss these questions in class, note down your thoughts and reactions. Finally, write a page or so for your instructor presenting your own thoughts about how the causal speculation affects our lives.

1. We've said that because causal explanation deals with possibilities instead of certainties, it must be somewhat tentative about its speculations. However, for causal argument to be convincing it can't be too timid. Compare the Fuchs and Dartnell essays. Which seems more assertive? What accounts for your response?

2. We've also said that if readers are not alert to the seductions of causal argument, they may begin to think that the explanation offered is the only possible one. Does either Fuchs or Dartnell present so seductive an argument that you find yourself accepting it without question?

3. Americans are often divided about whether individuals are primarily responsible for their circumstances or whether social, economic, and political conditions best explain people's difficulties and suffering. Where do Fuchs and Dartnell position themselves on this issue? Explore your own position, as well, focusing on the particular cases Fuchs and Dartnell write about. If you were to write about the causes of teen suicide or homelessness, which kinds of causes—individual or social—would you emphasize? Why?

4. Dartnell and Fuchs are writing causal arguments about social issues in which they are not personally involved and both rely totally on sources, rather than on their own personal experience. Notice also that both are white, middle class, and well-educated. How do their causal analyses reflect their own positions rather than the positions of the people they're writing about? Those directly affected by social problems seldom get to write causal analyses about their own plight; in our society, analysis is typically left to the experts. Imagine how extended interviews with suicidal young people and their families and with homeless people might have changed the causal arguments in these two essays. What is there about causal analysis as practiced in our society that invites experts to speculate about the lives of people who are very distant from them in terms of experience, income, education, and ethnicity?

■ For a history of science class, a student writes about the myth of the mad scientist in literature, focusing on two classic works: *Frankenstein* and *Dr. Jekyll and Mr. Hyde.* From her reading, she concludes that as a fictional figure, the mad scientist is socially isolated, obsessed with the desire for knowledge and power, and reckless of his own and others' safety. To develop her interpretation, the student quotes descriptions of the scientists in the two works and analyzes their words and actions.

■ A journalist writing about the American newspaper publisher William Randolph Hearst (1863–1951) decides to model his article on the classic film about a Hearstlike character, *Citizen Kane.* He organizes his piece around a series of imagined interviews with people who knew and worked for Hearst. Throughout the article, he draws parallels between Hearst and his film counterpart to support the point that Hearst is finally as unknowable as Kane.

■ In an introductory literature class, a student analyzes the structure and meaning of Edgar Allan Poe's poem "The Raven." As the thesis of her essay, she claims the poem's theme of inescapable despair is conveyed by its repetition of words and sounds as well as by its monotonous rhythm. As evidence for her conclusion, the student points to specific examples of repetition, alliteration, and rhythmic uniformity in the poem.

■ A freshman in a composition course explores the relationship between setting and action in William Faulkner's story "Dry September." He argues that the setting can be viewed meta- phorically, as a projection of the characters' emotions. To sup- port his point, he draws parallels between descriptions of the setting and descriptions of the characters.

■ For a political science course, a student writes a research paper arguing that the films Alfred Hitchcock made before, during, and after World War II appear to be pro-American, but actually question the as- sumption of American moral superiority. As evidence that the films represent the moral ambi- guity in world politics, he points to the way that Hitchcock makes viewers regard the enemy with sympathy and understand- ing in films like *Foreign Corre- spondent* and *Notorious,* and how he shows that the American government has as little regard for human life as its opponents in films like *North by Northwest* and *Torn Curtain.*

Interpreting Stories 10

■ After seeing Henrik Ibsen's *A Doll's House*, a student decides to write in her diary about the play's feminist themes. She is disturbed by the decision of the play's protagonist, Nora, to leave her home and children. If Nora felt she had never grown up or accepted responsibility, the student asks, why was she leaving her children? To answer this question, she attempts to examine Nora's character in light of the expectations Nora's husband and society in general have of women.

Stories have a special place in most cultures. Elders relate family and cultural history through stories; lessons are taught through moral fables and parables. The bonds of family and community are often strengthened by sharing stories. Even in a diverse society like ours, people come together to experience and discuss best-selling novels, popular films, and television shows.

Stories have the power to stimulate feeling and nourish the imagination, allowing us to escape our narrow routines and become aware of the wider world around us. They can lead us to look at others with new sensitivity and, for a brief time, to see the world through another person's eyes. They can also lead us to see ourselves differently, to gain insight into our innermost feelings and thoughts.

When we read stories on our own, we often look for an absorbing plot and characters we can relate to. Sometimes we read to escape ordinary life through fantasy and romance; at other times we seek stories that seem "true to life" and that enable us to see reflections of our own experience.

When we read stories for literature classes, however, the goals are somewhat different. Literature professors are not primarily concerned about whether a story is a "good read" or even whether it has a moral to teach. Instead of just experiencing the story, you are asked to analyze your reading experience. Instead of simply saying what the story means to you, you are asked to show how the words on the page led to your particular interpretation. Interpreting a story is a specialized kind of writing, one that is practiced by literature students and teachers interested in understanding not just *what* a story means, but also *how* it means. While this chapter focuses on interpreting short stories, the conventions you'll learn can be applied to interpreting films and television programs, as well as other literary works.

Like position papers, proposals, evaluations, and causal speculations, an essay interpreting a story presents an argument, making a claim about the story's meaning and providing evidence to convince readers that the interpretation is plausible. Since stories can be interpreted in different ways, writers of literary interpretations do not seek to prove that they have discovered the one correct or final meaning. Instead, they try to convince readers—instructors, classmates, or other students of literature—that they have analyzed the story carefully and thoughtfully and have found a plausible way of understanding it.

Writing in Your
Other Courses

In college, you will probably take literature courses in which you will be asked to write interpretive essays like these, as well as other types of analysis that examine works from different theoretical perspectives. The kind of close reading and writing demonstrated in this chapter teaches the fundamentals of such literary analysis. Other courses also may require you to analyze works of literature, film, or other media, as the following assignments suggest:

- *For a health course*: The media play a major role in educating people about difference. Analyze the portrayal of physical disability in a particular film or television program of your choice. (Some possibilities include the films *Rainman* and *Born on the Fourth of July* and the television programs *L. A. Law* and *Life Goes On*.)

- *For a philosophy course*: If war is hell, why is it so often glorified? Analyze the attitude toward war represented in one of the following novels: *War and Peace, Gravity's Rainbow, The Red Badge of Courage, All Quiet on the Western Front.*

- *For an American history course*: The study of history gives us many facts about the immigrant experience—when the great waves of immigration occurred, how many people came to America, where they came from, and where they settled. To fully understand the experience, however, you need the immigrant's perspective. Read one of the books on the reserve list in the library, and write an essay on the meanings you derive about the immigrant experience.

- *For a sociology course*: How are minorities represented in the media? Are they stereotyped or invisible, as some critics claim? To examine this situation, analyze one evening's worth of prime-time network television programs. Pay attention not only to the programs but to the commercials as well.

For Group Inquiry

This activity provides an introduction to interpreting stories. Reading and discussing a story with two or three other students should suggest a variety of possible interpretations. Your instructor may assign your group a story or may invite you to choose one from the following anthology. If there's time, you may enjoy having someone in the group read the story aloud.

After reading the story but before beginning to discuss it, do five minutes or so of exploratory writing on your own to discover what you think the story means. If you're unsure about anything that happens in the story or can't remember details that seem important, write down your questions.

Then, as a group, discuss the story for twenty minutes or so. Begin by going around the group, quickly telling the others what you think the story means. Spend the rest of the time in a free-flowing discussion of the story's possible interpretations.

Following your discussion of the story, take five more minutes to talk about the discussion itself by considering the following questions:

- Did the members of your group express different views? What led to the greatest disagreement? On what, if anything, did you agree?

- Roughly what proportion of your discussion was spent making general observations and sharing ideas and what proportion was spent rereading or analyzing particular passages?

- On which aspects of the story did you focus most: what it means, what happens, the characters, the setting, who tells the story, or anything else?

An Anthology of Short Stories

Following are four well-known short stories: "The Monkey Garden" by Sandra Cisneros, "The Use of Force" by William Carlos Williams, "The Hammer Man" by Toni Cade Bambara, and "Araby" by James Joyce. Your instructor may assign one or more of these for discussion and interpretation or allow you to choose one as the subject for your essay interpreting a short story.

■   ■   ■

Sandra Cisneros (b. 1954) has published the poetry collection *My Wicked Wicked Ways* and two short-story collections, *Woman Hollering Creek* and *The House on Mango Street*. As you read "The Monkey Garden," notice its fantastic setting—a child's imaginary garden based on the Chicago neighborhood in which Cisneros grew up.

THE MONKEY GARDEN
SANDRA CISNEROS

The monkey doesn't live there anymore. The monkey moved—to Kentucky— and took his people with him. And I was glad because I couldn't listen anymore to his wild screaming at night, the twangy yakkety-yak of the people who owned him. The green metal cage, the porcelain table top, the family that spoke like guitars. Monkey, family, table. All gone.

And it was then we took over the garden we had been afraid to go into when   2
the monkey screamed and showed its yellow teeth.

There were sunflowers big as flowers on Mars and thick cockscombs bleeding   3
the deep red fringe of theater curtains. There were dizzy bees and bow-tied fruit
flies turning somersaults and humming in the air. Sweet sweet peach trees. Thorn
roses and thistle and pears. Weeds like so many squinty-eyed stars and brush that
made your ankles itch and itch until you washed with soap and water. There were
big green apples hard as knees. And everywhere the sleepy smell of rotting wood,
damp earth and dusty hollyhocks thick and perfumy like the blue-blond hair of the
dead.

Yellow spiders ran when we turned rocks over and pale worms blind and afraid   4
of light rolled over in their sleep. Poke a stick in the sandy soil and a few blue-skinned
beetles would appear, an avenue of ants, so many crusty lady bugs. This was a garden, a wonderful thing to look at in the spring. But bit by bit, after the monkey left,
the garden began to take over itself. Flowers stopped obeying the little bricks that
kept them from growing beyond their paths. Weeds mixed in. Dead cars appeared
overnight like mushrooms. First one and then another and then a pale blue pickup
with the front windshield missing. Before you knew it, the monkey garden became
filled with sleepy cars.

Things had a way of disappearing in the garden, as if the garden itself ate them,   5
or, as if with its old-man memory, it put them away and forgot them. Nenny found
a dollar and a dead mouse between two rocks in the stone wall where the morning
glories climbed, and once when we were playing hide and seek, Eddie Vargas laid
his head beneath a hibiscus tree and fell asleep there like a Rip Van Winkle until
somebody remembered he was in the game and went back to look for him.

This, I suppose, was the reason why we went there. Far away from where our   6
mothers could find us. We and a few old dogs who lived inside the empty cars. We
made a club-house once on the back of that old blue pickup. And besides, we
liked to jump from the roof of one car to another and pretend they were giant
mushrooms.

Somebody started the lie that the monkey garden had been there before any-   7
thing. We liked to think the garden could hide things for a thousand years. There
beneath the roots of soggy flowers were the bones of murdered pirates and dino-
saurs, the eye of a unicorn turned to coal.

This is where I wanted to die and where I tried one day but not even the monkey   8
garden would have me. It was the last day I would go there.

Who was it that said I was getting too old to play the games? Who was it I   9
didn't listen to? I only remember that when the others ran, I wanted to run too, up
and down and through the monkey garden, fast as the boys, not like Sally who
screamed if she got her stockings muddy.

I said, Sally, come on, but she wouldn't. She stayed by the curb talking to Tito   10
and his friends. Play with the kids if you want, she said, I'm staying here. She could
be stuck-up like that if she wanted to, so I just left.

It was her own fault too. When I got back Sally was pretending to be mad . . .   11
something about the boys having stolen her keys. Please give them back to me, she
said punching the nearest one with a soft fist. They were laughing. She was too. It
was a joke I didn't get.

I wanted to go back with the other kids who were still jumping on cars, still 12
chasing each other through the garden, but Sally had her own game.

One of the boys invented the rules. One of Tito's friends said you can't get the 13
keys back unless you kiss us and Sally pretended to be mad at first but she said yes.
It was that simple.

I don't know why, but something inside me wanted to throw a stick. Something 14
wanted to say no when I watched Sally going into the garden with Tito's buddies
all grinning. It was just a kiss, that's all. A kiss for each one. So what, she said.

Only how come I felt angry inside. Like something wasn't right. Sally went behind 15
that old blue pickup to kiss the boys and get her keys back, and I ran up three flights
of stairs to where Tito lived. His mother was ironing shirts. She was sprinkling water
on them from an empty pop bottle and smoking a cigarette.

Your son and his friends stole Sally's keys and now they won't give them back 16
unless she kisses them and right now they're making her kiss them, I said all out of
breath from the three flights of stairs.

Those kids, she said, not looking up from her ironing. 17

That's all? 18

What do you want me to do, she said, call the cops? And kept on ironing. 19

I looked at her a long time, but couldn't think of anything to say, and ran back 20
down the three flights to the garden where Sally needed to be saved. I took three
big sticks and a brick and figured this was enough.

But when I got there Sally said go home. Those boys said, leave us alone. I felt 21
stupid with my brick. They all looked at me as if *I* was the one that was crazy and
made me feel ashamed.

And then I don't know why but I had to run away. I had to hide myself at the 22
other end of the garden, in the jungle part, under a tree that wouldn't mind if I lay
down and cried a long time. I closed my eyes like tight stars so that I wouldn't, but
I did. My face felt hot. Everything inside hiccupped.

I read somewhere in India there are priests who can will their heart to stop beat- 23
ing. I wanted to will my blood to stop, my heart to quit its pumping. I wanted to
be dead, to turn into the rain, my eyes melt into the ground like two black snails. I
wished and wished. I closed my eyes and willed it, but when I got up my dress was
green and I had a headache.

I looked at my feet in their white socks and ugly round shoes. They seemed far 24
away. They didn't seem to be my feet anymore. And the garden that had been such
a good place to play didn't seem mine either.

■   ■   ■

William Carlos Williams (1883–1963) is one of the most important poets
of this century, best known for his long poem *Paterson* (1946–58). He also
wrote essays, plays, novels, and short stories. "The Use of Force" was published initially in *The Doctor Stories* (1933), a collection loosely based on
Williams's experiences as a pediatrician.

THE USE OF FORCE
WILLIAM CARLOS
WILLIAMS

They were new patients to me, all I had was the name, Olson. Please come down 1
as soon as you can, my daughter is very sick.

When I arrived I was met by the mother, a big startled looking woman, very clean 2
and apologetic who merely said, Is this the doctor? and let me in. In the back, she
added. You must excuse us, doctor, we have her in the kitchen where it is warm. It
is very damp here sometimes.

The child was fully dressed and sitting on her father's lap near the kitchen table. 3
He tried to get up, but I motioned for him not to bother, took off my overcoat and
started to look things over. I could see that they were all very nervous, eyeing me
up and down distrustfully. As often, in such cases, they weren't telling me more than
they had to, it was up to me to tell them; that's why they were spending three dollars
on me.

The child was fairly eating me up with her cold, steady eyes, and no expression 4
to her face whatever. She did not move and seemed, inwardly, quiet; an unusually
attractive little thing, and as strong as a heifer in appearance. But her face was
flushed, she was breathing rapidly, and I realized that she had a high fever. She had
magnificent blonde hair, in profusion. One of those picture children often reproduced in advertising leaflets and the photogravure sections of the Sunday papers.

She's had a fever for three days, began the father and we don't know what it 5
comes from. My wife has given her things, you know, like people do, but it don't
do no good. And there's been a lot of sickness around. So we tho't you better look
her over and tell us what is the matter.

As doctors often do I took a trial shot at it as a point of departure. Has she had 6
a sore throat?

Both parents answered me together, No . . . No, she says her throat don't hurt 7
her.

Does your throat hurt you? added the mother to the child. But the little girl's 8
expression didn't change nor did she move her eyes from my face.

Have you looked? 9

I tried, said the mother, but I couldn't see. 10

As it happens we had been having a number of cases of diphtheria in the school 11
to which this child went during that month and we were all, quite apparently, thinking of that, though no one had as yet spoken of the thing.

Well, I said, suppose we take a look at the throat first. I smiled in my best pro- 12
fessional manner and asking for the child's first name I said, come on, Mathilda,
open your mouth and let's take a look at your throat.

Nothing doing. 13

Aw, come on, I coaxed, just open your mouth wide and let me take a look. Look, 14
I said opening both hands wide, I haven't anything in my hands. Just open up and
let me see.

Such a nice man, put in the mother. Look how kind he is to you. Come on, do 15
what he tells you to. He won't hurt you.

At that I ground my teeth in disgust. If only they wouldn't use the word "hurt" 16
I might be able to get somewhere. But I did not allow myself to be hurried or disturbed but speaking quietly and slowly I approached the child again.

As I moved my chair a little nearer suddenly with one catlike movement both her 17
hands clawed instinctively for my eyes and she almost reached them too. In fact she

knocked my glasses flying and they fell, though unbroken, several feet away from me on the kitchen floor.

Both the mother and father almost turned themselves inside out in embarrass- 18 ment and apology. You bad girl, said the mother, taking her and shaking her by one arm. Look what you've done. The nice man . . .

For heaven's sake, I broke in. Don't call me a nice man to her. I'm here to look 19 at her throat on the chance that she might have diphtheria and possibly die of it. But that's nothing to her. Look here, I said to the child, we're going to look at your throat. You're old enough to understand what I'm saying. Will you open it now by yourself or shall we have to open it for you?

Not a move. Even her expression hadn't changed. Her breaths however were 20 coming faster and faster. Then the battle began. I had to do it. I had to have a throat culture for her own protection. But first I told the parents that it was entirely up to them. I explained the danger but said that I would not insist on a throat examination so long as they would take the responsibility.

If you don't do what the doctor says you'll have to go to the hospital, the mother 21 admonished her severely.

Oh yeah? I had to smile to myself. After all, I had already fallen in love with the 22 savage brat, the parents were contemptible to me. In the ensuing struggle they grew more and more abject, crushed, exhausted while she surely rose to magnificent heights of insane fury of effort bred of her terror of me.

The father tried his best, and he was a big man but the fact that she was his 23 daughter, his shame at her behavior and his dread of hurting her made him release her just at the critical times when I had almost achieved success, till I wanted to kill him. But his dread also that she might have diphtheria made him tell me to go on, go on though he himself was almost fainting, while the mother moved back and forth behind us raising and lowering her hands in an agony of apprehension.

Put her in front of you on your lap, I ordered, and hold both her wrists.   24

But as soon as he did the child let out a scream. Don't, your hurting me. Let go 25 of my hands. Let them go I tell you. Then she shrieked terrifyingly, hysterically. Stop it! Stop it! You're killing me!

Do you think she can stand it, doctor! said the mother.   26

You get out, said the husband to his wife. Do you want her to die of diphtheria? 27

Come on now, hold her, I said.   28

Then I grasped the child's head with my left hand and tried to get the wooden 29 tongue depressor between her teeth. She fought, with clenched teeth, desperately! But now I also had grown furious—at a child. I tried to hold myself down but I couldn't. I know how to expose a throat for inspection. And I did my best. When finally I got the wooden spatula behind the last teeth and just the point of it into the mouth cavity, she opened up for an instant but before I could see anything she came down again and gripping the wooden blade between her molars she reduced it to splinters before I could get it out again.

Aren't you ashamed, the mother yelled at her. Aren't you ashamed to act like 30 that in front of the doctor?

Get me a smooth-handled spoon of some sort, I told the mother. We're going 31 through with this. The child's mouth was already bleeding. Her tongue was cut and she was screaming in wild hysterical shrieks. Perhaps I should have desisted and come back in an hour or more. No doubt it would have been better. But I have seen at least two children lying dead in bed of neglect in such cases, and feeling that I must get a diagnosis now or never I went at it again. But the worst of it was that I too had got beyond reason. I could have torn the child apart in my own fury and enjoyed it. It was a pleasure to attack her. My face was burning with it.

The damned little brat must be protected against her own idiocy, one says to 32
one's self at such times. Others must be protected against her. It is a social necessity. And all these things are true. But a blind fury, a feeling of adult shame, bred of a longing for muscular release are the operatives. One goes on to the end.

In a final unreasoning assault I overpowered the child's neck and jaws. I forced 33
the heavy silver spoon back of her teeth and down her throat till she gagged. And there it was—both tonsils covered with membrane. She had fought valiantly to keep me from knowing her secret. She had been hiding that sore throat for three days at least and lying to her parents in order to escape just such an outcome as this.

Now truly she was furious. She had been on the defensive before but now she 34
attacked. Tried to get off her father's lap and fly at me while tears of defeat blinded her eyes.

■   ■   ■

Toni Cade Bambara was born in New York City in 1939. In addition to writing several collections of short stories (including *Gorilla, My Love* and *The Sea Birds Are Still Alive*) and the novel *The Salt Eaters*, she has been deeply involved in improving life in urban communities and recording African-American culture. The following story was originally published in 1966.

THE HAMMER MAN
TONI CADE BAMBARA

I was glad to hear that Manny had fallen off the roof. I had put out the tale that 1
I was down with yellow fever, but nobody paid me no mind, least of all Dirty Red who stomped right in to announce that Manny had fallen off the roof and that I could come out of hiding now. My mother dropped what she was doing, which was the laundry, and got the whole story out of Red. "Bad enough you gots to hang around with boys," she said. "But fight with them too. And you would pick the craziest one at that."

Manny was supposed to be crazy. That was his story. To say you were bad put 2
some people off. But to say you were crazy, well, you were officially not to be messed with. So that was his story. On the other hand, after I called him what I called him and said a few choice things about his mother, his face did go through some piercing changes. And I did kind of wonder if maybe he sure was nuts. I didn't wait to find out. I got in the wind. And then he waited for me on my stoop all day and all night, not hardly speaking to the people going in and out. And he was there all day Saturday, with his sister bringing him peanut-butter sandwiches and cream sodas. He must've gone to the bathroom right there cause every time I looked out the kitchen window, there he was. And Sunday, too. I got to thinking the boy was mad.

"You got no sense of humor, that's your trouble," I told him. He looked up, but 3
he didn't say nothing. All at once I was real sorry about the whole thing. I should've settled for hitting off the little girls in the school yard or waiting for Frankie to come

in so we could raise some kind of hell. This way I had to play sick when my mother was around cause my father had already taken away my BB gun and hid it.

I don't know how they got Manny on the roof finally. Maybe the Wakefield kids, 4
the ones who keep the pigeons, called him up. Manny was a sucker for sick animals and things like that. Or maybe Frankie got some nasty girls to go up on the roof with him and got Manny to join him. I don't know. Anyway, the catwalk had lost all its cement and the roof always did kind of slant downward. So Manny fell off the roof. I got over my yellow fever right quick, needless to say, and ventured outside. But by this time I had already told Miss Rose that Crazy Manny was after me. And Miss Rose, being who she was, quite naturally went over to Manny's house and said a few harsh words to his mother, who, being who she was, chased Miss Rose out into the street and they commenced to get with it, snatching bottles out of the garbage cans and breaking them on the johnny pumps and stuff like that.

Dirty Red didn't have to tell us about this. Everybody could see and hear all. I 5
never figured the garbage cans for an arsenal, but Miss Rose came up with sticks and table legs and things, and Manny's mother had her share of scissor blades and bicycle chains. They got to rolling in the streets and all you could see was pink drawers and fat legs. It was something else. Miss Rose is nutty but Manny's mother's crazier than Manny. They were at it a couple of times during my sick spell. Everyone would congregate on the window sills or the fire escape, commenting that it was still much too cold for this kind of nonsense. But they watched anyway. And then Manny fell off the roof. And that was that. Miss Rose went back to her dream books and Manny's mother went back to her tumbled-down kitchen of dirty clothes and bundles and bundles of rags and children.

My father got in on it too, cause he happened to ask Manny one night why he 6
was sitting on the stoop like that every night. Manny told him right off that he was going to kill me first chance he got. Quite naturally this made my father a little warm, me being his only daughter and planning to become a doctor and take care of him in his old age. So he had a few words with Manny first, and then he got hold of the older brother, Bernard, who was more his size. Bernard didn't see how any of it was his business or my father's business, so my father got mad and jammed Bernard's head into the mailbox. Then my father started getting messages from Bernard's uncle about where to meet him for a showdown and all. My father didn't say a word to my mother all this time; just sat around mumbling and picking up the phone and putting it down, or grabbing my stickball bat and putting it back. He carried on like this for days till I thought I would scream if the yellow fever didn't have me so weak. And then Manny fell off the roof, and my father went back to his beer-drinking buddies.

I was in the school yard, pitching pennies with the little boys from the elementary 7
school, when my friend Violet hits my brand-new Spaudeen over the wall. She came running back to tell me that Manny was coming down the block. I peeked beyond the fence and there he was all right. He had his head all wound up like a mummy and his arm in a sling and his leg in a cast. It looked phony to me, especially that walking cane. I figured Dirty Red had told me a tale just to get me out there so Manny could stomp me, and Manny was playing it up with costume and all till he could get me.

"What happened to him?" Violet's sisters whispered. But I was too busy trying 8
to figure out how this act was supposed to work. Then Manny passed real close to the fence and gave me a look.

"You had enough, Hammer Head" I yelled. "Just bring your crummy self in this   9
yard and I'll pick up where I left off." Violet was knocked out and the other kids
went into a huddle. I didn't have to say anything else. And when they all pressed
me later, I just said, "You know that hammer he always carries in his fatigues?" And
they'd all nod waiting for the rest of a long story. "Well, I took it away from him."
And I walked off nonchalantly.

Manny stayed indoors for a long time. I almost forgot about him. New kids   10
moved into the block and I got all caught up with that. And then Miss Rose finally
hit the numbers and started ordering a whole lot of stuff through the mail and we
would sit on the curb and watch these weird-looking packages being carried in, trying to figure out what simpleminded thing she had thrown her money away on
when she might just as well wait for the warm weather and throw a block party for
all her godchildren.

After a while a center opened up and my mother said she'd increase my allow-   11
ance if I went and joined because I'd have to get out of my pants and stay in skirts,
on account of that's the way things were at the center. So I joined and got to thinking about everything else but old Hammer Head. It was a rough place to get along
in, the center, but my mother said that I needed to be be'd with and she needed
to not be with me, so I went. And that time I sneaked into the office, that's when
I really got turned on. I looked into one of those not-quite-white folders and saw
that I was from a deviant family in a deviant neighborhood. I showed my mother
the word in the dictionary, but she didn't pay me no mind. It was my favorite word
after that. I ran it in the ground till one day my father got the strap just to show
how deviant he could get. So I gave up trying to improve my vocabulary. And I almost gave up my dungarees.

Then one night I'm walking past the Douglas Street park cause I got thrown out   12
of the center for playing pool when I should've been sewing, even though I had
already decided that this was going to be my last fling with boy things, and starting
tomorrow I was going to fix my hair right and wear skirts all the time just so my
mother would stop talking about her gray hairs, and Miss Rose would stop calling
me by my brother's name by mistake. So I'm walking past the park and there's ole
Manny on the basketball court, perfecting his lay-ups and talking with himself. Being
me, I quite naturally walk right up and ask what the hell he's doing playing in the
dark, and he looks up and all around like the dark had crept up on him when he
wasn't looking. So I knew right away that he'd been out there for a long time with
his eyes just going along with the program.

"There was two seconds to go and we were one point behind," he said, shaking   13
his head and staring at his sneakers like they was somebody. "And I was in the clear.
I'd left the man in the backcourt and there I was, smiling, you dig, cause it was in
the bag. They passed the ball and I slid the ball up nice and easy cause there was
nothing to worry about. And . . ." He shook his head. "I muffed the goddamn shot.
Ball bounced off the rim. . . ." He stared at his hands. "The game of the season.
Last game." And then he ignored me altogether, though he wasn't talking to me
in the first place. He went back to the lay-ups, always from the same spot with his
arms crooked in the same way, over and over. I must've gotten hypnotized cause I
probably stood there for at least an hour watching like a fool till I couldn't even see
the damn ball, much less the basket. But I stood there anyway for no reason I know
of. He never missed. But he cursed himself away. It was torture. And then a squad

car pulled up and a short cop with hair like one of the Marx Brothers came out hitching up his pants. He looked real hard at me and then at Manny.

"What are you two doing?"   14

"He's doing a lay-up. I'm watching," I said with my smart self.   15

Then the cop just stood there and finally turned to the other one who was just   16
getting out of the car.

"Who unlocked the gate?" the big one said.   17

"It's always unlocked," I said. Then we three just stood there like a bunch of   18
penguins watching Manny go at it.

"This on the level?" the big guy asked, tilting his hat back with the thumb the   19
way big guys do in hot weather. "Hey you," he said, walking over to Manny. "I'm
talking to you." He finally grabbed the ball to get Manny's attention. But that didn't
work. Manny just stood there with his arms out waiting for the pass so he could
save the game. He wasn't paying no mind to the cop. So, quite naturally, when the
cop slapped him upside his head it was a surprise. And when the cop started counting three to go, Manny had already recovered from the slap and was just ticking off
the seconds before the buzzer sounded and all was lost.

"Gimme the ball, man." Manny's face was all tightened up and ready to pop.   20

"Did you hear what I said, black boy?"   21

Now, when somebody says that word like that, I gets warm. And crazy or no   22
crazy, Manny was my brother at that moment and the cop was the enemy.

"You better give him back his ball," I said. "Manny don't take no mess from no   23
cops. He ain't bothering nobody. He's gonna be Mister Basketball when he grows
up. Just trying to get a little practice in before the softball season starts."

"Look here, sister, we'll run you in too," Harpo said.   24

"I damn sure can't be your sister seeing how I'm a black girl. Boy, I sure will be   25
glad when you run me in so I can tell everybody about that. You must think you're
in the South, mister."

The big guy screwed his mouth up and let one of them hard-day sighs. "The   26
park's closed, little girl, so why don't you and your boyfriend go on home."

That really got me..The "little girl" was bad enough, but that "boyfriend" was   27
too much. But I kept cool, mostly because Manny looked so pitiful waiting there
with his hands in a time-out and there being no one to stop the clock. But I kept
my cool mostly cause of that hammer in Manny's pocket and no telling how frantic
things can get what with a bigmouth like me, a couple of wise cops, and a crazy
boy too.

"The gates are open," I said real quiet-like, "and this here's a free country. So   28
why don't you give him back his ball?"

The big cop did another one of those sighs, his specialty I guess, and then he   29
bounced the ball to Manny who went right into his gliding thing clear up to the
backboard, damn near like he was some kind of very beautiful bird. And then he
swooshed that ball in, even if there was no net, and you couldn't really hear the
swoosh. Something happened to the bones in my chest. It was something.

"Crazy kids anyhow," the one with the wig said and turned to go. But the big   30
guy watched Manny for a while and I guess something must've snapped in his head,
cause all of a sudden he was hot for taking Manny to jail or court or somewhere
and started yelling at him and everything, which is a bad thing to do to Manny, I
can tell you. And I'm standing there thinking that none of my teachers, from kin-

dergarten right on up, none of them knew what they were talking about. I'll be damned if I ever knew one of them rosy-cheeked cops that smiled and helped you get to school without neither you or your little raggedy dog getting hit by a truck that had a smile on its face, too. Not that I ever believed it. I knew Dick and Jane was full of crap from the get-go, especially them cops. Like this dude, for example, pulling on Manny's clothes like that when obviously he had just done about the most beautiful thing a man can do and not be a fag. No cop could swoosh without a net.

''Look out, man,'' was all Manny said, but it was the way he pushed the cop   31 that started the real yelling and threats. And I thought to myself, Oh God here I am trying to change my ways, and not talk back in school, and do like my mother wants, but just have this last fling, and now this—getting shot in the stomach and bleeding to death in Douglas Street park and poor Manny getting pistol-whipped by those bastards and whatnot. I could see it all, practically crying too. And it just wasn't no kind of thing to happen to a small child like me with my confirmation picture in the paper next to my weeping parents and schoolmates. I could feel the blood sticking to my shirt and my eyeballs slipping away, and then that confirmation picture again; and my mother and her gray hair; and Miss Rose heading for the precinct with a shotgun; and my father getting old and feeble with no one to doctor him up and all.

And I wished Manny had fallen off the damn roof and died right then and there   32 and saved me all this aggravation of being killed with him by these cops who surely didn't come out of no fifth-grade reader. But it didn't happen. They just took the ball and Manny followed them real quiet-like right out of the park into the dark, then into the squad car with his head drooping and his arms in a crook. And I went on home cause what the hell am I going to do on a basketball court, and it getting to be nearly midnight?

I didn't see Manny no more after he got into that squad car. But they didn't kill   33 him after all cause Miss Rose heard he was in some kind of big house for people who lose their marbles. And then it was spring finally, and me and Violet was in this very boss fashion show at the center. And Miss Rose bought me my first corsage— yellow roses to match my shoes.

■   ■   ■

James Joyce (1882–1941), a native of Dublin, Ireland, is widely considered one of the most influential writers of the early twentieth century. The following story, one of his most often anthologized, appears in the collection *Dubliners*, published in 1914. Like his novel *Portrait of the Artist as a Young Man* published two years later, it relies for much of its detail on scenes of Joyce's own boyhood.

ARABY
JAMES JOYCE

North Richmond Street, being blind,[1] was a quiet street except at the hour when   1 the Christian Brothers' School set the boys free. An uninhabited house of two storeys stood at the blind end, detached from its neighbours in a square ground. The other

[1] A dead end. The young Joyce in fact lived for a time on North Richmond Street in Dublin.

houses of the street, conscious of decent lives within them, gazed at one another with brown imperturbable faces.

The former tenant of our house, a priest, had died in the back drawing-room. 2 Air, musty from having been long enclosed, hung in all the rooms, and the waste room behind the kitchen was littered with old useless papers. Among these I found a few paper-covered books, the pages of which were curled and damp: *The Abbot*, by Walter Scott, *The Devout Communicant* and *The Memoirs of Vidocq*.[2] I liked the last best because its leaves were yellow. The wild garden behind the house contained a central apple-tree and a few straggling bushes under one of which I found the late tenant's rusty bicycle-pump. He had been a very charitable priest; in his will he had left all his money to institutions and the furniture of his house to his sister.

When the short days of winter came dusk fell before we had well eaten our 3 dinners. When we met in the street the houses had grown sombre. The space of sky above us was the colour of ever-changing violet and towards it the lamps of the street lifted their feeble lanterns. The cold air stung us and we played till our bodies glowed. Our shouts echoed in the silent street. The career of our play brought us through the dark muddy lanes behind the houses where we ran the gauntlet of the rough tribes from the cottages, to the back doors of the dark dripping gardens where odours arose from the ashpits, to the dark odorous stables where a coachman smoothed and combed the horse or shook music from the buckled harness. When we returned to the street light from the kitchen windows had filled the areas. If my uncle was seen turning the corner we hid in the shadow until we had seen him safely housed. Or if Mangan's sister came out on the doorstep to call her brother in to his tea we watched her from our shadow peer up and down the street. We waited to see whether she would remain or go in and, if she remained, we left our shadow and walked up to Mangan's steps resignedly. She was waiting for us, her figure defined by the light from the half-opened door. Her brother always teased her before he obeyed and I stood by the railings looking at her. Her dress swung as she moved her body and the soft rope of her hair tossed from side to side.

Every morning I lay on the floor in the front parlour watching her door. The blind 4 was pulled down to within an inch of the sash so that I could not be seen. When she came out on the doorstep my heart leaped. I ran to the hall, seized my books and followed her. I kept her brown figure always in my eye and, when we came near the point at which our ways diverged, I quickened my pace and passed her. This happened morning after morning. I had never spoken to her, except for a few casual words, and yet her name was like a summons to all my foolish blood.

Her image accompanied me even in places the most hostile to romance. On Sat- 5 urday evenings when my aunt went marketing I had to go to carry some of the parcels. We walked through the flaring streets, jostled by drunken men and bargaining women, amid the curses of labourers, the shrill litanies of shop-boys who stood on guard by the barrels of pigs' cheeks, the nasal chanting of street-singers, who sang a *come-all-you* about O'Donovan Rossa,[3] or a ballad about the troubles in our native land. These noises converged in a single sensation of life for me: I imag-

[2] *The Devout Communicant* is a collection of religious meditations; *The Abbot* is a historical romance set in the court of Mary, Queen of Scots, a Catholic, who was beheaded for plotting to assassinate her Protestant cousin, Queen Elizabeth I; *The Memoirs of Vidocq* is a collection of sexually suggestive stories about a French criminal turned detective.

[3] A contemporary leader of an underground organization opposed to British rule of Ireland.

ined that I bore my chalice safely through a throng of foes. Her name sprang to my lips at moments in strange prayers and praises which I myself did not understand. My eyes were often full of tears (I could not tell why) and at times a flood from my heart seemed to pour itself out into my bosom. I thought little of the future. I did not know whether I would ever speak to her or not or, if I spoke to her, how I could tell her of my confused adoration. But my body was like a harp and her words and gestures were like fingers running upon the wires.

One evening I went into the back drawing-room in which the priest had died. It   6 was a dark rainy evening and there was no sound in the house. Through one of the broken panes I heard the rain impinge upon the earth, the fine incessant needles of water playing in the sodden beds. Some distant lamp or lighted window gleamed below me. I was thankful that I could see so little. All my senses seemed to desire to veil themselves and, feeling that I was about to slip from them, I pressed the palms of my hands together until they trembled, murmuring: *"O love! O love!"* many times.

At last she spoke to me. When she addressed the first words to me I was so   7 confused that I did not know what to answer. She asked me was I going to *Araby.* I forgot whether I answered yes or no. It would be a splendid bazaar, she said she would love to go.[4]

"And why can't you?" I asked.   8

While she spoke she turned a silver bracelet round and round her wrist. She   9 could not go, she said, because there would be a retreat that week in her convent. Her brother and two other boys were fighting for their caps and I was alone at the railings. She held one of the spikes, bowing her head towards me. The light from the lamp opposite our door caught the white curve of her neck, lit up her hair that rested there and, falling, lit up the hand upon the railing. It fell over one side of her dress and caught the white border of a petticoat, just visible as she stood at ease.

"It's well for you," she said.   10

"If I go," I said, "I will bring you something."   11

What innumerable follies laid waste my waking and sleeping thoughts after that 12 evening! I wished to annihilate the tedious intervening days. I chafed against the work of school. At night in my bedroom and by day in the classroom her image came between me and the page I strove to read. The syllables of the word *Araby* were called to me through the silence in which my soul luxuriated and cast an Eastern enchantment over me. I asked for leave to go to the bazaar on Saturday night. My aunt was surprised and hoped it was not some Freemason affair.[5] I answered few questions in class. I watched my master's face pass from amiability to sternness; he hoped I was not beginning to idle. I could not call my wandering thoughts together. I had hardly any patience with the serious work of life which, now that it stood between me and my desire, seemed to me child's play, ugly monotonous child's play.

[4]Such traveling bazaars—featuring cafés, shopping stalls, and entertainment—were common at the time. Araby was an actual English bazaar that visited Dublin when James Joyce was a boy.

[5]Freemason refers to a secretive fraternal order with a long history, whose members have included many artists, philosophers, and politicians, and to which the Catholic church has traditionally been opposed.

On Saturday morning I reminded my uncle that I wished to go to the bazaar in   13
the evening. He was fussing at the hallstand, looking for the hatbrush, and answered
me curtly:

"Yes, boy, I know."   14

As he was in the hall I could not go into the front parlour and lie at the window.   15
I left the house in bad humour and walked slowly towards the school. The air was
pitilessly raw and already my heart misgave me.

When I came home to dinner my uncle had not yet been home. Still it was early.   16
I sat staring at the clock for some time and, when its ticking began to irritate me, I
left the room. I mounted the staircase and gained the upper part of the house. The
high cold empty gloomy rooms liberated me and I went from room to room singing.
From the front window I saw my companions playing below in the street. Their cries
reached me weakened and indistinct and, leaning my forehead against the cool
glass, I looked over at the dark house where she lived. I may have stood there for
an hour, seeing nothing but the brown-clad figure cast by my imagination, touched
discreetly by the lamplight at the curved neck, at the hand upon the railings and at
the border below the dress.

When I came downstairs again I found Mrs. Mercer sitting at the fire. She was   17
an old garrulous woman, a pawnbroker's widow, who collected used stamps for
some pious purpose. I had to endure the gossip of the tea-table. The meal was prolonged beyond an hour and still my uncle did not come. Mrs. Mercer stood up to
go: she was sorry she couldn't wait any longer, but it was after eight o'clock and
she did not like to be out late, as the night air was bad for her. When she had gone
I began to walk up and down the room, clenching my fists. My aunt said:

"I'm afraid you may put off your bazaar for this night of Our Lord."   18

At nine o'clock I heard my uncle's latchkey in the halldoor. I heard him talking   19
to himself and heard the hallstand rocking when it had received the weight of his
overcoat. I could interpret these signs. When he was midway through his dinner I
asked him to give me the money to go to the bazaar. He had forgotten.

"The people are in bed and after their first sleep now," he said.   20

I did not smile. My aunt said to him energetically: 21

"Can't you give him the money and let him go? You've kept him late enough   22
as it is."

My uncle said he was very sorry he had forgotten. He said he believed in the old   23
saying: "All work and no play makes Jack a dull boy." He asked me where I was
going and, when I had told him a second time he asked me did I know *The Arab's
Farewell to his Steed*. When I left the kitchen he was about to recite the opening
lines of the piece to my aunt.

I held a florin tightly in my hand as I strode down Buckingham Street towards   24
the station. The sight of the streets thronged with buyers and glaring with gas recalled to me the purpose of my journey. I took my seat in a third-class carriage of a
deserted train. After an intolerable delay the train moved out of the station slowly.
It crept onward among ruinous houses and over the twinkling river. At Westland
Row Station a crowd of people pressed to the carriage doors; but the porters moved
them back, saying that it was a special train for the bazaar. I remained alone in the
bare carriage. In a few minutes the train drew up beside an improvised wooden
platform. I passed out on to the road and saw by the lighted dial of a clock that it
was ten minutes to ten. In front of me was a large building which displayed the
magical name.

I could not find any sixpenny entrance and, fearing that the bazaar would be   25
closed, I passed in quickly through a turnstile, handing a shilling to a weary-looking
man. I found myself in a big hall girdled at half its height by a gallery. Nearly all the
stalls were closed and the greater part of the hall was in darkness. I recognised a
silence like that which pervades a church after a service. I walked into the centre of
the bazaar timidly. A few people were gathered about the stalls which were still
open. Before a curtain, over which the words *Café Chantant*[6] were written in col-
oured lamps, two men were counting money on a salver. I listened to the fall of the
coins.

Remembering with difficulty why I had come I went over to one of the stalls and   26
examined porcelain vases and flowered tea-sets. At the door of the stall a young
lady was talking and laughing with two young gentlemen. I remarked their English
accents and listened vaguely to their conversation.

"O, I never said such a thing!"   27

"O, but you did!"

"O, but I didn't!"

"Didn't she say that?"

"Yes. I heard her."

"O, there's a . . . fib!"

Observing me the young lady came over and asked me did I wish to buy any-   28
thing. The tone of her voice was not encouraging; she seemed to have spoken to
me out of a sense of duty. I looked humbly at the great jars that stood like eastern
guards at either side of the dark entrance to the stall and murmured:

"No, thank you."   29

The young lady changed the position of one of the vases and went back to the   30
two young men. They began to talk of the same subject. Once or twice the young
lady glanced at me over her shoulder.

I lingered before her stall, though I knew my stay was useless, to make my in-   31
terest in her wares seem the more real. Then I turned away slowly and walked down
the middle of the bazaar. I allowed the two pennies to fall against the sixpence in
my pocket. I heard a voice call from one end of the gallery that the light was out.
The upper part of the hall was now completely dark.

Gazing up into the darkness I saw myself as a creature driven and derided by   32
vanity; and my eyes burned with anguish and anger.

Readings

In order to become familiar with the basic features of essays that interpret
stories, you will read two student essays interpreting "Araby," the preceding
short story by James Joyce. Your instructor may have the class discuss "Ar-

---

[6]A music hall.

aby'' before you read and analyze the student essays; or you may be asked to read "Araby" quickly and to focus your primary attention on the basic features of the essays interpreting it. In either case, the Commentary following the first student essay and the For Analysis questions following the second will help you see how essays interpreting stories are structured, how they center on a thesis, and how they use textual evidence to support that thesis.

■   ■   ■

Sally Crane composed the following essay after a class discussion of "Araby." As her title suggests, Crane focuses on the meaning of the final scene. Notice that she begins her essay by referring to a common interpretation of that scene, one with which she disagrees.

GAZING INTO THE DARKNESS
SALLY CRANE

Readers of "Araby" often focus on the final scene as the key to the story. They 1
assume the boy experiences some profound insight about himself when he gazes "up into the darkness." I believe, however, that the boy sees nothing and learns nothing—either about himself or others. He's not self-reflective; he's merely self-absorbed.

The evidence supporting this interpretation is the imagery of blindness and the 2
ironic point of view of the narrator. There can seem to be a profound insight at the end of the story only if we empathize with the boy and adopt his point of view. In other words, we must assume that the young boy is narrating his own story. But if the real narrator is the grown man looking back at his early adolescence, then it becomes possible to read the narrative as ironic, and to see the boy as confused and blind.

The story opens and closes with images of blindness. The street is "blind" with 3
an "uninhabited house . . . at the blind end. . . ." As he spies on Mangan's sister, from his own house, the boy intentionally limits what he is able to see by lowering the "blind" until it is only an inch from the window sash. At the bazaar in the closing scene, the "light was out," and the upper part of the hall was "completely dark." The boy is left "gazing up into the darkness," seeing nothing but an inner torment that burns his eyes.

This pattern of imagery includes images of reading, and reading stands for the 4
boy's inability to understand what is before his eyes. When he tries to read at night, for example, the girl's "image [comes] between him and the page," in effect, blinding him. In fact, he seems blind to everything except this "image" of the "brown-clad figure cast by [his] imagination." The girl's "brown-clad figure" is also associated with the houses on "blind" Richmond Street, with their "brown imperturbable faces." The houses stare back at the boy, unaffected by his presence and gaze.

The most important face he tries and fails to read belongs to Mangan's sister. 5
His description of her and interpretation of the few words she says to him can be seen as further evidence of his blindness. He sees only what he wants to see, the

"image" he has in his mind's eye. This image comes more from what he's read than from anything he's observed. He casts her simultaneously in the traditional female roles of angel and whore:

> While she spoke she turned a silver bracelet round and round her wrist. She could not go, she said, because there would be a retreat that week in her convent. . . . She held one of the spikes, bowing her head towards me. The light from the lamp opposite our door caught the white curve of her neck, lit up her hair that rested there and, falling, lit up the hand upon the railing. It fell over one side of her dress and caught the white border of a petticoat, just visible as she stood at ease.

Her angelic qualities are shown in her plans to attend a convent retreat and in her bowed head. Her whorish qualities come through in the way she flirtatiously plays with the bracelet, as if she were inviting him to buy her an expensive piece of jewelry at the bazaar. The "white curve of her neck" and the "white border of a petticoat" combine the symbolic color of purity, associated with the Madonna, with sexual suggestiveness. The point is that there is no suggestion here or anywhere else in the story that the boy is capable of seeing Mangan's sister as a real person. She only exists as the object of his adoring gaze. In fact, no one seems to have any reality for him other than himself.

He is totally self-absorbed. But at the same time, he is also blind to himself. He says repeatedly that he doesn't understand his feelings: "Her name sprang to my lips at moments in strange prayers and praises which I myself did not understand. My eyes were full of tears (I could not tell why). . . ." His adoration of her is both "confused" and confusing to him. He has no self-understanding.

The best insight we have into the boy comes from the language he uses. Much of his language seems to mimick the old priest's romantic books: "Her name sprang like a summons to all my foolish blood"; "I imagined that I bore my chalice safely through a throng of foes"; "my body was like a harp and her words and gestures were like fingers running upon the wires." Language like this sounds as though it comes out of a popular romance novel, something written by Danielle Steel perhaps. The mixing of romance with soft porn is unmistakable. Perhaps the boy has spent too much time reading the priest's "sexually seductive stories" from *The Memoirs of Vidocq.*

I think this language is meant to be ironic, to point to the fact that the narrator is not the young boy himself but the young boy now grown and looking back at how "foolish" he was. This interpretation becomes likely when you think of "Araby" as a fictionalized autobiography. In autobiographical stories, remembered feelings and thoughts are combined with the autobiographer's present perspective. The remembered feelings and thoughts in this story could be seen as expressing the boy's point of view, but we read them ironically through the adult narrator's present perspective. The romantic, gushy language the boy uses is laughable. It reveals the boy's blindness toward everyone, including himself. He sees himself as Sir Galahad, the chivalric hero on his own grail quest to Araby. The greatest irony comes at the end when his quest is shown to be merely a shopping trip; and Araby, merely a suburban mall.

Most people interpret the ending as a moment of profound insight, and the language certainly seems to support this interpretation: "Gazing up into the darkness I saw myself as a creature driven and derided by vanity; and my eyes burned with anguish and anger." But here again we see the narrator using inflated language that suggests an ironic stance. So even in the moment of apparent insight, the boy is still playing a heroic role. He hasn't discovered his true self. He's just as self-absorbed and blind in the end as he was at the beginning.

Commentary   This commentary offers a comprehensive overview of the main features and strategies of Sally Crane's essay interpreting "Araby." It prepares you to do your own analysis of the features and strategies of the next essay by David Ratinov, an essay which offers a different interpretation of "Araby."

Essays interpreting short stories are thesis-centered: they assert an interpretation of the story. Knowing that many interpretations are possible, writers nevertheless assert one interpretation. Crane's thesis can be found at the end of her first paragraph: "I believe . . . that the boy sees nothing and learns nothing—about himself or others. He's not self-reflective; he's merely self-absorbed."

A thesis relies on key terms that are used throughout the essay to develop the interpretation and keep readers on track. Crane's key terms are "sees nothing" (and its synonym "blind") and "self-absorbed." If you glance through the essay, you will see these terms repeated, especially in the concluding paragraph.

For more on thesis and forecasting statements, see Chapter 13.

A thesis statement, along with other introductory material, may forecast the main points that support the thesis. It may even reveal the order of the points, enabling readers to anticipate the sequence in which main points will come up. Crane tells us at the beginning of her second paragraph that there are two kinds of evidence supporting her thesis: "imagery of blindness" and "the ironic point of view of the narrator." Notice that in her essay she first presents the evidence detailing images of blindness (paragraph 3–6) and then the evidence supporting the idea that the adult narrator views his childhood experiences ironically (paragraphs 7 and 8).

For more on argument, see Chapter 19.

The argument supporting the thesis is the heart of an interpretive essay. The writer attempts to support the thesis—to justify the interpretation of the story—by presenting a logical, step-by-step argument. Argument is necessary because the writer cannot assume readers will accept the asserted meaning without questions or will see readily why the writer came up with that interpretation rather than some other. The argument must seem logical to readers part-by-part as well as sentence-by-sentence. A close look at the parts of Crane's essay and their relations reveals her plan. Here is a paragraph-by-paragraph scratch outline:

1. thesis: the boy is blind because he is so self-absorbed
2. two kinds of evidence supporting the thesis
3. images of blindness
4. images of "reading"
5. misreading Mangan's sister
6. the boy's lack of self-understanding

7. the boy's exaggerated language
8. the adult narrator's ironic use of language
9. reiteration of thesis

This is a logical plan because each part seems to follow naturally from the previous part. There are no gaps, puzzles, or surprises. While readers may have questions or reservations as they consider each step in the argument, they have no trouble following along from one step to the next. Within a paragraph, readers hope to find, sentence-by-sentence, the same logical progression. We sometimes refer to this as "coherence." Besides "inventive" and "convincing," we want an argument to be "logical" and "coherent." Consider paragraph 3 sentence-by-sentence. The first sentence announces the topic, that the story has "images of blindness" and forecasts that these images appear principally in the story's opening and closing. The second sentence presents imagery from the opening, the third from somewhere near the middle, and the fourth and fifth from the closing. Each sentence presents one or more images of blindness. Readers have no trouble following along; at no sentence do they pause and ask, "Now, why is the writer telling me this?"

For more on cohesive devices, see pp. 476–79.

Arguments supporting interpretations of literary texts require evidence from the text. This evidence can be paraphrased (stated in the interpreter's own words) or quoted directly from the text. Textual evidence must relate to the point, and it must be integrated smoothly into the writing. Looking again at paragraph 3, you can see that Crane succeeds in both these ways. Notice how she integrates quoted words and phrases into her sentences. She uses ellipsis (. . .) to indicate she has left some words out of her quotation either because they're not relevant to the point she's making or they don't fit grammatically into her sentence. In paragraph 4, you also can see how she uses brackets to change the form of quoted words to make them fit grammatically into her sentence: "the girl's image [comes] between him and the page." In the original, the verb is not "comes" but the past tense form "came." Since Crane is writing in the present tense, the conventional tense for writing about stories, she changes the tense of the word she's quoting and puts brackets around it to indicate the change. By carefully integrating quotes into her sentences, Crane supplies evidence for her ideas and makes her writing flow smoothly.

For more on quoting, see pp. 595–600.

Another important thing to notice about Crane's use of quotation is that she generally doesn't let the quoted words speak for themselves. She follows the quote with one or more sentences explaining precisely what the quoted words mean and how they support her point. You can see this most clearly in paragraph 5 after the long, indented quotation. (Following the style of the Modern Language Association, quotations of more than four lines are indented this way.) Crane uses paraphrase and quotation to point to specific language in the indented passage, and explains what she thinks this language signifies. Such explanation is especially important in interpreting stories because readers often interpret particular words and phrases differently. In writing an interpretive essay, you should assume that readers have read the story, but cannot expect them to understand it exactly as you do.

Contributing to the coherence of an argument are the cues writers provide their readers. One important kind of cue is the topic sentence, often the first sentence in the paragraph. The topic sentence announces the topic of the paragraph (or group of paragraphs). For example, look again at paragraph 3: "The story opens and closes with images of blindness." Another important cue is the transition connecting the topic of one paragraph with the topic of the next. A good example appears at the beginning of paragraph 6: "He is totally self-absorbed. But at the same time, he is also blind to himself." The first sentence reiterates the point of the preceding paragraph, while the second announces what the point will be of this new paragraph. Transitions may also appear within paragraphs, connecting ideas or examples. Notice, for example, near the end of paragraph 4: "In fact, he seems blind to everything except this 'image,' of the 'brown-clad figure cast by [his] imagination.' The girl's 'brown-clad figure' is also associated with. . . ." Here, the word "also" cues the reader that the writer is making an additional point about the phrase "brown-clad figure."

One final word about the conclusion. Crane frames the essay by coming back at the end to the point she made at the beginning: that readers who see the ending as a moment of insight are wrong. Her concluding paragraph repeats the essay's basic argument, so that there can be no confusion about the point she's making. Essays interpreting a story also may conclude on a more general note. They may suggest possible implications of the interpretation or extend the idea somewhat.

■   ■   ■

David Ratinov wrote the following essay for his freshman composition class. Like Sally Crane and most readers of "Araby," Ratinov wanted to understand what the narrator's final statement meant and what motivated it. Notice how his interpretation differs from Crane's.

FROM INNOCENCE TO INSIGHT: "ARABY" AS AN INITIATION STORY
DAVID RATINOV

"Araby" tells the story of an adolescent boy's initiation into adulthood. The story is narrated by a mature man reflecting upon his adolescence and the events that forced him to face the disillusioning realities of adulthood. The minor characters play a pivotal role in this initiation process. The boy observes the hypocrisy of adults in the priest and Mrs. Mercer; and his vain, self-centered uncle introduces him to another disillusioning aspect of adulthood. The boy's infatuation with the girl ultimately ends in disillusionment, and Joyce uses the specific example of the boy's disillusionment with love as a metaphor for disillusionment with life itself. From the beginning the boy deludes himself about his relationship with Mangan's sister. At Araby, he realizes the parallel between his own self-delusion and the hypocrisy and vanity of the adult world.

From the beginning, the boy's infatuation with Mangan's sister draws him away   2
from childhood toward adulthood. He breaks his ties with his childhood friends and
luxuriates in his isolation. He can think of nothing but his love for her: "From the
front window I saw my companions playing below in the street. Their cries reached
me weakened and indistinct and, leaning my forehead against the cool glass, I
looked over at the dark house where she lived." The friends' cries are weak and
indistinct because they are distant emotionally as well as spatially. Like an adult on
a quest, he imagines he carries his love as if it were a sacred object, a chalice: "Her
image accompanied me even in places the most hostile to romance. . . . I imagined
that I bore my chalice safely through a throng of foes." Even in the active, distracting
marketplace, he is able to retain this image of his pure love. But his love is not pure.

Although he worships Mangan's sister as a religious object, his lust for her is   3
undeniable. He idolizes her as if she were the Virgin Mary: "her figure defined by
the half-opened door. . . . The light from the lamp opposite our door caught the
white curve of her neck, lit up her hair that rested there, and falling, lit up the hand
upon the railing." Yet even this image is sensual with the halo of light accentuating
"the white curve of her neck." The language makes obvious that his attraction is
physical rather than spiritual: "Her dress swung as she moved her body and the soft
rope of her hair tossed from side to side." His desire for her is strong and undeniable:
"her name was like a summons to all my foolish blood"; "my body was like a harp
and her words and gestures were like fingers running upon the wires." But in order
to justify his love, to make it socially acceptable, he deludes himself into thinking
that his love *is* pure. He is being hypocritical, although at this point he does not
know it.

Hypocrisy is characteristic of the adults in this story. The priest is by far the most   4
obvious offender. What is a man of the cloth doing with books like *The Abbott* (a
romantic novel) and *The Memoirs of Vidocq* (a collection of sexually suggestive
tales)? These books imply that he led a double life. Moreover, the fact that he had
money to give away when he died suggests that he was far from saintly. Similarly,
at first glance Mrs. Mercer appears to be religious, but a closer look reveals that she
too is materialistic. Her church work—collecting used stamps for some "pious purpose" (presumably to sell for the church)—associates her with money and profit.
Even her name, Mercer, identifies her as a dealer in merchandise. In addition, her
husband is a pawnbroker, a profession that the church frowns upon. Despite being
linked to money, she pretends to be pious and respectable. Therefore, like the priest,
Mrs. Mercer is hypocritical.

The uncle, as the boy's only living male relative, is a failure as a role model and   5
the epitome of vanity. He is a self-centered old man who cannot handle responsibility. When the boy reminds him on Saturday morning about the bazaar, the uncle
brushes him off, devoting all his attention to his own appearance. After being out
all afternoon the uncle returns home at 9:00, talking to himself. He rocks the hallstand when hanging up his overcoat. These details suggest that he is drunk. "I could
interpret these signs" indicates that this behavior is typical of his uncle. The uncle is
the only character in the story the boy relies upon, but the uncle fails him. Only after
the aunt persuades him does the uncle give the boy the money he promised. From
the priest, Mrs. Mercer, and his uncle, the boy learns some fundamental truths about
adulthood, but it is only after his visit to Araby that he is able to recognize what he
has learned.

Araby to the adolescent represents excitement, a chance to prove the purity of 6
his love and, more abstractly, his hope; however, Araby fulfills none of these expectations. Instead, the boy finds himself in utter disillusionment and despair. Araby is anything but exciting. The trip there is dreary, and uneventful, lonely and intolerably slow—not the magical journey he had expected. When he arrives, Araby itself is nearly completely dark and in the process of closing. With his excitement stunted, he can barely remember why he came (to prove the purity of his love by buying a gift for Mangan's sister).

The young lady selling porcelain and her gentlemen friends act as catalysts, caus- 7
ing the boy to recognize the truth of his love for Mangan's sister. Their conversation is flirtatious—a silly lovers' game that the boy recognizes as resembling his own conversation with Mangan's sister. He concludes that his love for her is no different than the two gentlemen's "love" for this "lady." Neither love is pure. He too had only been playing a game, flirting with a girl and pretending that it was something else and that he was someone else.

His disillusionment with love is then extended to life in general. Seeing the last 8
rays of hope fading from the top floors of Araby, the boy cries: "I saw myself as a creature driven and derided by vanity; and my eyes burned with anguish and anger." At last he makes the connection—by deluding himself, he has been hypocritical and vain like the adults in his life. Before these realizations he believed that he was driven by something of value (such as purity of love), but now he realizes that his quest has been in vain because honesty, truth, and purity are only childish illusions and he can never return to the innocence of childhood.

For Analysis

1.   Find the thesis statement in Ratinov's essay, and underline its key terms. Next, find and circle each use of these key terms in the essay. Are they all carried forward throughout the essay, or do any drop out of sight?

2.   Look at paragraph 4. What part of the argument forecast in the first paragraph does this paragraph attempt to develop? Explain briefly how this part of the argument is developed.

3.   Underline the first sentence in each paragraph, beginning with paragraph 2. Look closely at these sentences to discover how they connect the previous paragraph to the paragraph they introduce. Bracket the words or phrase in the sentence that actually create this connection. Besides creating this connection, what other role do these opening sentences play?

4.   In an argument, not only does every paragraph lead to the next, but within a paragraph each sentence leads to the next. Notice that the topic of paragraph 2 has to do with drawing the boy away from childhood to adulthood. Look closely at each sentence to discover whether it is related to that topic and whether each sentence follows logically from the preceding sentence.

5.   Underline the quoted material in paragraph 3 in order to see what proportion of the paragraph uses quotations as evidence. Quotes can't just be dropped into an argument. The writer must indicate what the quotation

means and how it relates to the point being made. Quotations used as evidence must pass this relevance test. How does Ratinov indicate the relevance of the quotations in this paragraph?

6.   Look at the concluding paragraph. Compare it sentence by sentence to the opening paragraph in order to discover how it frames the essay. In particular, are the key terms repeated in the last paragraph? If so, how does this repetition and other aspects of the framing assist the reader? Does the concluding paragraph simply repeat the ideas in the opening paragraph, or does it also add something new to the argument? If so, what? If not, what could it add?

PURPOSE AND AUDIENCE

When you write an essay interpreting a story, your purpose is to present an idea about what the work means. This idea is your interpretation. Since your readers may favor other interpretations, your task is to convince them that yours is plausible and that it reflects close reading and thoughtful analysis of the story.

There is, then, no single or best interpretation. There are only interesting or plausible ideas, intriguing ideas presented convincingly. Consequently, in writing an essay interpreting a story you are not trying to win a contest or prove that only your idea should be taken seriously. Instead, you are trying to share your idea and to develop a reasonable and well-supported argument for it. Your readers will not immediately assume that they disagree with what you are about to say. Quite the contrary, as members of your community of readers, they will be anticipating a new intriguing idea about the story, one that may lead them to a new understanding and appreciation of it.

Your readers do not expect you to come up with a startling insight into the story, though they will be pleased if you do. What readers do expect is a logical argument supported by an interesting "reading" of the story. If you have been discussing the same story (like "Araby") or a group of stories by the same author (like Joyce's book *Dubliners*, in which "Araby" appears), they may even find your thesis predictable or similar to their own. But a predictable thesis can be argued in an interesting way, showing readers new ways to look at the story. Your readers will be disappointed only if you propose an unclear or unfocused thesis with unworkable terms, propose a thesis that can be challenged by evidence in the text, argue illogically, neglect to include numerous examples and quotations from the text, or fail to provide the necessary cues to keep readers on track. Readers will be especially disappointed if they think you are retelling the plot rather than developing your own interpretation of the story.

BASIC FEATURES OF ESSAYS INTERPRETING STORIES

Writing about stories generally has only two key ingredients: an interpretation and a convincing argument based on textual evidence.

The Writer's Interpretation	At the center of a literary interpretation lies the writer's analysis of the story's meaning. This interpretation provides the main focus for the essay. Without such a central idea, the essay would be just an accumulation of ideas about the story rather than a coherent interpretation of it.

At the center of a literary interpretation lies the writer's analysis of the story's meaning. This interpretation provides the main focus for the essay. Without such a central idea, the essay would be just an accumulation of ideas about the story rather than a coherent interpretation of it.

In literary interpretation, this main idea is usually given directly in a thesis statement. A focal point, the thesis brings the parts of the essay into perspective, helping readers to understand how the subordinate ideas relate to one another as well as how they combine to illuminate the story.

For example, Ratinov states his thesis in his opening paragraph: " 'Araby' tells the story of an adolescent boy's initiation into adulthood. . . . [A]t Araby, he realizes the parallel between his own self-delusion and the hypocrisy and vanity of the adult world." The key terms in Ratinov's interpretation—*initiation*, *self-delusion*, *hypocrisy*, and *vanity*—are clear, appropriate, and workable.

Although skilled literary critics may want their interpretation to account for subtleties in the work, they do not want their readers to have difficulty understanding their argument. No matter how complex their ideas, they strive to make their writing direct and clear. Therefore, they usually alert readers early to the points they will be making, giving readers a context in which to understand their interpretation. Ratinov, for example, forecasts in the last two sentences of the opening paragraph the points he develops in the essay.

A Convincing Argument

In addition to stating their interpretation, writers must try to present a convincing argument for it. They may sometimes assume that readers are familiar with the story, but never can they expect readers to see it as they do or automatically to understand—let alone accept—their interpretation of a literary work.

Writers argue for their interpretation not so much to convince readers to adopt it but rather to convince them that it makes sense. They must demonstrate to readers how they "read" the story, pointing out specific details and explaining what they think these details mean.

The primary source of evidence for literary interpretation, then, is the work itself. Writers quote and, to a lesser degree, summarize and paraphrase passages from the story. They do more than just refer to a specific passage, however: they explain the meaning of the passage in light of their thesis. Both

Crane and Ratinov, for example, quote from the story repeatedly throughout their essays. This textual evidence alternates with their serious and energetic explanation of its significance to their thesis.

Guide to Writing

THE WRITING ASSIGNMENT

Write an essay interpreting a short story. Aim to convince readers that your view is insightful and plausible, one based on a thoughtful and imaginative analysis of the story.

INVENTION

Choose a short story, analyze it carefully, formulate a tentative thesis, and find evidence in the story to support that thesis.

Choosing a Story

You may have chosen a story already, or your instructor may have assigned you one. If so, go on to the next section, Annotating the Story to Analyze Specific Features.

　　If you must still choose a story on your own, consider—and read—several stories before deciding on one to write about. Choose a story that impresses, surprises, or puzzles you, one that excites your interest and imagination. You should not expect to understand the story completely on the first reading; just be sure to select a story that you expect to enjoy thinking about and that will reward close study. You may want to consult with your instructor about your choice.

Annotating the Story to Analyze Specific Features

To develop your understanding of a story's possible meanings, you need to analyze its language and structure. This section offers guidance for analyzing a story. Basically, it will help you read and annotate the story, focusing on specific features; take inventory of your annotations to discover possible patterns of meaning; and write to develop your ideas.

　　A good way to focus your analysis of the story is to read it with an eye for certain key features—character, setting, plot, point of view, theme. Ideally, you should read the story several times, each time focusing on a different feature. Review the following features carefully, and choose one to begin with.

　　Annotate as you read, noting all signs of the feature you've chosen to focus on. Write directly on the text or in the margins. The discussion of the features below includes advice on what and how to annotate.

You will find an example of annotating in the A Writer at Work section on pp. 420–23.

Character. Find characters that interest you, and mark all the passages where they appear. Annotate references to their names, physical appearance, personality, and mannerisms; what they say, do, think, and feel; what the narrator and other characters say about them. Consider the possible significance of images and symbols associated with them; think of what each character might stand for, what role each plays in the story. Look for possible ironies in what characters say about themselves or about others. Compare what they say to what they actually think, feel, and do; compare how they think of themselves to how others think of them. Don't expect characters to fit into categories or to be consistent; look for ambiguities and contradictions.

■ *Interpret characters psychologically*: Examine their motivations, their inner conflicts and doubts, whether they change or learn from experience, whether they achieve their desires. Focus on their relationships. Compare and contrast characters. Look for doubles or opposites.

■ *Interpret characters ethically*: Compare and contrast their virtues and vices, their beliefs and values, how their actions correspond to their words.

■ *Interpret characters from a social perspective*: Consider how they fit into and are defined by society—in terms of class, ethnicity, gender, and so on. Ask who in the story has power and knowledge and whether the balance of power shifts at all. Examine any changes in the social dynamic, their possible causes, effects, and significances.

Setting. To analyze the significance of the setting, mark passages where place and time are indicated, noting any scene changes. Highlight visual and other sensory details (shape, color, texture, sounds, smells); references to the weather, season, time of day; patterns of opposition (light/dark, warm/cold, sound/silence, open/closed); figurative language (similes, metaphors, symbols, image patterns, repeated or related words).

■ *Interpret the setting in relation to the action and to the characters*: Consider how it signals what's happening and whether it comments (possibly ironically) on the action. Notice how the setting affects the mood—for example, how it heightens tensions or foreboding. Look for cause/effect connections between the setting and what characters are thinking, doing, or feeling.

■ *Interpret the setting historically or culturally*: Think of how the historical period or cultural context in which the story is set might affect what happens and doesn't happen, and what it all means. Imagine how the meaning might be different if the historical time or cultural situation were different.

■ *Interpret the setting metaphorically or symbolically*: Consider the setting as representing how one of the characters thinks and feels. What would it tell you about that character's state of mind? Also consider what it might imply if the setting symbolized the social or power dynamics in the story.

Plot Structure.   To analyze the plot and its possible meanings, think of the story as a play. Number each act, looking for clues to how it establishes, builds, complicates, or resolves a central conflict. Note where the action rises, where the climax or turning point occurs, and how the story is resolved. Note also whether there's foreshadowing or framing, flashbacks or flashforwards. If there's a subplot, see how it might relate to the main plot.

- *Interpret the plot's realism*: Consider the logic and consistency of the events and whether they can be understood in cause/effect terms. Compare the events to "real life" as you know it.

- *Interpret the plot's aesthetic quality or symbolism*: Think of it as a series of images, more like a collage or a dream than a realistic portrayal of actual events. Look for meaningful patterns in the arrangement of these images.

Point of View.   To analyze how the story's meaning is influenced by its narrative point of view, first identify the "voice" of the text. If the story is told by "I," a character involved in the plot, look closely at what you are told or can infer about her or him: examine what the character knows and how that information is acquired. If the story is narrated by an authorial voice that is not a character in the story, consider how much this narrator knows: Does the narrator have access to all the characters' thoughts, for example, or to only one character's thoughts, or none? What can you infer about the narrator's values and attitudes? Does the narrator seem to reflect or prefer one character's point of view over that of others? Highlight any statements or word choices that might imply the narrator's opinions and judgments. Don't assume consistency, but look for contradictions and apparent misjudgments. Notice what is emphasized and what is played down or omitted altogether.

- *Interpret the point of view in terms of its trustworthiness*: Consider whether the narrator might be blind or biased, where his or her sympathies might lie, what social position the narrator might fit into. Imagine how your interpretation might be affected if the story were narrated from the point of view of a different character—perhaps with a different gender, ethnicity, or social status—or by a narrator with different sympathies.

Traditional Literary Motifs and Themes.   Search the story for recognizable conventions: the rite of passage; the heroic quest for truth or salvation; the clash of cultures, genders, or generations; the fall from innocence; the making of the artist. Look also for traditional literary themes such as the conflict between reality and illusion, hope and disillusionment, the head and the heart, beauty and the beast, nature and society, free will and fate, the past and the present, chaos and order, justice and injustice, the individual and the community.

■ *Interpret the story in terms of the literary motif or theme*: Point to specific places where the motif or theme applies to the story, explaining what it enables you to see and understand about the story. If you are familiar with the motif or theme from other works you have read, you might compare this story to others in order to point out how this story elaborates or varies the motif or theme.

Taking Inventory of Your Annotations

You will find examples of inventorying in A Writer at Work on pp. 420–23 and in Chapter 12.

Look over your annotations and take inventory of them by listing related items in groups on a sheet of paper and then naming the groupings. Try out several different ways of grouping your annotations. By organizing and re-organizing your annotations in this manner, you will begin to discover different patterns of meanings in the story.

Writing to Develop Your Ideas

Analyze your inventory by writing at least a page about the connections and patterns you have discovered. This writing will record what you have learned and may also lead you to further discoveries. As you write, ask yourself what your inventory reveals about the story. Sometimes a story raises more questions than answers. Write down your general conclusions—ideas you can assert confidently as well as questions you cannot yet answer. These reflections may help lead you to a thesis about the story.

Formulating a Tentative Thesis

In approaching the story by examining several different features, you have begun the process of finding a focus for your essay. Your aim now is to consider the possible focuses you have discovered and to formulate a tentative thesis you can support with evidence from the story.

Listing Possible Ideas about the Story.   Try by reviewing the reflections you wrote as you examined each feature. Some will be in the form of ideas, while others will be questions. List the ones that most interest you, those that you would like to explore further. Add to this list any ideas that you now have. Consider how your ideas relate to one another.

Exploring Your Ideas.   Choose what seems to you now to be the most intriguing idea from your list and write about it for five minutes. Focus your exploratory writing on these questions:

■ What will this idea enable me to say about the story's meaning and significance?

■ What in the story will I be able to point to as evidence to support and develop my idea?

If at the end of five minutes you are not satisfied with your choice—satisfied that it allows you to say something intriguing or worthwhile about the story—try exploring another of your ideas. It may take a few tries before you settle on a focus worth taking.

Writing a Tentative Thesis Statement.   When you decide on a focus, put it in the form of a thesis statement. Formulating a thesis, even one that you know will undergo change, will help you to clarify your idea. Pay special attention to the key terms you use. These stand for important concepts you will need to explain and illustrate.

It may help to recall David Ratinov's thesis (the key terms are italicized): " 'Araby' tells the story of an adolescent boy's *initiation* into adulthood [by which] he realizes the parallel between his own *self-delusion* and the *hypocrisy* and *vanity* of the adult world."

For Group Inquiry

At this point you may find it helpful to get together with two or three other students and get some response to one another's thesis statements. One by one, read your thesis aloud, and ask the other members to say what the thesis leads them to expect will be argued in the essay. For example, if you were a member of a group with David Ratinov, you might have said it led you to expect his essay to demonstrate the following ideas: (1) that the boy is self-deluded, (2) that the adults are hypocritical or vain, and (3) that the boy ultimately realizes he is like the adults.

Finding Evidence

Having settled on a tentative thesis, you now need to marshal evidence to see whether you can support it. You will find this evidence in the story and in your annotations, inventories, and exploratory writings about the inventories. After identifying evidence, you can begin to organize and evaluate it.

With your thesis in mind, search for evidence that will support it. Note and annotate everything you can find that seems relevant to your thesis—dialogue, events, descriptive details, key words, images. If you find evidence that seems to contradict your thesis, do not ignore it. Instead, let it lead you to clarify and revise your thesis.

Organizing Your Evidence.   The evidence you've discovered already may be organized in a certain way. You may now, however, see different ways to organize it. Or you may have identified new evidence that you overlooked in your earlier work. Your goal is only to begin grouping evidence, rather than to organize it precisely, since you cannot predict the exact sequence of your argument at this point.

Evaluating Your Evidence.   Determine whether you have sufficient evidence to support your thesis and develop a convincing argument for your particular readers. Also test the fit between your ideas and the available evidence. If you have trouble supporting your thesis or fitting evidence to it logically, you will need to revise your thesis or try out a different one.

PLANNING AND DRAFTING

You now need to review your notes, set goals, and make an outline before writing a first draft.

Seeing What You Have

It's a good idea at this point to print out a hard copy of what you have written on a word processor for easier reviewing.

Review your notes. If you wish or need to, reread the story. As you review what you have discovered about it, ask yourself these questions:

- Can I express my thesis more clearly?
- What are my reasons for holding this thesis?
- Can my evidence be interpreted in some other way?
- Have I overlooked any important evidence?
- Have I glossed over or ignored any contradictions or problems?

Postpone starting to draft if you find problems that still need to be worked out.

Setting Goals

Before you start to draft, consider the special demands of literary interpretation and of the story you are interpreting. Let the following questions guide you in setting goals for what you want to achieve in your essay and how you can meet these demands:

Your Readers

- Are my readers likely to know this story? If not, how much of the plot should I relate? If so, how can I lead them to see the story as I do?
- How can I organize the essay so that my readers will find it easy to follow? What cues can I provide about my organization and sequence? How can I integrate quotations?
- What questions or objections might my readers raise about my interpretation?

The Beginning

- Must I begin by describing the work for readers who have not read it?
- Should I state my thesis and forecast my plan, as Crane and Ratinov do?

The Argument

■ Is my thesis clear enough to act as the focus for all parts of my argument? Have I used key terms that forecast ideas I will develop in my argument?

■ How can my argument be considered authoritative and at the same time thoughtful and reasonable?

■ Is the tentative organization of the main parts of my argument logical? Have I arranged the evidence so that each new bit of evidence will build on earlier ones, making the argument convincing as a whole?

■ How much textual evidence must I include in order for my argument to seem informed and convincing?

■ Should I acknowledge readers' possible objections to my argument or differing interpretations, as Crane does?

The Ending

■ Should I repeat my key terms, as the writers in this chapter do?

■ Should I restate my thesis?

■ Should I end with a provocative question suggested by an analysis of the story?

Outlining

Outlining on a word processor makes it easy to experiment with ways of ordering information.

At this point you should try to develop a plan for your draft. You may compose a formal outline, a simple list of key points, or a clustering diagram. Whichever method you choose, remember that an outline is only a tentative plan; if you have other thoughts while drafting, try them out.

Drafting

If you can shift between screens, you might call up invention material on an alternate screen as you draft on the main screen, shifting back and forth to cut and paste invention material into your draft.

If some time has gone by since you last read the story, reread it quickly. Then begin to draft, keeping in mind the two goals of all literary analysis: presenting your interpretation and supporting that interpretation with textual evidence. Try to be as direct as you can. Explain your ideas fully. Make the relations between the thesis, the points you use to develop it, and the supporting evidence explicit for readers. Remember that they will have different ways of understanding the passages you refer to. Show them how you are using specific evidence from the work to make your own point about it. You might want to review the general advice on drafting on pp. 12–14.

GETTING CRITICAL COMMENTS

Now is the time to try to get a good critical reading. All writers find it helpful to have someone else read and comment on their drafts, and your instructor may schedule such a reading as part of your coursework. Otherwise, you can ask a classmate, friend, or family member to read it over. If your campus has a writing center, you might ask a tutor there to read and comment on your draft. The guidelines that follow are designed to be used by *anyone* reviewing an essay interpreting a story. (If you are unable to have someone else read over your draft, turn ahead to the Revision section on pp. 416–19, which gives guidelines for reading your own draft with a critical eye.)

In order to provide focused, helpful comments, your reader must know your intended audience and purpose. The reader must also have read the story you were writing about. Attach a copy of the story to your draft if you think your reader may not already have one, and briefly write out answers to the following questions at the top of your draft:

Audience. What do you expect your readers will think about the story? How might they react to your interpretation?

Purpose. What do you want your readers to learn about the story from reading your essay?

Reading with a Critical Eye

Reading an essay critically means reading it more than once, first to get a general impression and then to analyze its basic features.

Reading for a First Impression.   Read first to grasp the interpretation. As you read, notice any passages that are particularly well-written and convincing as well as any that seem especially weak. After you've finished reading the draft, briefly write out your impressions. Summarize what you think the essay says about the story, and indicate whether you think this interpretation makes sense. If your view of the story differs, you might indicate briefly how you interpret it.

See Chapter 12 for a review of critical reading strategies.

See pp. 407–08 for an explanation of the basic features.

Reading to Analyze.   Now reread to focus on the basic features of interpretive writing.

Is the Thesis Clear and Effective?

Identify the thesis statement. Do any of the key terms seem unclear or unworkable? Number the ideas expressed in the thesis and then skim the rest of the essay, identifying by number where each idea is developed. Note any ideas that do not reappear or are only identified vaguely. Also note any important ideas that should be added to the thesis.

Is the Argument Developed and Supported Adequately?

Take each point in turn. Note where an idea could be developed further. Also note where evidence from the story is lacking or where the evidence could be more explicitly connected to the idea it is supposed to illustrate.

Is the Argument Logical?

Does any idea seem to contradict the thesis or other ideas? Note where logical connections between ideas could be strengthened. Also note any places where there are gaps in the logic, where connecting ideas appear to be left out.

Is the Organization Effective?

Note any places where the argument is confusing or hard to follow. Point out places where the order of the evidence weakens the argument because new ideas do not build on previously stated ones. Look again at the *beginning* and note whether it adequately anticipates the rest of the essay. Look at the *ending* and note whether it is too abrupt or raises too many new ideas.

What Final Thoughts Do You Have?

What do you find best about this draft? Which part of the draft needs the most work?

REVISING AND EDITING

This section will help you to identify problems in your draft and to revise and edit to solve them.

To identify problems in your draft, you need to get an overview of it, analyze its basic features, and study any critical comments you've received from other readers.

Identifying Problems

Getting an Overview.   First consider the draft as a whole, trying to see it objectively. Two simple steps will help you begin to look somewhat objectively at your own writing:

Even if your essay is saved to a computer file, reread from a hard copy, preferably draft quality. Onscreen or as letter-quality hard copy, a paper can look more "finished" than it really is. Add notes to yourself and quick revisions as you read through the draft.

Reread. If at all possible, put the draft aside for a day or two before rereading it. When you do, start by reconsidering your purpose. Then read the draft straight through, trying to see it as your intended readers will.

Outline. Make a scratch outline to get an overview of the essay's development. This outline can be sketchy—words and phrases instead of complete sentences—but it should identify the basic features as they appear.

Charting a Plan for Revision.   You may wish to make a chart like the one below to keep track of any problems you need to solve. The left-hand column lists the basic features of writing interpretations of stories. As you analyze your draft and study any comments you've gotten, note the problems you want to solve in the right-hand column next to the appropriate feature.

Basic Features	*Problems to Solve*
Thesis	
Argument	
Organization	

Analyzing the Basic Features of Your Draft.   Turn now to the questions for analyzing a draft on pp. 415–16. Using these as guidelines, identify problems in your draft. Note anything you need to solve on the preceding chart.

Studying Critical Comments.   Review any comments you've received from other readers, and add to the chart any points that need attention. Try not to react too defensively to these comments; by letting you see how others respond to your draft, they provide invaluable information about how you might improve it.

Solving the Problems

Before revising using a word processor, copy your original draft to a second file. Then, should you change your mind about material you delete while revising, it will still be available to you.

Having identified problems, you now need to discover solutions and carry them out. Basically, you have three ways of finding solutions: (1) review your invention and planning notes for additional information and ideas; (2) do further invention to answer questions your readers raised; and (3) look back at the readings in this chapter to see how other writers have solved similar problems.

Following are suggestions to get you started solving some of the problems common to writing interpretations of stories. For now, focus on solving those problems identified on your chart. Avoid tinkering with sentence-level issues; that will come later when you edit.

The Thesis

- If the thesis statement is hard to identify, make it more explicit. Be sure that you have announced your main idea somewhere in the essay.
- If the key terms in the thesis don't match the points developed in the argument, revise the thesis or consider adding, deleting, or revising something in the argument.

The Argument

- If an idea seems undeveloped, try discussing it more—break it into subordinate ideas and discuss them, say what it tells about the story as a whole, compare or contrast it with related ideas. Also consider providing a theoretical framework to help explain the idea—for example, discussing character development by using psychoanalytical terms or discussing the power relationships among characters by using Marxist terms.
- If evidence seems lacking, add detail by quoting, paraphrasing, or summarizing parts of the story. Consider using other kinds of evidence, such as information about the story's historical or cultural context.
- If the connection between an idea and evidence seems vague, clarify it by explaining why you think the evidence illustrates or supports the idea. Don't just quote from the story. Explain how you interpret the quotation, which words seem significant, and how they support the point you're making.

■ If there are contradictions in the argument or the evidence, you may need to rethink, reorganize, or rewrite whole sections of your essay. Consider whether you can eliminate apparent contradictions by explaining more clearly how your ideas support your thesis.

■ If there are gaps in the logic or missing connections, fill them in. Remember that your readers cannot follow your train of thought unless you lay it out for them.

The Organization

Use your word processor's cut-and-paste or block-and-move functions to shift material around. Make sure that transitions are revised so that material fits in its new spot.

■ If the essay is hard to follow, you may need to provide more explicit cues, such as topic sentences for paragraphs, transitions between paragraphs and sentences, or brief forecasts and summaries to let readers know where they're going and where they've been.

■ If the beginning doesn't adequately prepare readers, you may need to revise it to better forecast your ideas.

■ If the ending seems abrupt, you may need to tie all the strands of the essay together, reiterate your thesis, or discuss its implications.

Editing and Proofreading

Now is the time to check your draft for matters of usage, punctuation, mechanics, and style. Research into student papers done for this chapter has revealed two common problems worth checking for: parallel structure (a matter of style) and ellipses (a matter of punctuation). Following are some guidelines designed to help you check your draft for these common problems.

When you use your word processor's spell check function to aid in proofreading for spelling, keep in mind that it will not find all misspellings, particularly misused homonyms (such as there, their, and they're), typos that are themselves words (such as fro for for), and many proper nouns and specialized terms. Proofread these carefully yourself, using hard copy and a dictionary if necessary. Also proofread for words that should have been deleted when you edited a sentence.

Checking for Parallelism in Your Writing.   When you present similar items together, they should be presented in similar grammatical form. All items in a series should be parallel in form—all nouns, all prepositional phrases, all adverb clauses, and so on. See, for example, how Sally Crane edited her first-draft sentences to introduce parallel structure.

▶ I believe, however, that the boy sees nothing and ~~is incapable of learning~~ about himself or others ~~because he is so~~ self-absorbed.   *learns nothing —either* / *He's not self-reflective, he's merely*

▶ This image comes more from ~~his reading~~ than from ~~his actual observation.~~   *what he's read* / *anything he's observed.*

▶ The greatest irony comes at the end when his quest is exposed as merely a shopping trip, *and Araby as merely a suburban mall.*

The parallelism makes Crane's sentences easier to read and helps give emphasis to some of her points. The parallelism of "sees nothing" and "learns nothing" emphasizes the relationship between these two realities in a way that the first-draft wording did not; the same is true of "what he's read" and "anything he's observed." The final sentence shows an example of how Crane adds a parallel phrase to add an ironic comment. Following are several more examples, each edited to show ways of making writing parallel.

▶ To Kafka, loneliness, ~~being isolated,~~ *isolation,* and regrets are the price of freedom.

▶ Sarah really cares about her brother and ~~to maintain~~ *values* their relationship.

▶ She lets us know that she was injured by her mother's abuse but avoids saying what she felt after the incident, how others reacted to the incident, and ~~the~~ *what* physical pain she endured.

Checking Your Use of Ellipses.   Ellipses are three spaced periods. They are used to indicate that something has been omitted from quoted text. You will often quote other sources when you interpret a story, and you must be careful to use ellipses to indicate places where you delete material from a quotation. Look, for example, at some text from "Araby" and then at the way Sally Crane uses ellipses in quoting from it.

Original Text

North Richmond Street, being blind, was a quiet street except at the hour when the Christian Brothers' School set the boys free. An uninhabited house of two storeys stood at the blind end, detached from its neighbours in a square ground.

With Ellipses

The street is "blind," with an "uninhabited house . . . at the blind end. . . ."

The ellipses indicate two omissions—one in the middle of the sentence and one at the end. When you omit the last part of a quoted sentence, add a period before the ellipses—for a total of four dots.

There are just a few simple rules to remember about using ellipses:

- When you delete a full sentence or more in the middle of a quoted passage, use a period before the three ellipses.
- Never use ellipses at the beginning of a quotation.
- Use ellipses at the end of a quotation only when you cut some words from the end of the final sentence quoted.
- Single-space before and after each ellipsis point.
- Single words and brief phrases can be quoted without ellipses.

Here are some edited student sentences about "Araby":

▶ We learn that a former tenant of the boy's house, ". . . a priest, had died in the back drawing-room . . . He had been a very charitable priest; in his will he had left all his money to institutions and the furniture of his house to his sister."

▶ The boy lived on "a quiet street . . ."

▶ The light shone on ". . . the white border of a petticoat . . ."

A Writer at Work

ANNOTATING AND INVENTORYING A LITERARY WORK

Annotating and taking inventory of annotations are basic tools for understanding and interpreting short stories. Used with various traditional approaches to analyzing stories, they provide an instructive strategy of critical
reading, inquiry, and interpretation. Here you can see a portion of the results
of one student's annotation and inventory of "Araby." The student is David
Ratinov, whose essay appears earlier in this chapter on pages 403–05.

Ratinov chose two features to analyze in "Araby": (1) character and character change, and (2) literary motifs. Following the instructions in the Guide
to Writing, he reread the story and annotated it from these two perspectives,
took inventory to discover connections and ideas among his annotations,
wrote briefly about his discoveries, and then wrote several generalizations
asserting his ideas about the story. One of these generalizations led to the
thesis you see in his essay.

Here are Ratinov's annotations on paragraphs 13 through 24. Notice the
diversity of his annotations. On the text itself, he underlines key words, circles
words to be defined, and connects related words and ideas. In the margin,
he defines words, makes comments, poses questions, and expresses tentative
insights, personal reactions, and judgments.

2nd mention of uncle fussing—vain? irritable? rude	On Saturday morning I reminded my <u>uncle</u> that I wished to go to the bazaar in the evening. He was fussing at the hallstand, looking for the hatbrush, and answered me (curtly:)
always unkind to the boy? uncle's effect on the boy	"Yes, boy, I know." As he was in the hall I could not go into the front parlour and lie at the window. I left the house in bad humour and walked slowly towards the school. The air was pitilessly raw and already my <u>heart misgave me</u>.
uncle will be late	When I came home to dinner my uncle had not yet been home. Still it was early.
sudden change in mood: *big* contrast	I <u>sat staring</u> at the clock for some time and, when its ticking began to <u>irritate</u> me, I left the room. I mounted the staircase and gained the upper part of the house. The
liberated from uncle?	high cold empty gloomy rooms liberated me and I went from room to room singing. From the front window I saw my companions playing below in the street. Their cries
isolated from friends	reached me weakened and indistinct and, leaning my forehead against the cool glass, I looked over at the dark house where she lived. I may have stood there for an hour, seeing nothing but the brown-clad figure cast by my imagination, touched
romantic, even sensual	discreetly by the <u>lamplight</u> at the <u>curved neck</u>, at the hand upon the railings and at the border <u>below the dress</u>.

merchandise

talkative

hypocritically religious

boy doesn't seem to like
or trust the adults

uncle and Mercer both
try to give a false im-
pression
aunt seems pious too

boy knows uncle is
drunk
boy's fears are justified
excuses

aunt to the rescue

hypocritical
what a bore!
boy determined to go to
bazaar to buy girl a gift

boy focused on his task

language shows boy's
impatience

boy still isolated

When I came downstairs again I found Mrs. Mercer sitting at the fire. She was an old garrulous woman, a pawnbroker's widow, who collected used stamps for some pious purpose. I had to endure the gossip of the tea-table. The meal was prolonged beyond an hour and still my uncle did not come. Mrs. Mercer stood up to go: she was sorry she couldn't wait any longer, but it was after eight o'clock and she did not like to be out late, as the night air was bad for her. When she had gone I began to walk up and down the room, clenching my fists. My aunt said:

"I'm afraid you may put off your bazaar for this night of Our Lord."

At nine o'clock I heard my uncle's latchkey in the halldoor. I heard him talking to himself and heard the hallstand rocking when it had received the weight of his overcoat. I could interpret these signs. When he was midway through his dinner I asked him to give me the money to go to the bazaar. He had forgotten.

"The people are in bed and after their first sleep now," he said.

I did not smile. My aunt said to him energetically:

"Can't you give him the money and let him go? You've kept him late enough as it is."

My uncle said he was very sorry he had forgotten. He said he believed in the old saying: "All work and no play makes Jack a dull boy." He asked me where I was going and, when I had told him a second time he asked me did I know *The Arab's Farewell to his Steed*. When I left the kitchen he was about to recite the opening lines of the piece to my aunt.

I held a florin tightly in my hands as I strode down Buckingham Street towards the station. The sight of the streets thronged with buyers and glaring with gas recalled to me the purpose of my journey. I took my seat in a third-class carriage of a deserted train. After an intolerable delay the train moved out of the station slowly. It crept onward among ruinous houses and over the twinkling river. At Westland Row Station a crowd of people pressed to the carriage doors; but the porters moved them back, saying that it was a special train for the bazaar. I remained alone in the bare carriage. In a few minutes the train drew up beside an improvised wooden platform. I passed out on to the road and saw by the lighted dial of a clock that it was ten minutes to ten. In front of me was a large building which displayed the magical name.

Annotating the story to analyze the boy's character, Ratinov finds himself paying a lot of attention to the boy's relations with other characters. Taking inventory of these annotations for the entire story, he notices how negatively the narrator portrays the priest, Mrs. Mercer, and the uncle. He decides that what these characters have in common is hypocrisy. This notion would become a key term in his thesis and a major idea in his essay. In his essay, of course, he would have to prove with textual evidence that all these minor characters are hypocrites. In addition, he would have to be sure that no textual evidence challenged this idea.

Here Ratinov tries to organize his textual and marginal annotations in paragraphs 13 through 24 under the idea of hypocrisy:

```
adult hypocrisy
Mrs. Mercer
  name means "merchandise"
  pious--a religious hypocrite
  widow of pawnbroker--makes money by lending money to
      poor people for their possessions
  collected stamps--to sell for a church charity?
  gossip--talk about others behind their backs
Uncle
  a banker or manager
  brushes hat--obsessive about appearance
  fussy, vain, irritable, curt
  boy distrusts him, hides from him, seems to have no
      real relationship with him*
  lives in a big house only partly furnished and heated
  drinks, often drunk--Irish habit or stress of social
      pretense?
  "all work and no play"--uncle is the player--plays at
      social status, vain about appearance; also "plays"
      in bar (pub?) every night (most nights?)
  lets boy down--can't be trusted, irresponsible,
      insensitive to the boy's feelings, forgets,
      doesn't keep promises*

  *irresponsibility, not hypocrisy
```

You can see that Ratinov labels this portion of his inventory with the connection he makes among the adult characters. He then lists relevant annotations under the characters' names. (Ratinov also inventoried information about the priest, but it is not included here because the priest is not mentioned in paragraphs 13 through 24.) Many inventories of text annotations use labels and lists in this way. The labels indicate connections, patterns, or ideas about the story. The lists bring together annotations relevant to the labels.

To analyze his inventory, Ratinov writes these sentences about the section on hypocrisy:

```
Mrs. Mercer may be a good neighbor to the boy's aunt, but
the boy dislikes her.  Joyce plants many clues that she
```

```
is a hypocrite.  She thinks of herself as a good relig-
ious Christian, but she is pious (an exaggerated Chris-
tian, not a believable one), collects stamps to sell for
charity instead of doing good works firsthand (my guess),
and she is a gossip.  Her husband got his money in an un-
christian way.  Does the boy know all this or only the
narrator much later?  I'm sure the boy senses it.  He
says he has to endure Mrs. Mercer and her gossip with his
aunt.  Now that I look over the evidence for the uncle's
hypocrisy, it seems that his unguardianlike actions to-
ward the boy, his irresponsibility toward him, is just as
big a flaw as his hypocrisy.  He seems to be trying to
hide something by drinking and being obsessive about his
appearance--a failure to advance at work?  He tries to
impress people with a bigger house than he can afford.
Says he believes in things that don't apply to his own
actions.  I think I can show that he's a hypocrite like
Mrs. Mercer.  Because the boy distrusts him, he must
sense this hypocrisy.
```

Writing about this portion of his inventory enables Ratinov to try out his ideas about hypocrisy. He confirms that the term itself is workable for discussing the story and that the evidence in the text supports the idea of hypocrisy. He also makes the important discovery that some annotations listed under the uncle concern his irresponsibility, so he goes back to the inventory to asterisk these items. This discovery leads in his essay to a more complex presentation of the uncle as a flawed adult inadvertently teaching lessons the boy will discover at the Araby bazaar.

After completing his written analysis of his annotations about the boy's relations with other characters, Ratinov writes several concluding ideas about what he discovered.

```
All the adult characters are hypocrites.

If this is just a story about romance, then all the adult
characters wouldn't have to be so weak and flawed.

Mangan's sister is different from the adults, but through
her he has to face up to what the adult world is all
about.

The adults are initiating the boy into adulthood, but he
doesn't see it until the end of the story.

Growing up means being able to see the world for what it
actually is, not what you want it to be.
```

From these ideas about initiation, epiphany, romance, and hypocrisy, Ratinov devised the thesis for his essay.

Thinking Critically about What You've Learned

Having read and discussed several essays interpreting a story as well as having written such an essay yourself, you're in a good position now to think critically about what you've learned. What problems did you encounter as you were writing, and how did you solve them? How did the essays you read influence your own writing? How does the genre of literary interpretation reflect social and cultural attitudes about stories and their meanings?

REFLECTING ON YOUR WRITING

Begin by gathering your invention and planning notes, drafts and critical comments, revising plan, and final revision. Review these as you complete the following writing task. Identify *one* significant writing problem you encountered while writing the essay. Don't be concerned with sentence-level problems; focus on a problem specific to writing an interpretation. For example: Were you uncertain about which features to analyze? Did you wonder how best to state your thesis and forecast your argument? Did you have trouble deciding which passages from the story to quote as evidence?

- How did you first recognize this problem? Was it, for example, when you were trying to analyze the story, thinking about how to sequence your ideas, or getting critical comments on a draft? What called the problem to your attention? Looking back, do you see signs of it in your early invention work? If so, where specifically?

- Reflect on how you solved the problem. If it arose during invention, did you try looking at a different feature? Did you discuss the feature you were analyzing with another student or your instructor? If it arose during drafting, did you do further invention to solve the problem—perhaps rereading the story or examining your original annotations to see what you omitted or thinking of other ways to connect your ideas to one another? If you noticed the problem as you were revising, did you reword, reorganize, or simply cut the part that was problematic? Did you review your invention notes or reread a part of the story to analyze it further?

- Now, write a page or so explaining to your instructor what the problem was, how you discovered it, and how you went about solving it. Be specific by quoting from your invention writing, drafts, others' critical comments, your own revision plan, and your final revision. Show the various changes your writing and thinking underwent. If you're still uncertain about your solution, say so. The point is not to prove that you've solved the problem but to show what you've learned about solving problems in the process of writing.

REVIEWING WHAT YOU LEARNED FROM READING

You've read several essays interpreting a story—the two selections on "Araby" and possibly also one or more student drafts on another story. Reading essays interpreting a story has probably influenced the essay you wrote.

- To reflect on the possible influence your reading may have had on your own thinking and writing, review the readings in this chapter as well as your own essay. Consider whether any of the essays in the chapter or by your classmates influenced your choice of approach or your way of organizing the essay. Look for ideas you got from your reading or writing strategies you were inspired to try. For example, did one of the essays suggest a way you could state your thesis clearly and emphatically, forecast your main points, use quotations to support your argument, or anticipate readers' questions? Did one help you decide how to introduce your evidence or how to separate and develop each idea?

- Write a page or so explaining to your instructor how your writing has been influenced by others. You may focus on a single influence or discuss what you learned from parts of different essays. Give examples, showing how you've built on what you've seen other writers do. You might also point out anything you'd now change in your essay, based on this review of the other readings.

CONSIDERING THE SOCIAL DIMENSIONS OF ESSAYS INTERPRETING STORIES

Apart from the pleasure of a good read, perhaps the most compelling reason for reading stories is that it brings us more in touch with ourselves and with others. Sometimes we see in stories reflections of our own experience; we especially enjoy reading these stories because we identify with the characters and situations. Most of us also enjoy reading stories about other people and places. We take pleasure in expanding our horizon, getting a glimpse of how other people's experience differs from our own. Sometimes, however, stories don't simply divert us: they also challenge us—making us see how we could improve ourselves as well as the society in which we live.

If, like most people, you read stories primarily for pleasure, you may be wondering why you should go to all the trouble of analyzing and interpreting stories as demonstrated in this chapter. The more we read, the more we realize that the pleasures we take in reading a story include not only being moved by the plot and intrigued by the characters but also discovering "meanings" that lie beneath the surface. Serious literary texts are constructed with great care, with intense imagination, and with a sensitivity to nuances of language that may not even be consciously recognized by their writers. Thoughtful, analytical readers can tease out meanings that expand our appreciation of these works. Interpreting, as we hope you've discovered, can not only be rewarding, but also fun. It's a kind of intellectual play that can heighten the pleasure of reading. To see why this is so, we need to think about how language, particularly literary language, works and how we make sense of it.

Language and Meaning.   Readers often think of reading as deciphering the writer's message as if the black marks on the page were a code. Linguists have shown that this way of thinking about language is true—to some degree. Writers and readers who speak the same language, who belong to the same culture, do share a linguistic code, but that code is varied and complex. There is no simple, one-to-one correspondence between a word and its meaning. Words are by nature ambiguous; they have multiple meanings, and numerous shadings. No single meaning can be said to be exactly the *right* one although a case can be made for some meanings being more plausible or useful than others.

Even asking the author what he or she meant does not guarantee that we'll discover what the story *really* means. We know from our own writing experience that writers wrestle with words to figure out what they want to say and that their intended meaning may not be fully communicated to every reader or even clear to themselves. Writers generally expect readers to find a profusion of possible meanings in their stories.

Like writers, readers, in effect, rewrite the text as they read, constructing a mental representation of it based on their associations with particular words and images. This is especially true for literary writing, which is typically rich in figurative and evocative language.

Assumptions about Stories.   Interpreting stories leads us to make a number of assumptions about stories that should be examined with a critical eye. The most basic assumption is that stories do, in fact, convey meaning. Some artists and critics claim that a work of art doesn't convey anything; it just is. This idea might be easier to accept for abstract art than for stories that realistically portray life experience. When we read a story, we seem "naturally" to look for characters, situations, and themes we recognize and relate to. But in this case, what feels natural is really learned. From early childhood, we are taught to extract meaning from fairy tales, parables, fables, and family stories. We are taught to look for correspondences between stories and real life.

We are also taught that authors are authoritative, that their precepts are wise and worth following. This assumption about the author's authority encourages us to assume that if we could know what the author intended, we would understand the meaning of the story.

At the same time, it encourages us to be passive readers, playing the role of the child obediently taking in the author's wisdom. But if the process of interpretation, as we said before, inevitably involves the reader's construction of meaning, then we cannot be passive.

Interpreting, as we've suggested throughout this chapter, is anything but passive. As a reader, you may analyze the story's language for figurative as well as literal meanings. You may think critically about characters' motivations and relationships. You may question what you are told by a narrator (who seems to speak with the authority of the author). You may be suspicious of endings that seem too pat or reductive. You may think of meanings in broad social and political terms. In other words, you may discover no single, fixed meaning but rather multiple, perhaps contradictory, meanings. You may find this discovery exciting, but it may also leave you with more questions than answers.

Because readers assume that stories bear some relation to real life, they also assume characters will behave as we people do—in a way that makes sense psychologically and is consistent with their personality or "essential" self. You may remember that in thinking critically about autobiographical writing in Chapter 2, we invited you to consider the possibility that there is no single essence that defines the self. Instead, the self might be constituted by the many, different roles we play in different situations. If this way of thinking about the self is useful, then we might want to think of literary characters differently too. We might be less inclined to interpret characters in static terms and be more inclined to see them in terms of the social and cultural roles they play.

For Discussion

Following are some questions to stimulate your thinking and discussion about analyzing and interpreting stories. Note down your thoughts in case your instructor asks you to write a page reflecting on what you have learned.

1. In discussing the relation between language and meaning, we've suggested that the process of reading is inevitably a process of interpretation because language is essentially ambiguous. Words simply invite multiple meanings and associations, and this is especially true of "literary" language, which as we said is heavily nuanced and evocative. For some readers, interpreting is fun; but others find the uncertainty discomforting. They may be unhappy because they associate ambiguity with lack of clarity, having been taught to value clarity and coherence in writing. Another possible reason for discomfort is that readers may associate ambiguity with relativism in politics and morality.

Examine your own and your classmates' attitudes about ambiguity. To what degree are you uncomfortable with the possibility that a story has no single "right" meaning? How do you account for your own feelings about ambiguity? How do you understand other people's feelings?

2. If there's no one indisputably "right" interpretation—not even the author's—how do we decide which interpretations have merit? Reflect on your experience interpreting stories for high school and college classes, including those you read and wrote about for this assignment. When you were planning and writing your own essay, did you consider more than one interpretation? If so, how did you decide which one to develop? How do you think your instructor—and how do you—evaluate an interpretation of a story? What is the basis you think should be used for deciding whether an interpretation is strong or weak, more or less convincing?

3. Examine critically the related assumptions that stories represent real-life experience and that reading stories can tell us something about life. Use one of the stories you read in this chapter as a test case: ask yourself how the situation in this story differs from real life, and how the characters differ from real people. On reflection, what seem to be the limitations of thinking of this story as though it were the same as an experience that actually happened? How can we talk about a story's relation to social reality if we recognize that it is really only words on a page?

PART TWO

Critical Thinking Strategies

Writers are like scientists: they ask questions, systematically inquiring about how things work, what they are, where they occur, and how more information can be learned about them. Writers are also like artists using what they know and learn to create something new and imaginative.

The invention and inquiry strategies described in this chapter are not mysterious or magical. They are tricks of the trade available to everyone and should appeal to your common sense and experience in solving problems. Developed by writers, psychologists, and linguists, they represent the ways writers, engineers, scientists, composers—in fact, all of us—creatively solve problems.

Once you've mastered these strategies, you can use them to tackle any writing situation you encounter in college or on the job. The best way to learn them is to use them as you write an actual essay. Part I, Chapters 2–10, shows you when these strategies can be most helpful and how to make the most efficient use of them. The guides to invention and research in these chapters offer easy-to-use adaptations of these general strategies, adaptations designed to satisfy the special requirements of each kind of writing.

The strategies for invention and inquiry in this chapter are grouped into two categories:

Mapping: a brief visual representation of your thinking or planning

Writing: the composition of phrases or sentences to discover information and ideas and to make connections among them

These invention and inquiry strategies can give you powerful help in the thinking and planning you need to do as a writer. They will help you to explore and research a topic fully before you begin drafting and then to solve problems as you are drafting and revising. In this chapter strategies are arranged alphabetically within each of the three categories.

MAPPING

Mapping involves making a visual record of invention and inquiry. Many writers find their mapping helps them think about a topic. In making maps, they usually use key words and phrases to record material they want to remember, questions they need to answer, and even new sources of information

A Catalog of 11
Invention Strategies

they want to check. The maps show the ideas, details, and facts they are examining. They also show possible ways materials can be connected and focused. Maps might be informal graphic displays with words and phrases circled and connected by lines to show relationships, or they might be formal sentence outlines. Mapping can be especially useful because it provides visual representation of your thinking and planning. Mapping strategies include clustering, listing, and outlining.

Clustering

Clustering is a strategy for revealing possible relations among facts and ideas. Unlike listing (the next mapping strategy), clustering requires a brief period of initial planning. You must first come up with a tentative division of the topic into subparts or main ideas. Clustering works as follows:

1. In a word or phrase, write your topic in the center of a piece of paper. Circle it.

2. Also in a word or phrase, write down the main parts or central ideas of your topic. Circle these, and connect them to the topic in the center.

3. The next step is to generate facts, details, examples, or ideas related in any way to these main parts. Cluster these around the main parts.

Clustering can be useful for any kind of writing. You can use it in the early stages of planning an essay in order to find subtopics and to organize information. You may try and discard several clusters before finding one that is promising. Many writers use clustering to plan brief sections of an essay as they are drafting or revising. (A model of clustering is on the next page.)

Listing

Listing is a familiar activity. We make shopping lists and lists of errands to do or people to call. Listing can also be a great help in planning an essay. It enables you to recall what you already know about a topic and suggests what more you may need to find out. It is an easy way to get started doing something productive, instead of just worrying about what you will write. A list rides along on its own momentum, the first item leading naturally to the next.

Listing is a basic activity for writers, especially useful for those who have little time for planning—for example, reporters facing deadlines or college

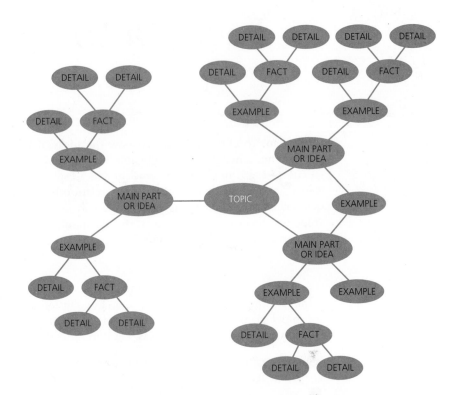

students taking essay exams. Listing lets you order your ideas quickly. It can also help as a first step in discovering possible writing topics.

Listing is a solitary form of brainstorming, a popular technique of problem solving in groups. If you were working with a group to generate ideas for a collaborative writing project, then you would be engaged in true brainstorming. Here is how listing works best for invention work: (1) Give your list a title that indicates your main idea or topic. (2) Write as fast as you can, in short phrases. (3) Include anything that seems *at all* useful. Do not try to be judgmental at this point. (4) After you have finished, or even as you write, reflect on the list and organize it in the following way. This is a very important step, for it may lead you to further discoveries about your topic.

Put an asterisk by the most promising items.

Number key items in order of importance.

Put items in related groups.

Cross out items that do not seem promising.

Add new items.

Outlining Outlining, like listing and clustering, is both a way of planning and a means of inventing. An outline may, of course, be used to organize an essay. Yet, as soon as you start making an outline, you begin to see new possibilities in your subject, discovering new ways of dividing or grouping information and seeing where you need additional information to develop your ideas. Outlining also lets you see at a glance whether your plan is appropriate.

There are three main forms of outlining: scratch, topic, and sentence. (Keep in mind that clustering is also a way of outlining.)

A scratch outline is an informal outline, really only a rough list of the main points (and sometimes subpoints as well) of an essay. You have no doubt made scratch outlines many times—both to clarify difficult reading and to plan essays or essay exams. As an example, here is a *scratch outline* for Victor Fuchs's essay in Chapter 9.

> SUICIDE AMONG YOUNG PEOPLE
>
> death rate rising for 15–24 years olds
>
> mainly more murders and suicides
>
> why more suicides?—not a result of new ways of reporting suicides or of Vietnam War or of bad economy
>
> causes probably in family—divorce, no discipline, loss of father
>
> increase in suicide really is unique to this age group
>
> no simple solution possible

Fuchs may have made such a scratch outline before he began drafting his essay. Notice that the items in a scratch outline do not necessarily coincide with paragraphs. Sometimes two or more items may be developed in the same paragraph or one item may represent two or more paragraphs. (A different scratch outline emphasizing strategies of causal analysis rather than content follows Fuchs's essay on p. 351.)

Scratch outlines are especially helpful for organizing information while you are still gathering it and for deciding how to revise an essay after it has been drafted. The writing guide for each chapter in Part I reminds you when you might use scratch outlining most profitably.

Topic and sentence outlines are more formal than scratch outlines. They follow a conventional format of numbered and lettered headings and subheadings. Some instructors require such an outline with term or research papers. Following is a *topic outline* of Fuchs's essay:

> SUICIDE AMONG YOUNG PEOPLE
>
> I. Increasing death rate in the 15–24 age group
> II. Increase explained by self-destructive behavior
>   A. Homicide
>   B. Suicide
> III. Unacceptable causes of the increase
>   A. Change in reporting of suicides
>   B. Attitudes toward Vietnam War
>   C. Unemployment and weak economy

IV. Probable causes of the increase
    A. Divorce or lack of discipline
    B. Loss of father
 V. Increase in suicides unique to 15–24 age group
VI. Challenge of this problem for public policy

Notice that the Roman numerals and capital letters are followed by periods. Topic outlines contain words or brief phrases, not sentences. Items are not followed by a period, but the first word is capitalized. It is customary for items at the same level of indentation to be grammatically parallel. Under item IV, for instance, the A and B items both begin with nouns:

A. *Divorce* or lack of discipline
B. *Loss* of father

The items would not be grammatically parallel if B began with an infinitive phrase (*to* plus a verb), like this:

A. *Divorce* or lack of discipline
B. *To lose* a father

Here is a *sentence outline* of Fuchs's essay. Each item is a complete sentence, the first word capitalized and the last word followed by a period.

SUICIDE AMONG YOUNG PEOPLE
   I. The death rate is rising only for Americans in the age group 15–24.
  II. This increase is a result of self-destructive behavior.
    A. The homicide rate is rising in the 15–24 age group, especially among blacks.
    B. The suicide rate is also increasing.
 III. Many explanations have been offered for the increasing suicide rate.
    A. The trend is not the result of a change in ways of reporting suicides.
    B. The trend cannot be explained by attitudes toward the Vietnam War.
    C. The trend cannot be explained by unemployment or a bad economy.
 IV. The causes of the trend can most probably be located in family situations.
    A. Children in families where little guidance is provided or where parents are divorced are more likely to commit suicide.
    B. Children who have lost a father are more likely to commit suicide.
  V. The increase in suicide rates is unique to the 15–24 age group.
 VI. Whatever the cause of the increasing suicide rate among youth, since there is no apparent solution, it is a serious challenge to public policy.

Sentence outlines can be considerably more detailed, to the point of containing most of the information in the essay; but for an essay the length of Fuchs's they are usually about as detailed as this one. Should you want to make a more detailed outline, you would probably need more levels of information than the preceding two outlines contain. A rule of thumb for subdividing topics is that there must be at least two items in every level. You would follow this convention for identifying levels:

I. (Main topic)
   A. (Subtopic of I)
   B.
      1. (Subtopic of I.B)
      2.
         a. (Subtopic of I.B.2)
         b.
            (1) (Subtopic of I.B.2.b.)
            (2)
               (a) (Subtopic of I.B.2.b.(2))
               (b)
               (c)

WRITING

Writing itself is a powerful tool for thinking. By writing, you can recall details, remember facts and ideas, find connections in new information you have collected, examine assumptions, and critically question what you know.

Unlike most mapping strategies, writing strategies of invention invite you to produce complete sentences. The sentence provides considerable generative power. Because sentences are complete statements, they take you further than listing or clustering. They enable you to explore ideas and define relationships, to bring ideas together or show how they differ, to identify causes and effects. Sentences can follow one another naturally and develop a logical chain of thought.

This section presents several invention and inquiry strategies which invite you to formulate complete sentences and thus produce brief exploratory pieces of writing. Some are guided, systematic strategies, while others are more flexible. Even though they call for complete sentences that are related to one another, they do not require planning or polishing.

These writing strategies include cubing, dialogues, diaries, dramatizing, quick drafting, journals, looping, and questioning.

Cubing

Cubing is useful for quickly exploring a writing topic. It lets you probe the topic from six different perspectives. (It is known as cubing because a cube has six sides.) Following are the six perspectives in cubing:

Describing. What does your subject look like? What size is it? Color? Shape? Texture? Name its parts.

Comparing. What is your subject similar to? Different from?

Associating. What does it make you think of? What connections does it have to anything else in your experience? Be creative here. Include any connection you can think of.

Analyzing. How is it made? Where did it come from? Where is it going? How are its parts related?

*Applying.*What can you do with it? What uses does it have?

Arguing. What arguments can you make for it? Against it?

Following are some guidelines to help you use cubing productively:

1. Select a topic, subject, or part of a subject. This can be a person, scene, event, object, problem, idea, or issue. Hold it in focus.

2. Limit yourself to three to five minutes for each perspective. The whole activity will then take no more than a half hour.

3. Keep going until you have written about your subject from *all six* perspectives. Remember that the special advantage of cubing is the quick *multiple* perspectives it provides.

4. As you write from each perspective, begin with what you know about your subject. However, do not limit yourself to your present knowledge. Indicate what else you need to know about your subject, and suggest where you might find that information.

5. Reread what you have written. Look for bright spots, surprises. Recall the part that was easiest for you to write and the part where you felt a special momentum and pleasure in the writing. Look for an angle or an unexpected insight. They may suggest a focus or a topic within a larger subject, or they may provide specific details to include in a draft.

Dialogues

A dialogue is a conversation between two or more people. You can use dialogue to search for topics, find a focus, explore ideas, critically evaluate opposing viewpoints, or evaluate the logic of arguments. As an invention strategy, writing a dialogue requires you to make up all parts of the conversation. Imagine two particular people talking, or hold a conversation yourself with some imagined person, or simply talk out loud to yourself. Follow these steps:

An example of dialogue used for invention is on pp. 57–58.

1. Write a conversation between two speakers. Label the speakers "1" and "2," or make up names for them.

2. If you get stuck, have one of the speakers ask the other a question.

3. Write brief responses in order to keep the conversation moving fast. Do not spend much time planning or rehearsing responses. Write what first occurs to you—just as in a real conversation, where people take quick turns to prevent any awkward silences.

Dialogues can be especially useful with personal experience and persuasive essays because they help you remember conversations and anticipate objections to your argument.

Dramatizing

Dramatizing is an invention activity developed by the philosopher Kenneth Burke as a way of thinking about how people interact and as a way of analyzing literature and the arts.

Thinking about human behavior in dramatic terms can be very productive for writers. Drama has action, actors, setting, motives, and methods. Since stars and acting go together, you can use a five-pointed star to remember these five points of dramatizing:

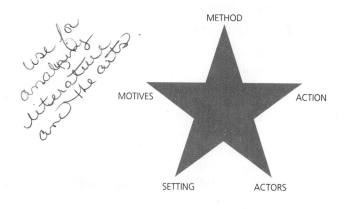

Each point provides a different perspective on human behavior. We can think of each point independently and in combination. Let us begin by looking at each point to see how it helps us analyze people and their interactions.

Action.   An action is anything that happens, has happened, will happen, or could happen. Action includes events that are physical (running a marathon), mental (thinking about a book you read), and emotional (falling in love). This category also refers to the results of activity (a term paper).

Actor.   The actor is involved in the action. He or she may be responsible for it or simply be affected by it. The actor does not have to be a person. It can be a force, something that causes an action. For example, if the action is a rise in the price of gasoline, the actor could be increased demand or short supply. Dramatizing may also include a number of co-actors working together or at odds.

Setting.   This is the situation, the background of the action. We usually think of setting as the place and time of an event, but it can be the historical background of an event or the childhood of a person.

Motive.   The motive is the purpose or reason for an action. It refers to the intention actors may have or the end an action serves.

Method.   Method is the way an action occurs, the techniques an actor uses. It refers to whatever makes things happen.

Each of these points suggests a simple invention question:

Action = What?
Actor = Who?
Setting = When and where?
Motive = Why?
Method = How?

This list looks like the questions reporters typically ask. But dramatizing goes further because it enables us to ask a much fuller set of invention questions generated by considering relations between these five elements. We can think about actors' motives, the effect of the setting on the actors, the relations between actors, and so on.

You can use this activity to learn more about yourself or about other significant people in your life. You can use it, as well, to explore characters in stories or movies you are analyzing or evaluating. Moreover, dramatizing is especially useful in analyzing readers you are trying to inform or convince.

To use dramatizing, imagine the person you want to understand better in a particular situation. Holding this image in mind, write answers to any questions in the following list that apply. You may draw a blank on some questions, have little to say to some, and a lot to say to others. Be exploratory and playful. Write quickly, relying on words and phrases, even drawings.

- What is the actor doing?
- How did the actor come to be involved in this situation?
- Why does the actor do what he or she does?
- What else might the actor do?
- What is the actor trying to accomplish?
- How do other actors influence—help or hinder—the main actor?
- What do the actor's actions reveal about him or her?
- What does the actor's language reveal about him or her?
- How does the event's setting influence the actor's actions?
- How does the time of the event influence what the actor does?
- Where did this actor come from?
- How is this actor different from what he or she used to be?
- What might this actor become?
- How is this actor like or unlike the other actors?

Quick Drafting

Sometimes you know basically what you want to say or don't have time for much invention. In these situations, quick drafting may be a good strategy. There are no special rules for quick drafting, but you should not rely on it unless you know your subject well, have had experience with the kind of writing you are doing, and will have a chance to revise your draft. Quick drafting can help you discover what you already know about the subject and what you need to find out. It can also help you develop and organize your thoughts.

Journals

Professional writers often use journals to keep notes, and so might you. It is quite easy to start a writer's journal. Buy a special notebook, and start writing. Here are some possibilities:

- Keep a list of new words and concepts you learn in your courses. You could also write about the progress and direction of your learning in particular courses—the experience of being in the course, your feelings about what is happening and what you are learning.

- Respond to your reading, assigned and personal. Write about your personal associations as you read, your reflections, reactions, evaluations. Summarize important passages. Copy memorable passages and comment on them. (Copying and commenting has been practiced by students and writers for centuries, in a special journal called a *commonplace book*.)

- Write to prepare for particular class meetings. Write about the main ideas you have learned from assigned readings and about the relation of these new ideas to other ideas in the course. After class, write to summarize what you have learned. List questions you have about the ideas or information discussed in class. Journal writing of this kind involves reflecting, evaluating, interpreting, synthesizing, summarizing, and questioning.

- Record observations and overheard conversations.

- Write for ten or fifteen minutes every day about whatever is on your mind. Focus these meditations on your new experiences and your understandings, interpretations, and reflections on them.

- Write sketches of people who catch your attention.

- Organize your time. You could write about your goals and priorities or list specific things to accomplish and what you plan to do.

- Keep a log over several days or weeks about a particular event unfolding in the news—a sensational trial, an environmental disaster, a political campaign, a campus controversy, the fortunes of a sports team.

If you begin a journal, there are many possibilities for using it. All of the writing in your journal has value for learning, observing experience closely, and organizing your life. It may also end up in other writing.

Looping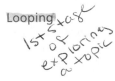

Looping—the strategy of timed, exploratory writing—is especially useful for the first stages of exploring a topic. From almost any starting point, no matter how general or unfocused, looping enables you to find a center of interest and eventually a thesis. The steps are simple:

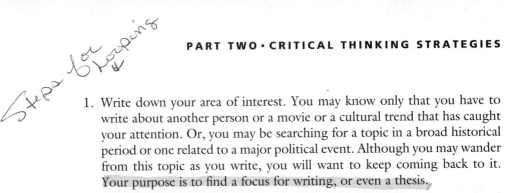

1. Write down your area of interest. You may know only that you have to write about another person or a movie or a cultural trend that has caught your attention. Or, you may be searching for a topic in a broad historical period or one related to a major political event. Although you may wander from this topic as you write, you will want to keep coming back to it. Your purpose is to find a focus for writing, or even a thesis.

2. Write nonstop for ten minutes. Start with the first thing that comes to mind. Write rapidly, without looking back to reread or to correct anything. *Do not stop writing. Keep your pencil moving.* That is the key to looping. If you get stuck for a moment, rewrite the last sentence. Trust the act of writing to lead you to new insights. Follow diversions and digressions, but keep returning to your topic.

3. At the end of ten minutes, pause to reread what you have written. Decide what is most important—a single insight, a pattern of ideas, an emerging theme, a visual detail, anything at all that stands out. Some writers call this a "center of gravity" or a "hot spot." To complete the first loop, express this center in a single sentence.

4. Beginning with this sentence, write nonstop for ten minutes.

5. Summarize in one sentence again to complete the second loop.

6. Keep looping until one of your summary sentences produces a focus or thesis. You may need only two or three loops; you may need more.

Questioning

Asking questions about a subject is a way to learn about it and decide what to write. However, when we first encounter a subject, our questions may be scattered. Also, we are not likely to think right away of all the important questions we ought to ask. The advantage of a basic list of questions for invention, like the ones for cubing and for dramatizing discussed earlier in this chapter, is that it provides a systematic approach to exploring a subject.

The questions here come from classical rhetoric (what the Greek philosopher Aristotle called "topics") and a modern approach to invention called *tagmemics.* Tagmemics, based on the work of American linguist Kenneth Pike, provides questions about all the ways we make sense of the world, all the ways we sort and classify experience and come to understand it.

Here are the steps in using questions for invention: (1) Think about your subject. (Subjects could be any event, person, problem, probject, idea, or issue—in other words, anything you might write about.) (2) Start with the first question, and move right through the list. Try to answer each question at least briefly with a word or phrase. Some questions may invite several sentences, or even a page or more of writing. You may draw a blank on a few questions. Skip them. Later, with more experience with questions for invention, you can start anywhere in the list. (3) Write your responses quickly, without much planning. Follow digressions or associations. Do not screen anything out. Be playful.

What Is Your Subject?

- What is your subject's name and what other names does it have, now or in the past?
- What aspects of the subject do these different names emphasize?
- Imagine a still photograph or moving picture of your subject. What would it look like?
- What would you put into a time capsule to stand for your subject?
- What are its causes and results?
- How would it look from different vantage points or perspectives?
- What particular experiences have you had with the subject? What have you learned?

What Parts or Characteristics Does Your Subject Have and How Are They Related?

- Name the parts or characteristics.
- Describe each one, using the questions in the preceding subject list.
- How is each part or characteristic related to the others?

How Is Your Subject Similar To and Different From Other Subjects?

- What is your subject similar to? In what ways are they alike?
- What is your subject different from? In what ways are they different?
- Of all the things in the world, what seems to you most unlike your subject? In what ways are they unlike each other? Now, just for fun, note how they are alike.

How Much Can Your Subject Change and Still Remain the Same?

- How has your subject changed from what it once was?
- How is it changing now—moment to moment, day to day, year to year?
- How much can it change and still remain the same?
- What are some different forms your subject takes?
- What does it become when it is no longer itself?

Where Does Your Subject Fit In the World?

- When and where did your subject originate?
- Imagine a time in the future when your subject will not exist.
- When and where do you usually experience the subject?
- What is this subject part of and what are its parts?
- What is the link between the subject and that of which it is a part?
- What do other people think of your subject?

A ll writers rely on information in books, articles, letters, and other documents. Working with such sources calls on you to be a writer *and* a reader—to gather, analyze, select, and organize the information you find.

This chapter presents strategies to help you read *with a critical eye*, not just to comprehend passively and remember what you read but also to scrutinize actively and evaluate it. When you read a text critically, you need to alternate between understanding and questioning—on the one hand, to understand the text on its own terms; on the other hand, to question its ideas and authority.

The reading strategies here complement and supplement strategies in Part I, Chapters 2–10. Critical reading is in fact central to your success with the writing assignments done in those chapters. The questions for discussion following each reading selection help you connect your own experience and awareness of social issues to the text and to reread it critically in light of those issues; the questions for analysis help you judge how well a text works. The writing guide in each chapter includes materials to help you read another student's draft and your own critically in order to see their problems and possibilities.

Reading is, after all, inextricably linked to writing, and the reading strategies in this chapter can help you in your work as both reader and writer. The strategies here include:

    annotating
    taking inventory
    contextualizing
    reflecting on challenges to your beliefs and values
    paraphrasing
    summarizing
    exploring the significance of figurative language
    looking for patterns of opposition
    evaluating the logic of an argument
    recognizing emotional manipulation
    judging the writer's credibility

These strategies can help you connect information from different sources and relate it to what you already know; distinguish fact from opinion; uncover hidden assumptions; examine your own beliefs and values; and subject both what you read and what you know to reasoned inquiry.

ANNOTATING

Annotations are the underlinings, highlightings, and comments you make directly on the text you're reading. Annotating can be used to record immediate reactions and questions, outline and summarize main points, evaluate and relate the reading to other ideas and points of view. Especially useful for studying and preparing to write, it is also an essential element of many other critical reading strategies. Your annotations can take many forms:

> writing comments, questions, definitions
> underlining or highlighting words or phrases
> circling or boxing words or phrases
> connecting related items with lines
> numbering a sequence of related items: points, examples, names
> bracketing parts of the text

AN ANNOTATED SAMPLE FROM "LETTER FROM BIRMINGHAM JAIL"
MARTIN LUTHER KING, JR.

Martin Luther King, Jr. (1929–1968) first came to national notice in 1955, when he led a successful boycott against back-of-the-bus seating of African Americans in Montgomery, Alabama, where he was minister of a Baptist church. He subsequently formed a national organization, the Southern Christian Leadership Conference, that brought people of all races from all over the country to the South to fight nonviolently for racial integration. In 1963, King led demonstrations in Birmingham that were met with violence; a black church was bombed, killing four little girls. King was arrested and, while in prison, wrote the famous "Letter from Birmingham Jail" to answer local clergy's criticism.

The following brief reading selection is excerpted from the letter and annotated to illustrate some of the ways you can annotate as you read. Since annotating is the first step for all critical reading strategies in this catalog, these annotations are referred to throughout the chapter. Add your own annotations in the right-hand margin. King begins by discussing his disappointment with the lack of support he's received from white moderates, such as the group of clergy who published their criticism in the local newspaper. As you read the selection, try to infer from King's written response what the clergy's specific criticisms might have been. Also, notice evidence of the tone King adopts in this selection. Does the writing seem to you to be apologetic, conciliatory, accusatory, or what?

1. White moderates block progress.

. . . I must confess that over the past few years I have been gravely disappointed with the white moderate. I have almost reached the regrettable conclusion that the Negro's [great stumbling block in his stride toward freedom] is not the White Citizen's Counciler or the Ku Klux Klanner, but the white moderate, who is more devoted to "order" than to justice; who prefers a negative peace which is the absence of tension to a positive peace which is the presence of justice; who constantly says: "I agree with you in the goal you seek, but I cannot agree with your methods of direct action"; who paternalistically believes he can set the timetable for another man's freedom; who lives by a mythical concept of time and who constantly advises the Negro to wait for a "more convenient season." Shallow understanding from people of good will is more frustrating than absolute misunderstanding from people of ill will. Lukewarm acceptance is much more bewildering than outright rejection.

order vs. justice

negative vs. positive
ends vs. means

treating others like children

1

2. Tension necessary for progress.

I had hoped that the white moderate would understand that law and order exist for the purpose of establishing justice and that when they fail in this purpose they become the [dangerously structured dams that block the flow of social progress.] I had hoped that the white moderate would understand that the present tension in the South is a necessary phase of the transition from an [obnoxious negative peace,] in which the Negro passively accepted his unjust plight, to a [substantive and positive peace,] in which all men will respect the dignity and worth of human personality. Actually, we who engage in nonviolent direct action are not the creators of tension. We merely bring to the surface the hidden tension that is already alive. We bring it out in the open, where it can be seen and dealt with [Like a boil that can never be cured so long as it is covered up but must be opened with all its ugliness to the natural medicines of air and light, injustice must be exposed, with all the tension its exposure creates, to the light of human conscience and the air of national opinion before it can be cured.]

2

Tension already exists anyway.

Simile: hidden tension like a boil

True?

3. Questions clergy's
logic: criticizing King =
blaming the victim,
Socrates, Jesus.

In your statement you assert that <u>our actions</u>, even 3
though peaceful, must be <u>condemned</u> because they precipitate violence. But is this a logical assertion? <u>Isn't this like</u>
<u>condemning</u> (a robbed man) because his possession of
money precipitated the evil act of robbery? <u>Isn't this like</u>
<u>condemning</u> (Socrates) because his unswerving commitment
to truth and his philosophical inquiries precipitated the act
by the misguided populace in which they made him drink
hemlock? <u>Isn't this like condemning</u> (Jesus) because his
unique God-consciousness and never-ceasing devotion to
God's will precipitated the evil act of crucifixion? We must
come to see that, as the federal courts have consistently af-
firmed, it is wrong to urge an individual to cease his efforts
to gain his <u>basic constitutional rights</u> because the question
may precipitate violence. [Society must protect the robbed
and punish the robber.]

Yes!

4. Justifies urgency

I had also hoped that the white moderate would reject 4
the <u>myth concerning time</u> in relation to the struggle for
freedom. I have just received a letter from a white brother
in Texas. He writes: "All Christians know that the colored
people will receive equal rights eventually, but it is possible
that you are in <u>too great a religious hurry</u>. It has taken
Christianity almost two thousand years to accomplish what
it has. The teachings of Christ take time to come to earth."

Quotes white moderate

Critiques assumptions

Such an attitude stems from <u>a tragic misconception of time,</u>
from the strangely irrational notion that there is something
in the very flow of time that will inevitably cure all ills. Actually, time itself is neutral; it can be used either destruc-
tively or constructively. More and more I feel that the people of ill will have used time much more effectively than
have the people of good will. We will have to repent in this
generation not merely for the [hateful <u>words and actions</u> of
the bad people] but for the [<u>appalling silence</u> of the good
people.] Human progress never rolls in on [wheels of inevitability;] it comes through the tireless efforts of men willing
to be co-workers with God, and without this hard work,
time itself becomes an ally of the forces of social (stagnation.)
[<u>We must use time creatively</u>, in the knowledge that <u>the</u>
<u>time is always ripe to do right.</u>] <u>Now is the time</u> to make real
the promise of democracy and transform our pending [na-
tional elegy] into a creative [psalm of brotherhood.] <u>Now is</u>
<u>the time</u> to lift our national policy from the [quicksand of
racial injustice] to the [solid rock of human dignity.]

Silence as bad as hateful
words and actions.

not moving
Time must be used

metaphors: quicksand
of racial injustice,
wheels of inevitability

5. King not an
extremist—between
two extremes.

You speak of our activity in Birmingham as <u>extreme</u>. At 5
first I was rather disappointed that fellow clergymen would
see my nonviolent efforts as those of an extremist. I began
thinking about the <u>fact</u> that <u>I stand in the middle of two</u>
<u>opposing forces in the Negro community.</u> One is a [force of

complacency,] made up in part of Negroes who, as a result of long years of oppression, are so drained of self-respect and a sense of "somebodiness" that they have adjusted to segregation; and in part of a few middle-class Negroes, who because of a degree of academic and economic security and because in some ways they profit by segregation, have become insensitive to the problems of the masses. The other [force is one of bitterness and hatred,] and it comes perilously close to advocating violence. It is expressed in the various black nationalist [groups that are springing up] across the nation, the largest and best-known being Elijah Muhammad's Muslim movement. Nourished by the Negro's frustration over the continued existence of racial discrimination, this movement is made up of people who have lost faith in America, who have absolutely repudiated Christianity, and who have concluded that the white man is an incorrigible "devil."

Malcolm X?

6. King offers better choice.

I have tried to stand between these two forces, saying   6
that we need emulate neither the "do-nothingism" of the complacent nor the hatred and despair of the black nationalist. For there is the more excellent way of love and nonviolent protest. I am grateful to God that, through the influence of the Negro church, the way of nonviolence became an integral part of our struggle.

7. King's movement has prevented racial violence. Threat?

If this philosophy had not emerged, by now many   7
streets of the South would, I am convinced, be flowing with blood. And I am further convinced that if our white brothers dismiss as "rabble-rousers" and "outside agitators" those of us who employ nonviolent direct action, and if they refuse to support our nonviolent efforts, millions of Negroes will, out of frustration and despair, seek (solace) and security in black-nationalist ideologies—a development that would inevitably lead to a frightening racial nightmare.

comfort

If . . . Then . . .
8. Revolution can't be stopped, only channeled, like a flood.

(Oppressed people cannot remain oppressed forever.)   8
The yearning for freedom eventually manifests itself, and that is what has happened to the American Negro. Something within has reminded him of his birthright of freedom, and something without has reminded him that it can be gained. Consciously or unconsciously, he has been caught up by the (Zeitgeist,) and with his black brothers of Africa and his brown and yellow brothers of Asia, South America and the Caribbean, the United States Negro is moving with a sense of great urgency toward the [promised land of racial justice.] If one recognizes this [vital urge that has engulfed the Negro community,] one should readily understand why public demonstrations are taking place. The Negro has many [pent-up resentments] and latent frustrations, and he must release them. So let him march; let him make prayer

spirit of the times

Worldwide uprising against injustice

pilgrimages to the city hall; let him go on freedom rides—and try to understand why he must do so. If his repressed emotions are not released in nonviolent ways, they will seek expression through violence; this is not a threat but a fact of history. So I have not said to my people: "Get rid of your discontent." Rather, I have tried to say that this normal and healthy discontent can be channeled into the creative outlet of nonviolent direct action. And now this approach is being termed extremist.

But though I was initially disappointed at being categorized as an extremist, as I continued to think about the matter I gradually gained a measure of satisfaction from the label. Was not Jesus an extremist for love: "Love your enemies, bless them that curse you, do good to them that hate you, and pray for them which despitefully use you, and persecute you." Was not Amos an extremist for justice: "Let justice roll down like waters and righteousness like an ever-flowing stream." Was not Paul an extremist for the Christian gospel: "I bear in my body the marks of the Lord Jesus." Was not Martin Luther an extremist: "Here I stand; I cannot do otherwise, so help me God." And John Bunyan: "I will stay in jail to the end of my days before I make a butchery of my conscience." And Abraham Lincoln: "This nation cannot survive half slave and half free." And Thomas Jefferson: "We hold these truths to be self-evident, that all men are created equal . . ." So the question is not whether we will be extremists, but what kind of extremists we will be. Will we be extremists for hate or for love? Will we be extremists for the preservation of injustice or for the extension of justice? In that dramatic scene on Calvary's hill three men were crucified. We must never forget that all three were crucified for the same crime—the crime of extremism. Two were extremists for immorality, and thus fell below their environment. The other, Jesus Christ, was an extremist for love, truth and goodness, and thereby rose above his environment. Perhaps the South, the nation and the world are in dire need of creative extremists.

I had hoped that the white moderate would see this need. Perhaps I was too optimistic; perhaps I expected too much. I suppose I should have realized that few members of the oppressor race can understand the deep groans and passionate yearnings of the oppressed race, and still fewer have the vision to see that injustice must be rooted out by strong, persistent and determined action. I am thankful, however, that some of our white brothers in the South have grasped the meaning of this social revolution and committed themselves to it. They are still all too few in quantity, but they are big in quality. Some—such as Ralph McGill,

Margin notes

Not a threat?

9. Justifies extremism for righteous ends.

Hebrew prophet

Christ's disciple

founded Protestantism
English preacher

freed the slaves

wrote Declaration of Independence

10. Disappointed in white moderate critics; thanks supporters.

9

10

Lillian Smith, Harry Golden, James McBride Dabbs, Ann Braden and Sarah Patton Boyle—have written about our struggle in eloquent and prophetic terms. Others have marched with us down nameless streets of the South. They have languished in filthy, roach-infested jails, suffering the abuse and brutality of policemen who view them as "dirty niggerlovers." Unlike so many of their moderate brothers and sisters, they have recognized the urgency of the moment and sensed the need for powerful "action" antidotes to combat the disease of segregation.

Who are they?

left unaided

framing—recalls boil

TAKING INVENTORY

An inventory is simply a list or grouping of items. Taking inventory helps you analyze your annotations for different purposes. For example, if you were reading the King excerpt to see how he answers the clergy's criticism, you might collect references to means and ends, look for a pattern in the authorities he names, or examine the images of sickness and healing. Taking inventory leads you to scrutinize the language patterns and think critically about the text's assumptions. It also prepares you to write about what you've found.

CONTEXTUALIZING

The texts you read were all written sometime in the past and often embody historical and cultural assumptions, values, and attitudes different from your own. To read critically, you need to become aware of these differences. Contextualizing is a critical reading strategy that enables you to make inferences about a reading selection's historical and cultural context and to examine the differences between its context and your own. To contextualize:

1. Annotate any language or ideas in the text that seem different to you—reflecting attitudes, assumptions, or values that strike you as somewhat foreign or out of style.

2. Reflect on what you know about the time and place in which the selection was written. Your knowledge may come from other reading, television or film, school, or elsewhere. (If you know nothing about the historical and cultural context, you could do some library research.)

3. In a paragraph or two, explore the differences you see between the writer's assumptions, values, and attitudes and those current in your culture today. Consider how these differences affect your understanding and judgment of the reading.

The excerpt from "Letter from Birmingham Jail" is a good example of a text that benefits from being read contextually. If you knew nothing about the history of slavery and segregation in the United States, if you had not heard of Martin Luther King, Jr., or the civil rights movement, it would be very difficult to understand the passion for justice and impatience with delay expressed in this selection. Most Americans have seen television documentaries of newsclips showing demonstrators being attacked by dogs, doused by fire hoses, beaten by helmeted police. Such images provide a sense of the violence, fear, and hatred that King was responding to. The Spike Lee film *Malcolm X* gives another point of view.

Comparing the context when King was in Birmingham Jail to present times reveals that things have changed since the sixties. Segregation has ceased to be legal. The term *Negro* is no longer used. Many African Americans hold powerful leadership positions. But then, the riots in Los Angeles after the police officers who beat Rodney King were exonerated tell us something is not right. As in Dr. King's time, many African Americans today are angry and demanding justice.

REFLECTING ON CHALLENGES TO YOUR BELIEFS AND VALUES

To read critically, you need to scrutinize your own assumptions and attitudes as well as those expressed in the text you're reading. The difficulty is that our assumptions and attitudes are so ingrained, we're usually not aware of them. A good strategy for getting at these underlying beliefs and values is to identify and reflect on the ways the text challenges you—makes you feel disturbed, threatened, ashamed, combative, or whatever.

1. Identify challenges by annotating the text, marking each point where you feel your beliefs and values are being opposed, criticized, or unfairly characterized.

2. Select one or two of the most troubling challenges you've identified and write a few paragraphs trying to understand why you feel as you do. Don't defend your feelings; but instead analyze them to see where they come from.

   For example, if you are disturbed (as many of his original readers were) by King's criticism in paragraph 1 of readers who are "more devoted to 'order' than to justice," consider why. Which do you value more: order or justice? How does your preference reflect your situation, upbringing, religious beliefs, gender, sexual orientation, social class, race, or ethnicity? For what purposes—if any—do you think it would be okay to disturb the peace other people enjoy? What should those who experience injustice do to remedy their situation?

PARAPHRASING

*Strategies for integrating
quoted material smoothly
into your writing are
demonstrated in Chapter
22.*

Paraphrasing is putting what you have read into your own words. As a critical reading strategy, paraphrasing can help to clarify the meaning of an obscure or ambiguous passage. It is one of the three ways of integrating other people's ideas and information into your own writing, along with *quoting* (reproducing exactly the language of the source text), and *summarizing* (distilling the main ideas or gist of the source text). You might choose to paraphrase rather than quote when the source's language is not especially arresting or memorable. You might paraphrase short passages but summarize longer ones.

Here is how one student paraphased the first five sentences of a paragraph from an article on Native American writing systems.

Original

The Native American groups which, despite all obstacles, have developed traditions of literacy in their own languages seem to share certain characteristics. All of them, of course, have preserved some sort of social organization, at least at the local community level. It would seem that such groups have also found one or more functions for their own literacy. Thus the spread of Fox, Winnebago, Cherokee, and Mahican literacy occurred at the same time that these several tribes were divided by migrations. In all four cases it seems reasonable to suppose that the first individuals to become literate were motivated by a desire to communicate with relatives who had departed for the west or, as the case may be, had lingered behind in the east.

Paraphrase

Native American groups had to overcome many obstacles in
order to develop writing systems in their own languages.
The groups that did develop writing are alike in several
ways: they maintained their social structure, and they
were able to put writing to good use. For example, writing became more common in the Fox, Winnebago, Cherokee,
and Mahican tribes after they were separated through migration. Tribal members probably wanted to write to relatives they could no longer see regularly.

The first thing to note about the paraphrase is that it contains *all* the information in the original. It is not just a summary. It is a complete reproduction in the student's own words. Although it has the same number of sentences as the original, the information is grouped into sentences in somewhat different ways. Without changing the information significantly, paraphrase aims to clarify and simplify the original.

SUMMARIZING

What Summary outline is.

Summarizing is a helpful strategy for understanding the content and structure of a reading. Many writers find it useful to outline text as a preliminary to summarizing. *Outlining* reveals the basic structure of the text, whereas summarizing synopsizes its main action, details, or argument.

Outlining may be part of your annotating process, or it may be done separately. Writing a brief outline in the margins of the text as you read and annotate makes it easier to find things later. Writing an outline on a separate piece of paper gives you more space to work with and therefore allows for more detail. Either way, your goal is to identify the text's main ideas.

Summary

The key to both outlining and summarizing is being able to distinguish between the main ideas and the supporting ideas and examples. The main ideas form the backbone, the strand that holds the various parts of the text together. Outlining the main ideas helps you discover this structure. As you outline, you will need to decide which are the most important ideas. Since importance is a relative term, different readers can make different—and equally reasonable—decisions based on what interests them in the reading. Outlining is further complicated when you use your own words rather than words from the text, for rephrasing can shift meaning or emphasis. Reading is never a passive or neutral act; the processes of outlining and summarizing show it to be a constructive one.

Paragraphs

You don't have to make a complicated outline with roman numerals and letters. An informal scratch outline that identifies the main idea of each paragraph will do. Paragraphs typically organize material around a single topic, with the topic usually stated in a word or phrase, and referred to throughout the paragraph. For example, the opening paragraph of the King excerpt makes clear that its topic is the white moderate.

Once you've found the topic of the paragraph, you need to figure out what is being said about it. To return to our example: if the white moderate is the topic of the opening paragraph, then what King says about it can be found in the second sentence, where he announces the conclusion he has come to—namely, that the white moderate is "the Negro's great stumbling block in his stride toward freedom." The rest of the paragraph specifies the ways the white moderate blocks progress.

When you outline a reading, it is best to use your own words. An outline of the King excerpt appears in the margins of the selection, with numbers for each paragraph. Here is the same outline, slightly expanded and reworded:

1. White moderates block progress in the struggle for racial justice.
2. Tension is necessary for progress.
3. The clergy's criticism is not logical.

```
 4. Time must be used to do right.
 5. Clergy accuse King of being extreme, but he stands
    between two extreme forces in the black community.
 6. King offers a better choice.
 7. King's movement has prevented racial violence by
    blacks.
 8. Discontent is normal and healthy but must be chan-
    neled creatively rather than destructively.
 9. Creative extremists are needed.
10. Some whites have supported King.
```

Summarizing goes beyond merely listing the main ideas, actually recomposing them to form a new text. Whereas outlining depends on close analysis of each paragraph, summarizing also requires creative synthesis. Putting the ideas together again—in your own words and in a condensed form—shows how reading critically truly is a constructive process of making meaning and can lead to deeper understanding of any text.

One reader's summary is likely to differ—sometimes significantly—from another reader's. By using their own words when they summarize and by focusing on different aspects of the text, two readers may summarize the same text differently. They may well have different purposes for reading. Also, there is no exact formula about how long and detailed a summary should be.

Following is a sample summary of the King excerpt. It is based on the outline above, but is much more detailed. Most important, it fills in connections between the ideas that King left for readers to make.

```
     King expresses his disappointment with white moder-
ates who, by opposing his program of nonviolent direct
action, have become a barrier to progress toward racial
justice.  He acknowledges that his program has raised
tension in the South, but he explains that tension is
necessary to bring about change.  Furthermore, he argues
that tension already exists.  But because it has been unex-
pressed, it is unhealthy and potentially dangerous.
     He defends his actions against the clergymen's crit-
icisms, particularly their argument that he is in too
much of a hurry.  Responding to charges of extremism,
King claims that he has actually prevented racial vio-
lence by channeling the natural frustrations of oppressed
blacks into nonviolent protest.  He asserts that extrem-
ism is precisely what is needed now—but it must be crea-
tive, rather than destructive, extremism.  He concludes
by again expressing disappointment with white moderates
for not joining his effort as many other whites have.
```

EXPLORING THE SIGNIFICANCE OF FIGURATIVE LANGUAGE

Figurative language—metaphor, simile, and symbol—enhances literal meaning by embodying abstract ideas in vivid images and by evoking feelings and associations.

Metaphor implicitly compares two different things by identifying them with each other. For instance, when King calls the white moderate "the Negro's great stumbling block in his stride toward freedom" (paragraph 1), he does not mean that the white moderate literally trips the Negro who is attempting to walk toward freedom. The sentence makes sense only if understood figuratively: the white moderate trips up the Negro by frustrating every effort to achieve justice. Similarly, King uses the image of a dam to express the abstract idea of the blockage of justice (paragraph 2).

Simile, a more explicit form of comparison, uses *like* or *as* to signal the relation of two seemingly unrelated things. King uses simile when he says that injustice is "like a boil that can never be cured so long as it is covered up" (paragraph 2). This simile makes several points of comparison between injustice and a boil. It suggests that injustice is a disease of society as a boil is a disease of the body and that injustice, like a boil, must be exposed or it will fester and worsen.

Symbolism compares two things by making one stand for the other. King uses the white moderate as a symbol for supposed liberals and would-be supporters of civil rights who are actually frustrating the cause.

How these figures of speech are used in a text reveals something of the writer's feelings about the subject as well as your own reading responses. Noting figures of speech as you annotate and taking inventory of any patterns can help you read between the lines of a text, to recognize meanings that may not be stated directly.

One systematic way to explore the patterns of figurative language follows:

1. Annotate and then list all the figures of speech you find in the reading—metaphor, simile, and symbol.

2. Group the figures of speech that appear to express similar feelings and attitudes, and label each group.

3. Try exploring the meaning of these patterns in writing. What do they tell you about the text?

Listing figures of speech in the King excerpt yields many examples, among them the following:

```
order is a dangerously structured dam that blocks the flow
social progress should flow
stumbling block in the stride toward freedom
injustice is like a boil that can never be cured
the light of human conscience and air of national opinion
```

```
time is something to be used, neutral, an ally, ripe
quicksand of racial injustice
the solid rock of human dignity
human progress never rolls in on wheels of inevitability
men are co-workers with God
groups springing up
promised land of racial justice
vital urge engulfed
pent-up resentments
normal and healthy discontent can be channeled into the
    creative outlet of nonviolent direct action
root out injustice
powerful action is an antidote
disease of segregation
```

Here is one way these figures can be grouped:

```
Sickness: segregation is a disease; action is healthy,
    the only antidote; injustice is like a boil
Underground: tension is hidden; resentments are pent-up,
    repressed; injustice must be rooted out; extremist
    groups are springing up; discontent can be channeled
    into a creative outlet
Blockage: forward movement is impeded by obstacles--the
    dam, stumbling block; human progress never rolls in on
    wheels of inevitability; social progress should flow
```

In writing about these patterns and thinking about what they mean, you might recognize patterns of blockage and underground as suggesting frustration and inertia. The simile of injustice being like a boil suggests something bad, a disease, inside society. The cure is to expose, to root out, the blocked hatred and injustice and release the tension or emotion that has so long been repressed. This implies that repression itself is the evil, not simply what is repressed.

LOOKING FOR PATTERNS OF OPPOSITION

All texts carry within themselves voices of opposition. These voices may echo the views and values of critical readers the writer anticipates or predecessors to which the writer is responding in some way; they may even reflect the writer's own conflicting values. Careful readers look closely for such a dialogue of opposing voices within the text.

When we think of oppositions, we ordinarily think of polarities: *yes* and *no*, *up* and *down*, *black* and *white*, *new* and *old*. Some oppositions, however, may be more subtle. The excerpt from "Letter from Birmingham Jail" is rich in such oppositions: *moderate* versus *extremist, order* versus *justice, direct action* versus *passive acceptance, expression* versus *repression*. These oppositions are not accidental; and they form a significant pattern that gives a critical reader important information about the essay. ·

A careful reading will show that one of the two terms in an opposition is nearly always valued over the other. In the King passage, for example, *extremist* is valued over *moderate* (paragraph 9). This preference for extremism is surprising. The critical reader should ask why, when white extremists like the Ku Klux Klan have committed so many outrages against black Southerners, King would prefer extremism. If King is trying to convince his readers to accept his point of view, why would he represent himself as an extremist? Moreover, why would a clergyman advocate extremism instead of moderation?

Studying the pattern of oppositions enables you to answer these questions. Then you will see that King sets up this opposition to force his readers to examine their own values and realize that they are in fact misplaced. Instead of working toward justice, he says, those who support law and order maintain the unjust status quo. Getting his readers to think of white moderates as blocking rather than facilitating peaceful change brings them to align themselves with King and perhaps even embrace his strategy of nonviolent resistance.

Here is a useful way to look for patterns of oppositions:

1. Divide a piece of paper in half lengthwise by drawing a line down the middle. In the left-hand column, list those words and phrases from the text that you annotated because they seem to indicate oppositions. Enter in the right-hand column the word or phrase that is the opposite of each word or phrase in the left-hand column. You may have to paraphrase or even supply this opposite word or phrase if it is not stated directly in the text.

2. For each pair of words or phrases, note which one the writer seems to prefer.

3. Study the words or phrases that seem to be valued. Do the same for the other list. What do they mean for your understanding—and acceptance—of the argument? What do they tell you about what the writer *wants* you to believe?

A list of oppositions in the King text might yield the following examples. The ones King seems to value are marked with asterisks.

```
white moderate        *extremist
order                 *justice
negative peace        *positive peace
absence of justice    *presence of justice
```

```
  goals                  *methods
*direct action            passive acceptance
*exposed tension          hidden tension
*robbed                   robber
*individual               society
*words                    silence
*expression               repression
*extension of justice     preservation of injustice
*extremist for love,      extremist for immorality
   truth, and justice
```

EVALUATING THE LOGIC OF AN ARGUMENT

An argument has two basic parts: a claim and support. The *claim* asserts a conclusion—an idea, an opinion, a judgment, or a point of view—that the writer wants readers to accept. The *support* includes *reasons* (shared beliefs, assumptions, and values) and *evidence* (facts, examples, statistics, and authorities) that give readers the basis for accepting the conclusion. Three conditions must be met for an argument to be considered logically acceptable—what we call the ABC test:

A. The support must be *appropriate* to the claim.
B. All of the statements must be *believable*.
C. The statements must be *consistent* with one another and not contradictory.

Testing for Appropriateness

As a critical reader, you must decide whether the statements intended to support the claim are actually appropriate and clearly related to it. To test for appropriateness, ask: How does each reason or piece of evidence relate to the claim? Is the connection between support and claim clear and compelling? Or is the support irrelevant or only vaguely related to the claim?

For more on invoking authority, see pp. 541–42; for more on analogy, see pp. 530–33.

Appropriateness of support comes most often into question when the writer is arguing by analogy or invoking authority. For example, in paragraph 2, King argues that if law and order fail to establish justice, "they become the dangerously structured dams that block the flow of social progress." The analogy asserts the following logical relationship: law and order is to progress toward justice what a dam is to water. If you do not accept this analogy, then the argument fails the test of appropriateness. King uses both analogy and authority in the following passage: "Isn't this like condemning Socrates because his unswerving commitment to truth and his philosophical inquiries precipitated the act by the misguided populace in which they made him drink hemlock?" (paragraph 3). You must not only judge the appropriateness of comparing the Greek populace's condemnation of Socrates to the white moderates' condemnation of King's actions, but you must also judge whether it is appropriate to accept Socrates as an authority on this subject. Since Socrates is generally respected for his teaching on justice, his words and actions are likely to be considered appropriate to King's situation in Birmingham.

There are several common flaws or fallacies in reasoning that cause an argument to fail the test of appropriateness:

- *False analogy*, when two cases are not sufficiently parallel to lead readers to accept the claim.

- *False use of authority*, when writers invoke as expert in the field being discussed a person whose expertise or authority lies not in the given field but in another.

- *Non sequitur* (Latin for "it does not follow"), when one statement is not logically connected to another.

- *Red herring*, when a writer raises an irrelevant issue to draw attention away from the central issue.

- *Post hoc, ergo propter hoc* (Latin for "after this, therefore because of this"), when the writer implies that because one event follows another, the first caused the second. Chronology is not the same as causality.

Testing for Believability

You also must look critically at each statement supporting the claim to see whether it is believable. While you may find some statements self-evidently true, the truth of others will be less certain. To test for believability, ask: On what basis am I being asked to accept this assertion as true? If it can't be proved true or false, how much weight does it carry?

In judging facts, statistics, examples, and authorities, consider the following:

Facts are statements that can be proven objectively to be true. The believability of facts depends on their *accuracy* (they should not distort or misrepresent reality), *completeness* (they should not omit important details), and the *trustworthiness* of their sources (sources should be qualified and unbiased). King, for instance, asserts as fact that the African American will not wait much longer for racial justice (paragraph 8). His critics might question the factuality of this assertion by asking: Is it true of all African Americans? How much longer will they wait? How does King know what African Americans will and will not do?

Statistics are often assumed to be factual but are really only interpretations of numerical data. The believability of statistics depends on the *comparability* of the data (apples cannot be compared to oranges), the *accuracy* of the methods of gathering and analyzing data (representative samples should be used and variables accounted for), and the *trustworthiness* of the sources (sources should be qualified and unbiased).

Examples and *anecdotes* are particular instances that if accepted as believable lead readers to accept the general claim. The believability of examples depends on their *representativeness* (whether they are truly typical and thus generalizable) and their *specificity* (whether particular details make them seem true to life). Even if a vivid example or gripping anecdote does not convince readers, it strengthens argumentative writing by clarifying the meaning and bringing home the point dramatically. In paragraph 5 of the King excerpt, for example, King supports his generalization that there are black nationalist extremists motivated by bitterness and hatred by citing the specific example of Elijah Muhammad's Muslim movement. Conversely, in paragraph 9, he refers to Jesus, Paul, Luther, and others as examples of extremists motivated by love. These examples support his assertion that extremism is not in itself wrong, that any judgment must depend on what cause one is an extremist for.

Authorities are people to whom the writer attributes expertise on a given subject. Such authorities not only must be appropriate, as mentioned earlier, but they must be believable. The believability of authorities depends on their *credibility*, on whether the reader accepts them as experts on the topic at hand. King cites authorities repeatedly throughout the essay. In the selection, for instance, he refers not only to religious leaders like Jesus and Luther but also to American political leaders like Lincoln and Jefferson. These figures are certain to have a high degree of credibility among King's readers.

In addition, you should be aware of the following fallacies in reasoning that undermine the believability of an argument:

- *Begging the question*, when the believability of the support itself depends on the believability of the claim. Another name for this kind of fallacy is *circular reasoning*.
- *Failing to accept the burden of proof*, when the writer asserts a claim but provides no support for it.
- *Hasty generalization*, when the writer asserts a claim on the basis of an isolated example.
- *Sweeping generalization*, when the writer fails to qualify the applicability of the claim and asserts that it applies to "all" instances instead of to "some" instances.
- *Overgeneralization*, when the writer fails to qualify the claim and asserts that it is "certainly true" rather than that it "may be true."

Testing for
Consistency

In looking for consistency, you should be concerned that all the support works together and that none of the supporting statements contradicts any of the other statements. In addition, the support, taken together, should provide sufficient reason for accepting the claim. To test for consistency, ask: Are any of the supporting statements contradictory? Do they provide sufficient support for the claim? Are there opposing arguments that are not refuted?

A critical reader might regard as contradictory King's characterizing himself first as a moderate between the forces of complacency and violence, and later as an extremist opposed to the forces of violence. King attempts to reconcile this apparent contradiction by explicitly redefining extremism in paragraph 9. Similarly, the fact that King fails to examine and refute every legal recourse available to his cause might allow a critical reader to question the sufficiency of his supporting arguments.

In evaluating the consistency of an argument, you should also be aware of the following fallacies:

- *Slippery slope*, when the writer argues that taking one step will lead inevitably to a next step, one that is undesirable.
- *Equivocation*, when a writer uses the same term in two different senses in an argument.
- *Oversimplification*, when an argument obscures or denies the complexity of the issue.
- *Either-or reasoning*, when the writer reduces the issue to only two alternatives that are polar opposites.
- *Double standard*, when two or more comparable things are judged according to different standards; often involves holding the opposing argument to a higher standard than the one to which the writer holds his or her own argument.

RECOGNIZING EMOTIONAL MANIPULATION

Many different kinds of essays appeal to readers' emotions. Tobias Wolff's remembered event essay may be terrifying to some readers, David Noonan's profile of brain surgery may be shocking, Donella Meadows's position paper may anger fans of talk-show host Rush Limbaugh whom she characterizes as "funny and pompous and a scape-goater and hatemonger."

Writers often try to arouse emotions in readers, to excite their interest, make them care, move them to take action. There's nothing wrong with appealing to readers' emotions. What's wrong is manipulating readers with false or exaggerated appeals. As a critical reader, you should be suspicious of writing that is overly or falsely sentimental, that cites alarming statistics and tries to enrage readers with frightening anecdotes, that demonizes others and identifies itself with revered authorities, that uses symbols (flagwaving) or emotionally loaded words (like *racist*).

King, for example, uses the emotionally loaded word *paternalistically* to refer to the white moderate's belief that "he can set the timetable for another man's freedom" (paragraph 1). In the same paragraph, King uses *symbolism* to get an emotional reaction from readers when he compares the white moderate to the "Ku Klux Klanner." To get readers to accept his ideas, he also relies on *authorities* whose names evoke the greatest respect, such as Jesus and Lincoln. You might consider the discussion of black extremists in paragraph 7 of the King excerpt to be a veiled threat designed to frighten readers into agreement. Or you might object that comparing King's crusade to that of Jesus and other so-called leaders of religious and political groups is pretentious and manipulative.

Following are some fallacies that may occur when the emotional appeal is misused:

- *Loaded or slanted language*, when the writer uses language that is calculated to get a particular reaction from readers.
- *Bandwagon effect*, when it is suggested that great numbers of people agree with the writer and if you continued to disagree, you would be alone.
- *False flattery*, when readers are praised in order to get them to accept the writer's point of view.
- *Veiled threat*, when the writer tries to alarm readers or frighten them into accepting the claim.

JUDGING THE WRITER'S CREDIBILITY

Writers often try to persuade readers to respect and believe them. Because readers may not know them personally or even by reputation, writers must present an image of themselves in their writing that will gain their readers' confidence. This image cannot be made directly but must be made indirectly, through the arguments, language, and the system of values and beliefs implied in the writing. Writers establish credibility in their writing in three ways:

By showing their knowledge of the subject

By building common ground with readers

By responding fairly to objections and opposing arguments

Testing for
Knowledge

Writers demonstrate their knowledge through the facts and statistics they marshal, the sources they rely on for information, the scope and depth of their understanding. As a critical reader, you may not be sufficiently expert on the subject yourself to know whether the facts are accurate, the sources reliable, and the understanding sufficient. You may need to do some research to see what others are saying about the subject. You can also check credentials—the writer's educational and professional qualifications, the respectability of the publication in which the selection first appeared, any reviews of the writer's work—to determine whether the writer is a respected authority in the field. King brings with him the authority that comes from being a member of the clergy and a respected leader of the Southern Christian Leadership Conference.

Testing for Common Ground

One way writers can establish common ground with their readers is by basing their reasoning on shared values, beliefs, and attitudes. They use language that includes their readers (*we*) rather than excludes them (*they*). They qualify their assertions to keep them from being too extreme. Above all, they acknowledge differences of opinion and try to make room in their argument to accommodate reasonable differences. As a reader, you will be affected by such appeals.

King creates common ground with readers by using the inclusive pronoun *we*, suggesting shared concerns between himself and his audience. Notice, however, his use of masculine pronouns and other references ("the Negro . . . he," "our brothers"). Although King addressed this letter to male clergy, he intended it to be published in the local newspaper, where it would be read by an audience of both men and women. By using language that excludes women, King misses the opportunity to build common ground with half his readers.

Testing for Fairness

Writers display their character by how they handle objections to their argument and opposing arguments. As a critical reader, you want to pay particular attention to how writers treat possible differences of opinion. Be suspicious of those who ignore differences and pretend everyone agrees with their viewpoint. When objections or opposing views are represented, you should consider whether they have been distorted in any way; if they are refuted, you want to be sure they are challenged fairly—with sound reasoning and solid evidence.

One way to gauge the author's credibility is to identify the tone of the argument, for it conveys the writer's attitude toward the subject and toward the reader. Examine the text carefully for indications of tone: is the text angry? sarcastic? evenhanded? shrill? positive? negative? Do you feel as if the writer is treating the subject—and you, one reader—with fairness? King's tone might be characterized as patient (he doesn't lose his temper), as respectful (he refers to white moderates as "people of good will"), as pompous (comparing himself to Jesus and Socrates).

Following are some fallacies that can undermine the ethical appeal:

- *Guilt by association*, when someone's credibility is attacked by associating that person with another person whom readers consider untrustworthy.
- *Ad hominem* (Latin for argument "against the man"), when the writer attacks his or her opponents personally instead of finding fault with their argument.
- *Straw man*, when the writer directs the argument against a claim that nobody actually holds or that everyone agrees is weak; often involves misrepresentation or distortion of the opposing argument.

ANALYZING THE WRITING IN OTHER DISCIPLINES

Each major or academic discipline has its own traditional ways of using writing to record and pass on what is already known as well as to establish new knowledge in that field. Students of literature do not use the same methods as laboratory scientists, for example. English instructors would be surprised to receive a paper in the form of a lab report just as scientists would be surprised to get an intepretive essay. And disciplines themselves often have different schools that disagree over things like methodology and the value of certain kinds of evidence. But, as a rule, the writing in one major differs from another, particularly across the broader disciplinary categories of the humanities, social sciences, and natural sciences.

As a college student taking general-education courses, you are required to take an array of courses from these areas to get a taste of the variety of ways knowledge is made in different disciplines. But it is not until you major in a field that you really come to appreciate what's special about the way scholars and researchers in that field think and construct texts.

To be a critical reader, you need to be aware of how the writing you are reading may be affected by disciplinary traditions. Following are some questions to guide you as you read texts in your major.

1. *What is the subject of study?* Is it a text? a natural phenomenon? a social trend? a set of documents or records? numbers or statistics?

2. *What kinds of statements tend to be made about subjects in this field?* For example, are they conjectures about causality, assertions of fact, interpretations of meaning, or something else? What generally seems to be the writer's purpose?

3. *What key concepts are necessary to make sense of the writing?* In broader terms, what assumptions are being made about your prior knowledge of the subject? What is taken for granted? How do such assumptions affect your understanding of the text? If key concepts are defined, should you question their definitions?

4. *What kinds of evidence carry weight in this field*—empirical data? statistics? textual quotation? authorities?

5. *If statistics or other numerical information is used, how is it typically presented*—in tables? charts? graphs? How does any numerical data serve the writer's purpose?

6. *How is any ethnographic or field research presented?* How do any interviews, direct observations, or questionnaires affect your understanding of the writer's point? Ask yourself whether some other data—interviews with *other* subjects, for instance—might change your understanding.

7. *How much of the writing is descriptive or narrative and how much interpretative or evaluative?* Whatever the writing strategies, how do they further the author's argument?

8. *If textual evidence is used, how are quotations cited?* Do quotations normally "speak for themselves," or does the writer analyze or otherwise interpret them for readers?

9. *How are other scholars cited?* If they are quoted or otherwise referred to, how does the writer handle competing claims or different methodologies? How are quotes documented?

10. *How is the author identified in the writing?* What kinds of credentials confer authority on the author? Are there multiple authors? If so, do you know enough about the team to understand "where they're coming from," or do you need to find out more?

11. *Where was the writing published?* If it is reprinted, where was it originally published? Which publication sources—professional journals or book publishers—are most important in your major field, and why?

12. *Which genres are most commonly written in your field*—lab reports? research reports? biography? position papers? proposals? How are they typically organized, and why?

PART THREE

Writing Strategies

In order to guide readers through a piece of writing, a writer can provide four basic kinds of cues or signals: (1) thesis and forecasting statements, to orient readers to ideas and organization; (2) paragraphing, to group related ideas and details; (3) cohesive devices, to connect ideas to one another and bring about coherence and clarity; and (4) transitions, to signal relationships or shifts in meaning. This chapter will examine how each of these cueing strategies works.

ORIENTING STATEMENTS

To help readers find their way, especially in difficult and lengthy works, you can provide two kinds of orienting information: thesis statements that declare the main point and forecasting statements that, in addition to stating the thesis, preview the way the thesis will be developed.

Thesis Statements

Although they may have a variety of forms and purposes, all essays are essentially assertive. That is, they assert or put forward the writer's point of view on a subject. We call this point of view the essay's *thesis*, or main idea.

To help readers understand what is being said about a subject, writers often provide a thesis statement early in the essay. The *thesis statement* is usually a single sentence that declares the essay's main idea. It operates as a cue by letting readers know which is the most important, general idea among the writer's many ideas and observations. Like the focal point of a picture, the thesis statement directs the reader's attention to the one idea that brings all the other ideas and details into perspective. Here are two thesis statements from essays in Part I:

> What seems on the surface to be irrational, intoxicated behavior is in fact part of nature's master strategy—a vital force that has helped humans survive, thrive, and multiply through thousands of years. –Anastasia Toufexis, Chapter 5

> Many of today's young people have a difficult time seeing any moral dimension to their actions. There are a number of reasons why that's true, but none more prominent than a failed system of education that eschews teaching children the traditional moral values that bind Americans together as a society and a culture.
> –William K. Kilpatrick, Chapter 6

Of the two preceding thesis statements, the first is expressed directly in a single sentence, while the second requires two sentences. Sometimes writers imply the thesis rather than state it directly. For example, William L. Kibler indicates that his proposal to combat plagiarism (Chapter 7) includes positive and negative reinforcement:

> The solution I propose, based on my recent research, is built on the concept that the most effective way to prevent cheating is to actively promote academic integrity, while at the same time effectively confronting those who do cheat.

Readers by necessity look for something that will tell them the point of an essay, a focus for the many diverse details and ideas they encounter as they read. The lack of an explicit thesis statement can make this task more difficult. Therefore, careful writers keep in mind the needs and expectations of readers in deciding whether or not to state the thesis explicitly.

A further important decision is where to place the thesis statement. Most readers expect to find some information early in the text that will give them a context for the essay. They expect essays to open with thesis statements, and they need such statements to orient them, particularly if they are reading about a new and difficult subject. A thesis statement placed at the beginning of an essay helps give readers a sense of control over the subject, enabling them to anticipate the content of the essay and more easily understand the relationship between its various ideas and details.

Occasionally, however, particularly in fairly short, informal essays and in some argumentative essays, a writer will save a direct statement of the thesis until the conclusion. Such a thesis is designed to bring together the various strands of information or evidence introduced over the course of the essay and to suggest the essay's overall point; in many cases, a concluding thesis is also used to point the way toward future developments or goals.

See Victor Fuchs's essay on pp. 351–54 for an example of a concluding thesis.

EXERCISE 13.1

Read an essay by Anastasia Toufexis (Chapter 5), William K. Kilpatrick (Chapter 6), or Stephen King (Chapter 9); then briefly explain how its thesis statement brings the ideas and details of the essay into perspective.

Forecasting Statements

A special kind of thesis statement, a *forecasting statement*, not only identifies the thesis but also gives an overview of the way that thesis will be developed. The opening paragraph of an essay by William Langer on the bubonic plague illustrates the role of the forecasting statement:

In the three years from 1348 through 1350 the pandemic of plague known as the Black Death, or, as the Germans called it, the Great Dying, killed at least a fourth of the population of Europe. It was undoubtedly the worst disaster that has ever befallen mankind. Today we can have no real conception of the terror under which people lived in the shadow of the plague. For more than two centuries plague has not been a serious threat to mankind in the large, although it is still a grisly presence in parts of the Far East and Africa. Scholars continue to study the Great Dying, however, as a historical example of human behavior under the stress of universal catastrophe. In these days when the threat of plague has been replaced by the threat of mass human extermination by even more rapid means, there has been a sharp renewal of interest in the history of the 14th-century calamity. <u>With new perspective, students are investigating its manifold effects: demographic, economic, psychological, moral and religious.</u>

–William Langer, ''The Black Death''

This paragraph informs us that Langer's article is about the effects of the Black Death. His thesis, however, is not stated explicitly. It is implied by the forecasting statement that concludes the paragraph. With this sentence, Langer states that the study of the plague currently is focused on five particular categories. As a reader would expect, Langer then goes on to divide his essay into analyses of these five effects, taking them up in the order in which they appear in the forecasting statement.

EXERCISE 13.2

Read an essay from Chapter 5, underlining the thesis and forecasting statements. If you do not find any sentences that perform these functions, try drafting them yourself. Reflect on the usefulness of these cueing devices.

PARAGRAPHING

Paragraph Cues

The indentation that signals the beginning of a new paragraph is a relatively modern printing convention. Old manuscripts show that paragraph divisions were not always marked. In order to make reading easier, scribes and printers began to use the symbol ¶ to mark paragraph breaks. Later, indenting became common practice, but even that relatively modern custom has changed in some forms of writing today. Instead of indenting, most writers in business now distinguish one paragraph from another by leaving an extra line of space above and below each paragraph.

The lack of paragraph cues makes reading extremely difficult. To illustrate this fact, the paragraph indentations have been removed from the following introductory section of a chapter in Stephen Jay Gould's book *Ever Since Darwin*. Even with proper paragraphing, this selection might be difficult because it includes unfamiliar information and technical language. Without paragraphing, however, Gould's logic becomes hard to follow, and the mind and the eye long for a momentary rest. (Each of the thirty sentences in the selection is numbered at the beginning.)

(1) Since man created God in his own image, the doctrine of special creation has never failed to explain those adaptations that we understand intuitively. (2) How can we doubt that animals are exquisitely designed for their appointed roles when we watch a lioness hunt, a horse run, or a hippo wallow? (3) The theory of natural selection would never have replaced the doctrine of divine creation if evident, admirable design pervaded all organisms. (4) Charles Darwin understood this, and he focused on features that would be out of place in a world constructed by perfect wisdom. (5) Why, for example, should a sensible designer create only on Australia a suite of marsupials to fill the same roles that placental mammals occupy on all other continents? (6) Darwin even wrote an entire book on orchids to argue that the structures evolved to insure fertilization by insects are jerry-built of available parts used by ancestors for other purposes. (7) Orchids are Rube Goldberg machines; a perfect engineer would certainly have come up with something better. (8) This principle remains true today. (9) The best illustrations of adaptation by evolution are the ones that strike our intuition as peculiar or bizarre. (10) Science is not "organized common sense"; at its most exciting, it reformulates our view of the world by imposing powerful theories against the ancient, anthropocentric prejudices that we call intuition. (11) Consider, for example, the cecidomyian gall midges. (12) These tiny flies conduct their lives in a way that tends to evoke feelings of pain or disgust when we empathize with them by applying the inappropriate standards of our own social codes. (13) Cecidomyian gall midges can grow and develop along one of two pathways. (14) In some situations, they hatch from eggs, go through a normal sequence of larval and pupal molts, and emerge as ordinary, sexually reproducing flies. (15) But in other circumstances, females reproduce by parthenogenesis, bringing forth their young without any fertilization by males. (16) Parthenogenesis is common enough among animals, but the cecidomyians give it an interesting twist. (17) First of all, the parthenogenetic females stop at an early age of development. (18) They never become normal, adult flies, but reproduce while they are still larvae or pupae. (19) Secondly, these females do not lay eggs. (20) The offspring develop live within their mother's body—not supplied with nutrient and packaged away in a protected uterus but right inside the mother's tissues, eventually filling her entire body. (21) In order to grow, the offspring devour the mother from the inside. (22) A few days later, they emerge, leaving a chitinous shell as the only remains of their only parent. (23) And within two days, their own developing children are beginning, literally, to eat them up. (24) *Micromalthus debilis*, an unrelated beetle, has evolved an almost identical system with a macabre variation. (25) Some parthenogenetic females give birth to a single male offspring. (26) This larva attaches itself to his mother's cuticle for about four or five days, then inserts his head into her genital aperture and devours her. (27) Greater love hath no woman. (28) Why has such a peculiar mode of reproduction evolved? (29) For it is unusual even among insects, and not only by the irrelevant standards of our own perceptions. (30) What is the adaptive significance of a mode of life that so strongly violates our intuitions about good design? —Stephen Jay Gould, *Ever Since Darwin*

A major difficulty in reading this selection is the need to hold the meaning of each sentence "in suspension" as you read ahead, because the meaning of an earlier sentence may be affected by the meaning of succeeding sentences. For instance, the second sentence clarifies the meaning of the first sentence by giving specific examples; the third sentence restates the idea, while sentences 4 through 7 clarify and illustrate it. Without paragraphing, you are forced to remember each sentence separately and even to anticipate such close connections among sentences in order to make sense of the text.

Paragraphing helps readers by signaling when a sequence of related sentences begins and ends. The use of such paragraph signals tells you when you can stop holding meaning in suspension. The need for this kind of closure is a major consideration of writers. Gould, for example, begins a new paragraph with sentence 8 in order to draw a sharp distinction between the examples and the general principle. Similarly, he begins a new paragraph with sentence 24 to signal a shift from a description of the reproductive mode of the cecidomyian gall midge to that of *Micromalthus debilis*. In this way, paragraphing keeps readers from being overloaded with information and at the same time helps them follow the development of ideas.

Paragraphing also helps readers judge what is most important in what they are reading. Writers typically emphasize important information by placing it at the two points where readers are most attentive—the beginning and ending of a paragraph. Many writers put information to orient readers at the beginning of a paragraph and save the most important information for last, as Gould does when he ends a paragraph with sentence 27.

See pp. 472–76 for discussion of topic sentences.

You can give special emphasis to information by placing it in a paragraph of its own. Gould, for example, puts sentences 11 and 12 together in a separate paragraph. These two sentences could have been attached to either the preceding or following paragraphs. But Gould gives them a separate paragraph in order to emphasize the general point he is making. In addition, this paragraph serves as an important transition between the general discussion of how science explains things that go against intuition and the specific example of the bizarre adaptation of the cecidomyian gall midge.

EXERCISE 13.3

Here is the way the Gould selection divides into its six original paragraphs: sentences 1–7, 8–10, 11–12, 13–23, 24–27, 28–30. Put a paragraphing symbol ¶ in your own book before the opening sentence of each paragraph. Later exercises will ask you to analyze aspects of Gould's paragraphing.

Paragraph
Conventions

Some writing situations call for fairly strict conventions for paragraphing. Readers may not be conscious of these conventions, but they would certainly notice if the custom were not observed. For example, readers would be surprised if a newspaper did not have narrow columns and short paragraphs.

This paragraphing convention is not accidental; it is designed to make newspaper reading easy and fast and to allow the reader to take in an entire paragraph at a glance. Business writing also tends to have short paragraphs. Memo readers frequently do not want an excess of details or qualifications. Instead, they prefer a concise overview, a capsule that is easy to swallow.

College instructors, on the other hand, expect students to qualify their ideas and support them with specifics. They care less about how long it takes to read a paragraph than about how well developed the writing is. Therefore, paragraphs in college essays usually have several sentences. In fact, it is not unusual to find quite long paragraphs, as this example from an undergraduate history essay on the status of women in Victorian England illustrates:

> A genteel woman was absolutely dependent upon the two men in her life: first her father, and then her husband. From them came her economic and social status; they were the center of her thoughts and the objects of any ambitions she might have. The ideal woman did not live for herself; she barely had a self, because her entire existence was vicarious. Legally, a woman had almost no existence at all. Until her marriage, a daughter was completely in the power of her father; upon her marriage, she was legally absorbed by her husband. Any money she had became his, as did all of her property, including her clothes and even those things that had been given her as personal gifts before her marriage. Any earnings she might make by working belonged to her husband. A woman could not be sued for debt separately from her husband because legally they were the same person. She could not sign a lease or sue someone in court without having her husband be the complainant, even in cases of long separation. In cases of a husband's enmity, she had almost no legal protection from him. Under English law, divorces could be obtained, in practice, only by men. A man could divorce his wife on the grounds of adultery, but the reverse was not the case.

If any rule for paragraphing is truly universal, it is this: paragraphs should be focused, unified, and coherent. That is, the sentences in a paragraph should be meaningfully related to one another, and the relationships among the sentences should be clear. The following sentences—although they may look like a paragraph—do not constitute a meaningful paragraph because they lack focus, unity, and coherence.

> Maturity and attitude go together because both determine why you want to become a model. I went to the university for two years, not because I wanted to but because I was pushed into it. I used to think models were thought of as dumb blondes, but after being here at the university I realized that people still have respect for modeling and know all the hard work put in it.

Even though each of these sentences mentions either modeling or the university or both, the two topics are not connected. With each sentence, the fous shifts—from the general desire to become a model, to the writer's attending university, to the attitude of people toward models. There is no unity because there is no single idea controlling the sentences. The various elements of the writing do not "stick together" to form a coherent meaning, and the reader may well become disoriented. The topic-sentence strategies discussed in the following section are useful for ensuring coherence.

EXERCISE 13.4

Look at the Gould passage earlier in this chapter. Analyze how Gould's paragraphing helps you follow his meaning. Is each paragraph focused, unified, and coherent? How could you have paragraphed this passage differently?

Topic-sentence Strategies

A *topic sentence* lets readers know the focus of a paragraph in simple and direct terms. It is a cueing strategy for the paragraph much as a thesis or forecasting statement is for the whole essay. Because paragraphing usually signals a shift in focus, readers expect some kind of reorientation in the opening sentence. They need to know whether the new paragraph is going to introduce another aspect of the topic or develop one already introduced.

Announcing the Topic.   Some topic sentences simply announce the topic. Here are a few examples taken from Barry Lopez's book *Arctic Dreams*:

> A polar bear walks in a way all its own.
>
> What is so consistently striking about the way Eskimos used parts of an animal is the breadth of their understanding about what would work.
>
> Distinctive landmarks that aid the traveler and control the vastness, as well as prominent marks on the land made inadvertently in the process of completing other tasks, are very much apparent in the Arctic.
>
> The Mediterranean view of the Arctic, down to the time of the Elizabethan mariners, was shaped by two somewhat contradictory thoughts.

These topic sentences do more than merely identify the topic; they also indicate how the topic will be developed in subsequent sentences—by citing examples, describing physical features, presenting reasons and evidence, relating anecdotes, classifying, defining, comparing, or contrasting.

Other strategies that can be used for paragraph development are discussed in Chapters 14 through 19.

Following is one of Lopez's paragraphs that shows how the topic in the first sentence is developed:

> What is so consistently striking about the way Eskimos used parts of an animal is the breadth of their understanding about what would work. Knowing that muskox horn is more flexible than caribou antler, they preferred it for making the side prongs of a fish spear. For a waterproof bag in which to carry sinews for clothing repair, they chose salmon skin. They selected the strong, translucent intestine of a bearded seal to make a window for a snowhouse—it would fold up for easy traveling and it would not frost over in cold weather. To make small snares for sea ducks, they needed a springy material that would not rot in salt water—baleen fibers. The down feather of a common eider, tethered at the end

of a stick in the snow at an aglu, would reveal the exhalation of a quietly sur-facing seal. Polar bear bone was used anywhere a stout, sharp point was re-quired, because it is the hardest bone.   –Barry Lopez, *Arctic Dreams*

EXERCISE 13.5

Read the Weisman essay in Chapter 7. Indicate which paragraphs begin with topic sentences, and explain how these sentences help you anticipate the par-agraph's topic and its method of development.

Forecasting Subtopics.   Other topic sentences actually give readers a detailed overview of subtopics that follow. In the following paragraph the subtopics mentioned in the opening sentence appear later in the paragraph. The sub-topics are <u>underscored</u> in the first sentence and then connected by lines to the point in the paragraph where they subsequently appear.

Notice that the subtopics are taken up in the same order as in the opening sentence: education first, followed by economic independence, power of of-fice, and so on. This correlation makes the paragraph easy to follow. Even so, one subtopic may be developed in a sentence while another requires two or more sentences. The last two subtopics—equality of status and recognition as human beings—are not directly brought up but are implied in the last sentence.

> <u>Oppressed groups are denied education, economic independence, the power of office, representation, an image of dignity and self-respect, equality of status, and recognition as human beings.</u> Throughout history women have been con-sistently denied all of these, and their denial today, while attenuated and partial, is nevertheless consistent. The <u>education</u> allowed them is deliberately designed to be inferior, and they are systematically programmed out of and excluded from the knowledge where power lies today—e.g., in science and technology. They are confined to conditions of <u>economic dependence</u> based on the sale of their sexuality in marriage, or a variety of prostitutions. Work on a basis of economic independence allows them only a subsistence level of life—often not even that. They do not hold <u>office</u>, are <u>represented</u> in no positions of power, and authority is forbidden them. The <u>image</u> of woman fostered by cultural media, high and low, then and now, is a marginal and demeaning existence, and one outside the human condition—which is defined as the prerogative of man, the male.
>
> –Kate Millett, *Sexual Politics*

Asking a Rhetorical Question.   Occasionally, writers put topic sentences in a question-answer format, posing a rhetorical question in one sentence which is then answered in the next sentence. Question-answer topic sentences do not always appear at the beginning of a paragraph. A question at the end of one paragraph may combine with the first sentence of the following para-graph. Here is a paragraph illustrating the rhetorical question strategy.

Why, then do so many people believe in astrology? One obvious reason is that people read into the generally vague astrological pronouncements almost anything they want to, and thus invest them with a truth which is not inherent in the pronouncements themselves. They're also more likely to remember true "predictions," overvalue coincidences, and ignore everything else. Other reasons are its age (of course, ritual murder and sacrifice are as old), its simplicity in principle and comforting complexity in practice, and its flattering insistence on the connection between the starry vastness of the heavens and whether or not we'll fall in love this month.

–John Allen Paulos, *Innumeracy: Mathematical Illiteracy and Its Consequences*

EXERCISE 13.6

Look at the selection by Anastasia Toufexis in Chapter 5 or by Mickey Kaus in Chapter 7. Where does the writer use the rhetorical question as a topic-sentence strategy? How well does it work? Explain briefly.

Making a Transition.　　Not all topic sentences simply point forward to what will follow. Some also refer back to earlier sentences. Such sentences work both as topic sentences, stating the main point of the paragraph, and as transitions, linking that paragraph to the previous one. Here are a few topic sentences from "Quilts and Women's Culture" by Elaine Hedges that use specific transitions (underscored) to tie the sentence to a previous statement:

Within its broad traditionalism and anonymity, however, variations and distinctions developed.

Regionally, too, distinctions were introduced into quilt making through the interesting process of renaming.

With equal inventiveness women renamed traditional patterns to accommodate to the local landscape.

Finally, out of such regional and other variations come individual, signed achievements.

Quilts, then, were an outlet for creative energy, a source and emblem of sisterhood and solidarity, and a graphic response to historical and political change.

Sometimes the first sentence of a paragraph serves as a transition, while a subsequent sentence—in this case the last—states the topic. The underscored sentences illustrate this strategy in the following example:

. . . What a convenience, what a relief it will be, they say, never to worry about how to dress for a job interview, a romantic tryst, or a funeral!

Convenient perhaps, but not exactly a relief. Such a utopia would give most of us the same kind of chill we feel when a stadium full of Communist-bloc athletes in identical sports outfits, shouting slogans in unison, appears on TV. Most people do not want to be told what to wear any more than they want to be told what to say. In Belfast recently four hundred Irish Republican prisoners "refused to wear any clothes at all, draping themselves day and night in blankets," rather than put on prison uniforms. Even the offer of civilian-style dress did not satisfy them; they insisted on wearing their own clothes brought from home, or nothing. <u>Fashion is free speech, and one of the privileges, if not always one of the pleasures, of a free world.</u>   –Alison Lurie, *The Language of Clothes*

Occasionally, whole paragraphs serve as transitions, linking one sequence of paragraphs with those that follow. See how the next transition paragraph summarizes what went before (evidence of contrast) and sets up what will follow (evidence of similarity):

Yet it was not all contrast, after all. Different as they were—in background, in personality, in underlying aspiration—these two great soldiers had much in common. Under everything else, they were marvelous fighters. Furthermore, their fighting qualities were really very much alike.

–Bruce Catton, "Grant and Lee: A Study in Contrasts"

Positioning the Topic Sentence.   Although topic sentences may occur anywhere in a paragraph, stating the topic in the first sentence has the advantage of giving readers a sense of how the paragraph is likely to be developed. The beginning of the paragraph is therefore the most commonly favored position for a topic sentence.

A topic sentence that does not open a paragraph is most likely to appear at the end. When placed in the concluding position, topic sentences usually summarize or generalize preceding information. In the following example, the topic is not stated explicitly until the last sentence.

Even black Americans sometimes need to be reminded about the deceptiveness of television. Blacks retain their fascination with black characters on TV: Many of us buy *Jet* magazine primarily to read its weekly television feature, which lists *every* black character (major or minor) to be seen on the screen that week. Yet our fixation with the presence of black characters on TV has blinded us to an important fact that *Cosby*, which began in 1984, and its offshoots over the years demonstrate convincingly: There is very little connection between the social status of black Americans and the fabricated images of black people that Americans consume each day. <u>The representation of blacks on TV is a very poor index to our social advancement or political progress.</u>

–Henry Louis Gates, Jr., "TV's Black World Turns—But Stays Unreal"

When a topic sentence is used in a narrative, it will often appear as the last sentence, often to evaluate or reflect on events:

I hadn't known she could play the piano. She wasn't playing very well, I guess, because she stopped occasionally and had to start over again. She concentrated intensely on the music, and the others in the room sat absolutely silently. My mother was facing me but didn't seem to see me. She seemed to be staring beyond me toward something that wasn't there. All the happy excitement died in me at that moment. <u>Looking at my mother, so isolated from us all, I saw her for the first time as a person utterly alone.</u>   –Russell Baker, *Growing Up*

In rare cases, the topic sentence for one paragraph will appear at the end of the preceding paragraph, as in this example:

> . . . And apart from being new, psychoanalysis was particularly threatening.
> French psychiatrists tended to look at the sufferings of their patients either as the result of organic lesions or moral degeneration. In either case, the boundary between the ''healthy'' doctor and the ''sick'' patient was clear. Freud's theory makes it hard to draw such lines by insisting that if the psychiatrist knew himself better, he would find more points in common with the patient than he might have thought. . . .   –Sherry Turkle, *Psychoanalytic Politics*

In addition, it is possible for a single topic sentence to introduce two (or more) paragraphs. Subsequent paragraphs in such a series consequently have no separate topic sentence of their own. Following is a two-paragraph sequence in which the topic sentence opens the first paragraph:

> Anthropologists Daniel Maltz and Ruth Borker point out that boys and girls socialize differently. Little girls tend to play in small groups or, even more common, in pairs. Their social life usually centers around a best friend, and friendships are made, maintained, and broken by talk—especially ''secrets.'' If a little girl tells her friend's secret to another little girl, she may find herself with a new best friend. The secrets themselves may or may not be important, but the fact of telling them is all-important. It's hard for newcomers to get into these tight groups, but anyone who is admitted is treated as an equal. Girls like to play cooperatively; if they can't cooperate, the group breaks up.
>
> Little boys tend to play in larger groups, often outdoors, and they spend more time doing things than talking. It's easy for boys to get into the group, but not everyone is accepted as an equal. Once in the group, boys must jockey for their status in it. One of the most important ways they do this is through talk: verbal display such as telling stories and jokes, challenging and sidetracking the verbal displays of other boys, and withstanding other boys' challenges in order to maintain their own story—and status. Their talk is often competitive talk about who is best at what.   –Deborah Tannen, *That's Not What I Meant!*

EXERCISE 13.7

Now that you have seen several topic-sentence strategies, look again at the Gould passage earlier in this chapter and identify the strategies he uses. Then evaluate how well his topic sentences work to orient you as a reader.

COHESIVE DEVICES

Certain cohesive devices can be used to guide readers, to help them follow a writer's train of thought by connecting key words and phrases throughout a passage. Among such devices are pronoun reference, word repetition, synonyms, repetition of sentence structure, and collocation.

Pronoun
Reference

One common cohesive device is pronoun reference. As noun substitutes, pronouns refer to nouns that either precede or follow them, and thus serve to connect phrases or sentences. The nouns that come before the pronouns are called antecedents. In the following paragraph, the pronouns (all *it*) form a chain of connection with their antecedent, *George Washington Bridge*.

> In New York from dawn to dusk to dawn, day after day, you can hear the steady rumble of tires against the concrete span of the George Washington Bridge. The bridge is never completely still. It trembles with traffic. It moves in the wind. Its great veins of steel swell when hot and contract when cold; its span often is ten feet closer to the Hudson River in summer than in winter.   —Gay Talese, "New York"

This example has only one pronoun-antecedent chain, and it comes first so all the pronouns refer back to it. When there are multiple pronoun-antecedent chains with references forward as well as back, writers have to be sure that readers will not mistake one pronoun's antecedent for another's.

Word Repetition

To avoid confusion, a writer will often repeat words and phrases. This device is used especially if a pronoun might confuse readers:

> The first step is to realize that in our society we have permitted the kinds of vulnerability that characterize the victims of violent crime and have ignored, where we could, the hostility and alienation that enter into the making of violent criminals. No rational person condones violent crime, and I have no patience with sentimental attitudes toward violent criminals. But it is time that we open our eyes to the conditions that foster violence and that ensure the existence of easily recognizable victims.   —Margaret Mead, "A Life for a Life: What That Means Today"

In the next example several overlapping chains of word repetition prevent confusion and help the reader follow the ideas:

> Natural selection is the central concept of Darwinian theory—the fittest survive and spread their favored traits through populations. Natural selection is defined by Spencer's phrase "survival of the fittest," but what does this famous bit of jargon really mean? Who are the fittest? And how is "fitness" defined? We often read that fitness involves no more than "differential reproductive success"—the production of more surviving offspring than other competing members of the population. Whoa! cries Bethell, as many others have before him. This formulation defines fitness in terms of survival only. The crucial phrase of natural selection means no more than "the survival of those who survive"—a vacuous tautology. (A tautology is a phrase—like "my father is a man"—containing no information in the predicate ["a man"] not inherent in the subject ["my father"]. Tautologies are fine as definitions, but not as testable scientific statements—there can be nothing to test in a statement true by definition.)
>
> —Stephen Jay Gould, *Ever Since Darwin*

Notice that Gould uses repetition to keep readers focused on the key concepts of "natural selection," "survival of the fittest," and "tautology." These key terms may vary in form—*fittest* becomes *fitness* and *survival* changes to *surviving* and *survive*—but they serve as links in the chain of meaning.

Synonyms

In addition to repeating the same word, you can also use synonyms, words with identical or very similar meanings, to connect important ideas. In the following example, the author develops a careful chain of synonyms and word repetitions:

> Over time, small bits of knowledge about a region accumulate among local residents in the form of stories. These are remembered in the community; even what is unusual does not become lost and therefore irrelevant. These narratives comprise for a native an intricate, long-term view of a particular landscape. . . . Outside the region this complex but easily shared "reality" is hard to get across without reducing it to generalities, to misleading or imprecise abstraction.
>
> –Barry Lopez, *Arctic Dreams*

Note the variety of synonym sequences: "region," "particular landscape"; "local residents," "community," "native"; "stories," "narratives"; "accumulate," "remembered," "does not become lost," "comprise"; "intricate long-term view," "complex . . . reality," "without reducing it to generalities." The result is a coherence of paragraph development that constantly reinforces the point the author is making.

Sentence-structure Repetition

Writers occasionally repeat the same sentence structure in order to emphasize the connections among their ideas. For example:

> But the life forms are as much part of the structure of the Earth as any inanimate portion is. It is all an inseparable part of a whole. If any animal is isolated totally from other forms of life, then death by starvation will surely follow. If isolated from water, death by dehydration will follow even faster. If isolated from air, whether free or dissolved in water, death by asphyxiation will follow still faster. If isolated from the Sun, animals will survive for a time, but plants would die, and if all plants died, all animals would starve.   –Isaac Asimov, "The Case against Man"

From the third sentence to the last, Asimov repeats the "If this . . . then that" sentence structure to emphasize the various points he is making.

Collocation

Words collocate when they occur together in expected ways around a particular topic. For example, in a paragraph on a high school graduation, a reader might expect to encounter words such as *valedictorian, diploma, commencement, honors, cap and gown,* or *senior class.* Collocations occur quite naturally to a writer, and they usually form a recognizable network of meaning for readers. The paragraph that follows uses five collocation chains:

1. housewife—cooking—neighbor—home
2. clocks—calculated cooking times—progression—precise
3. obstinacy—vagaries—problem
4. sun—clear days—cloudy ones—sundial—cast its light—angle— seasons—sun—weather

5. cooking—fire—matches—hot coals—smoldering—ashes—go out—
   bed-warming

> The seventeenth-century housewife not only had to make do without thermom-
> eters, she also had to make do without clocks, which were scarce and dear
> throughout the sixteen hundreds. She calculated cooking times by the progres-
> sion of the sun; her cooking must have been more precise on clear days than
> on cloudy ones. Marks were sometimes painted on the floor, providing her with
> a rough sundial, but she still had to make allowance for the obstinacy of the sun
> in refusing to cast its light at the same angle as the seasons changed; but she
> was used to allowing for the vagaries of sun and weather. She also had a prob-
> lem starting her fire in the morning; there were no matches. If she had allowed
> the hot coals smoldering under the ashes to go out, she had to borrow some
> from a neighbor, carrying them home with care, perhaps in a bed-warming pan.
>
> —Waverly Root and Richard de Rouchement, *Eating in America*

EXERCISE 13.8

The preceding section illustrates the following cohesive devices: pronoun reference, word repetition, synonyms, sentence-structure repetition, and collocation. Look again at the Gould passage on adaptation earlier in the chapter,
and identify the cohesive devices you find in it. How do these cohesive devices
help you to read the essay and make sense of it?

TRANSITIONS

The final type of cueing discussed in this chapter is the transition. A *transition*,
sometimes called a connective, serves as a bridge, connecting one paragraph,
sentence, clause, or word with another. Not only does a transition signal a
connection, it also identifies the kind of connection by indicating to readers
how the item preceding the transition relates to that which follows it. Transitions help readers anticipate how the next paragraph or sentence will affect
the meaning of what they have just read. Following is a discussion of three
basic groups of transitions, based on the relationships they indicate: logical,
temporal, and spatial.

**Logical
Relationships**

Transitions help readers follow the logic of an argument. How such transitions work is illustrated in this tightly—and passionately—reasoned paragraph by James Baldwin:

> The black man insists, by whatever means he finds at his disposal, that the white
> man cease to regard him as an exotic rarity <u>and</u> recognize him as a human being.
> This is a very charged and difficult moment, <u>for</u> there is a great deal of will power
> involved in the white man's naivete. Most people are not naturally malicious, <u>and</u>

the white man prefers to keep the black man at a certain human remove <u>because</u> it is easier for him <u>thus</u> to preserve his simplicity <u>and</u> to avoid being called to account for crimes committed by his forefathers, <u>or</u> his neighbors. He is inescapably aware, <u>nevertheless</u>, that he is in a better position in the world <u>than</u> black men are, <u>nor</u> can he quite put to death the suspicion that he is hated by black men <u>therefore</u>. He does not wish to be hated, <u>neither</u> does he wish to change places, <u>and</u> at this point in his uneasiness he can scarcely avoid having recourse to those legends which white men have created about black men, the most unusual effect of which is that the white man finds himself enmeshed, so to speak, in his own language which describes hell, <u>as well as</u> the attributes which lead one to hell, <u>as being</u> black as night.

—James Baldwin, "Stranger in the Village"

Transitions Showing Logical Relations

To introduce another item in a series: first, second; in the second place; for one thing . . . for another; next; then; furthermore; moreover; in addition; finally; last; also; similarly; besides; and; as well as.

To introduce an illustration or other specification: in particular; specifically; for instance; for example; that is; namely.

To introduce a result or a cause: consequently; as a result, hence; accordingly; thus; so; therefore; then; because; since; for.

To introduce a restatement: that is; in other words; in simpler terms; to put it differently.

To introduce a conclusion or summary: in conclusion; finally; all in all; evidently; clearly; actually; to sum up; altogether; of course.

To introduce an opposing point: but; however; yet; nevertheless; on the contrary; on the other hand; in contrast; still; neither . . . nor.

To introduce a concession to an opposing view: certainly; naturally; of course; it is true; to be sure; granted.

To resume the original line of reasoning after a concession: nonetheless; all the same; even though; still; nevertheless.

Temporal Relationships

In addition to showing logical connections, transitions indicate sequence or progression in time (temporal relationships), as this example illustrates:

<u>That night,</u> we drank tea and <u>then</u> vodka with lemon peel steeped in it. The four of us talked in Russian and English about mutual friends and American railroads and the Rolling Stones. Seryozha loves the Stones, and his face grew wistful <u>as we spoke</u> about their recent album, "Some Girls." He played a tape of "Let It Bleed" <u>over and over,</u> until we could translate some difficult phrases for him; <u>after that,</u> he came out with the phrases <u>at intervals during the evening,</u> in a pretty decent imitation of Jagger's Cockney snarl. He was an adroit and oddly formal host, inconspicuously filling our teacups and politely urging us to eat bread and cheese and chocolate. <u>While he talked to us,</u> he teased Anya, calling her "Piglet," and she shook back her bangs and glowered at him. It was clear

that theirs was a fiery relationship. <u>After a while,</u> we talked about ourselves. Anya told us about painting and printmaking and about how hard it was to buy supplies in Moscow. There had been something angry in her dark face <u>since the beginning of the evening</u>; I thought <u>at first</u> that it meant she didn't like Americans; but <u>now</u> I realized that it was a constant, barely suppressed rage at her own situation.   —Andrea Lee, *Russian Journal*

Temporal Transitions

To indicate frequency: frequently; hourly; often; occasionally; now and then; day after day; again and again.

To indicate duration: during; briefly; for a long time; minute by minute.

To indicate a particular time: now; then; at that time; in those days; last Sunday; next Christmas; in 1995; at the beginning of August; at six o'clock; first thing in the morning; two months ago.

To indicate the beginning: at first; in the beginning; since; before then.

To indicate the middle: in the meantime; meanwhile; as it was happening; at that moment; at the same time; simultaneously; next; then.

To indicate the end and beyond: eventually; finally; at last; in the end; subsequently; later; afterwards.

Spatial Relationships

Spatial transitions orient readers to the objects in a scene, as illustrated in this paragraph:

<u>On</u> Georgia 155, I crossed Troublesome Creek, then went <u>through</u> groves of pecan trees aligned <u>one with the next</u> like fenceposts. The pastures grew a green almost blue, and syrupy water the color of a dusty sunset filled the ponds. <u>Around</u> the farmhouses, <u>from</u> wires strung high <u>above</u> the ground, swayed gourds hollowed out for purple martins.

   The land rose <u>again on the other side</u> of the Chattahoochee River, and Highway 34 went to the ridgetops where long views <u>over</u> the hills opened <u>in all directions</u>. <u>Here</u> was the tail of the Appalachian backbone, its gradual descent <u>to</u> the Gulf. <u>Near</u> the Alabama stateline stood a couple of LAST CHANCE! bars. . . .

—William Least Heat Moon, *Blue Highways*

Transitions Showing Spatial Relationships

To indicate closeness: close to; near; next to; alongside; adjacent to; facing.

To indicate distance: in the distance; far; beyond; away; there.

To indicate direction: up or down; sideways; along; across; to the right or left; in front of or behind; above or below; inside or outside.

EXERCISE 13.9

Return to the Gould passage on page 469, and underline the logical, temporal, and spatial transitions. How do they help to relate the many details and ideas?

Narration is a basic writing strategy for presenting action. You can use narration for a variety of purposes: to illustrate and support ideas with anecdotes, entertain readers with suspenseful or revealing stories, analyze causes and possible effects with scenarios, and explain procedures with process narrative. This chapter focuses on narrative techniques—how to sequence narrative action, shape narrative structure, and present the narrative from various points of view. Finally, it looks at one special narrative form, how to present a process.

SEQUENCING NARRATIVE ACTION

Narration presents a sequence of actions taking place over a period of time. The most common way of ordering a narrative is to present the actions chronologically, beginning with the first action and going straight through to the last.

On occasion, however, writers complicate the narrative sequence by referring to something that occurred earlier, with a *flashback*, or to one that will occur later, with a *flashforward*.

The following excerpt from "Death of a Pig," an essay by E. B. White, shows how writers typically organize narratives chronologically. The essay from which the passage is taken tells us what happened when the pig White was raising became ill and died. This passage is referred to often in the pages that follow to illustrate the ways writers control readers' sense of passing time in a narrative and shape actions into meaningful stories.

> It was about four o'clock in the afternoon when I first noticed that there was something wrong with the pig. He failed to appear at the trough for his supper, and when a pig (or a child) refuses supper a chill wave of fear runs through any household, or ice-household. After examining my pig, who was stretched out in the sawdust inside the building, I went to the phone and cranked it four times. Mr. Dameron answered. "What's good for a sick pig?" I asked. (There is never any identification needed on a country phone; the person on the other end knows who is talking by the sound of the voice and by the character of the question.)
>
> "I don't know, I never had a sick pig," said Mr. Dameron, "but I can find out quick enough. You hang up and I'll call Henry."
>
> Mr. Dameron was back on the line again in five minutes. "Henry says roll him over on his back and give him two ounces of castor oil or sweet oil, and if

that doesn't do the trick give him an injection of soapy water. He says he's almost sure the pig's plugged up, and even if he's wrong, it can't do any harm.''

I thanked Mr. Dameron. I didn't go right down to the pig, though. I sank into a chair and sat still for a few minutes to think about my troubles, and then I got up and went to the barn, catching up on some odds and ends that needed tending to. Unconsciously I held off, for an hour, the deed by which I would officially recognize the collapse of the performance of raising a pig; I wanted no interruption in the regularity of feeding, the steadiness of growth, the even succesion of days. I wanted no interruption, wanted no oil, no deviation. I just wanted to keep on raising a pig, full meal after full meal, spring into summer into fall. I didn't even know whether there were two ounces of castor oil on the place.

Shortly after five o'clock I remembered that we had been invited out to dinner that night and realized that if I were to dose a pig there was no time to lose. The dinner date seemed a familiar conflict: I move in a desultory society and often a week or two will roll by without my going to anybody's house to dinner or anyone's coming to mine, but when an occasion does arise, and I am summoned, something usually turns up (an hour or two in advance) to make all human intercourse seem vastly inappropriate. I have come to believe that there is in hostesses a special power of divination, and that they deliberately arrange dinners to coincide with pig failure or some other sort of failure. At any rate, it was after five o'clock and I knew I could put off no longer the evil hour.

When my son and I arrived the pigyard, armed with a small bottle of castor oil and a length of clothesline, the pig had emerged from his house and was standing in the middle of his yard, listlessly. He gave us a slim greeting. I could see that he felt uncomfortable and uncertain. I had brought the clothesline thinking I'd have to tie him (the pig weighed more than a hundred pounds) but we never used it. My son reached down, grabbed both front legs, upset him quickly, and when he opened his mouth to scream I turned the oil into his throat—a pink, corrugated area I had never seen before. I had just time to read the label while the neck of the bottle was in his mouth. It said Puretest. The screams, slightly muffled by oil, were pitched in the hysterically high range of pig-sound, as though torture were being carried out, but they didn't last long; it was all over rather suddenly, and, his legs released, the pig righted himself.

–E. B. White, ''Death of a Pig''

EXERCISE 14.1

Think of something memorable you did that lasted a few hours. You might recall a race you ran in, an unusual activity you participated in, or an adventure in a strange place. Reflect on what you did, listing the events in the order in which they occurred. Then, write a brief, one-page narrative following the chronological sequence set out in your list.

Narrative Time Signals

Writers basically rely on three methods of sequencing actions for their readers: time markers, verb tense markers, and references to clock time.

Time Markers. A common way of showing the passage of time is with temporal transitions, words and phrases that locate an action at a particular point in time or that relate one point to another. Some familiar time markers inclue *then, when, at that time, before, after, while, next, later, first,* and *second.* Look back at the passage from "Death of a Pig" to see how White uses time markers. Notice, for example, that *when* in the first sentence labels the initial point at which he recognized something was seriously wrong. *After* in the third sentence signals the relationship between two actions—examining the pig and calling for advice.

Time markers are particularly crucial when explaining procedures to be followed or analyzing the steps in a complicated process, as you can see in this passage from an explanatory essay about the predatory relationship between wasps and tarantulas.

> When the grave is finished, the wasp returns to the tarantula to complete her ghastly enterprise. First, she feels it all over once more with her antennae. Then her behavior becomes more aggressive. She bends her abdomen, protruding her sting, and searches for the soft membrane at the point where the spider's legs join its body—the only spot where she can penetrate the horny skeleton. From time to time, as the exasperated spider slowly shifts ground, the wasp turns on her back and slides with the aid of her wings, trying to get under the tarantula for a shot at the vital spot. During all this maneuvering, which can last for several minutes, the tarantula makes no move to save itself. Finally the wasp corners it against some obstruction and grasps one of its legs in her powerful jaws. Now at last the harassed spider tries a desperate but vain defense. The two contestants roll over and over on the ground. It is a terrifying sight and the outcome is always the same.   —Alexander Petrunkevitch, "The Spider and the Wasp"

EXERCISE 14.2

Skim the White passage, underlining all the time markers. In each case, consider whether your understanding of the narrative would be hampered if the time marker had been left out.

Verb Tense Markers. Verb tense also plays an important role in presenting time in narrative. It indicates when the actions occur and whether they are complete or in progress. White, for example, sets most of his narrative in the simple past tense, complicating his narrative only when he reports actions occurring simultaneously: "When my son and I arrived at the pigyard, . . . the pig had emerged from his house and was standing in the middle of his yard. . . ." To convey the time relations among these actions, he uses three past tenses in one sentence: *simple past*, to indicate a completed action: "my son and I arrived"; *past perfect*, to indicate the action occurred before another action: "the pig had emerged"; *past progressive*, to indicate an ongoing action that had been in progress for some time: the pig "was standing."

Note that, in addition to these past tense forms, White also uses the present tense, to distinguish habitual, continually occurring, actions: "When a pig (or a child) refuses supper a chill wave of fear runs through any household." In fact, whole narratives may be written primarily in the present tense. This is generally the case for process narratives, as illustrated by the excerpt from "The Spider and the Wasp" in the preceding discussion. In addition, contemporary writers of profiles often use the present tense to give their writing a sense of "you-are-there" immediacy.

The pieces by Catherine Manegold and David Noonan in Chapter 4 are good examples of this use of the present tense.

Verb tense and temporal transitions can be used in various ways to distinguish actions that occurred repeatedly from those that occurred only once. In the following passage, for example, Willie Morris uses the tense marker *would* along with the time markers *many times* and *often* to indicate recurring actions. When he moves from action which occurred repeatedly to action which occurred only once, he shifts to the simple past tense, signaling this shift with the phrase *on one occasion*.

> Many times, walking home from work, I would see some unknowing soul venture across that intersection against the light and then freeze in horror when he saw the cars ripping out of the tunnel toward him. . . . Suddenly, the human reflex would take over, and the pedestrian would jackknife first one way, then another, arms flaying the empty air, and often the car would literally *skim* the man, brushing by him so close it would touch his coat or his tie. . . . On one occasion, feeling sorry for the person who had brushed against the speeding car, I hurried across the intersection after him to cheer him up a little. Catching up with him down by 32nd I said, "That was good legwork, sir. Excellent moves for a big man!" but the man looked at me with an empty expression in his eyes, and then moved away mechanically and trancelike, heading for the nearest bar.
> —Willie Morris, *North toward Home*

Clock Time. Most writers use clock time sparingly to signal the passage of time in a narrative, but it is a valuable device. White uses clock time to orient readers and to give a sense of duration. He tells us that the action lasted a little over an hour, beginning at about four o'clock and ending a little after five. He indicates that he called Mr. Dameron as soon as he had assessed the situation and then had to wait five minutes for him to call back. More important, he makes clear that once he learned what to do, he spent most of the hour avoiding the task.

In the following brief example, clock time serves the writer's purpose by making readers aware of the speed with which actions were taken:

> 9:05 P.M. An ambulance backs into the receiving bay, its red and yellow lights flashing in and out of the lobby. A split second later, the glass doors burst open as a nurse and an attendant roll a mobile stretcher into the lobby. When the nurse screams, "Emergent!" the lobby explodes with activity as the way is cleared to the trauma room. Doctors appear from nowhere and transfer the bloodied body of a black man to the treatment table. Within seconds his clothes are stripped away.   –George Simpson, "The War Room at Bellevue"

EXERCISE 14.3

Look back at any of the essays in Chapter 2. Read the essay to see how the writer signals the passage of time in the narration. How many time markers, verb tense markers, and references to clock time do you find? Identify any places where a signal should be added and any place where it seems unnecessary. What can you conclude from analyzing this particular essay about the importance of signaling in narrative?

EXERCISE 14.4

Look back at the narrative you wrote for Exercise 14.1. Did you use time markers, verb tense markers, or clock time? If you did, try to explain what they add. If you did not, how would your writing be improved if you added some of them? Which ones would you add, and where? Explain why you would add these particular transitions at these places.

SHAPING NARRATIVE STRUCTURE

In addition to clear sequencing of action, writers of effective narrative create a structure to give their stories interest and to focus the action. They shape the narrative around a central conflict, building tension by manipulating the narrative pace.

Conflict
and Tension

The basic device writers use to turn a sequence of actions into a story is *conflict*. Conflict adds the question "So what?" to "What happened next?" It provides motivation and purpose for the actions of characters. In this way, conflict gives narrative its dramatic structure.

The conflict in most narrative takes the form of a struggle between the main character and an opposing force. This force may take many forms—another person or creature, nature, society's rules and values, internal characteristics such as conflicting values or desires.

Conflict focuses the action toward some purpose. Instead of the simple "and then—and then—and then" structure that a time line gives, conflict provides a one-thing-leads-to-another structure. Along with conflict in a narrative comes *tension*, and this tension or suspense is what makes readers want to read on to find out what will happen. Tension in narrative does not refer to hostility or anxiety, but to tautness. This sense of *tension* comes from its Latin root, *tendere*, meaning "to stretch." By setting up an unresolved conflict, a writer can stretch the narrative line, creating a sense of tautness or suspense. Readers thus are involved in the action because they care about the ultimate resolution of the conflict, looking forward to the climax, the highest point of tension where the conflict is most focused and explicit.

We can see these concepts illustrated in the excerpt from "Death of a Pig." The opposing forces seem to be the man and the pig, but the conflict is really more elemental—between health and illness or life and death. We see the conflict as an internal drama within the narrator himself, who initially resists acknowledging that the routine of his life—not to mention the pig's—has been disrupted. Tension grows as he begins to face reality and consider what he can do to save the pig. In the pages that follow, we see how his efforts to forestall the inevitable are hopeless. The climax of the excerpt occurs when the narrator finally takes action, but the climax of the story does not occur until the pig dies.

EXERCISE 14.5

Look back at the essay you read for Exercise 14.3 and try to identify its conflict and climax. At what points do you feel the tension grow? When do you have a sense of anticipation or suspense? How do these feelings affect your enjoyment of the story?

Narrative Pace

Although you may place actions in the context of clock time, few writers really try to reproduce time as it is measured by clocks. Clock time moves at a uniform rate. If everything were emphasized equally, readers would be unable to distinguish the importance of particular actions. Such a narrative would be monotonous and unnatural.

Pacing techniques allow writers to represent the passage of narrative time. You can pace narratives by emphasizing more important actions and deemphasizing less important ones. To emphasize a sequence of action, you can heighten tension, thus making the action last longer or seem more intense. Common techniques for doing this are to concentrate on specific narrative action, to present action through dialogue, and to vary sentence rhythm.

Specific Narrative Action. The writer George Plimpton participated in the Detroit Lions football training camp in order to write a book about professional football. In this passage from his book, Plimpton tells what happened when he had his big chance in a practice scrimmage.

> Since in the two preceding plays the concentration of the play had been else-where, I had felt alone with the flanker. Now, the whole heave of the play was toward me, flooding the zone not only with confused motion but noise—the quick stomp of feet, the creak of football gear, the strained grunts of effort, the faint *ah-ah-ah*, of piston-stroke regularity, and the stiff calls of instruction, like exhalations. "Inside, inside! Take him inside!" someone shouted, tearing by me, his cleats thumping in the grass. A call—a parrot squawk—may have erupted from me. My feet splayed in hopeless confusion as Barr came directly toward me, feinting in one direction, and then stopping suddenly, drawing me toward him for the possibility of a buttonhook pass, and as I leaned almost off balance toward him, he turned and came on again, downfield, moving past me at high speed, leaving me poised on one leg, reaching for him, trying to grab at him despite the illegality, anything to keep him from getting by. But he was gone, and by the time I had turned to set out after him, he had ten yards on me, drawing away fast with his sprinter's run, his legs pinwheeling, the row of cleats flicking up a faint wake of dust behind.   —George Plimpton, *Paper Lion*

Although the action lasted only a few moments, Plimpton gives a closeup of it. He focuses on what we are calling *specific narrative action*—specific and concrete movements, gestures, and activities. Instead of writing "Someone ran by me shouting," he writes:

> "Inside, inside! Take him inside!" someone shouted, (verb) tearing by me, (par-ticipial phrase) his cleats thumping in the grass. (absolute phrase)

The underlined verbs and verb phrases identify a player's specific actions: shouting, tearing by, thumping cleats. In the long fifth sentence Plimpton gives us another series of specific narrative actions: "feet splayed," "came directly toward me," "feinting in one direction," "stopping suddenly," "drawing me toward him," "leaned almost off balance," "turned and came on again," and then "moving/leaving/reaching/trying" in quick succession. The specific actions slow the narrative pace and heighten the tension. In addition, because they are concrete, they enable us to imagine what is happening.

EXERCISE 14.6

Look at the selection by Maya Angelou in Chapter 3. Note particularly what happens in paragraph 18. How does Angelou's use of specific narrative action here contribute to the overall effectiveness of the selection?

EXERCISE 14.7

Look back at the narrative you wrote for Exercise 14.1. How effectively have you used specific narrative action to pace your narrative and make it concrete?

Choose a sentence or a series of sentences to revise, emphasizing a particular part of your narrative by adding specific narrative action. Then, compare the two versions, analyzing the different effects of pacing.

Dialogue. Another way of dramatizing narrative action is dialogue. Writers use it to reveal conflict directly, without the narrator's intruding commentary. Dialogues are not mere recordings of conversation, but pointed representations of conversation. Through dialogue, readers gain insight into the personality and motives of the characters.

Richard Wright uses dialogue to show what happened when a white man confronted a black delivery boy. Notice that the dialogue does not have the free give-and-take of conversation. Instead, it is a series of questions which get evasive answers: "he said" . . . "I lied" . . . "he asked me" . . . "I lied." The dialogue is tense, revealing the extent of the boy's fear and defensiveness.

> I was hungry and he knew it; but he was a white man and I felt that if I told him I was hungry I would have been revealing something shameful.
>
> "Boy, I can see hunger in your face and eyes," he said.
>
> "I get enough to eat," I lied.
>
> "Then why do you keep so thin?" he asked me.
>
> "Well, I suppose I'm just that way, naturally," I lied.
>
> "You're just scared, boy," he said.
>
> "Oh, no, sir," I lied agan.
>
> I could not look at him. I wanted to leave the counter, yet he was a white man and I had learned not to walk abruptly away from a white man when he was talking to me. I stood, my eyes looking away. He ran his hand into his pocket and pulled out a dollar bill.
>
> "Here, take this dollar and buy yourself some food," he said.
>
> "No, sir," I said.
>
> "Don't be a fool," he said. "You're ashamed to take it. God, boy, don't let a thing like that stop you from taking a dollar and eating."
>
> The more he talked the more it became impossible for me to take the dollar. I wanted it, but I could not look at it. I wanted to speak, but I could not move my tongue. I wanted him to leave me alone. He frightened me.
>
> "Say something," he said.   –Richard Wright, Black Boy

Wright does not try to communicate everything through dialogue. He intersperses information which supports the dialogue—description, reports of the boy's thoughts and feelings, as well as some movement—in order to help readers understand the unfolding drama.

You can also use dialogue to reveal a person's character and show the dynamics of interpersonal relationships. Notice the way Lillian Hellman uses dialogue to write about a long-time friend, Arthur W. A. Cowan:

> . . . Cowan said, "What's the matter with you? You haven't said a word for an hour." I said nothing was the matter, not wishing to hear his lecture about what was. After an hour of nagging, by the repetition of "Spit it out," "Spit it out,"

I told him about a German who had fought in the International Brigade in the Spanish Civil War, been badly wounded, and was now very ill in Paris without any money and that I had sent some, but not enough.

Arthur screamed, "Since when do you have enough money to send anybody a can to piss in? Hereafter, I handle all your money and you send nobody anything. And a man who fought in Spain has to be an ass Commie and should take his punishment."

I said, "Oh shut up, Arthur."

And he did, but that night as he paid the dinner check, he wrote out another check and handed it to me. It was for a thousand dollars.

I said, "What's this for?"

"Anybody you want."

I handed it back.

He said, "Oh, for Christ sake take it and tell yourself it's for putting up with me."

"Then it's not enough money."

He laughed. "I like you sometimes. Give it to the stinking German and don't say where it comes from because no man wants money from a stranger."

—Lillian Hellman, *Pentimento*

This dialogue is quite realistic. It shows the way people talk to one another, the rhythms of interactive speech and its silences. But the dialogue does something more: it gives readers real insight into the way Hellman and Cowan were with each other, their conflicts and their shared understanding. Such dialogue allows readers to listen in on private conversations.

The Hellman passage also exemplifies two methods of presenting dialogue: quoting and summarizing. In summarizing, writers choose their own words instead of quoting actual words used; this allows them to condense dialogue as well as to emphasize what they wish. When Hellman writes "I told him about a German . . . ," she is summarizing her actual spoken words.

EXERCISE 14.8

Turn to Chapter 3 and read Gerald Haslam's essay about his great-grandmother, paying attention to his use of dialogue. What does the dialogue reveal about the great-grandmother's character, and about the boy's relationship with her?

EXERCISE 14.9

Write several paragraphs of narrative, including some dialogue. Write about an incident that occurred between you and someone you consider a close friend or associate—a friend, a relative, an enemy, a boss. Try to compose a dialogue that conveys the closeness of your relationship.

Read over your dialogue, and reflect on the impression it gives. In a sentence or two, state what you think the dialogue reveals about your relationship with this person.

Sentence Rhythm.   Sequences of short sentences and phrases also contribute to narrative pace. You can see how this works in the following paragraph by Russell Baker about taking a flight test. See how the pace quickens until it reaches an apex in the dramatic series of quick phrases that make up the last sentence:

> The wheels were hardly off the mat before I experienced another eerie sensation. It was a feeling of power. For the first time since first stepping into an airplane I felt in complete mastery of the thing. I'd noticed it on takeoff. It had been an excellent takeoff. Without thinking about it, I'd automatically corrected a slight swerve just before becoming airborne. Now as we climbed I was flooded with a sense of confidence. The hangover's residue of relaxation had freed me of the tensions that had always defeated me before. Before, the plane had had a will of its own; now the plane seemed to be part of me, an extension of my hands and feet, obedient to my slightest whim. I leveled it at exactly 5,000 feet and started a slow roll. First, a shallow dive to gain velocity, then push the stick slowly, firmly, all the way over against the thigh, simultaneously putting in hard rudder, and there we are, hanging upside down over the earth and now—keeping it rolling, don't let the nose drop—reverse the controls and feel it roll all the way through until—coming back to straight-and-level now—catch it, wings level with the horizon, and touch the throttle to maintain altitude precisely at 5,000 feet.   –Russell Baker, *Growing Up*   *control of flying.*

TAKING A POINT OF VIEW

In narrative writing, point of view refers to the narrator's relation to the action at hand. Basically, writers use two points of view: first person and third person.

First person is used to narrate action in which the writer participated. For instance, when Piri Thomas writes, "Big-mouth came at me and we grabbed each other and pushed and pulled and shoved," he is using a first-person point of view. Third person, on the other hand, is used to narrate action performed by people other than the narrator. When Paul Theroux writes, "The Suns fought for it. One man gained possession, but he was pounced upon and the ball shot up and ten Suns went tumbling after it," he is using a third-person point of view. Because they are telling about their own experiences, autobiographers typically write first-person narrative, using the first-person pronouns *I* and *we,* as Piri Thomas does. When writers tell another person's story, as in biography, they use the third-person pronouns *he, she,* and *they* instead of the first-person *I* or *we.*

Of course, first-person narrators often observe and report on the actions of others. In such cases they may shift, perhaps for long stretches, into what seems to be primarily a third-person point of view. This is especially true when the writer is neither participating in the action nor introducing personal thoughts or feelings. However, the presence of the narrative "I" at any point in a piece of writing suggests a first-person point of view throughout.

EXERCISE 14.10

In Chapter 4, compare the profiles written by David Noonan and by Brian Cable, noting particularly each writer's point of view, first-person or third-person. Take a paragraph from each profile and rewrite it, using another point of view. What is the effect of the change of point of view in each case?

EXERCISE 14.11

Think of a brief incident involving you and one other person. Write about the incident from your own, first-person, point of view. Then write about the incident from the third-person point of view, as though another person is telling it. What impact does a change in point of view have on your story?

PRESENTING A PROCESS

Process narrative typically explains how something is done or how to do it. For example, in *Oranges*, a book about the Florida citrus industry, John McPhee tells how the technical operation of bud grafting is done. He is not writing directions for readers to follow. If he were, his narrative would be much more detailed and precise. Instead, he tells us as much as he thinks nonspecialists need or want to know.

> One of Adams' men was putting Hamlin buds on Rough Lemon stock the day I was there. He began by slicing a bud from a twig that had come from a registered budwood tree—of which there are forty-five thousand in groves around Florida, each certified under a state program to be free from serious virus disease and to be a true strain of whatever type of orange, grapefruit, or tangerine it happens to be. Each bud he removed was about an inch long and looked like a little submarine, the conning tower being the eye of the bud, out of which would come the shoot that would develop into the upper trunk and branches of the ultimate tree. A few inches above the ground, he cut a short vertical slit in the bark of a Rough Lemon liner; then he cut a transverse slit at the base of the vertical one, and, lifting the flaps of the wound, set the bud inside. The area was bandaged with plastic tape. In a couple of weeks, Adams said, the new shoot would be starting out of the bud and the tape would be taken off. To force the growth of the new shoot, a large area of the bark of the Rough Lemon would be shaved off above the bud union. Two months after that, the upper trunk, branches, and leaves of the young Rough Lemon tree would be cut off altogether, leaving only a three-inch stub coming out of the earth, thick as a cigar, with a small shoot and a leaf or two of the Hamlin flippantly protruding near the top.   –John McPhee, *Oranges*

Hanging from the ceiling there was a heavy glass chandelier on which the dust was so thick that it was like fur. And covering most of one wall there was a huge hideous piece of junk, something between a sideboard and a hall-stand, with lots of carving and little drawers and strips of looking-glass, and there was a once-gaudy carpet ringed by the slop-pails of years, and two gilt chairs with burst seats, and one of those old-fashioned armchairs which you slide off when you try to sit on them. The room had been turned into a bedroom by thrusting four squalid beds in among the wreckage.   —George Orwell, *The Road to Wigan Pier*

EXERCISE 15.1

Write a paragraph or two describing a room where you have spent a lot of time. Describe the room in a way that conveys its atmosphere. Then write a few sentences describing the dominant impression you want your description to make, explaining your purpose in describing the room this way.

NAMING

All writers point to and name things they wish to describe. In the following passage, for example, Annie Dillard identifies the face, chin, fur, underside, and eyes of a weasel she once encountered in the woods:

He was ten inches long, thin as a curve, a muscled ribbon, brown as fruitwood, soft-furred, alert. His <u>face</u> was fierce, small and pointed as a lizard's; he would have made a good arrowhead. There was just a dot of <u>chin</u>, maybe two browns hairs' worth, and then the pure white <u>fur</u> began that spread down his <u>underside</u>. He had two black <u>eyes</u> I didn't see, any more than you see a window.

—Annie Dillard, *Teaching a Stone to Talk*

The underscored nouns name the parts of the weasel on which Dillard focuses her attention. The nouns she uses are concrete: they refer to actual, tangible parts of the animal. They are also fairly specific: they identify parts of one particular animal, the weasel she saw.

In looking for the right word to name something, you can usually choose from a variety of words. Some words may be concrete (referring to tangible objects or actual instances), while others are abstract (referring to ideas or qualities). *Nose*, *tooth*, and *foot* are concrete words, whereas *love*, *faith*, and *justice* are abstract.

Some words may be specific (referring to a particular instance or individual), while others are general (referring to a class which includes many particular instances). *Specific* and *general* are relative terms. That is, the specificity of a word cannot be measured absolutely but only by contrasting it with other words that could be substituted for it. For example, *vegetable* is more specific than *food* but more general than *carrot.*

If you compare the following description to Dillard's, you will see how each writer has made particular word choices:

> The expression of this snake's <u>face</u> was hideous and fierce; the <u>pupils</u> consisted of a vertical slit in a mottled and coppery <u>iris;</u> the <u>jaws</u> were broad at the base, and the <u>nose</u> terminated in a triangular projection.
>
> —Charles Darwin, *The Voyage of the Beagle*

Like Dillard, Darwin uses the word *face*, though he specifies the *expression* on the snake's face. He could have used *eyes*, as Dillard does, but he uses the more specific *pupils* and *iris* instead. *Chin*, however, would not substitute for *jaws* because *jaws* refers to the bone structure of the lower face, while *chin* refers to something different—the prominence of the lower jaw. Darwin could have used the technical terms *maxilla* and *mandible*, the names of the upper and lower jaw bones. He chose not to use these words, even though they are more specific than *jaws*, possibly because they might be unfamiliar to readers or more specific than necessary. As a rule of thumb, most writers prefer more specific nouns for naming, but they adjust the degree of specificity to the particular needs of their readers.

In addition to naming perceivable objects and features, writers name sensations (*stink* and *plunk*) and qualities (the *sweetness* of the lumber):

> When the sun fell across the great white pile of the new Telephone Company building, you could smell the stucco burning as you passed; then some liquid <u>sweetness</u> that came to me from deep in the rings of the freshly cut lumber stacked in the yards, and the fresh plaster and paint on the brand-new storefronts. <u>Rawness,</u> sunshiny <u>rawness</u> down the end streets of the city, as I thought of them then—the hot ash-laden <u>stink</u> of the refuse dumps in my nostrils and the only sound at noon the resonant metal <u>plunk</u> of a tin can I kicked ahead of me as I went my way.   —Alfred Kazin, *A Walker in the City*

EXERCISE 15.2

This is an exercise in close observation and naming. Go to a place where you can sit for a while and observe the scene. It might be a landscape or a cityscape, indoors or outdoors, crowded or solitary. Write for five minutes, listing everything in the scene that you can name.

Then, for each noun on your list, try to think of two or three other nouns you could use in its place. Write these other names down.

Finally, write a paragraph describing the scene. Use the nouns you think go together best, assuming your readers are unfamiliar with the scene.

EXERCISE 15.3

Read "Father," the essay by Jan Gray in Chapter 3, and notice how much naming she does in her description. In a few sentences explain why you think Gray uses so much naming in this passage. What impression does it make on you? How specific is her naming? How subjective or objective is it?

DETAILING

Although nouns can be quite specific, adding details is a way of making them more specific, and thus describing something more precisely. Naming answers the questions "What is it?" and "What are its parts or features?" Detailing answers questions like these:

- What size is it?
- How many are there?
- What is it made of?
- Where is it located?
- What is its condition?
- What is its use?
- Where does it come from?
- What is its effect?
- What is its value?

To add details to names, add modifiers—adjectives and adverbs, phrases and clauses. Modifiers make nouns more specific by supplying additional information about them. See how many modifying details about size, shape, color, texture, value, and number Annie Dillard provides in this passage about a weasel.

> He was ten inches long, thin as a curve, a muscled ribbon, brown as fruitwood, soft-furred, alert. His face was fierce, small and pointed as a lizard's; he would have made a good arrowhead. There was just a dot of chin, maybe two brown hairs' worth, and then the pure white fur began that spread down his underside. He had two black eyes I didn't see, any more than you see a window.
>
> –Annie Dillard, *Teaching a Stone to Talk*

Like names, details can be more or less specific. For example, because "ten inches long" is a measurable quantity, it is more precise than the relative term *small*. Other detailing words like *good* and *pure* are also relative. Even *brown*, although it is more precise than the general word *color*, could be specified further, as Dillard does, by comparing it to the color of fruitwood.

Modifiers are also used to identify a person's character traits, as the following passage illustrates:

> By no amount of agile exercising of a wishful imagination could my mother have been called <u>lenient</u>. <u>Generous</u> she was; <u>indulgent,</u> never. <u>Kind,</u> yes; <u>permissive,</u> never. —Maya Angelou, *Gather Together in My Name*

EXERCISE 15.4

Choose something which you can examine closely, such as a car, vacuum cleaner, sofa, or desk. Study this object for at least five minutes. Then describe it for someone who has never seen it, using as many specific naming and detailing words as you can.

EXERCISE 15.5

Look at Gerald Haslam's description of his great-grandmother in Chapter 3. What modifiers does he use? How does this detailing contribute to the overall impression the selection gives you of her?

COMPARING

Whereas naming and detailing call on the power of observation, comparing brings the imagination into play. Comparison makes language even more precise and description more evocative. Look again at Annie Dillard's description of a weasel to see how she uses comparison:

> He was ten inches long, <u>thin as a curve, a muscled ribbon, brown as fruitwood,</u> soft-furred, alert. His face was fierce, <u>small and pointed as a lizard's; he would have made a good arrowhead.</u> There was just a dot of chin, maybe two brown hairs' worth, and then the pure white fur began that spread down his underside. He had two black <u>eyes I didn't see, any more than you see a window.</u>
>
> —Annie Dillard, *Teaching a Stone to Talk*

This passage illustrates two kinds of comparison: simile and metaphor. Both figures of speech compare things that are essentially dissimilar. A *simile* directly expresses a similarity by using the words *like* or *as* to announce the comparison. Dillard uses a simile when she writes that the weasel was "thin as a curve." A *metaphor*, on the other hand, is an implicit comparison by which one thing is described as though it were the other. Dillard uses a metaphor when she describes the weasel as "a muscled ribbon."

Here are more examples of comparison used descriptively:

Sometimes I rambled to pine groves, standing like temples, or like fleets at sea, full-rigged, with wavy boughs, and rippling with light. . . .

–Henry David Thoreau, *Walden*

On the walls are white spiders like tight buttons of surgical cotton suspended on long hairy legs.   –Barry Lopez, "Perimeter".

Comparing enhances a description by showing readers that which is being described in a surprising new way that can be suggestive and revealing. Although this strategy is called comparing, it includes both comparing and contrasting because differences can be as illuminating as likenesses. Once two things are compared, they are put into a context that causes them to play off each other in unexpected ways.

Useful as comparison is, there are a few pitfalls to avoid with this strategy. Be sure that the connection between the two things being compared is clear and appropriate to your description. Avoid using clichéd expressions, comparisons that are so overused that they have become predictable and consequently do not reveal anything new. Following are some examples of comparisons that have been worn out and thus do not enrich a description:

The kiss was as sweet as honey.

I am as busy as a bee.

That picture stands out like a sore thumb.

EXERCISE 15.6

Most writers use comparison only occasionally to achieve particular effects. Look at David Noonan's "Inside the Brain" in Chapter 4. Mark each metaphor and simile. Then reflect on how these comparisons contribute to your understanding of the human brain and the procedure being performed.

EXERCISE 15.7

Take five minutes to list as many clichés as you can think of. Then, pair up with another student, and discuss your lists to decide whether the entries are all clichés. When you are done, figure out what turns a comparison into a cliché for you, and together write a sentence defining a cliché.

EXERCISE 15.8

Turn to Jan Gray's essay about her father in Chapter 3. Reread the essay, noting the use of naming, describing, and comparing. What impression do you get of Gray's father from this description? How do these three strategies contribute to this impression?

USING SENSORY DESCRIPTION

If there are three basic descriptive strategies—naming, detailing, and comparing—there are many language resources, and some limitations, for reporting sense impressions. These resources help convey sights, sounds, smells, touches, and tastes.

In describing, the sense of sight seems to have primacy over the other senses. *Describere*, the Latin root for describe, even means "to sketch or copy." In general, people rely more on the sense of sight than on the other senses. Certainly our vocabulary for reporting what we see is larger and more varied than our vocabulary for reporting any other sense impression.

For the other senses, quite a few nouns and verbs designate sounds; a smaller number of nouns, but few verbs, describe smells; and very few nouns or verbs convey touch and taste. Furthermore, these nonvisual sensations do not invite as much naming as sights do because they are not readily divided into constituent features. For example, we have many names to describe the visible features of a car, but few to describe the sounds a car makes. Nevertheless, writers detail the qualities and attributes of nonvisual sensations—the loudness or tinniness or rumble of an engine, for instance.

The Sense of Sight

When people describe what they see, they identify the objects in their field of vision. As the following passages illustrate, these objects may include animate as well as inanimate things and their features. Details may range from words delineating appearance to those evaluating it.

The first selection, by Henry David Thoreau, depicts a nature scene with a lot of activity; the second passage, by Tracy Kidder, describes Mrs. Zajac, a grade school teacher.

> As I sit at my window this summer afternoon, hawks are circling about my clearing; the tantivy of wild pigeons, flying by twos and threes athwart my view, or perching restless on the white pine boughs behind my house, gives a voice to the air; a fish hawk dimples the glassy surface of the pond and brings up a fish; a mink steals out of the marsh before my door and seizes a frog by the shore; the sedge is bending under the weight of the reed-birds flitting hither and thither. . . .   —Henry David Thoreau, *Walden*

> She was thirty-four. She wore a white skirt and yellow sweater and a thin gold necklace, which she held in her fingers, as if holding her own reins, while waiting for children to answer. Her hair was black with a hint of Irish red. It was cut short to the tops of her ears, and swept back like a pair of folded wings. She had a delicate cleft chin, and she was short—the children's chairs would have fit

her. . . . Her hands kept very busy. They sliced the air and made karate chops to mark off boundaries. They extended straight out like a traffic cop's, halting illegal maneuvers yet to be perpetrated. When they rested momentarily on her hips, her hands looked as if they were in holsters.   —Tracy Kidder, *Among Schoolchildren*

EXERCISE 15.9

Using Kidder's description of Mrs. Zajac as a model, write a few sentences describing one of your teachers or friends. Do not rely on memory for this exercise: describe someone who is before you as you write. You can even look in the mirror and describe yourself. Then read what you have written and identify the dominant impression of this description. Which words contribute most to creating the impression? Which words, if any, seem to contradict or weaken it?

The Sense of Hearing

In reporting auditory impressions, writers seldom name the objects from which the sounds come without also naming the sounds themselves: the murmur of a voice, the rustle of the wind, the squeak of a hinge, the sputter of an engine. *Onomatopoeia* is the term for names of sounds that echo the sounds themselves: *squeak, murmur, hiss, boom, tinkle, twang, jangle, rasp*. Sometimes writers make up words like *plink, chirr, sweesh-crack-boom*, and *cara-wong* to imitate sounds they wish to describe. Qualitative words like *powerful* and *rich* as well as relative terms like *loud* and *low* often specify sounds further. Detailing sounds sometimes involves the technique called *synesthesia*, applying words commonly used to describe one sense to another, such as describing sounds as *sharp* and *soft*.

To write about the sounds along Manhattan's Canal Street, Ian Frazier uses many of these describing and naming techniques. He also uses comparison when he refers metaphorically to the horns getting "tired and out of breath":

The traffic on Canal Street never stops. It is a high-energy current jumping constantly between the poles of Brooklyn and New Jersey. It hates to have its flow pinched in the density of Manhattan, hates to stop at intersections. Along Canal Street, it moans and screams. Worn break shoes of semitrucks go "Ooohhhh nooohhhh" at stoplights, and the sound echoes in the canyons of warehouses and Chinatown tenements. People lean on their horns from one end of Canal Street to the other. They'll honk nonstop for ten minutes at a time, until the horns get tired and out of breath. They'll try different combinations shave-and-a-hair-cut, long-long-long, short-short-short-long. Some people have musical car horns; a person purchasing a musical car horn seems to be limited to a choice of four tunes "La Cucaracha," "Theme from *The Godfather*," "Dixie," and "Hava Nagila."   —Ian Frazier, "Canal Street"

EXERCISE 15.10

Find a noisy spot—a restaurant, a football game, a nursery school, a laundry room—where you can perch for a half hour or so. Listen attentively to the sounds of the place and make notes about what you hear. Then, write a paragraph describing the place through its sounds. When you are done, read your description and identify the dominant impression. Which words contribute most to creating this impression and which detract from it?

The Sense of Smell

The English language has a meager stock of words to express the sense of smell. In addition to the word *smell*, only about ten commonly used nouns name this sensation: *odor, scent, vapor, aroma, fragrance, perfume, bouquet, stench, stink.* Although there are other, rarer words like *fetor* and *effuvium,* few writers use them, probably for fear their readers will not know them. Few verbs describe receiving or sending odors—*smell, sniff, waft*—but a fair number of detailing adjectives are available: *redolent, pungent, aromatic, perfumed, stinking, musty, rancid, putrid, rank, foul, acrid, sweet,* and *cloying.*

In the next passage, Conroy uses comparing in addition to naming and detailing. Notice how he describes the effect the odor has on him:

> The perfume of the flowers rushed into my brain. A lush aroma, thick with sweetness, thick as blood, and spiced with the clear acid of tropical greenery. My heart pounded like a drowning swimmer's as the perfume took me over, pouring into my lungs like ambrosial soup.   –Frank Conroy, *Stop-time*

Naming the objects from which smells come can also be very suggestive:

> My mother worked on and off, primarily as a *costurera* or cleaning homes or taking care of other people's children. We sometimes went with her to the houses she cleaned. They were nice, American, white-people homes. . . . The odor of these houses was different, full of fragrances, sweet and nauseating. On 105th Street the smells were of fried lard, of beans and car fumes, of factory smoke and home-made brew out of backyard stills. There were chicken smells and goat smells in grassless yards filled with engine parts and wire and wood planks, cracked and sprinkled with rusty nails. These were the familiar aromas: the funky earth, animal and mechanical smells which were absent from the homes my mother cleaned.   –Luis J. Rodriguez, *Always Running: Gang Days in L. A.*

EXERCISE 15.11

Go someplace with noticeable, distinctive smells where you can stay for ten or fifteen minutes. You may choose an eating place (a cafeteria, a donut shop), a place where something is being manufactured (a saw mill, a bakery), or some other place that has distinctive odors (a fishing dock, a garden, a locker room). Take notes while you are there on what you smell, and then write a paragraph describing the place through its smells. What is the dominant impression you were trying to create in your description?

The Sense of Touch

Writers describing the sense of touch tend not to name the sensation directly or even to report the act of feeling. Probably this omission occurs because only a few nouns and verbs name tactile sensations besides words like *touch, feel, tickle, brush, scratch, sting, itch, tingle.* Nevertheless, a large stock of words describe temperature (*hot, warm, mild, tepid, cold, arctic*), moisture content (*wet, dry, sticky, oily, greasy, moist, crisp*), texture (*gritty, silky, smooth, crinkled, coarse, soft, leathery*), and weight (*heavy, light, ponderous, buoyant, feathery*). Read the following passages with an eye for descriptions of touch.

> The midmorning sun was deceitfully mild and the wind had no weight on my skin. Arkansas summer mornings have a feathering effect on stone reality.
>
> —Maya Angelou, *Gather Together in My Name*

> It was an ordeal for me to walk the hills in the dead of summer for then they were parched and dry and offered no shade from the hot sun and no springs or creeks where thirst could be quenched.   —William O. Douglas, *Go East, Young Man*

EXERCISE 15.12

Briefly describe the feel of a cold shower, a wool sweater, an autumn breeze, bare feet on hot sand, or some other tactile sensation. What is the dominant impression you were trying to create with this description?

The Sense of Taste

Other than *taste, savor,* and *flavor,* few words name the gustatory sensations directly. Certain words do distinguish among the four types of taste—*sweet* (*saccharine, sugary, cloying*); *sour* (*acidic, tart*); *bitter* (*acrid, biting*); *salty* (*briny, brackish*), while several other words describe specific tastes (*piquant, spicy, pungent, peppery, savory,* and *toothsome*).

In addition to these words, the names of objects tasted and other details may indicate the intensity and quality of a taste. Notice Hemingway's descriptive technique in the following selection.

> As I ate the oysters with their strong taste of the sea and their faint metallic taste that the cold wine washed away, leaving only the sea taste and the succulent texture, and as I drank their cold liquid from each shell and washed it down with the crispy taste of the wine, I lost the empty feeling and began to be happy and to make plans.   —Ernest Hemingway, *A Moveable Feast*

EXERCISE 15.13

Describe the taste of a particular food or meal as Hemingway does above. What dominant impression were you trying to create?

EXERCISE 15.14

Turn to "Uncle Willie" in Chapter 3. Reread the essay and bracket any instances where Angelou uses sensory language to describe the scene and people. What is the dominant impression you get from this description? How do you think sensory description helps create this impression?

ASSUMING A VANTAGE POINT

Writing effectively about a scene requires taking a vantage point—that is, selecting the point or position from which to describe the scene. By presenting objects and features from a particular vantage point, the writer creates a perspective by which readers can enter the scene.

A Stationary Vantage Point

A writer of description who stays still assumes a fixed or stationary vantage point. In the following passage, the author takes a position in a subway station and describes what he sees without moving around the station:

> Standing in a subway station, I began to appreciate the place—almost to enjoy it. First of all, I looked at the lighting: a row of meager electric bulbs, unscreened, yellow, and coated with filth, stretched toward the black mouth of the tunnel, as though it were a bolt hole in an abandoned coal mine. Then I lingered, with zest, on the walls and ceiling: lavatory tiles which had been white about fifty years ago, and were now encrusted with soot, coated with the remains of a dirty liquid which might be either atmospheric humidity mingled with smog or the result of a perfunctory attempt to clean them with cold water; and, above them, gloomy vaulting from which dingy paint was peeling off like scabs from an old wound, sick black paint leaving a leprous white subsurface. Beneath my feet, the floor was a nauseating dark brown with black stains upon it which might be stale oil or dry chewing gum or some worse defilement; it looked like the hallway of a condemned slum building. Then my eye traveled to the tracks, where two lines of glittering steel—the only positively clean objects in the whole place—ran out of darkness into darkness above an unspeakable mass of congealed oil, puddles of dubious liquid, and a mishmash of old cigarette packets, mutilated and filthy newspapers, and the debris that filtered down from the street above through a barred grating in the roof. As I looked up toward the sunlight, I could see more debris sifting slowly downward, and making an abominable pattern in the slanting beam of dirt-laden sunlight. I was going on to relish more features of this unique scene: such as the advertisement posters on the walls—here a text from the Bible, there a half-naked girl, here a woman wearing a hat consisting of a hen sitting on a nest full of eggs, and there a pair of girl's legs walking up the keys of a cash register—all scribbled over with unknown names and well-known obscenities in black crayon and red lipstick; but then my train came in at last. . . .   –Gilbert Highet, "The Subway Station"

Although Highet stays still, he shifts his field of vision, using these shifts to order the description of what he sees, looking first at the lights, then at the walls and ceilings, at the floor, at the tracks, toward the sunlight, and finally at the posters on the wall. He seems to describe things as they catch his attention. Sometimes writers give details in a more orderly pattern—for example, from left to right, top to bottom, big to small.

A Moving
Point of View

Instead of remaining fixed in one spot, a writer may move through a scene. Such is the case with the following description of what one writer sees as he drives along a highway:

> The highway, without warning, rolled off the plateau of green pastures and entered a wooded and rocky gorge; down, down, precipitously down to the Kentucky River. Along the north slope, man-high columns of ice clung to the limestone. The road dropped deeper until it crossed the river at Brooklyn Bridge. The gorge, hidden in the table and wholly unexpected, was the Palisades. At the bottom lay only enough ground for the river and a narrow strip of willow-rimmed houses on stilts and a few doublewides rose from the damp flats like toadstools. Next to one mobile home was a partly built steel boat longer than the trailer.
>
> –William Least Heat Moon, *Blue Highways*

See pp. 479–81 for a discussion of transitions and a list of those commonly used to indicate spatial relations.

Notice how the writer uses spatial transitions like *down*, *along*, *from*, and *next* to orient readers to his movements.

Combined
Vantage Points

Sometimes writers use more than one stationary vantage point or combine stationary and moving vantage points. In these cases, the important thing is to orient the readers to any change in position. See how Willie Morris begins with a moving vantage point and then uses several stationary points.

> One walked up the three flights through several padlocked doors, often past the garbage which the landlords had neglected to remove for two or three days. Once inside our place, things were not bad at all. There was a big front room with an old floor, a little alcove for a study, and to the back a short corridor opening up into a tiny bedroom for my son and a larger bedroom in the back. The kitchen was in the back bedroom. I had not been able to find a view of an extensive body of water at popular prices, but from the back window, about forty-yards out, there *was* a vista of a big tank, part of some manufacturing installation in the building under it, and the tank constantly bubbled with some unidentified greenish substance. From this window one could see the tarred rooftops of the surrounding buildings, and off to the right a quiet stretch of God's earth, this being the parking lot next door.   –Willie Morris, *North toward Home*

EXERCISE 15.15

Look back at the paragraph you wrote for Exercise 15.1. What vantage point did you take in that description? How do you think your choice of vantage point contributes to the dominant impression the description creates? Try rewriting a few sentences taking another vantage point. How does this vantage point change the dominant impression?

EXERCISE 15.16

Look at Brian Cable's profile, "The Last Stop," in Chapter 4. Mark places in the text where you notice that a particular vantage point is used or that a vantage point shifts. What effect does the use of a vantage point have on Cable's descriptions of the mortuary?

Defining is an essential strategy for all kinds of writing. Autobiographers, for example, must occasionally define objects, conditions, events, and activities for readers likely to be unfamiliar with particular terms. The following example (with definitions underlined) is from Chapter 3.

> My father's hands are grotesque. He suffers from psoriasis, <u>a chronic skin disease that covers his massive, thick hands with scaly, reddish patches that periodically flake off, sending tiny pieces of dead skin sailing to the ground.</u> –Jan Gray, "Father"

Writers sharing information or explaining how to do something must very often define important terms for readers who are unfamiliar with the subject. This example comes from Chapter 4.

> After the scalp and the skull, the next layer protecting the brain is the dura. <u>A thin, tough, leathery membrane that encases the brain,</u> the dura (<u>derived from the Latin for *hard*</u>), is dark pink, almost red. –David Noonan, "Inside the Brain"

To convince readers of a position or an evaluation or to move them to act on a proposal, a writer must often define concepts important to an argument. This example comes from Chapter 6.

> What I hear every day on talk radio is America's lack of education—and I don't mean lack of college degrees. I mean lack of the basic art of democracy, <u>the ability to seek the great truths that can come only by synthesizing the small truths possessed by each of us.</u>
> —Donella H. Meadows, "Rush and Larry, Coast to Coast: This Is Not Democracy in Action"

As these examples illustrate, there are many kinds of definitions and many forms that they can take. This chapter illustrates the major kinds and forms of definitions, from dictionary definitions to various forms of sentence definition. This type of definition, the most common form in writing, relies on various sentence patterns to provide concise definitions. Following this are illustrations of multi-sentence extended definitions, including definition by etymology, or word history, and by stipulation.

DICTIONARY DEFINITIONS

The most familiar source of definitions is the dictionary, where words are defined briefly with other words. In a short space, dictionaries tell us a lot about words: what they mean, how they are pronounced, how they look in context in a sample phrase or clause, where they originated, what forms they take as they function differently in sentences. Here is an example from *The American Heritage Dictionary:*

definition ——————————————————————

part of speech ——————————————————

syllabification ——————————————————

                         in-trep-id (ĭn-trĕp′ĭd) *adj.* Marked by reso-

pronunciation ——————————————————

                         lute courage; fearless and bold: *an intrepid*

illustrative use ——————————————————

                         mountaineer. [Fr. *intrépule* < Lat. *intrepidus*

etymology ——————————————————

                         : *in-*, not + *trepidus,* alarmed.]—in′tre-pid′i-

                         ty (-trə-pĭd′ĭ-tē), in-trep′id-ness *n.* —in-

                         trep′id-ly *adv.*

other forms ——————————————————

Other dictionary entries may include still more information. For example, if a word has more than one meaning, all of its meanings will be presented. From the context in which you read or hear the word, you can nearly always tell which meaning applies.

A good dictionary is an essential part of your equipment as a college student. It should always be within reach when you are reading so that you can look up unfamiliar words in order to understand what you read and to expand your vocabulary. When you are writing, you can use a dictionary to check spellings and the correct forms of words as well as to make sure of the meanings of words you might not have used before.

You may want to ask your instructor for advice about which dictionary to buy in your college bookstore. A good current dictionary like *The American Heritage Dictionary* or *Webster's New Collegiate Dictionary* is most useful. Though a hardback dictionary version will cost two or three times more than a paperback, it will be a sound and relatively inexpensive investment (about twenty dollars). Hardback dictionaries usually have the advantages of more entries, fuller entries, larger type, and a thumb index.

To present a great deal of information in a small space, dictionaries have to rely on many abbreviations, codes, and symbols. These differ somewhat from one dictionary to the next, but you can learn the system of abbreviations in your dictionary by reading the front matter carefully. You will also find a range of interesting topics and lists in the front and end matter of some dictionaries: articles on usage and language history, reviews of punctuation rules, biographical entries, and geographical entries.

Any dictionary you are likely to buy for desk use would be an *abridged* dictionary, which does not include many technical or obsolete words. Much larger *unabridged* dictionaries contain every known current and obsolete word in the language. Two unabridged dictionaries are preeminent: *Oxford English Dictionary* and *Webster's Third New International Dictionary*, the latter the standard reference for American English. Libraries have these impressive dictionaries available for specialized use.

A special dictionary called a *thesaurus* can be useful for a writer, but only if it is used judiciously. It is a dictionary of synonyms, words with identical or very similar meanings. The motive for searching out synonyms should be to use just the right word, not to impress readers. Straining to impress readers with unusual words will more often than not lead to the embarrassing use of a word in the wrong context.

Here is an example from *Roget's II, The New Thesaurus*. It offers alternatives to *brave*, used as an adjective. Among the synonyms for *brave* is *intrepid*, noted in the dictionary definition on the preceding page.

> **brave** *adjective*
> Having or showing courage: *a brave effort to rescue the drowning child.* **Syns:** audacious, bold, courageous, dauntless, doughty, fearless, fortitudinous, gallant, game, gutsy (*Informal*), gutty, heroic, intrepid, mettlesome, plucky, stout, stouthearted, unafraid, undaunted, valiant, valorous.

Some thesauri also offer antonyms, words opposite in meaning to the word of interest. (An antonym of *brave*, for example, would be *cowardly*.)

The great limitation of a thesaurus is that it does not tell you which synonym is most appropriate for a particular writing situation. *Brave* and *intrepid* are not simply interchangeable. Which word you might use would depend on your readers, your purpose, your subject, and the exact meaning you hoped to convey with the sentence in which the word appears. In the preceding list the only clue to appropriateness is the information that *gutsy* is informal. Checking each word in a good dictionary would be necessary to select the most appropriate word from a set such as the preceding one. A thesaurus is most useful, therefore, in reminding you of a synonym whose shades of meaning you are already closely familiar with.

A solution to the limitations of a thesaurus is a dictionary of synonyms with words in a set like the preceding one but with each synonym defined, contrasted, and illustrated with quotations. An excellent source is *Webster's New Dictionary of Synonyms*, which provides enough information to let you make an appropriate choice among words with similar meanings. Your college bookstore will have this book for about the cost of a hardback dictionary. This volume's entry for *brave*, for example, notes eleven common synonyms for *brave* as an adjective, ranging from *courageous* to *audacious*. Each synonym is defined and then quoted in context from a respected source, as this portion of the entry shows:

brave *adj* **Brave, courageous, unafraid, fearless, intrepid, valiant, valorous, dauntless, undaunted, doughty, bold, audacious** are comparable when they mean having or showing no fear when faced with something dangerous, difficult, or unknown. **Brave** usually indicates lack of fear in alarming or difficult circumstances rather than a temperamental liking for danger ⟨the *brave* soldier goes to meet Death, and meets him without a shudder—*Trollope*⟩ ⟨he would send an explosion ship into the harbor . . . a *brave* crew would take her in at night, right up against the city, would light the fuses, and try to escape—*Forester*⟩ **Courageous** implies stouthearted resolution in contemplating or facing danger and may suggest a temperamental readiness to meet dangers or difficulties ⟨I am afraid . . . because I do not wish to die. But my spirit masters the trembling flesh and the qualms of the mind. I am more than brave, I am *courageous*—*London*⟩ ⟨a man is *courageous* when he does things which others might fail to do owing to fear—*Russell*⟩ **Un-**afraid simply indicates lack of fright or fear whether because of a courageous nature or because no cause for fear is present ⟨enjoy their homes *unafraid* of violent intrusion—*MacArthur*⟩ ⟨a young, daring, and creative people—a people *unafraid* of change—*MacLeish*⟩ **Fearless** may indicate lack of fear, or it may be more positive and suggest undismayed resolution ⟨joyous we too launch out on trackless seas, *fearless* for unknown shores—*Whitman*⟩ ⟨he gives always the impression of *fearless* sincerity . . . one always feels that he is ready to say bluntly what every one else is afraid to say—*T. S. Eliot*⟩ **Intrepid** suggests either daring in meeting danger or fortitude in enduring it ⟨with the *intrepid* woman who was his wife, and a few natives, he landed there, and set about building a house and clearing the scrub—*Maugham*⟩ ⟨the *intrepid* guardians of the place, hourly exposed to death, with famine worn, and suffering under many a perilous wound—*Wordsworth*⟩

This entry shows that *brave* and *intrepid* are very close in meaning, but that *intrepid* would be the better choice if you wanted to suggest "daring in meeting danger" rather than "lack of fear" in facing danger when it comes. You might call a person setting off on a solo sea voyage in a small craft an *intrepid* sailor, but a flight attendant who faced down a potential hijacker is better described as *brave*.

To summarize our advice about dictionaries: buy a respected hardback dictionary for looking up the meanings of new words you encounter and for checking spellings and correct usage. Buy an inexpensive paperback thesaurus for a quick look at sets of synonyms. Buy a respected hardback dictionary of synonyms in order to discriminate among synonyms and pick the most appropriate word. These resources will enable you to write essays with correct spellings and verb forms and with just the right words.

SENTENCE DEFINITIONS

Every field of study and every institution and activity has its own unique concepts and terms. Coming to a new area for the first time, a participant or a reader is often baffled by the many unfamiliar names for objects and activities. In college, a basic course in a field often seems like an entire course in definitions of new terms. In the same way, a sport like sailing requires newcomers to learn much specialized terminology. In such cases, writers of textbooks and sailing manuals rely on brief sentence definitions, involving a variety of sentence strategies.

Following are some sentence strategies from one widely used introductory college biology text, Sylvia Mader's *Inquiry into Life*. These examples illustrate some of the sentence strategies an author may use to name and define terms for readers.

The most obvious sentence strategies simply announce a definition. (In each of the following examples the word being defined is in italics, while the definition is underlined.)

> *Homo habilis* means handyman.
>
> *Somatic mutations* are mutations that affect the individual's body cells.
>
> At the time of ejaculation, sperm leaves the penis in a fluid called *seminal fluid*.
>
> Thus an ecosystem contains both a *biotic* (living) and *abiotic* (nonliving) environment.
>
> The human blastula, termed the *blastocyst*, consists of a hollow ball with a mass of cells—the inner cell mass—at one end.

The sentence strategies illustrated so far all declare in a straightforward way that the writer is defining a term. Other strategies, signaled by certain sentence relationships, are less direct but still quite apparent.

> *Fraternal twins*, which originate when two different eggs are fertilized by two different sperm, do not have identical chromosomes.
>
> *Hemophilia* is called the bleeders disease because the afflicted person's blood is unable to clot.
>
> When a mutagen leads to an increase in the incidence of cancer it is called a *carcinogen*.
>
> If the thyroid fails to develop properly, a condition called *cretinism* results.

These sentence definitions—all of them relying on subordinate clauses—play an important role in sentences by adding details, expressing time and cause, and indicating conditions or tentativeness. In all these examples from *Inquiry into Life*, however, the clauses have a specific defining role to play in the sections of the text where they appear. In this specialized way, they are part of a writer's repertoire for sentence definitions.

There are, in addition, several other defining strategies. One of the most common is the appositive phrase. Here one noun defines another noun in a brief inserted phrase called an appositive. Sometimes the appositive contains the definition; other times it contains the word to be defined.

> Sperm are produced in the testes, but they mature in the *epididymus*, a tightly coiled tubule about twenty feet in length that lies just outside each testis.
>
> Breathing consists of taking air in, *inspiration*, and forcing air out, *expiration*.

Finally, in a comparative definition, two or more terms are defined in part by comparison or contrast with each other. For these multiple definitions, writers rely on a great variety of syntactic and stylistic strategies including the two illustrated below: (1) a series of phrases following either the main verb or a colon and (2) contrasting clauses beginning with words or phrases like *even though*, *in spite of*, or *whereas*. The various parts of the comparison are always grammatically parallel, that is, similar in form.

> The special senses include the *chemoreceptors* for taste and smell, the *light receptors* for sight, and the *mechanoreceptors* for hearing and balance.
>
> Whereas a *miscarriage* is the unexpected loss of an embryo or fetus, an *abortion* is the purposeful removal of an embryo or fetus from the womb.

EXERCISE 16.1

Look up any three of the following words in a dictionary. Define each one in a sentence. Try to use a different sentence pattern, like those illustrated above, for each of your definitions.

clinometer	senile dementia	buyer's market
ecumenism	caricature	Shakespearean sonnet
harangue	mnemonic	edema
ectomorph	testosterone	samba

EXERCISE 16.2

Turn to the essay by David Noonan in Chapter 4, and analyze the sentence definitions in paragraphs 2, 6, 9, 13, and 18. (Some of these paragraphs contain more than one sentence definition.) Classify each definition as one of the preceding sentence types. What is the purpose of all these definitions in the selection as a whole?

EXTENDED DEFINITIONS

Rather than a brief sentence definition, a writer may need to go further and provide readers with a fuller definition extending over several sentences. Here, for example, is how Earl Shorris defines a common Spanish term:

> Fulano is a very old Spanish word for someone of uncertain identity, a so-and-so, that less than memorable person the English call a bloke or a chap, the one known in American English as a guy or you-know (as in whatsisname). Fulano, zutano, and mangano play the role of Tom, Dick, and Harry or the butcher, the baker, the candlestick maker. Fulano isn't real, no one bears that name; Fulano doesn't play first base or marry your niece; he pays no taxes, eats no food, and leaves no mess behind; he's nobody. If by some error of madness, alcohol, or utter failure of the imagination, a child were named Fulano, his life would be a trial, for he would be no one and everyman, rich and poor, short and tall, Columbian, Cuban, Dominican, Mexican, Puerto Rican, Spanish, and so on.
>
> —Earl Shorris, *Latinos: A Biography of the People*

This extended definition relies on a variety of strategies—word history, comparisons, examples, even a hypothetical "incorrect" usage of the word.

A linguistics text provides another example of the way important concepts may require extended definition:

> **Prosodic meaning.** The way a sentence is said, using the prosody of the language, can radically alter the meaning. Any marked change in emphasis, for example, can lead to a sentence being interpreted in a fresh light. Each of the following sentences carries a different implication, as the stress (indicated by capitals) moves:
>
> John's bought a red CAR (not a red bicycle).
> John's bought a RED car (not a green one).
> JOHN'S bought a red car (not Michael).
>
> The prosody informs us of what information in the sentence can be taken for granted (is "given") and what is of special significance (is "new").
>
> —David Crystal, *The Cambridge Encyclopedia of Language*

Extended definitions may also include *negative definition*—that is, some explanation of what the thing being defined is *not*:

> It's important to be clear about the reverse definition, as well: what dinosaurs are not. Dinosaurs are not lizards, and vice versa. Lizards are scaly reptiles of an ancient bloodline. The oldest lizards antedate the earliest dinosaurs by a full thirty million years. A few large lizards, such as the man-eating Komodo dragon, have been called "relics of the dinosaur age," but this phrase is historically incorrect. No lizard ever evolved the birdlike characteristics peculiar to each and every dinosaur. A big lizard never resembled a small dinosaur except for a few inconsequential details of the teeth. Lizards never walked with the erect, long-striding gait that distinguishes the dinosaurlike ground birds today or the birdlike dinosaurs of the Mesozoic. —Robert T. Bakker, *The Dinosaur Heresies*

As a writer drafting an essay, your choice of appropriate definition strategies will be guided by what you want to accomplish and by your knowledge of who your readers will be. You need not even be consciously aware of particular choices while you are writing a first draft. Later, though, when you are revising this draft, you will have a special advantage if you can look critically at the way you have defined key terms. If your repertoire of defining strategies includes all the variations illustrated in this chapter, you will be able to revise with confidence and power.

Though it happens fairly rarely, some published essays and reports are concerned primarily with the definition of a little understood or problematic concept or thing. Usually, however, definition is only a part of an essay. A long piece of writing, like a term paper or a textbook or a research report, may include many kinds of brief and extended definitions, all of them integrated with other writing strategies.

EXERCISE 16.3

Choose one term that names some concept or feature of central importance in an activity or subject you know well. Choose a word with a well-established definition. Write an extended definition of several sentences for this important term. Write for readers your own age who will be encountering the term for the first time when they read your definition.

EXERCISE 16.4

Read "Inside the Brain," David Noonan's essay in Chapter 4, and analyze the extended definition of *sterile field* in paragraph 6. How does he define this term? What purpose does the definition have within the whole selection?

HISTORICAL DEFINITIONS

Occasionally a writer will trace the history of a word—from its first use, to its adoption into other languages, to its shifting meanings over the centuries. Such a strategy can be a rich addition to an essay, bringing to the definition of an important concept a surprising depth and resonance. A historical definition usually begins with the roots of a word, but it extends well beyond that to trace the word's history over a long period of time. Such a history should always serve a writer's larger purpose, as the example here shows.

In this example, from a book discussing the recent rise of witchcraft and paganism in America, the writer uses a historical definition of the word *pagan* as background to her own definition and also as a way of instructing us in how we should feel about the new pagans.

Pagan comes from the Latin *paganus*, which means a country dweller, and is itself derived from *pagus*, the Latin word for village or rural district. Similarly, *heathen* originally meant a person who lived on the heaths. Negative associations with these words are the end result of centuries of political struggles during which the major prophetic religions, notably Christianity, won a victory over the older polytheistic religions. In the West, often the last people to be converted to Christianity lived on the outskirts of populated areas and kept to the old ways. These were the Pagans and heathens—the word *Pagan* was a term of insult, meaning "hick."

Pagan had become a derogatory term in Rome by the third century. Later, after the death of Julian, the last Pagan emperor, in 362 A.D. the word *Pagan* came to refer to intellectual Pagans like Julian. Gore Vidal, in his extraordinary novel *Julian*, wrote a fictional description of this event in which the Pagan orator Libanius, after attending the funeral of a Christian notable, writes in his journal: "There was a certain amount of good-humored comment about 'pagans' (a new word of contempt for us Hellenists) attending Christian services. . . ." Julian, by the way, has long been one of Neo-Paganism's heroes, and an early Neo-Pagan journal was called *The Julian Review*. Centuries later the word *Pagan* still suffers the consequences of political and religious struggles, and dictionaries still define it to mean a godless person or an unbeliever, instead of, simply, a member of a different kind of religion.

Pagan is also often associated with hedonism. This makes some sense, since many ancient Pagan religions incorporated sexuality into ecstatic religious practice. One scholar, writing on the use of mystical experience by young people in the 1960s, observed that a characteristic of many groups was "the idea of paganism—the body is a temple in which there is nothing unclean, a shrine to be adorned for the ritual of love." New attitudes toward sexuality play a part in some, but not all, Neo-Pagan groups, and the old Pagan religions had their share of ascetics, but generally, Neo-Pagans seem to have healthy attitudes toward sex.

I use *Pagan* to mean a member of a polytheistic nature religion, such as the ancient Greek, Roman, or Egyptian religions, or, in anthropological terms, a member of one of the indigenous folk and tribal-religions all over the world. People who have studied the classics or have been deeply involved with natural or aboriginal peoples are comparatively free of the negative and generally racist attitudes that surround the word *Pagan*.   –Margot Adler, *Drawing Down the Moon*

EXERCISE 16.5

Any good dictionary tells the origins of words. Historical, or etymological, dictionaries, however, give much more information, enough to trace changes in use of a word over long periods of time. The preeminent historical dictionary of our language is the *Oxford English Dictionary*. Less imposing is *A Dictionary of American English*, and even less imposing is *A Dictionary of Americanisms*. Look up the historical definition of any one of the following words in *A Dictionary of Americanisms*, and write several sentences on its roots and development.

basketball	bonanza	eye-opener	picayune
bazooka	bushwhack	filibuster	podunk
bedrock	canyon	gerrymander	rubberneck
blizzard	carpetbag	jazz	sashay
bogus	dugout	pep	two bits

STIPULATIVE DEFINITIONS

The historical definition of pagans in the preceding section concludes with a stipulative definition: "I use *Pagan* to mean a member of a polytheistic nature religion. . . ." *To stipulate* means to seek or assert agreement on something. A stipulative definition is one in which the writer declares a certain meaning, generally not one found in the dictionary.

Stipulative definitions have a variety of important functions, several of which are illustrated here. In the next example, a prominent historian of science proposes a stipulative definition of the word *ecology*.

> Ernst Haeckel, the great popularizer of evolutionary theory in Germany, loved to coin words. The vast majority of his creations died with him a half-century ago, but among the survivors are "ontogeny," "phylogeny," and "ecology." The last is now facing an opposite fate—loss of meaning by extension and vastly inflated currency. Common usage now threatens to make "ecology" a label for anything good that happens far from cities or anything that does not have synthetic chemicals in it. In its more restricted and technical sense, ecology is the study of organic diversity. It focuses on the interactions of organisms and their environments in order to address what may be the most fundamental question in evolutionary biology: "Why are there so many kinds of living things?"
>
> –Stephen Jay Gould, *Ever Since Darwin*

Important concepts in technical fields like biology may gradually take on fuzzy or overly broad popular definitions. The specialists may then have to rescue a concept by redefining it, as Gould does here. He is asking his readers to agree with him that *ecology* means "the study of organic diversity." He stipulates a redefinition and asks us to use the word only as he defines it, at least for the duration of his book.

Another use of stipulative definition is to sort through alternative definitions of a problematic concept—*pure breed of cats* in the next example—in order to reject these definitions and argue for another.

> What is a pure breed of cats, and what constitutes a pure-bred animal? These terms can have a number of meanings. One of the simplest is merely to regard as pure-bred a cat that has been properly registered with a responsible body (such as the Governing Council of the Cat Fancy [GCCF] in Britain, or the Cat Fanciers' Association [CFA] or one of the other similar associations in the United States). Such a cat will have a pedigree of similarly registered parents, grand-

parents and so on for a given number of generations—normally at least four. This ensures that the cat has "respectable" parentage and is likely to be a representative specimen of the breed—though it says nothing about its quality.

However, the process of registration and the writing of pedigrees is, in a sense (and without meaning to be derogatory), merely window dressing. They simply set a seal upon a more fundamental definition of pure breeds of cats. This relates to the characteristics of the individuals constituting a recognized breed and how these may differ from those of other cats: from alley cats and from other recognized breeds. In one sense, a breed is a group of animals that sufficient people are mutually agreed to recognize as such. This is not enough in itself, however; the group must have coherent distinguishing features that set them apart from all other cats, and hence distinctive underlying genetic characteristics.   –Michael Wright and Sally Walters, *The Book of the Cat*

EXERCISE 16.6

In his Chapter 7 proposal about birth control in the schools, Adam Paul Weisman offers a stipulative definition of the role schools play in students' lives (paragraph 11). Read the essay, paying particular attention to this definition. What function does it serve in the essay as a whole?

EXERCISE 16.7

Write several sentences of a stipulative definition for one of the following.

1.   Define in your own way game shows, soap operas, police dramas, or horror movies. Try for a stipulative definition of what these (or some other form of entertainment) are generally like. In effect, you will be saying to your readers, other students in your class who are familiar with these shows, "Let's for now define X this way."

2.   Do the same for some hard-to-define concept—such as *loyalty, love, bravery, shyness, sportsmanship, male chauvinism,* or *worthwhile college courses.*

3.   Think of a new development or phenomenon in contemporary romance, music, television, leisure, fashion, or eating habits. Invent a name for it, and write a stipulative definition for it.

In a variety of writing situations, you will be faced with the task of sorting various scattered materials into an orderly presentation. A common strategy for doing so is *classifying*—combining items into a number of discrete groupings and then labeling each new group. In many instances classifying is a matter of *dividing* something into its constituent parts in order to consider the elements of each part separately.

In using classification and division, you will be particularly concerned with organization, principles of division, and coherence.

ORGANIZATION

As a strategy, classification and division serves primarily as a means of organization, of creating a framework for the presentation of information, whether in a few paragraphs of an essay or an entire book. Other strategies—definition, illustration, contrast—are often used to develop a topic in detail.

In the following passage, for example, Thomas Sowell uses classification as an organizing strategy in his discussion of immigrants in the United States. He classifies American immigrant groups into four discrete categories (refugees, sojourners, settlers, and captives):

> It has often been said that we are a nation of immigrants. In a sense that is true; but the blanket term "immigrants" covers over many important distinctions among the various peoples who came to America. The famine Irish and the east European Jewish victims of pogroms were essentially refugees who fled in whole family units, burning their bridges behind them, and arrived in the United States committed to becoming Americans. Others have come as sojourners, mostly men, and with the intention of returning to their native lands, so that Americanization in language, culture, or citizenship had a low priority for them. The earliest emigrations from Italy, China, Japan, and Mexico were largely of this character, as is much of today's migration back and forth between Puerto Rico and the mainland of the United States. There were also immigrants who were neither refugees nor sojourners, but simply people who chose to come to the United States to settle at a place and time of their choice. Such immigrants—the Germans or Scandinavians, for example—were far less likely to concentrate in the port cities where they landed and more likely to choose a long-run settlement cite suited to their conditions. Finally, there were those who did not choose to come at all but who were brought as captives—African slaves—and whose geographic distribution and occupational roles were suited to the convenience of others. —Thomas Sowell, *Ethnic America: A History*

The division of a topic into parts can be used for a variety of purposes. See how Ernest Hemingway uses the strategy to open a chapter in *Death in the Afternoon*, his classic book on bullfighting in Spain. To help us understand how a bullfight develops, Hemingway describes it as divided into three acts, each of which is named for the major action (the trial of the lances, the banderillas, and the death). Hemingway subdivides the third act further, into three parts (or scenes, to continue his analogy between a bullfight and a play). Finally, he summarizes his discussion in terms of a three-act "tragedy."

There are three acts to the fighting of each bull and they are called in Spanish los tres tercios de la lidia, or the three thirds of the combat. The first act, where the bull charges the picadors, is the suerte de varas, or the trial of the lances. Suerte is an important word in Spanish. It means, according to the dictionary: Suerte, f., chance, hazard, lots, fortune, luck, good luck, haphazard; state, condition, fate, doom, destiny, kind, sort; species, manner, mode, way, skillful manœuvre; trick, feat, juggle, and piece of ground separated by landmark. So the translation of trial or manœuvre is quite arbitrary, as any translation must be from the Spanish.

The action of the picadors in the ring and the work of the matadors who are charged with protecting them with their capes when they are dismounted make up the first act of the bullfight. When the president signals for the end of this act and the bugle blows the picadors leave the ring and the second act begins. There are no horses in the ring after the first act except the dead horses which are covered with canvas. Act one is the act of the capes, the pics and the horses. In it the bull has the greatest opportunity to display his bravery or cowardice.

Act two is that of the banderillas. These are pairs of sticks about a yard long, seventy centimetres to be exact, with a harpoon-shaped steel point four centimetres long at one end. They are supposed to be placed, two at a time, in the humped muscle at the top of the bull's neck as he charges the man who holds them. They are designed to complete the work of slowing up the bull and regulating the carriage of his head which has been begun by the picadors: so that his attack will be slower, but surer and better directed. Four pair of banderillas are usually put in. If they are placed by the banderilleros or peones they must be placed, above all other considerations, quickly and in the proper position. If the matador himself places them he may indulge in a preparation which is usually accompanied by music. This is the most picturesque part of the bullfight and the part most spectators care for the most when first seeing fights. The mission of the banderilleros is not only to force the bull by hooking to tire his neck muscles and carry his head lower but also, by placing them at one side or another, to correct a tendency to hook to that side. The entire act of the banderillas should not take more than five minutes. If it is prolonged the bull becomes discomposed and the fight loses the tempo it must keep, and if the bull is an uncertain and dangerous one he has too many opportunities to see and charge men unarmed with any lure, and so develops a tendency to search for the man, the bundle, as the Spanish call him, behind the cloth when the matador comes out for the last act with the sword and muleta.

The president changes the act after three or at most four pairs of banderillas have been placed and the third and final division is the death. It is made up of three parts. First the brindis or salutation of the president and dedication or toasting of the death of the bull, either to him or to some other person by the matador, followed by the work of the matador with the muleta. This is a scarlet serge cloth which is folded over a stick which has a sharp spike at one end and a handle at the other. The spike goes through the cloth which is fastened to the other end of the handle with a thumbscrew so that it hangs in folds along the length of the stick. Muleta means literally crutch, but in bullfighting it refers to the scarlet-serge-draped stick with which the matador is supposed to master the bull, prepare him for killing and finally hold in his left hand to lower the bull's head and keep it lowered while he kills the animal by a sword thrust high up between his shoulder blades.

These are the three acts in the tragedy of the bullfight, and it is the first one, the horse part, which indicates what the others will be and, in fact, makes the rest possible. It is in the first act that the bull comes out in full possession of all of his faculties, confident, fast, vicious and conquering. All his victories are in the first act. At the end of the first act he has apparently won. He has cleared the ring of mounted men and is alone. In the second act he is baffled completely by an unarmed man and very cruelly punished by the banderillas so that his confidence and his blind general rage goes and he concentrates his hatred on an individual object. In the third act he is faced by only one man who must, alone, dominate him by a piece of cloth placed over a stick, and kill him from in front, going in over the bull's right horn to kill him with a sword thrust between the arch of his shoulder blades.　–Ernest Hemingway, *Death in the Afternoon*

The way a topic is divided can be illustrated with a diagram showing its parts and subparts. Here is such a diagram of the organization of Hemingway's excerpt:

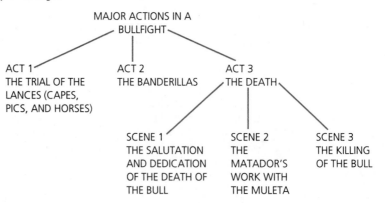

Using this division, the various actions of the bullfight can be classified according to the "act" in which they occur.

PRINCIPLES OF DIVISION

When you divide materials, be sure the division meets several basic requirements. First, it must be appropriate to your writing purpose. You shouldn't divide material simply to have smaller bits of information; rather, it should help you make a point about your topic. In addition, your divisions should be consistent, exclusive, and complete. These may be defined as follows:

Consistency—Resulting parts must be based on the same principle of division.

Exclusiveness—Parts resulting from the division should not overlap.

Completeness—No important parts should be omitted in the division.

The Hemingway excerpt illustrates each of these requirements. The *point* of Hemingway's division is to suggest the formalized, tragic drama of a bullfight and to highlight the contribution of the key action in each act to the noble defeat of the bull. This division is *consistent* in that the parts, or acts—the trial of the lances, the banderillas, and the death—are all formed on the same principle. Each one is a primary segment of the drama and revolves around a particular major action. The division is *exclusive* because there is no overlap: actions in one act do not usually occur again in other acts. It is *complete* because Hemingway's acts include all the actions responsible for the defeat of the bull. (Note that the subdivision of the third act into the major activities of the matador fulfills these same requirements.)

The principle of division you use depends on your purpose. Most topics can be divided in a number of ways. For example, based on the purpose of the study, sociologists might divide a survey's respondents according to age, education, income, or geographic location. Similarly, a gardener choosing deciduous trees for a midwestern park might be concerned, among other matters, with variations in leaf coloration or in shade-giving characteristics and thus divide the subject into the following groupings:

DECIDUOUS TREES OF THE MIDWEST

LEAF COLORS

PALE GREEN	GREY GREEN	DEEP GREEN	PURPLE	SILVER	BRONZE

SHADE-GIVING CHARACTERISTICS

FULL SHADE	MOTTLED SHADE	LIGHT SHADE

Writers likewise divide topics according to principles based on their purposes for writing. The division itself results from the writer's analysis of the topic and of all information gathered regarding the topic plus any ideas or insights he or she may have. Only full and thoughtful analysis of the topic and a carefully defined principle of division can assure that the division or system of classification will be consistent, exclusive, and complete.

EXERCISE 17.1

Diagram the division in the first example in this chapter, the selection by Thomas Sowell. Then decide whether the division is consistent, exclusive, and complete. What would you say is the point of the division?

EXERCISE 17.2

Pick at least two of the following topics, and divide them according to two or three different principles of division: teachers, dreams, crimes, poets, lies, restaurants, movies, popular music groups, ways of avoiding writing, football offenses, field hockey defenses. Diagram each division, and then state its point. Be sure that each division is consistent, exclusive, and complete.

MAINTAINING COHERENCE

Anytime you divide information into parts, you have to take care to present the material in a way that readers can follow easily. Biologist Sylvia Mader's *Inquiry into Life* includes many good examples of cues a writer can provide to bring coherence to a discussion and to guide readers sufficiently. In the following example from that book, Mader offers a straightforward three-part division to identify the parts of the human ear. In the larger context of the chapter in which it appears, its purpose is to name and classify the parts so that readers will be able to follow a discussion of how the ear functions.

The ear has three divisions: outer, middle, and inner. The **outer ear** consists of the **pinna** (external flap) and **auditory canal**. The opening of the auditory canal is lined with fine hairs and sweat glands. In the upper wall are modified sweat glands that secrete earwax to help guard the ear against the entrance of foreign materials such as air pollutants.

The **middle ear** begins at the **tympanic membrane** (eardrum) and ends at a bony wall in which are found two small openings covered by membranes. These openings are called the **oval** and **round windows**. The posterior wall of the middle ear leads to many air spaces within the **mastoid process**.

Three small bones are found between the tympanic membrane and the oval window. Collectively called the **ossicles**, individually they are the **hammer** (malleus), **anvil** (incus), and **stirrup** (stapes) because their shapes resemble these objects. The hammer adheres to the tympanic membrane, while the stirrup touches the oval window. . . .

Whereas the outer ear and middle ear contain air, the inner ear is filled with fluid. The **inner ear,** anatomically speaking, has three areas: the first two, called the vestibule and semicircular canals, are concerned with balance; and the third, the cochlea, is concerned with hearing.

The **semicircular canals** are arranged so that there is one in each dimension of space. The base of each canal, called the **ampulla,** is slightly enlarged. Within the ampullae are little hair cells.

The **vestibule** is a chamber that lies between the semicircular canals and the cochlea. It contains two small sacs called the **utricle** and **saccule.** Within both of these are little hair cells surrounded by a gelatinous material containing calcium carbonate granules, or **otoliths.** . . .   –Silvia Mader, *Inquiry into Life*

Mader's plan for her division is a *spatial* one, moving from outside to inside. (Note, in contrast, that Hemingway's division of the bullfight into three acts follows a *temporal* plan, moving across time.) In the initial statement of the division, Mader forecasts the plan of the presentation and names the three divisions in the order in which she will take them up: outer, middle, and inner ear. Each division is then introduced in a new paragraph and always with the same syntax at the beginning of a sentence: "The outer ear . . . The middle ear . . . The inner ear . . . ." Such strategies help readers to understand and to follow an explanation easily and without confusion.

General strategies for coherence are discussed on pp. 476–81.

EXERCISE 17.3

Look again at the second example in this chapter (by Ernest Hemingway) to examine the strategies the writer uses to present a coherent division of information. Does the initial statement of the division name all the groups and forecast the order in which they will be discussed? What other writing strategies does the writer use to steer the reader through the presentation?

USING CLASSIFICATION WITH OTHER WRITING STRATEGIES

This example is from a book explaining the new physics to nonphysicists.

There are two kinds of mass, which means that there are two ways of talking about it. The first is gravitational mass. The gravitational mass of an object, roughly speaking, is the weight of the object as measured on a balance scale. Something that weighs three times more than another object has three times more mass. Gravitational mass is the measure of how much force the gravity of the earth exerts on an object. Newton's laws describe the effects of this force, which vary with the distance of the mass from the earth. Although Newton's laws describe the effects of this force, they do not define it. This is the mystery of action-at-a-distance. . . .

The second type of mass is inertial mass. Inertial mass is the measure of the resistance of an object to acceleration (or deceleration, which is negative acceleration). For example, it takes three times more force to move three railroad cars from a standstill to twenty miles per hour (positive acceleration) than it takes to move one railroad car from a standstill to twenty miles per hour. . . . Similarly, once they are moving, it takes three times more force to stop three cars than it takes to stop the single car. This is because the inertial mass of the three railroad cars is three times more than the inertial mass of the single railroad car.

Inertial mass and gravitational mass are equal. This explains why a feather and a cannonball fall with equal velocity in a vacuum. The cannonball has hundreds of times more gravitational mass than the feather (it weighs more) but it also has hundreds of times more resistance to motion than the feather (its inertial mass). Its attraction to the earth is hundreds of times stronger than that of the feather, but then so is its inclination not to move. The result is that it accelerates downward at the same rate as the feather, although it seems that it should fall much faster.

The fact that inertial mass and gravitational mass are equal was known three hundred years ago, but physicists considered it a coincidence. No significance was attached to it until Einstein published his general theory of relativity.

–Gary Zukav, *The Dancing Wu Li Masters: An Overview of the New Physics*

This example illustrates the relation of classification and division to other essential writing strategies. Zukav divides his topic into two kinds of mass: gravitational and inertial. Then he defines each one. In the first paragraph, to define gravitational mass, he relies in part on the illustration of an ordinary balance scale. In the second paragraph, to define inertial mass, he contrasts the action of three railroad cars with that of one railroad car. These two paragraphs show how naturally dividing and classifying work together with definition, illustration, and contrast.

Dividing his material into two parts serves to emphasize his point: that inertial mass and gravitational mass (the two parts) are equal. This point is then illustrated by contrasting a feather with a cannonball.

As this example and the others in this chapter indicate, classification and division is basically an organizational strategy rather than one for development. Only when used together with other writing strategies can it be used to *explain* a topic.

EXERCISE 17.4

Analyze the following classifications, each from a selection in Part I of this book. First, within the context of the whole selection, decide the point of the division and the principle used. Then decide whether the division is consistent, exclusive, and complete. To focus your analysis, you might want to diagram the division.

Chapter 7. "Birth Control in the Schools," paragraphs 2–5

Chapter 7. "A Comprehensive Plan for Promoting Academic Integrity," paragraphs 2 and 11

Chapter 9. "Suicide among Young People," paragraph 2 and table

EXERCISE 17.5

Choose one of the following writing activities. Each one asks for some division; state briefly what point your division might make. Be sure, in addition, that your groupings have consistency, exclusiveness, and completeness. Include in your writing appropriate strategies of coherence: forecasting, paragraphing (optional in a brief piece), repeated sentence patterns, and so on.

1. Write several sentences in which you identify the major periods in your life. Label and briefly define each period.

2. Describe a familiar activity (running, sleeping, eating Chinese food) in a new way by dividing it into stages. Label and define each stage.

3. Develop in writing one of the classification systems you created in Exercise 17.2.

When you analyze and evaluate two or more things, you compare those things. You might compare two people you know well, three motorcycles you are considering buying for a cross-country tour, four Stephen King novels, three tomato plants being grown under different laboratory conditions, or two theories about the causes of inflation and unemployment. But as soon as comparison begins, contrast edges its way in, for rarely are two things totally alike. The contrasts, or differences, between the three motorcycles are likely to be more enlightening than the similarities, many of which may be so obvious as to need no analysis. *Comparison*, then, brings similar things together for examination, to see how they are alike. *Contrast* is a form of comparison that emphasizes their differences.

Comparison and contrast is more than a writing strategy, of course. It is a basic way of thinking and learning. A basic principle of learning theory says that we acquire new concepts most readily if we can see how they are similar to or different from concepts we already know.

Professional writers say that comparison and contrast is a basic strategy they would not want to be without. For some writing situations (like the ones above) it has no substitute. Indeed, some writing is essentially extended comparison. But for all kinds of writing, comparison and contrast regularly alternates with other writing strategies in presenting information.

Chances are that you will confront many test questions and essay assignments asking you to compare and contrast—two poems, three presidents, four procedures. This is a popular format in all academic disciplines, for it is one of the best ways to challenge students intellectually.

TWO WAYS OF COMPARING AND CONTRASTING

There are two ways to organize comparison and contrast in writing: in chunks and in sequence. In *chunking*, each object of the comparison is presented separately; in *sequencing*, the items are compared point by point. For example, a chunked comparison of two motorcycles would first detail all pertinent features of the Pirsig 241X and then consider all features of the Kawazuki 500S, whereas a sequenced comparison would analyze the Pirsig and the Kawazuki feature by feature. In a chunked comparison discussion is organized around each separate item being compared. In a sequenced comparison it is organized around characteristics of the items being compared.

Comparing and Contrasting 18

Look now at an example of chunked comparison, one that contrasts popular nineteenth-century "sentimental" novels with the "Western" novels that provided a reaction against them:

> . . . The female, domestic, "sentimental" religion of the best-selling women writers—Harriet Beecher Stowe, Susan Warner, Maria Cummins, and dozens of others—whose novels spoke to the deepest beliefs and highest ideals of middle-class America, is the real antagonist of the Western.
>
> You can see this simply by comparing the main features of the Western with the sentimental novel. In these books . . . a woman is always the main character, usually a young orphan girl, with several other main characters being women too. Most of the action takes place in private spaces, at home, indoors, in kitchens, parlors, and upstairs chambers. And most of it concerns the interior struggles of the heroine to live up to an ideal of Christian virtue—usually involving uncomplaining submission to difficult and painful circumstances, learning to quell rebellious instincts, and dedicating her life to the service of God through serving others. In these struggles, women give one another a great deal of emotional and material support, and they have close relationships verging on what today we would identify as homosocial and homoerotic. There's a great deal of Bible reading, praying, hymn singing, and drinking of tea. Emotions other than anger are expressed very freely and openly. Often there are long, drawn-out death scenes in which a saintly women dies a natural death at home. . . .
>
> The elements of the typical Western plot arrange themselves in stark opposition to this pattern, not just vaguely and generally but point for point. First of all, in Westerns (which are generally written by men), the main character is always a full-grown adult male, and almost all of the other characters are men. The action takes place either outdoors—on the prairie, on the main street—or in public places—the saloon, the sheriff's office, the barber shop, the livery stable. The action concerns physical struggles between the hero and a rival or rivals, and culminates in a fight to the death with guns. In the course of these struggles the hero frequently forms a bond with another man—sometimes his rival, more often a comrade—a bond that is more important than any relation he has with a woman and is frequently tinged with homoeroticism. There is very little free expression of the emotions. The hero is a man of few words who expresses himself through physical action—usually fighting. And when death occurs it is never at home in bed but always sudden death, usually murder. . . .
>
> —Jane Tompkins, *West of Everything: The Inner Life of Westerns*

The two parts of the comparison—sentimental novels and Westerns—are discussed separately, first one and then the other. The shift from the first

527

discussion to the contrasting one is signaled by a transitional sentence that begins a new paragraph. Each point of contrast is presented in the same order.

Schematically, a chunked comparison looks simple enough. As the preceding example shows, it is easy to block off such a discussion in a text and then provide a clean transition between the various parts. And yet it can in fact be more complicated for a writer to plan than a sequenced comparison. Sequenced comparison may be closer to the way people perceive and think about similarities or differences in things. For example, while your awareness that two navy blazers are different might come all at once, you would identify the specific differences—buttons, tailoring, fabric—one at a time. A sequenced comparison would point to the differences in just this way—one at a time—whereas a chunked comparison would present all the features of one blazer and then do the same for the second. Thus the chunked strategy requires that a writer organize all the points of comparison before starting to write. With sequencing, however, it is possible to take up each point of comparison as it comes to mind.

In the next example, from a natural history of the earth, sequencing is used to contrast bird wings and airplane wings:

> Bird wings have a much more complex job to do than the wings of an aeroplane, for in addition to supporting the bird they must act as its engine, rowing it through the air. Even so the wing outline of a bird conforms to the same aerodynamic principles as those eventually discovered by man when designing his aeroplanes, and if you know how different kinds of aircraft perform, you can predict the flight capabilities of similarly shaped birds.
>
> Short stubby wings enable a tanager and other forest-living birds to swerve and dodge at speed through the undergrowth just as they helped the fighter planes of the Second World War to make tight turns and aerobatic manoeuvres in a dog-fight. More modern fighters achieve greater speeds by sweeping back their wings while in flight, just as peregrines do when they go into a 130 kph dive, stooping to a kill. Championship gliders have long thin wings so that, having gained height in a thermal up-current they can soar gently down for hours and an albatross, the largest of flying birds, with a similar wing shape and a span of 3 metres, can patrol the ocean for hours in the same way without a single wing beat. Vultures and hawks circle at very slow speeds supported by a thermal and they have the broad rectangular wings that very slow flying aircraft have. Man has not been able to adapt wings to provide hovering flight. He has only achieved that with the whirling horizontal blades of a helicopter or the downward-pointing engines of a vertical landing jet. Hummingbirds have paralleled even this. They tilt their bodies so that they are almost upright and then beat their wings as fast as 80 times a second producing a similar down-draught of air. So the hummingbird can hover and even fly backwards.
>
> –David Attenborough, *Life on Earth*

The important thing to note about this example is the limited, focused basis for the comparison: the shape of wings. Attenborough specifies this basis in the second sentence of the passage (underscored here). Though birds and planes both fly, there is almost nothing else they have in common. They are so obviously different that it would even seem silly to compare them in writing. But Attenborough finds a valid—and fascinating—basis for comparison and develops it in a way that is both informative and entertaining. A successful comparison always has these qualities: a valid basis for comparison, a limited focus, and information that will catch a reader's attention.

EXERCISE 18.1

Pick any one of the following subjects and write several sentences comparing and contrasting. Be careful to limit the basis for your comparison, and underline the sentence that states that basis.

> two ways of achieving the same goal (travel by bus or subway, using flattery or persuasion to get what you want)
>
> two seemingly unlikely subjects for comparison (a child and an old man, soccer and ballet)
>
> two sports or theories

EXERCISE 18.2

Analyze the specified comparisons in the following selections from Part I. How is each comparison organized? (It may or may not be neatly chunked or sequenced.) Why do you think the writer organizes the comparison in that way? What is the role of the comparison in the whole piece? How effective do you consider the comparison?

> *Chapter 2.* "On Being a Real Westerner," Tobias Wolff, paragraphs 3, 4
>
> *Chapter 4.* "Inside the Brain," David Noonan, paragraphs 21–23
>
> *Chapter 5.* "Love," Anastasia Toufexis, paragraph 14.
>
> *Chapter 8.* "Searing, Nervy and Very Honest," David Ansen, paragraph 3
>
> *Chapter 9.* "Suicide among Young People," Victor Fuchs, paragraph 2

EXERCISE 18.3

Some of the selections in Part I are organized around comparisons. Identify and evaluate the comparisons in the Bellah piece in Chapter 5 and the one by Kibler in Chapter 7. (Remember that the comparison may be stated or implied.)

ANALOGY

One special form of comparison is the *analogy*, in which one part of the comparison is used simply to explain the other. See how John McPhee uses two different analogies—the twelve-month calendar and the distance along two widespread arms—to explain the duration of geologic time.

> In like manner, geologists will sometimes use the calendar year as a unit to represent the time scale, and in such terms the Precambrian runs from New Year's Day until well after Halloween. Dinosaurs appear in the middle of December and are gone the day after Christmas. The last ice sheet melts on December 31st at one minute before midnight, and the Roman Empire lasts five seconds. With your arms spread wide again to represent all time on earth, look at one hand with its line of life. The Cambrian begins in the wrist, and the Permian Extinction is at the outer end of the palm. All of the Cenozoic is in a fingerprint, and in a single stroke with a medium-grained nail file you could eradicate human history. Geologists live with the geologic scale. Individually, they may or may not be alarmed by the rate of exploitation of the things they discover, but, like the environmentalists, they use these repetitive analogies to place the human record in perspective—to see the Age of Reflection, the last few thousand years, as a small bright sparkle at the end of time.   –John McPhee, *Basin and Range*

Scientists have always made good use of analogy–in both their thinking and their writing. Physics, in particular, is full of concepts that strain the comprehension of the nonscientist. One such concept is the uncertainty principle, a concept that is very difficult for anybody but a physicist to define. See how Gary Zukav does so with an analogy—likening the uncertainty principle to a movie projector that is always slightly out of focus.

> The uncertainty principle reveals that as we penetrate deeper and deeper into the subatomic realm, we reach a certain point at which one part or another of our picture of nature becomes blurred, and there is no way to reclarify that part without blurring another part of the picture! It is as though we are adjusting a moving picture that is slightly out of focus. As we make the final adjustments, we are astonished to discover that when the right side of the picture clears, the left side of the picture becomes completely unfocused and nothing in it is recognizable. When we try to focus the left side of the picture, the right side starts to blur and soon the situation is reversed. If we try to strike a balance between these two extremes, both sides of the picture return to a recognizable condition, but in no way can we remove the original fuzziness from them.
>
> The right side of the picture, in the original formulation of the uncertainty principle, corresponds to the position in space of a moving particle. The left side of the picture corresponds to its momentum. According to the uncertainty principle, we cannot measure accurately, at the same time, both the position *and* the momentum of a moving particle. The more precisely we determine one of these properties, the less we know about the other. If we precisely determine the position of the particle, then, strange as it sounds, there is *nothing* that we

can know about its momentum. If we precisely determine the momentum of the particle, there is no way to determine its position.

–Gary Zukav, *The Dancing Wu Li Masters: An Overview of the New Physics*

Notice what a strong visual image Zukav's analogy produces—it is very easy to imagine alternating sides of the movie screen going in and out of focus. Explanatory analogies almost always use very familiar objects for comparison, probably because they are trying to explain something very unfamiliar.

Analogies can also be used for subjects other than abstract, scientific concepts. Indeed, writers often offer analogies to make nontechnical descriptions of explanations more vivid and entertaining. Here is a sports analogy from a sociological study of Hamilton, Ohio. It comes from a chapter describing a hearing held to examine a school board's decision to fire one teacher, Sam Shie. In it, the writer uses analogy to describe Shie's three lawyers, comparing them to an aggressive basketball team.

> The cross-examination of Dr. Helms was conducted by Randy Rogers, the young associate of Holbrock's. Rogers was tall and strongly built, lacking by only a couple of inches the height of a professional basketball player who weakens the opposition by fouling often and drawing fouls in return. This was close to the function Rogers performed for the defense. With Hugh Holbrock, Robert Dunlevey, and Randy Rogers all ranged against Carl Morgenstern, it was sometimes hard to tell just who the underdog was at the hearings. Sam Shie, to be sure, was a lone teacher up against a community's educational establishment which was trying to purge him. But at the hearings themselves, almost all the spectators were on Shie's side; he was being supported by the Ohio Education Association, and he had three articulate, variously styled lawyers who disputed virtually everything Carl Morgenstern or one of his witnesses said. Each came at Morgenstern from a different angle with a new tactic, trying to wear him down the way a basketball team will use a full-court press, a fast break, the setting of a pick or screen, the switching of defensive assignments to bewilder an opponent. Hugh Holbrock made long, arcing, oratorical shots from outside the key, Robert Dunlevey dribbled spectacularly around any position Morgenstern took, and Randy Rogers would try to provoke Morgenstern into exchanges of anger and procedural wrangles. Rogers was surly to Morgenstern, who would respond by being loftily sardonic. A few times Morgenstern slipped and got mad at Rogers, who was polite to witnesses but steeled himself to a single pitch of fury when he was addressing Morgenstern. The rest of the time Rogers sat moodily at the defense table—in effect on the bench—while Holbrock and Dunlevey performed their own specialties.   –Peter Davis, *Hometown*

Analogies are tricky. They may at first seem useful, but actually it is a rare analogy that is consistently useful at all the major points of comparison. Some are downright misleading.

Thus, most writers exercise caution with analogy. Nevertheless, you will run across analogies regularly; indeed, it would be hard to find a book without one. For certain very abstract information as well as some writing situations, analogy is the writing strategy of choice.

EXERCISE 18.4

Choose a principle or process that you know well. You might select a basic principle from the natural or social sciences; or you could consider a bodily movement, a physiological process, or a process of social change.

Write an analogy of several sentences that explains this principle or process to a reader who is unfamiliar with it. Look for something very familiar to compare it with that will help the reader understand the principle or process without a technical explanation.

he word *arguing* connotes a dispute—raised voices, doors slammed, names called. As a writing strategy, however, arguing means something quite different. It means presenting a carefully reasoned, well-supported argument that takes into account other points of view. Arguing here, then, connotes both inquiry and advocacy, presenting a position in a thoughtful and convincing way.

Reasoned argument need not assume reasonable readers, however. Sometimes readers you want to reach may hold inflexible and dogmatic views or may feel angered or cornered by your argument. Sometimes, through reasoned argument, such readers can be convinced to take your views seriously. If you suspect they cannot, then you could try addressing your argument to readers who are in a position to influence or constrain those you want to reach or challenge. For example, if you oppose an elected official's views on some issue, you could aim a reasoned argument at voters who might be convinced to vote for someone else. In your argument you could pointedly challenge the official's views, attempting to refute them by showing them to be foolish or dangerous.

You may find yourself in a writing situation where you believe that confrontation or contentiousness seem more justified than reason. This chapter, however, illustrates only strategies of reasoned argument, appropriate for those situations where you believe your readers amenable to thoughtful arguing and calm counterarguing.

This chapter presents the basic argumentative strategies available to a writer, focusing first on the structure of an argument—making claims, offering supporting reasons and evidence, and anticipating readers' concerns—and then on common abuses or errors in argumentation.

MAKING A CLAIM

Central to any writer's argument is a claim. The claim is whatever view or thesis or conclusion the writer puts forth about the subject. Argumentative essays present the claim in a thesis statement.

Here are some claims that appear as thesis statements in argumentative essays in Part I of this book:

When overzealous parents and coaches impose adult standards on children's sports, the result can be activities that are neither satisfying nor beneficial to children. —Jessica Statsky, "Children Need to Play, Not Compete" (Chapter 6)

Unfortunately, there is no quick fix, no single or simple solution to the problem of student cheating. . . . Institutions must adopt a comprehensive approach involving the entire institution—students, faculty members, and administrators. . . . Confronting cheating should include sanctions that respond to the behavior as well as educational programs or seminars that address developmental issues. —William L. Kibler, "A Comprehensive Plan for Promoting Academic Integrity" (Chapter 7)

Lee's conscience-pricking movie is bracing and necessary; it's the funkiest and most informed view of racism an American filmmaker has given us.
—David Ansen, "Searing, Nervy and Very Honest" (Chapter 8)

The mythic horror movie, like the sick joke, has a dirty job to do. It deliberately appeals to all that is worst in us. It is morbidity unchained, our most base instincts let free, our nastiest fantasies realized . . . and it all happens fittingly enough, in the dark. —Stephen King, "Why We Crave Horror Movies" (Chapter 9)

"Araby" tells the story of an adolescent boy's initiation into adulthood. . . . From the beginning, the boy deludes himself about his relationship with Mangan's sister. Through this self-delusion, he increasingly resembles the adult characters, and later, at Araby, he realizes the parallel between his own self-delusion and the hypocrisy and vanity of the adult world.
—David Ratinov, "From Innocence to Insight: 'Araby' as an Initiation Story" (Chapter 10)

Claims can be classified according to the kinds of questions they seek to answer. Each of the preceding thesis statements, for example, illustrates a different kind of claim:

Claim of judgment: What is your position on the issue? (Statsky)
Claim of policy: What should be done to solve the problem? (Kibler)
Claim of value: What is something worth? (Ansen)
Claim of cause: Why is something the way it is? (King)
Claim of interpretation: What does something mean? (Ratinov)

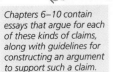

Chapters 6–10 contain essays that argue for each of these kinds of claims, along with guidelines for constructing an argument to support such a claim.

Successful claims must be arguable, clear, and appropriately qualified. Following is a discussion of each of these characteristics of successful claims.

Basically your thesis

Arguable
Statements

To be arguable, a claim must have some probability of being true. It should not, however, be generally accepted as true. In addition, a claim must be arguable on grounds shared by writer and readers.

Facts are unarguable as claims because they are objectively verifiable. Facts are easy to verify—whether by checking an authoritative reference book, asking an authority, or observing it with your own eyes. For example, these statements assert facts:

Jem will be twenty-four years old on May 6, 1995.

I am less than five feet tall.

Eucalyptus trees were originally imported into California from Australia.

Each of these assertions can be easily verified. To find out Jem's age, you can do many things, including asking him and looking up his school records. To determine a person's height, you can use a tape measure. To discover where California got its Eucalyptus trees, you can refer to a source in the library. There is no point in arguing over such statements (though you might question the authority of a particular source or the accuracy of someone's measurement). If a writer were to claim something as fact and attempt to support the claim with authorities or statistics, the essay would not be considered an argument but a report of information. Facts, as you will see in the next section, are used in arguments as evidence to support a claim and not as claims themselves.

Like facts, expressions of personal feelings are not arguable claims. While facts are unarguable because they can be definitively proven true or false, feelings are unarguable because they are purely subjective. Personal feelings can be explained, but it would be unreasonable to attempt to convince others to change their views or take action solely on the basis of your personal feelings.

You can declare, for example, that you love rocky road ice cream or that you detest eight o'clock classes, but you cannot offer an argument to support such claims. All you can do is explain why you feel as you do. You might explain that the combination of chocolate, marshmallow, and nuts in rocky road feels good in your mouth. Similarly, even though many people undoubtedly share your dislike of eight o'clock classes, it would be pointless to try to convince others to share your feelings. If, however, you were to restate the claim as "Eight o'clock classes are counterproductive," you could then construct an argument to support your claim that does not depend solely on your subjective feelings, memories, or preferences. Your argument could be based on reasons and evidence that apply to others as well as to yourself. For example, you might argue that students' ability to learn is at an especially low ebb after breakfast and provide scientific as well as statistical evidence as support, in addition, perhaps, to personal experience and informal interviews with your friends.

Clear and
Exact Wording

The way a claim is worded is as important as whether or not it is arguable. The wording of a claim, especially its key terms, must be clear and exact. Two common kinds of imprecision are vagueness and ambiguity.

Consider the following claim: "Democracy is a way of life." The meaning of this claim is vague and uncertain. The problem stems both from the abstractness of the word *democracy* and the inexactness of the phrase *way of life*. Abstract ideas like democracy, freedom, and patriotism are by their very nature hard to grasp, and they become even less clear with overuse. Too often, such words take on connotations that may obscure their original meaning. *Way of life* suffers from fuzziness: What does it mean? Moreover, can a form of government be a way of life? It depends on what is meant by *way of life*. Does it refer to daily life, to a general philosophy or attitude toward life, or to something else?

A related problem is ambiguity. While a claim is considered vague if its meaning is unclear, it is ambiguous if it has more than one possible meaning. For example, the statement "my English instructor is mad" can be understood in two ways: The teacher is either angry or insane. Obviously, these are two very different claims. You wouldn't want readers to think you mean one when you actually mean the other.

In any argumentative writing, you should pay special attention to the way you phrase your claims and take care to avoid vague and ambiguous language.

Appropriate
Qualification

In addition to being arguable and clear, the forcefulness with which a writer asserts a claim should be appropriate to the writing situation. If you are confident that your case is so strong that readers will accept your argument without question, you will want to state your claim emphatically and unconditionally. If, however, you expect readers to challenge your assumptions or conclusions, then you will want to qualify your statement. Qualifying the extremity or forcefulness of a claim makes it more likely that readers will take it seriously. Expressions like *probably*, *very likely*, *apparently*, *it seems* all serve to qualify a claim.

EXERCISE 19.1

Write a claim of judgment that asserts your position on one of the following controversial issues: restrictions on hate speech on college campuses, working part time during college, couples' remaining married for the good of the children, gays and lesbians in the military. These issues are complicated and have been debated for a long time. Constructing a persuasive argument would obviously require careful deliberation and probably some research as well. For practice in writing claims, however, try simply to construct a claim that is arguable, clear, and appropriately qualified.

EXERCISE 19.2

Find the claim in any one of the selections in Chapter 6 and read the entire essay. Then decide whether the claim meets the three requirements of a successful claim: that it be arguable, clear, and appropriately qualified.

SUPPORTING CLAIMS WITH REASONS AND EVIDENCE

Claims are supported with reasons and evidence. Whether you are taking a stand, proposing a solution, making an evaluation, speculating about causes, or interpreting a literary work, you need reasons and evidence to construct a convincing argument.

Reasons can be thought of as the main points supporting a claim. Often they are the answers to the question "Why do you make that claim?" For example, you might value a movie highly *because* of its challenging ideas, unusual camera work, and memorable acting. You might oppose restrictions on students' speech at your college *because* they would make students reluctant to enter into frank debates on important issues, offensive speech is hard to define, and restrictions violate the free-speech clause of the First Amendment. These *because* phrases are the reasons you make your claim. You may have one or many reasons for a claim, depending on your subject and writing situation. These reasons need evidence in order for them to be convincing and in order for your whole argument to succeed with your readers.

The main kinds of evidence writers use to construct arguments include facts, statistics, authorities, anecdotes, scenarios, cases, and textual evidence. Following is a discussion of each one, along with criteria for judging the reliability of that particular kind of evidence and examples from published works. In each example, you will be able to see readily how the evidence supports a main point or reason in a larger argument.

Facts

Facts may be used as supporting evidence in all types of arguments. A fact is generally defined as a statement accepted as true. Facts refer to a reality that can be measured or verified by objective means. The reliability of facts depends on their accuracy (they should not distort or misrepresent reality), completeness (they should not omit important details), and the trustworthiness of their sources (sources should be qualified and unbiased). Facts come from such sources as almanacs, encyclopedias, and research studies as well as from our own observations and experience.

In this example, a scholar who studies Mexican migration to the United States uses facts to argue against three assumptions about illegal migrants, assumptions he asserts are false.

 The case for a more restrictive immigration policy is based on three principal assumptions: that illegal aliens compete effectively with, and replace, large numbers of American workers; that the benefits to American society resulting from the aliens' contribution of low-cost labor are exceeded by the "social costs" resulting from their presence here; and that most illegal aliens entering the United States eventually settle here permanently, thus imposing an increasingly heavy, long-term burden upon the society.

There is as yet no direct evidence to support any of these assumptions, at least with respect to illegal aliens from Mexico, who still constitute at least 60 to 65 percent of the total flow and more than 90 percent of the illegal aliens apprehended each year.

Thesis

Where careful independent studies of the impact of illegal immigration on local labor markets have been made, they have found no evidence of large-scale displacement of legal resident workers by illegal aliens. Studies have also shown that Mexican illegals make amazingly little use of tax-supported social services while they are in the United States, and that the cost of the services they do use is far out-weighed by their contributions to Social Security and income tax revenues.

There is also abundant evidence indicating that the vast majority of illegal aliens from Mexico continue to maintain a pattern of "shuttle" migration, most of them returning to Mexico after six months or less of employment in the United States. In fact, studies have shown that only a small minority of Mexican illegals even aspire to settle permanently in the United States.

While illegal aliens from countries other than Mexico do seem to stay longer and make more use of social services, there is still no reliable evidence that they compete effectively with American workers for desirable jobs. The typical job held by the illegal alien, regardless of nationality, would not provide the average American fmaily with more than a subsistence standard of living. In most states, it would provide less income than welfare payments.

conclusion

Certainly in some geographic areas, type of enterprises, and job categories, illegal aliens may depress wage levels or "take jobs away" from American workers. But there is simply no hard evidence that these effects are as widespread or as serious as most policy-makers and the general public seem to believe.

–Wayne A. Cornelius, "When the Door Is Closed on Illegal Aliens, Who Pays?"

key words to convince

Notice that Cornelius refers to facts as "hard evidence." They are considered hard or solid evidence because once accepted, a fact carries a great deal of weight in an argument. To encourage readers to accept his statements as fact, Cornelius says they come from "careful independent studies." Although he does not cite the sources of these studies here, they are included in the list of works cited at the end of the book in which this selection appears. Citing sources is especially important when your facts are not commonly accepted. Skeptical readers can review the research cited, as well as other relevant research, and draw their own conclusions.

Any facts you include in an argument should be current because what is accepted as "the facts" does change as new observations and studies are completed. In addition, you should use only those facts relevant to your argument, even if it means leaving out interesting peripheral information. Cornelius, for example, does not include facts about the kind of transportation

Mexican illegals rely on because he wants to keep the focus on their brief periods of employment in the United States.

EXERCISE 19.3

Select one essay from Chapters 6–9 and evaluate its use of fact. Identify the statements presented as fact and comment on their reliability.

Statistics

In many kinds of arguments about economic, educational, or social issues, statistics may be essential. When you use statistics in your own arguments, you will want to ensure that they come from reliable sources. Your readers will expect you to explain the statistics clearly and present them fairly.

The following selection comes from an argument urging that fathers take on a larger role in raising their children. Notice how the writer uses statistics from several studies to suggest the extent of what she sees as the problem:

> In terms of *time* alone, the typical American father has a long way to go to achieve parity parenthood. One famous study found that the average father interacts with his baby for less than 38 seconds a day. In 38 seconds, you cannot even change a crib sheet or sing three verses of "The Farmer in the Dell." The *most* that any father in this sample devoted to his infant in one day was 10 minutes, 26 seconds—barely time enough for a bottle and a burp.
>
> Other fathers studied have logged up to 15 minutes daily feeding their babies, compared to one and a half hours daily for mothers; almost half these fathers said that they had *never* changed the baby's diapers, and three out of four had no regular care-giving responsibilities whatsoever. With one-year-olds, fathers spend between 15 and 20 minutes per day, and although no one is quite sure how to measure father involvement with older children, we have only to look at children's survey responses to learn that it is not enough. In one study:
>
> - half the preschool children questioned preferred the TV to their fathers;
> - one child in 10 (age 7 to 11) said that the person they fear most is their father;
> - half the children wished their fathers would spend more time with them;
> - among children of divorce, only one third said that they see their fathers regularly.
>
> –Lettie Cottin Pogrebin, "Are Men Discovering the Joys of Fatherhood?"

Chapter 21 provides help finding statistical data at the library.

Whenever possible, use sources in which statistics first appeared rather than summaries or digests of others' statistics. For example, you would want to get medical statistics from a reputable and authoritative professional periodical like the *New England Journal of Medicine* rather than from a popular news weekly. If you are uncertain about the most authoritative sources, ask a reference librarian or a professor who is a specialist on your topic.

EXERCISE 19.4

Analyze the use of statistics in one of the following selections from Part I:

Chapter 7. "Birth Control in the Schools," Adam Paul Weisman
Chapter 9. "Suicide among Young People," Victor Fuchs
Chapter 9. "Where Will They Sleep Tonight?," Kim Dartnell

1. Identify the sources of the statistics. Do they seem to be the original sources? How might you find out whether they are authoritative and reputable?

2. How does the writer integrate the statistics into the text? By direct quotation from the source? By paraphrase or summary? In tables or figures?

3. What part do the statistics play in the selection? Do you find the statistics convincing?

Authorities

To support their claims and reasons, writers do not hesitate to cite authorities. They establish their authorities' credentials and quote them. Quoting a respected authority on a topic generally adds weight to an argument.

From Loretta Schwartz-Nobel's book on starvation in America comes a typical example. The writer cites an authority, a researcher at a well-known oceanographic institute, to support her argument that we now have technical resources to eliminate hunger in America.

> Dr. John Ryther, a highly respected and well-known marine biologist at the Woods Hole (Massachusetts) Oceanographic Institution, points out that there are about one billion acres of coastal wetlands in the world. If only one-tenth of these wetlands were used to raise fish, the potential yield of fish using improved methods of production would be one hundred million tons a year. This is the equivalent of the yield from the entire world's commercial fisheries.
>
> Dr. Ryther has also devised a complex continuous culture system which produces oysters, seaweed, worms, flounder, and abalone. It ultimately becomes a biological sewage treatment plant returning clean water to the sea.
>
> If this kind of system were implemented on a large scale it could produce a million pounds of shellfish a year from each one-acre production facility. By using advanced culture techniques like those developed at Woods Hole, Dr. Ryther estimates that the yield could well be multiplied tenfold within the next three decades.   –Loretta Schwartz-Nobel, *Starving in the Shadow of Plenty*

The writer could simply have mentioned a system for wetland culture, but instead she emphasizes that it comes from a respected expert—thereby adding to her own authority and to the credibility of her material. (After all, she is not an expert on all the technical aspects of her topic.) Instead of quoting the expert directly, she paraphrases the information from him.

EXERCISE 19.5

Analyze the way authorities are used in one of the following selections from Part I of this book. Decide whether you find the use of authorities convincing. How might you find out whether the authorities are respected? How does the writer establish each authority's credentials?

How does the writer integrate the authority's words or opinions into the text of the selection? By direct quotation? By paraphrase or summary? What role does the authority have in the piece as a whole?

> *Chapter 6.* "Children Need to Play, Not Compete," Jessica Statsky
> *Chapter 7.* "Birth Control in the Schools," Adam Paul Weisman
> *Chapter 9.* "Suicide among Young People," Victor Fuchs

Anecdotes

Anecdotes are brief stories that can very effectively provide evidence in an argument. Their specificity may be quite convincing if they seem to readers to be true to life.

> While attending a medical meeting about a year ago, I ran into a fellow I'd known in residency. "What are you doing here, Bill?" he asked. "Giving a talk on the responses to death," I replied. "It will cover the psychological value of funerals as well as—"
>
> "Funerals!" he exclaimed. "What a waste *they* are! I've made it plain to my wife that *I* don't want a funeral. Why spend all that money on such a macabre ordeal? And why have the kids standing around wondering what it's all about?"
>
> "Look, Jim," I said patiently, "I've seen case after case of depression caused by the inability of patients—young and old—to work through their feelings after a death. I've found that people are often better off if they have a funeral to focus their feelings on. That lets them do the emotional work necessary in response to the loss." My friend still looked doubtful. And, as we parted company, I wondered how many other physicians are also overlooking the psychological value of funerals.   –William A. Lamers, Jr., "Funerals Are Good for People"

Notice that the anecdote characterizes one particular occurrence. Anecdotes are different from generalized narratives, which summarize recurring or typical events. They are also different from scenarios, which tell about something that might happen, and cases, which summarize observations made over a period of time. Anecdotes make a special contribution to argument through their concreteness.

See Chapters 2 and 14 for more on writing anecdotes.

In the next example, a historian repeats a secondhand anecdote to argue that we should take extrasensory perception more seriously than we do:

> At six o'clock one evening Swedenborg, while dining with friends in the town of Gothenburg, suddenly became excited and declared that a dangerous fire had broken out in his native city of Stockholm, some three hundred miles away. He asserted a little later that the fire had already burned the home of one of his

neighbors and was threatening to consume his own. At eight o'clock of that same evening, he exclaimed with some relief that the fire had been checked three doors from his home. Two days later, Swedenborg's every statement was confirmed by actual reports of the fire, which had begun to blaze at the precise hour that he first received the impression.

Swedenborg's case is only one among hundreds of similar instances recorded in history and biography of the great, the near-great, and the obscure. At some time in their lives Mark Twain, Abraham Lincoln, Saint-Saëns, to name but a few, had, according to their biographers and in some cases their own accounts, strange sudden visions of events taking place at a distance, or events that took place, down to the last minute detail, months or years later in their own lives. In the case of Swedenborg the ability to see at a distance developed later into a powerful and sustained faculty; in most other cases, the heightened perceptivity seemed to arise only in a moment of crisis.   –Gina Cerminora, *Many Mansions*

EXERCISE 19.6

Analyze the use of anecdote in one of the following selections from Part I of this book. How long is the anecdote in relation to the length of the whole essay? Does the writer comment on the significance of the anecdote or leave it to the reader to infer its importance? What role does the anecdote play in the selection as a whole? Do you find the anecdote convincing?

Chapter 6. "Children Need to Play, Not Compete," Jessica Statsky, paragraphs 6, 8

Chapter 8. "Searing, Nervy and Very Honest," David Ansen, paragraph 1

Scenarios

While an anecdote tells about something that actually happened, a scenario is a narrative that describes something that might happen. Writers create scenarios to make their arguments more vivid and convincing. Scenarios raise and answer the question "What if?"

The first example comes from a book on illiteracy in America. To help readers understand illiterates' plight, the author creates a scenario from a dream:

Since I first immersed myself within this work I have often had the following dream: I find that I am in a railroad station or a large department store within a city that is utterly unknown to me and where I cannot understand the printed words. None of the signs or symbols is familiar. Everything looks strange: like mirror writing of some kind. Gradually I understand that I am in the Soviet Union. All the letters on the walls around me are Cyrillic. I look for my pocket dictionary but I find that it has been mislaid. Where have I left it? Then I recall that I forgot to bring it with me when I packed my bags in Boston. I struggle to remember the name of my hotel. I try to ask somebody for directions. One person stops and looks at me in a peculiar way. I lose the nerve to ask. At last I reach into my wallet for an ID card. The card is missing. Have I lost it? Then I remember that my card was confiscated for some reason, many years before. Around this point, I wake up in a panic.

This panic is not so different from the misery that millions of adult illiterates experience each day within the course of their routine existence in the U.S.A.

–Jonathan Kozol, *Illiteracy in America*

EXERCISE 19.7

Analyze the use of scenario in Patrick O'Malley's proposal for more frequent testing (reprinted in Chapter 7). What role does the scenario play in the selection as a whole? Do you find the scenario convincing?

EXERCISE 19.8

Writers often use scenarios to discuss the possible effects of trends or phenomena. Choose one of the following subjects, and write a scenario illustrating the possible effects.

1. The effects of cable TV's popularity on commercial and public TV
2. The effects of aerobic dancing and exercise on Americans
3. The effects of increasing tuition costs on college students
4. The effects on U.S. society if colleges were available only to the wealthy
5. The effects on U.S. culture if we actually ran out of gasoline

Cases

Like an anecdote, a case is an example that comes from a writer's firsthand knowledge. Cases summarize observations of people. They are meant to be typical or generalized. Case histories are an important part of the work of psychologists, doctors, and social workers. These cases may be quite lengthy, sometimes following the life of one individual over many months or years. In persuasive writing, however, cases are presented briefly as evidence for a claim or reason.

This example comes from a publication for school administrators. It was written by two sociologists studying the psychological problems of adolescents, particularly alienation. Notice how they use the John Kelly case both to define alienation and to argue that it is a serious problem.

Since the beginning of man's awareness of "self" and "other," alienation has frayed the fabric of social institutions. In recent decades the term has become a euphemism for every kind of aberrant behavior from drug use to rejection of the political system. Adolescents are especially affected by this malaise. Let us consider the case of John Kelly, for example.

When John Kelly was 10, he was curious and energetic, the mascot of his family. His inquisitiveness led him to railroad yards, museums, and bus adventures downtown alone. In school, he was charming, cooperative, and interested. At 13, John suddenly changed. His agreeable nature vanished as he quarreled endlessly with his older brothers. He became moody and sullen, constantly snapping at his parents. He began to skip school and disrupt class when he did attend. When he was finally expelled, his parents enrolled him in another junior high school, hoping the change would solve some of John's problems. Instead, his difficulties intensified as he dropped his boyhood friends, stopped communicating with his parents, and withdrew into himself. Now, 16-year-old John bears little resemblance to the loving, active child his family once knew. He has been suspended from yet another school, hangs out with an older crowd, and comes home only to sleep. His parents feel hurt, bewildered, frustrated, and frightened.

As John Kelly's case makes clear, adolescent alienation is a teenager's inability to connect meaningfully with other people. At its root is aloneness, a feeling that no one else is quite like you, that you are not what other people want you to be.

—James Mackey and Deborah Appleman, "Broken Connections:
The Alienated Adolescent in the 80s"

As examples and evidence in persuasive writing, cases are usually brief, rarely longer than this one. Writers nearly always know much more about their cases than they tell us. They select just the details from the case that will support the claim they are making.

To be effective, a case must ring true. Readers need specific details: dress, manner, personal history. Though the person in this case is an abstraction, meant to represent many people like him or her, we still recognize a real person.

EXERCISE 19.9

Evaluate the use of a case in "Where Will They Sleep Tonight?" by Kim Dartnell (Chapter 9). Decide whether the case is relevant to the argument and whether it rings true. What does the case contribute to the essay?

Textual Evidence

When you argue claims of value (Chapter 8) and interpretation (Chapter 10), textual evidence may be very important. If you are criticizing a controversial book that your readers have not yet read, you may want to quote from it often so that readers can understand why you think the author's argument is not credible. If you are interpreting a novel for one of your classes, you may need to include numerous excerpts to show just how you arrived at your conclusion. In both situations, you are integrating bits of the text you are evaluating or interpreting into your own text and building your argument on these bits.

In the following example, a literary critic uses textual evidence to support the claim that the main character in James Joyce's story "Araby" is involved in a "vivid waiting." As you read, notice how the writer continually refers to events in the story and also regularly quotes phrases from the story.

You can read "Araby" on pp. 393–97.

"Araby," wrote Ezra Pound, "is much better than a 'story,' it is a vivid waiting." It is true; the boy, suspended in his first dream of love, is also held up by circumstance, and the subjective rendering of this total experience is indeed vivid. . . .

Every morning the boy kept watch from his window until Mangan's sister appeared, and then with a leaping heart he ran to follow her in the street until their ways diverged, hers toward her convent school. Of an evening, when she came out on the doorstep to call her brother to tea, the boys at play would linger in the shadows to see whether she "would remain or go in"; then while she waited they would approach "resignedly," but while Mangan still teased his sister before obeying, the boy of this story "stood by the railings looking at her," seeing "her figure defined by the light from the half-opened door" and waiting upon a summons of another kind. He must wait too for his uncle's late return and for the money to fetch the girl a present from the bazaar Araby; then the special train, almost empty, waited intolerably and he arrived late. Still he drove toward his goal, paying a shilling to avoid further delay in looking for a sixpenny entrance. Once inside, he found the place half-darkened and the stalls mostly closed. Though there was nothing for him to buy, he lingered still, baffled, stultified, prolonging only pretense of interest. What awaits him as the lights are being put out is a facing "with anguish and anger" of his obsessive mood and its frustration, of himself as "a creature driven and derided by vanity"—like Stephen in *A Portrait* "angry with himself for being young and the prey of restless foolish impulses."   –Warren Beck, *Joyce's Dubliners*

EXERCISE 19.10

Select one of the essays on "Araby" in Chapter 10 and analyze its use of evidence. Identify where "Araby" is quoted, paraphrased, summarized, or merely referred to. Indicate whether the evidence is simply cited or explained in some way.

ANTICIPATING READERS' CONCERNS

Claims, reasons, and evidence are essential to a successful argument. Thoughtful writers go further, however, by anticipating their readers' objections, alternatives, challenges, or questions. To anticipate readers' concerns, try to imagine a reader's point of view on the subject, knowledge about the subject, and familiarity with the issues. Try also to imagine a reader's response to the argument as it unfolds step by step. What will readers be thinking and feeling? How will they react? This kind of concern is called counterargument. Successful arguments include reasons, evidence, and counterarguments.

Anticipating readers' concerns, writers rely on three basic strategies: acknowledging, accommodating, and refuting. They let readers know they are aware of their objections and questions (acknowledge), accept all or part of the objections into their argument (accommodate), or explicitly oppose (refute) the objections. Writers may use one or more of these strategies in the same essay. Research by communications specialists indicates that readers find arguments more convincing when writers have anticipated their readers in these ways.

At this point, you may have an objection: Isn't it manipulative to acknowledge and accommodate readers' objections or questions? In fact, cynical writers and speakers do try to manipulate their readers' responses. They may try to trick readers, sell something, ensure a donation, or win support for a policy based on lies and evasions. However, unless readers are especially ignorant or emotionally vulnerable and willing to grant uncritically the writer's credibility, readers recognize and scorn manipulation. Anticipating readers' concerns is convincing when it builds a bridge of shared concerns between writer and reader. The writer bases the anticipation (and the argument) on shared values, assumptions, goals, or criteria. This approach—acknowledging, accommodating, and refuting readers' concerns—wins readers' respect and attention—and sometimes even their agreement.

Acknowledging Readers' Concerns

The primary purpose of argumentative writing is to influence readers. Therefore, careful writers seek to influence their readers with each choice of a word, each choice of a sentence. Sometimes writers may even address their readers openly, both to build a bridge of shared concerns and to acknowledge their questions or objections.

The first example comes from a book on hunger in America. The writer seeks to enlist readers' sympathies for neglected elderly people.

> This is South Philadelphia—a microcosm of America, a place where people have gone to work, raised children, and then retired. Their daughters are our secretaries, clerks, and teachers. Their sons are our policemen, longshoremen, bankers, doctors, and lawyers. Economically these retired people once represented America's middle class. Yet in this typical urban neighborhood with its tap dance school, businessmen's association, American Cancer Society chapter, and local fire station, a two-year survey conducted by the Albert Einstein Medical Center's Social Service Division concluded that "very few if any of the elderly were without need."
>
> These are men and women who have worked all their lives. These are our uncles, our aunts, our grandparents, our mothers, and our fathers. They live in a world of old newspaper clippings, pictures, and photographs of relatives who never visit. —Loretta Schwartz-Nobel, *Starving in the Shadow of Plenty*

Here the writer seems to anticipate that readers—as citizens, voters, and taxpayers in any part of the country—might question whether they have any personal responsibility for elderly people in South Philadelphia. Her strategy is to counterargue that South Philadelphia is a representative American community, not a peculiar place with unique problems. She implies that we are one big American family, with familylike responsibilities for aging relatives. Since she eventually argues for a national solution to what she believes to be a widespread problem, her success depends on convincing readers of their personal responsibility for needy elderly people anywhere in America.

The next example acknowledges readers' possible concerns even more directly. These are the opening paragraphs in an article arguing that some of America's homeless have chosen that way of life. The writer knows that readers may immediately doubt this surprising claim. It seems inconceivable that people would choose to sleep on sidewalks and eat out of garbage cans. The writer acknowledges three different doubts.

> The homeless, it seems, can be roughly divided into two groups: those who have had marginality and homelessness forced upon them and want nothing more than to escape them, and a smaller number who have at least in part chosen marginality, and now accept, or, in a few cases, embrace it.
>
> I understand how dangerous it can be to introduce the idea of choice into a discussion of homelessness. It can all too easily be used for all the wrong reasons by all the wrong people to justify indifference or brutality toward the homeless, or to argue that they are getting only what they deserve.
>
> And I understand, too, how complicated the notion can become: Many of the veterans on the street, or battered women, or abused and runaway children, have chosen this life only as the lesser of evils, and because, in this society, there is often no place else to go.
>
> And finally, I understand how much that happens on the street can combine to create an apparent acceptance of homelessness that is nothing more than the absolute absence of hope.
>
> Nonetheless we must learn to accept that there may indeed be people on the street who have seen so much of our world, or have seen it so clearly, that to live in it becomes impossible.   –Peter Marin, "Go Ask Alice"

You might think that acknowledging readers' objections in this way—addressing readers directly, listing their possible objections, and discussing each one—would weaken an argument. It might even seem reckless to suggest objections that not all readers would think of. On the contrary, however, readers respond positively to this strategy. The writer appears to have explored the issue thoroughly. He seems thoughtful and reasonable, more interested in inquiry than advocacy, more concerned with seeking the truth about the homeless than in ignoring or overriding readers' objections in order to win their adherence to a self-serving claim. By researching your subject and analyzing your readers, you will be able to use this strategy confidently in your own argumentative essays.

EXERCISE 19.11

How does William K. Kilpatrick acknowledge his readers in the essay by him in Chapter 6?

Accommodating   Careful argumentative writers often acknowledge their readers' objections,
Readers' Concerns   questions, and alternative causes or solutions. Occasionally, however, they
                    may go even further. Instead of merely acknowledging their readers' objec-
                    tions, they accept them and incorporate them into their own arguments. You
                    can imagine how disarming this strategy can be to readers.

This example comes from an essay speculating about the causes of people's interest in jogging. Before proposing his own cause (later in the essay), the writer acknowledges and then accommodates causes proposed by philosophers and theologists.

> Some scout-masterish philosophers argue that the appeal of jogging and other body-maintenance programs is the discipline they afford. We live in a world in which individuals have fewer and fewer obligations. The work week has shrunk. Weekend worship is less compulsory. Technology gives us more free time. Satisfactorily filling free time requires imagination and effort. Freedom is a wide and risky river; it can drown the person who does not know how to swim across it. The more obligations one takes on, the more time one occupies, the less threat freedom poses. Jogging can become an instant obligation. For a portion of his day, the jogger is not his own man; he is obedient to a regimen he has accepted.
> Theologists may take the argument one step further. It is our modern irreligion, our lack of confidence in any hereafter, that makes us anxious to stretch our mortal stay as long as possible. We run, as the saying goes, for our lives, hounded by the suspicion that these are the only lives we are likely to enjoy.
> All of these theorists seem to me more or less right. As the growth of cults and charismatic religions and the resurgence of enthusiasm for the military draft suggest, we do crave commitment. And who can doubt, watching so many middle-aged and older persons torturing themselves in the name of fitness, that we are unreconciled to death, more so perhaps than any generation in modern memory?   —Carll Tucker, "Fear of Death"

Notice that this writer's accommodation is not grudging. He admits that the theorists (and any readers who favor them) are "more or less right," and he suggests reasons why they must be right. Considering alternative causes is very common in essays of causal analysis (see Chapter 9). Writers must include alternatives that their readers may be aware of and then either accommodate or refute these alternatives. To do anything less makes writers seem uninformed and weakens their credibility.

EXERCISE 19.12

Exactly how does Patrick O'Malley attempt to accommodate readers in his Chapter 7 essay on more frequent exams? What seems successful or unsuccessful in his argument? What do his efforts at accommodation contribute to the essay?

Refuting
Readers'
Objections

Readers' objections and views cannot always be accommodated. Sometimes they must be refuted. When writers refute likely objections, they assert that they are wrong and argue against them. Refutation does not have to be delivered arrogantly or dismissively, however. Writers can refute their readers' objections in a spirit of shared inquiry in solving problems, establishing probable causes, deciding the value of something, or understanding all the issues in a controversy. In argument, differences are inevitable. Argument remains centrally important in human discourse because informed, well-intentioned people disagree about issues and policies.

In this example, an economist refutes one explanation for the increasing numbers of women in the work force. First he describes a "frequently mentioned" explanation. Then he concedes a point ("there is little doubt") before beginning his refutation.

> One frequently mentioned but inadequately evaluated explanation for the surge of women into paid employment is the spread of time-saving household innovations such as clothes washers and dryers, frozen foods, and dishwashers. There is little doubt that it is easier to combine paid employment with home responsibilities now than it was fifty years ago, but it is not clear whether these time-saving innovations were the *cause* of the rise in female labor force participation or whether they were largely a *response* to meet a demand created by working women. Confusion about this point is most evident in comments that suggest that the rapid growth of supermarkets and fast-food outlets is a cause of women going to work. Similar time-saving organizations were tried at least sixty years ago, but with less success because the value of time was much lower then. The absence of supermarkets and fast-food eating places in low-income countries today also shows that their rapid growth in the United States is primarily a *result* of the rising value of time and the growth of women in the work force, not the reverse.   –Victor Fuchs, "Why Married Mothers Work"

This selection illustrates very well that refutations must be supported. Writers cannot simply dismiss readers' concerns with a wave of the hand. Fuchs refutes one proposed cause by arguing that it is actually an effect or result of the trend. The last two sentences support his refutation.

The second example comes from a publication arguing for a revised English curriculum in the schools. In this section, the writers attempt to refute a predictable objection. Notice how they describe the objection and then assert their refutation.

> [An] argument against the teaching of literature, which enjoyed greater currency in the late 1960s and 1970s than it does now, goes something like this: Literature is an "elitist" discipline, a subterfuge for imposing ruling-class values on oppressed groups so that they will cooperate in their own exploitation. According to this argument, minority students will encounter a world view in literature classes that is either irrelevant to their own heritage or downright destructive of it. The rebuttal to this argument is straightforward: It is wrong. The treasurehouse of literature is not oppressive; it is liberating—of the constraints of time, place,

and personal experience into which each of us as an individual is born. The real injustice would be to deny any child access to the wealth of insights that our best literature has to offer. To deny students the wisdom of our literary heritage may restrict their social mobility and limit the potential that schools have to create opportunities for students to develop their individual talents and to prepare for participation in our society.

Of course, in literature and the arts, local districts should adopt reading lists that recognize the natural desire of communities to maintain an ethnic identity. Quite rightly, black students are inspired by Alex Haley's *Roots* and Richard Wright's *Black Boy*; Hispanic students, by Rudolfo A. Anaya's *Bless Me, Ultima* and Peter Matthiessen's *Sal Si Puedes: Cesar Chavez and the New American Revolution*; Japanese-Americans, by Yoshiko Uchida's *Samurai of Gold Hill* and Monica Sone's *Nisei Daughter*; and so on. Like all great literature, these stories confer lasting benefits—intellectual, social, and spiritual—on those who read them. Furthermore, all students will profit from such literature to understand those whose experiences of America differ from theirs. The point is, far from being "elitist," the common culture belongs to all of us. And every child in the United States—rich or poor, male or female, black, Hispanic, Asian, or white—is entitled to experience it fully.

Our country was founded on the expectation that out of many traditions one nation could evolve that would be stronger and more durable than any single tradition. To argue that teaching a common core of literature in our pluralistic society is not feasible because there is no basis for consensus is to beg the question. It is, and always has been, precisely the task of the public schools to help form that consensus.

In a society that celebrates the prerogatives of the individual, the public schools are potentially one of the most meaningful forces for social cohesion. They are the modern equivalent of the village square—a forum for identifying the shared ethos of our diverse and cosmopolitan society; a place where all our children can come together and discover what it is that unites us as a people. Well-taught literature is an essential part of that consensus building.

–California State Education Department, *Handbook for Planning an Effective Literature Program*

This example and the previous one illustrate that effective refutation requires a restrained tone and careful argument. Although you may not accept the refutation, you can agree that it is thoughtfully argued. You do not feel attacked personally because the writers disagree with you.

The writers of the second article make an important concession in the second paragraph. They acknowledge the value of minority literature while still arguing for a common literature in school English programs. Here, accommodation blends with refutation.

EXERCISE 19.13

Analyze and evaluate the use of refutation in any one of the essays in Chapter 6. How does the writer manage the refutation? Does the objection seem to be clearly and accurately described? How is the refutation asserted and argued for? What seems most convincing and least convincing in the argument? What is the tone of the refutation?

EXERCISE 19.14

Briefly refute any of the refutations you analyzed in the preceding exercise. State the writers' refutation accurately, and argue your refutation of it convincingly. Try to use a restrained tone.

EXERCISE 19.15

Return to the claim you wrote in Exercise 19.1. Imagine how you might develop an essay arguing for this claim with reasons and evidence. Then identify one likely objection or question from your readers, and write a refutation of it. State the objection accurately, and argue your refutation in a way that will not alienate your readers.

LOGICAL FALLACIES

Fallacies are errors or flaws in reasoning. Although essentially unsound, fallacious arguments seem superficially plausible and often have great persuasive power. Fallacies are not necessarily deliberate efforts to deceive readers. They may be accidental, resulting from a failure to examine underlying assumptions critically, establish solid ground to support a claim, or choose words that are clear and unambiguous. Here, listed in alphabetical order, are the most common logical fallacies:

- *Begging the question.*   Arguing that a claim is true by repeating the claim in different words. Sometimes called circular reasoning.
- *Confusing chronology with causality.*   Assuming that because one thing preceded another, the former caused the latter. Also called *post hoc, ergo propter hoc* (Latin for "after this, therefore because of this").
- *Either/or reasoning.*   Assuming that there are only two sides to a question, and representing yours as the only correct one.
- *Equivocating.*   Misleading or hedging with ambiguous word choices.
- *Failing to accept the burden of proof.*   Asserting a claim without presenting a reasoned argument to support it.
- *False analogy.*   Assuming that because one thing resembles another, conclusions drawn from one also apply to the other.
- *Overreliance on authority.*   Assuming that something is true simply because an expert says so and ignoring evidence to the contrary.

- *Hasty generalization.* Offering only weak or limited evidence to support a conclusion.

- *Oversimplifying.* Giving easy answers to complicated questions, often by appealing to emotions rather than logic.

- *Personal attack.* Demeaning the proponents of a claim instead of their argument. Also called *ad hominen* (Latin for "against the man").

- *Red herring.* Attempting to misdirect the discussion by raising an essentially unrelated point.

- *Slanting.* Selecting or emphasizing the evidence that supports your claim and suppressing or playing down other evidence.

- *Slippery slope.* Pretending that one thing inevitably leads to another.

- *Sob story.* Manipulating readers' emotions in order to lead them to draw unjustified conclusions.

- *Straw man.* Directing the argument against a claim that nobody actually holds or that everyone agrees is very weak.

PART FOUR

Research Strategies

In universities, government agencies, and the business world, field research can be as important as library research or experimental research. In specialties such as sociology, political science, anthropology, polling, advertising, and news reporting, field research is the basic means of gathering information.

This chapter is a brief introduction to three of the major kinds of field research: observations, interviews, and questionnaires. The writing activities involved are central to several academic specialties. If you major in education, communication, or one of the social sciences, you probably will be asked to do writing based on observations, interviews, and questionnaire results. You will also read large amounts of information based on these ways of learning about people, groups, and institutions.

Observations and interviews are essential for writing profiles (Chapter 4). Interviewing could be helpful, as well, in documenting a trend or phenomenon and exploring its causes (Chapter 9)—for example, to consult an expert or conduct a survey to establish the presence of a trend. In proposing a solution to a problem (Chapter 7), you might want to interview people involved; or, if many people are affected, you might find it useful to do a questionnaire. In writing to explain an academic concept (Chapter 5), you might want to interview a faculty member who is a specialist on that subject.

OBSERVATIONS

This section offers guidelines for planning an observational visit, taking notes on your observations, writing them up, and preparing for follow-up visits. Some kinds of writing are based on observations from single visits—travel writing, social workers' case reports, insurance investigators' accident reports—but most observational writing is based on several visits. An anthropologist or sociologist studying an unfamiliar group or activity might observe it for months, filling several notebooks with notes. If you are profiling a place (Chapter 4), you almost certainly will want to make two or three (or more) observational visits, some of them perhaps combined with interviews.

Second and third visits to observe further are important because as you learn more about a place from initial observations, from interviews, or reading, you will discover new ways to look at it. Gradually you will have more and more questions that can only be answered by follow-up visits.

Field Research 20

Planning the Visit

To ensure that your observational visits are worthwhile, you must plan them carefully.

Getting Access.   If the place you propose to visit is public, you probably will have easy access to it. If everything you need to see is within view of anyone passing by or using the place, you can make your observations without any special arrangements. Indeed, you may not even be noticed.

However, most observational visits that are part of special inquiries require special access. Hence, you will need to arrange your visit, calling ahead or making a get-acquainted visit, in order to introduce yourself and state your purpose. Find out the times you may visit, and be certain you can gain access easily.

Announcing Your Intentions.   State your intentions directly and fully. Say who you are, where you are from, and what you hope to do. You may be surprised at how receptive people can be to a college student on assignment. Not every place you wish to visit will welcome you, and a variety of constraints on outside visitors exist in private businesses as well as public institutions. But generally, if people know your intentions, they may be able to tell you about aspects of a place or an activity you would not have thought to observe.

Taking Your Tools.   Take a notebook with a firm back so that you will have a steady writing surface. Remember also to take a writing instrument. Some observers dictate their observations into portable tape recorders. You might want to experiment with this method. We recommend, though, that for your first observations you record in writing. Your instructor or other students in your class may want to see your written notes.

Observing and Taking Notes

Following are some brief guidelines for observing and taking notes.

Observing.   Some activities invite multiple vantage points, whereas others seem to limit the observer to a single perspective. Take advantage of every perspective available to you. Come in close, take a middle position, and stand back. Study the scene from a stationary position and also try to move around it. The more varied your perspectives, the more you are likely to observe.

Your purpose in observing is both to describe the activity or place and to analyze it. You will want to look closely at the activity or place itself, but you will also want to think about what makes it special, what seems to be the point or purpose of it.

Try to be an innocent observer: pretend you have never seen anything like this activity or place before. Look for typical features as well as unusual features. Look at it from the perspective of your readers. Ask what details would surprise and inform and interest them.

Taking Notes.   You undoubtedly will find your own style of notetaking, but here are a few pointers.

- Write only on one side of the page. Later, when you organize your notes, you may want to cut up the pages and file notes under different headings.
- Take notes in words, phrases, or sentences. Draw diagrams or sketches, if they help you see and understand the place or activity.
- Note any ideas or questions that occur to you.
- Use quotation marks around any overheard conversation you take down.

Since you can later reorganize your notes in any way you wish, you do not need to take notes in any planned or systematic way. You might, however, want to cover these aspects of a place:

The Setting. The easiest way to begin is to name objects you see. Just start by listing objects. Then record details of some of these objects—color, shape, size, texture, function, relation to similar or dissimilar objects. Although your notes probably will contain mainly visual details, you might also want to record sounds and smells. Be sure to include some notes about the shape, dimensions, and layout of the place as a whole. How big is it? How is it organized?

The People. Record the number of people, their activities, their movements and behavior. Describe their appearance or dress. Record parts of overheard conversations. Note whether you see more men than women, more members of one nationality or ethnic group than of another, more older than younger people. Most important, note anything surprising or unusual about people in the scene.

Your Personal Reactions. Include in your notes any feelings you have about what you observe. Also record, as they occur to you, any hunches or ideas or insights you have.

Reflecting on
Your Observation

Immediately after your observational visit (within just a few minutes, if possible), find a quiet place to reflect on what you saw, review your notes, and add to your notes. Give yourself at least a half hour for quiet thought.

What you have in your notes and what you recall on reflection will suggest many more images and details from your observation. Add these to your notes.

Finally, review all your notes, and write a few sentences about your main impressions of the place. What did you learn? How did this visit change your preconceptions about the place? What surprised you most? What is the dominant impression you get from your notes?

Writing Up Your Notes

Your instructor may ask you to write up your notes as a report on the observational visit. If so, review your notes, looking for patterns and vivid details. You might find clustering (described in Chapter 11) or inventorying (described in Chapter 12) useful for discovering patterns and relationships in your notes.

Decide on the main impression you want readers to have of the place. Use this as the focus for your report.

See Chapter 15 for a full discussion of descriptive strategies.

Now draft a brief description of the place. Your purpose is to present a general impression of the place through a selection of the details in your notes. Assume your readers have never been to the place, and try to present a vivid impression of it.

Preparing for Follow-up Visits

Rather than repeat yourself in follow-up visits, try to build on what you have already discovered. You should probably do some interviewing and reading before another observational visit so that you will have a greater understanding of the subject when you observe it again. It is also important to develop a plan for your follow-up: questions to be answered, hypotheses to be tested, types of information you would like to discover.

INTERVIEWS

Like making observations, interviewing tends to involve four basic steps: (1) planning and setting up the interview, (2) taking notes, (3) reflecting on the interview, and (4) writing up your notes.

Planning and Setting Up the Interview

The initial step in interviewing involves choosing an interview subject and then arranging and planning the interview.

Choosing an Interview Subject. First, decide whom to interview. If you are writing about some activity or enterprise in which several people are involved, choose subjects representing a variety of perspectives—a range of different roles, for example. If you are profiling a single person, most, if not all, of your interviews will be with that person.

You should be flexible because you may be unable to speak to the person you initially targeted and may wind up with someone else—the person's assistant, perhaps. Do not assume this interview subject will be of little use to you. With the right questions, you might even learn more from the assistant than you would from the person in charge.

Arranging an Interview. You may be nervous about calling up a busy person and asking for some of his or her time. Indeed, you may get turned down. But if so, it is possible that you will be referred to someone who will see you, someone whose job it is to talk to the public.

Do not feel that just because you are a student you do not have the right to ask for people's time. You will be surprised how delighted people are to be asked about themselves, particularly if you reach them when they are not feeling harried. Most people love to talk—about anything! And, since you are a student on assignment, some people may feel that they are doing a form of public service to talk with you.

When introducing yourself to arrange the interview, give a short and simple description of your project. If you talk too much, you could prejudice or limit the interviewee's response. At the same time, it is a good idea to exhibit some enthusiasm for your project. If you lack enthusiasm, the person may see little reason to talk to you.

Keep in mind that the person you are interviewing is donating time to you. Be certain that you call ahead to arrange a specific time for the interview. Be on time. Bring all the materials you need, and express your thanks when the interview is over.

Planning for the Interview. The best interview is generally the planned interview. It will help if you have made an observational visit and done some background reading before the interview. In preparation for the interview, you should do two things in particular: consider your objectives and prepare some questions.

Think about your main objectives. Do you want an orientation to the place or your topic (the "big picture") from this interview? Do you want this interview to lead you to interviews with other key people? Do you want mainly facts or information? Do you need clarification of something you have heard in another interview or observed or read? Do you want to learn more about the person, or learn about the place or your topic through the person, or both? Should you trust or distrust this person?

The key to good interviewing is flexibility. You may be looking for facts, but your interview subject may not have any to offer. In that case, you should be able to shift gears and go after whatever your subject has to discuss.

Composing Questions. Take care in composing the questions you prepare in advance; they can be the key to a successful interview. Any question that places unfair limits on respondents is a bad question. Two specific types to avoid are forced-choice questions and leading questions.

Forced-choice questions are unsatisfactory because they impose your terms on your respondents. Consider this example: "Do you think rape is an expression of sexual passion or of aggression?" A person may think that neither sexual passion nor aggression satisfactorily explain rape. A better way to phrase the question would be to ask, "People often fall into two camps on the issue of rape. Some think it is an expression of sexual passion, while others argue it is really not sexual but aggressive. Do you think it is either of these? If not, what is your opinion?" This form of questioning allows you to get a reaction to what others have said at the same time that it gives the interviewee freedom to set the terms for his or her response.

Leading questions are unsatisfactory because they assume too much. An example of this kind of question is this: "Do you think the increase in the occurrence of rape is due to the fact that women are perceived as competitors in a severely depressed economy?" This question assumes that there is an increase in the occurrence of rape, that women are perceived (apparently by rapists) as competitors, and that the economy is severely depressed. A better way of asking the question might be to make the assumptions more explicit by dividing the question into its parts: "Do you think there is an increase in the occurrence of rape? What could have caused it? I've heard some people argue that the economy has something to do with it. Do you think so? Do you think rapists perceive women as competitors for jobs? Could the current economic situation have made this competition more severe?"

Good questions come in many different forms. One way of considering them is to divide them into two types: open and closed. *Open questions* give the respondent range and flexibility. They also generate anecdotes, personal revelations, and expressions of attitudes. For example:

■ I wonder if you would take a few minutes to tell me something about your early days in the business. I'd be interested to hear about how it got started, what your hopes and aspirations were, what problems you faced, and how you dealt with them.

■ Tell me about a time you were (name an emotion).

■ What did you think of (name a person or event)?

■ What did you do when (name an event) happened?

The best questions are those that allow the subject to talk freely but to the point. If the answer strays too far from the point, a follow-up question may be necessary to refocus the talk. Another tack you may want to try is to rephrase the subject's answer, to say something like "Let me see if I have this right," or "Am I correct in saying that you feel. . . ." Often, a person will take the opportunity to amplify the original response by adding just the anecdote or quotable comment you've been looking for.

Closed questions usually request specific information. For example:

■ How do you do (name a process)?

■ What does (name a word) mean?

■ What does (a person, an object, or a place) look like?

■ How was it made?

Taking Your Tools.   As for an observational visit, when you interview someone you will need a notebook with a firm back so that you can write on it easily without the benefit of a table or desk. You might find it useful to divide several pages into two columns with a line drawn about one-third of the width of the page from the left margin. Use the left-hand column to note details about the scene, the person, the mood of the interview, other impressions. Head this column DETAILS AND IMPRESSIONS. At the top of the right-hand column, write several questions. You may not use them, but they will jog your memory. This column should be titled INFORMATION. In this column, you will record what you learn from answers to your question.

See pp. 152–54 for an example of notes of this sort.

Taking Notes during the Interview

Because you are not taking a verbatim transcript of the interview (if you want a literal account, use a tape recorder or shorthand), your goals are to gather information and to record a few good quotable comments and anecdotes. In addition, because the people you interview may be unused to giving interviews and so will need to know you are listening, it is probably a good idea to do more listening than notetaking. You may not have much confidence in your memory, but, if you pay close attention, you are likely to recall a good deal of the conversation afterward. Take some notes during the interview: a few quotations; key words and phrases; details of the scene, the person, and the mood of the interview. Remember that *how* something is said is as important as *what* is said. Look for material that will give texture to your writing—gesture, verbal inflection, facial expression, body language, physical appearance, dress, hair, anything that makes the person an individual.

Reflecting on the Interview

As soon as you finish the interview, find a quiet place to reflect on it and review your notes. This reflection is essential because so much happens in an interview that you cannot record at the time. Spend at least a half hour, maybe longer, adding to your notes and thinking about what you learned.

At the end of this time, write a few sentences about your main impressions from the interview. What did you learn? What surprised you most? How did the interview change your attitude or understanding about the person or place? How would you summarize your impressions of the person?

Writing Up Your Notes

Your instructor may ask you to write up your notes. If so, review them for useful details and information. Decide what main impression you want to give of this person. Choose details that will contribute to this impression. Select quotations and paraphrases of information you learned from the person.

To find a focus for your write-up, you might try looping or clustering. Invention questions can also help you consider the person from different perspectives.

These strategies are discussed in Chapter 11.

QUESTIONNAIRES

Questionnaires let you survey the attitudes or knowledge of large numbers of people. You could carry out many face-to-face or phone interviews to get the same information, but questionnaires have the advantages of economy, efficiency, and anonymity. Some questionnaires, such as ones you filled out in applying to college, just collect demographic information: your name, age, sex, home town, religious preference, intended major. Others, such as the Gallup and Harris polls, collect opinions on a wide range of issues. Before elections, we are bombarded with the results of these kinds of polls. Still other kinds of questionnaires, ones used in academic research, are designed to help answer important questions about personal and societal problems.

This section briefly outlines procedures you can follow to carry out an informal questionnaire survey of people's opinions or knowledge, and then to write up the results.

Focusing
Your Study

A questionnaire study usually has a limited focus. You might need to interview a few people in order to find this focus.

Let us assume that you went to your campus Student Health Clinic (SHC) and had to wait over an hour to see a nurse. Sitting there with many other students, you decide this is a problem that needs to be studied. Furthermore, it seems an ideal topic for a proposal essay (Chapter 7) you have been assigned in your writing class.

To study this problem, you do not have to explore the entire operation of SHC. You are not interested in how nurses and doctors are hired or how efficient their system of ordering supplies is. You have a particular concern: how successful is SHC in scheduling appointments and organizing its resources to meet student needs? More specifically: do students often have to wait too long to see a nurse or doctor? You might also want to know *why* this is the case, if it is; but you can only seek an answer to that question by interviewing SHC staff. Your primary interest is in how long students usually wait for appointments, what times are most convenient for students to schedule appointments, whether SHC resources are concentrated at those times, and so on. Now you have a limited focus, and you can collect valuable information with a fairly brief questionnaire.

To be certain about your focus, however, you should talk informally to several students to find out whether they think there is a problem. You might also want to talk to people at SHC, explaining your plans and asking for their views on the problem.

Whatever your interest, be sure to limit the scope of your study. Try to focus on one or two important questions. With a limited focus, your questionnaire can be brief, and people will be more willing to fill it out. In addition, a study based on a limited amount of information will be easier to organize and report.

Writing Questions

Two basic forms of questions—closed and open—were introduced earlier in this chapter. In the following section are additional illustrations of how these types of questions may be used in the context of a questionnaire.

Closed Questions.   Following are examples of some forms of closed questions for a possible student questionnaire. You probably will use more than one form in a questionnaire, because you will have several kinds of information to collect.

Checklists

With your present work and class schedule, when are you able to visit SHC? (Check as many boxes as necessary.)

☐ 8–10 A.M.
☐ 10–12 A.M.
☐ noon hour
☐ 1–3 P.M.
☐ 3–5 P.M.

Which services do you expect to use at SHC this year?

☐ allergy desensitization
☐ immunization
☐ optometry
☐ dental care
☐ birth control
☐ illness or infection
☐ counseling
☐ health education

Two-way Questions

Have you made an appointment this year at SHC?
_____ yes
_____ no

Have you ever had to wait more than thirty minutes at SHC for a scheduled appointment?
_____ yes
_____ no

If you could, would you schedule appointments at SHC after 7:00 P.M.?
_____ yes
_____ no
_____ uncertain

Multiple-choice Questions

How frequently have you had to wait more than ten minutes at SHC for a scheduled appointment?

_____ always

_____ usually

_____ occasionally

_____ never

From your experience so far with SHC, how would you rate its services?

_____ inadequate

_____ barely adequate

_____ adequate

_____ better than adequate

_____ outstanding

Ranking Scales

With your present work and class schedule, which times during the day (Monday through Friday) would be most convenient for you to schedule appointments at SHC? Put a 1 by the most convenient time, a 2 by the next most convenient time, until you have ranked all the choices.

_____ mornings

_____ afternoons before 5 P.M.

_____ 5–7 P.M.

_____ 7–10 P.M.

Open Questions.   Open questions ask for a brief answer.

What services do you expect to need at SHC this year?

_____

_____

_____

From your experiences with appointments at SHC, what advice would you give students about making appointments?

_____

_____

_____

What do you believe would most improve services at SHC?

_____

_____

_____

You may want to use a combination of closed and open questions for your questionnaire. Both offer advantages: closed questions will give you definite answers, but open questions can give information you may not have expected as well as providing lively quotations for your report.

Trying Out the Questions.   As soon as you have a collection of possible questions, try them out on a few typical readers. You need to know which questions are unclear, which seem to duplicate others, which seem most interesting. These tryouts will enable you to assess which questions will give you the information you need. Readers also can help you come up with additional questions.

Designing the
Questionnaire

Write a brief, clear introduction stating the purpose of the questionnaire and explaining how you intend to use the results. Give advice on answering the questions, and estimate the amount of time needed to complete the questionnaire. If you are going to give the questionnaire to groups of people in person, you can give this information orally.

Select your most promising questions, and decide on an order. Any logical order is appropriate. You might want to begin with the least complicated questions or the most general ones. You may find it necessary or helpful to group the questions by subject matter or form. Certain questions may lead to others. You might want to place open questions at the end.

Design the questionnaire so that it looks attractive and readable. Make it look easy to complete. Do not crowd questions together to save paper. Provide plenty of space for readers to answer open questions, and remind them to use the back of the page if they need more space.

Testing the
Questionnaire

Make a few copies of your first design, and ask at least two or three readers to complete the questionnaire. Find out how much time they needed to complete it. Talk to them about any confusion or problems they experienced. Review their responses with them to be certain each question is doing what you want it to do. From what you learn, reconsider your design, and revise particular questions.

Administering the
Questionnaire

Decide who will fill out your questionnaire and how you can arrange for them to do it. The more readers you have, the better; but constraints of time and expense almost certainly will limit the number. You can mail questionnaires or distribute them to dormitories or workplace mailboxes, but the return will be low. It is unusual for even half the people receiving mail questionnaires to return them. If you do mail the questionnaire, be sure to mention the deadline for returning it. Give directions for returning the questionnaire, and include a stamped, addressed envelope.

You might want to arrange to distribute the questionnaire yourself to some groups in class, at dormitory meetings, or at work.

Note that if you want to do a formal questionnaire, you will need a scientifically representative group of readers (a random or stratified random sample). Even for an informal study, you should try to get a reasonably representative group. For example, to study satisfaction with the appointments schedule at SHC, you would want to have students who had been to SHC fairly often. You might even want to include a concentration of seniors rather than freshman readers because after four years seniors would have made more visits to SHC. If many students commute, you would want to be sure to have commuters among your readers.

Your report will be more convincing if you demonstrate that your readers represent the group whose opinions or knowledge you claim to be studying. As few as twenty-five readers could be adequate for an informal study.

Writing Up the Results

Now that you have the completed questionnaires, what do you do with them?

Summarizing the Results.   Begin by tallying the results from the closed questions. Take an unused questionnaire, and tally the responses next to each choice. Suppose you had twenty-five readers. Here is how the tally might look for the first checklist question.

With your present work and class schedule, when are you able to visit SHC? (Check as many boxes as necessary.)

- ☐ 8–10 A.M. 卌 卌 卌 ||| (18)
- ☐ 10–12 A.M. 卌 || (7)
- ☐ noon hour 卌 卌 ||| (13)
- ☐ 1–3 P.M. ||| (3)
- ☐ 3–5 P.M. 卌 |||| (9)

Each tally mark represents one response to that item. The totals add up to more than twenty-five because readers were asked to check *all* the times they could make appointments.

Next consider the open questions. Read all twenty-five answers to each question separately to see the kind and variety of response to each. Then decide whether you want to code any of the open questions so that you can summarize results from them quantitatively, as you would with closed questions. For example, you might want to classify the types of advice given as responses to an open question proposed earlier: "From your experiences with appointments at SHC, what advice would you give students about making appointments?" You could then report the numbers of readers (of your twenty-five) who gave each type of advice. For an opinion question ("How would you evaluate the most recent appointment you had at SHC?"), you might simply code the answers as positive, neutral, and negative and then tally the results accordingly for each kind of response. However, responses to open questions are perhaps most often used as a source of quotations for your report.

You can report results from the closed questions as percentages, either within the text of your report or in tables. (See the Fuchs essay in Chapter 9 for one possible format for a table. You can find other formats in texts you may be using or even in magazines or newspapers. Conventional formats for tables in social science reports are illustrated in the *Publication Manual of the American Psychological Association*, 3rd ed. [Washington, DC: American Psychological Association, 1983].)

See pp. 597–98 for strategies for integrating quoted material.

You can quote responses to the open questions within your text, perhaps weaving them into your discussion like quoted material. Or you can organize several responses into lists and then comment on them. Since readers' interests can be engaged more easily with quotations than with percentages, plan to use many open responses in your report.

There are computer programs that will provide quantitative results from closed questions and will even print out tables you can insert into your report. For a small informal study, however, such programs probably would not save you much time.

Organizing and Writing the Report.   In organizing the report of your results, you might want to consider a plan that usually is followed in the social sciences:

Statement of the problem
    context for your study
    your question
    need for your study
    brief preview of your study and plan for your report
Review of other related studies (if you know of any)
Procedures
    designing the questionnaire
    selecting the readers
    administering the questionnaire
    summarizing the results
Results: presentation of what you learned, with little commentary or interpretation
Summary and discussion: brief summary of your results, and discussion of their significance (commenting, interpreting, exploring implications, and comparing to other related studies)

A college library presents a complex challenge. Unlike a course—with its limited number of texts, easy-to-find classroom, and familiar activities—the library contains thousands of texts organized in various ways. Each new research project you undertake presents surprises and unexpected problems. Each project leads you to new catalogs, indexes, floors, corners. You may find yourself keyboarding commands to access a computer database, threading a microfilm reader, viewing a videodisc, or squinting at the fine print in an index. You may read the latest weekly magazine or a rare book hundreds of years old. You may breeze through an encyclopedia entry introducing you to a new subject or struggle with a just-published report of a highly technical research study on the same subject.

A library's resources are so immense and so diverse that complete mastery of them is something only professional librarians have. With the help of these librarians and the guidelines in this chapter, however, you will be able to manage all the research assignments in this text and in your other college courses as well.

One way to make your college library seem more manageable is to think of its diverse materials as two different types of resources: the actual materials for your research, and the resources that enable you to find these materials.

This chapter is designed to help you learn how to use your college library's resources. It gives advice on how to learn about the library, develop a search strategy, keep track of your research, locate sources, and read them with a critical eye. Chapter 22 provides guidelines for using and acknowledging these sources in an essay. It also presents a sample research paper, on home schooling, written in response to an assignment to write an essay speculating about the causes of a trend.

See Chapter 9 for more essays speculating about causes.

The search for research materials requires patience, careful planning, good advice, and even luck. The rewards are great, however. One of life's greatest intellectual pleasures is to learn about a subject and then be able to put diverse information together in a new way—for yourself and others.

ORIENTING YOURSELF TO THE LIBRARY

Make a point of taking a tour of the library. Then, when you first research a subject, be sure you understand your research task well. Consult a reference librarian if you need help.

Library Research 21

Taking a Tour

Your instructor may arrange a library orientation tour for your composition class. If not, you can join one of the regular orientation tours scheduled by the librarians. Unless you are already using the library frequently, a tour is essential because nearly all college libraries are more complex and offer more services than typical school or public libraries. On a library tour, you will learn how the library catalog and reference room are organized, how to access computer catalogs and databases, whom to ask for help if you are confused, and how to get your hands on books, periodicals, and other materials.

Pick up copies of any available pamphlets and guidelines. Nearly every library offers handouts describing the resources and services it provides. Also look for a floor map of materials and facilities. See whether your library offers any research guidelines, special workshops, or presentations on strategies for locating resources.

Consulting a Librarian

Think of college librarians as advisors whose job is to help you understand the library and get your hands on sources you need to complete your research projects. Think of them also as instructors who can help you with the business of learning. Librarians at the information or reference desk are there to provide reference services, and most have years of experience answering the very questions you are likely to ask. You should not hesitate to approach them with any questions you have about locating sources. Remember, however, that they can be most helpful if you can explain your research assignment clearly.

Knowing Your Research Task

Before you go to the library to start an assigned research project, learn as much as you can about the assignment. Should you need to ask a librarian for advice, it is best to have the assignment in writing. Ask your instructor to clarify any confusing terms and to define the purpose and scope of the project. Find out how you can narrow or focus the project once you begin the research. Asking a question or two in advance can prevent hours—or even days—of misdirected work.

A RECOMMENDED SEARCH STRATEGY

In order for your library research to be manageable and productive, you will want to work carefully and systematically. The search strategy presented in this chapter was developed by college librarians with undergraduate needs

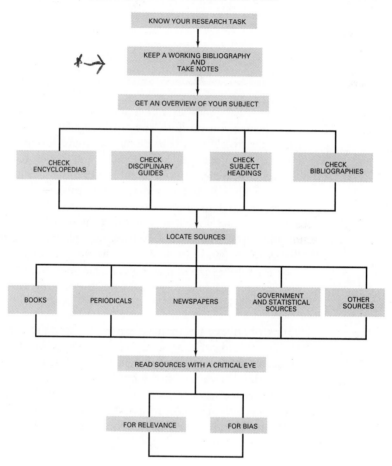

OVERVIEW OF A SEARCH STRATEGY

KNOW YOUR RESEARCH TASK

KEEP A WORKING BIBLIOGRAPHY
AND
TAKE NOTES

GET AN OVERVIEW OF YOUR SUBJECT

CHECK ENCYCLOPEDIAS | CHECK DISCIPLINARY GUIDES | CHECK SUBJECT HEADINGS | CHECK BIBLIOGRAPHIES

LOCATE SOURCES

BOOKS | PERIODICALS | NEWSPAPERS | GOVERNMENT AND STATISTICAL SOURCES | OTHER SOURCES

READ SOURCES WITH A CRITICAL EYE

FOR RELEVANCE | FOR BIAS

firmly in mind. Although specific search strategies may vary to fit the needs of individual research tasks, the general process presented here should help you get started, keep track of all your research, use library materials to get an overview of your subject, locate the sources you need, and read those sources with a critical eye.

KEEPING TRACK OF YOUR RESEARCH

As you research your topic, you will want to keep careful records of all your sources by setting up a working bibliography.

Keeping a
Working
Bibliography

A working bibliography is a preliminary, ongoing record of books, articles, pamphlets—all the sources of information you discover as you research your subject. In addition, you can use your working bibliography as a means of keeping track of any encyclopedias, bibliographies, and indexes you consult, even though you do not use these resources in an essay or a research review.

Practiced researchers keep their working bibliography on index cards, in a notebook, or in a computer file. They may keep bibliographical information separate from notes they take on the sources. Many researchers find index cards most convenient because they are so easily alphabetized. Others find them too easy to lose and prefer instead to keep everything—working bibliography, notes, and drafts—in one notebook. Researchers who use computers set up working bibliographies in word-processing programs or bibliographic management programs, such as Endnote Plus, that work in conjunction with word-processing programs. With these bibliographic programs, you enter a source's publication information, and the program then formats the information according to one of the preset documentation styles (MLA, APA, etc.) or a style you create. From the formatted listings, the program can create in-text citations and insert them into your essay, as well as format your final list of works cited. Some of these programs can interact with computer indexes and other databases, so you can download source information from the database right into your bibliographic file, which then correctly formats the information.

Whether you use cards, a notebook, or a computer, the important thing is to make your entries accurate and complete. If the call number for a book is incomplete or inaccurate, you will not be able to find the book in the stacks. If the volume number for a periodical is incorrect, you may not be able to locate the article. If the author's name is misspelled, you may have trouble finding the book in the library catalog.

Because you must eventually choose a documentation style for your essay, you may want to select it now at the beginning of your research so that all sources listed in your working bibliography will conform to the documentation style of your essay. Chapter 22 presents two different documentation styles, one adopted by the Modern Language Association (MLA) and widely used in the humanities, and the other advocated by the American Psychological Association (APA) and used in the social sciences. Individual disciplines often have their own preferred styles of documentation, which your instructor may wish you to use.

Taking Notes

Eventually, after you are oriented to your research topic and have found a way to focus it, you will want to begin taking notes from relevant sources. If you own the work or can photocopy the relevant parts, you may want to annotate right on the page. Otherwise, you can paraphrase, summarize, and

Outlining, paraphrasing, and summarizing are discussed on pp. 450–53 and quoting on pp. 595–600.

outline useful information as separate notes. In addition, you will want to write down quotations you might use in your essay.

You may already have a method of notetaking you prefer. Some researchers like to use index cards for notes as well as for their working bibliography. They use 3″ × 5″ cards for their bibliography and larger ones (4″ × 6″ or 5″ × 7″) for notes. Some even use a different color card for each of their sources. Other people prefer to keep their notes in a notebook, and still others enter their notes into a computer. Whatever method you use, be sure to keep accurate notes.

Care in notetaking is of paramount importance in order to minimize the risk of copying facts incorrectly or of misquoting. Another common error in notetaking is to copy the author's words without enclosing them in quotation marks. This error could lead easily to plagiarism, the unacknowledged use of another's words or ideas. Double-check all your notes, and be as accurate as you can.

See p. 602 for tips on avoiding plagiarism.

You might consider photocopying materials from sources that look especially promising. All libraries house a photocopy machine or offer a copying service. Photocopying can be costly, of course, so you'll want to be selective. It will facilitate your work, however, allowing you to reread and analyze important sources as well as to highlight material you may wish to quote, summarize, or paraphrase.

GETTING STARTED

"But where do I start?" is a question easily answered. You first need an overview of your topic. If you are researching a concept or an issue in a course you are taking, then your textbook or other course materials provide the obvious starting point. Your instructor can advise you about other sources providing overviews of your topic. If your topic is just breaking in the news, then current newspapers and magazines might be sufficient. For all other topics—and for background information—encyclopedias and disciplinary guides are often the place to start. They let you test your interest in a topic before you start gathering sources on it, and they introduce you to diverse aspects of a subject, from which you might find a focus for your research. In a typical college essay or research project, you do not have the time or space to summarize everything that is known on a subject, but you can inquire productively into some unusual or controversial aspect of it. Keep in mind that the key to a good research paper is choosing a topic you're interested in exploring.

Consulting Encyclopedias

Specialized encyclopedias can be a good place to start your research. General encyclopedias such as *Encylopedia Britannica* and *Encyclopedia Americana* cover many topics superficially, whereas specialized encyclopedias cover topics in the depth appropriate for college writing. In addition to providing an overview of a topic, a specialized encyclopedia will often include an explanation of issues related to the topic, definitions of specialized terminology, and selective bibliographies of additional sources.

As starting points, specialized encyclopedias have two further advantages: (1) they provide a comprehensive introduction to key terms related to your topic, terms that will be useful in identifying the "subject headings" that enable you to locate material in catalogs and indexes; and (2) by comprehensively presenting a subject, they enable you to see many possibilities for focusing your research on one aspect of it.

Following are some specialized encyclopedias in the major academic disciplines:

ART	*Encyclopedia of World Art.* 17 vols. 1987.
BIOLOGY	*Encyclopedia of Biological Sciences.* 1981.
CHEMISTRY	*Encyclopedia of Chemistry.* 1983.
COMPUTERS	*Encyclopedia of Computer Science and Technology.* 15 vols. 1975–80.
ECONOMICS	*Encyclopedia of Economics.* 1982.
EDUCATION	*Encyclopedia of Education.* 10 vols. 1971.
ENVIRONMENT	*McGraw-Hill Dictionary of Earth Sciences.* 1984.
FOREIGN RELATIONS	*Encyclopedia of American Foreign Policy.* 1978. *Encyclopedia of the Third World.* 1992.
HISTORY	*Harvard Guide to American History.* 2 vols. 1974. *New Cambridge Modern History.* 14 vols. 1957–80.
LAW	*Encyclopedia of Crime and Justice.* 4 vols. 1983.
LITERATURE	*Encyclopedia of World Literature in the 20th Century.* 4 vols. 1981–86.
MUSIC	*New Grove Dictionary of Music and Musicians.* 20 vols. 1980.
PHILOSOPHY	*Encyclopedia of Philosophy.* 4 vols. 1973.
PSYCHOLOGY	*Encyclopedia of Psychology.* 1979.
RELIGION	*Encyclopedia of Religion.* 16 vols. 1986.
SCIENCE	*McGraw-Hill Encyclopedia of Science and Technology.* 20 vols. 1987.
SOCIAL SCIENCES	*International Encyclopedia of the Social Sciences.* 8 vols. 1977.
WOMEN'S STUDIES	*Women's Studies Encyclopedia.* 2 vols. 1990.

You can locate any of these encyclopedias in the library by looking up its call number in the library catalog. Other specialized encyclopedias can be found by looking in the catalog under the subject heading for the discipline, such as "psychology," and the subheading "dictionaries and encyclopedias."

Two reference sources can help you identify other specialized encyclopedias covering your topic:

ARBA Guide to Subject Encyclopedias and Dictionaries. (1986). Lists specialized encyclopedias by broad subject category, with descriptions of coverage, focus, and any special features.

First Stop: The Master Index to Subject Encyclopedias. (1989). Lists specialized encyclopedias by broad subject category and also provides access to individual articles within them. By looking under the key terms that describe your topic, you will find references to specific articles in any of over four hundred specialized encyclopedias.

Consulting Disciplinary Guides

Once you have a general overview of your topic, you will want to consult one of the guides to research in that discipline. The following guides can help you identify the major handbooks, encyclopedias, bibliographies, journals, periodical indexes, and computer databases in the various disciplines. You need not read any of these extensive works straight through, but you will find them to be valuable references.

GENERAL	*Guide to Reference Books*, 10th ed. 1986. Edited by Eugene P. Sheehy.
HUMANITIES	*The Humanities: A Selective Guide to Information Sources*, 3rd ed. 1988. By Ron Blazek.
SCIENCE AND TECHNOLOGY	*Scientific and Technical Information Sources*, 2nd ed. 1987. By Ching-chih Chen.
SOCIAL SCIENCES	*Sources of Information in the Social Sciences: A Guide to the Literature*, 3rd ed. 1986. Edited by William H. Webb.
ANTHROPOLOGY	*Introduction to Library Research in Anthropology.* 1991. By John M. Weeks.
ART	*Visual Arts Research: A Handbook.* 1986. By Elizabeth B. Pollard.
EDUCATION	*Education: A Guide to Reference and Information Sources.* 1989. By Lois Buttlar.
FILM	*On the Screen: A Film, Television, and Video Research Guide.* 1986. By Kim N. Fisher.
HISTORY	*A Student's Guide to History*, 4th ed. 1987. By Jules R. Benjamin.
LITERATURE	*Reference Works in British and American Literature.* 1990. By James K. Bracken.
	Literary Research Guide, 2nd ed. 1983. By Margaret Patterson.
MUSIC	*Music: A Guide to the Reference Literature.* 1987. By William S. Brockman.

PHILOSOPHY *Philosophy: A Guide to the Reference Literature.* 1986. By Hans E. Bynagle.

POLITICAL SCIENCE *Information Sources of Political Science*, 4th ed. 1986. By Frederick L. Holler.

PSYCHOLOGY *Library Research Guide to Psychology: Illustrated Search Strategy and Sources.* 1984. By Nancy E. Douglas.

SOCIOLOGY *A Guide to Reference and Information Sources.* 1987. By Stephen H. Aby.

WOMEN'S STUDIES *Introduction to Library Research in Women's Studies.* 1985. By Susan E. Searing.

Checking Subject Headings

To carry your research beyond encyclopedias, you need to find appropriate subject headings. Subject headings are specific words and phrases used in libraries to categorize the contents of books and periodicals. As you read about your subject in an encyclopedia or other reference book, you will discover possible subject headings.

To begin your search for subject headings, consult the *Library of Congress Subject Headings* (LCSH), which usually can be found near the library catalog. This reference book lists the standard subject headings used in catalogs and indexes and in many encyclopedias and bibliographies. Following is an example from the LCSH:

> Home schooling *(May Subd Geog)*
> Here are entered works on the provision of compulsory education in the home by parents as an alternative to traditional public or private schooling. General works on the provision of education in the home by educational personnel are entered under Domestic Education.
>   UF Education, Home
>   Home-based education
>   Home education
>   Home instruction
>   Home teaching by parents
>   Homeschooling
>   Instruction, Home
>   Schooling, Home
>   BT Education
>   RT Education—Parent participation

In the LCSH, *UF* stands for "used for," *BT* for "broader term," *RT* for "related term," and, although not used here, *NT* for "narrower term" and *SA* for "see also." *May Subd Geog* means that place names may follow the heading. The subject headings provide you with various key words and phrases to use as you look through catalogs and indexes. For example, this entry proved particularly useful because when the student found nothing listed in the library catalog under "home schooling," she tried the other headings until "education—parent participation" and "education—United States" yielded information on three books. Similarly, when searching periodicals indexes, she found that one used "home education," whereas another used "instruction, home." Note, too, that this entry explains the *type* of articles that would be found under these headings—and those that would be found elsewhere. Keep in mind that the terms listed in the LCSH might not be the *only* ones used for your subject; don't be afraid to try terms that you think might be relevant.

Consulting Bibliographies

A bibliography is simply a list of publications on a given subject. Whereas an encyclopedia may give you only background information on your subject, a bibliography gives you an overview of what has been published on the subject. Its scope may be broad or narrow. Some bibliographers try to be exhaustive, including every title they can find, but most are selective. To discover how selections were made, check the bibliography's preface or introduction. Occasionally, bibliographies are annotated: that is, they provide brief summaries of the entries and, sometimes, also evaluate them. Bibliographies may be found in a variety of places: in encyclopedias, in the library catalog, and in research guides. All specialized encyclopedias and disciplinary research guides include bibliographies.

The best way to locate a comprehensive, up-to-date bibliography on your subject is to look in the *Bibliographic Index*. A master list of bibliographies that contain fifty or more titles, the *Bibliographic Index* includes bibliographies from articles, books, and government publications. A new volume is published every year. (Note that because this index is not cumulative, you should check back over several years, beginning with the most current volume.)

Even if you attend a large research university, your library is unlikely to hold every book or journal article a bibliography might direct you to. The library catalog and serial record (a list of the periodicals the library holds) will tell you whether the book or journal is available.

Determining the Most Promising Sources

As you follow a subject heading into the library catalog and bibliographic and periodical indexes, discovering many seemingly relevant books and articles, how do you decide which ones to track down and examine? With little to go on but author, title, date, and publisher or periodical name, you may feel at a loss; but these actually provide useful clues. Look, for example, at the entry from a card catalog on page 581. The entry shows the author, title, and subject cards for a book on home schooling. Note that from the author's birthdate and the publication date of the book, you can tell that he writes later in his career. He might, therefore, offer a historical perspective. From the physical description, you can see that the book includes a bibliography, which could lead you to other sources. Finally, from the subject headings, you can see that this book focuses on learning methods; you can also use "learning methods" to search for related books.

Now look at the following entry from *Education Index*, a periodical index:

Home schooling
Home schooling [litigation involving compulsory atten-
dance laws] P. A. Zirkel. *Phi Delta Kappan* 72:408-9
Ja '91
New taste for the homemade [United States] B. Norris.
Times Educ Suppl 3883[3884]:17 D 7 '90
Bibliography
Do-it-yourself books for parents [reviews] S. A. Moore
and D. W. Moore. *Read Teach* 44:62-3 S '90
Research
Home schooling: a question of quality, an issue of rights.
J. F. Rakestraw and D. A. Rakestraw. bibl *Educ Forum*
55:67-77 Fall '90

This entry lists articles that address different aspects of home schooling, briefly describing some of the articles. You can see that the first article deals with litigation, the second focuses on home schooling in the United States, and the third is a collection of reviews. The subheadings "bibliography" and "research" provide further help in identifying quickly whether these articles could be useful by telling you that the third article includes a list of books on the topics, while the fourth focuses on research into one particular aspect of the topic.

When you look in catalogs and indexes, consider the following to help you decide whether you should track down a particular source:

- *Relevance to your topic.* Do the title, subtitle, description, subject headings, abstract, or periodical title help you determine just how directly a particular source addresses your topic?

- *Publication date.* How recent is the source? For current controversies, emerging trends, and continuing technical or medical developments, you must see the most recent material. For historical or biographical topics, you will want to start with contemporary perspectives, but keep in mind that older sources offer authoritative perspectives.

- *Description.* Does the length indicate a brief or an extended treatment of the topic? Does the work include illustrations that may elaborate on concepts discussed in the text? Does the work include a bibliography that could lead you to other works or an index that could give you an overview of what is discussed in the text? Does the abstract tell you the focus of the work?

From among the sources that look promising, select at least one book, one research report in an academic journal, and one article in a popular magazine. Or select three or four publications that you can tell from their titles concern different aspects of your topic or approach it from different perspectives. In this first look beyond an encyclopedia, avoid selecting sources by the same author, from the same publisher, or in the same journal. Common sense will lead you to an appropriate decision about range.

LOCATING SOURCES

Following are guidelines to finding books; periodical articles; newspaper articles; government documents and statistical information; and other types of sources.

Finding Books

The primary source for books is the library catalog. Most libraries maintain a card catalog consisting of cards filed in drawers, but now nearly every college library also offers a computerized catalog, sometimes called an online catalog. The online catalog provides more flexibility in searching subject headings and may even tell you whether the book has already been checked out. Another distinct advantage it provides is the ability to print out source information, making it unnecessary for you to copy it by hand. Since an online catalog typically contains material received and catalogued only after a certain date, however, you need to check the card catalog as well.

Library catalogs organize sources by author, subject, and title. For each book there is a card or computer entry under the name of each author, under the title, and under each subject heading to which the book is related. Author, title, and subject cards or entries all give the same basic information.

1. The *call number*—always in the upper lefthand corner of cards in a card catalog, indicates the numerical code under which the book is filed in the library. Call numbers are assigned according to subject. Most college libraries use the Library of Congress subject headings and numbering system. Call numbers have at least two rows of numbers. The top row indicates the general subject classification, and the second row places the book within this classification. Subsequent rows identify the copyright and publication date for multiple editions. In an online catalog, the call number usually appears on a separate line.

2. The *author*—appears last name first, followed by birth and death dates. If there are multiple authors, there is an author card or entry under each author's name.

3. The *title*—appears exactly as it is printed on the title page of the book, except that only the first word and proper nouns and adjectives are capitalized.

4. The *publication information*—includes the place of publication (usually just the city), publisher, and year of publication. If the book was published simultaneously in the United States and abroad, both places of publication and both publishers are included.

5. The *physical description*—offers information about the book's length and size. A roman numeral indicates the number of pages used for front matter (such as a preface, table of contents, and acknowledgments).

6. *Notes*—indicate any special features (for example, a bibliography or an index).
7. *Subject headings*—indicate how the book is listed in the subject catalog. These may be headings you can use to find other books related to your subject.

Following are the author, title, and subject cards for a book on home schooling. The title and subject cards for a book are just like the author card except that they have headings printed at the top above the author's name. On the title card the heading is the title (which also appears again below the author's name). On a subject card the heading is one of the subject headings from the bottom of the card. Note that a separate catalog card or entry for a book will exist for each subject heading listed.

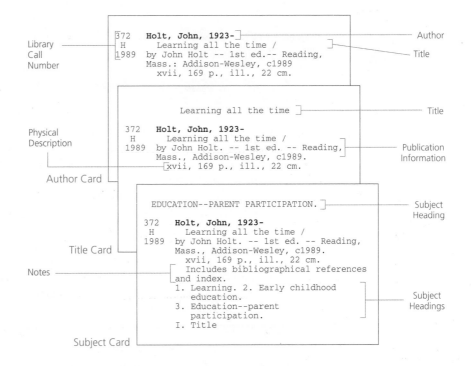

Here is one college library's online catalog display of the author entry for a more recent book on home schooling in its collection. Notice the call number along the bottom line.

AUTHOR: Guterson, David, 1951-
TITLE: Family matters: Why home schooling makes sense/
                David Guterson
EDITION: 1st Harvest ed.
PUBLISHER: San Diego: Harcourt Brace & Co., c1992
PHYSICAL DESC: x, 254 p.; 18 cm.

NOTES: Includes bibliographical references and index.
SUBJECTS: Education—United States
                Education—parent participation
                Teaching methods

LOCATION / CALL NUMBER   STATUS

UCSD Undergrad / 649.68 g 1993   Available

Finding
Periodical
Articles

The most up-to-date information on a subject usually is found not in books but in articles in magazines and journals, or periodicals. Articles in periodicals usually are not listed in the library catalog; to find them, you must instead use periodical indexes and abstracts. Indexes list articles, whereas abstracts summarize as well as list them. Library catalogs list the indexes and abstracts held in the library and note whether they are available in printed form, as microforms, or as computer databases. Those indexes listed in this section that are available as computer databases are labeled *O* (for online) and *CD-ROM* (for compact disc-read only memory). Names for these databases, if different from the print index, are also given. Check with a librarian to see what databases are available at your library.

Computer databases are discussed on pp. 585–86.

Periodical indexes and abstracts are of two types: general and specialized.

General Indexes.   These list articles in nontechnical, general-interest publications and cover a broad range of subjects. Most have separate author and subject listings as well as a list of book reviews. Following are some general indexes, beginning with one you may already be familiar with:

The Readers' Guide to Periodical Literature (1900–; O and CD-ROM, 1983–); updated quarterly. Covers about 200 popular periodicals and may help you start your search for sources on general and current topics. Even for general topics, however, you should not rely on it exclusively. Nearly all college libraries house far more than 200 periodicals, and university research libraries house 20,000 or more. *The Readers' Guide* does not even attempt to cover the research journals that play such an important role in college writing. Here is an example of an entry for "home education":

HOME EDUCATION
Home is where the school is. C. García-Barrio. il *Essence*
    22:104+ Ag '91
Home schooling [truancy convictions in Michigan] P. A.
    Zirkel. *Phi Delta Kappan* 72:408-9 Ja '91
Schooling in family values. T. Toch. il *U.S. News & World*
    Report 111:73-4 D 9 '91
Ten easy, at-home ways to make learning fun. A. Diamant.
    il *McCall's* 118:70+ S '91
When your home is the classroom [Andersen family] A.
    Cook. il *Money* 20:104-5+ S '91

Magazine Index. On microfilm (1988–), online (1973–), and on CD-ROM as part of InfoTrac (1973–); see below. Indexes over 400 magazines.

InfoTrac. On CD-ROM. Includes three indexes: the *General Periodicals Index* (current year and past four), which covers over 1,100 general-interest publications, incorporating the *Magazine Index* and including the *New York Times* and *Wall Street Journal;* the *Academic Index* (current year and past four), which covers 400 scholarly and general-interest publications, including the *New York Times;* and the *National Newspaper Index* (current year and past three), which covers the *Christian Science Monitor, Los Angeles Times, New York Times, Wall Street Journal,* and *Washington Post.* Some entries also include an abstract of the article.

Access: The Supplementary Index (1979–). Indexes magazines not covered by the *Readers' Guide,* such as regional and particular-interest magazines (the environment, women's issues).

Alternative Press Index (1970–). Indexes alternative and radical publications.

Humanities Index (1974–; also online and on CD-ROM). Covers archaeology, history, classics, literature, performing arts, philosophy, and religion.

Social Sciences Index (1974–; also online and on CD-ROM). Covers economics, geography, law, political science, psychology, public administration, and sociology.

Public Affairs Information Service Bulletin [PAIS] (1915–; also online and on CD-ROM). Covers articles and other publications by public and private agencies on economic and social conditions, international relations, and public administration. Subject listing only.

Specialized Indexes and Abstracts.   These list or abstract articles devoted to technical or scholarly research. The following example from *Sociological Abstracts,* which indexes and summarizes articles from a wide range of periodicals that publish sociological research, is typical of entries found in specialized indexes:

91X2727

Mayberry, Maralee & Knowles, J. Gary (Dept Sociology U Nevada, Las Vegas 89154), **Family Unity Objectives of Parents Who Teach Their Children: Ideological and Pedagogical Orientations to Home Schooling,** ᴜᴍ *The Urban Review,* 1989, 21, 4, Dec, 209-225. ¶ The objectives of parents who teach their children at home are examined, using results from 2 qualitative studies: (1) a study conducted in Ore in 1987/88, consisting of interview & questionnaire data (ɴ = 15 & 800 families, respectively); & (2) an ongoing ethnographic study being conducted in Utah (ɴ = 8 families). Analysis suggests that while families have complex motives for teaching their children at home, most respondents felt that establishing a home school would allow them to maintain or further develop unity within the family. It is concluded that a family's decision to home school is often made in an attempt to resist the effects on the family unit of urbanization & modernization. Policy implications are discussed. 36 References. Adapted from the source document. (Copyright 1991, Sociological Abstracts, Inc., all rights reserved.)

Here is a list of specialized works that cover various disciplines:

Accountant's Index (1944–).

American Statistics Index (1973–).

Applied Science and Technology Index (1958–). O, CD-ROM.

Art Index (1929–).

Biological and Agricultural Index (1964–). CD-ROM.

Education Index (1929–). O, CD-ROM.

Engineering Index (1920–).

Historical Abstracts (1955–).

Index Medicus (1961–). O, CD-ROM (called MEDLINE).

MLA International Bibliography of Books and Articles in the Modern Languages and Literature (1921–). O, CD-ROM.

Music Index. (1949–).

Philosopher's Index (1957–). O.

Psychological Abstracts (1927–). O (called PsycINFO), CD-ROM (PsycLIT).

Physics Abstracts (1898). O (called INSPEC).

Science Abstracts (1898–).

Sociological Abstracts (1952–). O, CD-ROM (called Sociofile).

Many periodical indexes and abstracts use the Library of Congress subject headings, but some have their own systems. *Sociological Abstracts*, for example, has a separate volume for subject headings. Check the opening pages of the index or abstract you are using to see how it classifies its subjects. Then look for periodicals under your chosen Library of Congress subject heading or the heading that seems most similar to it.

Computer Databases.   Your library may subscribe to *online* database networks and may own *CD-ROM* machines that are accessed through the library's computer terminals. Most research databases—like those noted in the lists above—are electronic indexes listing thousands of books and articles.

You may be able to use a CD-ROM database yourself, but you will probably need a librarian to conduct an online search. Although you can search a database by author or title, most likely you will use *descriptors*, or key words describing subjects. Make your descriptors as precise as possible so that your database search results in a manageable list of sources relevant to your topic. Most databases include a thesaurus of descriptors and a set of guidelines for combining terms to narrow your search.

Once you have typed in your descriptors, the computer searches the database and lists every reference to them it finds. You may be charged for access time and printing for an online search, or given a limit on time at the terminal and number of entries you can print from a CD-ROM database, so you may want to talk with a librarian before consulting a database. Also keep in mind that because most electronic indexes cover only the most recent years of an index, you may need to consult older printed versions as well.

In addition to the database versions of the indexes listed above, many libraries subscribe to computer services that provide abstracts and/or the full text of articles, either in the database so that you can see them on screen, or by mail or fax for a fee, and also list books in particular subject areas. The use of computers for scholarly research is becoming more widespread, with new technology being developed all the time, so be sure to check with a librarian about what's available in your library. Some of the more common services follow:

ERIC (*Educational Resources Information Center*) (1969–). Indexes, abstracts, and gives some full texts of articles from 750 education journals. Here is an example of a work on home schooling listed in ERIC:

SilverPlatter 3.1   **ERIC 1982-June 1993**
                                                             1 of 28

AN ACCESSION NUMBER: EJ442388
AU PERSONAL AUTHOR: Knowles,-J.-Gary; And Others
TI TITLE: From Pedagogy to Ideology: Origins and Phases of Home Education in the United States, 1970-1990.
PY PUBLICATION YEAR: 1992
JN JOURNAL CITATION: American Journal of Education; v100 n2 p195-235 Feb 1992
IS ISSN:0195-6744
AV AVAILABILITY: UMI
CH CLEARINGHOUSE: UD

FI SOURCE FILE: EJ
DT TYPE NUMBER: 080; 141
DT DOCUMENT TYPE: Journal Articles (080); Reports—Descriptive (141)
DE Descriptors: Civil—Liberties; Court—Litigation; Educational—Change;
Educational History—Home schooling; Ideology—Teaching methods
ID IDENTIFIERS: Social Movements
LA LANGUAGE: English
AB ABSTRACT: Examines issues of home education since 1970 by
surveying the home-schooling movement in the broader historical
context. The twenty-year growth period illustrates the fluid nature of
home education as a social movement. Contemporary home-
schooling is not closely tied to the liberal goals of home education.

Business Periodicals Ondisc (1988–) and ABI/INFORM (1988–). Provides the full text of articles from business periodicals. If your library has
a laser printer attached to a terminal, you can print out articles, including
illustrations.

PsycBooks (1987–). A CD-ROM database that indexes books and book
chapters in psychology.

Carl/Uncover (1988–). An online document delivery service that lists
over 3 million articles from 12,000 journals. For a fee, you can receive
the full text of the article by fax, usually within a few hours.

Interlibrary networks. Known by different names in different regions,
these networks allow you to search in the catalogs of colleges and universities in your area and across the country. In many cases, you can request a book by interlibrary loan.

Periodicals Representing Particular Viewpoints.   Some specialized periodical indexes tend to represent particular viewpoints and may help you identify different positions on an issue.

Index to Black Periodicals (1984–). An author and subject index to articles
of both a general and a scholarly nature about African-Americans.

Left Index. An author and subject index to over eighty periodicals with a
Marxist, radical, or left perspective. Listings cover primarily topics in the
social sciences and humanities.

Chicano Index (1967–). An index to general and scholarly articles about
Mexican-Americans. Articles are arranged by subject with author and title
indexes. (Before 1989 the title was *Chicano Periodical Index.*)

Another useful source for identifying positions is *Editorials on File*, described on page 587.

Locating Periodicals in the Library.   When you identify a promising magazine
or journal article in a periodical index, you must go to the library serial record

or online catalog to learn whether the library subscribes to the periodical and, if so, where you can find it. Recent issues of periodicals are usually arranged alphabetically by title on open shelves. Older issues are either bound like books and filed by call numbers or filmed and available in microform.

Finding Newspaper Articles

Newspapers provide useful information for many research topics in such areas as foreign affairs, economic issues, public opinion, and social trends. Libraries usually miniaturize newspapers and store them on microfilm (reels) or microfiche (cards) that must be placed in viewing machines to be read.

Newspaper indexes like the *Los Angeles Times Index, New York Times Index*, and the London *Times Index* will help you locate specific articles on your topic. College libraries usually have indexes to local newspapers as well.

Your library may also subscribe to newspaper article and digest services like the following:

National Newspaper Index. On microfilm (1989–), online (1979–), and on CD-ROM, as part of InfoTrac (see page 583). Indexes the *Christian Science Monitor, Los Angeles Times, New York Times, Wall Street Journal,* and *Washington Post.*

NewsBank (1970–). On microfiche and CD-ROM. Full-text articles from 500 U.S. newspapers. A good source of information on local and regional issues and on trends.

Newspaper Abstracts (1988–). An index and brief abstracts of articles from 19 major regional, national, and international newspapers.

Facts on File (Weekly). A digest of U.S. and international news events arranged by subject, such as foreign affairs, arts, education, religion, and sports.

Editorials on File (Twice monthly). Editorials from 150 U.S. and Canadian newspapers. Each entry includes a brief description of an editorial subject followed by fifteen to twenty editorials on the subject, reprinted from different newspapers.

Editorial Research Reports (1924–). Reports on current and controversial topics, including brief histories, statistics, editorials, journal articles, endnotes, and supplementary reading lists.

African Recorder (1970–). Articles on African issues from African newspapers.

Asian Recorder (1971–). Articles on Asian issues from Asian newspapers.

Canadian News Facts (1972–). A digest of current articles from Canadian newspapers such as the *Montreal Star, Toronto Star*, and *Vancouver Sun.*

Foreign Broadcast Information Service (*FBIS*) (1980–). Foreign broadcast scripts, newspaper articles, and government statements from Asia, Europe, Latin America, Africa, the Soviet Union, and the Middle East.

Current Digest of the Soviet Press (1963–). Articles on Soviet issues from Soviet and European newspapers.

Keesing's Contemporary Archives (Weekly). A digest of events in all countries, compiled from British reporting services. Includes speeches and statistics. Index includes chronological, geographical, and topical sections.

Finding Government and Statistical Information

Following is a description of some government publications and sources of statistical information that may help you find sources for a particular purpose or a particular kind of subject.

Sources for Political Subjects.   Two publications that report developments in the federal government can be rich sources of information on political issues. Types of material they cover include congressional hearings and debates, presidential proclamations and speeches, Supreme Court decisions and dissenting opinions, and compilations of statistics. These publications are not always included in catalogs but are shelved in the reference area or in a government documents department within some college libraries. If these works are not listed in the library catalog, ask a reference librarian for assistance.

Congressional Quarterly Almanac (Annual). A summary of legislation. Provides an overview of governmental policies and trends, including analysis as well as election results, records of roll-call votes, and the text of significant speeches and debates.

Congressional Quarterly Weekly Report. A news service that includes up-to-date summaries of committee actions, votes, and executive branch activities, as well as overviews of current policy discussions and activities within the federal government.

Chapter 9 provides guidance developing an argument speculating about the causes of a trend.

Sources for Researching Trends.   Research can help you identify trends to write about and, most important, provide the evidence you need to demonstrate the existence of a trend. The following resources can be especially helpful:

Statistical Abstract of the United States (Annual). Issued by the Bureau of the Census. Provides a variety of social, economic, and political statistics, often covering several years. Includes tables, graphs, and charts and gives references to additional sources of information.

American Statistics Index (1974–; annual with monthly supplements). Attempts to cover all federal government publications containing statistical information of research significance. Includes brief descriptions of references.

Statistical Reference Index (1980–). Claims to be "a selective guide to American statistical publications from sources other than the U.S. government." Includes economic, social, and political statistical sources.

World Almanac and Book of Facts (Annual). Presents information on a variety of subjects drawn from many sources. Includes such things as a chronology of the year, climatological data, and lists of inventions and awards.

The Gallup Poll: Public Opinion (1935–). A chronological listing of the results of public opinion polls. Includes information on social, economic, and political trends.

In addition to researching the trend itself, you may want to research others' speculations about its causes. If so, the reports of federal government activities described in the previous section may be helpful.

Finding Other Sources

Libraries hold a vast amount of useful materials other than books and periodicals. Some of the following sources and services may be appropriate for your research.

Vertical File. Pamphlets and brochures from government and private agencies.

Special collections. Manuscripts, rare books, materials of local interest, and the like.

Audio collections. Records, audiocassettes, and compact discs of all kinds of music, readings, and speeches.

Video collections. Slides, filmstrips, and videocassettes.

Art collections. Drawings, paintings, and engravings.

Interlibrary loans. Many libraries will borrow books from another library; be aware that interlibrary loans often take some time.

Computer resources. Many libraries house interactive computer programs that combine text, video, and audio resources in history, literature, business, and other disciplines.

READING SOURCES WITH A CRITICAL EYE

Suggestions for deciding which sources to consult at an early stage of your research are given on pp. 578–79.

From the beginning of your search, you will be evaluating sources to determine which to use in your essay. Obviously, you must decide which sources provide information relevant to the topic. But you also must read sources with a critical eye in order to decide how credible or trustworthy your sources are. Just because a book or essay appears in print does not necessarily mean the information or opinions in it are reliable.

Selecting Relevant Sources

Begin the evaluation of your sources by narrowing your working bibliography to the most relevant sources. Consider them in terms of scope, data, and viewpoint.

Scope and Approach.   To decide how relevant a particular source is, you need to examine it in depth. Do not depend on title alone, for it may be misleading. If the source is a book, check its table of contents and index to see how many pages are devoted to the precise subject you are exploring. You most likely will want an in-depth, not a superficial, treatment of the subject. Read the preface or introduction to a book or the abstract or opening paragraphs of an article and any biographical information given about the author to determine the author's basic approach to the subject or special way of looking at it. As you look at these elements, consider the following questions:

- Does the source provide a general or specialized view? General sources are helpful early in your research, but you then need the authority or up-to-dateness of specialized sources. Extremely specialized works, however, may be too hard to understand.
- Is the source long enough to provide adequate detail?
- Was the source written for general readers? specialists? advocates? critics?
- Is the author an expert on the topic? Does the author's way of looking at the topic support or challenge your own views?

Date of Publication.   Although you will always want to consult the most up-to-date sources available on your subject, older sources often establish the principles, theories, and data upon which later work rests and may provide a useful perspective for evaluating it. Since many older works are considered authoritative, you may want to become familiar with them. To determine which sources are authoritative, note the ones that are cited most often in encyclopedia articles, bibliographies, and recent works on the subject.

Viewpoint.   You will want your sources to represent a variety of viewpoints on the subject. Just as you would not depend on a single author for all of your information, so you do not want to use authors who all belong to the same school of thought. For suggestions on determining authors' viewpoints, see the next section, Identifying Bias.

Using sources that represent different viewpoints is especially important when developing an argument for one of the essay assignments in Chapters 6–10. During the invention work in those chapters, you may want to research what others have said about your subject to see what positions have been staked out and what arguments have been made. You will then be able to define the issue more carefully, collect arguments supporting your position, and anticipate arguments opposing it.

Identifying Bias

One of the most important aspects of evaluating a source is identifying any bias in its treatment of the subject. Although the word *bias* may sound like a criticism or drawback, it simply refers to the fact that most writing is not neutral or objective and does not try or claim to be. Authors come to their subjects with particular viewpoints, and in using sources you must consider carefully how these viewpoints are reflected in their writing and how these viewpoints affect the way authors present their arguments.

Although the text of the source will give you the most precise indication of the author's viewpoint, you can often get a good idea by looking at the preface or introduction or at the sources the author cites. When you examine a reference, you can often determine the general point of view it represents by considering the following elements:

Title. Does the title or subtitle indicate the text's bias? Watch for "loaded" words or confrontational phrasing.

Author. What is the author's title and/or affiliation? What is the author's perspective? Is he or she in favor of something or at odds with it? What has persuaded the author to take this viewpoint? What is the author's professional affiliation? How might the affiliation affect the author's perspective? What is the author's tone? Information on the author may also be available in the book or article itself or in biographical sources available in the library.

Presentation of Argument. Almost every written work has a position it takes, or an argument. To determine this position and the reason behind it, look for the main point. What evidence does the author provide as support for this point? Is the evidence from authoritative sources? Is the evidence persuasive? Does the author accommodate or refute opposing arguments?

Publication Information. Was the book published by a commercial publisher? by a corporation, government agency, or interest group? If so, what is that organization's position on the topic? Is the author funded by or affiliated with the organization?

Editorial Slant. What kind of periodical published the article? popular? academic? alternative? Knowing some background about the publisher or periodical can help determine bias, because all periodicals have definite editorial slants. In cases where the publication title does not indicate bias, there are reference sources that may help you to determine this information. Two of the most common are the following:

Gale Directory of Publications and Broadcast Media (1990). A useful source for descriptive information on newspapers and magazines. Entries often include an indication of intended audience and political or other bias. For example, the *San Diego Union* is described as a "newspaper with a Republican orientation."

Magazines for Libraries (1992). A listing of over 6,500 periodicals arranged by academic discipline. For each discipline there is a list of basic indexes, abstracts, and periodicals. Each individual listing for a periodical includes its publisher, the date it was founded, the places it is indexed, its intended audience, and an evaluation of its content and editorial focus. Here is one such listing:

> **4917.** *The Nation.* 1865. w. $40. Victor Navasky. Nation Assocs., Inc., P.O. Box 1953, Marion, OH 43305. Illus., index, adv. Circ: 50,000. Vol. ends: June/Dec. Microform: UMI.
>
> *Indexed:* BoRvI, PAIS, RG. *Bk rev:* 3–7, 1,400 words, signed, *Aud:* Hs, Ga, Ac.

Liberal to the left: first, foremost and always. That is the policy of the distinguished editor, who has given the journal new life with a series of investigative reports that often make headlines. The articles range from the Nicaraguan debate to abortion to Israel and the politics of Washington, D.C. It is partisan, yet witty and extremely intelligent. Some of the best stylists in journalism are regular columnists in the arts and entertainment sections, for example, Alexander Cockburn, I. F. Stone, Christopher Hitchens, Jefferson Morley, and Andrew Kopkind. The editorials are quite superior in both content and style. This is a required magazine for almost all types and sizes of libraries.

Much of the writing you will do in college requires you to use sources in combination with your own firsthand observation and reflection. Any time you get information and ideas from reading, interviews, lectures, and other nonprint material, you are using sources.

In college, using sources is not only acceptable, it is expected. No matter how original their thinking, educated people nearly always base their original thought on the work of others. In fact, most of your college education is devoted to teaching you what Matthew Arnold called "the best that has been thought and said," along with ways of analyzing and interpreting this information so that your own understanding is informed but not limited by what others have said. In other words, your education prepares you to take part in an ongoing conversation. When you use sources in your writing, you let readers in on the conversation so that they can see whose ideas and information have influenced your thinking on the subject. When you cite material from another source, you need to acknowledge the source, usually by giving the author and page or date (depending on the documentation system), in parentheses in your text and including a list of works cited at the end of your paper. This chapter provides guidelines for using sources effectively and acknowledging them accurately. It also presents a sample research paper that follows the Modern Language Association documentation style.

Guidelines for preparing parenthetical citations appear on pp. 603–04; for preparing the list of works cited, on pp. 605–12.

USING SOURCES

Writers commonly use sources by quoting directly as well as by paraphrasing and by summarizing. This section provides guidelines for deciding which of these three methods to use and how to carry them out effectively.

Deciding Whether to Quote, Paraphrase, or Summarize

As a general rule, quote only in these situations: (1) the wording of the source is particularly memorable or vivid or expresses a point so well that you cannot improve it without destroying the meaning; (2) the words of reliable and respected authorities would lend support to your position; (3) you wish to highlight the author's opinions; (4) you wish to cite an author whose opinions challenge or vary greatly from other experts'. Paraphrase those passages whose details you wish to note completely but whose language is not particularly striking. Summarize any long passages whose main points you wish to record selectively to provide background or general support for a point you are making.

Quoting

Quotations should duplicate the source exactly. If the source has an error, copy it and add "sic" (Latin for "thus") in brackets immediately after the error to indicate that it is not yours but your source's:

> According to a recent newspaper article, "Plagirism [sic] is a problem among journalists and scholars as well as students" (Berensen 62).

However, you can change quotations (1) to emphasize particular words by underlining or italicizing them, (2) to omit irrelevant information or to make the quotation conform grammatically to your sentence by using ellipses, and (3) to make the quotation conform grammatically or to insert information by using brackets.

Underlining or Italicizing for Emphasis.   Underline or italicize the words you want to emphasize, and add "emphasis added" at the end of the sentence. In his essay on youth suicide in Chapter 9, Victor Fuchs emphasizes that part of the quotation which refers specifically to suicide:

> In a review of psychosocial literature on adolescence, Elder (1975) concludes: "Adolescents who fail to receive guidance, affection, and concern from parents—whether by parental inattention or absence—are likely to rely heavily on peers for emotional gratification, advice, and companionship, *to anticipate a relatively unrewarding future*, and to engage in antisocial activities" (emphasis added).

Using Ellipses for Omissions.   An ellipsis, a set of three spaced periods (. . .), signals that something has been left out of a quotation. If you quote single words or a portion of a sentence, it will be obvious that you have left out some of the original so you don't need to use an ellipsis:

More specifically, Wharton's imagery of suffusing brightness transforms Undine before her glass into "some fabled creature whose home was in a beam of light" (21).

But when words are left out in the quotation, use an ellipsis to mark the missing words. When the omission occurs within the sentence, put a space *before*, *among*, and *after* the three periods:

> Hermione Roddice is described in Lawrence's *Woman in Love* as a "woman of the new school, full of intellectuality and . . . nerve-worn with consciousness" (17).

When the omission falls at the end of the sentence, place a sentence period *directly after* the last word, followed by three spaced periods, for a total of four periods:

> But Grimaldi's recent commentary on Aristotle contends that for Aristotle rhetoric, like dialectic, had "no limited and unique subject matter upon which it must be exercised. . . . Instead, rhetoric as an art transcends all specific disciplines and may be brought into play in them" (6).

A period plus an ellipsis can indicate the omission of the rest of the sentence as well as whole sentences, paragraphs, even pages.

When a parenthetical reference follows the ellipsis at the end of your sentence, place the three spaced periods after the quotation, and place the sentence period after the final parenthesis:

> But Grimaldi's recent commentary on Aristotle contends that for Aristotle rhetoric, like dialectic, had "no limited and unique subject matter upon which it must be exercised . . ." (6).

Using Brackets for Insertions or Changes.   Use brackets around an insertion or a change needed to make a quotation conform grammatically to your sentence, such as a change in verb tense or a change in the capitalization of the first letter of the first word of a quotation, or to replace an unclear pronoun. In this example from an essay on James Joyce's "Araby," reprinted in Chapter 10, the writer adapts Joyce's phrases "we played till our bodies glowed" and "shook music from the buckled harness" to fit the tense of her sentences:

> In the dark, cold streets during the "short days of winter," the boys must generate their own heat by "[playing] till [their] bodies glowed." Music is "[shaken] from the buckled harness" as if it were unnatural, and the singers in the market chant nasally of "the troubles in our native land" (30).

You may also use brackets to add or substitute explanatory material in a quotation:

> Guterson notes that among native Americans in Florida, "education was in the home; learning by doing was reinforced by the myths and legends which repeated the basic value system of their [the Seminoles'] way of life" (159).

Several kinds of changes necessary to make a quotation conform grammatically to another sentence may be made without any signal to readers: (1) the punctuation mark at the end of a quotation may be changed, and (2) double quotation marks (enclosing the entire quotation) may be changed to single quotation marks (enclosing a quotation within the longer quotation).

Integrating Quotations

A quotation may either be integrated into your text by enclosing it in quotation marks or set off from your text in a block without quotation marks.

In-text Quotations.   Incorporate brief quotations (no more than four typed lines of prose or three lines of poetry) into your text. You may place the quotation virtually any place in your sentence:

At the Beginning

"To live a life is not to cross a field," Sutherland quotes Pasternak at the beginning of her narrative (11).

In the Middle

Woolf begins and ends by speaking of the need of the woman writer to have "money and a room of her own" (4)—an idea that certainly spoke to Plath's condition, especially in her impoverished and harassed last six months.

At the End

In *The Second Sex*, Simone de Beauvoir describes such an experience as one in which the girl "becomes as object, and she sees herself as object" (378).

Divided by Your Own Words

"Science usually prefers the literal to the nonliteral term," Kinneavy writes, "—that is, figures of speech are often out of place in science" (177).

When you quote poetry, use a slash with spaces before and after (/) to signal the end of each line of verse:

Alluding to St. Augustine's distinction between the City of God and the Earthly City, Lowell writes that "much against my will / I left the City of God where it belongs" ("Beyond the Alps" lines 4–5).

Block Quotations.   Put in block form five or more typed lines of prose or four or more lines of poetry. Indent the quotation ten spaces from the left margin and double-space. *Do not* enclose the passage within quotation marks. Use a colon to introduce a block quotation, unless the context calls for another punctuation mark or none at all. When quoting a single paragraph or part of one, do not indent the first line of the quotation more than the rest. In quoting two or more paragraphs, indent the first line of each paragraph an additional three spaces.

In "A Literary Legacy from Dunbar to Baraka," Margaret Walker says of Paul Lawrence Dunbar's dialect poems:

> He realized that the white world in the United States tolerated his literary genius only because of his "jingles in a broken tongue," and they found the old "darky" tales and speech amusing and within the vein of folklore into which they wished to classify all Negro life. This troubled Dunbar because he realized that white America was denigrating him as a writer and as a man. (70)

Punctuating Introductory Statements

Statements that introduce quotations take a range of punctuation marks and lead-in words. Here are some examples of ways writers typically introduce quotations:

Introducing a Statement with a Colon

As George Williams notes, protection of white privilege is critical to patterns of discrimination: "Whenever a number of persons within a society have enjoyed for a considerable period of time certain opportunities for getting wealth, for exercising power and authority, and for successfully claiming prestige and social deference, there is a strong tendency for these people to feel that these benefits are theirs 'by right' " (727).

Introducing a Statement with a Comma

Similarly, Duncan Turner asserts, "As matters now stand, it is unwise to talk about communication without some understanding of Burke" (259).

Introducing a Statement Using *That*

Noting this failure, Alice Miller asserts <u>that</u> "the reason for her despair was not her suffering but the impossibility of communicating her suffering to another person" (255).

Introducing a Statement Using *As . . . said*

The token women writers authenticated the male canon without disrupting it, for <u>as</u> Ruth Bleier has <u>said</u>, "The last thing society desires of its women has been intellectuality and independence" (73).

Punctuating within Quotations

Although punctuation within a quotation should reproduce the original, some adaptations may be necessary. Use single quotation marks for quotations within the quotation:

Original

E. D. Hirsch also recognizes the connection between family and learning, suggesting in his discussion of family background and academic achievement "that the significant part of our children's education has been going on outside rather than inside the schools" (Guterson 16–17).

Quoted Version

Guterson claims that E. D. Hirsch "also recognizes the connection between family and learning, suggesting in his discussion of family background and academic achievement 'that the significant part of our children's education has been going on outside rather than inside the schools' " (16–17).

If the quotation ends with a question mark or an exclamation point, retain the original punctuation:

"Did you think I loved you?" Edith later asks Dombey (566).

But if a quotation ending with a question mark or an exclamation point concludes your sentence, put the parenthetical reference and sentence period outside the quotation marks:

Edith later asks Dombey, "Did you think I loved you?" (566).

Avoiding Grammatical Tangles

When you incorporate quotations into your writing, and especially when you omit words, you run the risk of creating ungrammatical sentences. Here are three common errors you should make an effort to avoid: verb incompatibility, ungrammatical omissions, and sentence fragments.

Verb Incompatibility.   When this error occurs, the verb form in the introductory statement is grammatically incompatible with the verb form in the quotation. When your quotation has a verb form that does not fit in with your text, it is usually possible to use just part of the quotation, thus avoiding verb incompatibility. In the following example, *The narrator suggests* and *I saw* do not fit together as the sentence is written; see how the sentence is revised for verb compatibility.

NOT   The narrator suggests his bitter disappointment when "I saw myself as a creature driven and derided by vanity" (35).

BUT   The narrator suggests his bitter disappointment when he describes seeing himself "as a creature driven and derided by vanity" (35).

An Awkward Omission.   Sometimes the omission of text from the quotation results in an ungrammatical sentence. In the following example, the quotation was awkwardly and ungrammatically excerpted. The revised sentences show two ways of correcting the grammar: first, by adapting the quotation (with brackets) so that its two parts fit together grammatically; second, by using only one part of the quotation.

NOT   From the moment of the boy's arrival in Araby, the bazaar is presented as a commercial enterprise: "I could not find any sixpenny entrance and . . . handing a shilling to a weary-looking man" (34).

BUT   From the moment of the boy's arrival at Araby, the bazaar is presented as a commercial enterprise: "I could not find any sixpenny entrance and . . . hand[ed] a shilling to a weary-looking man" (34).

OR   From the moment of the boy's arrival at Araby, the bazaar is presented as a commercial enterprise: he "could not find any sixpenny entrance" and so had to pay a shilling to get in.

An Incomplete Introductory Sentence.   Sometimes when a quotation is a complete sentence, writers will carelessly neglect the introductory sentence—often, for example, forgetting to include a verb. Even though the quotation is a complete sentence, the total statement is then a sentence fragment.

NOT   The girl's interest in the bazaar leading the narrator to make what amounts to a sacred oath: "If I go . . . I will bring you something" (32).

BUT   The girl's interest in the bazaar leads the narrator to make what amounts to a sacred oath: "If I go . . . I will bring you something" (32).

Paraphrasing and Summarizing

Chapter 12 offers a discussion of paraphrasing and summarizing as a critical reading strategy.

See p. 602 for more on plagiarism.

In addition to quoting their sources, writers have the option of paraphrasing or summarizing what others have written. In a *paraphrase*, writers accurately and thoroughly state in their own words all the relevant information from a passage, without any additional comments or elaborations. A paraphrase is useful for recording details of the passage when the order of the details is important but the source's wording is not. Because all the details of the passage are noted, a paraphrase is often about the same length as the original passage.

To avoid plagiarizing inadvertently, you must use *your own words and sentence structures* in a paraphrase, not simply synonyms for the author's words or an imitation of the author's style. If you include some of the author's words within the paraphrase, enclose them in quotation marks. Note that although paraphrases are in your own words, you need to include a parenthetical citation that identifies the original source.

In a *summary*, writers boil down a paragraph or long passages—several pages or even a whole chapter or work—and restate just the main ideas in their own words. Unlike a paraphrase, a summary conveys the gist of a source, using just enough information to record the main points or the points to be emphasized. In choosing which details to include in a summary, be sure not to distort the author's meaning. While the length of a summary depends on the length of the original and how much information you need, a summary is generally much shorter than the original passage.

Here is a passage from a book on home schooling and an example of a paraphrase of it.

Original Passage

Bruner and the discovery theorists have also illuminated conditions that apparently pave the way for learning. It is significant that these conditions are unique to each learner, so unique in fact, that in many cases classrooms can't provide them. Bruner also contends that the more one discovers information in a great variety of circumstances the more likely one is to develop the inner categories required to organize that information. Yet life at school, which is for the most part generic and predictable, daily keeps many children from the great variety of circumstances they need to learn well. –David Guterson, *Family Matters: Why Homeschooling Makes Sense* (p. 172)

Paraphrase

According to Guterson, the discovery theorists, particularly Bruner, have identified the "conditions" that allow learning to take place. Because these conditions are specific to each individual, many children are not able to learn in the classroom. According to Bruner, when people can explore information in different situations, they learn to classify and order what they discover. The general routine of the school day, however, does not provide children with the diverse activities and situations that would allow them to learn these skills (172).

Here is an example of a summary of the longer section that contains the original passage printed above:

In looking at different theories of learning that discuss individual-based programs (such as home schooling) versus the public school system, Guterson describes the disagreements among "cognitivist" theorists. One group, the discovery theorists, believe that individual children learn by creating their own ways of sorting the information they take in from their experiences. Schools should help students develop better ways of organizing new material, not just present them with material that is already categorized, as traditional schools do. Assimilationist theorists, on the other hand, believe that children learn by linking what they don't know to information they already know. These theorists claim that traditional schools help students learn when they present information in ways that allow children to fit the new material into categories they have already developed (171–75).

Introducing Cited Material

Notice in the preceding examples that the source is acknowledged by name. Even when you use your own words to present someone else's information, you generally must acknowledge the fact that you borrowed the information. The only types of information that do not require acknowledgment are common knowledge (John F. Kennedy was assassinated in Dallas), familiar sayings ("haste makes waste"), and well-known quotations ("All's well that ends well").

The documentation guidelines later in this chapter present various ways of citing the sources you quote, paraphrase, and summarize, but in general you should be sure your readers can tell where a source's words or ideas begin and end. You can accomplish this more easily by separating your words from those of the source's with phrases such as "As Jones asserts," "According to Smith," "Peters claims," and so on. When you cite a person for the first time, use the person's full name; afterwards, use just the last name.

Avoiding Plagiarism

Writers—students and professionals alike—occasionally misuse sources by failing to acknowledge them properly. The word *plagiarism*, which derives from the Latin word for "kidnapping," refers to the unacknowledged use of another's words, ideas, or information. Students sometimes get into trouble because they mistakenly assume that plagiarizing occurs only when another writer's exact words are used without acknowledgment. Keep in mind, however, that you need to indicate the source of any ideas or information you have taken note of in your research for a paper, even if you have paraphrased or summarized another's words rather than copied down direct quotations.

Some people plagiarize simply because they do not know the conventions for using and acknowledging sources. This chapter makes clear how to incorporate sources into your writing and how to acknowledge your use of those sources. Others plagiarize because they keep sloppy notes and thus fail to distinguish between what is their own and what is their source's. Either they neglect to enclose their source's words in quotation marks or do not indicate when they are paraphrasing or summarizing a source's ideas and information. If you keep a working bibliography and careful notes, you will not make this serious mistake.

See pp. 573–74 for tips on keeping a working bibliography and taking notes.

There is still another reason some people plagiarize: they feel unable to write the paper by themselves. They feel overwhelmed by the writing task or by the deadline or by their own and others' expectations of them. This sense of inadequacy is not experienced by students alone. In a *Los Angeles Times* article on the subject, a journalist whose plagiarizing was discovered explained why he had done it. He said that when he read a column by another journalist on a subject he was preparing to write about, he felt that the other writer "said what I wanted to say and he said it better." If you experience this same anxiety about your work, speak to your instructor. Don't run the risk of failing a course or being expelled because of plagiarizing.

ACKNOWLEDGING SOURCES

Although there is no universally agreed-upon system for acknowledging sources, there is agreement on both the need for documentation and the items that should be included. Writers should acknowledge sources for two reasons: to give credit to those sources, and to enable readers to consult the sources for further information.

Most documentation styles combine some kind of in-text citations keyed to a separate list of works cited. The information required in the in-text citations and the order and content of the works-cited entries vary across the disciplines, but two styles predominate: the author-page system, used in the humanities and advocated by the Modern Language Association (MLA), and the author-year system, used in the natural and social sciences and advocated by the American Psychological Association (APA). Be sure to check with your instructor about which style to use, or whether you should use another style.

This chapter presents the basic features of both these styles. In Part I of this book, you can find examples of student essays that follow MLA style (Jessica Statsky, Chapter 6; Kim Dartnell, Chapter 9) and APA style (Patrick O'Malley, Chapter 7).

If you find that you need more information about these documentation styles than we can offer in this chapter, consult the *MLA Handbook for Writers of Research Papers*, Third Edition (1988), or the *Publication Manual of the American Psychological Association*, Third Edition (1983).

Parenthetical Citation in Text

The MLA author-page system requires citations that include the author's last name and the page number of the original passage being cited. The APA author-year system calls for the last name of the author and the year of publication of the original work. If the cited material is a quotation, you also need to include the page number of the original.

MLA   Dr. James is described as a "not-too-skeletal Ichabod Crane" (Simon 68).

APA   Dr. James is described as a "not-too-skeletal Ichabod Crane" (Simon, 1982, p. 68).

Notice that the APA style uses a comma between author, year, and page as well as "p." for page (Simon, 1982, p. 68), whereas the MLA puts nothing but space between author and page (Simon 68). Note also that the citations in both cases come before the final period. With block quotations, however, the citation comes after the final period preceded by two spaces.

If the author's name is used in the text, put the page reference in parentheses as close as possible to the quoted material, but without disrupting the flow of the sentence. For the APA style, cite the year in parentheses directly following the author's name, and place the page reference in parentheses before the final sentence period.

MLA   Simon describes Dr. James as a "not-too-skeletal Ichabod Crane" (68).

APA   Simon (1982) describes Dr. James as a "not-too-skeletal Ichabod Crane" (p. 68).

To cite a source by two or three authors, the MLA uses all the authors' last names; for works with more than three authors, it uses all the authors' names or just the first author's name followed by "et al." For more than three authors, the APA uses all the authors' last names the first time the reference occurs and the last name of the first author followed by "et al." subsequently.

MLA　　　　Dyal, Corning, and Willows identify several types of students, including the "Authority-Rebel" (4).

APA　　　　Dyal, Corning, and Willows (1975) identify several types of students, including the "Authority-Rebel" (p. 4).

MLA　　　　The Authority-Rebel "tends to see himself as superior to other students in the class" (Dyal, Corning, and Willows 4).

APA　　　　The Authority-Rebel "tends to see himself as superior to other students in the class" (Dyal et al., 1975, p.4).

To cite one of two or more works by the same author(s), the MLA uses the author's last name, a shortened version of the title, and the page. The APA uses the author's last name plus the year and page. When more than one work being cited was published by an author in the same year, APA style uses letters with the date (1973a, 1973b).

MLA　　　　When old paint becomes transparent, it sometimes shows the artist's original plans: "a tree will show through a woman's dress" (Hellman, *Pentimento* 1).

APA　　　　When old paint becomes transparent, it sometimes shows the artist's original plans: "a tree will show through a woman's dress" (Hellman, 1973, p. 1).

To cite a work listed only by its title, both the MLA and the APA use a shortened version of the title.

MLA　　　　An international pollution treaty still to be ratified would prohibit all plastic garbage from being dumped at sea ("Awash" 26).

APA　　　　An international pollution treaty still to be ratified would prohibit all plastic garbage from being dumped at sea ("Awash," 1987, p. 26).

To quote material taken not from the original but from a secondary source that quotes the original, both the MLA and the APA give the secondary source in the list of works cited, and acknowledge that the original was quoted in a secondary source in the text.

MLA　　　　E. M. Forster says "the collapse of all civilization, so realistic for us, sounded in Matthew Arnold's ears like a distant and harmonious cataract" (qtd. in Trilling 11).

APA　　　　E. M. Forster says "the collapse of all civilization, so realistic for us, sounded in Matthew Arnold's ears like a distant and harmonious cataract" (cited in Trilling, 1955, p. 11).

List of Works Cited
or References

Providing full information for the parenthetical citations in the text, the list of works cited identifies all the sources the writer uses. Every source cited in the text must refer to an entry in the works cited list. And, conversely, every entry in the works cited list must correspond to at least one parenthetical citation in the text.

Whereas the MLA style uses the title "Works Cited," the APA prefers "References." Both alphabetize the entries according to the first author's last name. When several works by an author are listed, the APA provides these rules for arranging the list:

■ Same name single-author entries precede multiple-author entries:

```
Aaron, P. (1990).

Aaron, P., & Zorn, C. R. (1985).
```

■ Entries with the same first author and different second author should be alphabetized according to the second author's last name:

```
Aaron, P., & Charleston, W. (1987).

Aaron, P., & Zorn, C. R. (1991).
```

■ Entries by the same authors should be arranged by year of publication, in chronological order:

```
Aaron, P., & Charleston, W. (1987).

Aaron, P., & Charleston, W. (1993).
```

■ Entries by the same author(s) with the same publication year should be arranged alphabetically by title (according to the first word after *A*, *An*, *The*), and lowercase letters (*a*, *b*, *c*, and so on) should follow the year within the parentheses:

```
Aaron, P. (1990a). Basic . . .

Aaron, P. (1990b). Elements . . .
```

For multiple works by the same author (or group of authors), MLA style requires alphabetizing by title. The author's name is given for the first entry only; in subsequent entries, three hyphens and a period are used.

```
Vidal, Gore. Empire. New York: Random, 1987.

---. Lincoln. New York: Random, 1984.
```

The essential difference between the MLA and APA styles of listing sources is the order in which the information is presented. The MLA follows this order: author's name; title; publication source, year, and page. The APA puts the year after the author's name. Both systems call for two spaces after a period. The examples that follow indicate differences in capitalization and arrangement between the two documentation styles.

BOOKS

A Book by a Single Author

MLA   Guterson, David. *Family Matters: Why Homeschooling Makes Sense*. San Diego: Harcourt, 1992.

APA   Guterson, D. (1992). *Family matters: Why homeschooling makes sense*. New York: Harcourt Brace.

A Book by an Agency or Corporation

MLA   Association for Research in Nervous and Mental Disease. *The Circulation of the Brain and Spinal Cord: A Symposium on Blood Supply*. New York: Hafner, 1966.

APA   Association for Research in Nervous and Mental Disease. (1966). *The circulation of the brain and spinal cord: A symposium on blood supply*. New York: Hafner Publishing.

A Book by More Than One Author

MLA   Gottfredson, Stephen G., and Sean McConville. *America's Correctional Crisis*. Westport, CT: Greenwood, 1987.

APA   Gottfredson, S. G., & McConville, S. (1987). *America's correctional crisis*. Westport, CT: Greenwood.

MLA   Dyal, James A., William C. Corning, and Dale M. Willows. *Readings in Psychology: The Search for Alternatives*. 3rd ed. New York: McGraw, 1975.

APA   Dyal, J. A., Corning, W. C., & Willows, D. M. (1975). *Readings in psychology: The search for alternatives* (3rd ed.). New York: McGraw-Hill.

For works by more than three authors, MLA style lists all the authors' names or the name of the first author followed by "et al."

MLA   Nielsen, Niels C., Jr., et al. *Religions of the World*. 3rd ed. New York: St. Martin's, 1992.

A Book by an Unknown Author

Use title in place of author.

MLA   Rand McNally Commercial Atlas.   Skokie, IL: Rand,
           1993.

APA   Rand McNally commercial atlas.   (1993).   Skokie,
           IL: Rand McNally.

A Book with an Editor

APA   Arnold, M. (1966).   Culture and anarchy (J. Dover
           Wilson, Ed.).   Cambridge: Cambridge University
           Press.   (Original work published 1869)

If you refer to the text itself, begin with the author:

MLA   Arnold, Matthew.   Culture and Anarchy.   Ed. J.
           Dover Wilson.   Cambridge: Cambridge UP, 1966.

If you cite the editor in your text, begin with the editor:

MLA   Wilson, J. Dover, ed.   Culture and Anarchy.   By
           Matthew Arnold.   Cambridge: Cambridge UP,
           1966.

An Edited Collection

MLA   Carter, Kathryn, and Carole Spitzack, eds.   Doing
           Research on Women's Communication.   Norwood,
           NJ: Ablex, 1989.

APA   Carter, K. & Spitzack, C. (Eds.). (1989).   Doing
           research on women's communication.   Norwood, NJ:
           Ablex.

A Translation

APA   Tolstoy, L. (1972).   War and peace.   (C. Garnett,
           Trans.).   London: Pan Books. (Original work
           published 1868-1869)

If you are referring to the work itself, begin with the author:

MLA   Tolstoy, Leo.   War and Peace.   Trans. Constance
           Garnett.   London: Pan, 1972.

If you cite the translator in your text, begin the entry with the translator's
name:

MLA   Garnett, Constance, trans.   War and Peace.   By Leo
           Tolstoy.   London: Pan, 1972.

[handwritten notes at top of page: "Quotes or Berger 156-164 / Article 6 / English Text book" and "Kilborne, Jean. 'Beauty + Beast.' Reading Culture, ed. Diana George + John Trimbar. New York: Harper Collins, 1995. 152-155"]

A Work in an Anthology or Collection

MLA   Fairbairn-Dunlop, Peggy. "Women and Agriculture in Western Samoa." Different Places, Different Voices. Ed. Janet H. Momsen and Vivian Kinnaird. London: Routledge, 1993. 211-26.

APA   Fairbairn-Dunlop, P. (1993). "Women and Agriculture in Western Samoa." In J. H. Momsen & V. Kinnaird (Eds.), Different places, different voices (pp. 211-226). London: Routledge.

An Article in a Reference Book

MLA   Suber, Howard. "Motion Picture." Encyclopedia Americana. 1981 ed.

APA   Suber, H. (1981). Motion picture. Encyclopedia Americana.

An Introduction, Preface, Foreword, or Afterword

MLA   Holt, John. Introduction. Better Than School. By Nancy Wallace. Burnett, NY: Larson, 1983. 9-14.

APA   Holt, J. (1983). Introduction. In N. Wallace, Better than school (pp. 9-14). Burnett, NY: Larson.

A Government Document

MLA   United States. Cong. Senate. Subcommittee on Constitutional Amendments of the Committee on the Judiciary. Hearings on the "Equal Rights" Amendment. 91st Cong., 2nd sess. S. Res. 61. Washington: GPO, 1970.

APA   U.S. Department of Health, Education and Welfare. (1979). Healthy people: The surgeon general's report on health promotion. (DHEW Publication No. 79-55071). Washington, DC: U.S. Government Printing Ofice.

An Unpublished Doctoral Dissertation

MLA   Bullock, Barbara. "Basic Needs Fulfillment among Less Developed Countries: Social Progress over Two Decades of Growth." Diss. Vanderbilt U, 1986.

APA   Bullock, B. (1986). <u>Basic needs fulfillment among</u>
         <u>less developed countries: Social progress over</u>
         <u>two decades of growth</u>. Unpublished doctoral
         dissertation, Vanderbilt University, Nashville,
         TN.

ARTICLES

An Article from a Daily Newspaper

MLA   Burns, Jonathan F. "Afghans Seek Direct Talks with
         U.S. on Elections." <u>New York Times</u> 6 May
         1990: 4, 22.

APA   Burns, J. F. (1990, May 6). Afghans seek direct
         talks with U.S. on elections. <u>The New York</u>
         <u>Times</u>, pp. 4, 22.

An Article from a <u>Weekly</u> or <u>Biweekly</u> <u>Magazine</u>.

MLA   Glastris, Paul. "The New Way to Get Rich." <u>U.S.</u>
         <u>News & World Report</u> 7 May 1990: 26-36.

APA   Glastris, P. (1990, May 7). The new way to get
         rich. <u>U.S. News & World Report</u>, pp. 26-36.

An Article from a Monthly or Bimonthly Magazine

MLA   Rohn, Alfie. "Home Schooling." <u>Atlantic</u> Apr.
         1988: 20-25.

APA   Rohn, A. (1988, April). Home schooling. <u>Atlantic</u>,
         pp. 20-25.

An Article in a Scholarly Journal with Continuous Annual Pagination

MLA   Natale, Jo Anna. "Understanding Home Schooling."
         <u>Education Digest</u> 9 (1993): 58-61.

APA   Natale, J. (1933). Understanding home schooling.
         <u>Education Digest</u>, <u>9</u>, 58-61.

An Article in a Scholarly Journal That Paginates Each Issue Separately

MLA   Epstein, Alexandra. "Teen Parents: What They Need
         to Know." <u>High/Scope Resource</u> 1.2 (1982): 6.

APA   Epstein, A. (1982). Teen parents: What they need
         to know. <u>High/Scope Resource</u>, <u>1</u>(2), 6.

An Anonymous Article

MLA   "Awash in Garbage." <u>New York Times</u> 15 Aug. 1987,
            sec. 1: 26.

APA   Awash in garbage. (1987, August 15). <u>The New York</u>
            <u>Times</u>, section 1, p. A26.

An Editorial

MLA   "Stepping Backward." Editorial. <u>Los Angeles Times</u>
            4 July 1989, B6.

APA   Stepping backward. (1989, July 4). [Editorial].
            <u>Los Angeles Times</u>, section B, p. 6.

A Letter to the Editor

MLA   Rissman, Edward M. Letter. <u>Los Angeles Times</u> 29
            June 1989, B5.

APA   Rissman, E. M. (1989, June 29). [Letter to the
            editor]. <u>Los Angeles Times</u>, section B, p. 5.

A Review

MLA   Anders, Jaroslaw. "Dogma and Democracy." Rev. of
            <u>The Church and the Left</u>, by Adam Minchik. <u>New</u>
            <u>Republic</u> 17 May 1993: 42-48.

If you don't know the author, start with the title. If the review is untitled,
begin with the words "Rev. of" and alphabetize under the title of the work
being reviewed.

APA   Anders, J. (1993, May 17). Dogma and democracy
            [Review of <u>The church and the left</u>]. <u>The New</u>
            <u>Republic</u>, pp. 42-48.

OTHER SOURCES

Computer Software

MLA   <u>Nota Bene</u>. Vers. 3.0. Computer software. 1988.
            MS-DOS 2.0, 512 KB, disk.

APA   <u>SuperCalc 3 Release 2.1.</u> (1985). [Computer pro-
            gram]. San Jose, CA: Computer Associates, Micro
            Products Division.

Material from NewsBank

MLA   Sharpe, Lora. "A Quilter's Tribute." <u>Boston Globe</u>
            25 Mar. 1989. NewsBank [Microform], Social
            Relations, 1989, fiche 6, grids B4-6.

Material from a Computer Information Service

MLA　　　Belenky, Mary F. "The Role of Deafness in the
　　　　　　　Moral Development of Hearing Impaired Chil-
　　　　　　　dren." Teaching, Learning and Development.
　　　　　　　Ed. A. Areson and J. DeCaro. Rochester, NY:
　　　　　　　National Institute for the Deaf, 1984. 115-
　　　　　　　84. ERIC ED 248 646.

APA　　　Belenky, M. F. (1984). The role of deafness in the
　　　　　　　moral development of hearing impaired children.
　　　　　　　In A. Areson & J. DeCaro (Eds.), Teaching,
　　　　　　　learning and development (pp. 115-184). Roches-
　　　　　　　ter, NY: National Institute for the Deaf. (ERIC
　　　　　　　Document Reproduction Service No. ED 248 646)

Material from a Computer Service

MLA　　　Reece, Jerry S. "Measuring Investment Center Per-
　　　　　　　formance." Harvard Business Review 56.3
　　　　　　　(1978): 28-40. Dialog file 107, item 673280
　　　　　　　047658.

APA　　　Reece, J. S. (1978). Measuring investment center
　　　　　　　performance. Harvard Business Review 56(3), 28-
　　　　　　　40. (Dialog file 107, item 673280 047658)

Performances

MLA　　　Oleanna. By David Mamet. Dir. David Mamet.
　　　　　　　Orpheum Theatre, New York. 25 Oct. 1993.

APA　　　Mamet, D. (Playwright and Director). (1993, Octo-
　　　　　　　ber 25). Oleanna [play]. Orpheum Theatre, New
　　　　　　　York.

Records and Tapes

MLA　　　Beethoven, Ludwig van. Violin Concerto in D Major,
　　　　　　　op. 61. Cond. Alexander Gauk. U.S.S.R. State
　　　　　　　Orchestra. David Oistrikh, violinist. Alle-
　　　　　　　gro, ACS 8044, 1980.

　　　　　　Springsteen, Bruce. "Dancing in the Dark." Born
　　　　　　　in the U.S.A. Columbia, QC 38653, 1984.

APA　　　Beethoven, L. van. (Composer). (1980). Violin
　　　　　　　concerto in D major, op. 61. (Cassette
　　　　　　　Recording No. ACS 8044). New York: Allegro.

Springsteen, B. (Singer and Composer). (1984).
    Dancing in the dark. Born in the U.S.A. (Record
    No. QC 38653). New York: Columbia.

Interviews

MLA   Lowell, Robert. "Robert Lowell." With Frederick
            Seidel. Paris Review 25 (1975): 56-95.
                    speech delivered at NCC
         Franklin, Ann. Personal interview. 3 Sept. 1983.

APA   Lowell, R. (1975). [Interview with Frederick
            Seidel]. Paris Review, 25, pp. 56-95.

speeches →
↗

When using APA style, you do not need to list personal inteviews in your references list. Simply cite the person's name, "personal communication," and the date in parentheses in your text.

SOME SAMPLE RESEARCH PAPERS

As a writer, you will have many occasions when you will want or need to use sources. You may be assigned to write a research paper, complete with formal documentation of outside sources. Several of the writing assignments in this book present logical opportunities to do library or field research—in other words, to turn to outside sources. Among the readings in Part I, those listed below cite and document sources. (The documentation style each follows is given in the parentheses.)

"Schizophrenia: What It Looks Like, How It Feels," by Veronica Murayama, pp. 181–84 (APA)

"Children Need to Play, Not Compete," by Jessica Statsky, pp. 226–29 (MLA)

"More Testing, More Learning," by Patrick O'Malley, pp. 270–73 (APA)

"Suicide among Young People," by Victor Fuchs, pp. 351–54 (APA)

"Where Will They Sleep Tonight?" by Kim Dartnell, pp. 356–58 (MLA)

AN ANNOTATED RESEARCH PAPER

Here is a student research paper speculating about the causes of a trend—the increase in home schooling. The author cites statistics, quotes authorities, and paraphrases and summarizes background information and support for her argument. The student follows MLA documentation style.

Double-space

Paragraphs indented five spaces

Author named in text; parenthetical page reference falls at end of sentence

Author named and identified to introduce quotation

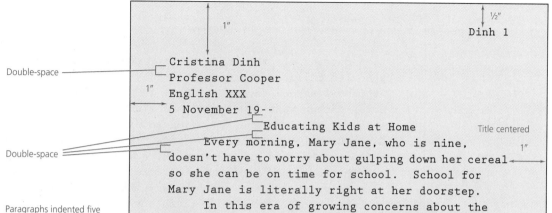

1″

½″

Dinh 1

Cristina Dinh
Professor Cooper
English XXX
5 November 19--

Educating Kids at Home   Title centered

Every morning, Mary Jane, who is nine,
doesn't have to worry about gulping down her cereal
so she can be on time for school. School for
Mary Jane is literally right at her doorstep.

In this era of growing concerns about the
quality of public education, increasing numbers
of parents across the United States are choosing
to educate their children at home. These parents believe they can do a better job teaching
their children than their local schools can.
Home schooling, as this practice is known, has
become a national trend over the past twenty
years. Patricia Lines, a senior research associate at the U.S. Department of Education, estimates that in 1970 the nationwide number of
home-schooled children was 15,000. By the
1990-91 school year, she estimates that the number rose to between 250,000 and 350,000 (5).
From 1986 to 1989, the number of home-schooled
children in Oregon almost doubled, from 2,671 to
4,578 (Graves B8). Home-school advocates believe that the numbers may even be greater; many
home schoolers don't give official notice of
what they are doing because they are still
afraid of government interference.

What is home schooling, and who are the
parents choosing to teach their children at
home? David Guterson, a high-school teacher
whose own children are home schooled, defines
home schooling as "the attempt to gain an educa-

1″

1″

Dinh 2

tion outside of institutions" (5). Home-
schooled children spend the majority of the conventional school day learning in or near their
homes rather than in traditional schools; parents or guardians are the prime educators.
Cindy Connolly notes that parents teach their
children the same subjects--math, science, music, history, and language arts--that are taught
in public schools but vary the way they teach
these subjects. Some home-schooling parents
create structured plans for their children,
while others prefer looser environments (E2).
While home schoolers are a diverse group--liber-
tarians, conservatives, Christian fundamental-
ists--most say they home school for one of two
reasons: they are concerned about the way children are taught in public schools or they are
concerned about exposing their children to secular education that may contradict their religious beliefs (Guterson 5-6).

The first group generally believes that
children need individual attention and the opportunity to learn at their own pace in order to
learn well. This group says that one teacher in
a classroom of twenty to thirty children (the
size of typical public-school classes) cannot
give this kind of attention. These parents believe they can give their children greater en-
richment and more specialized instruction than
public schools can provide. At home, parents
can work one-on-one with each child and be flexible about time, allowing their children to pursue their interests at earlier ages. Many of
these parents, like home-schooler Peter Bergson,
believe that

Author named in
parenthetical citation; no
punctuation between
name and page number

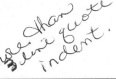

more than
3 line quote
indent.

Dinh 3

Quotation of more than
four lines typed as a
block and indented ten
spaces

home schooling provides more of an opportunity to continue the natural learning
process that's in evidence in all children.
[In school,] you change the learning process from self-directed to other-directed,
from the child asking questions to the
teacher asking questions. You shut down
areas of potential interest. (qtd. in
Kohn 22)

Brackets indicate addition
to quotation

Parenthetical citation falls
after period

Double-space

look at
on citation

The second, and larger, group, those who
home school their children for religious reasons, accounts for about 90 percent of all home
schoolers, according to the Home School Legal
Defense Association and the National Association
of State Boards of Education (Kohn 22). This
group is made up predominantly of Christian fun-
damentalists but also include Buddhists, Jews,
and black Muslims.

What causes underlie the increasing number
of parents in both groups choosing to home
school their children? One cause for this trend
can be traced back to the 1960s when many people
began criticizing traditional schools. Various
types of "alternative schools" were created, and
some parents began teaching their children at
home (Friedlander 20). As the public educational system has continued to have problems,
parents have seen academic and social standards
get lower. They mention several reasons for
their disappointment with public schools and for
their decision to home school. A lack of funding, for example, leaves children without new
textbooks. One day a mother found out her sons
were reading books that they read from the year
before (Monday C11). Many schools also cannot

Dinh 4

afford to buy laboratory equipment and other teaching materials. At my own high school, the chemistry teacher told me that most of the lab equipment we used came from a research firm he worked for. In a 1988 Gallup poll, lack of proper financial support ranked third on the list of the problems in public schools; poor curriculum and poor standards ranked fifth on the list (Gallup and Elam 34).

Parents also cite overcrowding as a reason for taking their kids out of school. Faced with a large group of children, a teacher can't satisfy the needs of all the students. Thus, a teacher ends up gearing lessons to the students in the middle level, so children at both ends miss out. Gifted children and those with learning disabilities particularly suffer in this situation. At home, parents of these children say, they can tailor the material and the pace for each child. Studies show that home-schooling methods seem to work well in preparing children academically. For example, in 1989, 74 percent of Oregon's home-schooled kids scored above the fiftieth percentile, and 22 percent above the ninetieth percentile, on standardized tests (Graves B9).

In addition, home-schooling parents claim that their children are more well-rounded than those in school. Because they don't have to sit in classrooms all day, home-schooled kids can pursue their own projects, often combining crafts or technical skills with academic subjects. Home schoolers participate in outside activities such as 4-H competitions, field trips with other children, parties, gym activities,

Source of statistic cited

Dinh 5

Christian pageants, and Boy Scouts or Girl
Scouts (Shenk D6). Some school districts even
invite home-schooled children to participate in
sports and to use libraries and computer facilities (Guterson 186).

Many home-schooling parents believe that
these activities provide the social opportunities kids need without exposing their children
to the peer pressure they would have to deal
with in school. Occasionally, peer values can
be good; often, however, students in today's
schools face many negative peer pressures. For
example, many kids think that drinking and using
drugs are cool. When I was in high school, my
friends would tell me a few drinks wouldn't hurt
and affect your driving. If I had listened to
them, I wouldn't be alive today. Four of my
friends were killed under the influence of alcohol. In 1975, according to the National Institute on Drug Abuse, 45 percent of high-school
seniors answered "yes" when asked if they had
"ever used" marijuana; in 1981, the number rose
to 60 percent, a 13 percent increase over six
years (Hawley K3). In 1986, 1987, and 1988 Gallup polls, use of drugs ranked first among the
problems in public schools, and the number of
students who use drugs was increasing (Gallup
and Elam 34).

Another reason many parents decide to home
school their kids is that they are concerned for
their children's safety. In addition to fears
that peer pressure might push their children
into using drugs, many parents fear drug-related
violence in and near public schools. There are
stories practically every week about drug-

related violence in schools--even in elementary schools. Home-schooling parents say they want to protect their children from dangerous environments. As Sam Allis notes about home-schooling parents, "There are no drugs in their bathrooms or switchblades in the hallways" (86).

The major cause of the growing home-schooling trend is Christian fundamentalist dissatisfaction with "godless" public schools. Maralee Mayberry, a professor of sociology at the University of Nevada, states in a 1987 survey that 65 percent of Oregon parents choose home schooling because they feel public schools lack Christian values (Graves B9). Kohn notes that Growing without Schooling, a secular home-schooling newsletter started by education critic John Holt, has 5,000 subscribers, whereas The Parent Educator and Family Report, a newsletter put out by Raymond Moore, a Christian home-school advocate and researcher, has 300,000 subscribers (22). Luanne Shackelford and Susan White, two Christian home-schooling mothers, claim that because schools expose children to "[p]eer pressure, perverts, secular textbooks, values clarification, TV, pornography, rock music, bad movies . . . [h]ome schooling seems to be the best plan to achieve our goal [to raise good Christians]" (160). Moore claims that children in public schools are more likely to "turn away from their home values and rely on their peers for values" (qtd. in Kilgore 24). Moore believes that home-schooled kids are less vulnerable to peer pressure because they gain a positive sense of self-worth fostered by their parents.

Paraphrase of original work cited by author in text and page number at end of sentence

Brackets used to change capitalization

Ellipsis used to indicate words left out of quotation

Quotation cited in another source

Dinh 7

In addition, those who cite the lack of "Christian values" are concerned about the textbooks used in public schools. For example, Kohn notes that Moore talks of parents who are "'sick and tired of the teaching of evolution in the schools as a cut-and-dried fact,' along with other evidence of so-called secular humanism" (21), such as textbooks that contain material that contradicts Christian beliefs. Moreover, parents worry that schools decay their children's moral values. In particular, some Christian fundamentalist parents object to sex education in schools, saying that it encourages children to become sexually active early, challenging values taught at home. They see the family as the core and believe that the best place to instill family values is within the family. These Christian home-schooling parents want to provide their children not only with academic knowledge but also with a moral grounding consistent with their religious beliefs.

Armed with their convictions, home-schooling parents, such as those who belong to the Christian Home School Legal Defense Association, have fought in court and lobbied for legislation that allows them the option of home schooling. In the 1970s, most states had compulsory attendance laws that made it difficult, if not illegal, to keep school-age children home from school. In 1993, thirty-two states permit home schooling, ten allow it with certain restrictions, while eight insist that the home school be a legal private school (Guterson 91). Because of their efforts, Mary Jane can start her school day without leaving the house.

Single quotation marks indicate a quotation within a quotation

Reference placed close to quotation, before punctuation

Dinh 8

Title centered

Double-space ——

Entries in alphabetical
order by author

Indent five spaces ——

Period after author, title,
and at end of entry

Works Cited

Allis, Sam. "Schooling Kids at Home." Time 22
    Oct. 1990: 84-85.

Connolly, Cindy. "Teen-agers See Advantages to
    Attending School at Home." Omaha World Her-
    ald 10 Sept. 1990. NewsBank [Microform],
    Education, 1990, fiche 106, grids E1-E3.

Friedlander, Tom. "A Decade of Home Schooling."
    The Home School Reader. Mark and Helen
    Hegener. Tonasket, WA: Home Education,
    1988.

Gallup, Alec M., and Stanley M. Elam. "The 20th
    Annual Gallup Poll: Of the Public toward
    the Public Schools." Phi Delta Kappan Sept.
    1988: 34.

Graves, Bill. "Home School: Enrollment In-
    creases in Oregon, Nation." Oregonian 4
    Nov. 1990 NewsBank [Microform], Education,
    1990, fiche 135, grids B8-B9.

Guterson, David. Family Matters: Why Home-
    schooling Makes Sense. San Diego:
    Harcourt, 1992.

Hawley, Richard A. "Schoolchildren and Drugs:
    The Fancy That Has Not Passed." Phi Delta
    Kappan May 1987: K1-K3.

Kilgore, Peter. "Profile of Families Who Home
    School in Maine." 1987. 1-47. ERIC ED 295
    280.

Kohn, Alfie. "Home schooling." Atlantic Apr.
    1988: 20-25.

Lines, Patricia. Estimating the Home School Ed-
    ucation Population. Washington, DC: U.S.
    Dept. of Education, 1991.

Monday, Susan McAtee. "In-House Education." San
    Antonia Light 18 Mar. 1990. NewsBank [Mi-

Dinh 9

croform], Education, 1990, fiche 27, grids
    C11, C13.
Shackelford, Luanne, and Susan White. <u>A Survi-</u>
    <u>vor's Guide to Home Schooling</u>. Westches-
    ter, IL: Crossway, 1988.
Shenk, Dan. "Parents Find Home-Schooling Has
    Special Rewards." <u>Elkhart Truth</u> 20 Mar.
    1988. NewsBank [Microform], Education,
    1988, fiche 41, grid D6.

PART FIVE

Writing for Assessment

E ven though the machine-scorable multiple-choice test has sharply reduced the number of essay exams administered in schools and colleges,
you can be certain that essay exams will continue to play a significant role in
the education of liberal arts students. Many instructors—especially in the
humanities and social sciences—still believe an exam that requires you to
write is the best way to find out what you have learned and, more important,
how you can use what you have learned. Instructors who give essay exams
want to be sure you can sort through the large body of information covered
in a course, identify what is important or significant, and explain your decision. They want to see whether you understand the concepts that provide
the basis for a course and whether you can use those concepts to interpret
specific materials, to make connections on your own, to see relationships, to
draw comparisons and find contrasts, to synthesize diverse information in
support of an original assertion. They may even be interested in your ability
to justify your own evaluations based on appropriate criteria and to argue
your own opinions with convincing evidence. Remember that your instructors hope they are encouraging you to think more critically and analytically
about a subject; they feel therefore that a written exam best allows you to
demonstrate that you are doing so.

As a college student, then, you will be faced with a variety of essay exams,
from short-answer identifications of a few sentences to take-home exams that
may require hours of planning and writing. You will find that the writing
activities and strategies discussed in Parts I and III of this book—particularly
narrating, describing, defining, comparing and contrasting, and arguing—as
well as the critical thinking strategies in Part II describe the skills that will
help you do well on all sorts of these exams. This chapter proposes some
more specific guidelines for you to follow in preparing for and writing essay
exams, and analyzes a group of typical exam questions to help you determine
which strategies will be most useful.

But you can also learn a great deal from your experiences with essay exams
in the past, the embarrassment and frustration of doing poorly on one and
the great pleasure and pride of doing well. Do you recall the best exam you
ever wrote? Do you remember how you wrote it and why you were able to
do so well? How can you be certain to approach such writing tasks confidently
and to complete them successfully? Keep these questions in mind as you
consider the following guidelines.

Essay Examinations 23

PREPARING FOR AN EXAM

First of all, essay exams require a comprehensive understanding of large amounts of information. Since exam questions can reach so widely into the course materials—and in such unpredictable ways—you cannot hope to do well on them if you do not keep up with readings and assignments from the beginning of the course. Do the reading, go to lectures, take careful notes, participate in discussion sections, organize small study groups with classmates to explore and review course materials throughout the semester. Trying to cram weeks of information into a single night of study will never allow you to do your best.

Then, as an exam approaches, find out what you can about the form it will take. There is little that is more irritating to instructors than the pestering inquiry, "Do we need to know this for the exam?"; but it is generally legitimate to ask whether the questions will require short or long answers, how many questions there will be, whether you may choose which questions to answer, and what kinds of thinking and writing will be required of you. Some instructors may hand out study guides for exams, or even lists of potential questions. However, you will often be on your own in determining how best to go about studying.

Try to avoid simply memorizing information aimlessly. As you study, you should be clarifying the important issues of the course and using these issues to focus your understanding of specific facts and particular readings. If the course is a historical survey, distinguish the primary periods and try to see relations among the periods and the works or events that define them. If the course is thematically unified, determine how the particular materials you have been reading express those themes. If the course is a broad introduction to a general topic, concentrate on the central concerns of each study unit and see what connections you can discover among the various units. Try to place all you have learned into perspective, into a meaningful context. How do the pieces fit together? What fundamental ideas have the readings, the lectures, and the discussions seemed to emphasize? How can those ideas help you digest the information the course has covered?

One good way to prepare yourself for an exam is by making up questions you think the instructor might give and then planning answers to them with classmates. Returning to your notes and to assigned readings with specific questions in mind can help enormously in your process of understanding. The important thing to remember is that an essay exam tests more than your memory of specific information; it requires you to use specific information to demonstrate a comprehensive grasp of the topics covered in the course.

READING THE EXAM CAREFULLY

Before you answer a single question, read the entire exam and apportion your time realistically. Pay particular attention to how many points you may earn in different parts of the exam; notice any directions that suggest how long an answer should be or how much space it should take up. As you are doing so, you may wish to make tentative choices of the questions you will answer and decide on the order in which you will answer them. If you have immediate ideas about how you would organize any of your answers, you might also jot down partial scratch outlines. But before you start to complete any answers, write down the actual clock time you expect to be working on each question or set of questions. Careful time management is crucial to your success on essay exams; giving some time to each question is always better than using up your time on only a few and never getting to others.

You will next need to analyze each question carefully before beginning to write your answer. Decide what you are being asked to do. It can be easy at this point to become flustered, to lose concentration, even to go blank, if your immediate impulse is to cast about for ideas indiscriminately. But if you first look closely at what the question is directing you to do and try to understand the sort of writing that will be required, you can begin to recognize the structure your answer will need to take. This tentative structure will help focus your attention on the particular information that will be pertinent to your answer. Consider this question from a sociology final:

> Drawing from lectures on the contradictory aspects of American values, discussions of the "bureaucratic personality," and the type of behavior associated with social mobility, discuss the problems of bettering oneself in a relatively "open," complex, industrial society such as the United States.

Such a question can cause momentary panic, but you nearly always can define the writing task you face. Look first at the words that give you directions: *draw from* and *discuss*. The term *discuss* is fairly vague, of course, but here it probably invites you to list and explain the problems of bettering oneself. The categories of these problems are already identified in the opening phrases: contradictory values, bureaucratic personality, certain behavior. Therefore, you would plan to begin with an assertion (or thesis) that included the key words in the final clause (bettering oneself in an open, complex, industrial society) and then take up each category of problem—and maybe still other problems you can think of—in separate paragraphs.

This question essentially calls for recall, organization, and clear presentation of facts from lectures and readings. Though it looks confusing at first, once it is sorted out, it contains the key terms for the answer's thesis, as well as its main points of development. In the next section are some further examples of the kinds of questions often found on essay exams. Pay particular attention to how the directions and the key words in each case can help you define the writing task involved.

SOME TYPICAL ESSAY EXAM QUESTIONS

Following are nine categories of exam questions, divided according to the sort of writing task involved and illustrated by examples. You will notice that, although the wording of the examples in a category may differ, the essential directions are very much the same.

All of the examples are unedited and were written by instructors in six different departments in the humanities and social sciences at two different state universities. Drawn from short quizzes, midterms, and final exams for a variety of first-year and sophomore courses, these questions demonstrate the range of writing you may be expected to do on exams.

Define or Identify   Some questions require you to write a few sentences defining or identifying material from readings or lectures. Such questions almost always allow you only a few minutes to complete your answer.

You may be asked for a brief overview of a large topic, as in Question 23.1. This question, from a twenty-minute quiz in a literature course, could have earned as much as 15 of the 100 points possible on the quiz:

Question 23.1

Name and describe the three stages of African literature.

Answering this question would simply involve following the specific directions. A student would probably *name* the periods in historical order and then *describe* each period in a separate sentence or two.

Other questions, like 23.2, will supply a list of specific items to identify. This example comes from a final exam in a communication course, and the answer to each part was worth as much as 4 points on a 120-point exam.

Question 23.2

Define and state some important facts concerning each of the following:
A. demographics
B. instrumental model
C. RCA
D. telephone booth of the air
E. penny press

With no more than three or four minutes for each part, students taking this exam would offer a concise definition (probably in a sentence). Then that definition would be briefly expanded with facts relevant to the main topics in the course.

Sometimes the list of items to be identified can be quite complicated, including quotations, concepts, and specialized terms; it may also be worth a significant number of points. The next example illustrates the first five items in a list of fifteen that opened a literature final. Each item was worth 3 points, for a total of 45 out of a possible 130 points.

Question 23.3

Identify each of the following items:
1. projection
2. "In this vast landscape he had loved so much, he was alone."
3. Balducci
4. *pied noir*
5. the Massif Central

Although the directions do not say so specifically, it is crucial here not only to identify each item but also to explain its significance in terms of the overall subject. In composing a definition or an identification, always ask yourself a simple question: Why is this item important enough to be on the exam?

Recall Details of a Specific Source

Sometimes instructors will ask for a straightforward summary or paraphrase of a specific source—a report, for example, on a book or film. Such questions hold the student to recounting details directly from the source and do not encourage interpretation or evaluation. In the following example from a sociology exam, students were allowed about ten minutes and required to complete the answer on one lined page provided with the exam.

Question 23.4

In his article "Is There a Culture of Poverty?" Oscar Lewis addresses a popular question in the social sciences. What is the "culture of poverty"? How is it able to come into being, according to Lewis? That is, under what conditions does it exist? When does he say a person is no longer a part of the culture of poverty? What does Lewis say is the future of the culture of poverty?

The phrasing here invites a fairly clear-cut structure. Each of the five specific questions can be turned into an assertion and illustrated with evidence from Lewis's book. For example, the first two questions could become assertions like these: "Lewis defines the culture of poverty as _____," and "According to Lewis the culture of poverty comes into being through _____." The important thing in this case is to stick closely to an accurate summary of what the writer said and not waste time evaluating or criticizing his ideas.

Explain the Importance or Significance

Another kind of essay exam question asks students to explain the importance of something covered in the course. Such questions require specific examples as the basis for a more general discussion of what has been studied. This will often involve interpreting a literary work by concentrating on a particular aspect of it, as in Question 23.5. This question was worth 10 out of 100 points and was to be answered in 75 to 100 words:

Question 23.5

> In the last scene in *The Paths of Glory*, the owner of a café brings a young German woman onto a small stage in his café to sing for the French troops, while Colonel Dax looks on from outside the café. Briefly explain the significance of this scene in relation to the movie as a whole.

In answering this question, a student's first task would be to reconsider the whole movie, looking for ways this one small scene illuminates or explains larger issues or themes. Then, in a paragraph or two, the student would summarize these themes and point out how each element of the specific scene fits into the overall context.

You may also be asked to interpret specific information to show that you understand the fundamental concepts of a course. The following example from a communication midterm was worth a possible 10 of 100 points and was allotted twenty minutes of exam time.

Question 23.6

> Chukovsky gives many examples of cute expressions and statements uttered by small children. Give an example or two of the kind of statements that he finds interesting. Then state their implications for understanding the nature of language in particular and communication more generally.

Here, the student must start by choosing examples of children's utterances from Chukovsky's book. These examples would then provide the basis for demonstrating one's grasp of the larger subject.

Questions like these are usually more challenging than definition and summary questions because you must decide for yourself the significance or importance or implications of the information. You must also consider how best to organize your answer so that the general ideas you need to communicate are clearly developed.

Apply Concepts

Very often courses in the humanities and social sciences emphasize significant themes, ideologies, or concepts. A common essay exam question asks students to apply the concepts to works studied in the course. Rather than providing specific information to be interpreted more generally, such questions will present you with a general idea and require you to illustrate it with specific examples from your reading.

On a literature final, an instructor posed this writing task. It was worth 50 points out of 100, and students had about an hour to complete it.

Question 23.7

Many American writers have portrayed their characters or their poetic speaker as being engaged in a quest. The quest may be explicit or implicit, external or psychological, and it may end in failure or success. Analyze the quest motif in the work of four of the following writers: Edwards, Franklin, Hawthorne, Thoreau, Douglass, Whitman, Dickinson, James, Twain.

On another literature final, the following question was worth 45 of 130 points. Students had about forty-five minutes to answer it.

Question 23.8

Several works studied in this course depict scapegoat figures. Select two written works and two films and discuss how their authors or directors present and analyze the social conflicts that lead to the creation of scapegoats.

Question 23.7 instructs students to *analyze*, Question 23.8 to *discuss*; yet the answers for each would be structured very similarly. An introductory paragraph would define the concept—the *quest* or a *scapegoat*—and refer to the works to be discussed. Then a paragraph or two would be devoted to each of the works, developing specific evidence to illustrate the concept. A concluding paragraph would probably attempt to bring the concept into clearer focus, which is, after all, the point of answering these questions.

Comment on a Quotation

On essay exams, an instructor will often ask students to comment on quotations they are seeing for the first time. Usually such quotations will express some surprising or controversial opinion that complements or challenges basic principles or ideas in the course. Sometimes the writer being quoted is identified, sometimes not. In fact, it is not unusual for instructors to write the quotation themselves.

A student choosing to answer the following question from a literature final would have risked half the exam—in points and time—on the outcome.

Question 23.9

Argue for or against this thesis: "In *A Clockwork Orange*, both the heightened, poetic language and the almost academic concern with moral and political theories deprive the story of most of its relevance to real life."

The directions here clearly ask for an argument. A student would need to set up a thesis indicating that the novel either is or is not relevant to real life, and then point out how its language and its theoretical concerns can be viewed in light of this thesis.

The next example comes from a midterm exam in a history course. Students had forty minutes to write their answers, which could earn as much as 70 points on a 100-point exam.

Question 23.10

"Some historians believe that economic hardship and oppression breed social revolt; but the experience of the United States and Mexico between 1900 and 1920 suggests that people may rebel also during times of prosperity."

Comment on this statement. Why did large numbers of Americans and Mexicans wish to change conditions in their countries during the years from 1900 to 1920? How successful were their efforts? Who benefited from the changes that took place?

Although here students are instructed to "comment," the three questions suggest evidence to be used in constructing an argument. Just as in Question 23.9, a successful answer will require a clear thesis stating a position on the views expressed in the quotation, specific reasons to support that thesis, and evidence from readings and lectures to argue for the reasons. In general, such questions don't require a "right" answer: whether you agree or disagree with the quotation is not as important as whether you can argue your case reasonably and convincingly, demonstrating a firm grasp of the subject matter.

Compare and Contrast

It could well be that instructors' most favored essay exam question is one that requires a comparison or contrast of two or three principles, ideas, works, activities, or phenomena. This kind of question requires you to explore fully the relations between things of importance in the course, to analyze each thing separately and then search out specific points of likeness or difference. Students must, thus, show a thorough knowledge of the things being compared, as well as a clear understanding of the basic issues on which comparisons and contrasts can be made.

Often, as in Question 23.11, the basis of comparison will be limited to a particular focus; here, for example, two works are to be compared in terms of their views of colonialism.

Question 23.11

Compare and analyze the views of colonialism presented in Memmi's *The Colonizer and the Colonized* and Pontecorvo's *The Battle of Algiers*. Are there significant differences between these two views?

Sometimes instructors will simply identify what is to be compared, leaving students the task of choosing the basis of the comparison, as in the next three examples from communication, history, and literature exams.

Question 23.12

In what way is the stage of electronic media fundamentally different from all the major stages that preceded it?

Question 23.13

> What was the role of the United States in Cuban affairs from 1898 until 1959? How did the U.S. role there compare with its role in the rest of Spanish America during the same period?

Question 23.14

> Write an essay on one of the following topics:
> 1. Squire Western and Mr. Knightley
> 2. Dr. Primrose and Mr. Elton

See Chapter 18 for more on comparing and contrasting.

Whether the point of comparison is stated in the question or left for you to define for yourself, it is important that your answer be limited to those aspects of similarity or difference that are most relevant to the general concepts or themes covered in the course.

Synthesize Information from Various Sources

In a course with several assigned readings, an instructor may give students an essay exam question that requires them to pull together (to synthesize) information from all the readings.

The following example was one of four required questions on a final exam in a course in Third World studies. Students had about thirty minutes to complete their answer.

Question 23.15

> On the basis of the articles read on El Salvador, Nicaragua, Peru, Chile, Argentina, and Mexico, what would you say are the major problems confronting Latin America today? Discuss the major types of problems with references to particular countries as examples.

See pp. 467–68 for information on forecasting statements.

This question asks students to do a lot in thirty minutes. They must first decide which major problems to discuss, which countries to include in each discussion, and how to use evidence from many readings to develop their answers. A carefully developed forecasting statement will be essential to developing a coherent essay.

Analyze Causes

In humanities and social science courses, much of what students study concerns the causes of trends, actions, and events. Hence, it is not too surprising to find questions about causes on essay exams. In such cases, the instructor expects students to analyze causes from readings and lectures. These examples come from mid-term and final exams in literature, communication, and sociology courses:

Question 23.16

> Why do Maurice and Jean not succumb to the intolerable conditions of the prison camp (the Camp of Hell) as most of the others do?

Question 23.17

Given that we occupy several positions in the course of our lives and given that each position has a specific role attached to it, what kinds of problems or dilemmas arise from those multiple roles, and how are they handled?

Question 23.18

Explain briefly the relationship between the institution of slavery and the emergence of the blues as a new African-American musical expression.

Question 23.19

Analyze the way in which an uncritical promotion of the new information technology (computers, satellites, etc.) may support, unintentionally, the maintenance of the status quo.

Chapter 9 presents strategies for analyzing causes.

These questions are presented in several ways ("way," "what kind of problem," "explain the relationship," "analyze the way"), but they all require a list of causes in the answer. The causes would be organized under a thesis statement, and each cause would be argued and supported with evidence from lectures or readings.

Criticize or Evaluate

Occasionally instructors will invite students to evaluate a concept or work. Nearly always they want more than opinion: they expect a reasoned, documented judgment based on appropriate criteria. Such questions not only test students' ability to recall and synthesize pertinent information; they also allow instructors to find out whether students can apply criteria taught in the course, whether they understand the standards of judgment that are basic to the subject matter.

On a final exam in a literature course, a student might have chosen one of the following questions about novels read in the course. Each would have been worth half the total points, with about an hour to answer it:

Question 23.20

Which has the more effective plot: *The Secret Agent* or *A Passage to India*?

Question 23.21

A Clockwork Orange and *The Comfort of Strangers* both attempt to examine the nature of modern decadence. Which does so more successfully?

To answer these questions successfully, students would obviously have to be very familiar with the novels under discussion. They would also have to establish criteria appropriate to evaluating an effective plot or a successful examination of modern decadence. Students would initially have to make a judgment favoring one novel over the other (although such a judgment need not cast one novel as a "terrible" and the other as a "perfect" illustration).

The answer would then give reasons for this judgment, argue each reason with evidence from the novels, and probably use the writing strategies of comparison and contrast to develop the discussion.

This next question was worth 10 of 85 points on a communication midterm. Students were asked to answer "in two paragraphs."

Question 23.22

> Eisenstein and Mukerji both argue that movable print was important to the rise of Protestantism. Cole extends this argument to say that print set off a chain of events that was important to the history of the United States. Summarize this argument, and criticize any part of it if you choose.

Evaluative questions like these involve the same sorts of writing strategies as those discussed in Chapter 8.

Here students are asked to criticize or evaluate an argument in several course readings. The instructor wants to know what students think of this argument and also, even though this is not stated, why they judge it as they do. Answering this unwritten "why" part of the question is the challenge: students must come up with reasons appropriate to evaluating the arguments and with evidence to support their reasons.

PLANNING YOUR ANSWER

The amount of planning you do for a question will depend on how much time it is allotted and how many points it is worth. For short-answer definitions and identifications, a few seconds of thought will probably be sufficient. (Be careful not to puzzle too long over individual items like theses. Skip over any you cannot recognize fairly quickly; often, answering other questions will help jog your memory.) For answers that require a paragraph or two, you may want to jot down several ideas and examples to focus your thoughts and give you a basis for organizing your information.

See pp. 431–35 for information on clustering and outlining.

For longer answers, though, you will need to develop a much more definite strategy of organization. You have time for only one draft, so allow a reasonable period—as much as a quarter of the time allotted the question—for making notes, determining a thesis, and developing an outline. Jotting down pertinent ideas is a good way to begin; then you can plan your organization with a scratch outline (just a listing of points or facts) or a cluster.

For questions with several parts (different requests or directions, a sequence of questions), make a list of the parts so that you do not miss or minimize one part. For questions presented as questions (rather than directives) you might want to rephrase each question as a writing topic. These topics will often suggest how you should outline the answer.

You may have to try two or three outlines or clusters before you hit on a workable plan. But be realistic as you outline—you want a plan you can develop within the limited time allotted for your answer. Hence, your outline will have to be selective—not everything you know on the topic, but what you know that can be developed clearly within the time available.

WRITING YOUR ANSWER

As with planning, your strategy for writing depends on the length of your answer. For short identifications and definitions, it is usually best to start with a general identifying statement and then move on to describe specific applications or explanations. Two sentences will almost always suffice, but make sure you write complete sentences.

For longer answers, begin by stating your forecasting statement or thesis clearly and explicitly. An essay exam is not an occasion for indirectness: you want to strive for focus, simplicity, and clarity. In stating your point and developing your answer, use key terms from the question; it may look as though you are avoiding the question unless you use key terms (the same key terms) throughout your essay. If the question does not supply any key terms, you will find that you have provided your own by stating your main point. Use these key terms throughout the answer.

If you have devised a promising outline for your answer, then you will be able to forecast your overall plan and its subpoints in your opening sentences. Forecasting always impresses readers and has the very practical advantage of making your answer easier to read. You might also want to use briefer paragraphs than you ordinarily do and signal clear relations between paragraphs with transition phrases or sentences.

Strategies for cueing the reader are presented in Chapter 13.

As you begin writing your answer, freely strike out words or even sentences you want to change by drawing through them neatly with a single line. Do not stop to erase, and try not to be messy. Instructors do not expect flawless writing, but they are put off by unnecessary messiness.

As you move ahead with the writing, you will certainly think of new subpoints and new ideas or facts to include later in the paper. Stop briefly to make a note of these on your original outline. If you find that you want to add a sentence or two to sections you have already completed, write them in the margin or at the top of the page, with a neat arrow pointing to where they fit in your answer.

Do not pad your answer with irrelevancies and repetitions just to fill up space. You may have had one instructor who did not seem to pay much attention to what you wrote, but most instructors read exams carefully and are not impressed by the length of an answer alone. Within the time available, write a comprehensive, specific answer without padding.

Watch the clock carefully to ensure that you do not spend too much time on one answer. You must be realistic about the time constraints of an essay exam, especially if you know the material well and are prepared to write a lot. If you write one dazzling answer on an exam with three required questions, you earn only 33 points, not enough to pass at most colleges. This may seem unfair, but keep in mind that instructors plan exams to be reasonably comprehensive. They want you to write about the course materials in two or three or more ways, not just one way.

If you run out of time when you are writing an answer, jot down the remaining main ideas from your outline, just to show that you know the material and with more time could have continued your exposition.

Write legibly and proofread. Remember that your instructor will likely be reading a large pile of exams. Careless scrawls, misspellings, omitted words, and missing punctuation (especially missing periods needed to mark the ends of sentences) will only make that reading difficult, even exasperating. A few minutes of careful proofreading can improve your grade.

MODEL ANSWERS TO SOME TYPICAL ESSAY EXAM QUESTIONS

Here we analyze several successful answers and give you an opportunity to analyze one for yourself. These analyses, along with the information we have provided elsewhere in this chapter, should greatly improve your chances of writing successful answers.

Short Answers

A literature midterm opened with ten items to identify, each worth 3 points. Students had about two minutes for each item. Here are three of Brenda Gossett's answers, each one earning her the full 3 points.

> Rauffenstein: He was the German general who was in charge of the castle where Boeldieu, Marical, and Rosenthal were finally sent in The Grand Illusion. He along with Boeldieu represented the aristocracy, which was slowly fading out at that time.
>
> Iges Peninsula: This peninsula is created by the Meuse River in France. It is there that the Camp of Hell was created in The Debacle. The Camp of Hell is where the French army was interned after the Germans defeated them in the Franco-Prussian War.
>
> Pache: He was the "religious peasant" in the novel The Debacle. It was he who inevitably became a scapegoat when he was murdered by Loubet, LaPoulle, and Chouteau because he wouldn't share his bread with them.

The instructor said only "identify the following" but clearly wanted both identification and significance of the item to the work in which it appeared. Gosset gives both and gets full credit. She mentions particular works, characters, and events. Although she is rushed, she answers in complete sentences. She does not misspell any words or leave out any commas or periods. Her answers are complete and correct.

Paragraph-length Answers

One question on a weekly literature quiz was worth 20 points of the total of 100. With only a few minutes to answer the question, students were instructed to "answer in a few sentences." Here is the question and Camille Prestera's answer:

> In *Things Fall Apart*, how did Okonkwo's relationship with his father affect his attitude toward his son?

> Okonkwo despised his father, who was lazy, cowardly, and in debt. Okonkwo tried to be everything his father wasn't. He was hard-working, wealthy, and a great warrior and wrestler. Okonkwo treated his son harshly because he was afraid he saw the same weakness in Nwoye that he despised in his father. The result of this harsh treatment was that Nwoye left home.

Prestera begins by describing Okonkwo and his father, contrasting the two sharply. Then she explains Okonkwo's relationship with his son Nwoye. Her answer is coherent and straightforward.

Long Answers

On final exams, at least one question requiring an essay-length answer is not uncommon. John Pixley had an hour to plan and write this essay for a final exam in a literature course.

Question

Many American writers have portrayed their characters or their poetic speaker as being engaged in a quest. The quest may be explicit or implicit, external or psychological, and it may end in failure or success. Analyze the quest motif in the work of four of the following writers: Edwards, Franklin, Hawthorne, Thoreau, Douglass, Whitman, Dickinson, James, Twain.

John Pixley's Answer

Americans pride themselves on being ambitious and on   1 being able to strive for goals and to tap their potentials. Some say that this is what the "American Dream" is all about. It is important for one to do and be all that one is capable of. This entails a quest or search for identity, experience, and happiness. Hence, the idea of the quest is a vital one in the United States, and it can be seen as a theme throughout American literature.

In eighteenth-century colonial America, Jonathan Ed-   2 wards dealt with this theme in his autobiographical and

*Key term (*quest*) is mentioned in introduction and thesis.*

First writer is identified immediately.

personal writings. Unlike his fiery and hard-nosed ser-
mons, these autobiographical writings present a sensitive,
vulnerable man trying to find himself and his proper, satisfying place in the world. He is concerned with his spiritual growth, in being free to find and explore religious
experience and happiness. For example, in Personal Narrative, he very carefully traces the stages of religious beliefs. He tells about periods of abandoned ecstasy,
doubts, and rational revelations. He also notes that his
best insights and growth came at times when he was alone in
the wilderness, in nature. Edwards's efforts to find himself in relation to the world can also be seen in his "Observations of the Natural World," in which he relates various meticulously observed and described natural phenomena to
religious precepts and occurrences. Here, he is trying to
give the world and life, in which he is a part, some sense
of meaning and purpose.

Although he was a contemporary of Edwards, Benjamin   3
Franklin, who was very involved in the founding of the
United States as a nation, had a different conception of the
quest. He sees the quest as being one for practical accomplishment, success, and wealth. In his Autobiography, he
stresses that happiness involves working hard to accomplish
things, getting along with others, and establishing a good
reputation. Unlike Edwards's, his quest is external and
bound up with society. He is concerned with his morals and
behavior, but, as seen in Part 2 of the Autobiography, he
deals with them in an objective, pragmatic, even statistical
way, rather than in sensitive pondering. It is also evident in this work that Franklin, unlike Edwards, believes so
much in himself and his quest that he is able to laugh at
himself. His concern with society can be seen in Poor Richard's Almanac, in which he gives practical advice on how
to find success and happiness in the world, how to "be
healthy, wealthy, and wise."

Still another version of the quest can be seen in the   4
mid-nineteenth-century poetry of Walt Whitman. The quest
that he portrays blends elements of those of Edwards and
Franklin. In "Song of Myself," which clearly is autobiographical, the speaker emphasizes the importance of finding,
knowing, and enjoying oneself as part of nature and the human community. He says that one should come to realize
that one is lovable, just as are all other people and all of
nature and life. This is a quest for sensitivity and
awareness, as Edwards advocates, and for great self-

Edwards's work and the details of his quest are presented.

Transition sentence identifies second writer. Key term is repeated.

Contrast with Edwards adds coherence to essay.

Another key term (*external*) from the question is included.

Franklin's particular kind of quest is described.

Transition sentence identifies third writer. Key term is repeated.

Comparison of Whitman to Edwards and Franklin sustains coherence of essay.

Whitman's quest is
defined.

confidence, as Franklin advocates. Along with Edwards,
Whitman sees that peaceful isolation in nature is important;
but he also sees the importance of interacting with people,
as Franklin does. Being optimistic and feeling good--both
in the literal and figurative sense--is the object of this
quest. Unfortunately, personal disappointment and national
crisis (i.e., the Civil War) shattered Whitman's sense of
confidence, and he lost the impetus of this quest in his own
life.

Transition: key term is
repeated and fourth
writer is identified.

Quest of James charac-
ter is described.

This theme of the quest can be seen in prose fiction as 5
well as in poetry and autobiography. One interesting example is "The Beast in the Jungle," a short story written by
Henry James around 1903. It is interesting in that the
principal character, John Marcher, not only fails in his
lifelong quest, but his failure comes about in a most subtle
and frustrating way. Marcher believes that something momentous is going to happen in his future. He talks about
his belief to only one person, a woman named May. May decides to befriend him for life and watch with him for the
momentous occurrence to come about, for "the beast in the
jungle" to "pounce." As time passes, May seems to know
what this occurrence is and eventually even says that it has
happened; but John is still in the dark. It is only long
after May's death that the beast pounces on him in his recognition that the "beast" was his failure to truly love May,
the one woman of his life, even though she gave him all the
encouragement that she possibly, decently could. Marcher
never defined the terms of his quest until it was too late.
By just waiting and watching, he failed to find feeling and
passion. This tragic realization, as someone like Whitman
would view it, brings about John Marcher's ruin.

Conclusion repeats key
term.

As seen in these few examples, the theme of the quest   6
is a significant one in American literature. Also obvious
is the fact that there are a variety of approaches to,
methods used in, and outcomes of the quest. This is an appropriate theme for American literature since Americans
cherish the right of "the pursuit of happiness."

This is a strong answer for two reasons: (1) Pixley has the information he
needs, and (2) he has organized it carefully and presented it coherently.

EXERCISE 23.1

The following essay was written by Don Hepler. He is answering the same
essay exam question as his classmate John Pixley. Analyze Hepler's essay to

discover whether it meets the criteria of a good essay exam answer. Review the criteria earlier in this chapter under "Writing Your Answer" and in the annotated commentary of John Pixley's answer. Try to identify the features of Hepler's essay that contribute to its success.

Don Hepler's Answer

The quest motif is certainly important in American literature. By considering Franklin, Thoreau, Douglass, and Twain, we can see that the quest may be explicit or implicit, external or psychological, a failure or a success. Tracing the quest motif through these four authors seems to show a developing concern in American literature with transcending materialism to address deeper issues. It also reveals a drift toward ambiguity and pessimism.

Benjamin Franklin's quest, as revealed by his Autobiography, is for material comfort and outward success. His quest may be considered an explicit one, because he announces clearly what he is trying to do: perfect a systematic approach for living long and happily. The whole Autobiography is a road map intended for other people to use as a guide; Franklin apparently meant rather literally for people to imitate his methods. He wrote with the assumption that his success was reproducible. He is possibly the most optimistic author in American literature, because he enjoys life, knows exactly why he enjoys life, and believes that anyone else willing to follow his formula may enjoy life as well.

By Franklin's standards, his quest is clearly a success. But his Autobiography portrays only an external, not a psychological success. This is not to suggest that Franklin was a psychological failure. Indeed, we have every reason to believe the contrary. But the fact remains that Franklin wrote only about external success; he never indicated how he really felt emotionally. Possibly it was part of Franklin's overriding optimism to assume that material comfort leads naturally to emotional fulfillment.

Henry David Thoreau presents a more multifaceted quest. His Walden is, on the simplest level, the chronicle of Thoreau's physical journey out of town and into the woods. But the moving itself is not the focus of Walden. It is really more of a metaphor for some kind of spiritual quest going on within Thoreau's mind. Most of the action in Walden is mental, as Thoreau contemplates and philosophizes, always using the lake, the woods, and his own daily actions as symbols of higher, more eternal truths. This spiritual quest is a success, in that Thoreau is able to appreciate the beauty of nature, and to see through much of the sham and false assumptions of town life and blind materialism.

Thoreau does not leave us with nearly as explicit a "blueprint" for success as does Franklin. Even Franklin's plan is limited to people of high intelligence, personal discipline, and sound character; Franklin sometimes seems to forget that many human beings are in fact weak and evil, and so would stand little chance of success similar to his own. But at least Franklin's quest could be duplicated by another Franklin. Thoreau's quest is more problematic, for even as great a mystic and naturalist as Thoreau himself could not remain in the woods indefinitely. This points towards the idea that the real quest is all internal and psychological; Thoreau seems to have gone to the woods to develop a spiritual strength that he could keep and take elsewhere on subsequent dealings with the "real world." 5

The quest of Frederick Douglass was explicit, in that he needed physically to get north and escape slavery, but it was also implicit because he sought to discover and redefine himself through his quest, as did Thoreau. Douglass's motives were more sharply focused than either Franklin's or Thoreau's; his very humanness was at stake, as well as his physical well-being and possibly even his life. But Douglass also makes it clear that the most horrible part of slavery was the mental anguish of having no hope of freedom. His learning to read, and his maintenance of this skill, seems to have been as important as the maintenance of his material comforts, of which he had very few. In a sense, Douglass's quest is the most psychological and abstract so far, because it is for the very essence of freedom and humanity, both of which were mostly taken for granted by Franklin and Thoreau. Also, Douglass's quest is the most pessimistic of the three; Douglass concludes that physical violence is the only way out, as he finds with the Covey incident. 6

Finally, Mark Twain's Huckleberry Finn is an example of the full range of meaning that the quest motif may assume. Geographically, Huck's quest is very large. But again, there is a quest defined implicitly as well as one 7

defined explicitly, as Huck (without consciously realizing it) searches for morality, truth, and freedom.
Twain's use of the quest is ambiguous, even more so than
the previous writers, because while he suggests success
superficially (i.e., the "happily-ever-after" scene in
the last chapter), he really hints at some sort of ultimate hopelessness inherent in society. Not even Douglass
questions the good or evil of American society as deeply
as does Twain; for Douglass, everything will be fine when
slavery is abolished; but for Twain, the only solution is
to "light out for the territories" altogether--and when
Twain wrote, he knew that the territories were no more.

     Twain's implicit sense of spiritual failure stands   8
in marked contrast to Franklin's buoyant confidence in
material success. The guiding image of the quest, however, is central to American values and, consequently, a
theme that these writers and others have adapted to suit
their own vision.

EXERCISE 23.2

Analyze the following essay exam questions in order to decide what kind of writing task they present. What is being asked of the student as a participant in the course and as a writer? Given the time constraints of the exam, what plan would you propose for writing the answer? Following each question is the number of points it is worth and the amount of time allotted to answer it.

1.   Cortazar is a producer of fantastic literature. Discuss first what fantastic literature is. Then choose any four stories by Cortazar as examples and discuss the fantastic elements in these stories. Refer to the structure, techniques, and narrative styles that he uses in these four stories. If you like, you may refer to more than four, of course. (Points: 30 of 100. Time: 40 of 150 minutes.)

2.   During the course of the twentieth century, the United States has experienced three significant periods of social reform—the progressive era, the age of the Great Depression, and the decade of the 1960s. What were the sources of reform in each period? What were the most significant reform achievements of each period as well as the largest failings? (Points: 35 of 100. Time: 75 of 180 minutes.)

3.   Since literature is both an artistic and ideological product, writers comment on their material context through their writing.

    a.   What is Rulto's perspective of his Mexican reality, and how is it portrayed through his stories?

b. What particular themes does he deal with, especially in these stories: "The Burning Plain," "Luvina," "They gave us the land," "Paso del Norte," and "Tell them not to kill me."

c. What literary techniques and structures does he use to convey his perspective? Refer to a specific story as an example.

(Points: 30 of 100. Time: 20 of 50 minutes.)

4. Why is there a special reason to be concerned about the influence of television watching on kids? In your answer, include a statement of:

a. Your own understanding of the *general communication principles* involved for any television watcher.

b. What's special about television and kids.

c. How advertisers and producers use this information. (You should draw from the relevant readings as well as lectures.)

(Points: 20 of 90. Time: 25 of 90 minutes.)

5. Analyze the autobiographical tradition in American literature, focusing on differences and similarities among authors and, if appropriate, changes over time. Discuss four authors in all. In addition to the conscious autobiographers—Edwards, Franklin, Thoreau, Douglass—you may choose one or two figures from among the following fictional or poetic quasi-autobiographers: Hawthorne, Whitman, Dickinson, Twain. (Points: 50 of 120. Time: 60 of 180 minutes.)

6. How does the system of (media) sponsorship work and what, if any, ideological control do sponsors exert? Be specific and illustrative! (Points: 33 of 100. Time: 60 of 180 minutes.)

7. Several of the works studied in this course analyze the tension between myth and reality. Select two written works and two films and analyze how their authors or directors present the conflict between myth and reality and how they resolve it—if they resolve it. (Points: 45 of 130. Time: 60 of 180 minutes.)

8. *Man's Hope* is a novel about the Spanish Civil War written while the war was still going on. *La Guerre est Finie* is a film about Spanish revolutionaries depicting their activities nearly thirty years after the Civil War. Discuss how the temporal relationship of each of these works to the Civil War is reflected in the character of the works themselves and in the differences between them. (Points: 58 of 100. Time: 30 of 50 minutes.)

9. Write an essay on one of these topics: The role of the narrator in *Tom Jones* and *Pride and Prejudice,* or the characters of Uncle Toby and Miss Bates. (Points: 33 of 100. Time: 60 of 180 minutes.)

A writing portfolio holds a representative sample of your best writing. Assembling a writing portfolio gives you the opportunity to show your best work. It challenges you to evaluate and reconsider your work and to think about what you have learned. The contents of a portfolio will of course vary from writer to writer—and may even be set by an instructor. Portfolios for college composition courses often include several pieces of work, a written statement about why they were chosen, and some reflection on what you've learned. This chapter provides guidelines for assembling a writing portfolio using the resources in *The St. Martin's Guide*.

WHAT PURPOSE DOES A PORTFOLIO SERVE?

Portfolios are widely used for many purposes, most generally to collect writing samples, art, or other documents. Artists present portfolios of their work to gallery owners and patrons. Designers and architects present portfolios of their most successful and imaginative work to show potential clients what they can do. Anyone applying for a position in which written communication plays an important role would be expected to submit representative samples of their writing. Some colleges request applicants to submit portfolios of high school writing; outstanding portfolios sometimes qualify students for college credit or placement in advanced courses. Some college majors require graduating seniors to submit a portfolio of their best work for evaluation, sometimes leading to special recognition or rewards. No matter what the specific purpose or occasion, a portfolio can present a rich opportunity to show what you can do.

You may as a student be required to assemble a portfolio of your work, either as part of a course or as part of an application to graduate school or for a job. Whether or not you are asked to turn in a writing portfolio, you might want to consider assembling one. You could create a portfolio from all the materials of your first-year writing course, for example. Probably you have produced many pages of very diverse materials, from journal entries to revised essays. Organizing it can help you reread and reflect on your written work and will serve as a valuable personal record of an important year in your intellectual development. You might even wish to add to it year by year, to include your best work from all your courses, or perhaps from all the courses

Assembling a Writing Portfolio 24

in your major. Such an effort should help you reflect on your learning—one of the key tasks in any education.

Pausing to reflect on your learning is sometimes referred to as *metacognition*, meaning roughly "thinking about your thinking." Such reflection helps consolidate what you have learned by reviewing the basic principles of a course. This review of your work can help you remember it and recognize connections to other courses.

In addition, it can develop your powers of judgment as you learn to evaluate your own work by the standards of judgment in various academic disciplines. It can increase your satisfaction with your courses as you become aware of the specific ways in which your knowledge is growing. Finally, it can give you insights into your own intellectual development, to recognize your strengths and weaknesses and to discover your interests.

ASSEMBLING A PORTFOLIO FOR YOUR COMPOSITION COURSE

Your instructor may ask you to assemble a writing portfolio as part of your course work. If so, the following guidelines will be helpful. They are designed to show you some resources in *The St. Martin's Guide* that can help you consider and assess your writing.

Your purpose in assembling such a portfolio is to show what you have learned in the course. In a writing course using *The St. Martin's Guide*, that goal probably means showing your work in various kinds of writing, including examples from all parts of the writing process. Following are guidelines to help you select work; revise one piece; consider what you've learned; and organize your portfolio.

Selecting Work
Your instructor will very likely specify a list of what to include in your portfolio. It may look something like the following list:

■ A selection of your best essays, including all of your work—invention, drafts, critical responses, final revisions. Your instructor will specify how many papers to include—some might want one essay, others may want several. To decide what among your writing is "best," consider response you've gotten from your instructor and other readers and review carefully the Basic Features discussion in relevant chapters of the *Guide*.

■ A further revision of this essay. Use the guidelines for Reading with a Critical Eye in the writing guide for that assignment to get ideas and the Revising and Editing section to establish a plan. You might also seek advice from your campus writing center or from friends or classmates.

■ Examples of your most imaginative, productive invention work completed for two or three other essays.

Reflecting on Your Work and Learning

Many instructors require a written statement about what you've learned about writing in the course. Some ask for this statement in the form of a letter; others may prefer an essay. Whatever form it takes, this kind of analysis is "thinking about thinking" *par excellence*. Following are some considerations in writing a thoughtful statement to your instructor about what you have learned.

■ *Describing the work.* Since you will need to refer to several works or parts of a work, be careful to name each one in a consistent way. In describing an essay, give its title and review briefly its purpose and topic.

■ *Justifying your choices.* Here begins the serious metacognitive work: when you justify what you see as your "best" work, you reveal what standards you have established for yourself about good work. These standards are fundamental to what you have learned. *The St. Martin's Guide* sets forth clear criteria for each kind of writing in the Basic Features sections in Chapters 2–10. You should review the discussion of those features to help you judge the success of your essay and refer to them as you explain your choice.

■ *Reflecting on your learning.* Your instructor may ask you to reflect on what you learned writing and revising a particular essay and also to consider what you have learned about managing the process of writing. In either case, it will help you to anchor your reflections in the specific work you've done using *The St. Martin's Guide.* Consider your work analyzing and discussing the readings; inventing; participating in group inquiry; planning and drafting; getting and giving critical comments; and revising. Look again at the sections on Thinking Critically about What You've Learned in Chapters 2–10. Here you will find help reflecting on how you solved problems in order to revise an essay, how reading influenced your writing, and how your writing can be situated and understood in a larger social context. You may well be able to use material you have already written for these sections in the statement about your learning.

Whatever materials you include, you have some important decisions to make, and these decisions reveal a lot about you as a writer. A portfolio presents you with the responsibility to assess your own work, a key step in taking charge of your own writing—and your own learning.

Organizing
the Portfolio

An inexpensive manila folder will do for presenting your portfolio. It need not be stapled; loose sheets will make it easier for your instructor to review your work and refer back and forth to the contents. You should include a separate table of contents, however; and take care to number all pages. You should also label all of your work in the upper right corner of each page. For example, write "Draft, 1" for page 1 of a draft; "Revision 2, 1" for page 1 of a second revision; "Invention, 1" for page 1 of your best invention materials; and so on. You should also date all work. Put everything in the sequence specified by your instructor.

HOW WRITING PORTFOLIOS ARE EVALUATED

Instructors read portfolios for an overall impression of student achievement. They look at how carefully the portfolio has been assembled: what choices have been made, the way the writer has justified those choices, the quality of the work, the success of revisions, and the insightfulness of reflections on the contents of the portfolio. They may not grade individual pieces of work, although they might comment on several pieces.

Your instructor will first determine whether your portfolio is complete, looking over the table of contents and skimming the portfolio to get an impression of the care with which it has been organized and presented. Labeling each piece carefully will help your instructor—or any reader— review your work.

The essays themselves will be read with certain expectations. Essays written for the assignments in *The St. Martin's Guide* will be evaluated on how appropriately they employ the available strategies of that kind of writing. In selecting work for your portfolio, therefore, and in evaluating the work yourself, you should review the Basic Features discussion of the appropriate chapter. You can expect as well that revisions will be compared to earlier drafts to assess how successfully you've solved any problems. In selecting this work for your portfolio, you should review the Identifying Problems and Solving the Problems sections in the Guide to Writing that kind of discourse. Finally, many instructors will consider how well the essay has been edited. The *Guide* includes tips for checking and editing several errors that often occur in each of its writing assignments; you might want to check for them in particular as you do any final revision for your portfolio.

Special attention is always given to the letter or essay of reflection on the portfolio contents. You can be sure your instructor will be curious to know why particular work was chosen and eager to see what rationale has been offered for the choices. A strong rationale shows that the student knows how to recognize good work and how to say precisely what makes it good. Instructors are particularly interested in student analysis of their revisions of drafts because recognizing and solving problems in a draft is a sign of a maturing writer.

Handbook

The process of generating ideas and discovering the most suitable form in which to present them, as we have described in the preceding sections of this book, is fundamental to the act of writing. As a draft is being revised into its final form, however, a writer must begin to be concerned with more precise editorial matters. Among the most important of these, of course, is the elimination of errors at various levels, but more is involved in thoughtful editing than simply correcting mistakes; serious editing requires looking at a draft with a fresh eye, shifting and adding or deleting material as necessary, rewriting sentences for clarity or expressiveness, adding or deleting punctuation where necessary to make one's meaning clear, and generally considering the potential effect on the reader of each word and every phrase. Then, at the very end of the editing process, when the final draft is complete, the writer should proofread for the sort of careless mistakes (such as transposing letters or leaving out a word) that can occur as a manuscript is being typed.

The purpose of this Handbook is to provide you with some reference tools you can use to edit and proofread effectively. In the remainder of this section, we offer an overview of the editorial and proofreading process, including a checklist of matters to keep in mind as you edit your own or another student's work. In the next section, we briefly review English sentence structure and the grammatical elements that make up sentences, in order to refresh your understanding of basic definitions and terminology. The sections that follow are concerned with various specific writing problems and generally accepted rules that you should be aware of as you edit: among these matters are a list of grammatical errors common to student writing and methods for correcting them (Editing for Problems of Standard Usage); suggestions for eliminating a variety of stylistic infelicities from your writing (Editing for Problems of Style); and a survey of punctuation usage that not only points out some common errors but also provides examples from a number of contemporary writers to demonstrate how the adroit management of punctuation can significantly expand one's ability to express ideas (Editing Punctuation). Next is a reference for such mechanical considerations as capitalization and hyphenation (Checking Mechanics).

Although you may choose or be assigned to read the whole of various sections of the Handbook, we expect that you will be more likely to use it selectively, either to find an answer to a question of grammar, usage, punctuation, or mechanics about which you are unsure, or to help correct a specific problem pointed out by your instructor or another student. Therefore, we

Guide to Editing and Proofreading

have organized each section in such a way that particular discussions can be readily located; in addition, you'll notice that each section begins with a list of topics discussed and that the inside back cover contains a list of correction symbols keyed to specific Handbook discussions.

EDITING

You may edit your writing at any stage. Whether to correct a misspelling, insert a missing comma, or rephrase a sentence, you will probably find yourself making corrections as you draft. Just by rereading your work as you go, you will see obvious problems that can be corrected quickly. Writers and researchers who have studied creativity and the writing process recommend editing very little in early drafts, however. Rather, they advocate directing full attention and energy to generating ideas, not correcting errors.

Eventually, though, you must turn to the task of editing your work. It is then that you will need to concentrate fully on perfecting your prose—finding and eliminating errors, modulating sentences for rhythm and emphasis, checking each word to be sure it is the best possible one for your intended meaning and desired effect. Editing your work effectively means becoming your own worst critic. For this reason, your editing session should take place some time after you have completed your final draft—preferably days or even a week. With such distance comes the objectivity necessary to discovering problems in your own writing. Try to read your essay as if for the first time, with the eyes of an objective, critical reader such as your instructor; this strategy can give you a better sense not only of what needs work, but also of what works best.

More difficult can be the task of editing for errors or stylistic problems that have become habitual to your writing, so that you often cannot even see them. The solution is to keep a record of the corrections made by your instructor. If, for example, papers typically come back to you with markings to indicate sentence fragments, dangling modifiers, incorrect verb forms, overuse of passive voice, or obvious statements, you could make a checklist of these sorts of problems to guide your editing. Look up each problem in the Handbook, read the explanation carefully, complete the exercises, and—if you are still uncertain—consult with your instructor. Then, before handing in each paper, proofread it for the problems on your checklist, making a separate read-through for each problem.

The following general checklist of points to consider when you are at the editing stage is meant as a diagnostic tool. It is basically in question form; by asking each question about your writing, you should be able to recognize editorial problems. Each question is then cross-referenced to a section of the Handbook that will provide help correcting the error.

This checklist can be used for editing your own work or someone else's. If you are editing someone else's work, you may wish to use the correction symbols found here and on the inside back cover of the book. If you are uncertain about how to recognize any of these problems, consult the appropriate discussion later in the Handbook.

Problems of Standard Usage

End-stop Error.   Are any independent clauses fused or run together without proper punctuation or a coordinating conjunction *(and, but, or)*? Are any independent clauses joined merely with a comma or a conjunctive adverb *(however, therefore, thus)*? If sentences are run together without proper punctuation or improperly spliced together with a comma, should the sentences be joined with proper punctuation or should they be broken into separate sentences? **(end)**

Sentence Fragments.   Are there any grammatically incomplete sentences, lacking either a subject or verb or beginning with a subordinate conjunction like *although*? If so, should they be integrated into adjoining sentences or should they be revised as complete, separate sentences? If any of these fragments are intentional, are they effective? **(frag)**

Mixed Constructions.   Does each sentence begin and end with the same structural pattern? **(mix)**

Faulty Predication.   Is there a logical match between the subject and predicate in each clause or sentence? Examine each sentence separately to see that the subjects and predicates make sense together. **(fp)**

Unclear Pronoun Reference.   Do all pronouns refer unambiguously to specific antecedents? Check that each pronoun has a clear antecedent. **(ref)**

Incomplete Comparison.   Are all comparisons complete? Are they all meaningful? **(comp)**

Dangling or Misplaced Modifiers.   Are all modifying words or phrases placed appropriately in relation to the words they modify? **(dang, mis)**

Subject-Verb Agreement.   Do all the subjects and verbs agree in number? Be certain that singular subjects have singular verbs, plural subjects plural verbs. Pay special attention to collective nouns and to sentences with *or, either . . . or,* or *neither . . . nor.* (**agr s/v**)

Pronoun-Antecedent Agreement. Do all pronouns agree with their antecedents in person, number, or gender? Pay special attention to indefinite pronouns. (**agr p/a**)

Inconsistencies in Verb Tense. Are there any unnecessary shifts in verb tense from one sentence to the next? From one clause to the next? (**vt**)

Confusion of Adjective and Adverb. Has an adverb been used to modify a noun or pronoun, particularly when used as a subject complement? Has an adjective been used to modify a verb, adjective, or adverb? (**adj/adv**)

Faulty Parallelism. Do all sentence elements in a series have the same grammatical form? (**para**)

Nonstandard Verb Form. Has an incorrect verb form been used? In particular, has an incorrect past participle of an irregular verb been used? (**vf**)

Wrong Words or Phrases. Look at each sentence word by word. Do your chosen words suit your meaning? Are any of the words or phrases you have used acceptable in conversation or informal writing, but not in a college assignment? Are there any homophones (words that sound alike but are spelled differently and have different meanings) that should be double-checked? Have any final consonants been dropped (*use to* for *used to,* for example)? Look especially at verb idioms—are the prepositions used properly? (**ww**)

Problems of Style

Strings of Prepositional Phrases. Is there an excess of prepositional phrases? Circle all prepositions. If you find three or more prepositional phrases within any one sentence, you may want to revise the sentence. (**prep**)

Overuse of *Be*. Are there too many main verbs that are forms of *be (is, are, am, was, were)*? Circle all main *be* verbs. Look at each one and try to replace it with another, more active verb. (**be**)

Overnominalization. Are the actions expressed in nouns rather than verbs? Examine each sentence, looking for *-ion* nouns *(completion, explanation)* and *be* or *has* main verbs. Revise the sentences as necessary to move the action to a verb *(complete, explain).* (**nom**)

Compound-noun Phrases. Are there any noun phrases with so many nouns strung together that the phrase requires unraveling? Consider your readers;

if they would have trouble understanding any such phrases, rewrite to simplify. **(comp noun)**

Overuse of the Passive Voice.   Is there excessive use of the passive voice? Is it unclear who the subject doing the action is? Read over your writing for passive constructions and then try rewriting each one in the active voice. Which is better? **(pass)**

Wordiness.   Is every word necessary? Examine each prepositional phrase—can any be reduced to single words? **(wrdy)** Are any words redundant? Read each sentence slowly, looking for unnecessary words. **(red)** Are there any unnecessary intensifiers *(very, really)* or hedges *(sort of, perhaps)*? **(intens or hedge)**

Vague or Obvious Statements.   Have you stated things most readers already know, statements that are unlikely to be interesting or new and that may lead readers to question your expertise? Consider in particular the first sentence in each paragraph—is it so general that it can simply be deleted? **(vague/ obvious)**

Inappropriate Words or Phrases.   Have you used words or phrases that are too colloquial or informal for college writing, or that seem unnecessarily formal given the writing situation? **(d)** Are the images you have invented suitable and unstrained, and have you avoided mixed metaphors that make comparisons that do not go together? **(image)** Have you avoided trite clichés? **(cliché)**

Punctuation

Periods.   Do you have periods wherever necessary? Are they included with the appropriate abbreviations, at the ends of all sentences, at the ends of indirect questions?

Question Marks.   Is every direct question (but not indirect question) followed by a question mark?

Exclamation Points.   Have you used exclamation points as necessary to show unusual emotion or strong emphasis? Examine each exclamation point in your work to be sure the sentence would not be better without it.

Ellipses.   Have you used them properly—three in the middle of a sentence and four at the end of a sentence?

Commas.   Are they used properly and well? Have you inserted commas before coordinating conjunctions, between items in a series, between coordinate adjectives, around parenthetical expressions? When necessary, have you put commas after transitional or introductory phrases and clauses? Are all non-restrictive clauses and phrases set off with commas? Are all final absolute phrases and contrast phrases set off with a comma? Commas pose so many difficulties that it is probably worth your time to examine each one carefully—just to be sure it belongs.

Semicolons.　Have you used semicolons correctly and wisely? If you have used this punctuation mark, examine each use to see whether a period, colon, or dash might be better.

Colons.　Examine your use of colons. Have you used a colon incorrectly following a phrase like *such as*? Would a period, comma, semicolon, dash, even ellipses be more effective? Are there places where a colon might effectively substitute for other punctuation?

Dashes.　Have you used dashes to set off any material from the rest of a sentence? If so, do they produce the desired effect? Or do they cast too much attention on the material? (Would parentheses be more subtle?) Are they overused? Be sure that you have not used dashes where other punctuation marks might be more appropriate or less intrusive. For each use, it might be helpful to ask yourself whether there is any good reason to use a dash instead of a comma.

Parentheses.　If you have used parentheses, are you sure they are the best way to punctuate the sentence? Look at the material they enclose—should it be integrated more closely in the sentence, perhaps with commas or dashes? Look also for any material that seems at all tangential to the discussion—should it be parenthesized? Within any parenthetical material, check to be sure that all other punctuation is correct.

Brackets.　Have any necessary editorial notes been enclosed in brackets? Has any parenthetical material within parentheses been enclosed in brackets?

Apostrophes.　Check all contractions and possessives to see that apostrophes are used correctly. For situations where you have a choice of using an apostrophe with or without an additional *s*, have you done so consistently?

Underlining.　Have you underscored all unusual foreign terms and words used as words? Have you correctly underlined all titles of books, newspapers, movies, paintings, and so forth?

Quotation Marks.　Have you used quotation marks where necessary to indicate direct quotations (but not indirect quotations)? Is your capitalization and punctuation within the quotation marks correct? Have you used quotation marks to punctuate titles of short written works?

Mechanics

Abbreviations. Have you used abbreviations? If so, are they appropriate and understandable by your readers? Are they spelled and punctuated as they are in the dictionary? Do they have to be defined on the first use? **(ab)**

Capitalization. Examine all capitalization to be sure it is proper and consistent. Have you capitalized proper names, all necessary words in titles, any historical events or periods that are commonly capitalized? **(cap)**

Hyphenation. Have you broken words properly at the end of a line? Have you inserted hyphens where necessary in compound words? If you are unsure about whether to hyphenate, close up, or treat a word as separate multiple words, check a dictionary. If you have a word that is not shown in the dictionary, decide for yourself and follow your usage consistently. Take a special look at all compound adjectives that precede nouns: Would hyphenating them help the reader? **(hyph)**

Numbers. Have you used numerals and words consistently? **(num)**

Spelling. Is anything misspelled? Never hesitate to reach for the dictionary, and be on the lookout for words that give everyone trouble—homophones, words with prefixes or suffixes, plurals. **(sp)**

EXERCISE

1. Look at a paper you wrote some time ago, perhaps for a class in high school. In a paragraph or two, summarize what you now see as the paper's strengths and weaknesses, indicating what you might do to improve it.

Choose one paragraph from the paper that strikes you as particularly in need of thoughtful editing—because it contains too many obvious statements or ideas in need of development, because there are sentences that need work on style, because there are errors of sentence structure or usage, and so forth. Type a clean copy of this paragraph exactly as it appears in the original paper, then mark up that copy with a pen or pencil to indicate the changes that need to be made. Finally, retype the paragraph, incorporating all of your changes into this final version.

2. From a paper you wrote in the past or one you are working on currently, bracket a sentence (or a series of shorter sentences) in which you have tried to express several different ideas or to present a fairly significant amount of information. Copy the sentence or sentences at the top of a piece of paper. Now, numbering down the page, rewrite the sentence(s) in as many different ways as you can (aim for ten) and still include all the ideas in the original. In doing so, experiment with different ways of using subordinate clauses and conjunctions, and shifting clauses and modifiers around; vary the punctuation, using dashes, colons, or parentheses in place of some periods, semi-

colons, or commas; recast verbs from passive to active voice and vice versa; delete or add words or phrases; and supply images as they occur to you. Once you've finished, evaluate each sentence in relation to the original: in what respects are the edited versions more or less effective?

3. Review as many papers as you can that you have written in the last six months or so. Bracket every sentence or phrase that has been marked by an instructor (or that you recognize) as in some way incorrect. These may include punctuation errors and those involving end-stop omissions and sentence fragments; awkward sentences that contain mixed constructions or predication problems; unclear or inconsistent grammatical relationships; incorrect verb forms; misspellings or misused words.

On the basis of this review, make a list of five to ten errors that occur most often in your written work. Be as specific in your listing as you can; the checklist at the beginning of this section provides a good example. Then, for each error, try to determine the cause of the problem: is it primarily carelessness, or are you having trouble understanding a particular point of usage? (If the latter, be sure to consult with your instructor or visit the campus writing lab.) Finally, devise strategies you can use to spot the error whenever it occurs in your work. Such strategies may take many forms, depending on the problem: you may need to circle every comma in a draft in order to check that stronger punctuation isn't required to indicate a full-stop, or review every verb to make sure its form is correct; you may want to read every sentence aloud, separately, to spot any awkwardness or inconsistency; you may need to compare every verb to its subject to make sure they are in agreement.

Such a checklist of problems and correction strategies can be a particularly useful tool as you edit drafts for habitual errors.

PROOFREADING

After editing and typing or writing your work, you must proofread the final copy. At this stage you are looking for careless errors—misspelled or omitted words, missing punctuation.

Proofreading requires examining your final copy word for word. Some proofreaders read a page backwards just so they can see each word separately. Others read aloud.

Read as slowly and carefully as you can, as though you are taking slow, precise steps on a hike down a dangerous trail. If possible, have someone else read your paper for mistakes and omissions.

A Brief Review
of Sentence Structure

As Parts I and II of this book show, there is more to writing than just making sentences. As you practice your writing, you will be concerned primarily with rhetoric, not sentence structure. You will be learning how to develop ideas, illustrate general statements, organize an argument, and integrate information. These and many other rhetorical matters will occupy your attention in Parts I and II.

Yet sentence structure is important. Writing clear and correct sentences is part of being a competent writer. This and the other sections in the Handbook will help you achieve that goal.

You may use this section as a quick, comprehensive review of sentence structure.[1] In addition, subsequent sections of the Handbook, particularly those dealing with problems of usage and style, will direct you to specific discussions in this review of sentence structure that will help explain the reasons and solutions for a number of common writing errors. For your own interest or information, you may want to read straight through this section as your writing course begins or before you use any of the other sections of the Handbook. On the facing page is a list of topics covered.

BASIC SENTENCE STRUCTURE

In considering basic sentence structure, we will look first at the elements that make up simple sentences and then at how simple sentences produce compound and complex sentences.

Words, Phrases, and Clauses

The basic building blocks of sentences are, of course, words, which can be combined into discrete groupings or *phrases*.

Words and phrases are further combined to create *clauses*. A clause is a group of at least two words that both names a topic and makes some point about that topic; every clause, then, can be divided into a *subject* and a *predicate*. The subject identifies the topic or theme of the sentence—what is being discussed—while the predicate says something about the subject and is the

---

[1]English sentence structure has been described with scientific precision by linguists. This brief review is based on an extraordinary sentence grammar, *A Grammar of Contemporary English* (New York: Harcourt, 1972). Two of its authors, Sir Randolph Quirk and Sidney Greenbaum, have written a shorter version, *A Concise Grammar of Contemporary English* (New York: Harcourt, 1973), which you might wish to consult for elaboration on any of the points discussed here.

focus of information in the clause. A clause can be either *independent* (that is, a complete idea in itself) or *dependent* (combined with an independent clause to create a complete idea). Dependent (or subordinate) clauses are discussed in a subsequent section on basic sentence elements.

Sentence Units

In order to introduce the principles of sentence structure, we will first consider *simple sentences,* those with only a single independent clause made up of a subject and a predicate.

Subject	Predicate
Native Americans	taught the New England settlers how to make Boston baked beans.
The native Americans	cooked their beans in maple sugar and bear fat.
The settlers	used molasses and salt pork instead.
Both baked bean dishes	were essentially the same.

The subject and the predicate may each be a single word or a group of words. In addition to its verb, the predicate may also include objects, complements, and adverbial modifiers. Simple sentences, then, are composed of some combination of these basic units: subject (S), verb (V), direct object (DO), indirect object (IO), subject complement (SC), object complement (OC), and adverbial modifier (A).

Of these seven units two—subject and verb—are required in every sentence. Note that subjects determine whether the verb in the predicate is singular or plural: in the last of the preceding examples, the plural subject *dishes* requires a plural verb *were.*

The basic sentence units can be defined as follows.

Subjects.   The simplest subject can be a single noun or pronoun; but a subject may also commonly consist of a noun phrase (including adjectives and other sentence elements) or even a noun clause. Subjects may also be *compound,* when two or more nouns or pronouns are linked by a conjunction. (See the next section, Basic Sentence Elements, for definitions and examples of these various elements.)

Verbs.   These can usefully be classified as *transitive,* when they occur with either a direct or indirect object, or *intransitive,* when they occur without an object. Intransitive verbs that occur with complements are often called *linking verbs.* Like subjects, verbs may be compound.

Objects.   These include direct and indirect objects, which, like subjects, can be nouns, noun phrases, noun clauses, or pronouns. Objects usually follow the subject and verb.

Complements.   These are either *subject complements* or *object complements:* subject complements refer to the subject, object complements to an object.

Like subjects and objects, complements can be nouns or pronouns, noun phrases or noun clauses (in which case, they are sometimes referred to as *predicate nominatives*). Complements can also be adjectives or adjective phrases (sometimes called *predicate adjectives*). Like objects, complements usually follow the subject and verb. They also follow any objects.

Adverbials.   These are modifiers that refer to the verb in the sentence. They can be adverbs, adverb phrases, or adverb clauses.

Types of Simple Sentences

The basic sentence elements listed above can be put together in various ways to produce seven general types of simple sentences.

(intransitive)
S	V
Steaks	sizzle.

(transitive)
S	V	DO
Americans	love	steak.

(transitive)
S	V	IO	DO
Families	serve	their guests	steak.

(linking) (adjective) (linking) (noun)
S	V	SC	S	V	SC
Steak	is	delicious.	It	is	an expensive meat.

(intransitive)
S	V	A
The best steak	comes	from the Midwest.

(transitive)
S	V	DO	OC
Vegetarians	consider	steak	unhealthy.

(transitive)
S	V	DO	A
They	prefer	lettuce	any day.

Combinations and Transformations

The various simple sentence patterns described above can be combined and transformed to produce all of the sentences writers of English need. Two or more clauses may be combined with a coordinating conjunction (such as *and* or *but*) or a pair of correlative conjunctions (such as *either/or*) to create a *compound sentence*. *Complex sentences* may be created when independent clauses are combined with a subordinating conjunction (such as *although* or *because*), or when two clauses are linked by a relative pronoun (such as *which* or *who*); clauses that contain subordinating conjunctions or relative pronouns are *dependent clauses,* and can no longer stand on their own as simple sentences. Clauses can also be combined to produce *compound-complex sentences* (that is, compound sentences that contain dependent clauses). Conjunctions and dependent clauses are discussed in more detail in the following section.

COMPOUND	Steak is delicious, but it is an expensive meat. Either Americans love steak, or they consider it unhealthy.
COMPLEX	Vegetarians consider steak unhealthy because it is high in cholesterol. Families who want to impress their guests serve them steak. Although steak is expensive, Americans love it.
COMPOUND-COMPLEX	Even though steak is unhealthy, it is a delicious meat, and Americans love it.

Simple sentences may also be transformed from *declarative* statements (as all those listed so far have been) into *questions, commands,* and *exclamations.* Sentences that are in the active voice (those that have transitive verbs and objects) can generally be transformed into *passive voice* sentences.

QUESTION	Do Americans consider steak unhealthy? Why is steak expensive? The steaks are sizzling, aren't they? The best steak comes from the Midwest?
COMMAND	Sizzle a steak on the grill.
EXCLAMATION	This steak is delicious!
PASSIVE	Steak is considered unhealthy by vegetarians. Guests are served steak when they come to dinner.

BASIC SENTENCE ELEMENTS

This section reviews the parts of speech and the types of clauses and phrases.

Parts of Speech

Although there are a number of difficulties with the traditional classification system for the parts of speech, most linguists continue to use it. It remains a very serviceable system for writers to use in analyzing and talking about their sentences.

There are ten parts of speech: nouns, pronouns, adjectives, adverbs, verbs, prepositions, conjunctions, articles, demonstratives, and interjections.

Nouns.　Nouns function in sentences or clauses as subjects, objects, and complements. They also serve as objects of various kinds of phrases and as appositives. They can be proper *(Burger King, Bartlett pear, Julia Child, General Foods)* or common *(tomato, food, lunch, cafe, waffle, gluttony).* Common nouns can be abstract *(hunger, satiation, indulgence, appetite)* or concrete *(spareribs, soup, radish, champagne, gravy).*

Nouns can be singular *(biscuit)* or plural *(biscuits),* and they may also be collective *(food).* They can be marked to show possession *(gourmet's choice, lambs' kidneys).* Nouns take determiners *(that lobster, those clams),* quantifiers *(many hotcakes, several sausages),* and articles *(a beer, the eggnog).* They can be modified by adjectives *(fried chicken),* adjective phrases *(chicken in a basket),* and adjective clauses *(chicken that's finger-licking good).*

Pronouns.   Pronouns come in many different forms and have a variety of functions in clauses and phrases.

Personal pronouns function as replacements for nouns and come in three case forms: (1) subjective, for use as subjects or subject complements: *I, we, you, he, she, it, they;* (2) objective, for use as objects of verbs and prepositions: *me, us, you, him, her, it, them;* and (3) possessive: *mine, ours, yours, his, hers, theirs.* Possessive pronouns also have a determiner form for use before nouns: *my, our, your, his, her, its, their.*

Calvin Trillin says the best restaurants in the world are in Kansas City, but <u>he</u> was born there.

If <u>you</u> ever have the spareribs and french-fried potatoes at Arthur Bryant's, <u>you</u> will never forget <u>them</u>.

<u>Your</u> memory of that lunch at Bryant's is clearer than <u>mine</u>.

Personal pronouns come in three persons (first person: *I, me, we, us;* second person: *you;* third person: *he, him, she, her, it, they, them*), three genders (masculine: *he, him;* feminine: *she, her;* neuter: *it*), and two numbers (singular: *I, me, you, he, him, she, her, it;* plural: *we, us, you, they, them*).

Reflexive pronouns, like personal pronouns, function as replacements for nouns, nearly always replacing nouns or personal pronouns in the same clause. Reflexive pronouns include *myself, ourselves, yourself, yourselves, himself, herself, oneself, itself, themselves.*

Susanna encouraged us to help <u>ourselves</u> to more strawberry shortcake.

Aunt Odessa prided <u>herself</u> on her chocolate sponge cake.

Reflexive pronouns may also be used for emphasis.

Barry baked the fudge cake <u>himself</u>.

Indefinite pronouns are pronouns that do not refer to a specific person or object: *each, all, every, everyone, everybody, everything, everywhere, both, some, someone, somebody, something, somewhere, any, anyone, anybody, anything, anywhere, either, neither, none, nobody, many, few, much, most, several, enough.*

Not <u>everybody</u> was enthusiastic about William Laird's 1698 improvement on apple cider—Jersey lightning applejack.

In the Colonies, <u>most</u> preferred rum.

Taverns usually served <u>both</u>.

Relative pronouns introduce adjective (or relative) clauses. They come in three forms: personal, to refer to people *(who, whom, whose, whoever, whomever),* nonpersonal *(which, whose, whichever, whatever),* and general *(that).*

In 1846 Nancy Johnson invented a small hand-operated machine, <u>which</u> was the forerunner of today's portable ice cream freezer.

It was Jacob Fussell of Baltimore <u>who</u> established the first wholesale ice cream business in 1851.

The fact <u>that</u> we had to wait until 1896 for someone (Italo Marchiony) to invent the ice cream cone is surprising.

Interrogative pronouns bear the same forms as relative pronouns, but have different functions. They serve to introduce questions.

<u>Who</u> invented the ice cream sundae?

Of chocolate and vanilla ice cream, <u>which</u> do you prefer?

The waiter asked, "<u>Whose</u> chocolate walnut sundae is this?"

Demonstrative pronouns are pronouns used to point out particular persons or things: *this, that, these, those.*

<u>This</u> is what Mandy likes best for brunch: pecan waffles with blueberry syrup.

Of everything on the menu, <u>these</u> must be most fattening.

Adjectives. Adjectives modify nouns and pronouns. Adjectives occur immediately before or after nouns they modify; or, as subject complements (sometimes called predicate adjectives), they may be separated by the verb from nouns or pronouns they modify.

<u>Creole</u> cooking can be found in <u>many</u> diners along the Gulf.

Bouillabaisse is a <u>spicy</u> stew.

Gumbo tastes <u>delicious</u>, and it is <u>cheap</u>.

Some adjectives change form in comparisons.

Bouillabaisse is <u>spicier</u> than crawfish pie.

Bouillabaisse is the <u>spiciest</u> of all Creole dishes.

Some words can be used as both pronouns and as adjectives; nouns are also sometimes used as adjectives.

    adj.   noun   pron.
<u>Many</u> people love <u>crawfish</u> pie, while <u>many</u> prefer bouillabaisse.

Adverbs. Adverbs may modify verbs *(eat well)*, adjectives *(very big appetite)*, and other adverbs *(extremely well done)*. They often tell when, how, where, why, and how often. A number of adverbs are formed by adding *-ly* to an adjective *(hearty* appetite, eat *heartily).*

Walter Jetton started the charcoal fires <u>early</u>. (when)

He basted the sizzling goat ribs <u>liberally</u> with marinade. (how)

Pots of beans simmered <u>nearby</u>. (where)

Like adjectives, adverbs can change form for comparison.

The sourdough biscuits cooked <u>fast</u>. (<u>faster</u> than the black-eyed peas, <u>fastest</u> of all the foods for dinner)

Adverbs ending in *-ly* enter comparison with the help of *more* and *most*:

Junior drank the first cold Lone Star beer <u>quickly</u>. (<u>more quickly</u> than Billy Joe, <u>most quickly</u> of all those at the bar)

A special kind of adverb—often called *sentence adverbs* or simply *connectives*—is used to connect the ideas in two sentences or independent clauses. Examples of these connectives include *consequently, however, therefore, similarly, besides*, and *nevertheless*.

The inspiration for Tex-Mex food came from Mexico. <u>Nevertheless</u>, it is considered a native American food.

Finally, adverbs may evaluate the information in a sentence.

Barbecue comes from *barbacoa*, a word the Spaniards <u>probably</u> picked up from the Arawak Indians.

Verbs.   As discussed in the section on sentence structure, verbs can be transitive (*Jerry <u>bakes</u> cookies.*) or intransitive (*Jerry <u>bakes</u> for a living.*); intransitive verbs that are followed by a subject complement (*Jerry <u>is</u> a fine baker, and his cookies always <u>taste</u> heavenly.*) are often called linking verbs.

Nearly all verbs have several forms (or principal parts), many of which may be irregular rather than follow a standard pattern. In addition, verbs have various forms to indicate tense (time of action or state of being), voice (performer of action), and mood (statement, command, or possibility). Studies have shown that because verbs can take so many forms, the most common errors in writing involve verbs.

Verb Phrases. Verbs divide into two primary groups: (1) main (or lexical) verbs and (2) auxiliary (or helping) verbs that combine with main verbs to create verb phrases. The three primary auxiliary verbs are *do, be*, and *have*, and all their forms:

do: does, did, doing, done
be: am, is, are, was, were, being, been
have: has, had, having

These primary auxiliaries can also act as main verbs in sentences. Other common auxiliary verbs *(can, could, may, might, shall, should, will, would, must, ought to, used to)*, however, cannot be the main verb in a sentence but are used in combination with main verbs in verb phrases. The auxiliary verb works with the main verb to indicate tense, mood, and voice. The following examples show how auxiliary verbs are used:

The favorite whiskey in the United States <u>has</u> always been bourbon.
Bourbon <u>should</u> be aged in new charred barrels for at least four years.
At least 51 percent of the mash <u>must</u> come from corn.

By the year 2000, Americans <u>will have been</u> drinking bourbon for nearly two hundred years.

Principal Parts of Verbs. All main verbs (as well as the primary auxiliary verbs *do, be,* and *have*) have five forms. The forms of a large number of verbs are regular, but many verbs have irregular forms.

Form	Regular	Irregular
Infinitive or base	sip	drink
Third person singular present (-*s* form)	sips	drinks
Past	sipped	drank
Present participle (-*ing* form)	sipping	drinking
Past participle (-*ed* form)	sipped	drunk

All new verbs coming into English have regular forms: *format, formats, formated, formating.*

For regular verbs, the past and past participle forms are the same: *sipped/ sipped.* Even though regular verbs have predictable forms, they pose certain spelling problems, having to do mainly with dropping or doubling the last letter of the base form before adding *-ing, -d,* or *-ed.*

Irregular verbs have unpredictable forms. (Dictionaries list the forms of irregular verbs under the base form.) Their *-s* and *-ing* forms are predictable, just like regular verbs, but their past and past participle forms are not.

Base	Past	Past Participle
do	did	done
begin	began	begun
lie	lay	lain
sit	sat	sat
throw	threw	thrown
come	came	come
cut	cut	cut
speak	spoke	spoken

A list of the principal parts of some of the most troublesome irregular verbs can be found in the section Editing for Problems of Standard Usage. The functions of infinitives and participles are explained in the discussion later in this section about phrases.

Tense. Native speakers of English know the tense system and use it confidently. They comprehend time as listeners and readers. As talkers, they use the system in combination with adverbs of time to identify the times of actions. As writers, however, even native speakers may encounter difficulty in putting together many sentences having time verbs: time may need to be expressed consistently from sentence to sentence, or shifts in time perspective may need to be managed smoothly. In addition, certain conventions permit time to be expressed in unusual ways: history can be written in present time to dramatize events, or characters in novels may be presented as though their actions are in present time. The following examples of verb tense provide only a partial demonstration of the complex system of time in English.

Present. There are three basic types of present time: timeless, limited, and instantaneous. Timeless present-tense verbs express habitual action.

Some Americans <u>grow</u> their own fruits and vegetables.

Limited present-tense verbs express an action in process and of limited duration.

The neighbors <u>are preparing</u> watermelon rind preserves this week.

Instantaneous present-tense verbs express action being completed at the moment.

Laura <u>is</u> now <u>eating</u> the last ripe strawberry.

Present tense verbs can also be emphatic.

I certainly <u>do enjoy</u> fresh strawberry preserves in the middle of winter.

Past. There are several kinds of past time. Some actions must be identified as having taken place at a particular time in the past.

While he <u>was waiting</u>, Jake <u>ordered</u> a ham sandwich on whole wheat bread.

In the present perfect tense, actions may be expressed as having taken place at no definite time in the past or as occurring in the past and continuing into the present.

Jake <u>has eaten</u> more ham sandwiches than he can count.

The Downtown Deli <u>has sold</u> delicious ham sandwiches on homemade bread for as long as he can remember.

Action can even be expressed as having been completed in the past prior to some other past action or event (the past perfect tense).

Before he <u>had taken</u> a bite, he dropped his sandwich on the floor.

Future. The English verb system has several different ways of expressing future time. Future action can be indicated with the modal auxiliary *will.*

Fast-food restaurants <u>will grow</u> in popularity.

A completed future action can even be viewed from some time farther in the future (future perfect tense).

Within a decade or two, Americans <u>will have given up</u> cooking their own meals.

Continuing future actions can be expressed with *will be* and the *-ing* form of the verb.

Americans soon <u>will be eating</u> every second meal away from home.

The right combination of verbs with *about* can express an action in the near future.

Jeremiah <u>is about to eat</u> his third apple turnover.

Future arrangements, commands, or possibilities can be expressed.

Junior and Mary Jo <u>are to be married</u> at McDonald's.
You <u>have to be</u> there by noon to get a good table.
If Junior <u>is to lose</u> weight, he must give up fried onion rings.

Voice. A verb is in the *active* voice when it expresses an action taken by the subject. A verb is said to be in the *passive* voice when it expresses something that happens to the subject.

In sentences with active verbs, it is apparent who is performing the action expressed in the verb.

The chef <u>disguised</u> the tasteless broccoli with a rich cheese sauce.

In sentences with passive verbs, it may not be clear who is performing the action.

The tasteless broccoli <u>was disguised</u> with a rich cheese sauce.

Adding a phrase *(by the chef)* would reveal the performer but would also create a clumsy sentence. Graceful, clear writing relies on active, rather than passive, verbs. Passive forms do fulfill certain purposes, however. They express the state of something, for example:

The broccoli <u>is disguised</u>.
The restaurant <u>was closed</u>.

Passives can give prominence to certain information by shifting it to the end of the sentence.

<u>Who</u> closed this restaurant? It was closed by <u>the Board of Health</u>.

Passives are also useful for shifting long noun clauses to the end to make a sentence more readable.

CHANGE   <u>That the chef disguised the tasteless broccoli</u> disgusted Elvira.
TO   Elvira was disgusted <u>that the chef disguised the tasteless broccoli</u>.

Mood. Mood refers to the writer's attitude toward his or her statement.

There are three moods: *indicative, imperative,* and *subjunctive.* Most statements or questions are in the indicative mood.

The chuck wagon <u>fed</u> cowboys on the trail.

<u>Did</u> cowboys ever <u>tire</u> of steak and beans?

Commands or directions are given in the imperative mood.

<u>Eat</u> those beans!

The subjunctive mood is mainly used to indicate hypothetical, impossible, or unlikely conditions.

If I <u>were</u> you, I'd compliment the cook.

If they <u>had been</u> here yesterday, they would have had hot camp bread.

Prepositions.   Prepositions always occur in phrases, followed by objects. (The uses of prepositional phrases are explained in the discussion of phrases later in this section.) Most prepositions are single words *(at, on, by, with, of, for, in, under, over, by)*, but some are two or three words *(away from, on account of, in front of, because of, in comparison with, by means of)*. They are used to indicate relations—usually of place, time, cause, purpose, or means—between their objects and some other word in the sentence.

I'll meet you <u>at</u> El Ranchero <u>for</u> lunch.

Their enchiladas are stuffed <u>with</u> cheese.

You can split an order <u>with</u> Georgette and me.

Objects of prepositions can be single or compound nouns or pronouns in the objective case (as in the preceding examples) or phrases or clauses acting as nouns.

Herman began making nachos <u>by</u> [grating the cheese].

His guests were happy <u>with</u> [what he served].

Conjunctions.   Like prepositions, conjunctions show relations between sentence elements. There are coordinating, subordinating, and correlative conjunctions.

Coordinating conjunctions *(and, but, for, nor, or, so, yet)* join logically comparable sentence elements.

Guacamole is made with avocados, tomatoes, onions, <u>and</u> chiles.

A little lemon <u>or</u> lime juice helps to keep the avocados fresh <u>and</u> green.

You may add salsa, <u>but</u> be careful not to add too much.

Subordinating conjunctions *(although, because, since, though, as though, as soon as, rather than)* introduce dependent adverb clauses.

As soon as the waitress came, Susanna ordered a club soda.

She dived into the salsa and chips because she was too hungry to wait for her No. 10 combination plate.

Correlative conjunctions come in pairs, with the first element anticipating the second *(both . . . and, either . . . or, neither . . . nor, not only . . . but also)*.

Charley wanted to order both the chile relleno and the enchiladas verdes.

Articles.   There are only three articles in English: *the, a,* and *an. The* is used for definite reference to something specific; *a* and *an* are used for indefinite reference to something less specific. *The Mexican restaurant in La Jolla* is different from *a Mexican restaurant in La Jolla*.

Demonstratives.   *This, that, these,* and *those* are demonstratives. Sometimes called demonstrative pronouns, they are used to point to (to "demonstrate") something:

Put one of these maraschino cherries at each end of the banana split.

The accident left pineapple frostee all over the front seat of that pickup!

Interjections.   Interjections indicate strong feeling or an attempt to command attention: *phew, shhh, damn, oh, yea, yike, ouch, boo.*

Dependent Clauses

Like independent clauses, all dependent clauses have a subject and a predicate (which may also have objects, complements, and adverbial modifiers). Unlike independent clauses, however, dependent clauses cannot stand as complete sentences by themselves; they always occur with independent clauses as part of either the subject or the predicate.

INDEPENDENT Ribbon-shaped pasta is popular in Northern Italy.

DEPENDENT   . . . while tubular-shaped pasta is popular in Southern Italy.

. . . , which is generally made by hand, . . .

. . . what is most popular in Northern Italy.

Although it originally comes from China, . . .

There are three types of dependent clauses: adjective, adverb, and noun.

Adjective Clauses.   Also known as relative clauses, adjective clauses modify nouns and pronouns in independent clauses. They are introduced by relative pronouns, adjectives, or adverbs *(who, whom, which, that, whose, where, when)*, and most often immediately follow the noun or pronoun they modify. Adjective clauses can be either *restrictive* (essential to defining the noun or pronoun they modify) or nonrestrictive (not essential to understanding the noun or pronoun); nonrestrictive clauses are set off by commas, while nonrestrictive clauses are not.

Vincent bought a package of anellini, <u>which is a pasta used in soup</u>.

We went back to the restaurant <u>where they serve that good vitello tonnato</u>.

Everyone <u>who likes Italian cooking</u> knows Romano cheese well.

Adverb Clauses. Introduced by subordinating conjunctions, adverb clauses nearly always modify verbs in independent clauses, although they may occasionally modify other elements (except nouns). Adverb clauses are used to indicate a great variety of logical relations with their independent clauses: time, place, condition, concession, reason, cause, circumstance, purpose, result, and so on. They are generally set off by commas.

<u>Although the finest olive oil in Italy comes from Lucca</u>, good quality olive oil is produced in other regions of the country. (concession)

<u>When the besciamella sauce comes to a boil</u>, reduce the heat and simmer. (time)

<u>If you know scampi</u>, you probably prefer them grilled to fried. (condition)

Ken drinks a double espresso every morning <u>because he likes a fast start</u>. (reason)

Noun Clauses. Like nouns, noun clauses can function as subjects, objects, or complements (or predicate nominatives) in independent clauses. They are thus essential to the structure of the independent clause in which they occur and so, like restrictive adjective clauses, are not set off by commas. Noun clauses usually begin with relative pronouns, but the introductory word may sometimes be omitted.

<u>That we preferred the valpolicella</u> surprised us. (subject of independent clause)

Harold did not know for sure <u>whether baloney came from Bologna</u>. (object of independent clause)

His assumption was <u>that it did</u>. (subject complement)

Hillary swears no one eats pizza in Italy. (direct object; relative pronoun *that* dropped)

Gnocchi may be flavored with <u>whatever fresh herbs are available</u>. (object of preposition *with*)

Phrases

Like dependent clauses, phrases can function as either nouns, adjectives, or adverbs in sentences. However, phrases are unlike clauses in that they do not contain both a subject and a verb. (Phrases, of course, cannot stand on their own but occur as part of independent clauses.) The six most common types of grammatical phrases are *prepositional, appositive, participial, gerund, infinitive*, and *absolute*.

Prepositional Phrases. Prepositional phrases function as either adjectives or adverbs.

Food <u>in Normandy</u> is noticeably different from that <u>in Provence</u>. (adjective phrases)

The perfect souffle is crisp <u>on the outside</u> and creamy <u>on the inside</u>. (adverb phrases)

Appositive Phrases.   Appositive phrases identify or give more information about a noun or pronoun just preceding. They take several different forms. Appositives may also be a single noun.

One kind of French bread, the petit Saint-Ouen, is named after a Paris bakery proprietor, M. Saint-Ouen.

The baguette, the most popular bread in France, is a loaf about two feet long.

The croissant, king of the breakfast rolls, is shaped like a crescent.

Our cook Marguerite makes superb croissants.

Participial Phrases.   Participles are verb forms used to indicate certain tenses (present: *sipping*; past: *sipped*). They can also be used as verbals—words derived from verbs—and function as adjectives.

For breakfast we were served steaming coffee and a simple buttered roll.

A participial phrase is an adjective phrase made up of a participle and any complements or modifiers it might have. Like participles, participial phrases modify nouns and pronouns in sentences.

Two-thirds of the snails consumed in France come from other countries.

Prepared in the Burgundian style, snails are served in shells in butter flavored with garlic and herbs.

Mopping up the herb butter with crusty French bread, Billy Joe thought to himself, "I could get used to this."

Gerund Phrases.   Like a participle, a gerund is a verbal. Ending in *-ing*, it even looks like a present participle; but it functions as a noun, filling any noun slot in a clause. Gerund phrases include complements and any modifiers of the gerund.

Roasting is the quickest way to cook a duck. (subject)

Preparing a cassoulet correctly takes several hours. (subject)

You begin by broiling the duck. (object of preposition)

Infinitive Phrases.   Like participles and gerunds, infinitives are verbals. Infinitives are the base forms of verbs, preceded by *to: to simmer, to broil, to fry*. Infinitives and infinitive phrases function as nouns, adjectives, or adverbs.

A cassoulet can be complicated to prepare. (adverb, modifying *complicated*)

To assemble the cassoulet, begin with a five-inch deep layer of beans. (adverb, modifying *begin*)

Remembering to peel the sausages is important. (noun, object of gerund phrase)

Anyone's first cassoulet is a meal to remember for a long time. (adjective, modifying *meal*)

Absolute Phrases.   Occupying a special place among phrases, the absolute phrase does not modify or replace any particular part of a clause, but modifies the whole clause. Nearly all modern prose writers rely on absolute phrases. Some style historians consider them a hallmark of modern prose.

Her eyes glistening, Lucy checked out the cases of donuts at Dunkin' Donuts.

She stood patiently in line, her arms folded to control her hunger and excitement, her hair in disarray, her book pack hanging off one shoulder.

When her turn finally came, she chose a maple bar and a chocolate donut, each one sensuously fat and rounded, each one glazed a satisfyingly rich dark color.

She walked slowly to a table, back straight, legs steady, each hand bearing a treasure.

FAULTY SENTENCE STRUCTURE

UNCLEAR GRAMMATICAL RELATIONSHIPS

INCONSISTENCY AMONG SENTENCE ELEMENTS

TROUBLESOME WORD FORMS

Editing for Problems
of Standard Usage

This section takes up the most common errors in terms of sentence structure, grammatical precision and consistency, and word choice. The common errors of sentence structure and grammar are each discussed in some detail, with suggestions for avoiding the error, several examples that illustrate the error, editing strategies for correcting the error, and one or more revised sentences; each topic is also followed by a brief exercise. The section on troublesome word forms provides a list of irregular verbs that are most likely to present problems and a glossary of commonly misused words.

Faulty Sentence Structure

end

END-STOP ERROR

End-stop errors include two kinds of problems. The first of these, the running together of two independent clauses with no punctuation, is called a *fused* or *run-on sentence*. The second end-stop problem, improperly using a comma to join together two independent clauses, is called a *comma splice*. These two problems are treated together here because underlying each error is the failure to signal appropriately the end of an independent clause.

Independent clauses in a single sentence should be linked by a comma and a coordinating conjunction, linked by a semicolon and a conjunctive adverb, or separated by a semicolon alone; alternatively, one clause may be made subordinate. Independent clauses may also be written as separate sentences.

When editing end-stop errors, keep the following editing strategies in mind, all of which are appropriate for both run-on sentences and comma splices.

Editing Strategies Treat the independent clauses as separate sentences, each ending with a period:

CHANGE   I asked the guard for directions she told me the time instead.

TO   I asked the guard for directions. She told me the time instead.

CHANGE   Most people don't realize the difficulties of working in a preschool, they've never tried to manage a room full of three year olds.

TO   Most people don't realize the difficulties of working in a preschool. They've never tried to manage a room full of three year olds.

Separate the independent clauses using coordinating conjunction (*and, but, for,* etc.) that is preceded by a comma (or a semicolon, if the individual clauses are particularly long and complex). This method is usual when the ideas in the different clauses are closely related and of equal importance:

OR   I asked the guard for directions, but she told me the time instead.

OR   Most people don't realize the difficulties of working in a preschool, for they've never tried to manage a room full of three year olds.

Separate the independent clauses using a semicolon, without a coordinating conjunction, to point up a close but implied connection between ideas:

OR   I asked the guard for directions; she told me the time instead.

          Most people don't realize the difficulties of working in a preschool; they've never tried to manage a room full of three year olds.

Make one clause subordinate by linking it to the independent clause with a subordinating conjunction (*when, although, because, since,* etc.). In this case, the subordinate (or dependent) clause in some way explains the central ideas presented in the main (or independent) clause:

OR   Although I asked the guard for directions, she told me the time instead.

OR   Most people don't realize the difficulties of working in a preschool because they've never tried to manage a room full of three year olds.

Link two independent clauses using a conjunctive adverb (*however, consequently, furthermore,* etc.), which must either be preceded by a semicolon or start a new sentence. The conjunctive adverb in such constructions separates the ideas in the clauses and emphasizes a very particular relationship between them:

OR   I asked the guard for directions; however, she told me the time instead.

OR   Most people have never tried to manage a room full of three year olds; consequently, they don't realize the difficulties of working in a preschool.

Remember that when a conjunctive adverb is used to link independent clauses, the clauses must be separated by a semicolon or written as separate sentences. This is also true of phrases such as *for example* and *in other words.*

CHANGE   By noon the temperature outside the compound hit 102 degrees, however, the climate control device kept the soldiers' living quarters comfortable.

TO   By noon the temperature outside the compound hit 102 degrees; however, the climate control device kept the soldiers' living quarters comfortable.

OR   By noon the temperature outside the compound hit 102 degrees. However, the climate control device kept the soldiers' living quarters comfortable.

EXERCISE

Rewrite each of the following sentences to remedy any end-stop errors.

1.   George Washington was born in 1732 in Virginia he was raised on a farm established by his great-grandfather.

2.   Washington had a big nose and pock-marked face, however he was still considered a handsome man.

3.   Washington said this about the war for independence: "Our cause is noble it is the cause of all mankind."

4.   At fifteen, Washington became a surveyor his first job was to survey the six-million-acre estate of his neighbor, Lord Fairfax.

5.   Washington wanted to return to Mount Vernon after the Constitutional Convention his colleagues persuaded him to become the country's first president.

6.   Washington's vice president John Adams was sworn in on April 21, 1789, Washington was sworn in as the first president on April 30, 1789.

7.   The British Parliament passed several measures unjust to the American colonists Washington became active in the resistance movement.

8.   Washington lost nearly all his teeth a French dentist made him a set from carved rhinoceros ivory.

9.   Washington held the first presidential barbecue in 1793, he roasted a five-hundred-pound ox for the party.

10.   Our national capital is named for him, many American colleges and towns bear his name.

frag   SENTENCE FRAGMENTS

A sentence fragment is an incomplete sentence or a dependent clause punctuated as a sentence, beginning with a capital letter and ending with a period.

For a group of words to be a complete sentence, it must have an independent clause with a subject and a predicate.

Editing Strategy

Connect the fragment to a complete sentence; or rewrite the fragment so that it is itself a complete sentence.

CHANGE   If you find that writing is hard, it's because it *is* hard. <u>One of the hardest things that people do.</u>

TO   If you find that writing is hard, it's because it *is* hard. It's one of the hardest things that people do.   –William Zinsser

OR   If you find that writing is hard, it's because it *is* hard—one of the hardest things that people do.

CHANGE   Stereotypes are a kind of gossip about the world. <u>A gossip that makes us prejudge people before we ever lay eyes on them.</u>

TO   Stereotypes are a kind of gossip about the world, a gossip that makes us prejudge people before we ever lay eyes on them.   –Robert L. Heilbroner

OR   Stereotypes are a kind of gossip about the world that makes us prejudge people before we ever lay eyes on them.

CHANGE   A new car simply presents a new set of troubles. <u>Which may be more disturbing than the beloved, familiar old troubles the old car presented.</u>

TO   A new car simply presents a new set of troubles, which may be more disturbing than the beloved, familiar old troubles the old car presented.
                                                                    –Russell Baker

OR   A new car simply presents a new set of troubles. These may be more disturbing than the beloved, familiar old troubles the old car presented.

CHANGE   Girls tend to drop out of math sooner than boys, and women experience an aversion to math and math-related activities that is akin to anxiety. <u>Although fear of math is not purely a female phenomenon.</u>

TO   Although fear of math is not purely a female phenomenon, girls tend to drop out of math sooner than boys, and women experience an aversion to math and math-related activities that is akin to anxiety.   –Sheila Tobias

OR   Girls tend to drop out of math sooner than boys, and women experience an aversion to math and math-related activities that is akin to anxiety. However, fear of math is not purely a female phenomenon.

Sometimes writers use fragments quite intentionally for emphasis or special effect. But, as a rule, you should avoid using sentence fragments in college writing.

The night was cold for this time in spring. No clouds. No wind.   –John McPhee

People in Stamps used to say that the whites in our town were so prejudiced that a Negro couldn't buy vanilla ice cream. Except on July Fourth. Other days he had to be satisfied with chocolate.   –Maya Angelou

Cans. Beer cans. Glinting on the verges of a million miles of roadways, lying in scrub, grass, dirt, leaves, sand, mud, but never hidden. Piels, Rheingold, Ballantine, Schaefer, Schlitz, shining in the sun or picked by moon or the beams of headlights at night; washed by rain or flattened by wheels, but never dulled, never buried, never destroyed. Here is the mark of savages, the testament of wasters, the stain of prosperity.
                                                                    –Marya Mannes

EXERCISE

Rewrite each of the following sentences to eliminate any fragments.

1. John Adams delivered the 1755 Harvard commencement oration in Latin. An accomplishment which earned him a job teaching Latin in a one-room country school.

2. Adams studied to become a lawyer. While he was teaching school.

3. After serving as minister to France and England; Adams returned to the United States. To serve two terms as Washington's vice president.

4. Adams distrusted the rising tide of Jeffersonian democracy in America. Because he was horrified by the French Revolution.

5. Adams lived ninety years. Longer than any other president. Long enough to see his son become the sixth president.

| mix | ## MIXED CONSTRUCTIONS |

A sentence should begin and end with the same structural pattern. Mixed constructions occur in a sentence when the writer starts out writing one sentence pattern and ends up writing another. The resulting sentence is illogical because the beginning and ending of the sentence do not go together. Consider this example:

By submitting to another person's authority is an acknowledgment of your own inadequacy.

The first modifying phrase *(By submitting to another person's authority)* cannot act as a subject for the predicate *(is an acknowledgment of your own inadequacy)*. The error can be corrected by changing the opening into a noun phrase.

Submitting to another person's authority is an acknowledgment of your own inadequacy.

It can also be corrected by rewriting the second part of the sentence to add a subject to the predicate.

By submitting to another person's authority, you acknowledge your own inadequacy.

Mixed constructions take many different forms, but they can all be corrected by choosing one structural pattern and using it consistently throughout the sentence.

Editing Strategy

Rewrite the sentence by choosing one structural pattern and using it consistently throughout the sentence.

CHANGE   Because Hemingway's style is simple makes his writing accessible to all readers.

TO	Because Hemingway's style is simple, his writing is accessible to all readers.
OR	Hemingway's simple style makes his writing accessible to all readers.
CHANGE	His latest book is funnier compared to his previous ones.
TO	His latest book is funnier than his previous ones.
OR	His latest book is funny compared to his previous ones.

EXERCISE

Rewrite the following sentences to correct any mixed constructions.

1. Because he wrote nine of the ten amendments that became the Bill of Rights is one reason James Madison is considered one of our most important founders.

2. By his active contributions to the Federal Constitutional Convention in 1785 earned Madison the title "master builder of the Constitution."

3. He was a stronger advocate of the Bill of Rights compared with many of the other delegates.

4. Because he kept a detailed journal at the Federal Constitutional Convention in 1787 is our best record of that historic event.

5. Although the British attacked Washington and burned the White House during Madison's first term did not prevent him from being elected to a second term.

6. By being only five feet four and never weighing over a hundred pounds did not keep Madison from being an authoritative president.

7. Madison's size was unimportant compared to his extraordinary political skills.

8. Noted for her charm and grace made Madison's wife, Dolley, as well known as her husband.

fp　　FAULTY PREDICATION

Faulty predication occurs when the predicate of a sentence is not compatible with its subject. If the subject cannot logically perform the action described in the predicate, then the sentence will be incoherent. Consider this example:

Neglect at home causes poorly behaved children at school.

The problem here is that neglect cannot *cause* children, poorly behaved or otherwise. A more logical statement is that neglect causes *poor behavior*, or that it causes children *to behave* in a certain way. Two ways the sentence might be revised, therefore, are as follows:

Neglect at home causes poor behavior in children at school.

Neglect at home causes children to behave poorly at school.

A minor but common predication error is the *is-when, is-because,* or *is-where* error. In sentences with this error, an adverb clause follows a form of *be* (usually *is* or *was*), which forces the adverb clause to function unnaturally as a noun. (For discussion of subject/predicate and adverb clauses, see the review of sentence structure.)

Remember, then, that the predicate of a sentence must be compatible in meaning with the subject.

Editing Strategies

Rewrite the sentence so that the subject and predicate fit together logically and are compatible in meaning.

CHANGE   Being able to express oneself on paper is a great sense of satisfaction.

TO   Being able to express oneself on paper provides a great sense of satisfaction.

OR   People who are able to express themselves on paper feel a great sense of satisfaction.

Rewrite the adverb clause as a noun clause, or revise the sentence to accommodate an adverb clause.

CHANGE   The reason her vocabulary is so large is because she studied Latin in high school.

TO   Her vocabulary is so large because she studied Latin in high school.

OR   The reason her vocabulary is so large is that she studied Latin in high school.

CHANGE   A placement examination is when you are tested to determine which course you should take.

TO   A placement examination is a test to determine which course you should take.

OR   A placement examination is given when you need to determine which course to take.

EXERCISE

Revise the following sentences to eliminate any faulty predication.

1. Andrew Jackson's presidency was when the first Democrat entered the White House.

2. One reason Jackson was elected president was because he was a popular general.

3. His great exploits on the battlefield were part of his popularity with the electorate.

4.   Jackson created the use of political patronage to reward supporters.

5.   The first assassination attempt on an American president was used against Jackson.

6.   During Jackson's first term the issue of South Carolina's secession posed a danger to the Union.

7.   Jackson's defeat of Henry Clay in 1832 caused another four-year presidential term.

Unclear Grammatical Relationships

<table>
<tr><td>

ref

</td><td>

UNCLEAR PRONOUN REFERENCE

</td></tr>
</table>

A pronoun must refer to a specific antecedent. Unclear pronoun reference takes several forms: the pronoun may lack an antecedent, it may refer ambiguously to two or more possible antecedents, or it may refer vaguely to a whole clause and not to a specific antecedent within the clause. Correcting errors in pronoun reference nearly always requires some writing; merely changing a word is rarely sufficient.

Editing Strategies   If a pronoun lacks an antecedent, rewrite the sentence without the pronoun.

CHANGE   Nora's car broke down in a rough neighborhood, <u>which</u> frightened her.

TO   The rough neighborhood where Nora's car broke down frightened her.

OR   Nora was frightened when her car broke down in a rough neighborhood.

OR   That her car broke down in a rough neighborhood frightened Nora.

If the pronoun refers vaguely to a clause or whole sentence but not to a specific antecedent, rewrite the sentence supplying a word or phrase to identify the antecedent.

CHANGE   The Bruins pulled away from the Trojans by ten points within the first five minutes of the game. <u>This</u> delighted the UCLA fans.

TO   The Bruins pulled away from the Trojans by ten points within the first five minutes of the game. This sudden lead delighted the UCLA fans.

If a pronoun refers ambiguously to two or more possible antecedents, rewrite the sentence to make the pronoun reference unambiguous.

CHANGE   <u>Phyllis</u> called <u>Becky</u> every day when <u>she</u> was on vacation.

TO   When <u>Phyllis</u> was on vacation, <u>she</u> called Becky every day.

Eliminate any vague uses of *it* or *they*.

CHANGE	In the last sentence of the essay it restates the thesis.
TO	The last sentence of the essay restates the thesis.
CHANGE	The fire in the library was finally put out. For a while, they thought an unhappy employee might have started it.
TO	The fire in the library was finally put out. For a while, the library staff thought an unhappy employee might have started it.

EXERCISE

Revise each of the following sentences to correct any unclear pronoun reference. The pronoun in question is underlined.

1. In 1845, Lucretia Mott was arguing that women should have the right to own property, which amazed nearly everyone at that time.

2. In 1848, Mott and Elizabeth Cady Stanton organized a meeting in Seneca Falls, New York. This turned into the first women's rights convention.

3. In the newspapers of the day it treated Mott and other women working to gain female suffrage with ridicule.

4. She knew that in Lincoln's White House they would oppose slavery.

5. Mott was a famous public speaker even though she didn't seek it.

comp INCOMPLETE COMPARISON

The most common error with comparison occurs when something is left out. By definition, a comparison establishes a connection between two or more things; yet sometimes people draw incomplete comparisons by failing to mention one of the items being compared. We have come to accept incomplete constructions in advertising *(Earn more on your savings)* and in conversation *(My cold is better today)*, but in writing they are not acceptable.

Comparisons in writing should be complete; all items of comparison should be named.

Editing Strategies

Rewrite the sentence to indicate all the things being compared.

CHANGE	This school offers a better education.
TO	This school offers a better education than all other schools in the state.

Rewrite the sentence to show that the stated item of comparison is a member of the group it is being compared to.

CHANGE	I found *Madame Bovary* more interesting than any French novel I've read.
TO	I found *Madame Bovary* more interesting than any other French novel I've read.

Revise the sentence to state the comparison fully.

CHANGE	His piano playing is like a professional.
TO	He plays piano like a professional.
OR	His piano playing is like that of a professional.
OR	His piano playing is like a professional's.
CHANGE	Mary is closer to Sue than Elizabeth.
TO	Mary is closer to Sue than she is to Elizabeth.
OR	Mary is closer to Sue than Elizabeth is.

EXERCISE

Rewrite the following sentences as necessary to make all comparisons complete and explicit.

1. Abraham Lincoln gave our country better leadership.
2. Lincoln is considered by many to be more eloquent than any president.
3. Lincoln was more like Jefferson than Madison.
4. Lincoln may have valued his stepmother as much, if not more than, his own mother.
5. Lincoln decided that preserving the Union was more important.
6. Lincoln's place in the American imagination is more like a spiritual father than a political leader.

dang | DANGLING MODIFIERS

A modifying phrase must clearly qualify the meaning of a particular word in the sentence. Phrases that do not modify a specific word in a sentence are called dangling modifiers. They usually occur at the beginning of sentences and are most often prepositional or participial phrases. In the following sentence, for instance, the phrase *having gone to bed late*, is dangling because it seems to modify *alarm*—clearly an illogical connection. There are two ways of revising the sentence to eliminate the dangling phrase:

CHANGE	Having gone to bed early, the alarm didn't awaken me when it went off.
TO	Having gone to bed early, I didn't awaken when the alarm went off.
OR	Even though I went to bed early, the alarm didn't awaken me when it went off.

Editing Strategies

Rewrite the sentence so that the word the phrase modifies immediately follows the phrase.

CHANGE   Disruptive in the classroom, a teacher may become exasperated with hyperactive children.

TO   Disruptive in the classroom, hyperactive children may exasperate a teacher.

Rewrite the sentence by changing the modifying phrase into a subordinate clause.

CHANGE   After leaving the stage, the audience's applause called the musicians back for an encore.

TO   After the musicians left the stage, the audience's applause called them back for an encore.

EXERCISE

Rewrite the following sentences to eliminate all dangling modifiers.

1. One of the most intelligent and talented men in American history, everything known at the time interested Thomas Jefferson.

2. With his remarkable skill as a writer, a colleague in the Continental Congress readily nominated Jefferson to draft the Declaration of Independence.

3. Appointed minister to France in 1785 to succeed Benjamin Franklin, five years in Europe spread Jefferson's influence and fame.

4. Retiring to Monticello in 1809 after two terms as president, the new University of Virginia occupied much of Jefferson's time.

5. A lover of good food and an enthusiastic cook, ice cream was introduced to America by Jefferson.

mis   MISPLACED MODIFIERS

Modifying words, phrases, or clauses should usually be placed next to or very close to the words they qualify. Words, phrases, or clauses that are placed too far away from the words they modify or that may be erroneously understood to refer to a preceding or following word are called misplaced modifiers. Although they do not generally distort a sentence's meaning, they can be confusing and should be avoided.

Editing Strategy   Move a misplaced word or phrase next to the word it modifies.

CHANGE   The guide <u>only</u> could take us to the edge of the swamp.

TO   The guide could take us <u>only</u> to the edge of the swamp.

OR   <u>Only</u> the guide could take us to the edge of the swamp.

CHANGE   Intruders broke into the laboratory and released more than 750 animals in masks and camouflage.

TO   Intruders in masks and camouflage broke into the laboratory and released more than 750 animals.

CHANGE   Many visitors have found gold coins and other pirate treasure scuba-diving in the lagoon.

TO   Many visitors scuba-diving in the lagoon have found gold coins and other pirate treasure.

EXERCISE

Rewrite these sentences, correcting the misplaced modifiers.

1.   Hull-House was the center of Jane Addams's work which she founded in 1889 in Chicago.

2.   Two of her books provide a comprehensive history of Hull-House, *Twenty Years at Hull-House* and *The Second Twenty Years at Hull-House*.

3.   During World War I in the United States, she collected food for European nations.

4.   She was the cofounder of the Woman's Peace Party and was elected its first national chairperson, with Carrie Chapman Catt.

5.   She helped the world comprehend the needs of the poor more fully.

6.   She sought reform in many different social areas with a firm commitment to principle and to her ideals.

7.   In 1931 Jane Addams was awarded for her decades of work for social betterment, civil rights, and world peace the Nobel Peace Price.

Inconsistency among Sentence Elements

agr s/v   LACK OF SUBJECT-VERB AGREEMENT

A verb must agree in number with its subject. If the subject of a sentence is singular—naming only one thing—then the verb in the predicate must be singular, too. If the subject is plural—naming two or more things—then the verb must be plural. Errors in agreement commonly occur under two circumstances: (1) when the subject is separated from its verb by several other words, especially if the subject is singular and a noun closer to the verb is plural; and (2) when the subject consists of two or more coordinated terms.

Editing Strategies

Rewrite the sentence, using a singular verb with a singular subject and with collective nouns that are regarded as units.

A Singular Subject

CHANGE   The worker in Japanese corporations are more efficient than American workers.

TO   The worker in Japanese corporations is more efficient than American workers.

Collective Nouns as Units

CHANGE   The group of children are ready.

TO   The group of children is ready.

Rewrite the sentence using a singular verb with two singular subjects that are joined by *or, either . . . or*, or *neither . . . nor*.

CHANGE   Tom or Jean need to speak with you.

TO   Tom or Jean needs to speak with you.

Rewrite the sentence using a singular verb when *either, neither*, or *each* is the subject.

CHANGE   Neither of these cars have the equipment you specified.

TO   Neither of these cars has the equipment you specified.

Rewrite the sentence, using a plural verb with a plural subject, with two or more singular subjects joined by *and*.

A Plural Subject

CHANGE   His parents was willing to take the blame for him.

TO   His parents were willing to take the blame for him.

Singular Subjects Joined by *And*

CHANGE   Tom and Jean looks great today.

TO   Tom and Jean look great today.

When a singular subject and a plural subject are joined by *or, either . . . or*, or *neither . . . nor*, rewrite the sentence using a verb that agrees in number with the subject closest to it.

CHANGE   Neither the president nor the cabinet ministers was at the meeting.

TO   Neither the president nor the cabinet ministers were at the meeting.

CHANGE   Either my parents or one of my siblings are nearly always at home.

TO   Either my parents or one of my siblings is nearly always at home.

Editing Strategy

When the subject comes after the verb, rewrite the sentence to make the subject and verb agree in number.

CHANGE   Even after so much has happened, there <u>is</u> still <u>people</u> who resist change.

TO   Even after so much has happened, there <u>are</u> still <u>people</u> who resist change.

EXERCISE

Complete each sentence by selecting the correct verb form.

1. Edward Steichen, as well as many other prominent photographers, (consider, considers) Dorothea Lange to be America's greatest documentary photographer.

2. Each of her books and magazine projects (was, were) done with the highest professional skill.

3. Neither text nor photographs (dominate, dominates) her early books.

4. Both scene and person (is, are) the subjects of her photographs.

5. From a California camp for migrant farm workers (come, comes) her most famous photograph, *Migrant Mother.*

6. Another collection of her photographs (deal, deals) with the Japanese internment during World War II.

7. Her photographs of Depression life still (has, have) a haunting power.

8. After her death in 1965, there (was, were) a special traveling exhibition of her photographs, as well as several memorials to her talent.

agr p/a   LACK OF PRONOUN-ANTECEDENT AGREEMENT

Pronouns and their antecedents must agree in three forms: in person (first, second, third), in number (singular, plural), and in gender (male, female). If the antecedent of a pronoun is singular—naming only one thing—then the pronoun must be singular. If the antecedent is plural, then the pronoun must be plural.

Editing Strategy

Rewrite the sentence, using a third-person pronoun *(one, it, he, she, he or she)* for a third-person antecedent.

CHANGE   If <u>one</u> wishes to participate in the political process, <u>you</u> can begin by voting regularly.

TO   If <u>one</u> wishes to participate in the political process, <u>one</u> can begin by voting regularly.

Or change the antecedent pronoun to a noun and rewrite the sentence.

People who wish to participate in the political process may begin by voting regularly.

Editing Strategy   Rewrite the sentence using a singular pronoun with a singular antecedent; with the antecedents *each, every,* or *neither;* and with indefinite pronouns (*everyone, anybody,* etc.).

CHANGE   This college has their own entrance requirements.

TO   This college has its own entrance requirements.

CHANGE   Each girl and boy must do their part to keep the home fires burning.

TO   Each girl and boy must do his or her part to keep the home fires burning.

CHANGE   Neither of the teams has their schedule resolved.

TO   Neither of the teams has its schedule resolved.

CHANGE   Everyone hoped to have their exams finished by Saturday.

TO   Everyone hoped to have his or her exams finished by Saturday.

OR   All the students hoped to have their exams finished by Saturday.

Editing Strategy   Use a plural pronoun for a plural antecedent.

CHANGE   Too often people either keep their feelings to themselves or take it out on others.

TO   Too often people either keep their feelings to themselves or take them out on others.

A special case of pronoun-antecedent agreement concerns the traditional use of masculine pronouns *(he, his,* or *him)* to refer to women as well as men. Many people now believe that such usage fosters stereotyping and thus discriminates against women. The pronoun *his* in the following sentence, for example, gives the impression that all attorneys are male.

A defense attorney has the responsibility of deciding whether or not his client should take the witness stand.

The stereotyping can be even more blatant, as in the next example:

Every job has its own special tools of the trade: the fireman has his hose, the judge his gavel, the accountant his calculator, and the nurse her thermometer.

The pronouns here are not used inclusively (to refer to men and women) but exclusively. They imply that certain jobs belong to men, and others belong to women. The language itself subtly suggests what is "normal" behavior for men and women.

It is a good idea to use the plural whenever possible when clearly referring to both men and women: judges have their gavels and nurses their thermometers. Otherwise, contemporary writers generally use phrases that include both masculine and feminine pronouns: *he or she, his or her, him or her.*

Editing Strategy

When referring to antecedents that clearly include both men and women, revise sentences to use both male and female pronouns or make the actual antecedents plural. In doing so, be careful that singular antecedents agree with singular pronouns.

CHANGE   Anyone arriving late for the concert was told to take <u>his</u> (or <u>their</u>) seat in the last two rows.

TO   Anyone arriving late for the concert was told to take <u>his or her</u> seat in the last two rows.

·OR   People arriving late for the concert were told to take <u>their</u> seats in the last two rows.

EXERCISE

Choose the correct pronoun in each of the following sentences.

1. Losing slaves from escapes north was a problem a slaveholder dreaded, and (he or she, they) would do almost anything to prevent (it, them).

2. Not every slave had the courage to find (their, his or her) way north along Harriet Tubman's Underground Railway.

3. Each of Tubman's fugitive slaves was grateful to be in (their, his or her) new northern home.

4. Neither New Yorkers nor Canadians disappointed Tubman in (his or her, their) support of the Underground Railway.

5. The government of Canada helped abolitionists in every way (they, it) could.

6. The Underground Railway seldom operated in an organized manner; it involved individuals working mostly on (their, his or her) own.

7. A citizen south of the Mason-Dixon line who aided the Underground Railway put (him or herself, themselves) in danger of prosecution.

8. Either a haystack or an attic could offer (its, their) protection to a fugitive slave.

9. A person like Harriet Tubman risked everything (they, he or she) had in the effort to free slaves.

10. One who wishes to learn more about the Underground Railway might check (your, their, his or her) library for a biography of Harriet Tubman.

vt

INCONSISTENCIES IN VERB TENSE

The English-language verb system lets us express many different times (tenses) of actions: past, present, future, continuing, completed, completed in the future, repeated in the past or present, just about to begin, and even future without the past. But problems arise when writers shift from one tense to another unnecessarily.

Verb tenses should not shift unnecessarily from sentence to sentence or within any one sentence.

Editing Strategy

Within a group of sentences, rewrite the main verbs in the same tense unless there is some reason for a shift.

CHANGE   The air conditioning hit them like a wall. Everybody's bone marrow congealed. It <u>makes</u> you feel like your teeth <u>are</u> loose.

TO   The air conditioning hit them like a wall. Everybody's bone marrow congealed. It made you feel like your teeth were loose.   –Tom Wolfe

CHANGE   As Dinah Washington was leaving with some friends, I overheard someone say she <u>is</u> on her way to the Savoy Ballroom where Lionel Hampton was appearing that night—she was then Hamp's vocalist.

TO   As Dinah Washington was leaving with some friends, I overheard someone say she was on her way to the Savoy Ballroom where Lionel Hampton was appearing that night—she was then Hamp's vocalist.   –Malcolm X

Another problem involving inconsistency in verb tense occurs in sentences that describe two actions that occurred at different times in the past. In general, the past perfect tense is used for the earlier of the two past actions.

Editing Strategy

Shift the verb referring to the earlier of the two actions from the past tense to the past perfect tense.

CHANGE   The researchers admitted that they <u>falsified</u> crucial data in the study.

TO   The researchers admitted that they <u>had falsified</u> crucial data in the study.

EXERCISE

Rewrite any of the following sentences in which there are unnecessary shifts in verb tense.

1.   Marian Anderson sang in her church choir from the age of six. She learned all four parts of hymns to fill in for absent singers. She was singing solos from the age of ten.

2.   Gertrude Stein's apartment in Paris became a magnet for artists. She was a great art collector and surrounded herself with works by contemporary artists, so visitors can see paintings by Picasso and Matisse on her walls.

3.   Pearl S. Buck, one of the most popular of all American novelists, was awarded a Nobel Prize in 1938, seven years after she won the Pulitzer Prize.

4.   In October 1916 Margaret Sanger opened the first birth control clinic in the United States. Sanger was regarded as a savior by the many women

who awaited the opening, but within twelve days she would be arrested. Later, when she was sent to jail, she went on a hunger strike.

5. If Amelia Earhart had not been lost at sea over the Pacific in 1937, she would be the first woman to fly around the world.

6. The 1932 Olympic Games made "Babe" Didrikson Zaharias a national figure. She was to set the world record in the javelin. She won the eighty-meter hurdle race, and she beat the world record in the high jump.

7. By the time she directed her final movie in 1940, Dorothy Arzner became one of the most successful women in Hollywood.

adj/adv   CONFUSION OF ADJECTIVE AND ADVERB

It is important to remember that adjectives and adverbs serve different grammatical functions and should not be used interchangeably. Adjectives modify nouns and pronouns, while adverbs modify verbs, adjectives, and other adverbs. One particularly common error to avoid is the use of an adverb as a subject complement after a sensory verb or the verb *be*. (See A Brief Review of Sentence Structure earlier in this Handbook for more detailed discussion of adjectives, adverbs, and subject complements.)

Editing Strategy   Change adjectives that modify verbs, adjectives, or other adverbs to their adverb form.

CHANGE   My mother and father, for their part, responded <u>different</u>, as their children spoke to them less.

TO   My mother and father, for their part, responded <u>differently</u>, as their children spoke to them less. –Richard Rodriguez

CHANGE   In my childhood days, a great deal of stock was put, in general, on the value of doing <u>good</u> in school.

TO   In my childhood days, a great deal of stock was put, in general, on the value of doing <u>well</u> in school. –Eudora Welty

Editing Strategy   Change adverbs that are subject complements modifying nouns to their adjective forms.

CHANGE   No matter what they say, most athletes feel <u>terribly</u> after losing a competition.

TO   No matter what they say, most athletes feel <u>terrible</u> after losing a competition.

CHANGE   My first loaf of bread smelled <u>wonderfully</u> as it was baking, but it looked <u>strangely</u> when it came out of the oven. It tasted <u>well</u>, however.

TO   My first loaf of bread smelled <u>wonderful</u> as it was baking, but it looked <u>strange</u> when it came out of the oven. It tasted <u>good</u>, however.

EXERCISE

In the following sentences, correct any faulty use of adjective or adverb.

1. One of America's foremost playwrights, Tennessee Williams has been praised most high for his portrayals of passion and delusion.

2. Among his greatest talents was his ability to make audiences feel sympathetically toward vain, self-centered characters.

3. His most famous creation, Blanche DuBois in *A Streetcar Named Desire*, is a particular good example.

4. She behaves manipulative and neurotic, but audiences admire her for both her strength and her sensitivity.

5. Although critics did not respond favorable to Williams's later plays, his reputation in the world theater is secure.

6. When performed well, his plays have the power to make us understand human nature fuller and more compassionate.

para   FAULTY PARALLELISM

Grammatical parallelism is a very important principle of usage and style. This sentence illustrates the principle:

It is this loftiness of sentiment, this purity, this dignity and self control, which make Scott's farewell letters—found under his body—such moving documents.

–Annie Dillard

The grammatical similarity of the three *this* phrases gives a strong signal to the reader that the phrases in this series are equally important, similar in meaning, and related in the same way to the rest of the sentence.

Thus, sentence elements that make up a series should be parallel in grammatical form (that is, each should be, for example, a noun phrase, a prepositional phrase, a subordinate clause, etc.).

Editing Strategy   Rewrite the sentence so that the items in the series have the same grammatical form.

CHANGE   Some of the less dangerous side effects of the drug are indigestion, mild headaches, and the hands may occasionally tremble.

TO   Some of the less dangerous side effects of the drug are indigestion, mild headaches, and occasional trembling of hands.

CHANGE   Despite all the evidence, experts continue to debate whether global warming exists, the extent of the problem, what the likely effects will be, and whether any remedy is possible.

TO   Despite all the evidence, experts continue to debate the existence of global warming, the extent of the problem, its likely effects, and the possibility of any remedy.

OR   Despite all the evidence, experts continue to debate whether global warming exists, how extensive the problem is, what the likely effects will be, and whether any remedy is possible.

EXERCISE

Rewrite these sentences to make the related items in the series parallel.

1.   Susan B. Anthony was born in 1820, raised in a Quaker family, and with training as a teacher.

2.   Traveling and with lectures, Susan B. Anthony spread the word about women's suffrage.

3.   She was instrumental in securing women's rights over their children, their property, and being able to keep their wages.

4.   In 1871 she traveled 13,000 miles and was to give 171 lectures.

5.   Anthony believed that slaves should be free, that drinking should be illegal, and in women having the right to vote.

6.   With determination, energy, and speaking eloquently, Anthony laid the groundwork for the Nineteenth Amendment, which gave American women the right to vote.

7.   In addition to organizing the Women's Loyal League, she was president of the National American Woman Suffrage Association, and *The History of Woman Suffrage* was compiled with her help.

Troublesome Word Forms

vf

LIST OF STANDARD VERB FORMS

The past and past participle for most verbs in English are formed by the simple addition of *-ed (walked, pretended, unveiled)*. However, a number of verbs have irregular forms, most of which are different for past and past participle. In particular, be careful to use the correct past participle form of irregular verbs. (For information about the uses of these forms, see the discussion of verbs in the section reviewing sentence structure and basic sentence elements.)

Listed here are the principal parts for fifty-one commonly troublesome irregular verbs. Check your dictionary for a more complete listing.

Present Tense	Past Tense	Past Participle
am, is, are	was, were	been
beat	beat	beaten
begin	began	begun
bite	bit	bitten
blow	blew	blown
break	broke	broken
bring	brought	brought
burst	burst	burst
choose	chose	chosen
come	came	come
deal	dealt	dealt
do	did	done
draw	drew	drawn
drink	drank	drunk
eat	ate	eaten
fall	fell	fallen
fly	flew	flown
freeze	froze	frozen
get	got	gotten
give	gave	given
go	went	gone
grow	grew	grown
have	had	had
know	knew	known
lay	laid	laid
lead	led	led
lie	lay	lain
lose	lost	lost
ride	rode	ridden
ring	rang	rung
rise	rose	risen
run	ran	run
say	said	said
see	saw	seen
set	set	set
shake	shook	shaken
sit	sat	sat
slink	slunk	slunk
speak	spoke	spoken
spring	sprang (sprung)	sprung
steal	stole	stolen
swear	swore	sworn
swell	swelled	swollen (swelled)

Present Tense	Past Tense	Past Participle
swim	swam	swum
take	took	taken
teach	taught	taught
tear	tore	torn
throw	threw	thrown
wear	wore	worn
win	won	won
write	wrote	written

WW   GLOSSARY OF FREQUENTLY MISUSED WORDS

A word or phrase may be wrong in many different ways. It might be wrong in form—*emigrant* used to mean *immigrant,* for example. It might be imprecise—*eager* used to mean *anxious.* It might be pronounced the same as the correct word (a homophone) and, consequently, easily confused—*principle* for *principal, council* for *counsel;* indeed, the incorrect use of many words in written work results from the fact that a mistaken usage sounds correct when spoken. It is also important to remember that some usages that have become common in informal situations and in advertising—such as the loss of a distinction between the words *less* and *fewer*—are still considered unacceptable in more formal writing situations.

In addition, problems can arise with idiomatic phrases, common everyday expressions that may or may not fit any rules. Many idioms are combinations of verbs and prepositions—*write down, write in, write off, write up* are just four examples using the verb *write.*

Finally, a word may be seen as used incorrectly because it does not precisely suit the context of the sentence. Such problems often arise from a misunderstanding on the part of the writer of a word's *connotative* meaning, those associations that it has in addition to its literal (or *denotative*) meaning. For example, while the adjectives *illegal, illicit, unauthorized, wrongful,* and *felonious* all have similar denotations ("not allowed," "against the law"), they cannot be used interchangeably. The connotations surrounding *unauthorized* are much less negative than those surrounding *felonious; illicit* implies an offensiveness or immorality that goes beyond what may be simply *illegal.* Be careful, particularly when using a thesaurus, that the word you choose is generally used to express exactly the meaning you have in mind.

Experts don't always agree regarding whether a particular usage is or is not acceptable; this is especially true of usages that have traditionally been viewed as nonstandard, but that have recently come into fairly wide use. This glossary steers away from such popular usages when they result in imprecision.

When editing for troublesome words, such as those that follow, it is a good idea to be aware of those you are likely to have difficulty with and watch carefully for them. Check this glossary or a dictionary whenever you are unsure of the meaning or spelling of a particular word.

accept/except *Accept* is a verb ("receive with favor"). *Except* may be a verb ("leave out") but is more commonly used as a preposition ("excluding"). Other forms: acceptance, acceptable; exception.

None of the composition instructors will <u>accept</u> late papers, <u>except</u> Mr. Siu.

Her <u>acceptance</u> of the bribe <u>excepts</u> her from consideration for the position.

adapt/adopt *Adapt* means "adjust in order to be more suitable." *Adopt* means "take on or in as one's own." Other forms: adaptable, adaptation; adoption.

To <u>adopt</u> a handicapped child, parents must be willing to <u>adapt</u> themselves to the child's needs.

advice/advise *Advice* is a noun; *advise* is a verb. Other forms: advisable, advisor.

Everyone <u>advised</u> him to heed the expert's <u>advice.</u>

affect/effect *Affect* is commonly used as a verb, most often meaning "influence"; in psychology, the noun *affect* is a technical term dealing with emotional states. *Effect* is generally a noun ("result or consequences"); it is only occasionally used as a verb ("bring about"), although the adjective form (effective) is common.

Researchers are studying the <u>effect</u> of stress.

How does stress <u>affect</u> the human body?

all right *All right* is generally the preferred spelling, rather than *alright*.

a lot A common expression meaning "a large number," *a lot* is always written as two words. Because of its vagueness and informality, it should be avoided altogether in college writing.

among/between *Among* is correct when the reference is to more than two objects; *between* should generally be limited to references to only two objects (although exceptions are sometimes made if the result of using *among* seems overly awkward).

It is hard to choose one winner <u>among</u> so many highly qualified candidates for the scholarship.

<u>Between</u> the two extreme positions lies a vast middle ground.

amount/number *Amount* refers to quantity of a unit ("amount of water," "amount of discussion"), while *number* refers to quantity of individual items ("number of papers," "number of times"). In general, use *amount* only before a singular noun.

anxious/eager   *Anxious* means "nervous" or "worried"; *eager* means "looking forward to [impatiently]." Avoid using *anxious* to mean *eager* in college writing.

The students were <u>eager</u> to learn their grades.

They were <u>anxious</u> for fear they wouldn't pass.

between/among   See **among/between.**

capital/capitol   *Capital* is the more common word and can have a variety of meanings; *capitol* refers only to a government building.

cite/sight/site   *Cite* as a verb means "refer to as proof" or "summon to appear in court." *Site* is a noun meaning "place or location." *Sight* may be a verb or a noun, always with reference to seeing or what is seen ("a sight for sore eyes").

Can you <u>cite</u> your sources for these figures?

A new dormitory will be built at this <u>site.</u>

When she <u>sighted</u> the speeding car, the officer <u>cited</u> the driver for recklessness.

complement/compliment   *Complement* refers to completion or the making of a satisfactory whole, while *compliment* indicates admiration or praise; both can be used as either nouns or verbs. *Complementary* means "serving to complete"; *complimentary* means "given free."

The dean <u>complimented</u> the school's recruiters on the full <u>complement</u> of students registered for the fall.

The designer received many <u>compliments</u> regarding the way the elements of the room <u>complemented</u> one another.

Buy a new refrigerator and receive a <u>complimentary</u> ice maker in a <u>complementary</u> color.

council/counsel   *Council* is a noun ("an assembly of people who deliberate or govern"). *Counsel* is a verb meaning "advise" or a noun meaning "advice." Other forms: councilor ("member of a council"); counselor ("one who gives advice").

The <u>council</u> on drug abuse has issued guidelines for <u>counseling</u> troubled students.

Before voting on the important fiscal issue, City <u>Councilor</u> Lopez sought the <u>counsel</u> of her constituents.

desert/dessert   As a noun or adjective, *desert* (dez'ərt) means "a dry, uncultivated region"; as a verb, *desert* (di·zurt') means "abandon." A *dessert* is a sweet dish served at the end of a meal.

The hunters were alone in the arid <u>desert, deserted</u> by their guides.

After a heavy meal, sherbet is the perfect <u>dessert.</u>

emigrant/immigrant　An *emigrant* moves out of a country; an *immigrant* moves into a country. Other forms: emigrate, emigration, emigré; immigrate, immigration.

Congress passed a bill to deal with illegal immigrants living in the United States.

Members of her family emigrated from Cuba to Miami, and Madrid.

enormity　Although often used incorrectly, *enormity* refers strictly to outrageous evil ("The *enormity* of Hitler's policies appalled the civilized world"). When referring to greatness of size, the better choice of word is *vastness* or *immensity* or *enormousness.*

etc.　An abbreviation of the Latin words *et cetera* ("and other things"), *etc.* should never be preceded by *and* in English. Also be careful to spell the abbreviation correctly (*not* "ect."). In general, *etc.* should be used very sparingly, if at all, in college writing.

except　See **accept/except.**

fewer/less　See **less/fewer.**

fortuitous/fortunate　Often used incorrectly, the adjective *fortuitous* means "by chance" or "unplanned" and should not be confused with *fortunate* ("lucky").

Josh and his ex-wife wished to avoid each other, so their fortuitous meeting in the parking lot was not a fortunate event for either.

himself/themselves　In nonstandard speech, "hisself" is sometimes used for *himself* and "theirselves" for *themselves,* but such usage is not acceptable in written work.

hopefully　In conversation, *hopefully* is often used as a convenient shorthand to suggest that some outcome is generally to be hoped for ("Hopefully, our nominee will win the election"); this usage, however, is not acceptable in most written work. Better substitutes include *I hope, let's hope, everyone hopes,* and *it is to be hoped that,* depending on one's meaning. The adverb *hopefully* ("full of hope") should always modify a specific verb or adverb.

I hope my brother will win the election.

We should all hope his brother will win the election.

Her sister is hopeful that she will win the election.

The candidate inquired hopefully about the results.

immigrant　See **emigrant/immigrant.**

its/it's　*Its* is a possessive pronoun; *it's* is the contraction for *it is.*

This job has its advantages.

When it's well grilled, there's nothing like a steak.

less/fewer *Less* should generally be used only before a singular noun ("less time," "less fat"); *fewer* is correct before a plural noun ("fewer minutes," "fewer calories"). In some popular writing, particularly in advertising, *less* is sometimes used incorrectly before plural nouns; but this use is avoided by more thoughtful writers.

lie/lay The verb *lie* ("recline") is intransitive; the verb *lay* ("put or place") is transitive. The past tense of *lie* is *lay*, and the past participle is *lain*. For *lay*, the past tense and the past participle forms are both *laid*. The most common error here is the incorrect use of *laid* as the past tense of *lie*. Other forms: lying, laying.

The lion lie in wait for the approach of its prey.

We expect the president to lay down the law on this matter.

Joseph laid down his shovel, took a shower, and lay down for a nap.

literally *Literally* means "exactly as stated, actually" and is often used to suggest that a cliché has in fact come true. However, to say, for example, "The movie made my hair literally stand on end," is to misuse the word (although a person who suffered a fatal heart attack brought on by a fearful shock might correctly be said to have *literally* died of fright).

loose/lose *Lose* is a verb ("mislay or fail to maintain"), while *loose* is most often used as an adjective ("not fastened tightly").

A loose button may make one lose one's pants.

of/have In standard speech "could have" and "would have" sound very much like "could of" and "would of"; however, the substitution of *of* for *have* in this construction is incorrect and should not be used in written work. The same holds true for "might of," "must of," "should of," "will of."

persecute/prosecute *Persecute* means "mistreat or oppress"; *prosecute* most often means "bring a legal suit or action against."

Minority groups in a community can easily be persecuted by the majority.

Only those who are accused of a crime can be prosecuted.

prejudice/prejudiced *Prejudice* is a noun or a verb. When used adjectivally, it should take the form of the past tense of the verb: *prejudiced*.

We should fight prejudice wherever we find it.

He was prejudiced against the candidate because of her dialect.

principal/principle *Principal* implies "first in rank, chief," whether it is used as an adjective ("the *principal* cities of the Midwest") or a noun ("the principal of a Midwestern high school"). *Principle* is generally a noun meaning "a basic law or truth."

In principle you are correct.

The principle of free speech will be the principal topic of discussion.

right/rite   *Right* has a number of meanings ("not left," "correct," "a justified claim"); *rite* means only "a solemn ritual." Although *rite* is sometimes substituted for *right* in very informal writing or advertising copy, this is not acceptable in college or other more formal writing situations.

sensual/sensuous   Both *sensual* and *sensuous* suggest the enjoyment of physical pleasure through the senses. However, *sensual* generally implies self-indulgence, particularly in terms of sexual activity; *sensuous* has a more positive meaning and suggests the ability to appreciate intellectually what is received through the senses. Other forms: sensuality; sensuousness.

When drunk, the emperor gave himself up to brutal sensuality.

Anyone can enjoy the sensuousness of a warm spring night.

set/sit   The difference between the verbs *sit* and *set* is similar to that between *lie* and *lay: sit* is generally intransitive ("rest on one's buttocks"), while *set* is transitive ("put [something] in a certain place"). *Set* also has a number of uses as a noun. The past tense and past participle forms of *sit* are both *sat;* these forms for *set* are both *set.*

He would rather sit than stand, and rather lie than sit.

He set his suitcase on the ground and then sat on it.

sight/site   See **cite/sight/site.**

stationary/stationery   *Stationary* is an adjective meaning "fixed, remaining in one place" ("Concrete will make the pole stationary"). *Stationery* refers to writing paper; one way to keep in mind the distinction is to associate the *-er* in *paper* with that in *stationery.*

that/which   When used as a subordinate conjunction, *that* always introduces a restrictive clause; *which* is generally used for nonrestrictive clauses. Although the use of *which* before a restrictive clause is not incorrect, *that* is generally preferred in order to clarify that the clause is restrictive. (See the discussion of restrictive and nonrestrictive clauses in the review of sentence structure and sentence elements on p. 670.)

Her first bid for the Senate was the only election that she ever lost.

Her first bid for the Senate, which was unsuccessful, brought her to prominence.

The Senate election that resulted in her defeat took place in 1968.

themselves   See **himself/themselves.**

to/too/two   *To* is a preposition; *too* is an adverb; and *two* is generally an adjective. The most common error here is the substitution of *to* for *too.*

It is too early to predict either of the two scores.

weather/whether   *Weather* is a noun ("atmospheric conditions"); *whether* is a conjunction.

The <u>weather</u> forecast indicates <u>whether</u> there will be sun or rain.

which   See **that/which.**

who's/whose   *Who's* is the contraction of *who is* or *who has; whose* is a possessive pronoun.

<u>Who's</u> up next?

She's the only student <u>who's</u> done her work correctly.

<u>Whose</u> work is this?

The man <u>whose</u> job I took has retired.

unique   To be precise, *unique* means "one of a kind, like no other." As such, careful writers do not use it loosely to mean simply "unusual or rare." Nor can it correctly take a comparative form *(most unique)*, although advertisers often use it this way.

The quality of compassion is not <u>unique,</u> although today it is increasingly rare.

This example of Mayan sculpture is apparently <u>unique;</u> none other like it has so far been discovered.

used to   In colloquial speech, *used to* is often sounded as "use to." However, *used to* is the correct form for written work.

My grandfather <u>used to</u> be a Dodgers fan until the team moved to Los Angeles.

READABILITY

CONCISENESS

APPROPRIATENESS

Editing for Problems of Style

We commonly think of proper usage as a requirement of good writing, but consider style to be mere decoration, a frill to make writing pretty or give it personality. Style, however, is as essential as usage—how well you communicate depends on both elements. The way you say something tells as much as what you say. Your words and the order you put them in not only decorate your meaning, but help create it.

What makes a style pleasing? Clarity and readability. A readable style is understandable, but it need not be simple or artless. You can call attention to your writing style, or you may choose to make your style transparent, hardly noticeable. Whether your writing style takes center stage or just serves to get your point across, it should be clear and readable.

A good writing style must also be concise, not wordy. This does not mean that your sentences should be short or your words no longer than two syllables. It means only that you should be careful to make every word count.

In addition, your writing style should be appropriate to the subject, the occasion, and the intended audience. For college writing, this most often involves carefully choosing suitable words and phrases to reflect a thoughtful respect for the work at hand, a reasonable presentation, and a high level of intellectual involvement.

Finally, a good writing style ought to be both vigorous and pleasing. Without vigor, writing can become impersonal and dull. A vigorous style embodies the natural rhythms of speech and employs active verbs and varied sentence structure. It is graceful, not stilted, emphatic, not monotonous. Moreover, writing should be fun to write and enjoyable to read. The writer who reaches for the memorable turn of phrase, who strives for humor or even elegance, knows that good writing can be aesthetically satisfying.

Good style is not simply a means of communicating. It is an art. As such, it cannot be taught through the study of rules. Writers develop a style by caring about the way they express themselves, by paying attention to the style of other writers, and by being willing to experiment with different possibilities for putting a thought into words.

Even so, there are a number of common stylistic problems that all writers need to become aware of and avoid. This section focuses on several of them: problems arising from pointless repetition; from the unthinking use of hackneyed words and phrases; from over-reliance on nouns, prepositional phrases, and *be* verbs; from failure to hear as well as see the patterns in your own style of writing. Many of the problems discussed here are interrelated—writing cluttered with nouns, for example, often includes strings of prepositional phrases and uses empty, inactive verbs. Resolving stylistic problems, therefore, can require recasting whole sentences, rethinking whole paragraphs, even overhauling a whole essay.

Readability

| prep | STRINGS OF PREPOSITIONAL PHRASES

Prepositional phrases indicate possession and location in time and space. Used well, they give writing good balance and clear emphasis. Consider, for example, the ringing phrases that conclude Lincoln's Gettysburg Address:

. . . and that government of the people, by the people, and for the people, shall not perish from the earth.

Too many prepositional phrases, however, can weigh down your prose. Writing dominated by strings of prepositional phrases tends to be wordy and monotonous, each sentence following the same da-da-dum rhythm. Look, for instance, at the following sentence:

In the absence of adequate and urgently needed research into the degree of actual prevalence of emotional illness in urban communities, one can do little more than speculate.

The string of prepositional phrases in this sentence makes it hard to read. By eliminating some of the prepositional phrases, we can substantially reduce the number of words and make the meaning clearer. The sentence could easily be reduced from twenty-eight words with six prepositional phrases to seventeen words with three prepositional phrases:

Without researching the rate of emotional illness in urban communities, one can do little more than speculate.

A simple way to monitor prepositional phrases in your writing is to circle all the prepositions. If you are stringing prepositional phrases together, you will probably find that eliminating some of the phrases will only improve your prose.

EXERCISE

Each of the following sentences contains far too many prepositional phrases. Revise them as necessary to improve the balance and sharpen the emphasis of the writing.

1.   There are still obstacles in the path of the achievement of an agreement on the control of nuclear weapons.

2.   All the water on the surface and water under the ground comes from the atmosphere in the form of rain, snow, or dew by means of the condensation of water vapor.

3.   The condensation of water vapor occurs when the temperature of air with a certain amount of water content falls to the critical degree known as the "dew point."

4.   The increase of smog in the air is attributed to the buildup of factories in areas of greatest contamination.

5.   Although the sexual revolution has resulted primarily in a change in the behavior of the female, neither the attitudes nor the behavior of the females has yet reached the level of liberality of the male in the samples studied.

6.   Historical surveys of members of the medical profession in the practice of working on a regular basis with patients afflicted with tuberculosis have shown no correlation between treatment methods and risk of personal infection.

7.   The potential for profit in the development of genetically engineered forms of plants for the purpose of increases in the size and in the yield of agricultural crops is great.

be

OVERUSE OF *BE*

The most common verb in the English language is the linking verb *be*. (See A Brief Review of Sentence Structure for further information on the use of linking verbs.) Its forms include *am, is, are, was, were, being, been. Be* is called a linking verb because it acts as an equal sign, connecting the subject with the predicate. As a verb, then, *be* actually carries little weight since it does not demonstrate an active relationship between the subject and the predicate. Consequently, writing dominated by *be* verbs is generally quite static. Consider this example:

A common characteristic of developing countries is an inadequate supply of food. Inadequate food supply is the leading cause of malnutrition. Malnutrition is the condition in which the immune system is weakened and resistance to disease is lowered. There are over 500 million children in developing countries who are malnourished. As a result, one in seven is dead before the age of five. Due to this high rate of infant mortality, in some societies naming of children is a ceremony that is not performed until the child has survived for some specified period of time.

Every sentence in this passage relies on a *be* verb. The next example shows how that passage might be rewritten with more active verbs:

Developing countries characteristically <u>lack</u> adequate food supplies. This inadequacy <u>causes</u> malnutrition, which <u>weakens</u> the immune system and <u>lowers</u> resistance to disease. Over 500 million children in developing countries <u>suffer</u> from malnutrition. As a result, one in seven <u>dies</u> before the age of five. Due to this high rate of infant mortality, some societies <u>postpone</u> naming children until the child has survived for some specified period.

Strengthening the verbs adds vigor to the writing, but it also does a good deal more. It reduces wordiness (in this case by about one third, from ninety-five words in the first version to sixty-five in the second) and it enhances clarity. Greater clarity results primarily from placing the action where it belongs—in the verb—instead of burying it in the subject.

Check your own writing—are you using too many *be* verbs? In your next essay, try circling them all. If you find them in every sentence, if your writing seems static, or if the action of each sentence is fuzzy rather than sharp, try finding other verbs that will better carry the action.

EXERCISE

Rewrite one of these passages to replace *be* verbs with more active verbs.

1.   The important point is that the warning lights were flashing early. By 1964, the first major investigation of the Concorde Supersonic aircraft was finished. The report was highly critical. The project was double its estimated cost and noise was already becoming a nagging problem. Worldwide protests were taking place and airports were looking closely at landing privileges.

2.   Totem poles are not religious artifacts. Although they are not used for worship, they are an important part of tribal life. They are historical records and monuments of honor. The poles are carved with pictures showing actual events and mythological legends. Many are made to honor a dead chief or other community personages. Mortuary posts are hollow and contain cremated remains. In Ketchikan, Alaska, there is a totem pole with a carving of Abraham Lincoln on top. He is wearing a frock coat and tall top hat. It is a tribute to Lincoln's freeing the slaves, including Indian slaves.

3.   The potato was not very popular in Europe as a whole until the nineteenth century. It was locally successful, however, at earlier dates. It was established in Ireland by the eighteenth century and was the almost exclusive diet of peasants. It was grown in England also, but for a long time it was mostly exported rather than being grown for home consumption. France was particularly backward as far as the potato was concerned; it continued to be disliked there until much later than in other countries.

4.   No one can predict how radically the personal computer is going to affect workers in the coming decades. Microcomputers are already in use by employees in homes and offices everywhere. Many who were fearful that com-

puters would be likely to eliminate jobs are now coming to realize that they were wrong and that computers are a tool that will be changing the face of the workplace for the better.

| nom |

OVERNOMINALIZATION

When action is repeatedly expressed in nouns instead of in verbs, writing becomes both stilted and wordy. Moreover, burying the action in nouns may obscure the action and who is performing it. For example:

The expectation of faculty opposition to the proposed tuition increase is high.

Here, the subject *expectation* embodies the action. But the actor is hidden: when you change the verb to *expects,* you discover that there is no clear subject: who expects? To make clear who exactly expects opposition to the proposed increase in tuition, you need to add information to the sentence:

Many administrators expect the faculty to oppose the proposed tuition increase.

Many students expect the faculty to oppose the proposed tuition increase.

Sentences beginning with *there is* and *there are* also tend to express action in nouns instead of in verbs. The *there is* and *there are* constructions are called expletives, or dummy subjects, because they stand in for the actual subject of the sentence. Consider this example:

There is resistance among students to the proposed increase in tuition.

The actual subject of this sentence is *students* and the actual action is hidden in the noun *resistance.* See how eliminating the expletives makes the sentence more direct and less wordy:

Students are resisting the proposed increase in tuition.

Overnominalization does not occur only with *be* verbs. Other weak verbs— *exist, occur,* and *have,* for instance—are often used to link one noun with another, thus hiding the real action of the sentence:

The need for an immediate solution to the problem exists.

The real action here is expressed in the noun *need,* and we see no obvious subject. To revise this sentence, we must add an appropriate subject:

We need to solve this problem immediately.

Overnominalization is a common problem in English and merits special attention. Check your writing by examining each sentence to identify what action is taking place and who is performing that action. If the action or subject is not clear, revise the sentence.

EXERCISE

Revise the following sentences as necessary to make the action and subject clear.

1. A thorough investigation of the problem is necessary before a solution can be found.

2. Students have no expectation that the faculty will get the administration to withdraw its proposal.

3. There is a pressing need for a re-examination of society's commitment to education.

4. The completion of the report has not yet occurred.

5. There was widespread disagreement among faculty over the report.

6. Parents of students at the college will be given notification of the proposal to increase tuition.

7. The university president would offer no explanation for the decision to postpone the tuition increase.

8. Students believe the decision to postpone the tuition increase was due to the fact that student discontent over the proposal was communicated to the president.

9. There are many on campus who would make a prediction that the funding for new dormitories will come from other sources.

10. The acquisition of contributions from business and industry will probably be the solution to this administration's funding problem.

**comp
noun**

COMPOUND-NOUN PHRASES

In a compound-noun phrase, nouns are used to modify other nouns. *Television program, faculty committee,* and *drunk-driving violation* are compound-noun phrases we use every day. They are economical in that they eliminate unnecessary prepositional phrases (program on television, committee of faculty, violation for drunk driving). But nouns strung together in this way often obscure the subject-verb relationship, making it hard to tell who is doing what in the sentence. In some cases, deciphering the compound-noun phrase takes more time and effort than reading countless prepositional phrases. Writing that requires word-by-word analysis is not likely to hold the attention of its readers. Consider one example:

Detroit assembly-line robotics utilization programs have been shown to impact negatively on the automobile industry employment opportunity picture.

Look at the first noun phrase: *Detroit assembly-line robotics utilization programs.* To decipher this phrase, we must break it into smaller units. *Detroit assembly-line* refers to Detroit's assembly lines. *Assembly-line robotics* means robotics on the assembly lines. So far we have *robotics on Detroit's assembly lines. Utilization programs* are probably plans for using the robotics. The resulting translation is, *Programs for utilizing robotics on Detroit's assembly lines.* We have spent almost five minutes so far—and made only a dent in the sentence. Given the option, many readers would read no further.

Compound-noun phrases are found most frequently in the writing of specialists. Nouns used in this way tend to become part of an official jargon, and no one in the field thinks twice about using them—and then using them together with other compound-noun phrases. The result: *Detroit assembly-line robotics utilization programs.* In most writing situations you will want to avoid compound-noun phrases.

EXERCISE
Rewrite each sentence to eliminate the compound-noun phrases.

1. Investor losses were attributed to stock-market-fluctuation prediction failure.

2. Consumer discontent led to product-safety reevaluation.

3. The network conducted a poll for candidate-voter appeal measurement.

4. Quality peer-verbal interaction produced measured intelligence gains in preschool children.

5. Registration delays resulted from data-processing malfunction.

6. Pentagon counterinsurgency-weapons-infiltration programs decontrol factors requisite to passification maintenance.

7. Tobacco fumigant inhalation is implicated in the occurrence of disorganized cell reproduction pathology.

8. The program objective is increased labor-market participation rates.

pass   OVERUSE OF THE PASSIVE VOICE

A passive construction is formed by combining the verb *be* or *get* with the past participle of another verb: *The project was designed by Jones and her associates.* Writers often use passive sentences when they desire anonymity or when they believe the action is more important than the actor. Many passive constructions do not even identify the agent performing the action. Thus, the passive predominates in scientific research reports in which the agent is assumed to be the experimenter, and repeatedly naming him or her would be redundant. For example:

Plants were grown in a greenhouse equipped with evaporative coolers with activated carbon filters for a filtered air supply. Full strength Hoagland's solution was applied weekly at the rate of 100 ml/pot. After six weeks, 40 uniform plants were randomly divided into four groups. The groups were designated I (50 mpphm/1h), II (50mpphm/2h), III (50mpphm/3h), and IV (ambients).

Some writers use passives to give a false impression of scientific objectivity or to hide the actor's identity and thereby avoid responsibility for the action. Because of the verbal smoke screen that passives construct, they are popular within impersonal institutions and large bureaucracies and those who seek to defend the indefensible:

Action to clean up toxic waste sites was not taken.

It has not been decided whether the most recently hired will be fired before other people.

It has been repeatedly shown that a stable community can be torn apart by the introduction of foreign elements. Threats have been issued, windows have been broken, bombs have been exploded, and other actions have been undertaken that are seen to pose a significant threat to the well-being of the citizenry. The best solution, therefore, is that communities be maintained according to the wishes of the majority.

In addition to fostering obscurity rather than clarity, passive constructions reverse the natural subject-verb order of English sentences, and when used excessively, make writing sluggish and difficult to read:

Last year it was recommended by the student government that a board of review be created so that students would be given a greater voice in campus governance. The proposal was accepted by the faculty, the president, and the board of trustees. A nine-member board of review was authorized, to be elected by students and faculty. College policies are reviewed by the board and, if they are determined to be inconsistent with the basic purpose of the college, must be revised unless the board's decision is vetoed by the president.

Revised to change passive verbs to active, this passage is far more vigorous and readable:

Last year the student government recommended that the school create a board of review to give students a greater voice in student governance. The faculty, the president, and the board of trustees accepted the proposal and authorized a nine-member board of review, elected by faculty and students. The board reviews college policies to determine whether any are inconsistent with the basic purpose of the college. The college must revise any policy the board recommends, unless the president vetoes the board's decision.

Rely on passives only when you must report information impersonally or when you do not want your readers to know who is responsible for an action. Otherwise, avoid the passive voice.

EXERCISE

Revise the following sentences to eliminate awkward or unnecessary passive constructions.

1.   Agreement can best be achieved if decisions are made by voice vote rather than by secret ballot.

2.   Awards are to be presented by the committee when its next meeting is held on Thursday.

3.   It is requested that all books be returned to the shelves from which they were taken and that all materials be removed from carrels by 9:30.

4.   Trouble is caused when people disobey rules that have been established for the safety of all.

5.   A campus rally was attended by more than a thousand students. Five students were arrested by campus police for disorderly conduct, while several others were charged by campus administrators with organizing a public meeting without being issued a permit to do so.

6.   The subjects that are considered most important by students are those that have been shown to be useful to them after graduation.

7.   Dr. Young has been criticized by a few patients who feel that they have not been adequately cared for, but he has been strongly defended by other patients who see the charges as having been motivated by personality conflicts.

8.   When a congressperson must vote on a controversial issue, concerns about reelection are conjured up.

Conciseness

wrdy

WORDY PHRASES

Many phrases are wordy because they use several words where one would do. You are no doubt familiar with many of these phrases—*due to the fact that* for *because, in the not too distant future* for *soon, in close proximity to* for *near*. As stock phrases, they come readily to mind; consequently, we use them without considering how well or poorly they express our ideas. Here are some of the most common wordy phrases and possible single-word alternatives:

Wordy Phrases	Single-word Alternatives
due to the fact that	
in view of the fact that	
the reason for	
for the reason that	for, because, why, since
this is why	
inasmuch as	
in light of the fact that	
on the grounds that	

Wordy Phrases	Single-word Alternatives
despite the fact that regardless of the fact that notwithstanding the fact that	although, though
as regards in reference to concerning the matter of where _____ is concerned with respect to	concerning, about, regarding
it is necessary that there is a need for it is important that	should, must
has the ability to is able to has the capacity for is in a position to	can
on the subject of	on, about
for the purpose of	to
in close proximity to	near
make contact with	meet
in the not too distant future	soon
as a matter of fact	actually
aware of the fact that	know
to the effect that	that
the way in which	how
in the event that	if, when

When you are editing or revising your writing, make a point to look for wordy phrases for which you can substitute single-word alternatives.

EXERCISE

Rewrite each sentence, substituting a single word for each wordy phrase.

1. He dropped out of school on account of the fact that it was necessary for him to help support his family.

2. In the event that you happen to be in agreement with me during the course of the meeting, please speak out.

3. Despite the fact that I was not prepared, I did well on the calculus exam.

4. Until such time as I have the opportunity to get help with this problem, I will have to cope with it myself.

5. In the not too distant future, college freshmen must all become aware of the fact that there is a need for them to make contact with an academic adviser concerning the matter of a major.

red

REDUNDANCY

Writing is redundant when it includes unnecessary repetition. The redundant words add nothing but useless padding and extra verbiage. Following are several kinds of redundancy you should make an effort to avoid:

Redundant Pairs.   Examples include *each and every, hopes and desires, first and foremost.* The words *each* and *every,* for instance, go together so naturally they seem inseparable. But neither word adds anything to the meaning of the other. Through habit, we use both when one would suffice.

Redundant Categories.   Phrases such as *blue in color, a hasty manner,* or *a period of time* are redundant because they give unnecessary information. Readers already know blue is a color; telling them something is blue in color repeats the obvious. Instead of *The shirt was blue in color,* write *The shirt was blue.* Instead of *I finished my homework in a hasty manner,* write *I finished my homework hastily.*

Be careful with the following words, which name categories and are often used redundantly: size *(large-sized),* color *(mauve in color),* manner *(a reluctant manner),* degree *(to an extreme degree),* state *(a helpless state),* type and situation *(a crisis-type situation),* area *(the area of population control),* kind *(passive kind of behavior).*

Redundant Modifiers.   Expressions such as *past memories, advance planning,* or *mix together* all contain unnecessary modifiers. All memories are of the past, planning is always done in advance, *mix* means "put together." Modifiers are redundant if they give information that is already in the word being modified.

Obvious Implications.   Expressions such as *the fact is true, bisect in half,* or *in my opinion, I believe* are redundant because they contain obvious implications. A phrase like *the fact is true* is redundant because *truth* is implied by the word *fact.* Similarly, the expression *in my opinion, I believe* says the same thing twice, since if you are giving your opinion, you must be saying what you believe.

Many of these redundancies—like wordy phrases—occur because they are so commonly used that we think of them as a unit. Some writers find it helpful to proofread with an eye for this kind of error; if you make a point of looking for unnecessary words you should rid your own writing of all redundancy.

EXERCISE

Rewrite each sentence as necessary to eliminate any redundancy.

1.   The ghost of Hamlet's father seemed unwilling to give a full and complete account of his murder.

2. It took a long period of time to complete the project.

3. Should we cut some wood for fuel purposes?

4. If you open a new account at Downtown Federal Savings, they will give you a free gift.

5. The incident was significant in several ways. One of the ways the incident was significant is that it was the first time I was totally and completely on my own.

6. Enclosed inside of this box are my high-school papers.

7. I have difficulty coping and dealing with pressure-type situations.

8. This newspaper article is factually true.

9. After a time interval of thirty seconds, a card that is red in color and round in shape is shown to the subject.

10. In today's modern world, it is very unusual to find someone who has never told a deliberate lie.

---

intens/ hedge

UNNECESSARY INTENSIFIERS OR HEDGES

We use intensifiers such as *very, really, clearly,* and *of course* to strengthen statements. The sentence *I am really hungry* suggests that the speaker is more than normally hungry. Using the intensifier here is fine, but substituting a more forceful word for *hungry* would be even more effective: *I am famished.*

Sometimes, intensifiers are unnecessary because the words to which they are attached are already as strong as possible. The sentence *It is very unique,* for example, makes no sense. Something either is or is not unique; it cannot be *very* or *slightly* unique.

In addition to intensifiers, many writers also use hedges such as *apparently, seem, perhaps, possibly, to a certain extent, tend,* and *somewhat* to qualify statements and allow exceptions. Writers use hedges to add subtlety to their prose—and to appear careful and thoughtful, as well as to suggest the real possibility of important exceptions to what they say. But when used excessively and for no specific reason, hedges make writing tentative and uncertain—and less worthy of a reader's attention.

EXERCISE

Rewrite each sentence to remove unnecessary intensifiers and hedges. Try to replace intensifiers with stronger words.

1. I was really happy to learn that the examination was postponed.

2. It is very likely possible that you might even enjoy the exam.

3. This is a very vital exam for me.

4.   It seems for the most part that those who study for exams tend to pass them more often than those who do not study.

5.   In my opinion, the exam may have been sort of difficult.

6.   Essay exams tend to be somewhat more difficult than objective tests, but to a certain extent they can perhaps allow greater room for error.

7.   It is very crucial that you study hard, no matter what form an exam may possibly take.

VAGUE OR OBVIOUS STATEMENTS

**vague/
obvious**

Editing for a vigorous and concise writing style means being on guard for statements that are either vague or obvious, such as the following:

Students who want to succeed in today's world face many challenges.

Some people believe in capital punishment, while other people are against it; there are many opinions on this subject.

Vague or obvious statements are common in initial drafts, where writers are working to establish a flow of ideas and put down on paper the first thoughts that come to mind. Most often, such thoughts lead to other, concrete statements that express the writer's particular ideas more specifically; but, it is important to remember that statements like these are not likely to encourage a reader's interest in what follows. Readers are easily bored by what they already know and are likely to question the expertise of a writer who makes vague assertions that add nothing to their understanding of the topic.

It is usually the case that vague or obvious statements can simply be deleted altogether. If the sentences that follow cannot be easily revised to create a more specific statement or transition, then you should probably return to the appropriate writing guide in Part I or to Chapter 11 to help you move beyond ideas that are not specific or are obvious to most readers.

Appropriateness

INAPPROPRIATE DICTION

d

Most problems of inappropriate diction involve colloquialisms, words or phrases that are generally accepted in informal conversation but are inappropriate in many writing situations. Examples include the following:

The kids [instead of students] in this research study kept careful records of the time spent studying the new words.

The president was <u>kind of</u> [instead of <u>somewhat</u>] irritated over leaks to the press.

The audience was <u>super-impressed</u> [instead of <u>stirred</u> or <u>amazed</u> or <u>strongly impressed</u>] by her valedictory address.

Diction ranges from very formal *(purloin, misappropriate)* to very informal *(rip-off, pinch)*; the appropriate level of diction is determined to a large extent by the audience for which one is writing, as well as the subject. In most academic writing, the best choice lies between the most formal and the most informal *(steal, rob, cheat)*.

INAPPROPRIATE IMAGE

image

An image is a figure of speech, such as a simile or metaphor, involving an imaginary comparison (or analogy) between generally unlike objects. When used effectively, images are vivid and original means of expressing an idea:

Old people moved along old sidewalks or pulled at greenery in old flowerbeds; they sat on old porches and shook the evening paper into obedience, or they rocked steady as old pendulums and looked into the old street as if reading something there. –William Least Heat Moon

The customary way to provide a convenient framework for one's thoughts is to compare the age of the universe with the length of a single earthly day. Perhaps a better comparison, along the same lines, would be to equate the age of our earth with a single week. On such a scale, the age of the universe, since the Big Bang, would be about two or three weeks. The oldest microscopic fossils (those from the start of the Cambrian) would have been alive just one day ago. Modern man would have appeared in the last ten seconds and agriculture in the last one or two. Odysseus would have lived only half a second before the present time. –Francis Crick

For a variety of reasons, images can be inappropriate. Most commonly, an image is inappropriate because it is strained or overly exaggerated or requires an imaginative leap that most readers are unable to make.

She burst with pride like an overfilled balloon.

Hamlet is as mixed up about his mother and father as a three-egg omelet.

In the wrong hands, guns are like a runaway train speeding out of control.

Another common problem is an image that is not carried through appropriately. Such an image, sometimes called a mixed metaphor, compares the topic of discussion with such a variety of unlike objects that the effect becomes ludicrous:

The stock market's tidal wave of speculation could soon be swept by a deadly undertow, and that's a branch you don't want to be on when it cracks.

Don't be afraid to use a clever or original image when it clearly and vividly communicates the idea you wish to express; writing devoid of images can be dull indeed. But be careful that your images are suitable to the subject and to the occasion.

| cliché |

CLICHÉS

Every language has expressions that at first sound fresh and vivid but then, due to overuse, lose their force and appeal. Such expressions are known as clichés. *Birds of a feather, hard as a rock, tried and true, last but not least* are some of the worst offenders in the English language. In conversation, clichés are perhaps inevitable (although those who use them consistently run the risk of appearing foolish). In any sort of thoughtful writing, however, clichés are inappropriate and seem unimpressive or even annoying.

Either way, they should be avoided. The solution is either to create a fresh expression of one's own (being careful that it is appropriate) or to rely on more literal expressions buttressed by specific, telling examples.

Editing Punctuation

This section illustrates the uses of punctuation marks. By giving sentences from prominent published writers for both examples and exercises, we hope to show the full range of possibilities for punctuation in contemporary writing. If you study the examples carefully, you will gain understanding of how to use each punctuation mark in your own writing. Besides learning how to use punctuation correctly, you will see how punctuation can give you the freedom to write new kinds of sentences and express ideas in more effective ways.

Surely there is one supreme rule: that punctuation is best which best serves to make writing subtle, supple, delicate, nuanced and efficient. Of course you can write using only periods and commas for punctuation. You can cook using only salt and pepper for seasoning. But why do it when there are so many seasonings pleasing to a mature palate?   –George Will

PERIODS

Periods are used to mark the end of declarative sentences.

I wish I owned a couple of acres of land now, in which case I would not be writing autobiographies for a living.   –Mark Twain

Periods are used to mark the end of indirect questions.

NOT   Junior asked Susanna whether she wanted any more pancakes?

BUT   Junior asked Susanna whether she wanted any more pancakes.

Periods are used with most abbreviations.

TITLES	Mr., Capt., Hon., Ms.
DEGREES	B.A., Ph.D., M.D., B.Sc.
STATES	Calif., N.Y., Tex. (But not in postal abbreviations—*CA, NY, TX*)
MONTHS	Sept., Oct., Nov., Dec.
NAMES	T. S. Eliot, John F. Kennedy
OTHER USES	A.M., B.C., A.D., vol., St., Ave.

If a sentence ends with an abbreviation, one period marks both the abbreviation and the end of the sentence.

Please give me a wake-up call at 6:00 A.M.

Notice that some abbreviations and acronyms do not have periods. Check a dictionary if you are not certain about a particular abbreviation or acronym.

mph, ft
UNESCO, UAW, SST, SW, NFL

Abbreviations are discussed more fully in the Checking Mechanics section of this Handbook. As you take courses in different disciplines, you will notice that each field has developed specialized abbreviations and conventions for punctuating them.

? QUESTION MARKS

Question marks are used after direct questions.

Can you count half of *Herzog* and a third of *Moby Dick* as one book?

–Gerald Nachman

Would you feel better as someone else?   –Alice Walker

Indirect questions and polite requests do not need a question mark.

Holly asked how to get to La Jolla Cove.
Will all of you please line up on the other side of the net.

Question marks are used to note a question about the accuracy of a preceding word or figure.

Socrates (470?–399 B.C.), the Greek philosopher and teacher, was condemned to death for his unpopular ideas.

Question marks should not be used to express irony or sarcasm.

NOT   Max's funny (?) comments spoiled the birthday party.
BUT   Max's clumsy attempts at humor spoiled the birthday party.

! EXCLAMATION POINTS

Exclamation points are used to show strong emotion or emphasis.

Call an ambulance!
Poor Columbus! He is a minor character now, a walk-on in the middle of American history.   –Frances FitzGerald

ELLIPSES

Ellipses are three spaced periods that are used to indicate omissions within quotations.

In his classic essay on James Fenimore Cooper's prose style, Mark Twain reminds us that ". . . an author's way of setting forth his matter is called his style. . . ."

The ellipses indicate that the writer is using only part of Twain's sentence. Notice that the final ellipsis includes an extra period to conclude the writer's own sentence.

Sometimes ellipses are used to show dramatic pauses in a sentence.

NASA had just announced that he no longer had . . . the right stuff. –Tom Wolfe

COMMAS

The comma is the most frequently used internal mark of punctuation. It has a great many functions—from separating the day and year in a date to marking divisions between clauses and phrases. This section uses examples from the works of established writers to illustrate the main uses of the comma.

Commas are used with full dates (month, day, and year) but are omitted with partial dates (month and year).

Gas had first been used by the Germans on October 27, 1914, when they fired a prototype of modern tear gas from an artillery near Ypres. –Paul Fussell

In England, in strange and almost sinister procession, the Archbishop of Canterbury, John Stratford, died in August 1348, his appointed successor died in May 1349, and the next appointee three months later, all three within a year. –Barbara Tuchman

In June 1985 Beth Henley was working on her fifth play.

Commas are required between most of the elements in place names and addresses. (The one exception is between state and zip code.)

Winnemucca, Nevada

Miami, Dade County, Florida

Writing Lab, University of California, Riverside

5625 Waverly Avenue, La Jolla, California 92037

In a complete sentence, a comma must follow the last element of place names or addresses.

He shot himself twice, once in the chest and then in the head, in a police station in Washington, D.C., with the cops looking on. –Red Smith

EXERCISE

In the following sentences, insert any commas needed with dates, place names, and addresses.

1.   The earthquake of October 9 1871 whose epicenter was near Wilmington Delaware delivered what for this area was the most intense earth shock in historical times.   –John McPhee

2.   I was in New Orleans when Louisiana seceded from the Union, January 26 1861 and I started north the next day.   –Mark Twain

3.   She lost her father, William Thomas Bishop, eight months after her birth on February 8 1911 in Worcester Massachusetts.   –Robert Giroux on Elizabeth Bishop

4.   On the morning of June 5 1962 the *Queen Elizabeth* brought my wife and me from Cherbourg to New York for the film première of *Lolita*.

–Vladimir Nabokov

5.   Miss Davis was born on April 5 1908 in Lowell Massachusetts in a gray clapboard house built on Chester Street by her grandfather Favor, who was descended from fighting Huguenots and was himself a belligerent abolitionist.   –Janet Flanner on Bette Davis

Commas are used before coordinating conjunctions (*and, but, for, yet, so, or,* and *nor*) that connect two or more independent clauses.

I used to help him out with his grammar and spelling after class, and he paid me back by lending me his battered collection of French postcards.   –Edward Rivera

Week after week and year after year the performance never changed, yet I don't remember anyone's ever remarking on her sincerity or readiness to sing.

–Maya Angelou

Winter brings blizzards, hot tornadic winds arise in the spring, and in summer the prairie is an anvil's edge.   –N. Scott Momaday

EXERCISE

In the following sentences, underline the coordinating conjunctions and insert a comma in the right place.

1.   Children have never been very good at listening to their elders but they have never failed to imitate them.   –James Baldwin

2.   I was now twelve years old and the thought of being *a slave for life* began to bear heavily on my heart.   –Frederick Douglass

3.   The Closerie des Lilas was the nearest good cafe when we lived in the flat over the sawmill at 113 rue Notre-Dame-des-Champs and it was one of the best cafes in Paris.   –Ernest Hemingway

4. One might argue that Carpenter had mishandled the re-entry but to accuse him of *panic* made no sense in light of the telemetered data concerning his heart rate and his respiratory rate.   –Tom Wolfe

5. People put up with less rockiness in a marriage now and the opportunity to dissolve a bad marriage in a rather easy fashion tips plenty of marriages that are not nearly all that bad into court.   –Edward Hoagland

Some very brief independent clauses may not require a comma.

We dickered and then we made a deal.   –Red Smith

I have seen the future and I'm tired of it.   –Gerald Nachman

If one or both of the independent clauses have internal punctuation (especially commas), a writer might choose to separate the two clauses with a semicolon and a coordinating conjunction so that the reader can easily see the main division in the sentence.

Genetically, we are nearly identical to mankind fifty thousand years ago; and some of us delight in the continuity represented by this, while others may be appalled.

–Edward Hoagland

A final note on using commas with coordinating conjunctions to join independent clauses: remember that coordinating conjunctions are also used to join many other sentence elements—modifiers (words or phrases), subjects, verbs, or complements. Rarely is a comma used before the conjunction in these cases, for it would separate closely related sentence elements, interrupt the rhythm of the sentence, and confuse the reader. Consider the following two sentences, for example.

As an adolescent I was a slammer of doors and a packer of suitcases.   –Eudora Welty

The conventional view of his time was that all species were immutable and that each had been individually and separately created by God.

–David Attenborough on Charles Darwin

Commas are used to separate three or more items in a series, including the last two items when they are joined by a coordinating conjunction.

Broad-canopied green, orange, purple, and red umbrellas shield produce from the sun.   –John McPhee

Deep in ice water that looked black as ink, murky shapes that would come up as Coca-Colas, Orange Crushes, and various flavors of pop, were all swimming around together.   –Eudora Welty

Without charging any illegal acts, without supplying the grounds for its proscription, without offering a machinery for individual reply, the government branded as putatively disloyal any citizen who belonged to a large number of organizations.

–Lillian Hellman on the McCarthy era

Sometimes writers will use a series that has no coordinating conjunction between the last two items.

Now she stops, turns, glowers. –John McPhee

Only the very young and the very old may recount their dreams at breakfast, dwell upon self, interrupt with memories of beach picnics and favorite Liberty lawn dresses and the rainbow trout in a creek near Colorado Springs. –Joan Didion

EXERCISE

Insert commas as necessary to separate items in series in the following sentences.

1. Our fire escapes were densely inhabited by mops short lines of washed socks geranium plants boxes of seltzer bottles and occasional dramatic scenes.

–Kate Simon

2. In the gaudy parade of liars killers pranksters boasters and boosters that fill up B. A. Botkin's *A Treasury of American Folklore,* Johnny Appleseed, along with Abe Lincoln and George Washington, occupies a tiny section entitled "Patron Saints." –Edward Hoagland

3. Meteorologists were commissioned to make detailed portraits of New Jersey's coastal temperatures humidity precipitation fogs thunderstorms tornado potentialities and "probable maximum hurricanes." –John McPhee

4. She had no confidence in books written in English paid almost nothing for them and sold them for a small and quick profit.

–Ernest Hemingway on Sylvia Beach

5. Every night for weeks there had been much preaching singing praying and shouting, and some very hardened sinners had been brought to Christ, and the membership of the church had grown by leaps and bounds.

–Langston Hughes

6. On the mornings that once throbbed with the dawn chorus of robins catbirds jays wrens and scores of other bird voices there was now no sound; only silence lay over the fields and woods and marsh. –Rachel Carson

7. It used to be understood that no matter how low your estimate of the public intelligence was how greedily you courted success or how much you debased your material in order to popularize it, you nevertheless tried to give the audience something. –Pauline Kael on contemporary movies

Commas are not required if the items in the series are all joined by coordinating conjunctions.

I'd like to be considered good and honest and reasonably accurate.

–Red Smith on sports writing

Fremont Street is lined with shops peddling cheap clothes and hideous souvenirs and zircon rings and pornography.   –A. Alvarez

Some writers omit the comma before the final item in the series if the item is preceded by a conjunction. This omission is acceptable if it does not cause any confusion. To avoid possible misreadings, however, it is a good idea not to omit this comma.

I would hold my laugh, bite my tongue, grit my teeth and seriously erase even the touch of a smile from my face.   –Maya Angelou

Commas are used between coordinate adjectives but are not used between noncoordinate adjectives.

I was a very shy, timid kid.   –Red Smith

The Committee room was almost empty except for a few elderly, small-faced ladies sitting in the rear.   –Lillian Hellman

The adjectives in this series are "coordinate" in that they have an equal modifying relation to the noun they modify. In some adjective series, however, one or two of the adjectives closest to the noun form a noun phrase, in effect making a noun for the remaining adjectives to modify. These adjective series are called "noncoordinate." In the following example, the phrase *red jasper boulders* is the noun. It is modified by one adjective—*huge*. Hence, there is no comma after *huge* or *red*.

Like the huge red jasper boulders and the tiny flecks of gold, Indiana's diamonds are glacial erratics.   –John McPhee

In your own sentences with adjective series, you can apply two tests to determine whether the adjectives are coordinate: the adjectives are coordinate and should be separated by commas if you can reorder the adjectives without changing the meaning, or if the word *and* can be inserted between the adjectives without changing the meaning. In the phrase *shy, timid kid,* you can reorder the adjectives to *timid, shy kid* without changing the meaning; and you can also join them with *and (shy and timid kid)*. Therefore, you would put a comma between the two adjectives.

Commas can be used to set off adjectives in special ways. Many contemporary writers use adjectives somewhat more freely than the examples shown so far in this discussion indicate. They may let adjectives follow the nouns they modify, or they may separate them from the nouns (still within the same sentence). Or, they may place adjectives before the noun but set them off in some way. The result is a particularly modern rhythm. This rhythm is marked by commas.

It was a Texas barbecue, Houston-style.   –Tom Wolfe

The few girls who managed it were never quite the same again, a little more defiant, a little more impudent. –Kate Simon

I remember the emeralds in shop windows, lying casually in trays, all of them oddly pale at the center, somehow watered, cold at the very heart where one expects the fire. –Joan Didion

EXERCISE

Insert commas to mark off the adjectives in the following sentences. In deciding where to put the commas, consider the rhythm and emphasis in the sentence.

1.   Lean ascetic possessed the anatomist stands before a dissecting table upon which lies the naked body of a man.   –Richard Selzer

2.   My mother was annoyed with me inattentive restless brooding darting toward the hallway whenever I thought I heard the Haskell door opening.

–Kate Simon

3.   Papi was almost eighteen now thin a little anemic but not as fragile as he looked.   –Edward Rivera

4.   I see the sky on the running river. Blue it chatters and pulls; blue it catches and pools behind a rock.   –Annie Dillard

5.   Mississippi State College for Women, the oldest institution of its kind in America poverty-stricken enormously overcrowded keeping within the tradition we were all used to in Mississippi was conscientiously and, on the average, well taught by a dedicated faculty remaining and growing there.

–Eudora Welty

6.   A school of minnows swam by, each minnow with its small individual shadow doubling the attendance so clear and sharp in the sunlight.

–E. B. White

7.   Names had great importance for us in the convent, and foreign names French German or plain English (which to us were foreign because of their Protestant sound) bloomed like prize roses among a collection of spuds.

–Mary McCarthy

8.   Contemptuous male laughter follows the boys in their robes towels about their heads sweating breathless.   –Joyce Carol Oates

Commas are used for setting off transitional expressions. Writers will sometimes use a transitional expression when moving from one sentence to the next to tell the reader the exact relation between the two sentences. (See Chapter 13 for a discussion of transitions.) These transitional expressions are set off with commas.

The determined will is rare, but it is not invariably benevolent. Furthermore, the American equation of success with the big time reveals an awful disrespect for human life and human achievement.   –James Baldwin

To say that all life is interconnected membrane, a weft linkage like chain mail, is truism. But in this case, too, the Galápagos islands afford a clear picture. On Santa Cruz island, for instance, the saddleback carapaces of tortoises enable them to stretch high and reach the succulent pads of prickly pear cactus.   –Annie Dillard

When transitional expressions join independent clauses, they must be preceded by a semicolon (to prevent an end-stop error) and followed by a comma.

As I have said, we lived in a slaveholding community; indeed, when slavery perished, my mother had been in daily touch with it for sixty years.   –Mark Twain

Commas are used for setting off parenthetical comments. Writers sometimes interrupt a sentence with a brief comment or aside. These interruptions are enclosed in commas, just as parentheses (hence, "parenthetical" elements) set off material from the rest of the sentence.

When granite forms under the earth's crust, great chunks of it bob up, I read somewhere, like dumplings.   –Annie Dillard

EXERCISE

Add commas as necessary to punctuate the transitional and parenthetical elements in the following sentences.

1.   Of course anyone fool enough to stand around in the asphalt mush of Downtown at noon watching a parade was obviously defective to begin with.
–Tom Wolfe

2.   Indeed Thanksgiving is the one day of the year (a fact known to everybody) when all thoughts of sex completely vanish from apartments, houses, condominiums, and mobile homes like steam from a bathroom mirror.
–Michael J. Arlen

3.   Many inanimate objects of course find it extremely difficult to break down. Pliers for example and gloves and keys are almost totally incapable of breaking down.   –Russell Baker

4.   Man by contrast is alone with the knowledge of his history until the day of his death.   –Loren Eiseley

5.   It was in short what one might searching for words call a beautiful land; it was more beautiful still when the ice cleared and the ice shone in the dark water.   –Annie Dillard

6.   It was I know a simple insight.   –Richard Rodriguez

7. It was no doubt about it a major occurrence in medicine, and a triumph for biological science applied to medicine but perhaps not a revolution after all, looking back from this distance. –Lewis Thomas

8. A little further on across the street was the house where the principal of our grade school lived—lived on, even while we were having vacation.

–Eudora Welty

9. Who were these saints? These crazy, loony, pitiful women? Some of them without a doubt were our mothers and grandmothers. –Alice Walker

10. Observing team sports teams of adult men one sees how men are children in the most felicitous sense of the word. –Joyce Carol Oates

Commas are used after introductory clauses and phrases. For clarity and ease of reading, some introductory clauses and phrases are set off by commas from the independent clauses that follow them. These include adverb clauses and phrases, participial phrases, absolute phrases, and appositive phrases.

ADVERB CLAUSE	Though we do not wholly believe it yet, the interior life is a real life, and the intangible dreams of people have a tangible effect on the world.

–James Baldwin

ADVERB PHRASE	For nearly a year, I sopped around the house, the Store, the school and the church, like an old biscuit, dirty and inedible. –Maya Angelou
PARTICIPIAL PHRASE	Flayed, unprotected against space, she felt pain return, focusing her body. –Maxine Hong Kingston
ABSOLUTE PHRASE	His hat pushed back on his forehead, he walked down the road whistling. –Maya Angelou
APPOSITIVE PHRASE	A student of human frailty, she probably knew deep in her soul that he was one of life's losers. –Russell Baker

EXERCISE

Insert commas as necessary after the introductory elements in each of the following sentences.

1. Partly walking partly gliding he straddles his machine. –John McPhee

2. When my breasts began to swell with horrifying rapidity I searched the sewing machine drawers for cloths and ribbons to tie around them, to stop them. –Kate Simon

3. With so many trees in the city you could see spring coming each day until a night of warm wind would bring it suddenly in one morning.

–Ernest Hemingway

4. A jangling medley of incompetent youth and aging competence the Red Sox were finishing in seventh place only because the Kansas City Athletics had locked them out of the cellar. –John Updike

5.   In my senior year in theological seminary I engaged in the exciting reading of various theological theories.   –Martin Luther King, Jr.

6.   When the conference was done there was only a small pattering of applause from the Press.   –Norman Mailer

7.   Slowly as though the engines were harnessed to elderly coolies we crept out of Granada.   –Truman Capote

8.   Like so much of this country Banyan suggests something curious and unnatural.   –Joan Didion

9.   Animated the face is quite attractive and at a distance youthful; particularly engaging is the crooked smile full of large porcelain-capped teeth.

–Gore Vidal on Ronald Reagan

10.   Always the school marm when it came to words my mother chided him for ignorance.   –Russell Baker

Nonrestrictive clauses and phrases are set off with commas; restrictive clauses and phrases are not. Clauses and phrases that provide information about the noun they modify but are not essential to understanding the meaning of the noun within its sentence are called *nonrestrictive*. That is, they are said *not* to restrict the meaning. Such clauses and phrases must be set off from the rest of the sentence with commas.

I borrowed books from the rental library of Shakespeare and Company, which was the library and bookstore of Sylvia Beach at 12 rue de l'Odeon.   –Ernest Hemingway

In this sentence the underlined adjective clause modifies the noun *Shakespeare and Company*. It provides information about the noun, but it seems to be added to the sentence, rather than being integral to its meaning. It does not affect the central idea of borrowing books. Hence, it is a nonrestrictive clause and must be set off with commas. Notice that adjective clauses or appositive phrases following a proper (capitalized) noun will nearly always be nonrestrictive and thus require commas.

Many clauses and phrases, however, are essential to understanding the meaning of the noun. These are called *restrictive* and are not set off with commas.

The glory which is built upon a lie soon becomes a most unpleasant encumbrance.

–Mark Twain

The Twain example has an adjective clause modifying the noun *glory*. The clause is restrictive because it identifies the particular kind of glory that soon becomes an encumbrance. Since the clause does restrict the meaning of the noun and is integral to the meaning of the sentence, it is not set off with commas. The restrictive-nonrestrictive distinction is one drawn with several sentence elements. Appositives and participial phrases, in particular, merit some examples.

Appositives

RESTRICTIVE   The surgeon and writer Richard Selzer read his latest work at the Iowa Writers' Workshop.

NON-RESTRICTIVE   Robert Bernstein, the president of Random House, runs a large book-publishing complex. –Frances FitzGerald

Astronomers say that when telescopes of greater range can be built, ones that can look down the distant curve of the universe billions of light-years away, they might show existence at the time of creation.
                                                –William Least Heat Moon

Participial Phrases

RESTRICTIVE   The tree silhouetted against the last light in the sky was a red fir.

NON-RESTRICTIVE   The very mechanism of scientific procedure, built up over the years, is designed to encourage doubt and to place obstacles in the way of new ideas. –Isaac Asimov

At three-thirty, quitting time, I would stand upright and slowly let my head fall back, luxuriating in the feeling of tightness relieved.
                                                –Richard Rodriguez

Commas are used for setting off contrast phrases. Some writers use a special sentence pattern that sets up an obvious contrast. These sentences generally end with a negative phrase (beginning with *not* or *no* or *nothing*). These negative phrases are always set off with commas.

Home in the rue Cardinal Lemoine was a two-room flat that had no hot water and no inside toilet facilities except an antiseptic container, not uncomfortable to anyone who was used to a Michigan outhouse. –Ernest Hemingway

She spoke with a slight accent, nothing like the cadences I heard on Lafontaine, not marked enough to mimic. –Kate Simon

Commas are used to set off final absolute phrases from their independent clauses.

The Loop has electronic sensors embedded every half-mile out there in the pavement itself, each sensor counting the crossing cars every twenty seconds. –Joan Didion

EXERCISE

In each of the following sentences, add commas as needed to set off all non-restrictive phrases, nonrestrictive clauses, and absolute phrases.

1. It didn't occur to me for many years that they were as alike as sisters separated only by formal education. –Maya Angelou

2. He stepped out of the dugout and faced the multitude two fists and one cap uplifted. –Red Smith on Reggie Jackson

3.   Vitus Bering shipwrecked in 1740 on Bering Island was found years later preserved in snow.   –Annie Dillard

4.   He apparently believed that the *astronaut* the passenger in the capsule was the heart and soul of the space program.   –Tom Wolfe

5.   Dawn is ruddy over Tappan Zee the far end of the great bridge indistinct in mist.   –John McPhee

6.   There were fierce, unspecified punishments for losing library books a sin as terrible as stealing or playing doctor.   –Kate Simon

7.   One Christmas we received gifts from our mother and father who lived separately in a haven called California where we were told they could have all the oranges they could eat.   –Maya Angelou

8.   It was from behind the lumber village of Tschagguns which was on the far edge of the valley that the good skiing went all the way up until you could eventually cross the mountains and get over the Silvretta and the Klosters area.   –Ernest Hemingway

9.   Manteo is the seat of Dare County and one of the few courthouse towns as the Carolinians call them on an island in the Atlantic Ocean.

–William Least Heat Moon

10.   The conclusions reached in science are always when looked at closely far more provisional and tentative than are most of the assumptions arrived at by our colleagues in the humanities.   –Lewis Thomas

11.   Fleas and rats which were in fact the carriers are not mentioned in the plague writings.   –Barbara Tuchman

12.   When the goods were divided among the family, three of the brothers took land, and the youngest my father chose an education.

–Maxine Hong Kingston

13.   I took along my son who had never had any fresh water up his nose and who had seen lily pads only from train windows.   –E. B. White

14.   Porcupines breed in December the male performing a clumsy, poignant, three-legged dance while clutching his testicles with one front paw.

–Edward Hoagland

SEMICOLONS

The semicolon is not simply an alternative to the period, colon, or comma. With it a writer can signal special relationships between independent clauses, and can increase the readability of long sentences that contain several commas.

Semicolons can be used to join independent clauses if the second clause restates or sets up a contrast to the first.

My academic record at Princeton was middling fair; I had entered college at fifteen, having been a bright enough high-school student, but then I turned into a moult of dullness and laziness, average or below average in the courses requiring real work.

–Lewis Thomas

We know through painful experience that freedom is never voluntarily given by the oppressor; it must be demanded by the oppressed.   –Martin Luther King, Jr.

Although a period would be acceptable in each of these examples, the semi-colon emphasizes how closely the two clauses fit together. A comma followed by *and* would be correct but misleading, because *and* signals additional information, not restatement or contrast. Similarly, the semicolon in the next example could be replaced with a comma and *but*, but the semicolon makes the contrast sharper and more immediate.

In winter there was always a refreshing breeze up through the puncheon floor; in summer there were fleas enough for all.   –Mark Twain

Semicolons may be used to join a series of independent clauses.

If you knew grammar you were special. You had prestige, power, access to magic; you understood a mystery; you were like a nuclear physicist.   –Peter Elbow

A slab bench is made of the outside cut of a saw-log, with the barkside down; it is supported on four sticks driven into augur holes at the ends; it has no back and no cushions.   –Mark Twain

Although a period could acceptably replace each semicolon in the two preceding examples, the semicolon lets the reader know that the information in each clause is part of a continuing series.

Semicolons are used before sentence adverbs (*however, nevertheless, moreover, consequently,* etc.) to join independent clauses.

The thymus is large in relation to the rest of the body during fetal development and childhood; however, it stops growing by puberty and then begins to atrophy and get progressively smaller.   –Sylvia Mader

Semicolons are used to separate independent clauses or items in a series having internal commas.

A million babies a year are born in Egypt; and Cairo, like Mexico City or Jakarta, is jammed with youngsters.   –Edward Hoagland

Everything was cheap: apples, peaches, sweet potatoes and corn, ten cents a bushel; chickens, ten cents apiece; butter, six cents a pound; eggs, three cents a dozen; coffee and sugar, five cents a pound; whisky, ten cents a gallon.   –Mark Twain

EXERCISE

Insert semicolons as needed in each of the following sentences.

1.   Westinghouse had put several dozen people to work on the concept General Electric had a team too—preparing to make eventual bids for the reactor contract.   –John McPhee

2.   A President's power over the bureaucracy depends, in part, on respect born of fear during the first term it depends, in part, on the idea that a President may run again.   –George Will

3.   At the arterial end of a capillary, blood pressure is greater than asmotic pressure therefore, water leaves the capillary along with oxygen and nutrients that diffuse from the capillary.   –Sylvia Mader

4.   Ice coats the deck, spars, and rigging the masts and hull shudder the sea freezes around the rudder, and then fastens on the ship.   –Annie Dillard

5.   To my astonishment there were no sentimentalities, no dramatics, no George Washington effects she was not moved in the least degree she simply did not believe me and said so!   –Mark Twain

6.   Now that I can have her only in memory, I see my grandmother in the several postures that were peculiar to her: standing at the wood stove on a winter morning and turning meat in a great iron skillet sitting at the south window, bent above her beadwork, and afterwards, when her vision failed, looking down for a long time into the fold of her hands going out upon a cane, very slowly as she did when the weight of age came upon her praying.

–N. Scott Momaday

7.   Women's rights is not only an abstraction, a cause it is also a personal affair.   –Toni Morrison

8.   We cannot establish instant security we can only build it step by step.

–Margaret Mead

9.   To take off a uniform is usually a relief, just as it is a relief to abandon official speech sometimes it is also a sign of defiance.   –Alison Lurie

10.   The Kiowas are a summer people they abide the cold and keep to themselves, but when the season turns and the land becomes warm and vital they cannot hold still an old love of going returns upon them.   –N. Scott Momaday

COLONS

Colons serve a variety of conventional purposes—separating hours from minutes when reporting time, chapter from verse when citing the Bible, titles from subtitles when identifying a book or article.

4:30 P.M.

Genesis 2:3, Matthew 4:1–6

The Living Planet: A Portrait of the Earth

Colons are used mainly to introduce specific details. The part of the sentence up to the colon makes a general statement, and the part after the colon adds specifics (often in a grammatically parallel list).

They thought of themselves as equals in their work: no boss, no peons, no unequal distribution of the labor.   —Edward Rivera

At Simpson Strait some Inuit had seen a very odd sight: the pack ice pierced by the three protruding wooden masts of the bark.   —Annie Dillard

However, a colon is not used before a series of specific details introduced by a phrase like *such as* or *for example*.

NOT   We will study important twentieth-century authors such as: D. H. Lawrence, Virginia Woolf, and E. M. Forster.

BUT   We will study a number of important twentieth-century English authors: D. H. Lawrence, Virginia Woolf, and E. M. Forster.

OR   We will study important twentieth-century English authors such as D. H. Lawrence, Virginia Woolf, and E. M. Forster.

Colons are also used to introduce a statement, sometimes adding special, even dramatic, emphasis.

It is a terrible, an inexorable law that one cannot deny the humanity of another without diminishing one's own: in the face of one's victim, one sees oneself.

—James Baldwin

Sometimes the information following the colon is anticipated by clues in the first clause.

We can summarize the weather forecast as follows: fog and drizzle.

A person had to see it to believe it: flocks of seagulls wheeling around in the air out in the middle of the high desert in the dead of winter and grazing on antediluvian crustaceans in the primordial ooze.   —Tom Wolfe

Colons are sometimes used to introduce quotations and questions. Commas may also be used, but a colon provides greater pause and emphasis.

When I wander into a place that is obviously out of bounds for me—hardware store, jewelry shop, florist—the clerk just grins, crosses his arms, and flashes a look that says: "Well, well—and who do we have here?"   —Gerald Nachman

And now it unblinkingly agreed that Eckert and his staff should explore the concept of the oceanborne nuclear plant, and spend enough time and money to answer the primary question: Is there any reason, technically, that it won't work?   —John McPhee

The first word following a colon is generally not capitalized. Some writers do capitalize the first word, however, when a complete sentence follows the colon. The most important thing here is to be consistent.

EXERCISE

Insert a colon as needed in each of the following sentences.

1. All the poisonous snakes known to North America were in residence there rattlers, copperheads, cottonmouths, and corals. –Tom Wolfe

2. She told one laughing story that appalled me for years there was a man who could neither sit nor stand nor lie down (this with elaborations of voice and gesture), so he found a solution—he hanged himself. –Kate Simon

3. We have been expected to lie with our bodies to bleach, redden, unkink or curl our hair, pluck eyebrows, shave armpits, wear padding in various places or lace ourselves, take little steps, glaze finger and toe nails, wear clothes that emphasized our helplessness. –Adrienne Rich

4. In perpetrating a revolution, there are two requirements someone or something to revolt against and someone to actually show up and do the revolting. –Woody Allen

5. Almost anything can trigger a specific attack of migraine stress, allergy, fatigue, an abrupt change in barometric pressure, a contretemps over a parking ticket. –Joan Didion

6. The Fifth Amendment is, of course, a wise section of the Constitution you cannot be forced to incriminate yourself. –Lillian Hellman

7. She is asked, point blank, a question which may lead into painful talk "How do you feel about what is happening between us?" –Adrienne Rich

8. To illustrate A student enters a laboratory which, in the pragmatic view, offers the student the optimum conditions under which an educational experience may be had. –Walker Percy

9. When an old woman in a nursing home was asked what she really liked to do, she answered in one word "Eat." –Malcolm Cowley

10. Our look was as if two lovers, or deadly enemies, met unexpectedly on an overgrown path when each had been thinking of something else a clearing blow to the gut. –Annie Dillard

11. When I asked who won all the money, I was given a neutral, poker player's answer "The cash got distributed pretty good." –A. Alvarez

12. After all, turkey tastes very similar to haddock same consistency, same quite remarkable absence of flavor. –Michael J. Arlen

13. I have even heard the claim as explanation for the drift of things in

modern art and modern music Nothing is left to contemplate except ran-
domness and senselessness; God is nothing but a pair of dice, loaded at that.

–Lewis Thomas

14.   The spitting incidents of 1957 and 1958 and the similar dockside cour-
tesies that Williams now and then extended to the grandstand should be
judged against the background the left-field stands at Fenway for twenty years
have held a large number of customers who have bought their way in primarily for the privilege of showering abuse on Williams.

–John Updike on former Boston Red Sox player Ted Williams

DASHES

Dashes are used for setting off material from the rest of a sentence. Whether
a list, a modifying phrase or clause, or an added explanation, the material set
off usually causes a noticeable break in the sentence's rhythm or meaning.
Dashes are used to set off text either in the middle or at the end of a sentence.
In very informal writing, such as quick notes or letters to close friends, the
dash can become a substitute for other punctuation. In most formal or college
writing, however, it is used sparingly—and then for special effect.

In typed or handwritten manuscript, a dash is generally represented by
two hyphens ("--") with no space before or after.

Dashes are used to introduce or set off a list of parallel items.

There are no holidays in August, which reveals the month for what it is—a complete
loser, a scandal of major proportions, a national embarrassment.   –Gerald Nachman

Not only are there many major categories of creatures—monkeys, rodents, spiders,
hummingbirds, butterflies—but most of those types exist in many different forms.

–David Attenborough

After a week in Glitter Gulch, I began to exhibit symptoms of physical deprivation—
nervous tension, disorientation, insomnia, loss of appetite—which seemed inappropriate in a town geared exclusively to self-indulgence.   –A. Alvarez on Las Vegas

Like commas, dashes can set off modifiers from the rest of the sentence, including single words, phrases, and whole clauses.

It rained all night at Seven Islands—heavily and steadily—but tapered in the early
morning to drizzle and mist.   –John McPhee

Maybe I'm all alone in my feeling about grape jelly—that it's an abhorrent slimy
substance—but is it possible all of America is that crazy for grape jelly?

–Gerald Nachman

Dashes are often used to set off material that defines terms in the main sentence.

The new container ships come equipped with bow thrusters and stern thrusters—extra propellers that, in effect, enable them to move sideways at will.

–Edward Hoagland

Dashes are sometimes used to signal the kind of pause for dramatic effect that a speaker might use.

It looked as if Carpenter had consumed all his fuel up there playing around—and had burned up. –Tom Wolfe

The dash can be used to punctuate a major sentence element that begins by repeating and defining some earlier word in the sentence. In these sentences the material set off by the dash is usually longer than the base sentence preceding it.

She had a slender, small body but a large heart—a heart so large that everybody's joys found welcome in it and hospitable accommodation. –Mark Twain

Only at the horizon do inky black mountains give way to distant, lighted mountains—lighted not by direct illumination but rather paled by flowing sheets of mist hung before them. –Annie Dillard

Dashes are often used to insert—and set off—a full sentence within a sentence. Generally such sentences contain commentary or explanation.

Scott did not stop talking and since I was embarrassed by what he said—it was all about my writing and how great it was—I kept on looking at him closely and noticed instead of listening. –Ernest Hemingway on F. Scott Fitzgerald

Darwin was far from being an atheist—he had, after all, taken a degree in divinity from Cambridge—but he was deeply puzzled by this enormous multiplicity of forms.

–David Attenborough

Dashes are used to set off brief personal comments writers sometimes insert for emphasis or transition.

What I find appalling—and really dangerous—is the American assumption that the Negro is so contented with his lot here that only the cynical agents of a foreign power can rouse him to protest. –James Baldwin

Our civilization is decadent and our language—so the argument runs—must inevitably share in the general collapse. –George Orwell

The dash or the comma?

In most of the preceding examples, the break in sentence rhythm seems to call for a dash. In some, however, a comma would be acceptable. Which is preferable depends on the writer's intent—whether he or she wants greater or lesser emphasis on the inserted material. In the following example, Hemingway decided to set off with commas an inserted clause that causes a strong break in the rhythm of the sentence. He might have used dashes—as he did often in his writing. Presumably he used commas in order to soften the break—dashes would have placed stronger emphasis on the inserted material.

Skiing was not the way it is now, the spiral fracture had not become common then, and no one could afford a broken leg. –Ernest Hemingway

EXERCISE

Insert dashes in the appropriate places in the following sentences.

1.   Both the streets and the lanes were paved with the same material tough black mud in wet times, deep dust in dry. –Mark Twain

2.   To profile the seabed, they cruised around in boats using seismic instruments high-resolution boomers, high-resolution sparkers. –John McPhee

3.   White folks couldn't be people because their feet were too small, their skin too white and see-throughy, and they didn't walk on the balls of their feet the way people did they walked on their heels like horses. –Maya Angelou

4.   Wherever we go, there seems to be only one business at hand that of finding workable compromises between the sublimity of our ideas and the absurdity of the fact of us. –Annie Dillard

5.   It might have been because I felt banished by my mother's absorption with my new baby sister no time to make me a new pongee sailor dress, no time to hear me sing "Over the Hill" with heart-breaking quavers that I spent more and more time with Fannie. –Kate Simon

6.   All the pupils brought their dinners in baskets corn dodger, buttermilk and other good things and sat in the shade of the trees at noon and ate them.

–Mark Twain

7.   The entrepreneur individualistic, restless, with vision, guile and courage has been the economists' only hero. –John Kenneth Galbraith

8.   All of those things rock and men and river resisted change, resisted the coming as they did the going. –William Least Heat Moon

9.   I would have evaded and for how long could I have afforded to delay? learning the great lesson of school, that I had a public identity.

–Richard Rodriguez

10.   Cells in those organs that suffer constant wear and tear as in the skin or in the intestinal lining grow and multiply all life long. –Isaac Asimov

11.   If I made myself American-pretty so that the five or six Chinese boys in the class fell in love with me, everyone else the Caucasian, Negro, and Japanese boys would too. –Maxine Hong Kingston

12.   Papa Santos was so good that whenever there wasn't enough food for everyone and that was often he used to steal chickens and vegetables from his neighbors.   –Edward Rivera

13.   Polar explorers one gathers from their accounts sought at the Poles something of the sublime.   –Annie Dillard

14.   She planted ambitious gardens and still does with over fifty different varieties of plants that bloom profusely from early March until late November.
–Alice Walker

15.   The fighters in the ring are time-bound is anything so excruciatingly long as a fiercely contested three-minute round? but the fight itself is timeless.
–Joyce Carol Oates

16.   My hair was whiter it may have been 1975 when a young woman rose and offered me her seat in a Madison Avenue bus.   –Malcolm Cowley

 ## PARENTHESES

Parentheses enclose interrupting material in sentences. Sometimes dashes and parentheses are interchangeable, but usually the dash is for material that causes a stronger break in the rhythm and meaning of the sentence. Parentheses have certain conventional, required uses. However, like dashes and colons, parentheses make possible new kinds of sentences. Although the material they enclose can be removed without changing the sentence's basic pattern, the material is not just incidental. It is essential material—defining, illustrating, elaborating—that changes the meaning of the sentence.

Parentheses are used to insert numbers, dates, and acronyms.

Berkeley is one of America's most lively, culturally diverse, and politically adventurous small cities (population 103,000).   –University of California Undergraduate Application Packet

The octagon and related geometry of the bay window were more fully expressed in the Theodore P. Gordon house (1897).   –Randall Makinson

In recent years, the Federal Government has made available low-interest educational loans through the Guaranteed Student Loan (GSL) program to undergraduates who are United States citizens or permanent residents.   –Yale University Bulletin

Parentheses are used for the numbers in numbered lists.

There should be a way to salvage your literary reputation by gaining points for (1) thumbing through a book enough to get the drift, (2) seeing the movie, and (3) soaking up the plot by hearsay, thus allowing you to venture bold opinions at parties.
–Gerald Nachman

Parentheses are used to insert facts, examples, and definitions. Parentheses enable a writer to insert facts, examples, and definitions into a sentence quickly and easily. The insertion can be a word, a phrase, or a sentence. The parenthetical insert in the first example is a sentence, but it is not punctuated as one; that is, it does not begin with a capital and end with a period.

In July Bob White had flown to 314,750 feet, or 59.6 miles, 9.6 miles into space (50 miles was now officially regarded as the boundary line) and well above the project's goal of 280,000 feet. –Tom Wolfe

The problem is that in the next quarter-century the population of Egypt will grow to something like seventy (from thirty-seven) million, with only an original skinny strip of six million tillable acres along the Nile—desert everywhere else.   –Edward Hoagland

My parents were skeptics and, bored with the spates of *bubbe meises* (grandmother's tales), preferred to tell pointed little stories about each other's relatives.   –Kate Simon

After practicing on an F-104 simulator, Yeager's students would take the ship up to 35,000 feet and open her up to Mach 2 (the boom), then aim her up at about forty-five degrees and try to poke a hole in the sky (the zoom).   –Tom Wolfe

Parentheses are sometimes used to enclose comments and elaboration.

He picks his moment, leaps, arches his back (ball behind his head), scores.
                                                                                              –John McPhee

We lived with our grandmother and uncle in the rear of the Store (it was always spoken of with a capital *S*), which she had owned some twenty-five years.
                                                                                              –Maya Angelou

The blue-back notebooks, the two pencils and the pencil sharpener (a pocket knife was too wasteful), the marble-topped tables, the smell of early morning, sweeping out and mopping, and luck were all you needed.   –Ernest Hemingway

Notice that parenthetical materials can be inserted anywhere after the first word in the sentence. Of course the placement must be appropriate and relevant to the sentence, and the inserted material must not be so long that it totally interrupts the reading of the sentence. Notice too that parentheses do not influence punctuation in the rest of the sentence. The parenthetical element concluding the Tom Wolfe sentence *(the zoom)* is placed inside the period that closes the sentence. Also, the parenthetical element in the Kate Simon sentence *(grandmother's tales)* is placed inside the comma that closes the larger participial phrase.

Toward the end he got Extreme Unction, that last-ditch sacrament. If you believed in that stuff, and who in those days didn't (Xavier perhaps?), then Xavier was on his way to paradise. –Edward Rivera

There were English round-trippers ("Oh, have you just come on board?"), and English who had flown to America only the day before. –Edward Hoagland

Although they do not affect punctuation in the sentences in which they are inserted, parentheses can have their own internal punctuation. A declarative or imperative sentence within parentheses need not be capitalized (nor does it need a period) if it is contained within another sentence.

Sometimes parenthetical text can be presented as a separate sentence.

I left America because I doubted my ability to survive the fury of the color problem here. (Sometimes I still do.) –James Baldwin

EXERCISE

Insert parentheses at the appropriate places in the following sentences.

1. There was a joy in going to town with money in our pockets Bailey's pockets were as good as my own and time on our hands. –Maya Angelou

2. Only a few months before Xavier's death, a "rare disease" my mother's mysterious phrase had knocked off his wife, Sara. –Edward Rivera

3. If current biological determinism in the study of human intelligence rests upon no new facts actually no facts at all, then why has it become so popular of late? –Stephen Jay Gould

4. The highest satisfaction of the sightseer not merely the tourist but any layman seer of sights is that his sight should be certified as genuine.

–Walker Percy

5. While students don't go to many movies they read even less and perhaps *that's* why they've been named the film generation, the few movies each year that they do care about they seem to take more *personally* than earlier generations of students did. –Pauline Kael

6. In Meridien I had only gone ninety miles from Jackson there was a wait of hours for the train that went from New Orleans to New York.

–Eudora Welty

7. He was the only father who wore penny loafers on business trips, a Mouseketeer hat to pick up my brother on his first movie date, and had the delicious gall to invite the richest girl in my class she had her own pool but an exclusive number of invitations to come on over to the house "When you're free, of course" and watch our lawn sprinklers. –Phyllis Theroux

8. *Police* pronounced PO-lice is a soul term, whereas *The Man* is merely slang for the same thing. –Claude Brown

9. In the weeks following, friends cautioned that I had no idea how hard physical labor really is. "You only think you know what it is like to shovel for eight hours straight." The objections seemed to me challenges.

–Richard Rodriguez

10. The ship had come from the Black Sea port of Caffa now Feodosiya in the Crimea, where the Genoese maintained a trading post. –Barbara Tuchman

[ ] BRACKETS

Brackets are used to insert editorial notations into a quotation and to enclose parenthetical material within text that is already in parentheses.

Perhaps Alvarez is justified in claiming, "He [Mark Twain] greatly exaggerates flaws in Cooper's prose style just to get an easy laugh from readers."

Soon after John Muir went away to college at the University of Wisconsin, he wrote home, "I was at once led and pushed and whirld [sic] and tossed about by new everythings everywhere."

We drove through Borrego Springs (years ago [maybe 1938] when we were still youngsters) on our way to Indio.

In the second sentence, *sic* indicates that the misspelling is in the original quoted material, not in the present writer's book or manuscript.

, APOSTROPHES

The apostrophe is used to mark the possessive form of nouns and some pronouns, the omission of letters or figures, and the plural of letters or figures.

Possessives

Marianne Moore's hats, a cheetah's habitat, writer's block, Laura's premonition

men's suits, children's books, the alumni's bulletin

Plural Nouns Ending in s

professors' retirement plan, students' parking lot

Singular Nouns Ending in s

When a singular noun ends in *s,* it is acceptable to use an apostrophe with or without an additional *s.* The important thing is to be consistent.

Charles's vacation *or* Charles' vacation

Massachusetts' laws *but probably not* Massachusetts's laws

Indefinite Pronouns

one's, anyone's, anybody's, someone's, everyone's, nobody's

Possessive forms of personal pronouns, however, do not have apostrophes: *my, mine, your, yours, hers, his, its, our, ours, their, theirs.*

Omitted Letters or Figures

we've, they've, he'll, won't, isn't

'86, class of '90, summer of '52, '67 Chevy

Plurals of Letters and Figures

Give me two 7's.

Write your *q*'s so they don't look like *g*'s.

Professor Oxfam gives too many *D*'s.

un   UNDERLINING

In print and with some word processors, words can be given special emphasis with a slanting type called *italic*. In handwritten or typewritten work, the same effect is achieved by underlining.

Names of airplanes, ships, and trains are underlined.

Lindbergh's <u>Spirit of St. Louis</u>

the liner <u>Mariposa</u>

Amtrak's <u>San Diegan</u>

Titles of books, newspapers, magazines, long poems, movies, television programs, and long musical compositions are underlined.

Hemingway's <u>For Whom the Bell Tolls</u>

the <u>Washington Post</u>

the newly designed <u>Harper's</u> magazine

<u>The Love Song of J. Alfred Prufrock</u>

<u>E.T.</u>

<u>60 Minutes</u>

Mozart's <u>The Magic Flute</u>

Note, however, that the Bible and its divisions are not underlined. Also, titles of book chapters, essays, articles, stories, and short poems are enclosed in quotation marks, not underlined. Song titles and paintings may be either enclosed in quotation marks or underlined.

Foreign words not commonly used in English are underlined.

He voted <u>in absentia</u>.

He longed for <u>la dolce vita</u>.

English borrows many words from other languages, but if a foreign word is used for a long time, it is eventually thought of as no longer foreign: *delicatessen* and *boutique,* for example. These familiar foreign words are not underlined.

Words, numbers, and letters used as themselves are underlined.

Marcella couldn't think of a synonym for <u>uxorious.</u>
Duke never could spell <u>committed</u> correctly.
Dominica rolled three <u>7</u>'s in a row.
Is this a <u>q</u> or a <u>g</u>?

Sometimes writers use underlining to emphasize a word.

Like most children, I thought if I could face the worst danger voluntarily, and <u>triumph</u>, I would forever have power over it.   –Maya Angelou

I <u>appear</u> to be taking it all in—nodding brightly, listening perkily—when in fact I'm not hearing a word being said.   –Gerald Nachman

Be conservative in underlining for emphasis. Too much underlining gives the impression that you are simply raising your voice. Good writers try to build the proper emphasis into their sentence structure, not to rely on underlining for emphasis.

QUOTATION MARKS

Quotation marks are used to indicate direct quotations, to punctuate some titles, and to mark words used in special ways. Double quotation marks (") are used for all purposes except quotations within quotations, which are marked by single marks ('). Quotation marks are always used in pairs: an opening mark and a closing mark.

Direct quotations must be set off with quotation marks.

In her introduction to *In Search of Our Mothers' Gardens,* Alice Walker writes, "I thank my friend June Jordan."

Indirect quotations are given without quotation marks.

In the introduction to *In Search of Our Mothers' Gardens,* Alice Walker wrote that she thanked her friend June Jordan.

When giving a direct quotation, a writer can put the speaker tag (*Alice Walker wrote*) before, inside, or after the quotation.

Alice Walker wrote, "My sense of the Cubans' spiritedness stayed with me."
"My sense of the Cubans' spiritedness," Alice Walker wrote, "stayed with me."
"My sense of the Cubans' spiritedness stayed with me," Alice Walker wrote.

Notice that the first word of the quotation is capitalized, but if the quotation is broken, as in the second example, the first word after the speaker tag is not capitalized unless it actually begins a new quoted sentence.

Speaker tags can be followed by commas, by colons, or by *that*.

Carl Sagan has said recently, "The price we pay for anticipation of the future is anxiety about it."

Carl Sagan has said recently: "The price we pay for anticipation of the future is anxiety about it."

Carl Sagan has said recently that "the price we pay for anticipation of the future is anxiety about it."

When using the word *that*, the first word of the quotation is not capitalized, even if it was so in the original source.

To punctuate the closing of quotations, commas and periods are always placed inside the closing mark; semicolons and colons are always placed outside.

Alice Walker wrote, "I thank my friend June Jordan."

Alice Walker wrote, "I thank my friend June Jordan," and then she went on to mention still others who had contributed to her book.

Alice Walker wrote, "I thank my friend June Jordan"; she noted, as well, Jordan's specific contributions to the book.

Alice Walker wrote, "I thank my friend June Jordan": acknowledgment of this sort is an old tradition in writers' prefaces.

Question marks and exclamation marks are placed inside closing quotations if the question or exclamation is made in the quotation itself, and outside if it is made in the writer's sentence that includes the quotation.

Susanna asked, "Are we going to improve the avocado's image?"

Did Susanna say, "We are going to improve the avocado's image"?

Notice that no period is necessary after the final word in either example.

Single quotation marks are used to set off quotations within quotations.

Susanna said, "Maybe we can improve the avocado's image if we return to our old 'slice it, chop it, mash it' slogan."

Titles of short works such as articles, chapters, essays, stories, poems, and songs are enclosed in quotation marks. The general principle is that titles of works published or performed by themselves are italicized or underlined, whereas the titles of *parts* of those works are enclosed in quotation marks. Hence, the title of an essay in a book would be enclosed in quotation marks, and the title of the book would be italicized or underlined.

''Under Glass'' is a story in Margaret Atwood's collection *Dancing Girls.*

Charley's instructor read several poems from Robert Frost's *In the Clearing,* including ''The Objection to Being Stepped On'' and ''Quandry.''

Outdoor sculptures, like Niki de Saint Phalle's ''The Sun God,'' are nearly always controversial.

Have you ever heard Ella sing ''Puttin' on the Ritz''?

Sometimes writers enclose in quotation marks words being defined or words used ironically.

Off and on as the years passed, I was briefly troubled by my ignorance of what ''contumely'' really was, but never, mind you, never troubled enough to open a dictionary. –Russell Baker

When I read William Saroyan's *The Human Comedy,* I was immediately pleased by the narrator's warmth and the charm of his story. But as quickly I became suspicious. A book so enjoyable to read couldn't be very ''important.'' –Richard Rodriguez

EXERCISE

Insert quotation marks and other punctuation marks as necessary in the following sentences.

1.   Maxine replied Unemployment won't decline unless interest rates do the same.

2.   Did Maxine reply Unemployment won't decline until interest rates do the same.

3.   Tropical storms Susanna declared do occur in Anza-Borrego in August and September.

4.   Chloe had this to say The semester ends Friday, and life begins on Saturday.

5.   I overheard Charley say Why don't we send a telegram that announces The deal can be closed if you double the advance.

Checking Mechanics

ab	## ABBREVIATIONS

Abbreviations are used frequently in informal writing, but few are appropriate for the more formal writing done in college. When you do have occasion to abbreviate, there are two important rules to follow: (1) use only abbreviations your readers will recognize, and (2) use the forms given in the dictionary.

If you use an abbreviation your readers may not know, use the full word for the first reference, followed by the abbreviation in parentheses. Then use the abbreviation for subsequent references:

In 1962, Watson and Crick won a Nobel Prize for discovering the structure of deoxyribose nucleic acid (DNA). They found that DNA has the form of a double helix.

Following are some conventions covering the acceptable use of abbreviations. Notice that some abbreviations have periods, and others do not. In general, abbreviations composed of all capital letters are written without periods or space between letters. When capital letters are separated by periods, do not skip a space after the period (B.A.), except for initials of a person's name (T. S. Eliot).

Abbreviate titles and degrees.

Dr. Albert Einstein, Mr. Roger Smith, Rev. Jesse Jackson, Ms. Martina Navratilova

Diana Lee, M.D., Ann Hajek, Ph.D.

Ring Lardner, Jr.

Abbreviate agencies and organizations.

FBI, IRS, CBS, NATO, NOW

Abbreviate common technical terms.

DNA, GNP, CPM

Do not abbreviate geographical names or designations in formal writing.

NOT	We moved from 5th Ave. in NY to Wilshire Blvd. in LA.
BUT	We moved from Fifth Avenue in New York to Wilshire Boulevard in Los Angeles.

Note, however, that it is acceptable to abbreviate geographical areas generally known by their abbreviations, such as U.S.S.R.

Do not abbreviate dates or measurements in formal writing.

NOT   The average American man is 5 ft. 9 in. tall and weighs 178 lbs.

BUT   The average American man is 5 feet 9 inches tall and weighs 178 pounds.

Abbreviate common Latin expressions.

cf.	compare
e.g.	for example
et al.	and others (used with people)
etc.	and so forth
i.e.	that is
vs. (or v.)	versus
c. (or ca.)	about (used with dates)

cap | CAPITALIZATION

Capitalize the first word of a sentence, including sentences enclosed in parentheses.

The Constitution provided that states be equally represented in the Senate, but that the House of Representatives be elected on the basis of population. (Slaves were counted as three-fifths of a person.)

Capitalize proper names.

Proper names are names of specific persons and places, as well as specific groups—religious denominations, ethnic groups, political parties, and so on.

Most of Shakespeare's plays were presented first at the Globe Theater in London.

Jerusalem is considered a holy city by Jews, Christians, and Moslems.

Many native American writers come from Texas and New Mexico.

The University of California has nine campuses.

Do not capitalize *university* or other kinds of institutions when the reference is general rather than specific.

Billy was fortunate enough to be admitted to several universities.

Capitalize titles preceding proper names.

Professor John Ganim, Aunt Alice, Reverend Fabricant

Do not capitalize titles when they follow proper names.

John Ganim, my professor; Alice Jordan, my favorite aunt

Capitalize titles of written works.

Capitalize first and last words, and all other words except for articles *(a, an, the)*, short conjunctions *(and, or)*, and prepositions *(between, on, of)*.

War and Peace, A Stranger in a Strange Land, "Lines Composed a Few Miles above Tintern Abbey," *The Grand Canyon Suite*

Capitalize historical events, periods, and monuments.

World War II, the Great Depression, Lincoln Memorial

Capitalize holidays, weekdays, and months.

Independence Day, Passover, Ramadan, Monday, January

Do not capitalize seasons.

summer vacation, last winter

Capitalize compass directions to refer to specific geographical areas.

the Northeast, Southerners

Do not capitalize compass directions when they are used generally.

southern exposure, western life

hyph   HYPHENATION

Hyphens have two uses: (1) to break a word at the end of a line; and (2) to join words to form a compound word.

Break words only between syllables.

If you are uncertain about syllabication, refer to your dictionary.

go-ing, height-en, mus-cu-la-ture

Break compound words between the joined words.

self-interest (not self-in-terest)

Break words with prefixes or suffixes between the root and the prefix or suffix.

re-vision, dis-satisfied, com-mitment, pro-crastinate

honor-able, philos-ophy, proba-tion, ego-ism

Some compound words are written as one word, others as separate words, and still others as hyphenated words. Some words have more than one acceptable spelling (*percent* and *per cent*, for example); the important thing is to use one spelling consistently.

moonshine, postmaster, shipboard

vice versa, place kick

like-minded, once-over, father-in-law, take-it-or-leave-it

Hyphenate compound modifiers before a noun.

after-school activities, cream-filled cupcakes, fast-growing business

Do not hyphenate compound modifiers that follow a noun.

activities after school, cupcakes that are cream filled

Do not hyphenate compound modifiers that are made up of an adverb ending in *-ly* and an adjective.

rapidly growing business

Hyphenate compound numbers used as modifiers or nouns.

a twenty-one gun salute

Thirty-five graduated with honors.

Hyphenate compounds made up of prefixes and proper nouns.

un-American, anti-American, pro-American

Hyphenate compounds beginning with *ex-* or *self-*.

ex-husband, self-motivated

num

NUMBERS

Numbers may be written as words (fourteen) or as numerals (14). In general, use words to express numbers one through nine and numerals for ten and over. You may have noticed that this book uses words to express numbers one to ninety-nine, and numerals to express numbers over 100. Either rule is acceptable. Choose one and use it consistently.

Use numerals with abbreviations and symbols, in addresses and dates, and for page references and text divisions.

3 cm., 185 lbs., $200, 99%, 5 A.M.

175 Lexington Avenue; May 6, 1970; the 1980s

page 44; chapter 22

Do not begin a sentence with a numeral.

> Fifty-six percent of those students failed.

BUT   He failed 56 percent of the class.

Express related numbers in the same form.

One out of ten *or* 1 out of 10 (*but not* 1 out of ten)

Use a combination of words and numerals to express very large, rounded numbers, or when two numbers are used as modifiers.

3.5 million dollars, nearly 14 million

eight 20-cent stamps, ten 3-year-olds

sp   SPELLING

Some spelling errors, like typing mistakes, are mechanical. The writer really knows how to spell the word, but somehow it comes out wrong. Letters may be transposed (*becuase*) or omitted (*becaus*). Occasionally, words are confused with homophones, or similar-sounding words (*than* for *then*). These are careless errors that all writers commit, but that good writers catch when they proofread their writing. Unfortunately, many spelling errors are hard to detect. The best advice may be simply to become aware of spelling. Proofread all your writing carefully, and check the dictionary for any words you are uncertain about. Pay special attention to words with prefixes and suffixes, for they cause many writers problems. Keep a list of words you often misspell. Try to pinpoint your own spelling problems, and take the time to study the spelling rules.

Proofread Carefully

Manage your time so that you can carefully check your spelling before handing in your writing. When you proofread for spelling, read the paper backwards, beginning with the last word. This strategy keeps you from reading for content and lets you focus on each word.

Use a Dictionary

The best aid to spelling is a good dictionary. When you are writing and doubt the spelling of a word, put a question mark by the word. Do not interrupt your writing to look up a word in the dictionary or to check usage and punctuation in a handbook. The proper time to worry about correcting is after, not during, drafting.

If you do not know the opening letters of a word, you may have difficulty finding the correct spelling in the dictionary. In this case, consult a misspeller's dictionary that lists words under their most common misspellings.

Keep a List of Words You Habitually Misspell

Misspelling nearly always follows a pattern. Writers may have difficulty with *-able* and *-ible* endings, or be unsure when to double the final consonant before *-ing*. If you keep a record of all the words you misspell, you will eventually detect your own misspelling patterns. When looking for a pattern, remember that you are not likely to consistently misspell every word of a particular type. You may spell *edible* and *manageable* correctly, but write *inevitible* for *inevitable* and *sensable* for *sensible*. Or you may spell the same word two different ways in the same essay.

Know the Spelling Rules and Their Exceptions

If you discover a pattern to your spelling errors, check to see if there is a spelling rule that applies. Be sure you know the exceptions as well as the rule. Also check the dictionary to make certain of the accepted spelling of the words giving you trouble. Some words have more than one accepted spelling (*benefitted* or *benefited*, *judgment* or *judgement*); but, in general, the following rules hold true:

I before *e* except after *c*.

Most people remember this rule because of the jingle "Write *i* before *e* / Except after *c* / Or when sounded like *ay* /As in *neighbor* and *weigh*."

EXCEPT   either, foreign, forfeit, height, leisure, neither, seize, weird

Add prefixes to a root without doubling or dropping letters.

distrust, dissatisfy

misbehave, misspell

unable, unnatural

Double the final consonant when adding a suffix beginning with a vowel if the word has a single syllable that ends in a single consonant preceded by a single vowel (or has a final stressed syllable that ends in a single consonant preceded by a single vowel).

begging, hidden, fitting

BUT NOT   acting, parted, seeming, or stooped

beginning, occurrence

In some cases, the stress shifts to the first syllable when a suffix is added. When it does, do not double the final consonant.

prefér—preférring, préference
          preférred, préferable

Drop a final silent *e* when adding a suffix that begins with *y* or a vowel.

achieving, icy, location, grievance, lovable, continual

However, keep the final silent *e* to retain a soft *c* or *g* sound, to prevent mispronunciation, or to prevent confusion with other words.

changeable, courageous, noticeable

eyeing, mileage, canoeist

dyeing, singeing

Keep a final silent *e* when adding a suffix that begins with a consonant.

achievement, discouragement, sincerely, extremely

EXCEPT   argument, awful, truly, wholly

Words ending in the sound "seed" are usually spelled *-cede*.

precede, recede, secede, intercede

EXCEPT   supersede, proceed, succeed

Pluralize singular nouns that end in a consonant followed by *y* by changing *y* to *i* and adding *-es*.

baby, babies

cry, cries

However, simply add an *-s* to proper names.

Mary, Marys

Pluralize singular nouns that end in a consonant and *o* by adding *-es*.

potato, potatoes

echo, echoes

veto, vetoes

EXCEPT   pianos, sopranos, dynamos, Eskimos, autos

Pluralize singular nouns that end in *-s*, *-ss*, *-sh*, *-ch*, *-x*, *-z* by adding *-es*.

Jones, Joneses

hiss, hisses

bush, bushes

match, matches

suffix, suffixes

buzz, buzzes

EXCEPT   The plural of *fish* is *fish;* the plural of *thesis* is *theses.*

Editing ESL Troublespots

This section provides advice about problems of grammar and standard usage that are particularly troublesome for speakers of English as a second language (ESL). For more on these and other matters of concern to students still mastering English as a second language, consult a comprehensive ESL grammar reference or dictionary.

art

ARTICLES

There are three articles in English: *a*, *an*, and *the*. These words are used before a common noun to indicate whether the noun refers to something specific (*the* moon) or whether it refers to something that is one among many or hasn't yet been specified (*a* planet, *an* asteroid). (Note that *a* is used before a consonant, *an* before a vowel.) For some nouns the absence of an article indicates that the reference is not specific, as described below. In deciding which article to use (or whether to omit the article), it is necessary to distinguish between *count nouns*, *noncount nouns*, and *proper nouns*.

Articles with Count Nouns

Count nouns refer to people and things that can be counted. Most count nouns have separate singular and plural forms: *one teacher, two teachers; one movie, several movies; one child, nine children.*

Use *a* or *an* before a singular count noun when it refers to one entity among many or when it refers to an entity that has not yet been specifically identified.

A good teacher is patient and explains each point carefully.

I saw an exciting movie last night.

Use no article before a plural count noun when it does not refer to a specific entity.

Good teachers are patient.

Adventure movies are popular all over the world.

Use *the* before a singular or plural count noun when it refers to a specific entity or entities.

When the teachers at my high school spoke, we listened.

The movie I saw was on television.

Note that after a first reference marked by *a* or *an*, subsequent references to a count noun, now specific, are generally marked by *the*:

I saw an exciting movie last night. The movie was on television.

However, there are exceptions:

I saw an exciting movie last night. It was a movie made for television. (The second reference is to one among many.)

In addition, a count noun acccompanied by a superlative adjective is always marked by *the*:

I saw the most exciting movie last night.

The best teachers are patient in their explanations.

Articles with Noncount Nouns

Noncount nouns refer to things or ideas that are not counted or are not countable, and they usually have no plural form in English. These include many natural phenomena (*thunder, steam, electricity*); natural elements (*gold, air, sand*); manufacturing materials (*steel, wood, cement*); fibers (*wool, cotton, rayon*); and general categories made up of a variety of specific items (*money, music, furniture, equipment*). Most nouns naming abstract ideas are noncount (*happiness, loyalty, adolescence, wealth*), as are most nouns naming liquids (*milk, gasoline, water*). Some nouns naming foodstuffs are always noncount (*pork, rice, broccoli*); others are noncount when they refer to food as it is eaten (*We ate chicken steamed in wine with fruit*), but count when they refer to individual items or varieties (*We bought a plump chicken, along with several fine wines and various exotic fruits*).

Use no article before a noncount noun when the reference is general.

Money cannot guarantee happiness; loyalty is worth more than gold.

Equipment manufactured of steel resists water.

Use *the* before a noncount noun when the reference is specific or when the noun is followed by a prepositional phrase beginning with *of*.

Where is the gold I asked you to buy? Did you lose the money I gave you?

The happiness of an employer depends on the loyalty of the company's employees.

The steel was carefully tested before being used in making the new equipment.

Note that both count nouns and noncount nouns referring to specific entities can also be introduced by possessive nouns or pronouns (*Maya's* friends, *her* money) or demonstrative pronouns (*these* friends, *that* money). Indefinite count and noncount nouns can also be introduced by words that indicate amount (*few* friends, *some* money).

Articles with Proper Nouns

In general, singular proper nouns are not preceded by an article: Dr. Livingston, New York City, Hawaii, Disneyland, Mount St. Helens, Union Station, Wrigley Field. *The*, however, is required before proper nouns that name (1) most bodies of water, except when the generic part of the name precedes the specific name (*the* Atlantic Ocean, *the* Red River, but Lake Erie); (2) geographic regions (*the* West Coast, *the* Sahara Desert, *the* Grand Canyon); (3) transport craft (*the* Concorde); (4) many named buildings and bridges (*the* World Trade Center, *the* Golden Gate Bridge); and (5) national or international churches (*the* Mormon Church), governing bodies preceded by a proper adjective (*the* British Parliament), titles of religious and political leaders (*the* Dalai Lama, *the* president), religious and historical documents (*the* Bible, *the* Magna Carta), and historical periods (*the* Gilded Age, *the* Civil War). *The* is also used before proper noun phrases that include *of* (*the* Rock of Gibraltar, *the* Gang of Four).

Most plural proper nouns require *the*: *the* United States, *the* Philippines, *the* Black Hills, *the* Clintons, *the* Los Angeles Dodgers. Exceptions include business names (Hillshire Farms, Miller Auto Sales).

verb VERBS

Like native speakers, speakers of English as a second language may encounter several basic problems with verbs covered elsewhere in the Handbook: subject-verb agreement (p. 686), inconsistencies in verb tense (p. 690), irregular verb forms (p. 694). This section focuses on some problems that are special troublespots for ESL writers.

Missing Verbs

In English, every sentence—with rare exceptions—should have both a subject and a verb (see p. 660). If your native language allows the omission of either subject or verb when the meaning is clear without them, check your drafts carefully to be sure that you include both.

CHANGE	The writer's point not hard to understand.
TO	The writer's point is not difficult to understand.
CHANGE	Are many ways to interpret the story.
TO	There are many ways to interpret the story.

Correct Verb
Forms with *Do*
and *Have*

After the auxiliary verbs *do*, *does*, and *did*, always use the base form of the main verb (see p. 694):

CHANGE   When does the committee expects to make a decision?

TO   When does the committee <u>expect</u> to make a decision?

CHANGE   Early observers did not understood the phenomenon.

TO   Early observers did not <u>understand</u> the phenomenon.

After the auxiliary verbs *have*, *has*, and *had*, always use the past participle form of the main verb (see p. 694):

CHANGE   Experts have argue over the effects of television for years.

TO   Experts have <u>argued</u> over the effects of television for years.

CHANGE   He has not visiting much since he started his new job.

TO   He has not <u>visited</u> much since he started his new job.

Conditional
Sentences

Sentences that contain subordinate clauses beginning with *if*, *unless*, and *when* generally indicate causal relationships or speculate about possible outcomes. In such cases the tenses of the verbs in the main clause and the conditional clause must be chosen with care to express a specific meaning.

To express general or specific truths or actions that happen together habitually, the verbs in both clauses are in the same tense (generally the present or the past).

When heat <u>is</u> applied to a solid, its molecules <u>vibrate</u>.

As a child, I never <u>missed</u> school unless a relative <u>died</u>.

To express future possibilities or predictions, the verb in the main clause is usually future, and the verb in the conditional clause is in the present.

Unless somebody <u>acts</u>, the problem <u>will continue</u>.

If we <u>learn</u> to love the Earth, our children <u>will thank</u> us.

When describing conditions that are unreal or contrary to fact, the verb in the main clause is generally *would* or *could* plus the base form of the verb, and the verb in the *if* clause is the past form (actually the subjunctive; see p. 668). Note that *if* clauses use *were* rather than *was*.

I <u>would help</u> you if I <u>could</u>.

If I <u>were</u> you, I <u>would save</u> my money.

When describing actions in the past that did not in fact occur, the verb in the main clause is formed with *would have*, *might have*, or *should have*

plus the past participle, and the verb in the *if* clause is the past perfect form.

If they <u>had started</u> sooner, they <u>would have finished</u> on time.

Two-Word Verbs

English has many verbs that are made up of a verb and some other word (generally a preposition or adverb) whose combined meaning cannot be understood literally. Consider the following examples:

I <u>ran into</u> Denise at the library. ("met by chance")
Nora <u>walked out on</u> her husband and children. ("abandoned")

Many two-word verbs have subtle differences in meaning and usage.

She <u>fell down</u>, and he <u>fell off</u> his bike.
Willie <u>argued with</u> his father <u>about</u> playing Nintendo.
We <u>look forward</u> to the ballet; he's <u>looking into</u> tickets.

Two-word verbs simply must be learned. When you are unsure of the meaning or usage of such verbs, the best advice is to consult a dictionary designed for nonnative speakers of English.

prep

PREPOSITIONS

Three of the most common prepositions in English—*in*, *on*, and *at*—can cause particular problems for nonnative speakers. All three are used to indicate both location and time.

Location

- *In* usually means *within a geographic place or enclosed area*: *in* Mexico, *in* a small town, *in* the park, *in* my bedroom, *in* a car.
- *On* means *on top of* (*on* the shelf, *on* a hill, *on* a bicycle) and is also used with modes of mass transportation (*on* a train, *on* the metro), streets (*on* Broadway), pages (*on* page 5), floors of buildings (*on* the tenth floor), and tracts of private land (*on* a farm, *on* the lawn).
- *At* refers to specific addresses and named locations (*at* 1153 Grand Street, *at* Nana's house, *at* Macy's), to general locations (*at* work, *at* home, *at* the beach), and to locations that involve a specific activity (*at* the mall, *at* the gym, *at* a party, *at* a restaurant).

Time

- *In* is used with months (*in* May), years (*in* 1997), and seasons (*in* the fall), as well as with *morning*, *afternoon*, and *evening* (*in* the morning).
- *On* is used with days of the week (*on* Monday) and dates (*on* June 2, 1984).
- *At* is used with specific times (*at* 7:30, *at* noon, *at* midnight) and with *night* (*at* night).

Appendix
Writing with a Word Processor

Prepared by the Daedalus Group

Do you compose your essays in longhand and then use a word processor to prepare a clean, nicely printed final copy for your instructor? Then this brief appendix is for you. Even the simplest and least expensive word processor provides many extremely powerful tools for writers. If you learn to use those tools well, you'll find that your word processor can help you with all the stages of the writing process, not just the final editing. This appendix will describe some word-processing techniques you can use for invention, drafting, revising, and editing. The specific techniques you use will depend partly on the particular word-processing software available to you, and partly on your own strategies as a writer. You may want to experiment with various techniques until you find the ones that work best for you.

WORD-PROCESSING BASICS

Composing with a word processor involves a few very basic steps. First you have to write something: in word-processing jargon, this is called "entering text." Once you've entered some text, you can do various things with it.

You can modify your text in various ways. For example, you can add to it. You can also delete part of what you've written. Or you can rearrange it, say by changing the order of your words or sentences or paragraphs. Once the text reads the way you like it, you can work with its format (that is, its physical appearance) and print it. A word processor allows you to do all these things on your screen without having to recopy or retype anything.

Creating Files

Whenever you enter text that you want to refer to or work on again—such as invention activities, notes from sources or a rough draft of an essay—you can store or "save" your work in the computer's hard disk or on floppy disks. To do so, you have to tell the computer to save your work in a "file." If you don't do this before you exit your word processor or turn your computer off, you'll lose everything you've written. To save your work, you give the word processor a command, usually the "save" command. The way to give this command varies with different word processors, so you'll need to check your program's manual to see how to do this.

Most word processors ask (or "prompt") you to type in a "file name" for work you want to save. Many word-processing programs ask you to do this after you enter text; a few require you to do so before you start entering text. This is so the computer will know how to identify your work so you can get access to it later.

What should you name your file? Your instructor may ask you to use a specific file name; if not, make up a name you can remember—ideally, one that indicates what's in the file. FILE 1 isn't a good name, for example, because it says nothing about what's in the file. The more information you can get into the file name, the better: the first draft of an essay on Martin Luther King, Jr., for instance, might be named KING 1.

File names are necessarily short. On IBM or IBM-compatible computers, they may have no more than eight letters or numbers. The rules for naming files vary, though, depending on what kind of computer you're using. If you're using an Apple Macintosh, for instance, you can give your files longer, and thus much clearer, names, like "KING ESSAY, DRAFT 1."

Once you've entered a file name, the computer will store what you've written in an electronic file. You need to save your work frequently, every fifteen minutes or so. This is necessary to guard against losing it accidentally—because of a power failure, for example. For work you especially don't want to lose, you might make backup copies on a separate floppy disk.

Entering Text

To enter text, simply start your word processor and, when the "editing screen" appears, begin typing. The cursor—in some programs, a blinking white line; in others, a solid rectangle—will indicate where on the screen the next character will appear. No need to press a carriage return key (or "enter" key) at the end of each line—the only time you'll need the carriage return key is when you want to begin a new paragraph.

Modifying Text

You can add, delete, or reorganize your work with a few simple keystrokes. Every word-processing system has its own strokes for particular commands; check your user's manual to find out which keystrokes to use for your particular program.

To add text, just move the cursor to the spot where you want the new text to go and begin typing. Most word processors will automatically insert the new text where you put it in the existing text.

To delete text, simply press the backspace key, which erases characters to the left of the cursor. On IBM-compatible computers, you can also use the "del," or delete key to remove the character indicated by the cursor.

Working with Blocks of Text

One of the greatest conveniences a word processor offers is the ability to work with and manipulate blocks of text. Simply mark off (or "define") the block of text you want to work on, and you can then do various things with it. For example, you can:

- "cut"—delete it completely
- "cut and paste"—delete it from one place in the text and insert it somewhere else

- "copy"—leave it where it is and also insert a copy of it somewhere else
- "reformat"—boldface or italicize it; adjust its spacing; and so on

The manual for your word processor will tell you the specific commands to use. Most word processors also have an "undelete" or "restore" command in case you make a mistake; be sure you learn how to use it.

Formatting and Printing

Formatting the text means arranging its physical appearance: justifying (or not justifying) the margins; determining the spacing (single, double, triple, etc.); adding page numbers. Some word processors allow for special formats—for setting off quotations, numbering footnotes, keeping bibliographic entries, and so on. It's probably best not to get too fancy; remember that your first obligation is to make your work clear and readable.

Once you think you've got the format right, print out a copy of your text. If your word processor permits it, "preview" the finished document onscreen so that you can make any necessary changes before printing.

SOME USEFUL TECHNIQUES

All word processors offer features that can well serve any writer. Following is a brief catalogue of some of the most useful features, ones you will want to try out if you are writing with a word processor.

Working with a Split Screen

Many word processors have a split-screen capability, allowing you to divide your screen into two (or sometimes more) "windows." You can use the windows for displaying various things—sections of your draft, invention notes, information from outside sources, an outline of your plan, whatever. For instance, you might use one window to display a section you're working on, and put some earlier section in another window. You might, for example, want to keep your introductory paragraph in one window while you work on a later paragraph in another window. Such a two-paragraph view can help you to keep your main point always in mind, and to avoid straying from that point as you draft.

Some word processors allow you to work with a different file in each window, thus letting you keep some of your notes in front of you as you draft. This would facilitate work with source materials—when inserting block quotations, for instance, or even when paraphrasing rather than quoting a source's words.

Cutting and Pasting

Cutting and pasting takes its name from a common method used by writers who work with pen and paper—namely, cutting up a text into little strips, arranging them in some order, and then pasting them down on a piece of paper. Word processors let you cut and paste electronically—that is, you can "cut" a block of text from one place in your text and "paste" it in somewhere else. It is so easy that you can arrange and rearrange your text many different ways before finally settling on any one way. Experienced writers say that this function allows them to revise more easily than ever before, and thus encourages them to do so more ambitiously.

To cut and paste, simply select the block of text you want to move and use the "cut" or "move" commands (depending on your word processor). If at any time you want to go back to your original arrangement, you can easily reverse the procedure, sometimes with a single "undo" command.

With some word processors, you can cut and paste between different windows on your screen, and even between files. Imagine, for example, that you discover a need for some dialogue or for a different example in your draft. If your system allows you to cut and paste between screens, you could, with a few keystrokes, move an anecdote (or an example) from the screen with your invention notes right into your draft.

You can also "copy" text, which means to leave it where it is in your draft or notes and at the same time to insert it elsewhere. This copying feature allows you to experiment with your materials, to try them out here and then there. Say, for instance, that you have one especially powerful quotation to use and you can't decide whether it should go at the beginning of your essay, to draw readers in, or at the end, to leave them with something memorable. Copying allows you to try it out in both places, see where it works better, and then decide.

Highlighting

With a word processor you can highlight portions of your text, either by underscoring or boldfacing. Highlighting can help you to check over your text for various things. You could, for example, decide to highlight all examples, and thus see at a glance whether there are any places in your draft with too many or not enough examples. You could do the same with other important elements—topic sentences, dialogue, anecdotes, whatever. Someone working on a typewriter could of course do the same, but a word processor allows you, with a keystroke or two, to make the highlighting go away once you've checked what you want to see.

Using the Search Function

"Searching" is one of the most useful functions a word processor can offer to a writer. By issuing a single command, you can locate particular words or punctuation marks or even kinds of spacing every time they occur in your text. You could, for instance, use the search function to find every use of the word *I*, perhaps to check that you not overuse it. Or you might want to find every instance of the word *he*, perhaps to check whether it should instead be *he or she*. You can also use the search function to check for consistency—to make sure you spell a word one way throughout, for instance, *theater* or *theatre*, not both.

In addition to making a search, your word processor will allow you to "search and replace"—in other words, to search for one word or other element and automatically replace it with another. Say, for instance, that you've named Shakespeare as the author of a play that was actually written by Ben Jonson. With a search-and-replace function, you simply instruct your word processor to find every occurrence of the word *Shakespeare* in your text and to replace it with the words *Ben Jonson*.

A word of warning, however. The search-and-replace function is merely a tool; *you* must be the one to do the actual checking. It can lead you to various elements; you still have to decide which elements to check and what's appropriate or inappropriate. Like all word-processing features, the search-and-replace function is but a tool. You are still the writer.

Spell Checkers

Most word processors include a spell checker. Spell checkers are simply functions that compare each word in your text to a list of words stored in the program's memory. It will question any of your words that it can't find on its list. Some spell checkers will also offer alternative spellings to replace the misspelled word, and most allow you to add your own words to the list, thus creating your own personal word list.

Be aware, however, that spell checkers are not human, and they aren't magic; they're simply programs that compare strings of letters without any understanding of what the letters mean. In fact, a spell checker can be wrong, and in various different ways. For instance, it may signal that a correctly spelled word is misspelled when it can't find it in its list of words. On the other hand, there are some spelling errors it will never recognize. For example, a spell checker will not call attention to mistaken usage of the possessive *its* or the contraction *it's*. Both are correct spellings, and the spell checker cannot tell whether you've *used* them correctly or not. You'll have the same difficulty with another often confused pair, *affect* and *effect*. The point is, don't assume that your draft has no spelling errors just because the spell checker doesn't find any.

Usage, Style, and Grammar Checkers

You can also find programs that check for usage, style, and, sometimes, grammar. Like spell checkers, these can be helpful tools that can alert you to some things you may want to check for—*be* verbs, extremely long sentences, instances of the passive voice, and so on. Properly used, such programs can help you to see your writing more critically by pointing out potential problems. But they are even more likely to mislead you than spell checkers because they can catch only some problems, and they sometimes flag nonexistent problems. Be aware of the limits of the programs if you use them; and don't expect miracles from them. Like spell checkers, usage, style, or grammar checkers don't correct with an eye for content. Only you can do that.

USING WRITER'S PROLOGUE

The St. Martin's Guide to Writing is accompanied by *Writer's Prologue*, a customized software package available for both IBM-compatible and Macintosh computers. Your instructor may request a copy to install on your campus network, or you may order a copy of your own through your college bookstore.

Writer's Prologue is an integrated software program designed to be used with *The St. Martin's Guide*. It contains a word processor to use as you complete the assignments in the *Guide*—and a series of prompts to help you as you write. These prompts provide you with step-by-step guidance through the invention and revision stages of your writing assignments. *Writer's Prologue* allows you to switch quickly between your responses in the prompt window and your draft document, and you can easily copy information between the two windows. For collaborative projects, you can load a companion's document and review it following special prompts for revision.

For specific information on how to use *Writer's Prologue* on your computer, consult the documentation provided with the software itself.

An Overview

After starting *Writer's Prologue*, you will first encounter the word processor. This program features text-formatting capabilities, cut-and-paste options, search-and-replace functions, and a 50,000-word spell checker. It also allows you to save and retrieve your work at any time, or to transfer files to any other word processor.

Writer's Prologue also includes a writing tutorial for use with *The St. Martin's Guide*. For each of its writing assignments (in Chapters 2–10), you will find on *Prologue* a series of prompts to help you as you draft and revise. Each prompt is accompanied by an Explain screen, which offers helpful information about the prompt and suggests where to look in the *Guide* for more information.

One of the most challenging aspects of writing is formulating a topic that's manageable and still stimulating. *Writer's Prologue* uses carefully designed and tested prompts to help you through all the challenges of invention. To start your work, select the first menu option under Invention and Planning for your current chapter assignment. You will notice that the prompt window is split in two with a question at the top and a response box below. After reading the question, use the response box to write any ideas or notes that will help you with your essay. At any time, you can switch to the word processor and work on your draft. You can save your responses in a file, print them out, or copy them into your draft. If you don't have time to address all the prompts, you can save what you've done and return to it later.

Once you have a rough draft, you will want to revise and edit it carefully before turning it in as a finished paper. *Writer's Prologue* includes prompts to help you revise your own work or to make suggestions for improving someone else's draft.

As you move on to the reading and revising prompts for each chapter assignment, you will discover that they work just like the Invention and Planning prompts. They will help you analyze how successfully the draft fulfills the writing assignment and to plot strategies for revision. You can save your responses, print them out, or copy them into your draft.

Writer's Prologue is designed to help you with your writing assignments. Use it however it works best for you. Do not feel compelled to respond to every prompt, and feel free to work out of sequence—beginning in the middle of the invention prompts if you already have a topic, abandoning a topic that isn't working for you and starting over, moving between your draft and your prompt responses in order to keep things moving. When you find an activity that works particularly well for you, be sure to see what else *The St. Martin's Guide* has to say about it.

Acknowledgments (continued from page ii)

Gerald Haslam. "The Horned Toad" from *New Arts Review*. Copyright © 1983 by Gerald Haslam. Reprinted by permission of author.

Ernest Hemingway. Reprinted with permission of Charles Scribner's Sons, an imprint of Macmillan Publishing Company, from *Death in the Afternoon* by Ernest Hemingway. Copyright © 1932 by Charles Scribner's Sons. Copyright renewed © 1960 by Ernest Hemingway.

"Home education." From *Reader's Guide to Periodical Literature*, 1991, page 940 (Home Education.) Copyright © 1992 by The H. W. Wilson Company. Material reproduced with permission of the publisher.

"intrepid." Copyright © 1991 by Houghton Mifflin Company. Reprinted by permission from *The American Heritage Dictionary, Second College Edition.*

James Joyce. "Araby," from *Dubliners* by James Joyce. Copyright 1916 by B. W. Heubsch. Definitive text Copyright © 1967 by the Estate of James Joyce. Used by permission of Viking Penguin, a division of Penguin Books USA Inc.

Mickey Kaus. "Street Hassle." Reprinted by permission of *The New Republic*, © 1993, The New Republic, Inc.

William L. Kibler. "Cheating: Institutions Need a Comprehensive Plan for Promoting Academic Integrity," by William L. Kibler, 1992, November 11, *The Chronicle of Higher Education*, pp. B1-2. Reprinted by permission of author.

William Kilpatrick. "Turning Out Moral Illiterates." From the *Los Angeles Times*, July 20, 1993. Reprinted by permission of the author. William Kilpatrick, a professor of education at Boston College, is the author of *Why Johnny Can't Tell Right from Wrong* (Simon & Schuster, 1992).

Martin Luther King, Jr. "Letter from Birmingham Jail" from *Letter from Birmingham Jail*. Reprinted by arrangement with The Heirs to the Estate of Martin Luther King, Jr., c/o Joan Daves Agency as agent for the proprietor. Copyright 1963 by Martin Luther King, Jr., copyright renewed 1991 by Coretta Scott King.

Stephen King. "Why We Crave Horror Movies." © Stephen King, All rights reserved, used with permission.

Charles Krauthammer. "Saving Nature, but Only for Man." Copyright 1991 Time Inc. Reprinted by permission.

Audre Lorde. "The Election." © 1982 by Audre Lorde, excerpted from *Zami: A New Spelling of My Name*, Crossing Press, Freedom California.

Sylvia S. Mader. From *Inquiry into Life*, 3rd edition, by Sylvia S. Mader. Copyright © 1982 Wm. M. Brown Communications, Inc., Dubuque, Iowa. Reprinted by permission. All rights reserved.

Catherine Manegold. "To Crystal, 12, School Serves No Purpose." Copyright © 1993 by The New York Times Company. Reprinted by permission.

Donella H. Meadows. "Rush and Larry, Coast to Coast: This Is Not Democracy in Action." From the *Los Angeles Times*, February 12, 1993. Reprinted by permission of author.

The New Yorker. "Soup." Originally titled "Slave." From "Talk of the Town" section of *The New Yorker*, January 23, 1989. © 1989 The New Yorker Magazine, Inc.

David Noonan. "Inside the Brain." From *Neuro* by David Noonan. Copyright © 1989 by David Noonan. Reprinted by permission of Simon & Schuster, Inc.

Anastasia Toufexis. "Love: The Right Chemistry." Originally titled "The Right Chemistry." Copyright 1993 Time Inc. Reprinted by permission.

Adam Paul Weisman. "Birth Control in the Schools: Clinical Examination." Reprinted by permission of *The New Republic*, © 1987, The New Republic, Inc.

William Carlos Williams. "The Use of Force." From *The Doctor Stories* by William Carlos Williams. Reprinted by permission of New Directions Publishing Corp.

Tobias Wolff. "On Being a Real Westerner." From the book *This Boy's Life* by Tobias Wolff, Copyright © 1989 by Tobias Wolff. Used with the permission of Grove/Atlantic Monthly Press.

Author and Title Index

Subject Index

Submitting Papers for Publication

To Students and Instructors

We hope that we'll be able to include essays from more colleges and universities in the next edition of the *Guide* and our accompanying anthology, *The Great American Bologna Festival and other student essays*. Please let us see essays written using *The St. Martin's Guide* you'd like us to consider. Send them with this Agreement Form to The Guide, St. Martin's Press, 175 Fifth Avenue, New York, NY 10010.

Instructor's Name _____

School _____

Address _____

Department _____

Student's Name _____

Course _____

Writing activity the paper represents _____

This writing activity appears in chapter(s) _____
of *The St. Martin's Guide to Writing*

Agreement Form

I hereby transfer to St. Martin's Press all rights to my essay,

(tentative title), subject to final editing by the publisher. These rights include copyright and all other rights of publication and reproduction. I guarantee that this essay is wholly my original work, and that I have not granted rights to it to anyone else.

St. Martin's Press representative: _____

Student's signature X: _____

Please type

Name: _____

Address: _____

_____

_____

Phone: _____

Correction Symbols

ab	ABBREVIATION	751
adj/adv	CONFUSION OF ADJECTIVE AND ADVERB	692
agr p/a	PRONOUN-ANTECEDENT AGREEMENT	688
agr s/v	SUBJECT-VERB AGREEMENT	686
art	ARTICLES	759
be	OVERUSE OF *BE*	707
cap	CAPITALIZATION	752
cliché	CLICHÉ	719
comp	INCOMPLETE COMPARISON	683
comp noun	COMPOUND-NOUN PHRASE	710
d	INAPPROPRIATE DICTION	717
dang	DANGLING MODIFIER	684
end	END-STOP ERROR	675
fp	FAULTY PREDICATION	680
frag	SENTENCE FRAGMENT	677
hedge	UNNECESSARY HEDGE	716
hyph	HYPHENATION	753
image	INAPPROPRIATE IMAGE	718
intens	UNNECESSARY INTENSIFIER	716